This book is due for return not later than the last
date stamped below, unless recalled sooner.

GERMAN
DIASPORIC
EXPERIENCES

German Diasporic Experiences

Identity, Migration, and Loss

Mathias Schulze,
James M. Skidmore,
David G. John,
Grit Liebscher, and
Sebastian Siebel-Achenbach,
editors

WLU

Wilfrid Laurier University Press

We acknowledge the financial support of the Government of Canada through the Book Publishing Industry Development Program for our publishing activities.

Library and Archives Canada Cataloguing in Publication

German diasporic experiences : identity, migration, and loss / Mathias Schulze ... [et al.], editors.

Proceedings of a conference at the University of Waterloo, August 24–27, 2006.
Co-published by: Waterloo Centre for German Studies.
Includes bibliographical references and index.

ISBN 978-1-55458-027-9

1. Germans — Foreign countries — Congresses. 2. Germans —Ethnic identity — Congresses. 3. Germany — Emigration and immigration — History — Congresses. I. Schulze, Mathias, 1963–   II. Waterloo Centre for German Studies

JV8010.G47 2008   305.83'1   C2007-907613-0

Co-published with the Waterloo Centre for German Studies

The front cover reproduces a painting titled *Centred* (1945), by the German American artist Hilla Rebay von Ehrenwiesen (1890–1967), who was the first director and curator of what would become the Solomon R. Guggenheim Museum in New York. All works of art by Hilla Rebay © The Hilla von Rebay Foundation used by permission. All rights reserved. Cover design by Blakeley Words+Pictures. Text design by P.J. Woodland.

∞

This book is printed on Ancient Forest Friendly paper (100% post-consumer recycled).

Printed in Canada

CONTENTS

The Speckled People

Hugo Hamilton

In his memoir, *The Speckled People*, Hugo Hamilton, an Irish writer and the son of a German mother and an Irish father, tells the story of an Irish German family in Dublin through the eyes of one family member, a young boy. The following excerpt recounts the Christmas visit of his German aunt, now living in Salzburg.

I couldn't breathe very well. My shoulders were going up and down trying to get air. My mother stroked my head and listened to the howling in my chest. She prayed that I would get better. She smiled at me and said everything would soon be fine again, because her oldest sister Marianne was coming with her daughter Christiane. And Tante Marianne was very good at helping people breathe. She helped people in Salzburg when it was hard to breathe.

For days and days my mother was cleaning the house. She polished the stairs and every piece of wood in the house was shining. She put fruit in a bowl on the table and baked a cake. Tante Marianne was going to get my room. It had no wallpaper any more, only pink plaster and some long cracks, but my mother said it looked clean and friendly, and that's all that mattered. And as soon as Marianne walked in the front door, she would see the old oak trunk that came from their house on the Buttermarkt and think she was at home.

My mother put on her blue suit with the big white collars. She put the big number 4711 on her wrists and wore the green Smaragd snake. We put on our best clothes, too, with no blue elbows, and kept looking out the window until Tante Marianne and Christiane arrived in a taxi with suitcases. Then my mother dropped her apron on the floor of the kitchen and ran all the way along the hallway smiling and crying at the same time. Tante Marianne was smiling and crying, too, as they embraced and stood back to look each other up and down.

"Ja, ja, ja," they kept saying. And then, "Nein, nein, nein."

They could not believe their own eyes. They shook their heads and wiped their tears and embraced each other again. Ja, ja, ja, and nein, nein, nein, and ja, ja, ja, until Tante Marianne turned around to look at us. She knew our names from letters and photographs, but she had to kneel down and look at us properly, one at a time. She knew everything. She knew about Maria's picture of my mother with the arms going all around the walls. She knew that I slapped the schoolteacher. And she knew about the mashed potato on the ceiling.

My father carried in the suitcases and smiled at everyone. Christiane talked to us and Tante Marianne talked to my mother as if they couldn't waste a minute. They went through each of the names one by one—Ta Maria, Elfriede, Adam, Lisalotte, Max, Minne and Wilhelm, and all the children, as if they had to travel around Germany in their heads until every question was asked and every story was told. My mother had to hear everything twice and clapped her hands around her face as if she could not believe what she heard.

Tante Marianne brought new perfume into the house. Everyone wanted to be close to her all the time and sit beside her at the table. Maria followed her everywhere. My mother and Tante Marianne could not be separated either, because they kept talking, even when they were not in the same room. Even when Tante Marianne was upstairs and my mother was in the kitchen, they kept remembering things out loud, calling up and down the stairs as if they were at home again in the house on the Butter-markt square. Tante Marianne called her Irmgard. We still called her Mutti, and it was like having two mothers in the house, because they had the same teeth and the same eyes and the same hair. They had the same words and the same way of laughing out loud until the tears came into their eyes. They had the same way of peeling an orange in strips along the side and the same trick of cutting the peel into the shape of teeth. Two mothers playing the monster with big orange teeth while my father was out getting coal for the boiler.

"Vooo, vooo, vooo, vooo …,' they both said. Then they started laughing so much that they couldn't stop any more. Laughing and shaking, so that my father stopped pouring coal into the boiler to come and see what was happening.

Tante Marianne's suitcase was full of toys and books for everyone. There were lots of gummi bears and chocolates and biscuits that you would never get in the shops in Ireland. She brought a spirit level for my father, and a toy train for me and Franz. Some other presents were wrapped and put away immediately, for Christmas. There were biscuits to be eaten now and biscuits to be kept for later. One by one, Tante Marianne took things out with great care, explaining where they came from. We were allowed to read the Mecki books immediately, about a hedgehog who travelled all over the world in a hot air balloon with his crew—Charlie Penguin, and a cat called Kater Murr. Nobody in Ireland knows about Mecki, and they laugh at us because we don't know who Red Riding Hood is and we don't realise it's the same as Rotkäppchen.

Everything in our house was German again.

ONE

Diaspora Experiences
German Immigrants and Their Descendants

Mathias Schulze
James M. Skidmore

"Diaspora Experiences: German Immigrants and Their Descendants" was the title of a conference organized by the Waterloo Centre for German Studies in 2006. From 24 to 27 August, about two hundred participants— researchers in history, literature and film, and linguistics as well as members of the interested public—discussed characteristics of Austrian, German, and Swiss identity in minority settings, aspects of the migration of German speakers from central Europe to many different countries of the world, and also painful experiences such as the loss of Heimat or one's native language.

WHEN WE WERE PLANNING THE CONFERENCE,[1] we wanted to facilitate an interdisciplinary discussion of the complex issues, perspectives, and aspects of German minorities worldwide under a broad thematic umbrella. Relatively early on and with some hesitation, we decided on the centrality of the notion of "diaspora" for this conference. The concept, applied to the German context of at least the last two centuries, is, of course, not unproblematic. In part this is due to problems with applying the distinct concept of diaspora to a variety of contexts in migration studies, but more importantly, problems stemming from the semantic, historical, political, and moral tensions between the adjective "German" and the noun "diaspora." We therefore decided to open up the word and return to its etymological roots—its Ancient Greek meaning of scattering, first of seeds and later of people—without ignoring its later application in Jewish and postcolonial contexts. This led to interesting and stimulating discussions during and after the conference presentations.

Of course, ours was not the first conference that facilitated an academic dialogue on German minorities. A number of recent conferences and publications have concentrated on Germans in Canada. For instance, the 2004 conference "Assimilation—Integration—Acculturation? The German-Canadian Case"—organized by Alexander Freund, chair in German-Canadian Studies at the University of Winnipeg—brought together scholars from history, linguistics, and literature. With a wide understanding of migration and post-migration experiences, the focus of this conference was clearly on German Canadians. Similarly, in their volume *A Chorus of Different Voices*, editors Angelika E. Sauer and Matthias Zimmer collected the contributions of participants to a 1996 workshop on German Canadian identity. The volume sought to problematize "the notion of German Canadians,"[2] indeed, as they note in their preface, "German Canadians defy definition." The contributors to that workshop and volume were, for the most part, historians who attempted to approach the topic of German Canadian culture from fresh disciplinary perspectives. The volume's explicit challenge to reflect on and reconsider the practice of studying the German diaspora in Canada—its problematization of German Canadian studies, in other words—sounded a clear warning to scholars that traditional approaches to the German diaspora in Canada would no longer suffice. *A Chorus of Different Voices* dealt specifically with German Canadians, and largely from a historiographical perspective, but its quarrel with established modes of understanding German diasporic identity was part of a larger shift in the scholarship of identity and culture.

This swing toward a more probing scholarly discourse is seen in the collection of essays *Theorizing Diaspora* edited by Jana Evans Braziel and Anita Mannur in 2003. An anthology of earlier and more contemporary texts, this volume's interdisciplinary and eclectic range covers a breadth of issues both theoretical and related to specific diasporas. One of the collection's most useful contributions with respect to the German diaspora is to espouse a very liberal view of the term "diaspora" itself, with some of the essays discussing diasporas as diverse as Jewish, Asian American, Afro-Caribbean, and gay Filipino. One of the highlights of the volume, a reprinting of Stuart Hall's important essay "Cultural Identity and Diaspora," reminds the reader of the fact that cultural identity undergoes constant negotiation and renegotiation, a finding that can be easily seconded by much of the research in the present volume. Although one might fault *Theorizing Diaspora* for its lack of disciplinary or content focus—issues of language remain largely unexplored, for example—the theoretical impulses contained in the collection will play a large role in future research.

Issues of language and society have also been discussed elsewhere. German-language islands in Europe and North America are examined in *Sprachinselwelten,* edited by Nina Berend and Elisabeth Knipf-Komlósi in 2006. The contributions of this book—based on a section meeting of the International Society for German Dialectology—concentrate on linguistic features of selected varieties spoken outside of the German-speaking areas in central Europe. With an exclusively European focus, but a wider consideration of sociolinguistic issues, the volume *National Varieties of German Outside Germany: A European Perspective,* edited by Gabriele Hogan-Brun, examines varieties of German after the sociopolitical transformations in central and eastern Europe. Of course, issues of minority languages, language contact and change, societal and individual bilingualism—to name but a few—have been discussed in relation to the German language and many others. The same could be said about (German) literature in minority settings (see chapter 14). It has been described, analysed, and interpreted under headings such as migrant literature, expatriate literature, and *Exilliteratur.* However, hardly ever have essays in linguistics and literature of German minorities appeared together and alongside essays on history, migration, and diaspora studies. The small conference "Assimilation— Integration—Acculturation? The German-Canadian Case" is a notable exception here.

German Diasporic Experiences thus breaks new ground by presenting in one volume linguistic, historical, literary, and cinematic scholarship on similar, overlapping, complementary, and sometimes contrasting aspects of German minorities worldwide. A representative selection of edited papers from this conference, as well as the keynote addresses, follow in this volume, divided into three main parts: identity, migration, and loss.

Identity

Janet Fuller begins Part 1 with her discussion of identity in and through language. Her focus is on German speakers—particularly Pennsylvania German—in the United States. Patrick Stevenson and Jenny Carl continue the discussion of language and the negotiation of identities, but focus on German-speaking communities in central Europe, e.g., Hungary and the Czech Republic. Doris Schüpbach discusses how immigrants to Australia from German-speaking Switzerland relate their migratory experience of building a new life in a different language. Staying with the Australian context, Sandra Kipp gives an overview of German and German speakers in Australia between 1939 and 2001. A similar overview—with a focus on identity and identity construction—is provided by Rolf Annas, who discusses the German-speaking people of Paarl in South Africa. In the first essay on Germans in Canada, Grit Liebscher

xvi MATHIAS SCHULZE, JAMES M. SKIDMORE

and Jennifer Dailey-O'Cain show how these speakers position themselves in German conversations.

Of course, the identity of immigrants and their descendants is not just constructed in language use. Andrea Strutz, for example, explores the memories that Austrian-Jewish refugees maintained over several generations in the United States. The identity of well-known German American journalists and newspaper editors, Pulitzer and Preetorius, is Jason Todd Baker's focus. Anne Löchte looks at the *Berliner Journal* (1859–1918) and asks what this Canadian German-language newspaper can tell us of the identity of its journalists and readership. Similarly influenced by "external" political events are the Russian German émigré activists during the interwar period in Germany, whom James Casteel discusses in the next essay. Christiane Harzig, on the other hand, is more interested in transcultural spaces when looking at how German American women in Chicago between 1889 and 1950 constructed their (cultural) identity. The last chapter of the first part looks at more recent historical events and how they affected the relationship of East German institutions with Canadians and German Canadians. Here, Manuel Meune investigates the role of the Gesellschaft Neue Heimat (1980–1990) and its representation of official East German identity in Canada.

Migration

Part II—Migration—encompasses a broad spectrum of subthemes, all of which have in common a focus on moving: migration from one country to another, the personal experience of changing places, as well as the metaphors of moving on and making progress in a particular area. It is the latter perspective James M. Skidmore takes when he argues for moving the study of expatriate German literature into the academic mainstream of German literary studies. Gisela Holfter takes a very different approach, providing an overview of German migration to Ireland at the time of the Third Reich. Looking back further, Nora Faires analyses evangelicalism among German immigrants newly arrived in Pittsburgh in the nineteenth century. Often German and other immigrants were recruited first in their homeland by so-called immigration agents, and Angelika Sauer looks at the attempt by three such agents to create a German diaspora in nineteenth-century Canada. By the twentieth century many countries had developed a set of immigration and recruitment policies, which Johannes-Dieter Steinert and Inge Weber-Newth examine in the British context, paying particular attention to the reception of German migrants. Another focus on migration is offered by Christin Pschichholz, who discusses the immigration of German-speaking people to the territory of Turkey between 1850 and 1918. The subsequent two chapters by Patrick

Farges and Pascal Maeder both talk about Sudeten Germans in Canada and their migration and acculturation. Anne Ribbert, when looking at German speakers in the Netherlands, shows that migration experiences can affect language use and competence. The next two essays both deal with the depiction of emigration in German film: Carsten Würmann looks at the fictional figure of the *Onkel aus Amerika* and Hanno Sowade describes the depiction of expellees in post-1945 West German film. A number of Christian Lieb's interviewees—German-speaking immigrants who came to British Columbia, Canada after 1945—have a lot in common with some of the fictional characters in these two films.

Numerous chapters concentrate on German-speaking migrants to continents other than North America. Stefan Engelberg discusses German-language politics of the colonial powers and attitudes toward German and the other languages spoken in the South Seas in the early twentieth century. Brigitte Bönisch-Brednich focuses on migration experiences of immigrants to New Zealand and highlights gender differences. Similarly, Karin Bauer looks at the role of Elisabeth Förster-Nietzsche in building a German colony in South America.

Loss

Part III is introduced by Hans Lemberg, who provides a historical overview of the expulsion of Germans from eastern and central Europe after World War II. Shifting the focus to the flight and expulsion of Jewish entrepreneurs from Frankfurt during the Third Reich, Benno Nietzel discusses the concept and realities of *Wiedergutmachung* in the postwar years. Dieter Buse directs the reader's attention to the dissolution of a German minority in Poland. The Russian German diaspora in Kazakhstan—their forced migration and suffering—is the centre of attention in J. Otto Pohl's essay. Similarly, the fate of a German-speaking minority—the case of Blumenau in South Brazil—at the mercy of national politics is what interests Méri Frotscher Kramer. However, not every loss has primarily a political or ideological cause. Jörg Meindl, for example, ponders the question whether the changes in Pennsylvania German in Kansas can be described as language loss. The ostensible loss of "memory" is what Monique Laney investigates in her chapter on Wernher von Braun and Arthur Rudolph. In her literary analysis and interpretation, Doris Wolf employs a similar approach to memory and *Vergangenheitsbewältigung* when she approaches Gertrud Mackprang Baer's personal narrative *In the Shadow of Silence*. Alexander Freund also looks at *Vergangenheitsbewältigung*, in his case by German migrants in Canada. The last two chapters of this collection deal with different kinds of loss: Natasha G. Wiebe interprets the loss of "community" and the changing cultural identity as depicted in the works of the Mennonite writer Di Brandt and Monika S. Schmid analyses aspects of and contributors to the loss of German by speakers in Vancouver.

In its thirty-eight chapters, this book provides a complex album of cultural, historical, and linguistic perspectives on many different aspects of German-speaking minorities on five continents—a collection that highlights the many different facets of current thinking on and knowledge of these minorities all over the globe.

We would like to thank all the authors for their insightful contributions to this book and for the very pleasant collaboration over the course of about two years. The editors of this book benefited greatly from help by Janet Vaughan at the University of Waterloo and from the support of the colleagues at Wilfrid Laurier University Press. Moreover, the conference on which the volume is based would not have been possible without the assistance of graduate students—here we would like to mention Peter Wood, Janice MacGregor, and Agata Monkiewicz in particular—as well as the immense work by staff at St. Paul's College at the University of Waterloo, especially Jodie Fitzgerald. Finally, all of us involved wish to express our appreciation to the conference's sponsors: the Social Sciences and Humanities Research Council of Canada, Eddie Koch, the Waterloo Centre for German Studies, the University of Waterloo, the Goethe Institute (Toronto), the German Canadian Chamber of Industry and Commerce (Toronto), the German Canadian Congress (Ontario), the German embassy (Ottawa), the Consulate General of Germany (Toronto), the Consulate General of Switzerland (Toronto), the Austrian Embassy (Ottawa), and Marga Weigel. Thank you all.

Waterloo, Ontario

Notes

1 For information follow the links on the website of the Waterloo Centre for German Studies at <www.wcgs.ca>.
2 Sauer and Zimmer, *Chorus*, ix.

Works Cited

Berend, Nina, Elisabeth Knipf-Komlósi, eds. *Sprachinselwelten: Entwicklung und Beschreibung der deutschen Sprachinseln am Anfang des 21. Jahrhunderts = The World of Language Islands: The Developmental Stages and the Description of German Language Islands at the Beginning of the 21st Century.* Frankfurt: Peter Lang, 2006.

Braziel, Jana Evans, and Anita Mannur. *Theorizing Diaspora: A Reader.* Malden, MA: Blackwell Publishing, 2003.

Freund, Alexander, ed. *Beyond the Nation? Immigrants' Local Lives in Transnational Cultures.* Toronto: University of Toronto Press, forthcoming.

Hogan-Brun, Gabrielle. *National Varieties of German Outside Germany.* Oxford: Peter Lang, 2000.

Sauer, Angelika E., and Matthias Zimmer, eds. *A Chorus of Different Voices. German-Canadian Identities.* New York: Peter Lang, 1998.

PART ONE

IDENTITY

TWO

Language and Identity in the German Diaspora

Janet M. Fuller

This chapter addresses the role of language in the construction of identity among German emigrants and their descendants living around the world. Speakers of Pennsylvania German are taken as a first example, with a focus on how characteristics of group identity are constructed through varieties of German and English. The chapter also addresses the role of social identity in language shift for different groups of Pennsylvania German speakers. It then integrates studies of other German enclaves in the Americas, Australia, Africa, and the former Soviet Union into the discussion to create a broader analysis of what German identity means in the diaspora, how different language varieties construct it, and how it is maintained without the German language.

Introduction

IN THIS CHAPTER, THE TERM DIASPORA is used to discuss people who left areas where German was the majority language in order to live in places where it was a minority language; thus the use here of "German" denotes a sociolinguistic group, not a national one. However, this use is far from unproblematic. Dirk Hoerder notes that while many people believe that social groups—both their own and others'—are monocultural, most emigrant groups, and particularly German emigrants, are not.[1] German emigrants left different regions with diverse cultural practices and distinct and sometimes mutually unintelligible varieties of German. In many cases, they left before a sense of German national identity had developed, and from areas that may or may not be part of contemporary Germany. In other words, emigrants left as Hessians, Mecklenburgers, or Alsatians; they arrived in their new homelands as simply Germans. Settlements in the new homeland may have been treated like enclosed, homogenous groups of immigrants, but were more likely to be heterogeneous and dispersed. The groups discussed in this chapter are those that settled in areas with other groups from their home area, and have continued to identify with that point of departure.

This chapter examines how, or if, these immigrants and their descendants use language to create a German identity for their group. Identity, or social identity as used here, is defined as the "linguistically [or socially] constructed membership in one or more social groups or categories."[2] Social identity includes ethnic identity, which will be the focus in this chapter, but also gender identity, age identity, etc. It is "socially constructed" because, although it is often perceived as something that is a basic physical reality, it is the product of cultural, including linguistic, behaviour and values.

The social identity of a group relies on contrast. In the context of the German diaspora, this means group members define themselves as distinct from the majority ethnic group in their new homeland and distinct from all other minority ethnic groups. However, the "performance" or "construction" of the contrasts may vary from situation to situation. For example, a German-heritage child in the diaspora may construct an identity as part of the mainstream while in the schoolyard, but may express that identity as part of the minority group—including but not limited to speaking German—at home or in the ethnic community. Social identity—for example, as a German Canadian—is thus not a characteristic someone possesses, but something repeatedly performed in different ways depending on the social setting, interlocutors, and location, among other factors.

While the variation in these examples takes a synchronous perspective, variable performance of identity can also be found diachronically. Significant for our discussion of the German diaspora is how group identification can change over time. A simple example of this is how a distinct German identity can, over three generations, be superseded by (for example) a mainstream U.S. American identity as language shift, exogamy, and integration take place. Although the third generation is often aware of their German heritage, this aspect of identity has become minor in comparison to their sense of belonging to other groups: Americans, Minnesotans, citizens of the town of New Ulm, or members of the local Rotary Club.

Another important aspect of social identity is how it matches, or does not match, social categories that are generally pre-existent and in use by people in a society. While the category of "German American" pre-exists for most people in the United States, people who have emigrated from Austria may be put into it despite their protests. There is also variation in the level of acceptance of such hyphenated terms in a society; while they are commonly used in North America; they are only beginning to gain acceptance in other countries (such as Germany itself, where labels such as "*Deutsch-Türken*" exist but are not in widespread use). Another issue in identity construction involves a speaker's wish to construct an identity that is narrower than the inclusive identity of being "German"—for example, if they want to construct themselves as Swabian—since this is less readily recognized by the mainstream culture.

As this last example indicates, part of social identity is not just the individual's sense of belonging to a category but also other people's acceptance of the individual as part of the social group. The person performing an identity must fit the criteria others have for that social group. An Afro German woman, for example, may not fit some people's idea of a German because of her physical appearance. Her stories of growing up in Germany may be followed by questions about where she is "really" from, a clear rejection of her construction of herself as German, while the focus is on the colour of a person's skin as a marker of social group identity.

The linguistic construction of identity, the focus of this chapter, is based on three particular aspects of language use. First and foremost, I am interested in language choice: to what extent, and in what circumstances and with what consequences, is German used in specific communities in the German diaspora? Second, the German dialect is another important aspect of language in the diaspora, particularly its structure, both as the dialect leaves Germany and after it has been spoken as a minority language for several generations. Language change in the context of differences in the varieties of Pennsylvania German is mentioned briefly. Third, this chapter will address how German-speaking immigrants and their descendants speak the majority language in the diaspora. In some cases the majority language is used to construct ethnic group boundaries. Although it is common for the children of immigrants to learn the majority language natively and be linguistically indistinguishable from other local users of that language, it is also possible for an ethnic variety of the majority language to develop. This process of language acquisition is intertwined with the maintenance and change of the German variety; thus all three of these aspects of language will be discussed here in terms of how they interact with each other and in terms of identity construction in the German diaspora. The first example is Pennsylvania German speakers.

Language and Identity in Pennsylvania German-
Speaking Groups

There are two main groups of Pennsylvania Germans (or Pennsylvania Dutch, as they are commonly called). The first and largest group today comprises Anabaptists, called "sectarian" or "Plain" Pennsylvania German speakers. The term "Anabaptist" includes both Amish and Mennonite groups. The concept of Plainness is a crucial one; it is a descriptor for core Anabaptist beliefs, in particular modesty and lack of participation in worldly mainstream culture. Community practices can be placed on a continuum of more or less Plain, with the more liberal Mennonite communities being the least Plain, and the most traditional Amish communities, called Old Order Amish communities, being the most Plain. It is in the Plainest communities that Pennsylvania German continues to be spoken.[3]

The second group of Pennsylvania German speakers is composed largely of Lutherans; this group is often called the "non-sectarian" or "non-Plain" Pennsylvania Germans. Beginning with heavy German emigration to Pennsylvania starting in the 1600s, these two groups—the Plain and the non-Plain—populated the same areas of Pennsylvania. Because many of the immigrants were from the Palatinate area of Germany, their dialect still bears a resemblance to the eastern Palatinate dialect. However, although a relatively uniform dialect of German arose in Pennsylvania, its speakers did not form their community based on a shared sense of connection to a specific community in Germany. Moreover, the sectarian and non-sectarian groups were separated by an important difference: religion. The non-sectarians did not differ greatly from their non-German neighbours in terms of religion, and thus slowly integrated into the mainstream anglophone society. Today, the only remaining speakers of non-Plain Pennsylvania German are elderly. However, this does not necessarily mean that they have lost their sense of German identity. Although they may refer to themselves as Dutch and their ways as "Dutchified," they are quite aware that their heritage is German, and historically this has been something that set them apart from mainstream society.[4] This distinct identity can be seen in their use of English, as discussed in a study by Achim Kopp.[5] His data show one part of what is called the "Pennsylvania German Paradox": although the non-Plain Pennsylvania German speakers are decidedly more integrated into mainstream society than those of the Plain group, their English shows more features of interference from German. The presence of these features in their English does decrease over generations, but the non-Plain speakers use more Dutchified features in their English than the Plain speakers, regardless of generation. In other words, the strength of a speaker's "Dutch" accent is not linked to dominance of Pennsylvania German in his or her linguistic repertoire; in fact, it is quite the opposite.

Kopp's explanation for this paradox is linked to both patterns of language maintenance and social identity. Since the non-Plain Pennsylvania Germans are shifting to English, they can no longer use German to draw group boundaries; with each generation, more and more group members would fail to qualify. Thus a distinctive variety of English develops that serves to identify them as Pennsylvania Dutch. The Plain Pennsylvania Germans, who continue to speak a variety of the German language and pass it on to their children, have no need of an English variety that distinguishes them, because they have a robust in-group language; thus their English tends to be closer to local non-Dutch norms. In this way, both groups use language to construct group membership, but the Plain use Pennsylvania German and the non-Plain use Pennsylvania German English.

The second part of the Pennsylvania German paradox has to do with the changes that are occurring in the German variety. According to many studies, the Plain variety is undergoing more change, while the non-Plain variety has been more conservative.[6] At first glance, this is the opposite of what is to be expected. The expectation is that the Plain speakers, who are religiously conservative and value isolation from the mainstream, would surely preserve their language carefully, while the non-Plain, who have a more open attitude to integration into the mainstream, could be expected to be similarly more open to linguistic convergence. But this is not the case; it is the Plain variety that contains the most innovative features—that is, is most conducive to change. The explanation can be linked to identity and language shift. Since non-Plain speakers frequently use English, there is no need for the German variety to adapt to new circumstances and increased bilingualism: when speakers have difficulty saying what they want to say in Pennsylvania German, they switch to English. In this way, the German variety retains features such as case marking, but eventually dies out due to language shift. In contrast, the Plain Pennsylvania German speakers—or at least the Old Order Amish—must continue to develop their language so that it remains viable within their community; their identities as Plain people depend upon it.

The number of Plain speakers of Pennsylvania German is actually growing, due to the high birth rate among the Old Order Amish (approximately seven children per family) and the high retention rate (80 percent) in their religious group.[7] The Amish, in particular the Old Order, value separation from the world in their charter, and this separation is clearly and explicitly linked to the maintenance of Pennsylvania German. It is also apparent that Pennsylvania German speakers have a sophisticated understanding of the importance of linguistic symbolism. It is not that they believe that Pennsylvania German is somehow inherently more Plain than other languages, but that English represents the outside world, which has no place in their home and community interactions.[8] Among Plain Pennsylvania German speakers, English can have different values. Karen Johnson-Wiener reports that some more liberal Anabaptist groups use English to mark their commitment to evangelism and their rejection of Old Order values. For former Amish who have joined Mennonite communities, the use of English carries symbolic significance; it marks their loyalty to a Mennonite, and not Amish, community.

In my own research, I examined values of Pennsylvania German in a tertiary community in South Carolina.[9] The speakers in this study grew up in secondary communities in the Midwest and moved as adults to found or join less conservative Beachy Amish Mennonite or Conservative Mennonite communities in South Carolina. The links between language and identity changed within the lifetimes of the people interviewed. Their discussion of the value of Pennsylvania German in their childhood Old Order communities shows a clear link between the Pennsylvania German language and Amish identity: see example 1.

EXAMPLE 1

Meist die Amische kenne schwetzte [can speak "Dutch"], *aber die Mennonites sin some wegkomme davon.* (F6)

The interesting aspect of these people's experience, however, is how they have come to realize that speaking Pennsylvania German is not intrinsically linked to being Plain. In their current communities, there are people from other regions in the United States who have equally Plain backgrounds, but Pennsylvania German language is less dominant. In example 2, one woman recognizes this.

EXAMPLE 2

We have one family that moved here from Montezuma, Georgia, and over there, they're actually, as far as Plain people are concerned, they'd probably be Plainer than we are. But they speak all English. (F5)

Thus the assumptions about the role of language in the construction of Plainness have been questioned in these communities. These speakers have been forced to recognize that while speaking Pennsylvania German may be a sign of being Plain, being Plain does not necessarily mean speaking Pennsylvania German.

With Pennsylvania German in the United States as an example, I discussed how language in the diaspora can be linked to identity in different ways. Among the Plain, a variety of the German language can be closely linked to group identity. The identity is not a German one (they view themselves as Americans), but rather a religious identity of Plain Anabaptists, in particular of Old Order Amish. Among the non-Plain, an ethnic variety of English is used to construct a Pennsylvania German identity. Any adoption of new features into the German variety is not a sign of openness to cultural change and convergence, but merely the linguistic consequence of the social practice of bilingualism.

This theme of religious identity as a strong support for language maintenance can be seen in other communities around the world. Peter Rosenberg reports that although most Germans in Latin America have not maintained the German language, the Mennonite communities in Mexico, Paraguay, and Belize continue to speak German varieties.[10] He also reports that Germans in Russia with a confessional identity tend to continue to speak German, while others have mixed languages or speak mostly Russian.[11] Similarly, the Hutterites in the United States and Canada have maintained their language in a similar fashion as the Amish.[12]

With regard to German emigrant communities that do not differentiate themselves sharply from the mainstream in their adopted country according to religion, three further intertwined aspects influence language and identity in the German diaspora: the forces of language shift, the nature of the German variety, and the nature of the identity that is represented.

Causes of Language Shift in German Diaspora Communities Worldwide

Although the conventional wisdom is that German in the United States began to decline during World War I, when it became associated with the enemy, and that World War II was then the death toll for any remaining German varieties, scholars of German in the United States have shown that this is largely untrue. While it is certainly true that German Americans had to negotiate their identities quite carefully throughout this period, in many communities language shift was already well underway by the advent of World War I.[13] Therefore it is not the case that German Americans constructed their identity through bilingualism until they suddenly had to choose between being German and being American, and would have enacted this change in identity linguistically by shifting to English.

What, then, are the factors that contribute to language shift?[14] Certainly tolerance of linguistic diversity in the country of immigration is not a negligible factor; studies of German in South America often mention the force of nationalization as one that leads to language shift.[15] However, the authors do not argue that nationalization movements were the direct cause of language shift, but rather the argument is that the social climate forced other cultural changes—such as the loss of German schools or bilingual education—that had more direct bearing on language use patterns.

Several factors that favour language maintenance are mentioned frequently in the literature on German diasporas: population density of the ethnic enclave, endogamy, isolation (rural areas being generally more conducive to language maintenance than urban ones), homogeneity of the immigrant community, and the presence of German-language or bilingual institutions (especially schools and churches, but also radio and TV stations, newspapers, etc.).[16] Clearly, these are interrelated factors, some of which may be seen to have causal relationships to others. This listing of factors helps to describe language shift; it does not, however, explain it.

Salmons claims that, in German diaspora communities in the United States, factors external to the German-language enclaves were the catalysts for shift. When control of institutions such as churches and schools began to move from the local to national organisations, the process of language shift also commenced. It has often been noted that minority-language (or bilingual) education is a key aspect of language maintenance;[17] the catalyst for language shift lies in the fact that as these institutions became nationalized, they became English domains, and slowly in the institutions locally and across public domains and private ones.

This position is supported by research on the decline of the German language in the Soviet Union, which Rosenberg (1994) explicitly links to the loss of administrative control over schools and other institutions.[18] Work on the Hutterites of the United States and Canada also supports the idea that language maintenance is linked to local control of various institutions. The Hutterites live in so-called Bruderhöfe, which are communal and insular colonies.[19] Peters's report from the 1970s indicates that they usually have their own school in their colony, which offers literacy instruction in High German in addition to the regular school curriculum. This control over the education of their children is doubtlessly integral to language maintenance.

While Salmons's position is that external factors lead to language shift, he does not claim that loss of the ethnic group language is necessarily tied to loss of ethnic group identity. Tony Waters's work on the maintenance of ethnic group identity presents a different perspective: language shift is seen as a sign of assimilation, which follows the loss of ethnic group solidarity; thus his framework stipulates that ethnic identity and language identity are lost or maintained together.[20] His claim, based on an analysis of data on six German immigrant groups in the United States and Russia, is that ethnic group identity was only maintained when it was essential for the inheritable economic base in the new homeland. Salmons's study suggests that the connection between language and identity can be loosened or cut; while macro-level factors may induce language shift, this does not mean the end of ethnic group identity. In contrast, Waters's study suggests that the bond between language and identity needs to remain intact; he assumes that language shift is a sign of loss of ethnic identity.

While the perspective in Waters's study is intriguing, it does not seem to be supported by the findings of most scholars studying the German diaspora. They describe communities in which ethnic identity remains after the language has been lost. An example is the development of a German club called Wiedergeburt in the Transcarpathian Region (in the present-day Ukraine) after the fall of the Soviet Union, at a point when little German was spoken in this area.[21] Rosenberg states that while there is a high level of language loyalty among Germans in the former Soviet Union, this may mean lip service to the language rather than actual use and maintenance.[22] He echoes Salmons in his claim that the communities in which German was preserved were those that were relatively homogenous and had stable structures within which speakers could continue to use German in public.

Rosenberg's study of German communities in Latin America shows that although the German language is rarely maintained over generations in German settlements in Latin America, contact to Germany is upheld through economic ties, trips back to the old country, and, in some cases, longer stays for continued education.[23] This sustained contact is somewhat unusual in the German diaspora, and is undoubtedly tied to an unrelenting sense of German identity. It does not, however, lead to continued use of German in the Latin American communities; language shift is the norm in these settlements. Similarly, Wilfried Schabus reports little language loyalty among mid nineteenth-century German immigrants to Peru, but the presence of a distinct ethnic identity.[24]

Constructions of Identity in the Diaspora: Ancestry, Trait, and Hybridity

The first question that arises is what exactly German identity, or German American, German Chilean, Volga German identity, etc., encompasses. It is not merely the knowledge of having German ancestors; many people have ancestors from Germany and do not consider themselves members of a social group based on their German ancestry. The reason may in part be frequent identification with much smaller regions than the large nation of Germany. Salmons writes explicitly about this phenomenon in German settlements in Wisconsin, giving the example that people consider themselves not German Americans but "Hessians from Rhine Township in Sheboygan County."[25] This "psychological identity with locality" is a critical and common experience among immigrants, and has direct bearing on how language plays a role in their identity.[26]

Since identity is socially constructed membership in a group or category, the features associated with this group or category, i.e., the cultural norms of the group and the characteristics of its members, are critical to the construction of identity. What traits are claimed by a person who expresses a German identity?

For many, Germanness is associated with a set of characteristics that are seen as distinct from the majority culture, in particular distinct from what are considered negative traits of the mainstream. John M. Coggeshall, in his study of a German American community in southwestern Illinois, found that the traits discussed by members of this group to describe themselves included cleanliness (e.g., keeping one's yard nice and tidy), thriftiness, and liking certain foods.[27] Although folk speech (i.e., an ethnic dialect of English) is mentioned as a trait of German Americans, it is best seen as the means with which this identity is constructed. Further to these traits, Schwarzkopf notes that in the nineteenth century, German immigrants were often credited with bringing classical German culture, such as music and literature, to the United States; thus being German was associated with the characteristic of being cultured and educated.[28] However, traits listed by her twentieth-century informants were primarily cleanliness and being hard-working.

An intriguing study by Katheryn Dietrich examines how the German American population in Fredericksburg, Texas, negotiated its ethnic group identity in the period from 1845 to World War I.[29] One theme that continues throughout this period is the link between German identity and morals. They considered their ability to resolve conflicts with "Indians" as a moral victory linked to their German heritage. They sided with the Union in the Civil War, and, although this alignment set them apart from other Texans, it set them on what they perceived as the moral high ground. In World War I, their patriotic sacrifices were described as due to their German morality. Thus German identity was constructed through moral values, not allegiance to Germany.

Another aspect of the identity construction discussed in Dietrich's study is how German Americans in Fredericksburg constructed a hybrid identity. Although they credited their success with the Native Americans to German morals, their frontier experience was quintessentially American. Their allegiance to the Union during the Civil War reinforced their position as Americans. In peacetime, they celebrated the Fourth of July, the day of U.S. independence, with German folk music and dancing. Little is said about language in this study, but other research done in this area reveals that German is still used by some elderly speakers in Fredericksburg today and bilingualism remained part of the German American tradition in Fredericksburg.[30]

Another study that exemplifies a hybrid identity is Ulrike Ziebur's study of a German community in the Llanquihue Region of Chile.[31] The people in this study describe themselves as Chileans of German descent, which emphasizes their Chilean identity while acknowledging German ethnicity. While Ziebur reports a strong identification with their German heritage and subgroup, German proficiency is claimed by only 39 percent of those surveyed, and the primary interlocutors are parents and grandparents, meaning the language is unlikely to be passed on. In this case, German identity is not constructed through the German language. The German population is well integrated; many of those self-identifying as Chileans of German descent have only one parent who is of German ancestry. However, they define Germanness according to a set of traits that they see as distinct from mainstream Chilean culture—Germans are hard-working, punctual, responsible, and orderly. Significantly, they also see their identity as Chileans of German descent as distinct from Germans in Germany, whom they describe as direct, hard, or strict; they describe themselves as more social, open, and friendly.

Finally, another issue that arises in German identity construction is racialized ethnicity. In the United States, early German immigrants often melted into the ethnically more neutral self-image of "old stock," which could include other European Americans, but the racial implications of this term clearly distinguished them from African Americans.[32] In Namibia, the racial aspect of German identity was even more apparent and explicit. Settlements began in 1884 when Germany occupied Namibia and, although many left in 1919 when Namibia became a mandate of the League of Nations, a settlement of some thousands has remained. Research from the 1990s describes German schools and use of the language in school, church, family, and friendship domains, indicating a robust German identity.[33] The link between whiteness and German identity was firmly established by the early twentieth century, and children born of the (illegal) union of a (white) German and a (black) African were denied an entry in German birth registries by a 1908 Berlin law. However, racialized ethnicity does not necessarily mean that whiteness is used for a group to align with other white groups. In some cases, language is used to draw boundaries between racialized social groups. Despite widespread trilingualism in German, English, and Afrikaans, the German language is used by (white) Germans in Namibia as a symbolic tool for maintaining their positions of power in society, and separates them from white South Africans.[34] The identity of Germans in Namibia as "Südwester" is in many ways a hybrid one, stressing both their Germany identity and their sense of belonging in southwest Africa, even though they cannot be said to be integrated into Namibian society. Similar to the Fredericksburg Germans in Texas, their identity is tied to both their German heritage and their experience in the diaspora.

The Role of the German Variety for Identity Construction

Different dialects of German, particularly High and Low German dialects, are often mutually unintelligible (to the extent that one can speak of intelligibility in binary terms). It is sometimes reported that dialect differences contribute to language shift, i.e., that German speakers in the United States will speak English to each other if their German varieties come from different areas.[35] However, Schwarzkopf indicates that the majority of speakers in her study of three communities in Wisconsin reported that most German speakers spoke Standard German in addition to their High or Low German dialect.[36] Standard German, and not English, was thus often used for communication across dialect groups. A similar situation is described by Werner Bausenhart for the Mennonites in Ontario, a group made up of those who went to Ontario via Pennsylvania and spoke Pennsylvania German (a High German variety), and those who immigrated to Canada via the Ukraine and Paraguay, bringing a Low German dialect with them. As with Schwarzkopf's study, these Mennonites also used a German variety for in-group interaction instead of English, presumably to distinguish themselves symbolically from the English-speaking mainstream.

While of course there are real and sometimes major linguistic differences between dialects, I suggest that differences in identity between groups in contact also contribute to the inability to communicate in their different German varieties. Groups who do not see themselves as Germans but as Mecklenburgers and Swabians will have little motivation to pool linguistic resources. Instead, they will interact with the other German minority group the way they would with any other non-German social group, i.e., in the language of the majority. This assumption is based on what is known about dialect levelling, i.e., the convergence of different dialects, which takes place when groups are in contact.[37] Thus when dialect levelling does not occur, distinct social grouping plays a role.

Conclusion: Language and Identity in the Diaspora

A review of German enclaves in the diaspora has shown that not all of those who claim German identity use the German language. While language is a convenient group marker, it is not easy to maintain, and depends on more than group identity. Although the final word about what causes language shift has not been spoken, it is clear that minority language use in the public is critical. Language maintenance is not necessary for a distinct social group identity to persist, but the reverse is true: without a distinct group identity, a minority language will not be maintained. As the Pennsylvania German example has shown, the identity need not be an explicitly German one; in fact, religious group identity has been shown to be more effective for language maintenance than ethnic group identity.

When a distinct German identity remains in the diaspora, the cultural traits that are associated with this group vary across communities and times. Some view Germanness as an indication of cleanliness and order, others as a badge of education and cultural knowledge or superior morality. It seems that in all cases, having ancestors from some German-language area in Europe is necessary to claim a German identity, but in many communities those with only one German-heritage parent or grandparent may still proudly consider themselves German and be an accepted member of a German community.

Moreover, not everyone who uses German is constructing the same type of social identity. The major reason for this is that German identity is no one entity, be it in Germany, in Canada, in Namibia, or in Brazil. Being German does not always mean love of good bread and beer any more than it always means a fondness for neat front gardens or classical music. In the diaspora, Germanness is a hybrid entity—individuals have identities that are German American, Russian German, Chilean of German descent, and so on. This hybridity is at the core of the German diaspora experience. Interestingly, it is this hybridity that ties the diaspora to present-day Germany: as Germany becomes the diaspora for emigrants from so many different parts of the whole world, for diaspora groups, such as *Russlanddeutsche,* it is increasingly becoming the case that Germany's population is characterized by hybrid identities, which raises new and interesting questions about language and identity both in the diaspora and in Germany itself.

Notes

1 Hoerder, "German Language Diasporas," 8–9.
2 Kroskrity, "Identity," 111.
3 The term "Pennsylvania German" somewhat mislabels these speakers: Anabaptists have moved on to secondary communities, particularly in the midwestern United States, and to tertiary communities—communities made up of people who have moved out of secondary communities—as well as to settlements in new regions such as South Carolina, Texas, and Georgia.

4 Louden, "Minority-Language Maintenance," 134.
5 Kopp, *Phonology of Pennsylvania German English.*
6 Bausch, "In Other Words"; Huffines, "Dying by Convergence?"; Huffines, "Case Usage"; Louden, "Variation in Pennsylvania German Syntax"; Louden, "Minority-Language Maintenance."
7 Louden, "Pennsylvania German."
8 Johnson-Wiener, "Community Identity."
9 Fuller, "Sociopragmatic Values."
10 Rosenberg, "Deutsche Minderheiten."
11 Rosenberg, "Varietätenkontakt und Varietätenausgleich."
12 Peters, "Hutterites," 127.
13 Salmons, "Community, Region, and Language Shift"; Schwarzkopf, *Deutsch als Muttersprache.*
14 Complicating the issue of what causes language shift is the lack of definition of what it means to know or use a language. It is not the case that speakers either speak a language or do not; there are many gradations between mastery of a language and no knowledge of it, and many ways to use a language that do not require constant or even fully competent production.
15 Bärnert-Fürst, "Conservation and Displacement Processes."
16 Louden, "Minority-Language Maintenance"; Salmons, "Language Shift in German-Speaking Wisconsin."
17 See, for example, Clyne, "What Can We Learn from Sprachinseln?"; Pauwels, "Swabian Speech Communities"; Bongart, "Deutsch in Ontario ii."
18 Rosenberg, "Varietätenkontakt und Varietätenausgleich."
19 Peters, "Hutterites."
20 Waters, "Towards a Theory."
21 Melika, "Spracherhaltung."
22 Rosenberg, "Deutsche Minderheiten."
23 Rosenberg, "Varietätenkontakt und Varietätenausgleich."
24 Schabus, "Beobachtungen zu Sprachkontakt."
25 Salmons, "Language Shift in German-Speaking Wisconsin," 170.
26 Warren, "The Community in America," qtd. in Salmons, "Language Shift in German-Speaking Wisconsin," 170.
27 Coggeshall, "One of Those Intangibles."
28 Schwarzkopf, "Beobachtungen zu Sprachkontakt," 28, 305.
29 Dietrich, "Nexus of American Ethnicity and Patriotism."
30 Gilbert, *Linguistic Atlas,* "English Loanwords."
31 Ziebur, "Die soziolinguistische Situation."
32 Luebke, Book Review.
33 Gretschel, "Status and Use of the German Language."
34 Pütz, "'Südwesterdeutsch' in Namibia."
35 See Johnson-Wiener, "Community Identity," for a discussion of this among Old Order Amish community members in Norfolk, Virginia; see Coggeshall, "One of Those Intangibles," for a discussion of attitudes of High and Low German speakers in southwestern Illinois.
36 Schwarzkopf, *Deutsch also Muttersprache,* 148.
37 See Schabus, "Beobachtungen zu Sprachkontakt," for a discussion of Rheinländisch and Tirolisch dialect levelling in Peru; see Rosenberg, "Varietätenkontakt," on German dialects among Russian Germans.

Works Cited

Bärnert-Fürst, Ute. "Conservation and Displacement Processes of the German Language in the Speech Community of Panambi, Rio Grande do Sul, Brazil." In S*prachinselforschung. Eine Gedenkschrift für Hugo Jedig*, edited by Nina Berend and Klaus J. Mattheier, 273–87. Frankfurt: Peter Lang, 1994.

Bausch, Karl-Heinz. "'In Other Words—Now How Do You Say That in English?': Observations on Pennsylvania German Today." *Sprachreport* 4 (1997): 1–6.

Bausenhart, Werner. "Deutsch in Ontario. I. Toronto und Ottawa; Deutsch bei den Mennoniten." In *Deutsch als Muttersprache in Kanada. Berichte zur Gegenwartslage. Deutsche Sprache in Europa und Übersee: Berichte und Forschung, Band 1*, edited by Leopold Auburger, Heinz Kloss, and Heinz Rupp, 15–24. Wiesbaden: Franz Steiner Verlag, 1977.

Bongart, Klaus. "Deutsch in Ontario II: Deutsch Sprache und Kultur in Kitchener-Waterloo." In *Deutsch als Muttersprache in Kanada. Berichte zur Gegenwarstlage. Deutsche Sprache in Europa und Übersee: Berichte und Forschung, Band 1*, edited by Leopold Auburger, Heinz Kloss, and Heinz Rupp, 25–32. Wiesbaden: Franz Steiner Verlag, 1977.

Clyne, Michael. "What Can We Learn from Sprachinseln? Some Observations on 'Australian German.'" In S*prachinselforschung. Eine Gedenkschrift für Hugo Jedig*, edited by Nina Berend and Klaus J. Mattheier, 105–22. Frankfurt: Peter Lang, 1994.

Coggeshall, John M. "'One of Those Intangibles': The Manifestation of Ethnic Identity in Southwestern Illinois." *Journal of American Folklore* 99, no. 392 (1986): 177–207.

Dietrich, Katheryn. "The Nexus of American Ethnicity and Patriotism." Paper presented at the annual meeting of the American Sociological Association, 14 August 2004. <www.allacademic.com/meta/p109514_index.html> (March 2008).

Fuller, Janet M. "The Sociopragmatic Values of Pennsylvania German ('Dutch'): Changes Across Time, Place, and Anabaptist Sect." In *ISB4: Proceedings of the 4th International Symposium on Bilingualism*, edited by James Cohen, Kara T. McAlister, Kelli Rolstad, and Jeff MacSwan, 800–07. Somerville, MA: Cascadilla Press, 2005.

Gilbert, Glen G. "English Loanwords in the German of Fredericksburg, Texas." *American Speech* 40 (1965): 102–12.

———. *Linguistic Atlas of Texas German*. Austin: University of Texas Press, 1972.

Gretschel, Hans-Volker. "The Status and Use of the German Language in Independent Namibia: Can German Survive the Transition?" In *Discrimination through Language in Africa? Perspectives on the Namibian Experience*, edited by Martin Pütz, 299–313. Berlin: Mouton de Gruyter, 1995.

Hoerder, Dirk. "The German-Language Diasporas: A Survey, Critique, and Interpretation." *Diaspora* 11, no. 1 (2002): 7–44.

Huffines, Marion Lois. "Case Usage among the Pennsylvania German Sectarians and Nonsectarians." In *Investigating Obsolescence: Studies in Language Contraction and Death*, edited by Nancy C. Dorian, 211–26. New York: Cambridge University Press, 1989.

————. "Dying by Convergence? Pennsylvania German and Syntactic Change." In *The German Language in America, 1683–1991*, edited by Joseph Salmons, 250–63. Madison, WI: Max Kade Institute for German-American Studies, 1993.

Johnson-Wiener, Karen. "Community Identity and Language Change in North American Anabaptist Communities." *Journal of Sociolinguistics* 2, no. 3 (1998): 375–94.

Kopp, Achim. *The Phonology of Pennsylvania German English as Evidence of Language Maintenance and Shift.* Selinsgrove, PA: Susquehanna University Press, 1999.

Kroskrity, Paul V. "Identity." *Journal of Linguistic Anthropology* 9 (1999): 111–14.

Louden, Mark. "Variation in Pennsylvania German Syntax: A Diachronic Perspective." In *Proceedings of the International Congress of Dialectologists in Bamberg, Germany, Volume 2: Historical Dialectology and Linguistic Change*, edited by Wolfgang Viereck, 169–79. Stuttgart: Franz Steiner Verlag, 1993.

————. "Minority-Language Maintenance 'by Inertia': Pennsylvania German among Nonsectarian Speakers." In *"Standardfragen." Festschrift für Klaus J. Mattheier zum 60 Geburtstag*, edited by Jannis Androutsopoulos and Evelyn Ziegler, 121–37. Frankfurt: Peter Lang, 2003.

————. "Pennsylvania German in the Twenty-First Century." In *Sprachinselnwelten— The World of Language Islands*, edited by Nina Berend and Elisabeth Knipf-Komlósi. Frankfurt: Peter Lang, 2006.

Luebke, Frederick. Review of *Becoming Old Stock: The Paradox of German American Identity*, by Russell A. Kazal. *Journal of American History* 92, no. 1 (2005): 251–52.

Melika, Georg. "Spracherhaltung und Sprachwechsel bei der deutschen Minderheit von Transkarpatien." In S*prachinselforschung. Eine Gedenkschrift für Hugo Jedig*, edited by Nina Berend and Klaus J. Mattheier, 289–301. Frankfurt: Peter Lang, 1994.

Pauwels, Anne. "Swabian Speech Communities in Melbourne: A Sociolinguistic Discussion." In S*prachinselforschung. Eine Gedenkschrift für Hugo Jedig*, edited by Nina Berend and Klaus J. Mattheier, 205–20. Frankfurt: Peter Lang, 1994.

Peters, Victor. "The Hutterites." *Deutsche Sprache in Europa und Übersee.* Volume 1. Wiesbaden: Franz Steiner Verlag, 1977.

Pütz, Martin. "'Südwesterdeutsch' in Namibia: Sprachpolitik, Sprachplanung und Spracherhalt." *Linguistische Berichte* 136 (1991): 455–67.

Rosenberg, Peter. "Varietätenkontakt und Varietätenausgleich bei den Russlanddeutschen: Orientierungen für eine moderne Sprachinselforschung." In *Sprachinselforschung. Eine Gedenkschrift für Hugo Jedig*, edited by Nina Berend and Klaus J. Mattheier, 123–64. Frankfurt: Peter Lang, 1994.

————. "Deutsche Minderheiten in Lateinamerika." In *Particulae particularum. Festschrift zum 60 Geburtstag von Harald Weydt*, edited by Theo Harden and Elke Hentschel, 261–91. Tübingen: Stauffenburg, 1998.

Salmons, Joseph. "Community, Region, and Language Shift in German-Speaking Wisconsin." In *Regionalism in the Age of Globalism: Volume 2: Forms of Region-*

alism, edited by Lothar Hönnighausen, Marc Frey, James Peacock, and Niklaus Steiner, 167–82. Madison: Center for the Study of Upper Midwestern Cultures, 2005.

Schabus, Wilfried. "Beobachtungen zu Sprachkontakt, Varietätenausgleich, Sprachloyalität und Sprachwechsel in Poxuxu (Peru) und bei den 'Ländlern' in Siebenbürgen." In S*prachinselforschung: Eine Gedenkschrift für Hugo Jedig,* edited by Nina Berend and Klaus J. Mattheier, 221–62. Frankfurt: Peter Lang, 1994.

Schwarzkopf, Christa. *Deutsch als Muttersprache in den Vereinigten Staaten, Teil III: German Americans, Die sprachliche Assimilation der Deutschen in Wisconsin.* Stuttgart: Franz Steiner Verlag, 1987.

Warren, Roland. *The Community in America.* Chicago: Rand-McNally, 1978. Quoted in Joseph Salmons, "Community, Region, and Language Shift in German-Speaking Wisconsin." In *Regionalism in the Age of Globalism: Volume 2: Forms of Regionalism,* edited by Lothar Hönnighausen, Marc Frey, James Peacock, and Niklaus Steiner, 167–82. Madison: Center for the Study of Upper Midwestern Cultures, 2005.

Waters, Tony. "Towards a Theory of Ethnic Identity and Migration: The Formation of Ethnic Identity by Migrant Germans in Russia and North America." *International Migration Review* 29, no. 2 (1995): 515–44.

Ziebur, Ulrike. "Die soziolinguistische Situation von Chilenen deutscher Abstammung." *Linguistik Online* 7 (2000). <www.linguistik-online.de/3_00/ziebur .html> (March 2008).

THREE

Language and the Negotiation of Identities among German-speaking Diasporic Communities in Central Europe

Patrick Stevenson
Jenny Carl

This chapter develops recent work in linguistic anthropology on language ideologies and the negotiation of identities in a study of the language biographies of German speakers in central Europe. Based on interviews conducted in 1995 and 2005 with three generations of German speakers in Hungary and the Czech Republic, it focuses on the analysis of the participants' formulated responses to the changing positions of German speakers in these two countries. Using the framework of positioning theory, the chapter explores the relationship between individual narratives and the changing public discourses surrounding their telling on the one hand and their points of reference on the other: how do individual speakers position themselves and others by drawing on their experiences with language in the present and in the past? By investigating speakers' (re-)evaluations of their language repertoires, this analysis reveals a more complex and differentiated set of representations than is often proposed through generalized categories such as language maintenance and shift. It aims to show the complexity and instability of relationships between different varieties of the German language and ethnicity and how different processes of identification are manifested in the participants' narratives.

Introduction

THE RESHAPING OF CENTRAL EUROPEAN space in the years after 1989 and the transformation of the region's political economy have led to the "recontextualization" of the relationship between ethnolinguistic minorities and majority communities.[1] This chapter draws from an extensive study involving more than seventy interviews conducted in 1995 and 2005 in six locations in Hungary and the Czech Republic in order to explore what it means today to be a "German speaker" in a context of double marginalization (in relation to the majority Magyar and Czech populations on the one hand, and to German and Austrian citizens in the neighbouring "mother lands" on the other). These interviews constitute, in part, "language biographies," in which individuals reflect on their experiences with language in relation to salient moments in their lives.[2] The aims in this chapter are, first, to show how language becomes relevant to individuals in the course of conversations in which they (inter)actively develop a sense of self by constructing narrative accounts of their own and their families' lives and, second, to investigate how they position their "selves" in relation to others in the present and to their selves in the past.

Theoretical and Conceptual Orientation

A growing body of literature on the relationship between language and ethnicity is devoted to attempts to mediate between macro and micro levels of analysis by exploring ways in which changes in social and political conditions are refracted through personal experience and emerge in individual narratives as expressions of personal (re)alignment in relation to time and place. Much of this work has been concerned with the elaboration of theoretical perspectives on the evaluation and representation of language clustered under the conceptual umbrella of "language ideologies,"[3] which have been defined variously as, for example, "sets of beliefs about language articulated by users as a rationalization or justification of perceived language structure and use"[4] and "the cultural system of ideas about social and linguistic relationships, together with their loading of moral and political interests."[5] Common to such definitions is the contention that views about language are not just shared among members of a community but are organized as a point of reference around which people build moral and social judgments. Focusing on ideas about linguistic differentiation and ways in which these are reflected in understandings of particular language users, Judith Irvine and Susan Gal develop this argument by identifying specific semiotic processes through which language ideologies function, two of which—iconization and erasure— are particularly relevant to the present discussion.[6] Iconization is a process by which an indexical relationship between a particular linguistic feature or variety and its users is transformed so that the linguistic form is perceived as an iconic representation of the social group that uses it (for example, the iconization in which for many Germans before 1989 Sächsisch came to be not merely indexical of certain East Germans but an iconic representation of the social conditions and political relations in the German Democratic Republic [GDR]). Erasure involves "simplifying the sociolinguistic field" so that people or (socio)linguistic features or practices are rendered invisible: "Facts that are inconsistent with the ideological scheme either go unnoticed or get explained away. So, for example, a social group or a language may be imagined as homogeneous, its internal variation disregarded."[7]

This work on language ideology also underlies recent poststructuralist studies on the negotiation of identities in multilingual contexts.[8] Aneta Pavlenko and Adrian Blackledge argue that "in multilingual settings, language choice and attitudes are inseparable from political arrangements, relations of power, language ideologies, and interlocutors' views of their own and others' identities" and assert that "in post-modern societies ... languages may not only be 'markers of identity' but also sites of resistance, empowerment, solidarity, or discrimination."[9] The studies in their volume adopt a broad conceptualization of "positioning theory."[10] Positioning is a discursive process, through which participants situate themselves and others in relation to particular subject positions that are made available within specific discourses. Bronwyn Davies and Rom Harré define subject positions as entailing a personal act of locating our self in terms of our own "subjective lived histories."[11] In the course of conversational interaction, individuals adopt a subject position and see the world "in terms of the particular images, metaphors, story lines and concepts which are made relevant within the particular discursive practice in which they are positioned."[12]

Pavlenko and Blackledge further argue that positioning (whether of the self or of others) may be subject to contestation or negotiation, either between or "within" individuals, and that the process of positioning is always contingent on the social and historical conditions in which it occurs. They propose three types of identity that positioning may give rise to under different circumstances: "*imposed identities* (which are not negotiable in a particular time and place), *assumed identities* (which are accepted and not negotiated), and *negotiable identities* (which are contested by groups and individuals)."[13]

Our interest here is in how individuals use linguistic categories (whether applied to linguistic forms, such as Deutsch, Muttersprache, or Schwäbisch, or to their users, as in Ungarndeutsche[r] or Schwob) discursively to position themselves and others as well as to contest or reject ways in which others position them and to deny ways in which others position themselves. The chapter will focus on the biographical or autobiographical location of speakers' selves in the context of social and historical conditions that make various (ethnic) identifications *possible* through the (self-)allocation to a group on the basis of language knowledge or use, where this may or may not be considered *desirable*. The issue, then, is not simply whether individuals are or are not "German speakers," but rather whether or not they position themselves as such and, furthermore, whether or not this self-attribution is contingent on the perceived validity of specific ethnic categories.[14]

Being a German Speaker in Central Europe

Interviewed in 1995, participants in both Hungary and the Czech Republic (especially members of the older generation) frequently highlighted the impact of the hostile social conditions under which German speakers lived in the postwar years. Frau B., in example 1, was born in Budapest during the war and recalls the political consequences of positioning oneself as an Ungarndeutsche(r).

EXAMPLE 1

Durch die politischen Ereignisse werden sich nie so viele bekanntgeben, wie sie wirklich da sind [d.h. Ungarndeutsche], auch heute nicht … Eben diese schlimmen Erfahrungen mit der Volkszählung 1941 hat so tiefe Spuren hinterlassen, dass die Leute es nie wieder tun werden, sich bloßlegen.

In the 1941 census, people were required for the first time not only to declare their mother tongue but also their nationality, so that "not only the counting itself, but also the political activity preceding it, had the effect of forcing a change in respondents' understanding of what it meant to be speaking a language … Language choice was no longer a local matter, but one with much broader political significance."[15] The census data were used as the basis for drawing up deportation lists after the war and for Frau B. this politicization of the relationship between language and ethnicity entails a form of imposed identity that members of this community accepted at their peril.

The question of language use is explicit in the story of Frau M., who was born in Prague in 1933 to a Czech German father and a Czech Austrian mother (her parents were divorced in 1938 and she did not see her father again). After the war, her mother initially continued to speak German with her but gradually switched to speaking Czech, a decision which Frau M. explains in the following way.

EXAMPLE 2

Wissen Sie, meine Mutter hatte solche panische Angst gehabt, es kann einen Augenblick kommen, wo jemand kommen kann und kann sie in ein Lager nehmen. Es war schreckliche Zeit … Ich durfte nicht Matura machen, nicht nur weil ich Deutsche

war, sondern weil wir wohnten in eigenem Zinshaus, und eine
Hausmeisterin hat geschrieben in meine Schule, dass wir
Bourgeoisie sind, dass wir arbeiterklassefeindlich sind, und ich
durfte nicht Matura machen.

Since the subject position "German-speaking Czech" appears not to
have been available in the prevailing political discourse in postwar Czechoslovakia, her mother's strategy of self-censorship in no longer speaking German to her daughter seems to have been an attempt to resist being positioned as an undesirable other and to position herself instead as a Czech
through speaking Czech.[16]

Although the German population of Czechoslovakia was radically
reduced through deportations in the postwar years, residual pockets of German speakers remained but with low visibility and no formal status as a recognized minority group. Herr S., a seventy-five-year-old man interviewed
in 2005, talks about the impossibility of establishing a German-medium
school after the war, even though there were sufficient numbers to make
this feasible.

EXAMPLE 3

Wie überhaupt wir nie als Minderheit anerkannt wurden, die
deutsche Sprache war sozusagen tabu und die Existenz der
deutschen Minderheit ist immer umstritten worden. Auch
schon in den Verträgen zwischen der DDR und der Tschechoslowakei ... ist immer gesagt worden, das Problem existiert nicht
mehr, gibt's nicht mehr ... Da war alle Minderheiten, waren die
Minderheitenrechte zuerkannt, in Schulbildung, in Religion
und dergleichen mehr, nur die Deutschen waren ganz einfach
nicht präsent. [To his daughter:] Na, was hast du mit der
deutschen Sprache zu tun? (Alle lachen.)

Herr S. not only collocates the (German) minority and the German language in his narrative, but he also associates the silencing of the language
with the denial of the existence of a German minority. His ironic quip to
his daughter, who obviously speaks German, suggests that, while the capacity to speak the language may have been transmitted to individual members of her generation, this was not sufficient to sustain the political presence of an entire German community. Where German survived within
the family under these conditions, it has often been only in the form of
fragments associated with particular domestic practices. Herr L., a sev-
enty-year-old man, is married to a Czech woman and has three children,
all of whom acquired some knowledge of German through his mother, but
only "words," not "a language."

EXAMPLE 4

Das sind noch so Begriffe ja, wenn die Großmutter gesagt hat „anziehen" oder so, aber das [ist] keine Sprache. Das ist, würde ich sagen, typisch. Das ist bei anderen Familien auch so, drum sag ich ja als Muttersprache ist das mit uns [i.e., with his generation] zu Ende.

However, like Frau M.'s mother in example 2, other Czech Germans of that generation actively contributed to the erasure of this aberrant category by speaking only Czech with their children and making no reference to their German background. Herr P., for example, was born in Prague in 1974 and began to learn German only when he started university in 1992. Interviewed three years later, he said:

EXAMPLE 5

Mein Vater hat mir erst vor drei Jahren gesagt, daß ich deutsch-stämmig bin, weil er wollte nicht, dass ich die Probleme habe. Weil er selbst konnte nicht z.B. an der Hochschule studieren, weil er Deutscher war... Mein Großvater ist im Konzentrations-lager gestorben, aber als Deutscher. Meine Großmutter konnte hier bleiben und sie haßte die Deutschen. (Interviewer: War sie Tschechin?) Nein, auch Deutsche. Und sie wollte nicht, meinen Vater Deutsch zu lernen, weil hier waren schlechte Bedingun-gen für Leute und sie war nicht sicher, wollte mein Vater schon emigrieren... Ich wohne in einem sehr kommunistischen Dorf, und mein Vater hat vor zehn Jahren eine sehr schöne[?] gebaut, und da kamen viele anonyme Briefe, daß er in Hitler-Jugend war, aber er war vier Jahre alt, nach dem Weltkrieg.

The use (or avoidance) of German in Herr P.'s family seems to be strongly associated with particular places and institutions. Being "German" had prevented his father from studying at university and in order to protect his son from similar problems he not only brought him up monolingually but even concealed his German ethnicity. His grandmother had also seen a threat in the possibility of her son learning German, but in this case apparently because it might have given him the opportunity to leave the country in search of a better life. However, although the family stayed in Czechoslovakia, even their radical efforts at assimilatory denial of their Germanness appear not to have been sufficient to shield them, in their "very communist village," from accusations of having a fascist past.

In the interviews conducted in 2005, especially with younger participants, the iconic associations of German with the fascist past still appear but are now more often in an attenuated form. Herr Z., for example, is in his late thirties and grew up in Pécs, in southern Hungary, first as a monolingual German dialect speaker, before being required to learn Hungarian at kindergarten.

EXAMPLE 6

Also ich zuhause Schwäbisch, bis zum Kindergarten habe ich nur Deutsch gekannt [lacht] also Mundart, und dann im Kindergarten, dadurch dass man im—das war noch der Kommunismus [lacht]—dass man da nicht Deutsch sprechen durfte, obwohl alle Kindergärtnerinnen Ungarndeutsche waren, aber offiziell durften sie das nicht machen. Da habe ich in zwei Wochen Ungarisch gelernt [lacht], und bin nach Hause gekommen und habe gesagt „reden wir ordentlich" zu meinen Eltern und Großeltern, weil wir lebten zusammen, und ordentlich hieß auf Ungarisch.

His rather jocular manner, indicated by the frequent (self-)ironic laughter, and the straightforwardly explanatory (almost didactic) narrative mitigate the severity of the image constructed of the young child returning from his nursery school, where his teachers were all Ungarndeutsche, to his parents and grandparents, who spoke German dialect in the home, and declaring that they should "speak properly," by which he meant in Hungarian and not in Standard German. The self-consciously quoted cliché "das war noch der Kommunismus" provides a formulaic historical rationalization of the erasure of German from the classroom, and the transfer to the home domain of the simple message with its condensed import of symbolic subordination is accomplished in the uncomplicated syntax of everyday narrative ("Da habe ich ... und bin nach Hause gekommen und habe gesagt,... und ordentlich hieß ...").

This unproblematized account of language choice within the family belies a process of negotiation that was often fraught with tension and feelings of embarrassment and estrangement induced by differing levels of linguistic competence. Frau F., a young woman in her early twenties interviewed in Hungary in 1995, spent most of her pre-school years with her maternal grandparents, who at that time spoke only German dialect in the home; her mother is bilingual in German dialect and Hungarian, but her father speaks only Hungarian.

EXAMPLE 7

Das führte zu Komplikationen in der Familie und deshalb hat sich meine Mutter entschlossen, daß wir zu Hause Ungarisch lernen ... Weil sie sich vor mir schämt, seitdem ich die Hochsprache lerne, weil sie einfach Angst hat. Sie redet mich in der Mundart an, aber dann kann ich in der Mundart nicht mehr antworten, und das stört sie, dann wechselt sie sofort auf

Hochdeutsch. Sie kann's zwar, sie versucht es, aber sie bleibt nicht bei der Mundart. Meine Großeltern sprechen jetzt auch untereinander nicht mehr die Mundart, weil eben die ungarische Sprache viel leichter ist für sie, weil sie im öffentlichen Leben nur die ungarische Sprache verwenden.

The linguistic ecology of this extended family incorporates three varieties, but the choices individuals make are neither random nor consistent and are associated with conditions that are, at least in part, external to the family. Her younger sister, on the other hand, never spoke German dialect with her grandparents, but is now learning (Standard) German.

EXAMPLE 8

Sie bemüht sich jetzt, weil sie eben nach Deutschland will. Sie versteht zwar sehr viel, aber nicht weil meine Großeltern mit ihr Deutsch gesprochen haben, sondern durch Fernsehen. Sie sieht sehr oft die Satelliten-Programme, also das hat mit der Minderheit nichts mehr zu tun.

While Frau F.'s own socialization was coloured by linguistic patterns that she associates with a Hungarian German ethnicity, she positions her sister as a member of a different category of young Hungarians not learning local German dialect through the traditional means of transmission within the family, but rather learning Standard German through modern, non-local technologies. Her parents, too, now want to learn German (i.e., Standard German—her mother has always been a dialect speaker) and they are now encouraging her to use Standard German with them.

Other participants also show how different options have become available through the changing social and political conditions of the more recent past. Frau C., for example, was born in Berlin in 1962 but moved to Prague as a baby. Her mother is German, her father was Czech, and she had become accustomed to speaking Czech with her mother. By the mid 1990s, though, in her early thirties, she had begun to speak German with her again.

EXAMPLE 9

Anlass dazu war eigentlich diese neue Freundin, die aus Berlin stammt, und dass ich sozusagen wieder mehr zu meiner deutschen Identität zurückgekehrt bin. Das hat mich so beeinflusst, dass ich jetzt mit meiner Mutter auch fast ausschließlich Deutsch spreche.

She attributes her changed conversational practice to a new personal relationship with a woman from Berlin, which seems to have reactivated a dormant sense of Germanness that she conceptualizes in spatial terms, as a "place" where she had once been and to which she has now "returned."[17] Through this experience she reflexively repositions herself as someone with—among other forms of identification—a German identity[18]; adopting this position in turn permits (or even encourages) her to resume speaking German with her mother and thereby to restyle their relationship. After many years of living within an "assumed identity" as a Czech speaker, she is now able to negotiate alternatives for herself, and recalibrating the components of her linguistic repertoire is part of this process: for her, German is now upgraded as a valued variety, but not for instrumental purposes nor for purely local affective reasons.

Asserting the positive value of ties with the past is also often a motivation for policy decisions within families that take them in the opposite direction from those who sought shelter in assimilatory monolingualism. Frau S. in Hungary, for example, says she and her husband (who is also a German speaker), both now in their mid forties, decided to bring their children up bilingually.

EXAMPLE 10

Und unsere Kinder, als sie zur Welt gekommen sind, haben wir gleich besprochen, dass wir möchten, dass sie auch zwei-sprachig sind. Wir möchten diese ganze, unser Geschichte nicht ver- ver- vergessen. Ich denke, soviel bin ich meine Großeltern schuldig, irgendwo ... Und wenn sie manchmal sagen, das ist zu schwer, weil sie muss das auf eine andere Sprache lernen, und das ist manchmal wirklich nicht leicht, dann sage ich ihnen immer, sie sollen das nicht vergessen, dass einmal meine Urgroßmutter, die sie auch gekannt haben, so gesprochen hat damals, und zweitens, dass das sehr wichtig ist heutzutage, über-haupt dass wir in die EU gekommen sind, denke ich, ist das überhaupt wichtig, solche Sprachen zu kennen, wo da in Mitteleuropa Leute, sehr viele Leute reden.

In Frau S.'s narrative, the pragmatic value of bilingualism for her children as citizens of an EU member state is emphatically acknowledged but is only of secondary importance. She identifies and legitimates her parental decision first on personal and moral grounds in terms of a debt owed to her grandparents, and only subsequently as a generalized responsibility toward her children. She recognizes that this imposes a heavy burden on her children but this is outweighed by her sense of bearing a duty to maintain a knowledge of German in the family as a means to securing continuity across the generations. At first, she expresses this desire as a somewhat unfocused wish "not to forget our history," but she then refines this by referring specifically to language and saying how she exhorted her children not to forget that her (their?) great grandmother "used to speak like that in those days."

This curiously non-specific reference to a way of speaking rather than to a language is also symptomatic of ambiguities and contradictions in individual discourses about language among our participants. The variety of German that Frau S.'s children learned in school is the standard form, while the variety spoken by her great grandmother was the local dialect. Therefore, the children were clearly not learning to speak the way their forebears "used to speak." However, the apparent lack of coherence in her story can be understood (if not resolved) in the context of her internal struggle, earlier in the interview, to negotiate her own relationship with the linguistic varieties in her repertoire:

EXAMPLE 11

Normalerweise wäre meine Muttersprache, ich denke, die deutsche Sprache. Schwäbische Sprache gibt's nicht als Sprache, also muss es die deutsche Sprache sein. Weil es ist ganz interessant, das haben sie oft von mir gefragt in meinem Leben, schon als Kind her, wie ist, welche ist deine Muttersprache? Ich eh bis fünf Jahre konnte ich nicht Ungarisch, ich bin in Ungarn gelebt aber ich konnte nicht Ungarisch ... Dann haben sie gefragt, welche habe ich am ersten gesprochen. Am ersten habe ich Schwäbisch gesprochen, also ist meine Muttersprache Deutsch.

Like Herr Z. (example 6), Frau S. grew up monolingual in her local German dialect until she went to kindergarten. But when confronted with the need to categorize the components of her linguistic repertoire, she wrestles with uncomfortable terminology. Her discussion in the interview has a symmetrical pattern, suggesting that this "struggle" is something she has encountered before. The same assertion marks the beginning and end, encompassing a narrative in which she recounts how the recurring question "what is your mother tongue?" has been a motif running through her life. The question evidently constituted a challenge to her that required her to conduct an internal negotiation. The term "mother tongue" is a notoriously intransigent concept;[19] but this is only one part of her difficulty. A more fundamental problem for her lies in determining which linguistic varieties can be accorded the status of "a language."[20] She has evidently internalized the ideology that only certain varieties meet the criteria required for "language" status, although she does not articulate what these might be. At all events, Schwäbisch is "what she spoke first" and is the way she spoke as a young child, but it is not "a language." However, she does see this variety in a dependent relationship with "the German language," because she is able to conclude that "first I spoke Schwäbisch, *therefore* my mother tongue is German."

Conclusions

In this chapter, we have tried to uncover some of the complexity of ways in which individuals position themselves and others by reference to particular linguistic varieties in the context of specific social and historical conditions in Central Europe and in relation to prevailing language ideologies. Drawing on ethnographic interviews conducted in 1995 and 2005 in several locations in Hungary and the Czech Republic with members of different generations, all of whom include at least one form of what they refer to as "German" in their linguistic repertoires, we have explored ways in which experiences with language are articulated in biographical and autobiographical narratives dealing with challenges confronting individuals and their families in periods of social change. While those interviewed typically use the same two moments of social transformation—the years following 1945 and 1989 respectively—as points of orientation in their narratives and common motifs recur, the analysis of individual stories has enabled us to isolate a range of ways in which linguistic forms are represented and evaluated and how these narrative practices function in the process of accepting, resisting, and negotiating forms of identification or social categorization.

This project is supported by a Research Grant from the UK Arts and Humanities Research Council.

Notes

1 See especially Gal, "Codeswitching," "Cultural Bases," "Diversity," and "Migration."
2 See, for example, Nekvapil, "Language Biographies."
3 Blommaert, *Language Ideological Debates, Discourse*; Gal and Woolard, *Languages and Publics*; Irvine and Gal, "Language Ideology and Linguistic Differentiation"; Schieffelin, Woolard, and Kroskrity, *Language Ideologies*; Woolard and Schieffelin, "Language Ideology."
4 Silverstein, "Language Structure," 193.
5 Irvine, "When Talk Isn't Cheap," 255.
6 Irvine and Gal, "Language Ideology and Linguistic Differentiation," 35–39.
7 Irvine and Gal, "Language Ideology and Linguistic Differentiation," 38.
8 See, for example, Pavlenko and Blackledge, *Negotiation of Identities*, and Meinhof and Galasiński, *Language of Belonging*.
9 Pavlenko and Blackledge, "Introduction," 1, 4.
10 Davies and Harré, "Positioning and Personhood."
11 Davies and Harré, "Positioning and Personhood," 41–42.
12 Davies and Harré, "Positioning and Personhood," 35.

13 Pavlenko and Blackledge, "Introduction," 20–21.
14 See also Giampapa, "Politics of Identity," on Italian Canadians in Toronto.
15 Gal, "Diversity," 345.
16 See Nekvapil, "On Non-Self-Evident Relationships."
17 See Gal, "Migration, Minorities, and Multilingualism."
18 See Moghaddam, "Reflexive Positioning."
19 See, for example, Mills, "Mothers and Mother Tongue."
20 See Gal, "Migration, Minorities, and Multilingualism." ·

Interview Sources

The data in this chapter are taken from nine interviews conducted by the authors in 1995 and 2005 in several locations in Hungary and the Czech Republic (Budapest, Pécs, Sopron, Prague, and Ústí nad Labem). Original recordings are in the possession of the authors.

Works Cited

Blommaert, Jan, ed. *Language Ideological Debates.* Berlin: Mouton de Gruyter, 1999.

Blommaert, Jan. *Discourse: A Critical Introduction.* Cambridge: Cambridge University Press, 2005.

Davies, Bronwyn, and Rom Harré. "Positioning and Personhood." In *Positioning Theory: Moral Contexts of Intentional Action,* edited by Rom Harré and Luk van Langenhove, 32–52. Oxford: Blackwell Publishing, 1999.

Gal, Susan. "Codeswitching and Consciousness in the European Periphery." *American Ethnologist* 14, no. 4 (1987): 637–53.

———. "Cultural Bases of Language Use amongst German-speakers in Hungary." *International Journal of the Sociology of Language* 111 (1995): 3–102.

———. "Diversity and Contestation in Linguistic Ideologies: German Speakers in Hungary." *Language in Society* 22, no. 3 (1993): 337–59.

———. "Migration, Minorities, and Multilingualism: Language Ideologies in Europe." In *Language Ideologies, Policies, and Practices: Language and the Future of Europe,* edited by Clare Mar-Molinero and Patrick Stevenson, 13–27. Basingstoke: Palgrave, 2006.

Gal, Susan, and Kathryn Woolard, eds. *Languages and Publics: The Making of Authority.* Manchester: St. Jerome, 2001.

Giampapa, Frances. "The Politics of Identity, Representation, and the Discourses of Self-Identification: Negotiating the Periphery and the Center." In *Negotiation of Identities in Multilingual Contexts,* edited by Aneta Pavlenko and Adrian Blackledge, 192–218. Clevedon: Multilingual Matters, 2004.

Irvine, Judith. "When Talk Isn't Cheap." *American Ethnologist* 16, no. 2 (1989): 248–67.

Irvine, Judith, and Susan Gal. "Language Ideology and Linguistic Differentiation." In *Regimes of Language: Ideologies, Polities, and Identities,* edited by Paul Kroskrity, 35–83. Santa Fe, NM: School of American Research Press, 2000.

Meinhof, Ulrike Hanna, and Dariusz Galasiński. *The Language of Belonging.* Basingstoke: Palgrave, 2005.

Mills, Jean. "Mothers and Mother Tongue: Perspectives on Self-Construction by Mothers of Pakistani Heritage." In *Negotiation of Identities in Multilingual Contexts,* edited by Aneta Pavlenko and Adrian Blackledge, 161–91. Clevedon: Multilingual Matters, 2004.

Moghaddam, Fathali. "Reflexive Positioning: Culture and Private Discourse." In *Positioning Theory: Moral Contexts of Intentional Action,* edited by Rom Harré and Luk van Langenhove, 74–86. Oxford: Blackwell Publishing, 1999.

Nekvapil, Jirí. "Language Biographies and the Analysis of Language Situations: On the Life of the German Community in the Czech Republic." *International Journal of the Sociology of Language* 162 (2003): 63–83.

———. "On Non-Self-Evident Relationships between Language and Ethnicity: How Germans Do Not Speak German, and Czechs Do Not Speak Czech." *Multilingua* 19, no. 1–2 (2000): 37–53.

Pavlenko, Aneta, and Adrian Blackledge. "New Theoretical Approaches to the Study of Negotiation of Identities in Multilingual Contexts." Introduction. In *Negotiation of Identities in Multilingual Contexts,* edited by Aneta Pavlenko and Adrian Blackledge, 1–33. Clevedon: Multilingual Matters, 2004.

Pavlenko, Aneta, and Adrian Blackledge, eds. *Negotiation of Identities in Multilingual Contexts.* Clevedon: Multilingual Matters, 2004.

Schieffelin, Bambi, Kathryn Woolard, and Paul Kroskrity, eds. *Language Ideologies: Practice and Theory.* New York: Oxford University Press, 1998.

Silverstein, Michael. "Language Structure and Linguistic Ideology." In *The Elements,* edited by Paul R. Clyne, William F. Hanks, and Carol L. Hofbauer, 193–247. Chicago: Chicago Linguistic Society, 1979.

Woolard, Kathryn, and Bambi Schieffelin. "Language Ideology." *Annual Review of Anthropology* 23 (1994): 55–82.

FOUR

German-speaking Swiss in Australia
Typical Swiss, Model Immigrants, or a Sonderfall *Abroad?*

Doris Schüpbach

This chapter explores how fifteen immigrants to Australia from German-speaking Switzerland relate their migratory experience of building a new life in a different language. The analysis of written and oral life-story data focuses on two aspects: First, the language practices and attitudes discussed show that the linear pattern of language and identity construction in German-speaking Switzerland is superseded by a much more complex and more varied pattern in Australia. Second, an examination of how the participants use language to make sense of their lives reveals a number of shared stories that connect the individual to the larger social, cultural, and historical contexts. The Swiss myth of *Sonderfall* is identified as unifying many shared stories. The participants present themselves as exceptional Swiss while retaining the notion of Switzerland as a *Sonderfall* and as exceptional immigrants in Australia without aligning themselves completely with the Anglo-Australian mainstream.

Introduction

PEOPLE OF SWISS GERMAN BACKGROUND are a very small, mostly unnoticed group in Australia,[1] Most twentieth-century emigrants left Switzerland of their own free will rather than out of economic or political necessity. They are usually well integrated into the host society. Their diverse language background makes them particularly interesting to language and identity research. They come from the German-speaking part of an officially multilingual country, where a diglossic situation prevails, i.e., where the use of languages and language varieties is tied to specific functions and contexts. Swiss German immigrants can be seen as a distinct subgroup within the German speech community in Australia, where German prevails as a significant language, in terms of numbers of immigrant speakers as well as in terms of its importance as a second language taught at school.

The Language Background

Switzerland has four national languages distributed on a territorial principle. German is spoken in the northern, central, and eastern parts of the country, French in the west, Italian in the south, and Rhaeto-Romansh in the southeast. According to the Swiss census of 2000, Switzerland has 64 percent or 4.64 million residents who have a variety of German as their first language; 20 percent or 1.48 million speak French; 6.5 percent or 0.5 million list Italian; and 0.5 percent or 35,000 identify Rhaeto-Romansh as their first language, while the other 9 percent represent speakers of immigrant languages. Consequently, Switzerland does not have a common language, but "linguistic pluralism is one of the most salient features of its national image."[2] However, this societal multilingualism does not translate into universal individual multilingualism. In fact, the vast majority of Swiss are initially raised monolingually and acquire other languages they may speak at school or as adults.[3]

A diglossic situation prevails in the German-speaking part of Switzerland. One variety, (Swiss) Standard German, is used for written discourse and orally in certain formal contexts, such as the federal parliament, at university, and in most news broadcasts. The other variety, denoted by the umbrella term Swiss German, actually consists of a set of highly differentiated, mostly Alemannic dialects that are in general mutually intelligible. Thus, Swiss German does not exist as a common, standardized variety but as a set of different local and regional varieties, which are used in everyday oral communication but are hardly ever written. This diglossic situation has been stable for some time, but during the twentieth century the use of Swiss German expanded into more formal domains such as radio, TV, church services, and local parliaments. Even more importantly, its prestige has increased significantly. For an overwhelming majority of Swiss Germans, the dialects express spontaneity, intimacy, and interaction, i.e., identification, whereas Standard German stands for authority, distance, and formality, i.e., alienation. Swiss German "is the vehicle of personal identity and in-group communication" and constitutes probably the most powerful marker of local or regional identity, rather than national identity.[4] In summary and following Richard Watts, the Swiss identity can be described—in language terms—as constructed from the bottom up.[5]

Swiss Germans feel that their local dialect is the primary linguistic marker of their identity. On another level, the diglossia between Swiss Standard German and a Swiss German dialect marks their regional identity as Swiss from the German-speaking part of the country and a more general Swiss identity is marked by (real or imagined) multilingualism.

Methodology

The approach taken in this study is based on the premise that identities are constructed in and through language; i.e., language choices and language practices construct and express people's identities. These choices, in turn, are informed by language attitudes and language ideologies. Language is thus not a purely individual and private affair but is also influenced by beliefs held in the wider community.

This study takes a narrative approach that posits that people make sense of their experiences by telling stories. These stories therefore provide more than purely factual information, since they also show how people recount their lives and significant events. In addition, personal stories are not only expressions of the individual but are informed by the larger social, cultural, and historical contexts just as individual stories inform and help create a communal story.[6] Thus, narratives—and life stories in particular—are social constructs as well as sites of identity construction. For these reasons, life stories are well suited for investigating how people make sense of migratory experiences, of building a new life in a new environment and in a new language.

The fifteen participants—five women and ten men—were born between 1918 and 1969. They moved away from Switzerland between 1937 and 1991 and arrived in Australia between 1940 and 1998. While this is an extremely wide distribution over time, there are clusters: A total of nine participants arrived in Australia during the period of assimilationist policies from 1945 to 1973, which at the same time was the period when immigration was most encouraged by the Australian government.[7] The average age of the participants was fifty-eight (for both men and women) and they had lived in Australia for an average of thirty-one years (thirty-four and a half for men, twenty-six for women). A wide variety of occupations are represented, including farming, trades, teaching, and academia, but none of the participants is an unskilled worker. Six have university degrees and four are retired.

The participants self-selected for this study, i.e., they responded to an advertisement in the Australian edition of the *Swiss Review*, a quarterly publication sent to Swiss citizens abroad. At the outset of the project they were asked to write an autobiographical sketch or personal memoir in the language variety of their choice. They were aware that they were writing for a researcher and fellow Swiss in Australia and for a research project focusing on language. No specific topic was set for the memoir—they were asked to write about the events in their lives they considered important and memorable. This was followed some months later by an interview that focused more explicitly on language-related issues (language use, shift, learning, etc.) but also asked questions about migration and about the memoir. The written texts varied considerably in length, from sketches of about two hundred and fifty words to almost book-length texts that had been written for other purposes; eleven memoirs were in English, three in Standard German, and one participant used both languages. The interviews lasted between one and three hours; six were in English, six in Swiss German, and two in both languages.[8]

The Written Memoirs

Despite the diversity of the participants, a potentially typical life course emerges from the data: leaving Switzerland in one's twenties, possibly moving back and forth between countries before settling down in Australia around the age of thirty. This is in line with the notion of *Lehr- und Wanderjahre*, a period of one's life spent abroad for language study or working holidays, as part of further education and/or career development.

The themes addressed in the memoirs cover what could be expected in life stories written for an unknown person. Unlike a curriculum vitae for official purposes (e.g., job application), they include some personal detail. However, very personal thoughts and events are generally omitted. Topics addressed by all participants to a considerable extent include family background, working life, professional career, and reasons for migration. Five other topics—place of birth, schooling, study or professional training, partner, and children—are also mentioned by all participants but only marginally by some. These themes are no surprise as they constitute the backbone of a biography: family background sets the scene and illustrates one's origin; the topic cluster of schooling, study or training, and professional career reflects the general focus on one's working life in western society. The reason for migration, finally, is an essential component of an immigrant life story to create coherence by linking the here and the there, the old and the new countries.

In terms of structure, all memoirs are roughly organized in chronological order, reflecting the preference for the temporal order in western cultures as the most important organizing principle of narratives.[9] Consequently, a three-part structure emerges quite clearly from all memoirs: pre-migration, migration, and post-migration.

Language Biographies and Language Identities

A typical language biography, which focuses on the commonalities in the language-related life courses of the participants, is described below.[10]

The participants were brought up as monolinguals by their German-speaking parents in German-speaking Switzerland, with German as their first language. In particular, they acquired the Swiss German dialect of the area and were exposed to Swiss Standard German at school (if not before) when they learned to read and write. The first foreign language they learned at school was French, and toward the end of compulsory schooling they were first exposed to some English. They then started an apprenticeship that would not involve much use of languages other than the German varieties. After the apprenticeship and a few years of full-time employment they realized that in order to further their careers they needed to broaden their horizons, to gain additional experience and to improve their English. This fitted nicely with their wish to see the world before settling down. Thus migration was initially intended to be temporary. They arrived in Australia on their own with rather limited knowledge of English. Initially, they had considerable difficulties with local pronunciation, regionalisms, and colloquialisms, but were eager to adapt. They immersed themselves in the new language environment as they believed this to be the best way to learn a language. They also enrolled in short-term language classes where they hoped to improve their accuracy and to learn more about cultural differences. They made new friends and soon met their (Anglo-Australian) partner who helped them to further improve their English. English became the couple's language even if the partner had some knowledge of German or French. The couple decided to settle in Australia, which seemed to provide more opportunities and be a better place to bring up children. Within the family, English developed from the couple's language into the family language. The children were brought up in English with a limited amount of Swiss German. More than language, some Swiss traditions were cultivated within the family (in addition to Australian customs) and the right to Swiss citizenship was preserved for the children. Despite the children's limited knowledge of Swiss German, many eventually went to live and work in Switzerland for some time. Today the immigrants from German-speaking Switzerland use the German varieties mainly to communicate with old friends and family in Switzerland. Cheaper and more convenient intercontinental telecommunication and more affordable air travel have led to an increased use of Swiss German in oral interaction, whereas previously the use of German was limited to Swiss Standard German in occasional letters; this variety is used in emails today. In Australia, Swiss German is used for oral interaction with Swiss visitors from overseas and with a few, selected people (family or friends); Standard German is only used receptively (e.g., to listen to or read news in German) and so are the other languages learned (French in particular).

Given the diversity of the participants—they cover a wide age range and several migration vintages and live in rather different circumstances—this language biography does not apply equally neatly to all of them. It most closely matches the five males born around 1945 who migrated to Australia in the 1960s and it is also largely representative for most of the other five participants born before 1939. The five participants born after 1950, however, do not fit the biography as neatly. In addition, there is more variation between them, so that it is difficult to establish a single alternative language biography for them.

Overall, this typical language biography shows linguistically well-integrated immigrants in Australia even though this linguistic integration takes different forms and varies in depth. It needs to be emphasized that participation in the study alone shows that the participants identify to some extent as Swiss and that they accept Swiss Germanness as their background and heritage. However, language is clearly of divergent importance in constructing their identity. If language practices are considered to be acts of identity, the participants can be allocated to four identity types that are each associated with particular communicative practices (or linguistic acts of identity).[11] These are summarized in Table 1.

TABLE 1 Identity types and associated acts of identity among German-speaking Swiss in Australia

	Language use in		L1 trans-mission	Impor-tance of language	Symbolic value of Swiss German	Identity based on
	public	private				
Assimilated immigrants	L2	L2	no	low	low	host community
Integrated immigrants	L2	L1/L2	no	low	high	host community and heritage
Hybrid immigrants	L2	L1	yes	high	high	both communities
Multilinguals A	L2	L1/L2	yes	high	high	both communities
Multilinguals B	L2	L1/L2	no	high	low	superordinate entity

Note: L1 = first language (German varieties); L2 = second language (English).

1 The assimilated immigrants or Swiss-born Australians (three participants) use only English in Australia and do not transmit their first language to their children. Their identity is based primarily on the host community (as immigrants in an immigrant society). Language is not particularly important to them and Swiss German carries only low symbolic value.

2 The integrated immigrants or Australian Swiss (two participants) use English in public and English and/or (Swiss) German in private domains but do not transmit their first language. Their identity is based on integration into the host community while maintaining a strong sense of heritage. While language as such is not important to them, Swiss German has retained high symbolic value.

3 The hybrid immigrants or Swiss Germans in Australia (two participants) use English in public and Swiss German in private wherever possible. They transmit Swiss German to the next generation. Their identity is based on both communities equally. Language generally is seen as important and Swiss German has high symbolic value.

4 The multilinguals in Australia fall into two subtypes that share the following practices: they use English in the host community and Swiss German only to a limited extent in private domains and they all attribute high importance to language in general. Type A (five participants) raise their children bilingually and attribute high symbolic value to Swiss German. Their identity is based on both communities equally. Type B (three participants) do not transmit their first language to the next generation. Their identity is based on a superordinate entity, linked not to a specific language but to their own multilingualism (e.g., "citizen of the world," European in Australia); consequently, Swiss German has only low symbolic significance.

The three levels of the original Swiss German language identity in Switzerland—local (dialect), regional (diglossia), national (multilingualism)—are recast in Australia, enacted and perceived differently in different contexts. In interactions with the researcher, the three levels were acknowledged but not always enacted in language: English has replaced Standard German for writing in many instances but the functional separation of the two German language varieties was recognized by the participants, and so was the significance of Swiss German for the language identity of the German-speaking Swiss at least within Switzerland. In actual conversations with most Australians, however, some of these identity levels become meaningless (e.g., the local identification as person from Bern or Basel) or are confusing (e.g., the functionally separated use of Standard

German and Swiss German) and are therefore no longer enacted or mentioned.

In sum, in Australia, the participants have more language identity options available to them than in Switzerland but these are less structured and less hierarchical. The Swiss German dialect is still seen by participants "as a badge of Swissness" and as an overt symbol of "non-Germanness."[12] This is particularly apparent in the frequent use of the term "Swiss" to denote Swiss German, so as to avoid any confusion with German.

Common Experiences and Shared Stories

The participants in this study share the experience of migrating to Australia from German-speaking Switzerland, but they do not share a unified story about the experience, circumstances, and consequences. There are, however, some similarities and commonalities—in short, shared stories.

The concept of shared stories is used to highlight patterns of sense making and identity construction within the life stories of this rather disparate group of migrants from a similar background. One of the major premises of the narrative approach is that identities are constructed in narratives, and the identities as well as the narratives are situated, variable, and influenced by sociohistorical circumstances and available discourses. The term "shared stories" has appeared in different contexts, in various disciplines.[13] Here, stories are seen as able to be shared in terms of content, form, manner of narration, and/or purpose. The notion of shared story can refer to common features at a variety of levels, including plot, elements of content, and formal features.

Some stories shared by the participating immigrants from German-speaking Switzerland have already been mentioned: the typical life course including the notion of *Lehr- und Wanderjahre*, a typical language biography (which is complemented by shorter shared stories of language shift, language learning, and intergenerational language transmission, which are not discussed here), the chronological organization of the life stories, their three-part structure mentioned earlier, and their predictable content in terms of conventional landmark events including, of course, the reasons for and circumstances of migration.

In fact, migration gives rise to several shared stories in the data. While its central position in the life story is shared by all participants, its allocated status differs. Two divergent stories emerge: one group presents migration as a major turning point, the other views it as a minor break.

For a group of five participants, migration was an escape from Switzerland, associated with liberation and a new beginning, and most intended

it to be permanent from the outset. A rather lengthy justification for turning their backs on the country of origin and the old life—generally including a description of their difficulties and negative experiences there—
highlights the need to explain the discontinuity. This indicates that this
kind of migration is a marked event outside the accepted life course from
a Swiss point of view. Not surprisingly then, these participants also present themselves as outsiders in Switzerland.

The other group of ten participants presents migration as a minor
break in their lives or as a continuation of their previous life plans, in line
with their intentions and a purposeful action to fulfill their ambitions—
language learning and professional and personal development. Migration was intended to be temporary and they do not reflect negatively on
Switzerland; the short purposeful explanations indicate that this type of
migration is seen as more acceptable by Swiss standards. However, the
reason for settling in Australia requires an explanation. This is normally
provided in terms of opportunities or family reasons and, in most instances,
takes the form of an argument, where advantages and disadvantages are
weighed against each other, highlighting not only the rationality of the decision but also the sense of purpose behind it. Nevertheless, this decision
sets these participants apart from the majority of Swiss who return to
Switzerland after their *Lehr- und Wanderjahre.*

After settling in Australia, integration into the host society is seen as
a requirement and as a positive act. This view is implicitly shared by all participants and it is apparent in the reported language shift to English,
which is characterized as unmarked and desirable, and through comparisons with other immigrants in Australia who are less proficient in English
or less inclined to adapt. The participants thus present themselves as having done "the right thing," as model immigrants, and they set themselves
apart from other, less integrated immigrants.

Despite being well integrated, the participants have maintained some
ties to their country and culture of origin, albeit to different extents and
in different ways. A shared story emerges with regard to citizenship. With
two exceptions, the participants maintained their Swiss citizenship while
becoming naturalized Australians. Adopting a second nationality is seen
as unproblematic, as advantageous, and as desirable. Had naturalization
involved giving up Swiss citizenship, however, this view would have been
different, as is implied in many comments and apparent in the findings
about preferred citizenship of Swiss immigrants.[14] In addition, many participants emphasize that they ensured their spouse and children were
granted Swiss citizenship. This is also part of another shared story reflecting an ongoing attachment to the country of origin: most participants

highlight that the second generation is aware, even proud, of their Swiss background and heritage, and many present this as their personal achievement, whether accompanied by language transmission or not.

Shared comparisons or "shared evaluative points" are also found in the life stories.[15] They are concerned with presumably typical Swiss characteristics, such as punctuality or reliability and the Swiss work ethic, which are contrasted with Australian counterparts—sometimes humorously (e.g., in stereotypical anecdotes) but nevertheless evaluated positively. Another, more general set of comparisons between the two countries is often mentioned when participants write or talk about visits to Switzerland. While Australia is associated with openness, the counterpart for Switzerland is narrowness, and in both instances the terms are used topographically as well as metaphorically. In fact, "*eng*" (narrow, often bearing the additional connotation of narrow-minded) is the word most often used to describe the participants' impressions of Switzerland—a shared story in a single word. A second set of adjectives frequently used to characterize Switzerland and the Swiss includes "conservative" and "static," whereas Australia is described as dynamic and flexible, adaptable and capable of change. Thus the participants distance themselves from the perceived "typical" Swiss in Switzerland, claiming that they have overcome the narrow-mindedness and conservatism associated with the old country. Simultaneously however, they also distance themselves from the perceived "typical" Australian by maintaining what they perceive as Swiss characteristics and by contrasting Australian Ockerism (archetypical rather rough, working class, male-dominated Australian culture) with a more refined but generic European identity that they present more positively.

A *Sonderfall* Abroad

The notion of Switzerland as a *Sonderfall* can be seen as a higher-order shared story or as a myth. Myths tell the story of larger sociocultural groups and help reconstruct and validate them. Myths are "essentially fictive, but they always contain elements of reality … they can be changed, altered, lost, abandoned, inverted etc., i.e. they are continually reproduced and reconstructed socially."[16]

Richard Watts outlines some important Swiss myths that can all be linked to the overarching myth of Switzerland as a *Sonderfall*. The country is often portrayed and perceived as special, different, and exceptional—both from within and from the outside. It is seen and sees itself as industrious, economically savvy, and fiercely independent. It is thus often viewed as the outsider and an anachronism in today's Europe. With regard to language, the myth of a multilingual and multicultural Switzerland alludes to the linguistic and cultural diversity that, in reality, may exist less on a concrete everyday level than on an institutional or even ideological level. In the eyes of many Swiss, it nevertheless makes the country a model for the peaceful cohabitation of cultural minorities. Its political system—strongly decentralized and federalist, based on consensus, and often termed the oldest democracy in the world—is equally seen as contributing to the country's status as a potential role model. As a consequence of the status of Switzerland as a *Sonderfall*, many Swiss see themselves as exceptional.

The participants present themselves as a *Sonderfall* within the *Sonderfall*. While they use their distancing from Switzerland to demonstrate that they were able to step out of Switzerland and to overcome its perceived narrowness, this leaves the myths of Switzerland as a *Sonderfall* intact. This is reminiscent of Ingrid Piller's argument (regarding national stereotypes) that "by claiming exception to a stereotype, the stereotype remains intact" and one saves face simultaneously.[17] This strategy thus allows the participants to assert their difference without challenging the myth.

In the shared stories identified above the participants present themselves as exceptional, as a *Sonderfall* in various ways: as different from other immigrants in Australia and from mainstream Australians, and as different from the perceived "typical" Swiss German in Switzerland. They distance themselves from both by highlighting their difference—as exceptional immigrants and as atypical Swiss—and present themselves as a *Sonderfall*.

Notes

1   Australia's 2001 census reports 10,753 Swiss-born in a total Australian population of just under nineteen million; it is unknown how many of them are from German-speaking Switzerland.
2   Stevenson, *German-Speaking World*, 22.
3   Dürrmüller, "Multilingualismus der Gesellschaft," 218.
4   Clyne, *German Language*, 44.
5   Watts, "Ideology of Dialect," 69.
6   Denzin, *Interpretive Biography*, 73.
7   See also Chapter 5.
8   Only fourteen participants could be interviewed.
9   Ochs, "Narrative."
10 See Nekvapil, "Sprachbiographien."
11 Le Page and Tabouret-Keller, *Acts of Identity*; Lüdi, "Internal Migrants."
12 Watts, "Ideology of Dialect," 75, 83.
13 See, for example, Johnstone, "Discourse Analysis"; Linde, *Life Stories*; and Steffen, "Life Stories."
14 Wegmann, *Swiss in Australia*, 133–34.
15 Linde, "Narrative in Institutions," 522.
16 Watts, "Ideology of Dialect," 73–74.
17 Piller, *Bilingual Couples Talk*, 211.

Interview Sources

Fifteen written memoirs, correspondence to the author, 14 November 2001 to 13 May 2002.

Fourteen interviews, conducted by the author, 1 April 2003 to 15 November 2003.

Works Cited

Clyne, Michael G. *The German Language in a Changing Europe.* Cambridge: Cambridge University Press, 1995.

Denzin, Norman K. *Interpretive Biography.* Newbury Park, CA: Sage, 1989.

Dürrmüller, Urs. "Multilingualismus der Gesellschaft." In *Mehrsprachigkeit—Eine Herausforderung,* edited by Hans Bickel and Robert Schläpfer, 209–45. Aarau: Sauerländer, 1994.

Johnstone, Barbara. "Discourse Analysis and Narrative." In *The Handbook of Discourse Analysis,* edited by Deborah Schiffrin, Deborah Tannen, and Heidi E. Hamilton, 635–49. Oxford: Blackwell Publishing, 2001.

Le Page, R.B., and Andrée Tabouret-Keller. *Acts of Identity: Creole-Based Approaches to Language and Ethnicity.* Cambridge: Cambridge University Press, 1985.

Linde, Charlotte. *Life Stories: The Creation of Coherence.* New York: Oxford University Press, 1993.

———. "Narrative in Institutions." In *The Handbook of Discourse Analysis,* edited by Deborah Schiffrin, Deborah Tannen, and Heidi E. Hamilton, 518–35. Oxford: Blackwell Publishing, 2001.

Lüdi, Georges. "Internal Migrants in a Multilingual Country." *Multilingua* 11, no. 1 (1992): 45–73.

Nekvapil, Jirí. "Sprachbiographien und Analyse der Sprachsituationen: Zur Situation der Deutschen in der Tschechischen Republik." In *Leben mit mehreren Sprachen. Sprachbiographien/Vivre avec plusieurs langues: Biographies langagières,* edited by Rita Franceschini and Johanna Miecznikowski, 147–72. Bern: Peter Lang, 2004.

Ochs, Elinor. "Narrative." In *Discourse as Structure and Process. Discourse Studies: A Multidisciplinary Introduction, Volume 1,* edited by Teun A. van Dijk, 185–207. London: Sage, 1997.

Piller, Ingrid. *Bilingual Couples Talk: The Discursive Construction of Hybridity.* Amsterdam: John Benjamins, 2002.

Steffen, Vibeke. "Life Stories and Shared Experience." *Social Science and Medicine* 45, no. 1 (1997): 99–111.

Stevenson, Patrick. *The German-Speaking World: A Practical Introduction to Sociolinguistic Issues.* London: Routledge, 1997.

Watts, Richard. "The Ideology of Dialect in Switzerland." In *Language Ideological Debates,* edited by Jan Blommaert, 67–103. Berlin: Mouton de Gruyter, 1999.

Wegmann, Susanne. *The Swiss in Australia.* Grüsch: Rüegger, 1989.

FIVE

Migration, Language Use, and Identity

German in Melbourne, Australia,
since World War II

Sandra Kipp

This chapter presents an overview of the German language in Australia, concentrating on the period from 1939 to 2001 and using census and interview data. Australian national census data are used to provide the large-scale context for family case studies of a number of subgroups of German-speaking immigrants to Australia, namely prewar Jewish refugees, members of the Temple Society deported from Palestine to Australia in 1941, refugees from Europe arriving between 1947 and 1954, and economic migrants from the Federal Republic of Germany and Austria during the 1950s and '60s. Relative levels of language maintenance or shift are related to factors in the homeland, at the time of migration, and within the developing context of multiculturalism in Australia.

Introduction

THE GERMAN LANGUAGE HAS HAD A PRESENCE in Australia since the early days of European settlement. The nineteenth century in particular saw the rapid growth of German-speaking communities in the developing cities as well as in rural areas, largely due to the network of Lutheran settlements that were established across southern Australia, as well as in Queensland, from the 1830s to the early twentieth century. Before the federation of states into the Commonwealth of Australia in 1901, the prevailing attitudes toward languages other than English and their speakers tended to be laissez-faire, and many communities, including the German-speaking ones, established their own schools (often taught through the medium of their own language), their own print media, and their own social and religious institutions. Federation (in 1901) ushered in a period of aggressive monolingualism, with assimilation the social policy of choice. The White Australia Policy instituted at that time meant the cessation of migration from Asia or from any other part of the world considered incompatible with the developing national ethos—that of a monocultural, British-oriented society, albeit with a distinctive Australian character based on egalitarianism and informality.[1] This monocultural bias was demonstrated by the strong opposition to an influx of southern European migrants in the 1920s and resurfaced in the wake of World War II, when the migration boom engineered to boost population (in case of attack from Australia's northern neighbours and for the growing industrial sector) failed to produce the mostly British migrants that had been promised.[2]

World War I had already seen the suspension of print media in German, the changing of place names, and radical state intervention in community schooling. In South Australia, for example, the Lutheran schools were closed and several important representatives within the Lutheran church were interned. In Victoria, as in some other Australian states, the community schools remained open but an amendment to the Education Act in 1916 prohibited the teaching through the medium of any language other than English in registered (i.e., non-state) schools. It was a period of intense hostility toward those of German background (including third-generation Australians) and the use of German in public places was met with censure and abuse. The result was a rapid acceleration of language shift, even in the rural enclaves, which had been particularly successful in maintaining German over three, and sometimes four, generations.

While there was a limited amount of German-speaking immigration between the wars, the next significant wave of German-speaking immigrants came in the wake of World War II. By the 1970s arguably the most dramatic attitudinal shift since European settlement was underway. It came about largely as the result of the fundamental demographic transformation that had been set in motion by the postwar immigration boom (1947–60) from all parts of Europe, but increasingly from the south as first British sources, then northern and western European sources, dried up. After fundamental reforms to the immigration system instituted by a new reformist government, the 1970s also saw the recommencement of Asian migration, first from Vietnam and then from eastern and northeast Asia. A strong grassroots reform movement, supported by academics and teachers and accompanied by the change of government and a number of other facilitating developments, saw the prevailing monocultural mindset and assimilationist policies replaced by a multicultural model that emphasized the social and economic benefits of diversity.[3] While policies on language and diversity have continued to evolve, and do in fact appear to be in crisis at the beginning of the twenty-first century, Australia's current linguistic demography still reflects the events of the late twentieth century;[4] Vietnamese, Arabic, and Chinese varieties continue to gain ground on Italian, Greek and German, the strongest languages of the postwar period.

In the years after World War II, German speakers would thus have arrived in a country committed to the ethos of assimilation and seen the climate change over the succeeding decades to one that placed a much greater value on diversity. This change brought with it funding opportunities for language-maintenance institutions and a much higher profile for "ethnic minorities." The change did not take effect, however, until many of the postwar immigrants' children and the Australian-born children of the early migrants were themselves adults. It is worth noting here that although German language and cultural studies had been established at major universities and some secondary schools taught German, the emphasis had been firmly on second-language acquisition rather than on the maintenance or development for "background" language speakers. Such speakers were, in fact, actively discriminated against in the examination process.

Distribution and Maintenance of German in Australia

Large-scale home language-use data from the Australian Bureau of Statistics for 1976, 1986, 1991, 1996, and 2001 can be cross-tabulated with place of residence, birthplace, year of arrival, and age to provide an overall demographic picture of German speakers in the Australian context. In addition, language use and birthplace data can be analysed to establish language shift rates in the first and second generations of immigrants.

In 2001, 76,303 people resident in Australia claimed to speak German regularly at home. This represents a 23 percent decrease from 1996, and a 33 percent decrease from 1991. Of these, most lived in New South Wales (29 percent) and Victoria (27 percent), followed by Queensland (18 percent), and South Australia (12 percent). The majority lived in the state capitals, although significant minorities lived in other parts of Queensland (11 percent), New South Wales (10 percent), and Victoria (6 percent). Within the capital cities, German speakers have been one of the least concentrated language groups.[5] The few slight concentrations that do occur in Sydney and Melbourne are on the rural-urban fringes where not many other speakers of languages other than English are found—to the east in Melbourne and to the north and west in Sydney.

Of those who reported using German at home in 2001, 54 percent were born in Germany, 9 percent in Austria, and 5 percent in Switzerland. The vast majority of the German and Austrian born arrived before 1986 (87 percent and 83 percent respectively), while the Swiss migration is somewhat more recent, with only 59 percent arriving before 1986. German speakers in Australia are usually older, with 31 percent of speakers aged over 65 in 2001. Only five language communities have a larger proportion of older speakers: Hungarian (33 percent), Dutch (39 percent), Ukrainian (43 percent), Lithuanian (51 percent), and Latvian (54 percent).

Language shift has been calculated as the proportion of immigrants born in a non-English speaking country (and their children) who now use only English at home.[6] German- and Austrian-born immigrants have consistently had very high rates of language shift—surpassed only by the Netherlands born—in both the first and second generations (see Table 1).

As well as the relatively high rates of language shift for both the German- and Austrian-born immigrants, Table 1 shows an increase in shift between 1996 and 2001 for these two groups. Exogamous marriages result in uniformly higher shift rates in the second generation. It is unfortunately not possible to compare the second-generation shift rate for 1996 with 2001, as the census question detailing birthplace of parents had been replaced with a binary distinction of "born in Australia versus born outside Australia." Language shift in different age groups of the overseas born since 1986 can nonetheless be compared (see Table 2).[7]

TABLE 1 Language shift: 1996, 2001

Birthplace	Percent shift (1st generation 2001)	Percent shift (1st generation 1996)	Percent shift (2nd generation 1996)		
			Endogamous	Exogamous	Aggregated
Austria	54.4	48.3	80.0	91.1	89.7
Germany	54.0	48.2	77.6	92	89.7
Greece	7.1	6.4	16.1	51.9	28.0
Italy	15.9	14.7	42.6	79.1	57.9
Netherlands	62.6	61.9	91.1	96.5	95.0
PR China	4.3	4.6	17.1	52.8	37.4
Turkey	7.1	5.8	5.0	46.6	16.1

Source: Australian Bureau of Statistics.

TABLE 2 Language shift by age among German and
Austrian born in Australia, 1986–2001

Birthplace	Year	0–14	15–24	25–34	35–44	45–54	55–64	65+
Austria	2001	25.2	32.1	46.1	59.6	70.4	56.9	45
	1996	24.2	33.4	53.1	63.0	61.9	43.4	33.6
	1986	25.4	39.5	55.8	53.0	38.1	29.0	24.5
Germany	2001	26.3	39.5	48	56.7	69.1	55.4	42.7
	1996	29.5	37.7	50.5	59.9	62.9	38.3	31.7
	1991	25.7	30.4	46.2	60.8	42.4	29.4	24.7
	1986	27.9	40.9	54.3	54.4	32.7	28.5	23.9

Source: Australian Bureau of Statistics.

It is clear from Table 2 that the oldest and youngest age groups show the lowest level of shift overall, although the numbers in the youngest age group are generally quite small, given that the German-speaking immigration had decreased by the 1970s. The shift in the oldest age group does, however, increase over time, reflecting the passing of the earliest adult arrivals. The pattern of the highest shift for Austria and Germany would suggest that it is the (overseas-born) children of the original settlers who have shifted most. This temporal shift pattern reflects the influx of Austrian and German families as economic migrants in the 1950s. Some families may have arrived from German refugee camps as early as the late 1940s.

Groups of German Speakers, Interview Data, and Focus

The indications from the large-scale census data prompted the collection of qualitative data to complement the big picture, particularly given the heterogeneous nature of the German-speaking migration. The German speakers are unusual among twentieth-century immigrants in that they do not have a readily identifiable point of origin. An overview of German-speaking migration to Australia over the second half of the twentieth century or so would have to include at least the groups listed in Table 3.

TABLE 3 Groups of German speakers in Australia
from 1938 to the present

Year(s) of immigration	Groups of German Speakers
1938–39	Refugees from Nazi Germany and Austria (largely Jewish)*
1941	Members of the Temple Society deported from Palestine to Australia*
1947–54	Displaced persons from central and eastern Europe, many of whom either had German as their first language or used it as a lingua franca*
1948– early 1950s	German speakers entering Australia under special employment schemes
1950s & 1960s	Economic "assisted migrants" from Germany and Austria*
1970s– present	Ongoing and non-assisted migration from German-speaking countries (Germany, Austria, Switzerland)

*These groups are discussed in this chapter.

Each one of these groups has had differing relationships with the German-speaking motherland as well as somewhat different experiences within Australia, as shown below in the discussion of interviews with seventeen families from different groups. Where possible, interviews included three immigrant generations with at least one subject from each interviewed in each family. The families were selected to include the major German-speaking groups of immigrants outlined in Table 3.

The analysis of the interviews focuses on why people made the language choices they made, and whether the choices made by prewar migrants, for example, were markedly different from those made by Templers or postwar migrants. The particular position of the overseas-born children of all groups raised the additional question of how the complex processes of identity negotiation typical of this age group were played out in the country of migration and how they have been reflected in linguistic behaviour.

The following discussion concentrates specifically on the first and second generations and addresses the following questions, with particular attention to their implications for language use:

- For the first generation, what were the main priorities in a new country?
- What were the "dimensions of difference" perceived by the second generation between themselves and their "Australian" peers, and how did they respond to them?

First Generation

Prewar Immigrants

Two of the three prewar immigrant families were refugees from Nazism, one from Berlin and one from Vienna. In both cases there was almost total disruption of family connections, family fortunes, and career paths. Both families were accustomed to material comforts and high cultural pursuits, and while success in monetary terms was slowly won in Australia and never quite reflected what was left behind, both families immediately set about becoming part of an active cultural circle, gathering about them artists, musicians, and academics of all sorts. This phenomenon has already been noted by Michael Clyne.[8]

> **EXAMPLE 1**
>
> So my mother had a circle ... she got to know a lot of very interesting people and kept up friendship with them ... we had a subtenant who was a cousin of Boris Pasternak, the famous Russian author, we had another subtenant who was a widow of, um, one of the librettists for Franz Leonhard, the great operetta composer, [laughs] ... we were all quite amazed and ... yeah, things that, you know ... illustrious kind of, sort of, um ...
> (PWR1C2)
>
> I didn't understand that at first, but I remember knowing when I was older, and understanding that that was the one thing that couldn't be taken ... no matter how wealthy someone was, it counted for nothing, but that was the one thing that was valued ... so I remember hearing all the stories of what happened, and having that understanding later, and then knowing "oh, gee, there's why all these people ..." there's dentists and doctors and this and that ... you know, you'd meet someone in Omy's lounge room, and this was someone who was the first ... female doctor, or whatever it was, and I know she likes to always surround herself with ... educated or cultured and that sort of thing. (PWR2G3)

German was the language of choice for the first generation in the families interviewed, although this was not universal in their networks, bearing out the potential ambivalence toward the German language within this group, who may have chosen to distance themselves from all things German or to consider themselves the bearers of "true" German culture in exile.

EXAMPLE 2
They mixed with people of their generation ... they only spoke German, but there were some in that group who thought it was not the done thing, so they always spoke English, which was very strange. (PWR2G2)

The third family had not come as refugees, but rather to escape an increasingly nationalistic and, to their mind, dangerous Europe, and were committed to an inclusive lifestyle based on Christian principles. Their social networks were increasingly non-German-speaking and their language choice was English from the earliest days.

Templers

For the Templers—transported as a unit from Palestine—the family group and the preservation of their own particular type of community were paramount. As Barbara Imberger reports, although a number of individuals and families opted to start a new life away from the Templers, deliberately speaking only English, the majority eventually returned, finding the *Gemeindeleben* (community life) and common ethnic background supportive and important to their lifestyle.[9]

The Temple Society was clearly not just a religious organization; it provided a comprehensive social life for its members:

EXAMPLE 3
When I was growing up, the Temple society was larger than it is now, and there were very big balls and dances and that sort of thing, and we'd get together and decorate the halls, or if somebody got married, the young girls would be asked to come as waitresses and help set up the thing, and we still run Sunday school and children's camps and teenage camps and ... so I guess there's a lot happening, even it's a very small group of people. Ladies' guilds, men's groups ... I mean, recently in the last few years we've been trying to organise small forums for specific groups. (TS1G2)

The maintenance of German was supported not only by the many activities offered in the language, but also by the decades of experience in language maintenance in Palestine and the ongoing presence of the grandparent generation, most of whom were not comfortable in English. As a group, the Templers were the most patriotically "German" of those who immigrated around the time of World War II. Therefore, they had a fairly uncomplicated relationship with the German language and the culture it represented. Dorit Monheit confirms the relative success of the Temple Society in transmitting German to the second and third generations when compared with postwar German-speaking families.[10]

Displaced Persons

For the displaced persons, coming from the dislocation and losses of war, the establishment of a family house came up again and again in the interviews:

> **EXAMPLE 4**
>
> I stepped from that ship, and I went on the train, and the train was gone like the devil himself, and I looked out the window, and I said yeah, and I saw the houses, one day I will have a house like that, and I felt free, like, I could breathe, somehow … and as soon as I had that roof over my head, so nobody can chuck me out anymore, and I'm happy. Happy about that … (DP1G1)

> Dad lost everything, so that definitely comes through in our family, especially the hoarding mentality, and the wanting to build and impress and build something that's substantial again. (DP2G2)

Language use patterns depended to some extent on the "type" of the displaced person. Some individuals from occupied homelands had a strong interest in preserving language and culture (not always German) while others, particularly those from mixed marriages, often opted for a completely new start, including using English, away from the horrors of the recent past.

The hard work involved in making the dream materialize often meant in purely practical terms that there was little interpersonal interaction:

> **EXAMPLE 5**
>
> I became one of these latch-key kids—parents both at work, shift work, and you didn't actually see your parents, so, I mean, that's another reason you wouldn't use a lot of … I wouldn't have spoken a lot of German because there was no one to speak to. (DP1G2)

It was often not until homes had been established and careers regained that such migrants felt free to look about them and develop real ties to their adopted country:

> **EXAMPLE 6**
>
> And eventually … it probably took maybe fifteen years, because I remember I would have been about fourteen or fifteen, that there was a complete turnaround, and my father had requalified as a doctor, and he found such pleasure in going out to the Australian bush, the blinkers were taken off and he actually thought Australia was an exquisitely beautiful place to be. (DP3G2)

Economic Migrants

The migrants who came a little later for economic reasons were clearly also very committed to the dream of home ownership, although in their case it was more upgrading from apartment or rental living to a more leisured lifestyle.

> **EXAMPLE 7**
>
> I couldn't have afford it back home, just a flat, and now, you know, you step out and have already other people, hardly a space ... but now here, I feel like I have a piece of paradise. Even if I have to work hard for it, you know. But no, no, I think that's why it's really nice. (POWA1G1)

Language choice tended to be dictated by pragmatic factors, such as occupational patterns and degree of contact with the homeland.

Second Generation

The second generation identified many dimensions of difference between themselves and their Australian peers, and recounted them with great passion and depth of feeling, even forty or fifty years after the event. Common to all groups were memories of the clothes they wore to school and, particularly, the school lunch. German names were also an issue, particularly boys' names, as was the embarrassment caused by parents' use of German within earshot of school friends or the general public.

> **EXAMPLE 8**
>
> But, ah, I hated my Vienna loaf bread with jam and my dad must have cut them about two inches thick ... but gee, I really would have liked to have those white sandwiches and the neatly cut off crusts and all that silly stuff. (DP4G2)
>
> First of all, we had a very German name, as German as they come. My brother's name was Holger ... and it was like ... "who?" Oh, he hated it. He hated it with a passion. (POWG1G2)
>
> I think the difference never went away. Um, certainly, my mother didn't help. She always made me look as different as she possibly could. She had my aunt send out lovely, um, tights, that I could wear, of all different lovely woollen colours, while all the Australian children had white or brown or grey socks that stopped at the ankles and mottled blue legs, I had nice woolly warm coloured ones [laughs] ... (DP5G2)
>
> My parents would try to speak German to us on the streets, but we'd respond "Speak English! Don't you dare! Don't ever talk

to us in German on the street! Ever!" We were mortified. It was terrible. (POWG1G2)

The informants responded to, and coped with, this difference in a variety of ways. For the following informants a significant element of defiance accompanied the obvious embarrassment about appearances:

EXAMPLE 9

One of the things was my bread, the bread at school. Now, I remember actually hiding it in a brown paper bag and sort of nibbling out the edge because other kids made fun, but I remember thinking "this tastes good, and I'm not giving it up," like, "I don't care what you say." (DP1G2)

So unfortunately, at that time you couldn't change the oath, you had to say oath of allegiance, but what I did was cross my fingers, okay, so I was quite happy to be an Australian citizen, but be damned if I was going to be obey the Queen in any shape or form. (DP1G2)

For one informant, the overall reaction was one of stoicism:

EXAMPLE 10

Growing up, I never looked at it as a down or upside. It was what it was, and there was no changing it, and I accepted it. I never thought about changing it. It was how my life was, and that was that, and I had to make the best of it. (DP3G2)

Some members of this generation were able to "compartmentalize" their lives and to live reasonably happily in several camps:

EXAMPLE 11

He was quite happy to come here in the Austrian club, but outside of that, at the footy club, at the tennis club, at school, he really didn't want it to be known. He kept those two parts of his life separate. (POWA3G1)

It was separate, kind of. It was.... there was school and ... sort of the Australian community and then on weekends, that was family and, um, family and Templer stuff. But it was sort of separate. It kind of ... they didn't cross over, really, I don't think. (TS2G2)

In all of these families (examples 9–11), the language of the home has survived remarkably well, unless or until countered by exogamous marriages and other external circumstances. However, where the wish to conform was uppermost, the language and culture fared less well:

EXAMPLE 12

Well, the thing of it is, I didn't want to carry it on. I wanted to really become Australian, so I did very little of that while I was growing up. (DP4G2)

It made me extremely polite to everyone. Um, it also made me, me personally, um, quite self-reliant in my own way. I was never lacking for friends … I was also a, a good little student, a good child, I didn't make waves, I didn't cause disruptions … there was no way I enjoyed being different, and I wasn't going to stand out there and say "listen to me, I can speak a different language." It was the last thing I wanted to do. I wanted to fit in. (DP5G2)

In neither of these families has any German been transmitted to the third generation. This strategy—belonging to the host society at the expense of the original culture—is not necessarily successful, however, as demonstrated by the informants below, who were ultimately unable to fit in and did in fact revert to a culture and a language that they had once rejected.

EXAMPLE 13

It was pretty hard as kids. That's why we refused to speak one word of it. We tried to be so Australian it was disgusting. We couldn't even play tennis in our local town. There were four churches, and we belonged to the Methodist church, and we couldn't even get into the Methodist tennis team. It's impossible. I was so glad to leave that town, and I thought "you can all go and jump" … I think it made me, when I left school, I have this natural urge … I mean, I'm not anti-Australian but I have got this absolute natural urge to want to be around Europeans or foreigners. And because I've only had one son and I've brought him up by myself, I have insisted on him being German. I said "be proud of this, Nick, we were never allowed to be proud of ours." (POWG1G2)

Embarrassment is one of the key things that I've been aware of … when I grew up, I was fairly shy, because, um, I really don't, or didn't have an identity completely … I feel neither Australian nor German, and that's probably why I was happy when I met Hans, because he was … he spoke German. I wouldn't have felt comfortable in a completely Australian household. (PW2G2)

In the first case in example 13, German was embraced out of defiance, in the latter more by default. Both informants share a feeling of alienation from mainstream Australian society.

Conclusion

The Templers have been identified as a group with a very successful record of language maintenance in Australia, a status that this
study confirms. Facilitating factors for language maintenance among the
Templers include relative geographical concentration, a central focus
with symbolic weight (the Temple Society), families that remained intact
over a number of generations, and a fairly uncomplicated commitment
to the German state as well as a history shared with it. Other groups and
individuals in this study may demonstrate some of these attributes, but
no other group displays all of them. In particular, a strong community
language social life and the presence of non–English-speaking family
members provided an ongoing context for German use among Templers;
the children accepted this context alongside their Australian networks, leading to a high degree of functional specialisation or diglossia, a condition
that Joshua Fishman and his colleagues have described as vital to successful language transmission.[11] All groups acknowledged a growing acceptance of bilingualism and biculturalism within Australian society, although
this often happened too late for transmission to continue uninterrupted,
and some informants felt that German, in particular, remained stigma-
tised. There is, however, some evidence of a renewed interest in language
as the second generation reached adulthood (often prompted by a visit
to the homeland), and biculturalism, if not bilingualism, is now seen by
most informants as attainable and comfortable. For some this came as a
revelation; for others it has been a more gradual process. The study also
suggests that attitudes developed by children out of a perception of difference can inform their linguistic and cultural behaviour for life. In particular, the importance of group membership is highlighted.

The author would like to acknowledge the Australian Research Council,
which funded the research on which this chapter is based.

Notes

1 Clyne, *Australia's Language Potential*; Jupp, *Arrivals and Departures.*
2 Lack and Templeton, *Bold Experiment.*
3 Clyne, *Community Languages.*
4 Clyne, *Australia's Language Potential.*
5 Clyne and Kipp, "Language Concentrations."
6 As the census has never included a question on language first spoken, birthplace
   has been used as a (not entirely satisfactory) surrogate.
7 The age structure of the 1976 census is not directly comparable to those from
   1986 onward. There was no language question in 1981.
8 Clyne, "Thirty Years Later."
9 Imberger, *Language Use.*

10 Monheit, *Role of the German Ethnic School.*
11 Fishman et al., *Rise and Fall.*

Works Cited

Australian Bureau of Statistics. *Australian National Census,* 1976, 1986, 1996, 2001. Canberra.

Clyne, Michael, and Sandra Kipp. "Language Concentrations in Metropolitan Areas." *People and Place* 6, no. 2 (1998): 50–60.

Clyne, Michael. "Thirty Years Later: Some Observations on 'Refugee German' in Melbourne." In *Lexicography and Dialect Geography: Festgabe for Hans Kurath,* edited by Harald Scholler and John Reidy, 96–106. Wiesbaden: Steiner, 1973.

———. *Australia's Language Potential.* Sydney: University of New South Wales Press, 2005.

———. *Community Languages: The Australian Experience.* Cambridge: Cambridge University Press, 1991.

Fishman, Joshua, et al. *The Rise and Fall of the Ethnic Revival: Perspectives on Language and Ethnicity.* Berlin: Mouton de Gruyter, 1985.

Imberger, Barbara. *Language Use and Language Maintenance in a Small German Religious Community: A Study of Trilingualism and Triglossia in the Temple Society, with Special Reference to Mixed Marriages.* BA thesis, Monash University, 1979.

Jupp, James. *Arrivals and Departures.* Melbourne: Cheshire-Lansdowne, 1966.

Lack, John, and Jacqueline Templeton, eds. *Bold Experiment: A Documentary History of Australian Immigration Since 1945.* Melbourne: Oxford University Press, 1995.

Monheit, Dorit R. "The Role of the German Ethnic School in Maintaining the German Language in Melbourne." BA thesis, Monash University, 1975.

SIX

Language and Identity

The German-speaking People of Paarl

Rolf Annas

Paarl is the third-oldest town in South Africa, situated approximately sixty kilometres from Cape Town, and many Germans have settled there over the last three hundred years. This chapter provides an overview of the history of the German-speaking immigration to Paarl and reports on a series of interviews in which German-speaking people of the town were asked about their German origins, the ways in which they try to preserve their language and culture, and how they would describe their primary identity. Since its founding in 1876, the Lutheran congregation of the town has served as a focal point for German community life. As the flow of immigrants slowed down in recent years and as German speakers became more integrated into the larger South African community, in cases where their spouses were not German speakers or their children could no longer speak the language, the church tried to adapt to the circumstances by becoming a multilingual entity. In addition, there is a split between Germans who have moved to Paarl in recent years and those of longer standing, since the former do not identify with the religious and cultural values of the latter and prefer not to socialize with them but find their contacts in the broader community.

Introduction

IDENTITY IS WIDELY REGARDED TODAY AS A PROCESS, resulting in a "discursive construct," whereby people use and create boundaries such as language, nationality, and social group to distinguish between the self and the other.[1] In South Africa, the question of language has always been a contentious topic and an important element in defining group identity. In the early days of European occupation, first Dutch and later English were the only recognized official languages. Later, during apartheid, when Afrikaans became the compulsory medium of instruction in certain subjects in schools attended by blacks, this caused the riots in 1976. In the present day, the University of Stellenbosch is publicly criticized by certain members of the community for not doing enough to promote and preserve the Afrikaans language. German has had an equally turbulent history, which will be discussed in the next section, while the second half of this chapter will examine how Germans living in Paarl today see themselves, their identity, and the preservation of their language and culture.

The German Community in Paarl: A Brief History

Since 1996, South Africa has eleven official languages (see Table 1). According to the constitution, the state is responsible for promoting indigenous languages as well as those languages spoken by other communities in the country. German is explicitly mentioned alongside Greek, Portuguese, Arabic, and other languages.[2] German is also one of seven non-official languages that students may choose for the highest level of the country's new National Senior Certificate (NSC) examination.[3] The promotion of German, which is spoken as a mother tongue by approximately sixty thousand inhabitants, is thus even entrenched in the South African constitution.[4]

TABLE 1   First home-language speakers in South Africa

Language	Speakers (in millions)
Zulu	10.7
Xhosa	7.9
Afrikaans	6.0
Sepedi	4.2
Setswana	3.7
English	3.7
Sesotho	3.6
Tsonga	2
Swati	1.2
Venda	1
Ndebele	0.7

Source: "Census 2001: Primary tables," Statistics South Africa, 2004.

Paarl, South Africa's third-oldest town after Cape Town and Stellen-bosch, is the second largest industrial centre in Western Cape province. It is regarded as the birthplace of the Afrikaans language for it is here that the first Afrikaans newspaper, *Die Afrikaanse Patriot*, was published in 1876. Coincidentally in the same year, the German Lutheran congregation in the town was formed.

The visitor who approaches the town from Cape Town is met by a vista of the majestic Klein Drakenstein Mountains on the one side and the granite Paarl Rock on the other side of the valley, from which the Afrikaans Language Monument looms, which was unveiled in 1975 to commemo-rate the origin and growth of Afrikaans. The second largest of the three towers of this monument represents the contribution of European lan-guages, especially Dutch and German, to the development of Afrikaans.

Paarl was established in 1687 when the governor, Simon van der Stel, allotted farms to twenty-three farmers along the banks of the Berg River. According to G.C. de Wet, ten of the 116 farmers who settled in the Dra-kenstein area during the seventeenth century (which included Paarl, Dal Josafat, and Franschhoek) were of German origin.[5] During the time of the first occupation by the Dutch East India Company (1652–1795) Dutch was the only official language at the Cape, and Lutherans were not per-mitted to hold their own services. As a result, German immigrants did not maintain their mother tongue for long.

One of the old farms, Berlyn (Berlin), which used to be situated along Paarl Main Road and is now a central residential district, was owned by Carl Heinrich Richter, originally from Berlin, who arrived in the Cape in 1773 as soldier in the service of the Dutch East India Company. Four years later he sold the farm to another German, Johann G. Stegmann, born in Plauen, who arrived at the Cape in 1769 as a soldier. Both married women of Dutch, rather than German, origin. Similarly, the minister of the Paarl Drakenstein Dutch Reformed Church, Reverend Johan Wilhelm Geb-hart—born in Mannheim, who arrived in South Africa in 1810—was mar-ried to an English woman, Sarah Margareta Payne.

The history of the Germans at the Cape is very much a part of the his-tory of the Lutherans, who played a major role in maintaining the German language. The first Lutheran Church at the Cape (*Evangelische Luthersche Kerk*) was founded in 1779, and although 372 of the 442 founding mem-bers were from Germany, the language in which the services were held was Dutch.[6] The congregation in the city centre was served by both Dutch and German ministers, and also had members of both language groups, and it seems that communicating never really was a problem.

In the middle of the nineteenth century, German immigration to the Cape was encouraged by Governor Sir George Grey. Most Germans settled in the Eastern Cape region of Caffraria; others were required as agricultural workers on the large farms in the Western Cape areas of Malmesbury, Paarl, and Worcester. It was only in 1871 that a separate German Evangelical Lutheran congregation was founded in Cape Town. The split did not come about because of language but as a result of theological differences among members of the congregation. It was the *"verwaschene und unschriftmässige Predigtweise"* of the minister that led to the founding of the new German St. Martini congregation, in which both Dutch and German were used initially.[7]

In September 1875, the new minister of the St. Martini congregation, Pastor Carl Hugo Hahn, went to visit the German immigrants in Paarl and held the first church service for them in German. According to the census of 1875, there were 168 German immigrants in Paarl, 95 of whom were Lutheran.[8] In the following month, forty-seven adults drew up a petition that they presented to Pastor Hahn expressing their need for a German congregation for the reason:

> dass in kurzer Zeit eine Vermehrung von Arbeitskräften auf dem Gebiet der Deutsch-Evangelisch Lutherischen Kirche am Kap der Guten Hoffnung zu erwarten ist, richten sie hiermit an ihn [Pastor Hahn] die Bitte, sich der hiesigen Deutschen, die bis jetzt vom Gehör Göttlichen Wortes in der Muttersprache und dem Gebrauch der Heiligen Sakramente … entblösst waren, anzunehmen und ihnen kirchliche Pflege angedeihen zu lassen.[9]

The congregation was established on 21 February 1876, as a sub-congregation of St. Martini with local chemist, Hermann Parisius, brother of the founder of St. Martini, appointed as *Lektor* to hold services until a minister could be found.

In 1879, the congregation received land from the municipality *"dank des Ansehens des Apothekers Parisius und des Arztes Dr. Fismer."*[10] During the following year, the church was built. In 1882, a minister was appointed, a manse was built, and, in 1883, the congregation became independent with the son of the St. Martini minister, also called Pastor Carl Hugo Hahn, as its first minister.

At the turn of the century and up to the outbreak of World War I, the German community at the Cape experienced a rich cultural life, as is apparent from reports and advertisements in the biweekly newspaper *Südafrikanisches Gemeindeblatt*, later known as the *Deutscher Evangelischer Volksbote für Südafrika*. Mention is also made of a German *Volksliederverein*, *Jünglingsverein*, *Posaunenchor*, *Gesangchor*, and *Nähverein* in Paarl, where the congregation between 1897 and 1914 consisted of approximately two hundred and fifty members.

Looking after and maintaining their mother tongue was an important aspect in the history of the congregation. Already in 1879 a small private school, started by a relative of Mr. Parisius, had been taken over by the congregation. Keeping the school going was an enormous financial burden, but teaching children German and teaching them in German was regarded a necessity for the survival of the congregation. As W.H.C. Hellberg maintains:

> Die Erhaltung des Luthertums war durch die Kenntnis der Muttersprache bedingt. War diese unzulänglich, dann entzogen sich die ihm unterstellten Menschen seiner Seelsorge. Daher veranlassten so viele Pastoren die Gründung deutscher Gemeindeschulen. Sie mussten unablässig hart um ihre Erhaltung kämpfen und, bei Mangel an geeigneten Lehrkräften, selbst einspringen.[11]

Similar German schools were established by other congregations for the same reason. In and around Cape Town, three German schools were founded: one in Philippi in 1882, another at St. Martini in 1883, and a third in Wynberg in 1895. Of these, only the one in Cape Town, now known as the Deutsche Internationale Schule Kapstadt, still exists.

In 1900, the church synod considered that—with the financial assistance of the German Reich—its schools should become independent of the local school system. In Paarl, however, it was decided that "*die Schule solle nicht deutsche, sondern coloniale Erziehung geben.*" [12] The school survived both World War 1 as well as the Spanish influenza epidemic, and, in 1920, it became fully funded by the state. Only two years later, the new minister, Pastor F. Lührs, had to contend with threats by the authorities to close it down because of insufficient numbers. Eventually, he could increase the number of children from twenty-eight to forty-one. In 1924, the school was again threatened with closure due to a decline in the number of students. However, inspired by a change in government under General J.B.M. Hertzog, a church delegation took courage to see the new minister for education, Dr. D.F. Malan, who promised government support for the German "unionists" of the country and gave them the right to teach German Afrikaans children in German, as long as the official languages were also taught.[13]

This meeting must have encouraged Pastor Lührs to come up with the preposterous idea to found the Deutsches Institut Paarl. He envisaged a German school leading up to the Abitur, "*um so die weitesten Kreise des südafrikanischen Volkes mit deutscher Kultur in Verbindung zu bringen.*" [14] He even had his plans published in the "*Mitteilungen*" of the Deutsche Akademie, requesting donations for the erection of school buildings on a property of thirty-two hectares on the slopes of Paarl Mountain.[15] In

1929, Pastor Lührs's plans were discussed with the church committee, which felt that he invested too much time in the school project rather than in the congregation, and so their ways parted. He returned to Germany after having served the congregation for seven years. Although it can safely be assumed that a school project of this size would never have succeeded in such a small town, where it had been impossible—even in the best of times—to find more than fifty pupils for the German school, the decision by the church committee represents an understanding that still exists in the Paarl congregation until fairly recently: that the pastor should work primarily, if not exclusively, in and for the congregation.

In 1933, the school's fiftieth anniversary was celebrated and, with the support of the German consul, a teacher was sent from Germany whose presence brought about a change in German identity in the town. Hellberg makes the following observation:

> Danach trat eine Änderung in der Haltung des Deutschtums in Paarl ein. Bis dahin war die Kirche Mittelpunkt aller deutschen Veranstaltungen gewesen. Der Pastor galt als der Repräsentant des Deutschtums. Das änderte sich mit einem Schlage, als das deutsche Konsulat in Kapstadt erklärte, dass nicht die Kirche, sondern die NSDAP das Deutschtum verträte. Der Pastor galt nicht mehr als der Repräsentant desselben.[16]

The teacher, a Mr. Kurt Falck, became the new representative of what was German in Paarl. The German consulate, which up to then had cooperated with the church, now worked with the leadership of the National Socialist German Workers Party (NSDAP). The annual report of the school for 1938 lamented the idea that the education of the children had to be oriented toward Germany. Parents felt that this might alienate the children from their new country, South Africa.[17] When the question of employing a different teacher at the school was discussed, the congregation was adamant that it should not be somebody from Germany, not even someone local who had received his training in Germany.

At the outbreak of World War II, Mr. Falck immediately returned to Germany to join the war, whereas Pastor Johl allowed two of his sons to join the South African forces against Germany. When the second son joined the war against Germany, this proved too much for most of the congregation and led to Pastor Johl's resignation in 1943. Circumstances here seemed to replicate those of World War I, when Pastor Hahn's sons fought on the side of the English. Both ministers wanted to stay out of politics and felt they had to remain loyal to the government of the day. As Pastor Johl was born on a mission station at Embizeni in 1881 and only went to Germany for his theological training, he seemed to identify more with South Africa than with Germany.

Not only did the congregation lose its minister during World War II, but the school was closed at the end of 1939, after only two children had enrolled for the following year. During World War II, the Germans in town kept a very low profile. Evidence of this was, for example, that they held their annual bazaar in the church hall rather than in the town hall. As most of the German men in South Africa were interned during the war, the congregation was only able to appoint a new minister in 1947.

From 1947 onward, there was again a steady stream of immigrants to South Africa. As government policy favoured immigrants from western Europe, especially trained craftspeople, many of the Lutheran congregations benefited from the arrival of large numbers of Germans. Many of those found employment in Paarl for its proximity to Cape Town and its opportunities in the textile, engineering, and wine industries. Just as the local Germans did, the new immigrants also benefited from the apartheid laws introduced after 1948 which gave whites special privileges in terms of education, housing, and employment, as well as language and culture. Having had only 261 members in 1947, the St. Petri congregation grew steadily, doubling its membership to 530 by 1962.

Most of the post–World War II immigrants in Paarl were single young men in their early twenties who had received their vocational training in Germany. This was the time when the German Club was relaunched after the war and the German male voice choir was founded.[18] Through these organizations, activities were arranged that were enjoyed by young people at the time, such as dances, outings, festivals, and opportunities for young men to meet. As most of the young men could not speak English or Afrikaans, they relied on one another for company and these organizations provided them with a platform to find their feet. A seventy-one-year-old German resident still remembers that, when he arrived at the town in 1959, there were twenty-seven German craftsmen in Paarl, including a baker, butcher, bookseller, and a tailor.

Among the Germans who settled in Paarl, a few became famous throughout the country, and even internationally, including the Berlin-born Willi Voigt who founded an engineering business in 1893 that supplied the South African agricultural sector with diesel engines, pumps, and other machinery. Also among them were the winemaker Johann Georg Graue, who introduced the system of cold fermentation on his wine farm Nederburg after World War II, and Günter Brözel, who made Nederburg wines world famous during his thirty-three years as cellar master of the estate.[19]

As far as could be ascertained, the Germans in Paarl were highly regarded in the community. At the commemoration of the centenary of the German Lutheran St. Petri congregation in 1976, an editorial appeared in the local newspaper glorifying the members as "loyal and faithful members of the Paarl community as a whole" and as "hardworking and certainly a big asset to the town."[20] In a similar vein, a publication from 1924 with contributions by high school students, carried the following:

> If it is noteworthy that the English preserve their identity in Paarl, still more is this the case with the Germans, for they are in the vast minority ... One is made aware of their presence chiefly by the activities of their Church—the Lutheran Church—and of their Primary School. The Germans are amongst the most diligent people of the town. Work to them seems play, and play is work.[21]

The present-day visitor to the town will find hardly any reference to German.[22] Along the Hoofstraat, the longest main road in the country, there is a small sign pointing to the Lutherse kerk and on the approach from the eastern side, there is one that reads Deutscher Klub. In the Paarl Mall, the recently built shopping centre for the town, there is a shop called Herr Wurst, where one can purchase "German" produce such as Thüringer Bratwurst, Sauerkraut, and Brötchen from an Afrikaans-speaking woman.

In recent years, the flow of immigrants has slowed down and German speakers have become integrated into the larger (white) community, since their spouses are often not German speaking and many children can no longer speak the language. In effect, the German institutions tried to adapt to these circumstances by becoming multilingual entities. For example, the Lutheran congregation has been offering services in three languages for many years now: Afrikaans was introduced in 1972, and services have also been held in English since 1995. The German male voice choir has an Afrikaans-speaking conductor and rehearses and performs in three languages (German, Afrikaans, and English). German functions are still held by the club and attended by people from other communities. However, all three institutions (the Lutheran Church, the choir, and the German club) continue to function exclusively within the white community and also rarely attract young people, new immigrants, and visitors from Germany.[23]

Interviews with Germans in Paarl

In order to examine how the Germans of Paarl see themselves, how they define their primary identity, and how important the preservation of their language and culture is to them, interviews were conducted with seventeen German-speaking people who live in the town: men and women, young and old; some were born in Paarl, while others arrived there only recently.[24]

Seven of the interviewees arrived in Paarl in their early twenties between 1954 and 1976. They all were and still are, to a greater or lesser extent, involved in the activities of the German Club. They still regard themselves very much as Germans, although those men who arrived here single all married South African women. Two of these men, Rainer (fifty-nine) and Harald (seventy-one), regularly engage in social activities with other Germans but German is not spoken at home. Rainer wanted his children to grow up with only one language, and thus only Afrikaans, the language of his wife, is spoken in the home. Harald, who has a Scottish wife, speaks mostly English at home and his children also do not speak German.

The long-term viability and survival of the German language in Paarl was already questioned by Pastor Hahn in 1905 when he suggested in a report on the German School that the Germans did not have enough character to maintain their language in foreign surroundings: "*Besässen Deutsche die Characterfestigkeit, in fremder Umgebung ihre Muttersprache in Haus und Familie zu erhalten, dann würde unter hiesigen Verhältnissen die Anzahl der Deutschstunden genügen.*"[25] However, not even using the language in the home and family seems to ensure its survival. Alfred (forty-nine), who arrived in South Africa in 1977, married a German-speaking South African. They have two daughters and only speak German at home. They are active members in the congregation and in the club; however, although their daughters are, to some extent, trilingual, they now speak only English to one another and do not socialize with other Germans. In this case, not even German parents and a German church or club could preserve the language for the next generation. In fact, children whose parents force them to speak German might hate the language and refuse to speak it. This certainly was the case with Inge, whose father came from Pomerania and whose mother was a cousin of one of the founders of the congregation. As she went to an Afrikaans school, she did not want to be seen as different from her peers and refused to speak German to her father. It was only when she met her husband, Dieter, a textile merchant from Germany, that she rediscovered her roots and became an active member of the German community of the town.

Yet another case is Herbert (forty-nine) whose parents both emigrated to South Africa and were married in Paarl in 1956. Herbert's wife is a South African who learnt German at school and regards herself as having been "born with a German soul." They speak German, English, and Afrikaans in the home, and during the interview, at which their young son was also present, they frequently switched between all three languages. Herbert, who is an artist by profession, regards Germany as his cultural home, but the family does not socialize with Germans in the town and has hardly any German cultural traditions. Only during Christmas do they feel strongly connected to their German roots, when they go to church and unpack their Christmas decorations and nativity figures, which Herbert's grandparents brought along from Germany.

Some of the interviewees—Michael (forty-four) and Doris (forty-three) with son Jörg (seventeen)—are part of a new generation of Germans who have to purchase large properties and invest in the country in order to qualify as immigrants. They arrived in Paarl in 1998 to establish a business in the tourism industry. Doris, who grew up in a small town near Stuttgart, felt very homesick during the first few years. She did not feel comfortable in the Lutheran church. At the German club, people spoke mainly Afrikaans, a language she could not understand, and some held racist views and fears she did not share. Her contacts now are mainly with English-speaking South Africans, recent German immigrants, and, through her husband, members of the local cycling club.

Another new immigrant from Germany is Jan (twenty-nine), marketing manager in an up-market hotel in the town. He was invited to work at the hotel for three months but enjoyed Paarl so much that he extended his contract for another six years. He loves the town, the surroundings and has both English- and German-speaking friends. He is involved with the local tourism board but has no desire to go to church, nor would he go to any German event. Through his work, he is able to visit Germany twice a year and this way maintains contacts with his friends and family. He feels it is important to maintain a cosmopolitan culture in Paarl with German culture as one part, since he would love to buy German rolls and cold meats and have a German-speaking doctor.

In summary, the new generation of German immigrants seems to choose Paarl for the lifestyle it offers: the weather, the natural environment, the wine, the tourism potential with top class restaurants, hotels, and recreation facilities. As far as integration with the local South African community is concerned, the older immigrants took the route of inviting speakers of other languages to join their institutions, whereas Germans who arrived in Paarl more recently get involved in local institutions such as the tourism board, a community school, or a sports club. The church and the company of other German speakers are not important to these recent immigrants, and what the German club promotes as "*ein kleines Stück der alten Heimat*" is both a concept and a way of life they would rather want to get away from.[26] It seems, therefore, that German cultural institutions in South Africa, especially those outside the main city centres, are not able to attract new immigrants because, despite the common language, their perceptions of what German is are too diverse.

Notes

1 Meinhof and Galasiński, *Language of Belonging*, 7.
2 Constitution of the Republic of South Africa, ch. 1, sec. 6, cl. 5.
3 The NSC is the new school leaving certificate, which will be written for the first time in 2008. Learners must take at least two official languages, one of which must be taken at the highest level (home language level).
4 Böhm, *Deutsch in Afrika*, 613–14.
5 De Wet, "White Settlement," 18.
6 Hellberg, "Die deutschen evangelisch-lutherischen Kirchengemeinden," 11.
7 Hellberg, "Die deutschen evangelisch-lutherischen Kirchengemeinden," 35.
8 Hellberg, "Die deutschen evangelisch-lutherischen Kirchengemeinden," 228.
9 Hellberg, "Die Frühzeit," 10.
10 Hellberg, "Die Frühzeit," 13.
11 Hellberg, "Die deutschen evangelisch-lutherischen Kirchengemeinden," 266.
12 Münchmeyer, "Die deutsche Schule," 30.
13 Münchmeyer, "Die Schule," 40.
14 Münchmeyer, "Die Schule," 41.
15 "Das Deutsche Institut in Paarl," 864–65.
16 Hellberg, "Die deutschen evangelisch-lutherischen Kirchengemeinden," 259.
17 Münchmeyer, "Die Schule," 44.
18 The German club dates back to 1926 when it was known as the Deutscher Turnverein. In 1936, the German cultural organisations of the town amalgamated to form the Deutscher Verein, in which Mr. Kurt Falck played a prominent role. The club existed until 1939, was re-established in 1953, and became known as Deutscher Klub Paarl in 1967.
19 Simons and Proust, *Nederburg*, 106–19; Ambrosi, Grünewald, and von Dürckheim, *Deutsche im Kapweinbau*, 76.
20 "Paarl's German Community."
21 Maré and Sands, *Valley of the Berg*, 100.
22 Paarl currently has approximately 100,000 inhabitants. Only about three hundred are German speaking.
23 Efforts by Pastor M. Löhde, who served St. Petri between 1984 and 1990, to forge closer links with the black community of Paarl were not appreciated by the congregation.
24 Names have been changed to protect the identities of the people who were interviewed.
25 Hahn, "Bericht," 7.
26 Fleitmann, "Vorwort," 2.

Interview Sources

Seventeen German-speaking residents of Paarl, interviews by Rolf Annas, Stellenbosch University, June 2006.

Works Cited

Ambrosi, Hans, Hildemarie Grünewald, and Max Graf von Dürckheim. *Deutsche im Kapweinbau*. Wiesbaden: Gesellschaft für Geschichte des Weines, 1999.
Böhm, Michael Anton. *Deutsch in Afrika. Die Stellung der deutschen Sprache in Afrika vor dem Hintergrund der bildungs- und sprachpolitischen Gegebenheiten sowie der deutschen auswärtigen Kulturpolitik*. Frankfurt: Peter Lang, 2003.

"Census 2001: Primary tables South Africa: Census '96 and 2001 compared. Pretoria: Statistics South Africa, 2004. <www.statssa.gov.za/census01/html/RSAPrimary.pdf>.

Constitution of the Republic of South Africa Act 108 of 1996. As adopted on 8 May 1996 and amended on 11 October 1996 by the Constitutional Assembly; and amended by the Constitution of the Republic of South Africa Amendment Act, 1997. <www.info.gov.za/documents/constitution> (March 2008).

"Das Deutsche Institut in Paarl (Südafrika)." *Mitteilungen der Deutschen Akademie zur wissenschaftlichen Erforschung und zur Pflege des Deutschtums* 19 (1928): 864–65.

De Wet, G.C. "White Settlement in the Drakenstein Valley up to 1700." In *Paarl Valley 1687–1987*, edited by Arie Gerhardus Oberholster, 13–22. Pretoria: Human Sciences Research Council, 1987.

Fleitmann, Richard. "Vorwort." In *Deutscher Klub Paarl 1976–2001*, 2. Paarl: Intermedia Printers, 2001.

Hahn, Carl Hugo. "Bericht über die Schule." In *Südafrikanisches Gemeindeblatt*, 26 January 1905, p. 7.

Hellberg, W.H.C. "Die deutschen evangelisch-lutherischen Kirchengemeinden im Westen des Kaplandes." DLitt diss., Stellenbosch University, 1957.

———. "Die Frühzeit—Filialgemeinde von Kapstadt." In *Deutsche Evangelisch-Lutherische St. Petri-Gemeinde Paarl. 100 Jahre 1876–1976. Festschrift zum hundertjährigen Bestehen der Gemeinde*, edited by Christoph Brandt, 9–14. Paarl: Paarl Printing Company, 1976.

Maré, B.J., and G.W. Sands, eds. *In the Valley of the Berg or The Romance of a South African Town by the Gymnasium Senior Matriculation Class of 1924*. Paarl: Paarl Printing Company, 1924.

Meinhof, Ulrike Hanna, and Dariusz Galasiński. *The Language of Belonging*. Hampshire: Palgrave Macmillan, 2005.

Münchmeyer, M. "Die deutsche Schule (1878–1920)." In *Deutsche Evangelisch-Lutherische St. Petri-Gemeinde Paarl. 100 Jahre 1876–1976. Festschrift zum hundertjährigen Bestehen der Gemeinde,* edited by Christoph Brandt, 26–32. Paarl: Paarl Printing Company, 1976.

———. "Die Schule (1920–1939)." In *Deutsche Evangelisch-Lutherische St. Petri-Gemeinde Paarl. 100 Jahre 1876–1976. Festschrift zum hundertjährigen Bestehen der Gemeinde,* edited by Christoph Brandt, 40–46. Paarl: Paarl Printing Company, 1976.

"Paarl's German Community." *Paarl Post*, 12 March 1976.

Simons, Phillida Brooke, and Alain Proust. *Nederburg: The First Two Hundred Years*. Cape Town: Struik Publishers, 1992.

SEVEN

Canadian German
Identity in Language

Grit Liebscher
Jennifer Dailey-O'Cain

Whenever speakers of one language move to a place where a different language is spoken, language contact phenomena are to be expected. This chapter investigates such phenomena within the social context of language use and, in particular, links them to questions of identity. It bases its analysis on interviews and conversations with German-speaking immigrants and their descendants in Kitchener-Waterloo and Edmonton, Canada. By considering the emic perspective, this chapter contributes to the reconstruction of what it means to be German in the diaspora from the participants' point of view. It uses the concept of positioning to explore how speakers, through their linguistic choices, form the groups with which they create alliances or from which they set themselves apart, most notably German, Canadian, and German Canadian.

Introduction

FOR DECADES, LINGUISTS HAVE BEEN WORKING on German speech island dialects in North America and elsewhere, addressing the various ways in which the language has been affected by such an intense and prolonged contact with English. An extensive body of literature has developed that identifies contact features at all levels of language.[1] At the same time, other scholars have investigated the larger question of the maintenance of the German language in Canada, making use of census data to show the extent to which German has given way to English, especially in the urban areas.[2] The binary view of identity taken up by this kind of work, however, can force researchers into a position of projecting categories onto their subjects: if speakers' German is being influenced by English, they are assumed to be becoming "less German," and if the domains in which they use German are gradually shifting in favour of English, they are assumed to be becoming "more Canadian." This chapter instead adopts a qualitative analytical approach based on conversation analysis, through which the complexity of these speakers' identities can be addressed in a way that is not possible through an analysis of census data or contact influence.

More specifically, the interest here is in the ways in which German immigrants in Canada and their direct descendants construct their identities through their use of language. While research on language contact phenomena provides insights into the structural changes in the language of individuals and groups, it does not draw attention to the ways in which these phenomena become interactional resources that position speakers in relation to the social categories that exist in their societies. In a similar vein, while census data provides a general picture of people's beliefs about language use and their membership in preconceived groups (e.g., German, Canadian, etc.), those data do not detail actual language use and how this use relates to a German Canadian identity. If identity categories are viewed as constructed through interaction rather than as fixed, the different roles played by various contact phenomena and the use of English can be revealed.

The research presented here is part of a larger project about German Canadian language and identity. This chapter will focus on three speakers out of a larger corpus of twenty speakers from Kitchener-Waterloo, Ontario, and twelve speakers from Edmonton, Alberta: one from Edmonton and two from Kitchener-Waterloo. Taken as a group, the German of all of these speakers exhibits features typical of contact with English, such as code-switching or code-mixing, frequent borrowings and loan translations, and both morphological and syntactic influence. However, each speaker also distinguishes himself or herself on the basis of the identity construction that can be perceived in the interaction.

The Cities: Edmonton and Kitchener-Waterloo

In the early 1900s, the provincial capital city of Edmonton and its sister city, Strathcona (they were amalgamated in 1912), were the destination of the largest number of Alberta's immigrants from German-speaking countries. According to the 2001 census, the city of Edmonton has nearly 26,000 inhabitants of German ethnic origin, a community that maintains its own schools and stores, its own newspaper, and many clubs and activities. Use of German as a home language, however, declined by

57.2 percent in Edmonton between 1971 and 1991. In 2001, a large majority of Edmonton's home-language German speakers were over age fifty-five. This indicates that while the German ethnic affiliation remains strong in the city, most of the native speakers are not passing their language on to the later generations.[3]

The twin cities of Kitchener-Waterloo, despite being much smaller in terms of overall population, have an even larger community of German ethnic origin. In the nineteenth century, Waterloo County was known as "New Germany," and even today the area still stands out nationally as the centre of German Canadian culture.[4] The 2001 census data reveals that 32,910 inhabitants of German ethnic origin still live in the Waterloo Regional Municipality, and, as in Edmonton, the community has a strong cultural presence through supplementary schools and activities such as the yearly Oktoberfest, which attracts 700,000 people. As in Edmonton, however, there is also evidence of a shift from German to English among the Kitchener-Waterloo German Canadians. Just shy of 7,500 of the aforementioned group of Waterloo Regional Municipality residents of German ethnic origin still speak German as a home language, and nearly 60 percent of those are over age fifty-five. While there are proportionally more people of German ethnic origin in Kitchener-Waterloo than in Edmonton, these data suggest that even among New Germany's Germans the actual use of the language is rapidly declining.[5]

Identity and Positioning

Two forms of identity are pertinent both to this chapter and to the larger project of which it is a part. The first form, and the most immediately obvious, is personal identity, which is built upon the particular life history of each individual person.[6] This form of identity consists of biographical facts about people, such as where they live and have lived, who their family and friends are, and what languages they speak. One of its aspects is the exposure to a certain linguistic environment and the kinds of (linguistic) contacts a person has. Social identity, as a second form, can be defined as a way of describing the groups into which people categorize themselves and others.[7] Some groups that may be relevant for this discussion are those that can be distinguished by labels such as "German," "Canadian," and "Canadian with German background." When individuals interact, they bring with them a cognitive awareness of the various social identities by which they may categorize themselves or be categorized by others. It is only through this interaction that certain aspects of people's identities are highlighted and social identities become relevant. In an analysis of this kind of interactive identity construction, identity is not viewed as limited to any preconceived categories that social scientists may regard as important, but is co-constructed by all conversation participants.[8] Identity in that sense is changing, often from one moment to the next—something that can be particularly relevant in a situation of migration.

The process by which interactants make personal and social identities relevant at any given point in a conversation is called positioning.[9] People carry out positioning by using various linguistic and interactional resources, thereby constructing personal and social identities on the spot. People can position both themselves and others, often through the same utterance, and positioning can be either unconscious and subtle or conscious and deliberate. While positioning is a natural and unavoidable process of conversation, the positioning of interactants, whether subtle or deliberate, is an expression of their identities.

Data Analysis

Language use in interaction can indicate how people see themselves and others in light of their relationships to social groups, as can be illustrated by analysing data drawn from conversations and interviews. How the interviewer's perceived identity may play a role in the interview, as Janet Fuller points out, is also relevant.[10] Typical contact phenomena are a part of this analysis, but the focus is on how these phenomena emerge in the interaction and affect the construction of identities rather than on listing them all for each speaker.

The first example, which is from the Edmonton corpus, is an excerpt of a conversation between the research assistant at the University of Alberta, who is called Diana here, and the Edmonton speaker, a woman with the pseudonym NS, who is a first-generation immigrant.[11] NS came to Canada in the mid 1970s, where she met her Austrian husband. They moved to Austria but returned to Canada after six months. The conversation is about NS's initial immigration to Canada and her workplace, a house in the neighbourhood where she used to work as a nanny and still works as a housekeeper. The analysis here draws attention to the ways in which NS positions herself with respect to a German Canadian identity.

EXAMPLE 1:

NS: *jetzt im September dreißig Jahr, ja*
Diana: wow
NS: *wenn ich kam zu Kanada—also nach Kanada. neunzehnhundert*
              und fünfundsiebzig,
Diana: *hmm*
NS: *ich kam hier am zwölften Februar, ich bin allein gekommen mit meiner*
              Tochter, weil ich n Bruder hier hatte

The passage in example 1 is preceded in the conversation by NS telling her experience in a variety of German that does not show any transfer from English. Here transfer means the influence of one language on another, which, in this case, would be the influence of English on German or vice versa.[12] The first time such evidence of transfer is seen is in the phrase "*zu Kanada*," which is a loan translation from the English "to Canada." This phrase is non-standard German (or grammatically incorrect, if judged against norms of the standard), but not uncommon among Germans who live outside Germany. In this particular case, it may be triggered by the English word order of the construction "*wenn ich kam zu Kanada*" ["when I came to Canada"], which contrasts with standard German "*als ich nach Kanada kam*," where the verb is at the end. NS performs a self-correction in which she marks the non-standard "*zu Kanada*" as wrong and presents the standard version "*nach Kanada*" as correct. Corrections of any sort, or more generally repairs, are common in all conversation and are defined by conversation analysts as trouble in speaking, hearing, or understanding.[13] Sometimes, as is the case here, a link can be drawn between the repair and the constructed identity of the speaker. Gail Jefferson has drawn attention to the use of repair as "a resource for negotiating and perhaps reformulating a current set of identities."[14] The use of the loan translation "*zu Kanada*" invokes NS's identity as a German speaker living outside of Germany, specifically in an English-speaking environment. In reformulating using standard German "*nach Kanada*," she repositions herself as a standard speaker of German, not invoking her immigration history. In fact, through the use of the reformulation marker "*also*," NS marks the non-standard as an error. The correction is spoken more softly and quietly, by which NS marks it as an aside, as if to apologize for the "mistake." In correcting herself, she makes an extra effort to speak standard German and to show her awareness of what is correct, even though she would likely have been understood using the non-standard version. It seems important to her to present the correct form, that is to position herself as somebody who knows the correct standard German alternative.

As Fuller points out, the interviewer's perceived identity may play an important role in language use and the ways in which the participants position each other.[15] NS's correction may be influenced by the fact that she is talking to a native speaker of German who is also a relative stranger. Whereas NS constructs her use of non-standard German as something worthy of correction, Diana neither comments on nor orients to this correction, which indicates that Diana neither sees NS's use of non-standard German as wrong nor does she particularly require her to use a standard form. In fact, there are other instances in NS's language use during this brief excerpt that show influence from the English, which are not corrected, for example "*ich kam hier*" for standard German "*ich kam hierher.*" NS may, in fact, know the standard German in all these cases but chooses not to correct herself. In terms of her identity, NS positions herself as a German living abroad through the English-influenced forms (rather unconscious and subtle), but still shows an attempt (conscious and deliberate positioning) to pass as a standard German speaker through the correction. She thus positions herself flexibly, foregrounding her German Canadian identity at times by showing evidence of transfer, and at other times showing her ties to the German mainland, by exhibiting awareness of standard German.

Thus the analysis of interactional phenomena such as repair can provide insights into the way speakers see themselves and want to be seen with respect to social identity. The analysis of language use in interaction informs a different complexity of identity than either-or identifications such as that requested by the census. The discussion will now turn to two excerpts taken from the same conversational interview from the Kitchener-Waterloo corpus.[16] These excerpts are used for contrast to show that the naming of a social identity for oneself may differ or in fact contrast with identities as they emerge through language use in the interaction. The interviewer, called Maria, is an English-German bilingual speaker who is herself from the fourth generation of a German-speaking immigrant family. The interview is with a couple from the Kitchener-Waterloo area who are both in their seventies. The husband, here called DS, is of the first generation, was born in the former Yugoslavia and has lived in several European German-speaking areas. He moved to Canada in the late 1940s, when he was about fifteen years old, and only started learning English at that point. He met his wife, CS, in Canada. She was born in Canada to German-speaking parents and considers German her first language. The fact that she is of the second generation and he is of the first generation does not immediately present itself through the language use (for example, through contact phenomena) in the interview. One would have to go beyond the analysis here to detect any differences in their language use that could be traced back to differences in generation, which would be an interesting question on its own. Both individuals chose to speak their variety of German right from the beginning of the interview, after the interviewer asked them in English to speak "English German whatever." The interviewer also used German after the couple started speaking German and the interview continued mostly in German.

The discussion of examples 2 and 3 focuses on the ways in which the speakers position themselves in regard to the social identities "German," "Canadian," etc. Here the complexities of these social identities and changing positioning coming with a multiplicity of identities are exhibited. In

example 2, the interviewer Maria directly asks about CS's and DS's identities in a way that the census may pose such question.

EXAMPLE 2

Maria: *würden Sie sagen, dass Sie Kanadier sind, oder einer anderen Natio-*
        nalität oder Mischung aus Kanadier und was anderes?
DS: *ob wir Kanadier sind?*
Maria: *nja also was würden Sie sagen was für eine Nationalität haben Sie*
        oder Identität
CS: *bei mir ist e—, bei mir, weil ich doch da geboren bin in Kanada, bin*
        ich kanadisch zuerst und deutsche Abstammung, des is so, so antworte
        ich, bei dir ist es
DS: well *ich bin deutsch und bin*
CS: Canad—
DS: *kanadischer Staatsbürger halt*

DS's confirmation question after Maria's initial request shows a preference to approach this question through a single category. Maria refor-
mulates her question without the term "Canadian" to indicate an openness for other categories. However, her new focus on nationality gives
identity a rather specific definition usually associated with citizenship. CS
then describes herself in terms of her citizenship (by birth place) as Canadian with German heritage. In contrast to CS, her husband DS puts his Germanness first, although the answer does not come to him easily, as indicated by the fact that he starts with the hesitation or disagreement marker
"well." He further hesitates in describing his Canadianness, which is why
his wife can make a suggestion using the English pronunciation for "Canadian." DS then describes himself in German as *"kanadischer Staatsbürger
halt."* Two aspects are noteworthy about this description. First, the Canadianness is formulated purely in terms of citizenship, which contrasts with
"ich bin deutsch," leaving open whether this implies feeling German or
being a German citizen or speaking German. Second, the discourse marker
"halt" makes the description of Canadian citizenship an essentiality that
comes for example with living in the country and applying for citizenship
rather than a matter of identification. Given the contradiction between policy (citizenship) and matters of identification, the question arises which
aspects of Canadianness or Germanness determine these categories.

Example 3 from the same interview indicates some of the ways that
the categories German and Canadian are negotiated and deconstructed.
In this example, CS and DS are trying to describe Kirchweih, a traditional
German festival, after Maria has admitted that she does not know what
it is.

EXAMPLE 3

DS: *und dann wie die Zeit war für Kirchweih un da war die Zeit das*
        ist meistens die so wie Erntedank es ist so wie ähnliches wie also der
        harvest time.

CS: well, *Kirchweih wie die Kirche eingeweiht wurde.*

DS: *Kirch und dann in Herbst im Herbst waren die Früchte wie soll ich*
        sage die alles das alles

CS: *ja*

DS: your Thanksgiving.

Maria: *ja*

DS: *so etwas. meistens um die Zeit war das.*

The excerpt starts with DS and CS trying to explain to Maria what Kirch-weih is, with DS suggesting "*Erntedank*" and "harvest time" as alternatives. CS provides a reformulation in terms of the original meaning of Kirchweih, the consecration of a church. After DS situates Kirchweih in the fall, CS switches to English in comparing it to Thanksgiving. Through the formulation "like your Thanksgiving," CS positions the interviewer ("your") as part of the group that she associates with Thanksgiving, presumably contrasting this group with the one she associates with Kirch-weih. The choice of "your" instead of "our" also indicates that CS does not see herself as part of the interviewer's group. For her, then, Kirch-weih is part of her own identity construction, whereas she associates Thanksgiving with whatever the interviewer stands for: the younger generation of Canadians, Canadians in general as opposed to German Cana-dians/Germans, or fourth-generation German Canadians. The reference to the last group is especially interesting because it clearly shows that CS does not recognize Maria as part of the same German Canadian group as herself, maybe not even as fourth-generation German Canadian at all but as Canadian. Although there may be other interactional circum-stances when Maria may be constructed as part of CS's group, it is not with the kind of experiences, knowledge, and values associated with Kirchweih.

Conclusion

The contribution of this chapter to linguistic research on the German diaspora lies in providing an interactional, conversation analyt-ical perspective, which investigates how participants in the interaction construct each others' identities by positioning themselves and others through language use. This includes the fact that speakers make (con-scious or unconscious) linguistic choices that relate to the ways a speaker wants to or will be seen. The chapter also discusses the influence of the conversational partner for certain types of positioning and, in fact, the co-construction of identity by all participants. An analysis of interaction reveals that identity construction in the interaction is more complex and more flexible than the answers to specific questions about nationality or identity, for example on a census. By making the emic, or insiders' perspective relevant, "German Canadian" as a single category is reconstructed through analyses such as the ones provided here. However, since identity construction, suggested through this perspective, is an ongoing process, there will never be a finite definition of such a category.

This chapter is based on research supported by a number of grants from the universities of Alberta and Waterloo.

Notes

1 Burridge, "Throw the Baby"; Clausing, *English Influence*; Clyne, *Dynamics of Language Contact*; Fuller, "The Principle"; Goss and Salmons, "Evolution of a Bilingual Discourse Marking System"; Johnson, "Structural Aspects"; Louden, "Patterns of Sociolinguistic Variation."
2 Prokop and Bassler, *German Language Maintenance.*
3 Prokop and Bassler, *German Language Maintenance.*
4 Prokop and Bassler, *German Language Maintenance,* 240.
5 Prokop and Bassler, *German Language Maintenance.*
6 Ricker, *Migration, Sprache und Identität,* 9.
7 Gumperz, *Language and Social Identity.*
8 Antaki and Widdicombe, *Identities in Talk.*
9 Harré and van Langenhove, "Varieties of Positioning"; van Langenhove and Harré, "Positioning and Autobiography."
10 Fuller, "Language Choice."
11 Names have been changed to protect the identities of the people who were interviewed.
12 Clyne, *Dynamics of Language Contact.*
13 Schegloff, Jefferson, and Sacks, "The Preference for Self-Correction."
14 Jefferson, "Error Correction."
15 Fuller, "Language Choice."
16 Heffner, "Heritage Languages."

Works Cited

Antaki, Charles, and Sue Widdicombe. *Identities in Talk.* London: Sage, 1998.
Burridge, Kate. "Throw the Baby from the Window a Cookie: English and Pennsylvania German in Contact." In *Case, Typology, and Grammar: In Honor of Barry J. Blake.* Edited by Anna Siewierska and Jae Jung Song, 71–93. Amsterdam: John Benjamins, 1998.
Clausing, Stephen. *English Influence on American German and American Icelandic.* New York: Peter Lang, 1986.
Clyne, Michael. *Dynamics of Language Contact.* Cambridge: Cambridge University Press, 2003.

Fuller, Janet. "Language Choice and Speaker Identity: The Influence of a Researcher's Linguistic Proficiency in Interviews." *Southern Journal of Linguistics* 24, no. 1 (2000): 91–102.

———. "The Principle of Pragmatic Detachability in Borrowing: English-Origin Discourse Markers in Pennsylvania German." *Linguistics* 39, no. 2 (2001): 351–69.

Goss, Emily L., and Joseph C. Salmons. "The Evolution of a Bilingual Discourse Marking System: Modal Particles and English Markers in German-American Dialects." *International Journal of Bilingualism* 4, no. 4 (2000): 469–84.

Gumperz, John J. *Language and Social Identity: Studies in Interactional Sociolinguistics.* Cambridge: Cambridge University Press, 1983.

Harré, Rom, and Luk van Langenhove. "Varieties of Positioning." *Journal for the Theory of Social Behaviour* 21, no. 4 (1991): 393–407.

Heffner, Lori. *Heritage Languages: The Case of German in Kitchener-Waterloo.* MA thesis, University of Waterloo, 2002.

Jefferson, Gail. "Error Correction as an Interactional Resource," *Language in Society* 3, no. 2 (1974): 181–99.

Johnson, D. Chris. "Structural Aspects of the Volga German Dialect of Schoenchen, Kansas." In *The German Language in America, 1683–1991,* edited by Joseph C. Salmons, 158–87. Madison: Max Kade Institute for German-American Studies, University of Wisconsin, 1993.

Louden, Mark L. 1993. "Patterns of Sociolinguistic Variation in Pennsylvania German." In *The German Language in America, 1683–1991,* edited by Joseph C. Salmons, 284–306. Madison: Max Kade Institute for German-American Studies, University of Wisconsin, 1993.

Prokop, Manfred, and Gerhard Bassler. *German Language Maintenance across Canada. A Handbook.* Sherwood Park, AB: M. Prokop, 2004.

Ricker, Kirsten. *Migration, Sprache und Identität. Eine biographieanalytische Studie zu Migrationsprozessen von Französinnen in Deutschland.* Bremen: Donat Verlag, 2000.

Schegloff, Emanuel A., Gail Jefferson, and Harvey Sacks. "The Preference for Self-Correction in the Organization of Repair in Conversation." *Language,* 53, no. 2 (1977): 361–82.

van Langenhove, Luk, and Rom Harré. "Positioning and Autobiography: Telling Your Life." In *Discourse and Lifespan Identity,* edited by Nikolas Coupland and Jon F. Nussbaum, 81–99. London: Sage, 1993.

EIGHT

"Memories from Afar"

Aspects of Memories Spanning Several Generations in Families of Austrian Jewish Refugees

Andrea Strutz

How did Austrian Jewish refugees remember their former home and culture, and what memories and narratives did they pass on to later generations? The research in this chapter is based on interviews with children and grandchildren of Austrian Jewish refugees in New York with at least one Jewish grandparent who had been expelled from Austria in 1938. The memories of the first generation of Austrian Jewish refugees concerning the expulsion from Austria in 1938 and the Holocaust were not dominant, although the grandparents had been traumatized. Even though cultural heritage or the German language became formative in the identies and memories of the second and third generations, the research discovered that Austrian cuisine dominated the memories of second- and third-generation refugees, creating for them a positive emotional bond with their ancestors' former home.

HOW DOES ONE REMEMBER THE PAST, and how are memories passed on? How do Austrian Jewish refugees remember their former home and culture? What memories and narratives do they pass on to younger generations? These are key questions of the video history project titled "Erinnerungen aus der Ferne."[1] This is a follow-up investigation to the project "Emigration: Austria–New York," whose goal was the collection and analysis of experiences and memories of Austrian Jews who were expelled from Austria in 1938–39, took refuge in the United States, and could not (or did not want to) return after World War II.

"Emigration. Austria–New York" focused on New York City, where more than 70,000 Austrian and German fugitives from Hitler populated Washington Heights in Manhattan—called the "Fourth Reich on the Hudson"—and Riverdale in the Bronx.[2] "Since so many of the Austrians were city-dwellers from Vienna, it was not surprising that a very large proportion of them settled first in New York."[3] Twenty-three qualitative interviews were videorecorded with Austrian Jewish refugees in 1996 in New York City.[4] An essential part of the project was to explore the relationship of Austrian Jewish refugees with their former home country and to find out in particular what images and memories about Austria the interviewees had preserved. The video documentation *continental divide.geteilte leben* features the life stories of these interviewees and the crucial moments in their lives, and also the relationship with their former home and their reminiscences of Austria.[5] The video gives Austrian Jewish refugees a voice to express themselves and shows the various ways of coming to terms with the past.[6]

"Memories from Afar" continued these research activities, but concentrated on the second and third generations of families of Austrian Jewish refugees. In his investigation of collective memory, Jan Assmann differentiates between cultural memory and communicative memory.[7] Cultural memory preserves a group's pool of knowledge. This knowledge is, at the same time, reconstructed for the actual situation, and memory is culturally moulded and handed down to later generations via rites, texts, memorials, and history books. While cultural memory, according to Assmann, stretches over long periods with certain fixed points, collective memory is defined by a limited and accompanying time span of three to four generations and also describes the period of investigation of oral history. Communicative memory, on the other hand, is based on everyday conversation: "Personal memory is built up from this type of conversation ... it is a) socially conveyed and b) group related. Each individual memory is constituted in a combination with the other." Therefore, this project aims to explore the communicative memory in the families of refugees. The interviews with the first generation of Austrian refugees had revealed, besides terror and the resulting nightmares, depictions of Austria and especially Vienna with certain nostalgia. The apartments of these interviewees are decorated with drawings, photographs, books, calendars, and other souvenirs of Austria. During the interviews with the first generation of refugees, their grandchildren in particular showed enormous interest in the grandparents' former home country as well as in their memories.

Being carriers of cultural codes and images, migrants have important functions in mechanisms of reception and reflexion. The "Memories from Afar" project investigates how Austrian Jewish refugees remembered their former home and culture and what memories and narratives they passed on to their descendants. How were these memories and narratives transformed, and what memories are dominant in the second and third generations? For that reason, the relationship between the first generation of refugees and their descendants was most interesting, as was the latter group's knowledge of the fate and the personal history of their grandparents. Further questions concerned the identity of the second and third generations, specifically if Austrian heritage and maybe the German language played a significant part in their lives and/or family history, and if this heritage shaped their identity in any way. A special issue was the relationship of the second and third generations to Austria and their images of Austria, either because of their own experiences and/or because of the memories and narratives that were passed on to them.

For logistical reasons, interviewees for "Memories from Afar" were sought in the greater New York area; they had to have at least one Austrian Jewish grandparent who was forced to flee in 1938–39. Six persons were selected, three women and three men, who, at the time of the interviews, were between twenty-eight and fifty years of age and had grown up in New York or its suburbs. All but one lived and worked in the greater New York area. Five had a grandfather as well as a grandmother who were Austrian, more precisely Viennese; in one case, the grandmother was from Vienna and the grandfather was from Germany. The interviews were conducted in English in 2001. As with the previous investigation, semi-structured interviews were used. It was assumed that the images of Austria would be influenced by the narratives of the first generation of refugees, the American socialization of the descendants, and possibly by actual Austrian political issues (for example, matters of restitution or coming to terms with the National Socialist past).

Austria, the home country of the first generation, was of variable importance in the growing-up process of the descendants. The fact that sometimes grandparents as well as parents of the interviewees were part of the emigrant generation caused certain problems, as the threads of tradition could not always be clearly followed. However, it is not surprising that for this group of interviewees an aggregation of fragments of memory and behaviour can be noticed, as grandparents as well as parents had experienced a European socialization, as illustrated by example 1.

EXAMPLE 1

I think a lot of what I learned, it would be hard to say was directly from my grandparents or from my parents. I can no longer sort that out. I know since I was tiny, since I was my children's age, I read everything I could read about the Holocaust … I cannot remember not knowing about it. So that is

what is so strange to me, as I said earlier that to me for people
not to know and not to share, I cannot remember not
knowing.[8]

The stories of the first generation sank deep into the memory of the
second and third generations. Austria is a regular element in all their
family stories. It is not always the most important issue, but it is constantly
present as the country from which the family was expelled. In this regard
Lisa Mehl says: "Austria is a topic as far as the Holocaust is involved: it is
a very emotional topic for my grandparents, approached often. They speak
about it like it was yesterday.... It is important for the family tradition."[9]
In addition, some of the interviewees associated Austria firstly with hurt-
ful personal loss and also material loss that the family had experienced as
victims of the Nazi persecution.

> **EXAMPLE 2**
>
> Sadness and fear, I in a sort think of my history being gone. My
> family had significant roots there, had a nice big apartment and
> a business and dance teachers and music teachers, a real com-
> munity that they had known. I feel kind of ripped off, sad that I
> never got a part of it. The pictures look wonderful. Yes, sadness
> and a bit of anger, I guess, are the first thing I think of.[10]

Nevertheless, neither the expulsion from Austria nor the Holocaust
dominated the memories that the first generation passed on to their children and grandchildren. Personal experiences and the strength of relations with Austria in the second and third generations depended on the
frequency and intensity of visits to the country.

> **EXAMPLE 3**
>
> As a little boy, I travelled with my father, who had a sabbatical.
> I was just five years old, and I have not been back since that.
> I would like to go sometime and check it out. That would be
> interesting ... I have mixed feelings about going to Austria.
> There is a part of me that stays away ... but it gives me a little
> bit of a creepy feeling to think my family was basically running
> for their lives from their own homes. I would go, but kind of
> cautiously.[11]

For others trips to Austria were a natural part of their lives that would
profoundly mould their image of Austria.

> **EXAMPLE 4**
>
> We went to Austria almost once a year. Some people in this
> country go to the mountains. We had gone to Austria. In my
> case, Austria was so embedded in our lives. It just sort of hap-

pened…. In London, we were visitors. My father did not consider us visitors when we were in Vienna. Trips to Vienna were more a family visit. By the time I was ten, I knew where my father fell when he was five…. I have spent enough time in Austria to not have the picture of the von Trapp family. I go to Germany and Austria so often. I get an Austrian newspaper on my email every week.[12]

The same diversity could be observed with respect to German-language skills. Some of the interviewees understand single words while others grew up in a bilingual environment.[13] It was striking that the German mother tongue of the grandparents inspired only a small number of the children or grandchildren to study German in school, even though German (more specifically the Viennese dialect) played an important part in the everyday conversations of the generations who lived together. In some families German was used as a "secret language" by the older generation.[14]

EXAMPLE 5

I did not learn German. But I tell you this: growing up we used to speak German in the house. I did, to count, things like that, eins, zwei, drei … my father speaks a little bit and understands everything. As a family, it was English, Viennese, German. English, but the grandkids always said speak English, speak English. My parents grew up in a household that was bilingual. For us it was different. The language was just part of us growing up. Even now my grandmother will speak Viennese to me just like in the middle of the sentence. And I know what she is saying and she does not realize it.[15]

Quite different approaches to the use of the German language within one generation could be observed in families of Austrian Jewish refugees:

EXAMPLE 6

My parents spoke English to us. You have to remember my mother had been here a long time before I was born. My sisters were born in New York City but I was born in the Catskill Mountains because the mountains reminded them of the Austrian Alps. My sisters did not speak German until later and my older sister still does not speak German very well. She went to the University of Vienna for one summer. I think she had a radically different experience than I did and never learned German particularly well. My middle sister studied German in school and actually learned to speak correctly but never very easily. For neither of them is it a comfort language. For me it is a comfort language and maybe that's because the age I was when my grandmother moved in with us.[16]

Nevertheless, those who had frequent contact with the Austrian culture in their everyday life, including frequent trips to Austria, developed expertise in German. In one case German and English blended in the everyday conversation.

EXAMPLE 7

My father and I were the best for Dschinglish. We would throw words, whatever the easiest word was ... I didn't get taught, it was spoken ..., it was spoken to me and when I was hungry and wanted Palatschinken I guess, I realized, it was smarter to say: Ich bin hungrig, würdest du ... I used German especially when I wanted to get good food from my grandmother. It is so engrained, it is hard to separate ... occasionally I find words I know in German and not in English.[17]

However, all the families of Austrian Jewish refugees used German loanwords. All grandparents are addressed with the German words for grandparents, a memento from where they came.

EXAMPLE 8

My grandparents were Oma and Opa. There are German constructions, language constructions that even when you speak perfect English—for example, a small one is—Americans say my parents or your parents or our parents but in German man sagt: die Eltern and Americans of German descent say the parents, did you call them parents? I call the parents, mom and dad ... Mutti and Vati, well, when my kids have children, I will certainly be Opa. And my parents are Opa and Oma to my children.[18]

Diverse formative cultural impacts shaped the identities and memories of the descendants of Austrian Jewish refugees.

EXAMPLE 9

My identity is probably heritage and culturally Austrian. Religiously Jewish. Culturally gay too. Citizenship American. Wohnort New York.... I feel that Austria is one of my homes. I feel it is funny since there are no more relatives there who welcome me home there, it feels not so much as home ... the people sort of make the home.... It is a very special country. I consider myself Austrian. There is no question. I was brought up with enough cultural identification to identify in both directions.[19]

EXAMPLE 10

My identity is mixed. I see myself in one way as first-generation survivor of the Holocaust. So in that way I feel kind of different from American society at large, but I am also very
American. I grew up on a diet of baseball and New York. I am
pretty much a New York guy. It is a strange question to ask in
New York, you know, everyone has a little bit of a different
sprinkling or something. I see myself in part as European. I
carry this name almost by accident, Wiener, but I have a mother
with a German accent, so I see myself with a little bit of an
Austrian spin sprinkled in there. And Jewish. An American Jew.
It is tough to put that all together.[20]

EXAMPLE 11

I am certainly an American. In 1974, I was making an application to be admitted to a particular program and part of the
application form was, you had to write a short autobiographical
sketch. And the first sentence of what I wrote was: I am the only
son of Jewish refugees who fled from Nazi Europe. And that is
certainly an important part of my identity. If you say: are you an
American? The answer is: Ja. I am an American. I was born
here, I went to school here, and I know the idiom. But it is an
important part of my identity that I am the son of Jewish
refugees. But my construction of that would be my family is
Jewish, not my family is Austrian.[21]

The statements above show the blending of components that affected
the interviewees' identities.[22] Above all, if there had been several generations of Austrian Jewish refugees living together, it was possible to cultivate and hand down en passant memories of the old home, habits, or cultural items. This could be done with everyday activities such as cooking
meals, singing Austrian children's songs, reading Austrian children's books
and literature, looking at photographs and pictures, telling childhood
stories, or listening to European music.

A surprising finding of the study was to learn that one everyday activity would actually have the strongest influence on the interviewees' rap-
port with their Austrian heritage: cooking. Throughout all conversations
with the second and third generations it became apparent that Austrian
cooking and food culture had become an elementary ingredient of their
memories, regardless of the great variety of individual connections with
Austria and the variety of their emotional bonds with the country that
had expelled their families. Wiener Schnitzel, Sachertorte, or fruit dumpling
featured in all stories.

EXAMPLE 12

I love Wiener Schnitzel. My grandmother makes the best. My
mother made it; my mother learned a lot of recipes from my
grandmother. Wiener Schnitzel and spinach. I am serious.
That's what we wanted … Wiener schnitzel, on the bone or without the bone, with potatoes and with spinach for me, for her
Lisi. I wanted spinach, creamed spinach of course.[23]

EXAMPLE 13

The Austrian habit—if you want to say habit—I have taken over
is culinary. Is that I cook. And you know, much of what I cook
are Viennese recipes from my grandmother. And the cookbook
on my shelf is the Heß cookbook.[24] My kids are used to
Apfelkuchen mit Mürbeteig und Linzertorte, strudel. You know,
my son who was born in June, knows that for his birthday he
gets Marillenknödel. And for my birthday it is August, so we get
Zwetschkenknödel. I mean, the habit that I have taken over
from my grandparents is in the food area.[25]

The conceptions of meals and eating habits became substantial, distinguishing features of an emigration culture, although the first generation declared many times their appreciation for admission into the United
States.

EXAMPLE 14

We had a lot of Austrian cooking and my grandmother used to
make Apfelstrudel on the table upstairs and she had a plastic
covering and she would role out the dough paper thin. My
mother, something I have said to her repeatedly, I do not know
how she would work all day, come home, and make the food
she would make. I can come home and cook some lamb chops
or Backhendl or Wiener schnitzel, but I am not talking about
that. I am talking about the sauces, the Paprikahendl, and all
the different things that she could get on the table and all the
vegetables. What I did think about when I would go to my
friend's houses: my God how boring their food is. It is just
broiled meat. They would have a vegetable, a potato, and some
broiled meat and I would think how not dinner that is. It is
nothing here, just a non-event. Food was very much part of our
lives … it was such an important part and that was when family
sat down, it was very much the centre of Sunday dinners.[26]

Recipes and cookbooks from the first generation became a precious
good and were passed on to the next generation. They are an essential component of their family traditions.

EXAMPLE 15

So, I still have my grandmothers' cookbook, with her fathers' handwritten pages and hand binding in it. But you know, also her handwritten recipes and in fact, what my oldest son wanted for his graduation present from me ... was, he wanted me to give him all of those family recipes in his own cookbook. So I went to the store and for one dollar bought a blank notebook and copied all of my Oma's recipes into the cookbook for him. So he has them all.[27]

Concerning the discussion about different forms of memory, the social psychologist Harald Welzer states that "ein gemeinsames Merkmal von 'kulturellem' und 'kommunikativem Gedächtnis' liegt darin, daß beide Gedächtnisformen vorwiegend intentional mit der Vergangenheit umgehen; es geht hier um bewusste oder zumindest bewußtseinsfähige Praktiken der Kommunikation und Formung von Vergangenheit."[28] In this respect, he advocates considering other forms of relaying memory, namely unintentional relaying. He calls this type of unplanned propagation "social memory." Welzer argues that our own memory cannot be separated from the social and historical framework that gives form to our perceptions and memories. Many aspects of the past influence current feelings and decisions, and there are forms of trans-generational transmission of experience that touch on the biochemical and neuronal processing of children and grandchildren.[29] The familial memory usually does not consist of grand narratives but is composed of many little stories and circumstantial items such as clothing or individual's arbitrary preferences.[30] Family history is related as dialogue and constituted through the social interaction of all participants by continuous acts of collective remembering. Since emotional colouring also plays a role in the narrative process, "muß der emotionalen Qualität von Erinnerungen besondere Aufmerksamkeit gewidmet werden, da diese nicht nur die Grundierung für die Bedeutsamkeit und Dauerhaftigkeit von Erinnerungen liefert, sondern auch im Prozeß der Tradierung eine enorm große Rolle spielt."[31]

Surprisingly, the memories of the expulsion from Austria and of the Holocaust did not dominate the memories that were passed on to the second and third generations of Austrian Jewish refugees, although parents and/or grandparents in the group interviewed had been victims of the Nazi persecution and had been traumatized by their own forced emigration from Austria and the loss of family members. Quite different aspects formed their decedents' memories and identities. The greatest influence in the trans-generational transmission of memories and narratives came through social interaction within the families, which created a positive emotional bond and thus was an unintentional form of relaying memories: in exile, the grandmothers kept on preparing Austrian cuisine, using cookbooks from their former home, writing down recipes, and passing them on to their children and grandchildren. Why it was especially Austrian food that dominated the memories of the second and third generations in such a strong way might be explained by the fact that, with all three generations sometimes living together in the same home, the selected interview partners had strong familial ties. And all interviewees had remarkably good relationships with their grandmothers.[32]

It became evident in all interviews that the representative value of meals and cooking habits was particularly important for the succeeding generations of the Austrian Jewish refugees. These values were handed down to the later generations, who accepted them. "Food has tremendous representational value, something you can recreate without being there, it has that possibility, you can't be there, but you can recreate."[33]

Notes

1 "Erinnerungen aus der Ferne" was part of the research program "Transformations of Society Recall: Interdisciplinary Research on the History of Austrian Memory in the Second Republic," which was funded by Austria's Ministry of Science within the framework of Cultural Studies; see Gerbel et al., *Transformationen*.

2 See Winkler, "Metropole New York," 179.

3 Spaulding, *Quiet Invaders*, 88.

4 The team consisted of Manfred Lechner and Andrea Strutz, Ludwig Boltzmann Institut für Gesellschafts- und Kulturgeschichte (Cluster Geschichte) located at the Department of History, University of Graz, Austria.

5 Lechner and Strutz, *continental divide.geteilte leben*. Parts of the video documentation are available at <www-gewi.uni-graz.at/zg/cd/cd1.htm>.

6 Strutz and Lechner, "drehbuch 'continental divide.geteilte leben.'"

7 Assmann, "Kollektives Gedächtnis," 10.

8 Lederer-Plaskett, interview. Interviews have been edited slightly to improve the readability.

9 Mehl, interview.

10 Wiener, interview.

11 Wiener, interview.

12 Spira, interview.

13 The use of German language in the first generation of Jewish refugees is ambivalent. Some refugees spoke only English and stopped talking German (mainly because they did not want to speak the "language of the murderer"), while others learned English only to a certain extent. It seems that for some refugees German functioned as a residue to preserve their former home and identity; see Dokumentationsarchiv des österreichischen Widerstandes, *Österreicher im Exil*, 243–45.

14 In some families of post–World War II labour migrants from Austria to the United States, German was also used as a secret language; see Horvarth, "'I bin Amerikaner,'" 560.

15 Mehl, interview.

16 Lederer-Plaskett, interview.
17 Spira, interview.
18 Elmer, interview.
19 Spira, interview.
20 Wiener, interview.
21 Elmer, interview.
22 See other research concerning intergenerational transmission: Inowlocki, "Grand-mothers"; Goodman, "Memory."
23 Mehl, interview.
24 Heß, *Die moderne Kochkunst.*
25 Elmer, interview.
26 Lederer-Plaskett, interview.
27 Elmer, interview.
28 Welzer, "Das soziale Gedächtnis," 15.
29 Welzer, "Das soziale Gedächtnis," 11.
30 See Welzer, "Erinnern und Weitergeben."
31 Welzer, "Das soziale Gedächtnis," 20.
32 In many cases, the grandfathers died quite early, some even during their escape or within the first years in New York City.
33 Spira, interview.

Interview Sources

All interviews conducted by Andrea Strutz and Manfred Lechner and are in the possession of the interviewers.

Elmer, Jerry (born 1951). New York, NY, 17 June 2001.
Lederer-Plaskett, Catherine (born 1955). Hartsdale, NY, 22 June 2001.
Mehl, Lisa (born 1973). New York, NY, 25 May 2001.
Spira, Jonathan (born 1961). New York, NY, 25 May 2001.
Wiener, Willy (born 1965). New York, NY, 6 June 2001.

Works Cited

Assmann, Jan. "Kollektives Gedächtnis und kulturelle Identität." In *Kultur und Gedächtnis*, edited by Jan Assmann and Tonio Hölscher, 9–19. Frankfurt: Surkamp, 1988.
continental divide.geteilte leben. S-VHS. Graz: Department of Contemporary History at the University of Graz, 1997.
Dokumentationsarchiv des österreichischen Widerstandes. *Österreicher im Exil. USA 1938–1945. Eine Dokumentation.* Vienna: Österreichischer Bundesverlag, 1995.
Gerbel, Christian, Manfred Lechner, Dagmar C.G. Lorenz, Oliver Marchart, Vrääth Öhner, Ines Steiner, Andrea Strutz, and Heidemarie Uhl, eds. *Transformationen gesellschaftlicher Erinnerung. Studien zur "Gedächtnisgeschichte" der Zweiten Republik.* Vienna: Turia + Kant, 2005.
Goodman, Ruth. "Memory, Family Stories, and Intergenerational Communication." In *Die Lebendigkeit der Geschichte. (Dis-)Kon-tinuitäten in Diskursen über den Nationalsozialismus*, edited by Eleonore Lappin and Bernhard Schneider, 180–96. St. Ingbert: Röhrig Universitätsverlag, 2001.

Heß, Olga. *Die moderne Kochkunst.* Vienna: Steiner, 1908.

Horvarth, Traude. "'…I bin Amerikaner…oba fühlen tua i wia a Österreicher.' Burgenländische Auswanderung nach 1945." In *Auswanderungen aus Österreich. Von der Mitte des 19. Jahrhunderts bis zur Gegenwart*; mit einer umfassenden Bibliographie zur österreichischen Migrationsgeschichte, edited by Traude Horvath and Gerda Neyer, 549–67. Vienna: Böhlau Verlag, 1996.

Inowlocki, Lena. "Grandmothers, Mothers, and Daughters. Intergenerational Transmission in Displaced Families in Three Jewish Communities." "Between Generations. Family Models, Myths and Memories," edited by Daniel Bertaux and Paul Thomson. Special issue, *International Yearbook of Oral History and Life Stories* 2 (1993): 139–53.

Lechner, Manfred, and Andrea Strutz, "continental divide/geteilte leben." Universität Graz, 2007. <www-gewi.uni-graz.at/zg/cd/cd1.htm> (March 2008).

Spaulding, E. Wilder. *The Quiet Invaders. The Story of the Austrian Impact upon America.* Vienna: Österreichischer Bundesverlag, 1968.

Strutz, Andrea, and Manfred Lechner. "Drehbuch 'continental divide/geteilte leben.'" In *multiple choice: Studien, Skizze, und Reflexionen zur Zeitgeschichte*, edited by Abteilung Zeitgeschichte, 155–81. Graz: Leykam, 1998.

Welzer, Harald. "Das soziale Gedächtnis." In *Das soziale Gedächtnis. Geschichte, Tradition, Erinnerung*, edited by Harald Welzer, 9–21. Hamburg: Hamburger Edition 2001.

———. "Erinnern und weitergeben. Überlegungen zur kommunikativen Tradierung von Geschichte." *BIOS* 11, no. 2 (1998): 155–70.

Winkler, Michael. "Metropole New York." "Metropolen des Exils," edited by Wulf Koepke, Claus-Dieter Krohn, Erwin Rotermund, Lutz Winckler, and Irmtrud Wojak. Special issue, *Exilforschung. Ein internationales Jahrbuch* 20 (2002): 178–98.

NINE

Pulitzer, Preetorius, and the German American Identity Project of the *Westliche Post* in St. Louis

Jason Todd Baker

Divided by imported regional prejudices, religious differences, political affiliations, and spread in pockets across the city, the Germans in nineteenth-century St. Louis comprised the city's largest immigrant ethnicity and possibly its least cohesive. An examination of the Midwest's largest German-language daily, *Die Westliche Post*, illustrates the tension between competing models of German American identity as embodied by the editorial and political practices of Joseph Pulitzer and the Preetorius family. The story of the paper's fortunes, from its founding on the eve of the American Civil War through its struggle to retain readership in the face of generational attrition and linguo-cultural assimilation, mirrors the plight of German-language media in the United States and that of the German American identity movement as a whole.

IN 1900, ST. LOUIS WAS THE FOURTH-LARGEST CITY in the United States. The city, founded in 1764 as a French colonial outpost, witnessed a population explosion in the nineteenth century, booming from 2,447 residents in 1800 to 600,000 in 1900. German-speaking immigrants constituted the largest of the immigrant populations in Missouri and St. Louis proper.[1] Due to the dense concentration of German-speaking immigrants in the region, the St. Louis Germans enjoyed considerably more cultural and political influence than did other ethnic groups. Indeed, St. Louis was perceived nationally as something of a "German city in the middle of America."[2] The decisive role played by the city's German immigrants in preventing Missouri's secession (1861) merely confirmed this perception. The Civil War era not only provided area Germans with an opportunity to prove their loyalty to the republic (effectively countering nativist arguments of immigrant infelicity), but also gave birth to the city's most important German-language newspaper, *Die Westliche Post*.

Carl Dänzer founded the newspaper after difficulties with his employer, the volatile Heinrich Boernstein, who ousted him from his job at the *Anzeiger des Westens*, the city's major German-language daily.[3] During the Civil War, an upstart Republican Party daily called *Die Neue Zeit*—under the direction of Carl Schurz, William Stengel, and Emil Preetorius—merged with the *Westliche Post* and took the latter's name.[4] Preetorius, like his better-known colleague Schurz, was a Forty-Eighter, an immigrant fleeing political persecution after the failed revolution. Like Schurz, he developed a keen interest in American politics and was even elected to the state legislature in 1862. After assuming the editorship of the *Post* in 1864, Preetorius was able to establish the paper as the most financially successful German-language news organ in the country. In addition to serving as the primary news organ of the local German community, Preetorius recruited prominent European political correspondents, including Karl Blind, Arnold Ruge, Otto Lüning, and Fanny Lewald, to keep his readers abreast of international developments. The fact that Preetorius solicited political commentary from European revolutionaries (many of whom were then living in foreign exile) is indicative of the *Post*'s ardent republican activism under his tenure.

It is also no surprise, considering the paper's political leanings, that Preetorius established Carl Schurz as co-owner and editor in 1867. Schurz's oratorical skill and bilingual abilities made him an ideal operative for the peddling of political influence, and his allegiance to the ideals of the Republican Party helped soften that party's flirtations with nativism a decade prior, which in turn made the party significantly more appealing to German immigrants.[5]

Preetorius's most significant personnel decision was the hiring of a penniless "street beat" reporter in 1868.[6] Joseph Pulitzer was a generation younger than his editors, having been born in 1847 in Makó, Hungary. Although of Hungarian and Jewish descent, Pulitzer was primarily educated in the German language as part of Austria's attempted eradication of the Magyar movement. After being rejected by three European armies (owing to his young age, odd physique, and bad eyesight), Pulitzer travelled to Hamburg and committed himself to the service of the Union Army in 1864. Upon his discharge, the destitute Pulitzer headed west, arriving in St. Louis in October 1865. After a series of odd jobs, he found his calling as an investigative reporter. His obsessive approach to reporting irrevocably altered journalism in the city. Editors of the city's English-language papers, after being repeatedly scooped by "Joey the German," began instructing their newshounds to imitate Pulitzer's tactics.[7] Pulitzer's stock was rising within the *Westliche Post* as well, and in 1869 Schurz and Preetorius appointed him editor for St. Louis news and politics.

Pulitzer's interest in politics prompted him to accept the Radical Republican nomination for the state legislature in 1869 (despite being technically underage and in a traditionally Democratic Party ward that his party had little hope of carrying). Instead of having a laugh at his own expense, Pulitzer took his candidacy seriously, using the city page of the *Westliche Post* as a bully pulpit to endorse his candidacy and beat down his Democratic opponents. Pulitzer's campaign rhetoric introduced a new tenor to the fiery but civilized *Post*. Instead of running on principles and platforms, he attacked his opponents' character, their social standing, potential Confederate sympathies, business acumen, and—most significantly—their ethnicity. The young Pulitzer made it a point to draw his readers' attention to the fact that his opponents in the ward were almost exclusively Irish.[8] He routinely played up the burgeoning rivalry between the two immigrant groups, portraying the Irish as a feeble-minded herd of brawling drunkards who would vote for whichever Democrat their corrupt party leaders told them to. Against all expectations, and aided by a crippling ice storm that prevented all but the most motivated voters from turning out at the polls, the traditionally Democratic fifth ward elected Republican Joseph Pulitzer to the state legislature.

Up for re-election the following year, Pulitzer again exploited his position as newspaper editor to aid his campaign and garner support for the ticket of the newly created Liberal Republican Party. U.S. senator Schurz and state representative Pulitzer were instrumental in forming the new party—the result of a state-wide Republican schism over former Confederates' enfranchisement—and both occupied high positions in the faction.[9] The state schism became a national schism and Pulitzer delivered German-language speeches for the party's candidates across the Midwest.[10] Where Pulitzer had previously flirted with ethnic rhetoric, he now openly attempted to usher Germans to the polls as an ethnic block. By claiming that his opponents intended to forsake the German vote in favour of that of the newly enfranchised African-American population, Pulitzer insinuated that his opponents considered the Germans inferior to the "*Neger*."[11] This attempt to goad German Americans into voting on the basis of alleged racial superiority did not aid Pulitzer in his own re-election campaign, as he fell victim to what he repeatedly referred to in the *Post* as an "*irisch-französischer Negersieg.*"[12]

Following his recall from Jefferson City to St. Louis, Pulitzer devoted much of his time to organizing and publicizing the (first and only) Liberal Republican Party national convention in Cincinnati. Although the party had been founded and defined in Missouri by German American newspaper editors, it became more of a bi-partisan reservoir for malcontents as it grew at the national level. Despite the considerable energies of Pulitzer, Schurz, and Preetorius to rally the German vote, the election was a bust. The party disbanded, its presidential candidate, Horace Greeley, went mad and died, and the *Westliche Post*, which had bound its fortunes to the new party's success, suffered a marked drop in advertising revenue.

In the wake of the Liberal Republican demise, Schurz and Preetorius allowed Pulitzer an unprecedented degree of control over newspaper policy. Given free rein, the *Post* under Pulitzer became much more sensational and less given to substantial coverage of current political events: "Fires, burglaries, white slavery, assaults, mysterious murders, embezzlings, inheritance feuds—these became the main diet for the *Westliche Post* reader."[13] In short, the paper became less of a mediator for the German American community and more of a vehicle for entertainment and titillation. And it sold. Well enough, at least, that the advertising revenues rebounded and the Forty-Eighter editors once again viewed their paper as a financially tenable venture. The apparent conflict of journalistic styles was not lost on Preetorius and Schurz; in 1873, they offered Pulitzer 30,000 dollars for his interest in the *Post*.[14]

But Pulitzer's stay at the newspaper had exploded some of the paper's fundamental myths: one being that the St. Louis German community preferred sober coverage of current events to the salacious scandals of the penny dreadfuls. Moreover, Pulitzer's frustrated attempts at ethnic and race baiting proved that the St. Louis Germans were too diverse politically to be a reliable ethnic voting block. He briefly owned the St. Louis *Staats-Zeitung*, but after reselling it almost immediately and turning a handsome profit, Pulitzer devoted the rest of his life to English-language journalism. Despite the significant German cultural influence in St. Louis, Missouri, and the Midwest, English was the lingua franca of power brokers, politicians, and influential cultural figures at the national level. Pulitzer's ambition precluded provincialist complacency and, after increasing his power and prestige at the helm of his own paper, the *St. Louis Post and Dispatch*, he left for New York in 1883.[15]

Following the departure of the *enfant terrible* from the *Westliche Post*, the paper entered into a relatively staid period of community-oriented, partisan, German-language journalism. Schurz, who never really acquired a taste for the newspaper trade, moved on to Washington, DC, and the national political stage.[16] With Pulitzer and Schurz gone, the *Post* bore the stamp of only one hand, that of Emil Preetorius.

In New York, Pulitzer stirred the English-speaking melting pot via *The World* with sensational news engineered for mass consumption. Yet, in some ways, Preetorius faced a more challenging undertaking with his more modest newspaper. As the political activism of the 1870s illustrated, the German American community in St. Louis could not be counted on to vote as an ethnic block.[17] In fact, they could not be relied upon to do much of anything as a group. St. Louis served (and still does) as the seat of the Lutheran Church Missouri Synod, a conservative American Lutheran confession, and their local strength led to friction with Germans of other faiths. These Lutherans did not traffic much with the sizable German Catholic population of the city, who often shared their houses of worship and political stances with the Irish. The small rabbinical German Jewish community remained insular. The Freethinkers, atheists, socialists, et al., had little use for any of these groups. In addition, the Germans, while heavily concentrated in a few pockets of north and south St. Louis, were spread across the city proper and into the larger countryside.[18]

The cultural battle waged by the proponents of a German American identity was made much more difficult by the heterogeneity of its constituency.[19] Instead of rallying around indices of identification such as religion, location, and politics, the Germans were forced to turn to intangibles to build an imaginary community.[20] As Audrey Olson puts it, "a desire to retain a physical German community, therefore, could not play a part in the ethnic self-consciousness of the Germans because this community had never existed."[21]

The German Americans could, however, rally around a common language, albeit with some dialect difficulty. This explains the panic with which the *Westliche Post*, and German American identity proponents in general, viewed the encroaching Anglo-Saxon assimilation and the disinterest for the German language in the younger generations. German-language instruction had been introduced into the St. Louis public school system in 1864 and remained in the curriculum (for all students) alongside English until 1887 as part of an effort to aid the assimilation of immigrant children.[22] Voluntary after-school and weekend classes continued until 1917, although attendance had been tapering off for decades.

Rather than focusing on the linguistic bond, the St. Louis Germans rallied around what both Audrey Olson and David Detjen refer to as "intangibles."[23] The sense of *Deutschtum* and *Gemütlichkeit* associated with the German *Vereine*, fondness for social alcohol consumption, and "continental" Sundays fuelled the German American identity project more than did linguistic identification. Divided by geography, religion, political affiliation, and class, and lacking the initiative or desire to maintain use of their common language, the Germans could and did still speak of a "German way of life" or German *Gemütlichkeit,* by which they meant the internal group cohesion afforded them by social interaction in their clubs and activities.[24] It also then follows that the anti-hyphenate movement of World War I (which virtually eradicated German community bonding from the public sphere) and Prohibition (which hurt the habitual beer or wine drinker more than the consumer of hard liquor) would virtually eradicate all vestiges of this community project.[25]

An investigation of the *Westliche Post*'s fortunes circa 1900 offers an intriguing example of German American cultural attrition and provides a counterpoint to the assimilated Pulitzer's success. By the time of the last great German immigration boom in the 1880s, Preetorius's *Westliche Post* was the dominant German-language daily in St. Louis. To reduce the competition in an ever-shrinking market, Preetorius merged his paper with the *Anzeiger des Westens* and the smaller *St. Louis Tageblatt* and formed the German-American Press Association in June 1898.[26] Shortly after the merger, the association issued a press release to potential advertisers in the English-speaking business community: "If you want to reach the Germans of St. Louis, the West, and the entire Southwest, you must use the publications of the German-American Press Association, [which runs] the largest German publications in the world.... Our motto is, 'We aim to satisfy READERS and ADVERTISER, and WE DO IT.'"[27] While this statement bears the mark of hyperbole—as did virtually all American advertising discourse at the turn of the century—it makes clear the position that the association sought to occupy: an intermediary between the German American and Anglo-American communities. The very fact that Preetorius needed to appeal to the English-language business community underscores that the German American community was not a self-sufficient economic or cultural entity. Despite the large role played by German American businesses in the St. Louis economy (one needs only to think of beer giant Anheuser-Busch), advertising revenue from the non-German business community was essential to the success of Preetorius's risky publishing venture.

The St. Louis World's Fair of 1904 brought much needed revenue for the city, and the papers of the German-American Press Association were intimately involved in planning and covering the almost year-long event. The highlight of the fair for the *Post* was the 7 October 1904, 58-page *Sonderausgabe* on 7 October 1904, which covered the events of the fair's German Day.[28] The venerable Preetorius served as chairman of the national committee for German Day and was instrumental in the execution of the celebration. Understandably, the events (at least as they were reported in the *Post*) bear witness to the peculiar brand of German American identity politics espoused for decades by Preetorius and Schurz, who was a guest of honour. The allegorical mural that prefaced the coverage served to reinforce the sense of pride and mutual loyalty central to the German American identity project. It depicts female allegories of Germania and Columbia framed by an arch with the Deutsches Haus and Fair pavilions in the background.[29] Under the banner of the paper's title, the *Post* offers a telling and unmistakable stand on its identity project. Above two cherubim holding a scroll that reads *"UNSER MOTTO"* stands the phrase *"EWIGE LIEBE DEM ALTEN VATERLAND—EWIGE TREUE DEM NEUEN VATERLAND—EWIGE FREUNDSCHAFT FÜR BEIDE!"* This motto echoed the popular familial metaphor of "Germany our mother, Columbia our bride." Preetorius had made a more direct distinction in subsequent remarks: "We are, and mean to stay, American. If war were to be declared against Germany, we would take up our guns, though it would be with bleeding hearts."[30] For Preetorius and the *Westliche Post*, the loyalty to the idea of American citizenship supplanted any emotional ties to one's country of origin.

Preetorius also delivered a speech on German Day that offered a moving negotiation of these conflicting devotions. While he encouraged German Americans to retain the best aspects of their cultural heritage, he insisted that the project before them was to better their adopted homeland through civic and cultural engagement:

> Wahrlich, wir brauchen hier, um gute Amerikaner zu sein, keine schlechte Deutsche [*sic*] zu werden. Im Gegentheil: Die besten Deutschen sind auch die besten Amerikaner! Je treuer wir hier's germanische Erbtheil bewahren und in Sprache und Sitte die höchsten Schätze des Geistes und Herzens hüten für Mit- und Nachwelt, desto werthvolleres Edelmetall werfen wir in den Schmelztiegel, worin sich hier der Assimilirungsprozeß der Nationalitäten vollzieht.[31]

Interestingly, Preetorius spoke to the issue of assimilation with a rather non-contentious argument. In his speech, cultural assimilation, the march of which would inevitably destroy the *Post* and the visibility of an ethnically distinct German American community, is portrayed as a foregone conclusion, even as a positive and natural development. It would behoove the German American, according to Preetorius, to influence the larger American culture by bringing to the table *"die höchsten Schätze des Geistes und Herzens,"* a modified German cultural heritage. The retention of the German language is a necessary component for maintaining this cultural heritage. Preetorius encouraged active and deliberate cultural "agitation" to impart idealized German cultural attributes to a protean American culture.

Shortly after the 1904 World's Fair both the elder statesmen of the *Westliche Post*, Carl Schurz and Emil Preetorius, fell ill and died. Operations of the paper were officially turned over to Preetorius's fluently bilingual, American-born son, Edward. With subscription rates in a steady decline (owing to immigration caps and the ease of assimilation through the advent of a collective mass culture), Edward Preetorius floated an English-language publication, the *St. Louis Times,* from the offices of the German-American Press Association.[32] He was not able to stop the financial hemorrhaging, though, and went so far as to flirt with the Hohenzollern sympathies of such popular groups as the Deutsch-Amerikanischer National-Bund (DANB) in attempts to boost circulation. He committed suicide shortly after the inauguration of the Naked Truth monument, a thirty-thousand-dollar tribute to the St. Louis German American press, on 24 May 1914.[33]

The Naked Truth monument depicts a seated female nude holding aloft twin torches to symbolize the twin fires of German and American enlightenment. Above the seated bronze figure, the names of Schurz, Preetorius, and Dänzer are carved into the granite. Beer baron Adolphus Busch, who did not live to see its dedication, funded the monument and commissioned its sculptor, Berlin artist Wilhelm Wandschneider. The rear of the monument bears an inscription, fittingly in both English and German. The German reads:

> Als Deutschamerikaner und Führer ihrer Landsleute im öffentlichen Leben hatten sie stets das hohe Ziel vor Augen, ihrem Adoptivvater-lande treu zu dienen. Unabhängige Charaktere, für alles Große und Schöne begeistert, brachten sie die edelsten Güter der Kultur Germanias mit sich und legten sie zum Segen aller künftigen Geschlechter in den Schoß Columbias. In neidloser Anerkennung ihre dankbaren Mitbürger.[34]

In its celebration of these three pioneers of the St. Louis German-language press, the St. Louis German American community created ethnic heroes of men whose calls for cultural solidarity it had not always heeded.

The glaring omission on the monument is Joseph Pulitzer, who had passed away in 1911. Pulitzer was certainly the brighter light in the St. Louis newspaper industry and had a much greater impact on American journalism and culture as a whole. His introduction of the colour supplement, banner headlines, funny papers, investigative reporting, and populist reform crusades provided a template for newspapers across the country. But Pulitzer never became an icon for the German American identity movement. Although he was of Jewish descent (which he disputed), anti-Semitism has little to do with it. Pulitzer was the embodiment of successful (predominantly Anglo-Saxon) assimilation and identified with the German American movement only when it served his purposes. Pulitzer often found himself on the other side of issues from his Forty-Eighter mentors, usually on the more profitable and popular side. Additionally, Pulitzer actively cultivated an image of himself as a wholly self-made individual—that is to say, as an American success story. German American identity politics, with its conceit of ethnic community, was of little value to this image of rugged individualism.

During his St. Louis years, Pulitzer realized that the fractured German community (in St. Louis and nationally) was no match for encroaching linguo-cultural assimilation. Subsequently, he embraced this assimilation and built an English-language publishing empire that redefined the face of American journalism. The Preetorius family, on the other hand, consolidated virtually every German-language newspaper in the region, championed civic activism, and even flirted with German imperial chauvinism in their failed attempts to preserve their paper's slipping cultural influence and fiscal viability. Most existing studies posit that World War I–era anti-German sentiment sounded the death knell for the German American community in St. Louis. An examination of the fortunes of the *Westliche Post* suggests that the unstable community had already forfeited cultural dominion and had been steadily crumbling for decades.

Notes

1   Faust, *The German Element*, 447–48.
2   Detjen, *The Germans in Missouri*, 6.
3   Hofacker, *German Literature*, 4. For a detailed account of Boernstein's relationship with Dänzer, as well as an anti-clerical sketch of the St. Louis German milieu circa 1860, see Boernstein, *Memoirs of a Nobody*.
4   Dänzer later returned to the *Anzeiger* and landed in the rather bizarre position of actively competing for subscriptions with the newspaper he had founded. The *Anzeiger* and the *Westliche Post*, under Dänzer and Preetorius respectively, would remain competitors for the next thirty-five years.
5   Schurz's decision to move back to St. Louis and co-publish the *Post* was a concession to his political ambitions. Missouri, with its powerful German American lobby, presented a better opportunity for elected office than did Michigan. Additionally, the paper provided Schurz with a daily forum to denigrate his opponents and assist his own campaign.
6   There is some disagreement as to when Pulitzer actually started working for the paper. In 1867 Pulitzer was active as the secretary for the Deutsche Gesellschaft, an immigrant assistance organization run by Preetorius and Schurz. Pulitzer may have already begun submitting items for the paper at this time; existing biographies begin his employment at the *Post* in 1868.
7   Swanberg, *Pulitzer*, 10.
8   *Westliche Post*, "Die Wahl."
9   *Westliche Post*, "Die amerikanische Union."
10 Seitz, *Joseph Pulitzer*, 73.
11 *Westliche Post*, "Die deutschen Namen."
12 *Westliche Post*, "Deutsch."
13 Saalberg, "The *Westliche Post* of St. Louis," 224.
14 Pulitzer also switched political allegiances and became an opposition Democrat, which likely sped his departure from the paper.
15 Although Pulitzer left the German-language press, he was still wary of nativist leanings in the English-language press. On the other hand, he used the pages of

the *Post-Dispatch* to plead the case for "Americanization" of German immigrant children via the public school system—by means of the gradual eradication of German-language instruction (Rammelkamp, *Pulitzer's Post-Dispatch*, 262–63).

16 After his appointment as secretary of the interior under President Rutherford B. Hayes in 1877, Schurz gave up any lingering affiliation with the paper.

17 Additionally, many elected German American officials were not necessarily ethnic leaders. Political, business, and legal ambitions (in short, careerism) often superseded ethnic loyalties, especially at the national level. At the local level, Walter Kamphoefner points out that "St. Louis elected more German mayors relative to its population than any other [American] city" ("German and Irish Big City Mayors," 236). This statistic should not be read as evidence of the strength of the German voting block, but rather as a testament to the ability of "Americanized" German American politicians to curry favour across ethnic lines.

18 Consider, as a counter example, the St. Louis Irish in the city's Kerry Patch: nearly uniformly Catholic, Democrat, and physically localized.

19 Russell Kazal notes that this phenomenon was not unique to St. Louis Germans: counter-productive heterogeneity was the hallmark of German America (*Becoming Old Stock*, 18).

20 The concept of "imaginary communities" is derived here from Benedict Anderson's criticism of national consciousness of the same name (*Imagined Communities*). Instead of constructing an "imagined" nation, the Germans in St. Louis built up an "imagined" ethnic community to transcend the deep divisions (regional, political, religious) within their group.

21 Olson, "St. Louis Germans," 90.

22 This attempt at bilingualism prevailed as long as the German Americans held a majority on the school board. But in 1887, the board, citing budgetary concerns, cut the funding for public school instruction of German unilaterally (Olson, "St. Louis Germans," 99).

23 Olson, "St. Louis Germans"; Detjen, *The Germans in Missouri*.

24 Olson, "St. Louis Germans," 167–68.

25 Ronnenberg, *The Politics of Assimilation*, 8–9.

26 Hofacker, *German Literature*, 7–8.

27 Saalberg, "The *Westliche Post*," 305.

28 For an in-depth examination of the Imperial German participation at the St. Louis World's Fair as well as the local German American community's negotiation of this presence (and, by proxy, their own hybrid identities), see Paul Michael Lützeler and Graduate Students, "The St. Louis World's Fair."

29 Germania, to the left, holds the German flag. A garland of oak leaves on her head and to her feet. Her appearance is fairly martial, much more so than on the mural for the "First Anniversary Edition." She wears a breastplate, sash, and shield, all emblazoned with the black eagle. To her right stands Columbia, clutching the Stars and Stripes. At her feet sits an eagle with wings outstretched, a bundle of arrows in its talons. The pair are joined in holding a laurel wreath with three ribbons that read "ACHTUNG," "FREUNDSCHAFT," and "EWIGER FRIEDE."

30 Quoted in Detjen, *The Germans in Missouri*, 26.

31 *Westliche Post*, "Ansprache von Dr. Preetorius."

32 Erik Kirschbaum documents 488 operational German-language newspapers (dailies and weeklies) in the United States in 1910 (*Eradication of German Culture*, 40, 71). A decade later there were only 152 and they had suffered a 60 percent decrease in total circulation. Hysterical war propaganda and the concomitant

persecution of German-language news organs accounted for much of this loss, but he notes that American-born German Americans were already much less likely to renew subscriptions.

33 Saalberg, "The *Westliche Post* of St. Louis," 336.

34 *Westliche Post*, "Denkmalweihe."

Works Cited

Anderson, Benedict. *Imagined Communities: Reflections on the Origin and Spread of Nationalism*. London: Verso, 1983.

Boernstein, Henry. *Memoirs of a Nobody: The Missouri Years of an Austrian Radical*. Trans. Steven Rowan. St. Louis: Missouri Historical Society Press, 1997.

Detjen, David W. *The Germans in Missouri, 1900–1918*. Columbia, MO: University of Missouri Press, 1985.

Faust, Albert Bernhardt. *The German Element in the United States*, Volume 1. New York: Houghton Mifflin, 1909.

Hofacker, Eric P. *German Literature as Reflected in the German-Language Press of St. Louis Prior to 1898*. St. Louis: Washington University, 1946.

Kamphoefner, Walter D. "German and Irish Big City Mayors: Comparative Perspective on Ethnic Politics." In *German-American Immigration and Ethnicity in Comparative Perspective*, edited by Wolfgang Helbich and Walter D. Kamphoefner, 221–42. Madison: Max Kade Institute for German-American Studies, 2004.

Kazal, Russell A. *Becoming Old Stock: The Paradox of German-American Identity*. Princeton: Princeton University Press, 2004.

Kirschbaum, Erik. *The Eradication of German Culture in the United States: 1917–1918*. Stuttgart: Akademischer Verlag, 1986.

Lützeler, Paul Michael, and Graduate Students. "The St. Louis World's Fair of 1904 as a Site of Cultural Transfer: German and German-American Participation." In *German Culture in Nineteenth-Century America: Reception, Adaptation, Transformation*, edited by Matt Erlin and Lynne Tatlock, 59–88. Rochester, NY: Camden House, 2005.

Olson, Audrey L. "St. Louis Germans, 1850–1920: The Nature of an Immigrant Community and Its Relation to the Assimilation Process." PhD diss., University of Kansas, 1970.

Rammelkamp, Julian S. *Pulitzer's Post-Dispatch: 1878–1883*. Princeton: Princeton University Press, 1967.

Ronnenberg, Herman W. *The Politics of Assimilation: The Effect of Prohibition on the German Americans*. New York: Carlton Press, 1975.

Saalberg, Harvey. "The *Westliche Post* of St. Louis: A Daily Newspaper for German Americans, 1857–1938." PhD diss., University of Missouri, 1967.

Seitz, Don C. *Joseph Pulitzer: His Life and Letters*. New York: Simon & Schuster, 1924.

Swanberg, W.A. *Pulitzer*. New York: Charles Scribner's Sons, 1967.

Westliche Post. "Ansprache von Dr. Preetorius," 7 October 1904.

———. "Denkmalweihe gestaltet sich zu gewaltiger Kundgebung," 25 May 1914.

———. "Deutsch," 11 November 1870.

————. "Die amerikanische Union," 4 September 1870.

————. "Die deutschen Namen," 3 September 1870.

————. "Die Wahl in der fünften Ward," 18 December 1869.

TEN

"We dont want Kiser to rool in Ontario"

*Franco-Prussian War, German Unification,
and World War I as Reflected in the Canadian
Berliner Journal (1859–1918)*

Anne Löchte

For a long time the *Berliner Journal* was the mostly widely read German-language newspaper in Canada. It stands out because of its nationwide reach and its long period of publication. For nearly sixty years the *Berliner Journal* was published weekly in Berlin (later Kitchener) before it was banned in 1918 due to World War I. Throughout its existence, both the situation of German immigrants in Canada and political developments in Germany were important issues in the *Journal*. It followed the Franco-Prussian War and German unification in 1870–71 with passionate patriotism. But the editors also thought of themselves as loyal citizens of Canada who deeply appreciated the assets of their "adopted fatherland." With the beginning of World War I this double loyalty was put to the test. This chapter deals with how the *Berliner Journal* reported these events, especially in view of the standing of the German-speaking immigrants and their descendants.

The *Berliner Journal*: A German-Language Newspaper in Canada

THE PUBLICATION OF A GERMAN-LANGUAGE NEWSPAPER like the *Berliner Journal* was not exceptional in Ontario. In the nineteenth century the Germans were the third-largest immigrant group in Canada after the English and the French. In the first half of the nineteenth century a wave of German-speaking immigrants from all parts of Germany, Austria, Switzerland, and Pennsylvania settled in southwest Ontario. Berlin, today's

Kitchener, and the place of publication of the *Berliner Journal*, was the centre of that immigration. The city proudly titled itself "Canada's German capital" or "Canada's Kaiser City." A flourishing newspaper scene resulted from the stream of immigrants. Newspapers supported these non–English-speaking newcomers with practical help, provided them with news from the old and the new world, and made them familiar with Canada. The era of a wide range of German-language newspapers came to an end in 1918 with the ban of all newspapers in languages of "the foe." Most German-language newspapers would not recover from this blow.

The *Berliner Journal* held a special position in the German-language press of Ontario. While many of the smaller newspapers had to cease publication after a short period, the *Journal* appeared for nearly sixty years and had appeal well beyond Berlin. It had subscribers in Toronto, Ottawa, Halifax, Montreal, as well as in British Columbia and the northern United States. It extended its readership and increased its subscription numbers from about one thousand in the beginning to more than five thousand in 1908, giving it the largest readership among German-language newspapers in Canada. During a difficult phase after 1900, the owners of the *Berliner Journal* bought up a number of smaller newspapers, which stabilized their subscription numbers. The continuity of the newspaper's editorship was also remarkable. The founders, John Motz, an immigrant from Thuringia, and Friedrich Rittinger from Baden, jointly led the paper for nearly forty years before their sons took it over in 1899.

The editors of the *Berliner Journal* took great interest in the lives of German immigrants in Canada and in developments in Germany. Two events in particular had a major impact: the Franco-Prussian War and subsequent German unification 1870–71, and World War I. Both had enormous consequences for German immigrants and their descendants in Canada. While unification strengthened their self-esteem and raised the reputation of Germans in Canada, the World War I did exactly the opposite, leading in 1918 to the cessation of the newspaper. The following chapter discusses the portrayal of these events in the *Journal*.

The Franco-Prussian War and German Unification 1870–71

In the years leading up to 1870, the *Berliner Journal* already held a sympathetic view toward the Danish-Prussian War and the Austro-Prussian War but the interest it took in the events of 1870–71 was much more heightened. Just like German immigrants in the United States, German Canadians were overwhelmed by nationalism because an end to German division seemed to be at hand.[1] Reports on the war dominated the columns of the *Journal* from July 1870 until the peace agreement in May 1871.

Because of the great interest demonstrated by their readers, Rittinger and
Motz published an extra evening paper to keep them informed about the
latest developments.

The tone of the articles was euphoric. Some articles argued that the
moment for Germany to become a world power had arrived. France, in its
"outrageous boisterousness," had declared war on Prussia, while nearly
"the whole civilized world" hoped for a Prussian victory.[2] The *Journal*
noted approvingly that the English-language press was on Prussia's side.
They quoted the Toronto *Leader* and the *Telegraph*, which claimed that
Prussia was acting in a "steadfast, dignified and cool" manner while
"offended, challenged and insulted" by despotic France.[3] They reported
in glowing terms on the German troops that were thrusting into France
for the knock-out blow. This time Napoleon was not dealing with "nearly
starved Mexicans, badly armed bandits or half-wild Africans . . . , but with
a unified, strong, brave people, willing to make sacrifices, who were superior to [France's] bewitched subjects in every respect." After the decisive
battle of Sedan, the *Journal* reported triumphantly that France was lying
"nearly defenceless at Germany's feet," and now had to pay for its impu-
dence. Such actions were unique in world history: "We are filled with
amazement and admiration but we are unable to find suitable words to
do justice to the triumph of German arms. It is as difficult to grasp the great
achievement of the Germans as it is to describe them. Only a fighting-fit,
heroic people in arms under wise and brave leaders could have undertaken
such an action." The *Journal* suggests that the German victories were due
in part to a cultural and moral superiority of the Germans over the French.

The *Journal* reported a spontaneous celebration in Waterloo following the victory at Sedan. The "marvellous news of the victory" had resulted
in "enthusiastic cheering among the German citizens." A number of German citizens gathered in a bar to "celebrate the victory." "Hearty speeches"
were given and the "national song was sung"repeatedly.[4] At ten o'clock
there was a torchlight procession through the main streets of Waterloo,
the town neighbouring Berlin.

The events in Europe were always seen through the lens of the standing of Germans in North America. *Journal* editorials suggested that this
war would have a lasting influence on the reputation of German immigrants. Finally the Germans had proven themselves courageous, driven,
and desirous of unification, and had shown the French arch-enemy its limits. A French victory would have had terrible consequences for German
Canadians:

> If the arrogant French people had been successful, the Germans would
> have been treated like Indians or Negros. Not only Celts and Anglo-Sax-
> ons, even certain Germans, who don't want to be German and fight

against their own flesh and blood, would have looked down on us pity-
ingly and scornfully. Therefore, honour to our German brothers: by
fighting for their fatherland they fought for the honour of the German
name around the world.[5]

In March the German citizens of Berlin decided like many other German North Americans to celebrate the German victory with a major festival. The celebration was held on 2 May 1871. The *Journal* reported extensively in two issues on the event.[6] Berlin welcomed on that occasion more
than ten thousand visitors from all over Ontario and from the United
States. The city was festively decorated with wreaths and garlands, with
German, English, and American flags and triumphal arches. Banners were
hung with pictures of William I, Otto von Bismarck, and Helmuth von
Moltke; on others were slogans such as "Long live a united Germany" or
"Alsace-Lorraine, rejoice that you are German again." Tobacco factory
owners extended to "all people the pipe of peace" on their banner, and
one citizen had hung a huge sausage from his apartment with the rhymed
German couplet: "What this sausage is among sausages / so is Emperor
William among rulers."

The celebration began with rumbling of guns and drum rolls. The
bells of the German churches rang and afterward services were held.
There was a long procession to Waterloo. An oak as the symbol of "German greatness, strength, and dignity" was planted (it ironically died later),
and choirs sang "Was ist des Deutschen Vaterland" and "Die Wacht am
Rhein."[7] The speeches, parts of which the *Journal* printed, show the enormous interest German Canadians took in German unity and the victory
over the French.[8] The "joy about the unification of our people, who for
so long lived in [a situation of] powerless fragmentation" and the "delight
about the peace with honour won after bloody struggles" were articulated
in impassioned speeches. Germany had gotten rid of its "century-long
oppressor" and was praised as the "first nation of the world." The *Journal*
claimed that Germany as a cultural nation was superior to the decayed
France. The French people were morally depraved, internally rotted, and
incapable of survival, all of which had led to the glorious victory of the Germans. The moment had come for Germany to be the first power in Europe:
"This nation, which has not become enraptured with its victory, a victory
that in its completeness is unique in world history, deserves to have all
others look up to her and listen to her, the arrogant with fear, the weak
with trust." The *Journal* reported that this speech was "often interrupted
by loud and sustained cheering," and that it "enthused the crowd."[9]

In a more moderate speech, Otto Klotz, a prominent school trustee in
Preston, Ontario, discussed the significance of German unity for Germans
in Canada. Finally the "provincial conceit" was overcome, the new "pow-

erful phrase of unity" was: "We all are Germans!" Klotz stated that the glorious events must have consequences for the self-confidence of Germans in Ontario. They had to work with combined efforts so that Germans in Canada earned the respect they deserved as the "sons of the great, enlightened Germany." He also turned to the Alsatians in the audience. At last they again belonged to the German Reich, from which they had been separated through "robbery, betrayal, and iniquities."[10] It would not be long before their German roots would be embedded in the consciousness of Alsatians.

Another speaker, Pastor Salinger from St. Jacobs, expressed the hope that the events would increase the national consciousness of Germans abroad and that it would lead to better care of the German language. He regretted that at the school in his city, in which Germans were predominant, the German language was deprecated. He urged his audience: "Folks, do you hear the German tongue among yourselves, in your homes and schools? Can the German brother feel at home with you because he hears his marvellous, beautiful, extremely rich language? Or are you also ashamed … of the beloved dear mother tongue?" At this point, reported the *Journal*, the speaker heard a loud "No" from the audience.[11]

The euphoria about the founding of the Reich soon subsided and was superseded by sharp criticism of developments in Germany. Only a few years later the *Journal* reported that the ambitious political hopes Germans in America had associated with the founding of the Reich proved elusive. They criticized in particular the absence of parliamentary rights and of freedom of speech. Canada and the United States appeared to be the lands of political freedom and participation from which Germany could learn. Despite this negative development, the euphoria of 1870–71 had a lasting impact on the self-confidence of German Canadians. For the Germans of Berlin the great success of the peace celebration was especially important. For the first time German immigrants appeared as one ethnic group before the greater public, and the positive response in the English press encouraged them in their new self-esteem. The *Journal* acknowledged the North American peace celebrations in whole as "the most important event in the history of American Germanness," and years later they remembered the local peace celebration as the high point of the German history of Berlin.[12]

World War I and the Ban of the *Berliner Journal*

When World War I broke out forty-three years later, the natural pride with which Berlin presented itself after 1871 as a German city in Canada was irreparably damaged. The city not only had to deal with internal tensions, accusations, and riots, but it also had to fight for its reputation.[13] Berlin saw itself forced to oppose through several measures the suspicion that its inhabitants were disloyal and that they sided with Germany. The most important was renaming Berlin to Kitchener in 1916. The break with the German tradition of Berlin due to the World War I was irreversible. Historians John English and Kenneth McLaughlin state: "The war years had assured that Kitchener could never again be Berlin."[14] For the *Berliner Journal* the most difficult time in its existence had begun.

From the beginning of the war the *Berliner Journal* stressed that the loyalty of all German Canadians had to be with Canada. The first of these articles came out immediately after Germany had joined the war in August 1914. The *Journal* launched an "appeal to the Germans in Ontario," reminding them of their loyalty, and discussed the difficult situation of Germans. For those Germans and their descendants who had become Canadians, the stress of the outbreak of the war was even more acute: "The love for our old fatherland is innate, and the admiration of our new homeland should not bring us into inner conflict … Canada … has invited us to make a home here. We mustn't forget the years of peace and prosperity we have experienced under the British flag.… The 'Union Jack' has fluttered above us, our children were born under it. Germany's victory or defeat will not change anything in our relations to our adopted fatherland, to our new home.… Don't allow yourselves to be driven to demonstrations of any kind, avoid arguments with citizens of other nations. Be silent, bear this difficult time with dignity and show that you are true Germans, grateful to the country that accommodated you and in which you found a new home."[15] Again and again the *Journal* reminded new immigrants that they had sworn loyalty to Canada and claimed that Germans, by their very nature faithful and honest, would never break that oath. Nevertheless, it was only natural that German immigrants sympathized with their "old fatherland," because "the heart could not be torn from the breast." Some of these Germans, however, expected the *Berliner Journal* to take the German side. Such a suggestion, the *Journal* stated, was as irresponsible as it was incompatible with the political attitude of the editors. On the one hand, the publishing of "British-hostile articles" would be suicidal for the newspaper. On the other, the editors were "born Canadians." The sons of Rittinger and Motz, who had taken over the newspaper from their fathers in 1899, were born and raised in Canada. Although they stressed how proud they were of their "German origins," they considered themselves Canadian. They said that they had made it their duty "to publish only officially approved telegrams in the war news." Obviously they could not please everyone. For many, the *Journal* was too pro-British, for others it was too pro-German, as the reasons for subscription cancellations show. One subscriber wrote: "We dont want Kiser Williams paper in canada we want King George papers we dont want Kiser too rool in Ontario we have inglish paper too find out whats going on. You better get out too Germany there you can print what you like."[16] But the editors of the *Berliner Journal* also saw themselves forced to justify their clear commitment to Canada. In an article published on 9 September 1914, they turned to recent German immigrants who were irritated by the sympathies Canadian-born descendants of German immigrants had for the British.

> The German immigrant thinks that his Canadian-born German compatriot has the same deep feelings for the old fatherland that he feels himself, but we mustn't forget that our local German fellow citizens are by now the second, third, even fourth generation to be born under the British flag. We have to consider that the education system has influenced them, and even though they preserve and nurture the German language and customs, everything around them makes them feel British politically.[17]

Therefore one should not expect "the same love for the old fatherland."[18] In a similar vein, the *Journal* justified its stance to U.S. German-language newspapers that reproached the *Journal*. Baltimore's *Deutsche Korrespondent* accused the *Berliner Journal* of "grovelling before England," as the *Journal* reported.[19] The *Journal* countered that it would be ungrateful if it "denigrated the land in which we enjoy complete freedom as well as protection of life and property."[20] The editors had shown their loyalty with an appeal in the fall of 1914 to Germans in Canada to contribute to the Patriotic Fund. Nobody, it said, should refuse to participate in this "deed of compassion." German Canadians enjoyed the protection of the Canadian government and were permitted to conduct their affairs. They should therefore show their gratitude by willingly donating money.[21]

The difficult situation of the *Berliner Journal* brought on by World War I can also be seen in its circulation figures. In 1908, the *Journal* had more than five thousand subscribers. Ten years later, when it ceased publication, it had just thirty-two hundred. In an appeal in February 1916 the *Journal* asked its readers for support. They should shop primarily at establishments that advertised in the *Berliner Journal* and should also voice their appreciation of their support of the German Canadian press.[22] The tense situation also caused several rumours that the publication of the *Journal* would cease. In March 1916 the *Journal* assured its readers that every edition was examined by the official censor in Ottawa and that there had not been any complaints as yet: "On the contrary, more than once he had made us understand unequivocally his appreciation of the good patriotic attitude of the newspaper. As already said, we are Canadians and British, and our loyalty is innate. They should expect nothing less from us."[23] The *Berliner Journal* was always eager to maintain good working relations with the community and was therefore careful not to exaggerate anti-German incidents. It stressed in particular the reliability of the government. There was little that could be done about insults and offences of the "mob" and the government appreciated and protected German immigrants.

The increasingly critical situation following the sinking of the British passenger steamer *Lusitania* by a German submarine on 7 May 1915 was also reflected in the *Berliner Journal*. It stated: "The dislike of the Germans became worse" after that day. It reported several incidents in Vancouver, British Columbia, and in St. Catharines and Preston in Ontario, and on the closing of German clubs in Berlin, Toronto, Hamilton, and Montreal. The *Journal* adopted a conciliatory approach. It was "only natural ... that the Canadian soul was stirred to its deepest depths." Nevertheless, the conduct of the Canadian government toward Germans had been "exemplary." The *Journal* denied the rumour of a Toronto newspaper that "a number of German citizens had celebrated the sinking of the *Lusitania* with an opulent dinner, at which the catastrophe had been met with cheering."[24]

The renaming of Berlin as Kitchener in 1916, which the *Berliner Journal* had vigorously opposed, was the last political debate in which the newspaper participated. After this battle had been lost, the number of critical political articles diminished. The *Journal* still printed long news summaries, but the editorial articles, which had been few to begin with, became fewer and fewer. In the summer of 1917, the newly named *Ontario Journal* now filled its columns with neutral articles with titles like "On Getting Up Early," "Nervous Parents," or "About Cold Baths."[25] Articles that dealt critically with the Canadian war policy, such as those that had been published in 1915, had become unthinkable. If the editors wanted to express their opinion, they did it by translating English newspaper articles. The difficult situation of German Canadians was discussed one last time in the spring of 1918. What prompted the discussion was a bill to ban the use of the German language in schools, churches and public institutions. The *Journal* editors confessed that they would have remained silent on this "bill, dictated by blind hatred," but there was unexpected criticism from some "Anglo-Canadians."[26] In the editorial the pent-up frustration about the tense situation of the war broke through: "We Canadians of German descent had to suffer under this blind hatred without daring to justify ourselves, even though our loyalty was equal in every way to that of the British-born Canadians and even though we bear no guilt for the war. We would have also quietly accepted this latest offence, but there arose a fair judgement from a source where we had hardly expected it, from Anglo-Canadians." The *Journal* reported that leading authorities from arts and science, being able to differentiate between German politics and German science, had spoken up for the study of the German language:

These words are a tonic for us Canadians of German descent. We have been faithful to the beautiful country that we or our parents chose as our home. We have made efforts to help the country to thrive, and when the disastrous war broke out we did not shy away from sacrifice. But nothing helped because we were and stayed targets of fanatic hatred, and everywhere we went, every move we made, we were often exposed to the coarsest insults. Is that going to change? ... Do we German Canadians have to bear this burden until the end of the war and maybe even longer?[27]

The ban on German newspapers in October 1918 caught the editors of the *Journal* off guard. Although they had feared a possible ban since the beginning of the war, the actual Order-in-Council came rather abruptly. In the last German-language issue of 2 October the editors were still optimistic that they could continue publication in German even though there were rumours of a ban. A press release of 26 September stated that the Canadian government had passed an Order-in-Council according to which all Canadian newspapers in languages of the enemy would have to be published in English or French. The editors of the *Journal* had been "considerably agitated," but their inquiries had not suggested an impending ban. They were confident they could acquire a special licence but their optimism proved unfounded. The next issue had to be published in English: no exceptions were made. Shortly after the end of the war bilingual newspapers were permitted. German-only newspapers were forbidden, but they were allowed to publish if every article had an English or French translation. The editors of the *Journal* rejected this as impractical.[28] With that the nearly sixty-year history of the *Journal* as a German-language newspaper in Canada came to its final end.

This chapter is based on a research conducted by the author as a guest researcher of the Waterloo Centre for German Studies in 2005–06. For the complete results, see Löchte, Das "Berliner Journal."

Notes

1   On the situation in the United States see Trefousse, "Deutschamerikanische Einwanderer."
2   All English translations of the German texts in the *Berliner Journal* are by the author.
3   *Berliner Journal*, 21 July 1870.
4   *Berliner Journal*, 8 September 1870.
5   *Berliner Journal*, 2 February 1871.
6   *Berliner Journal*, 4 and 11 May 1871.
7   *Berliner Journal*, 11 May 1871.
8   Speeches printed in the *Berliner Journal*, 4 and 11 May 1871.
9   *Berliner Journal*, 11 May 1871.
10 *Berliner Journal*, 11 May 1871.

11 *Berliner Journal,* 4 May 1871.
12 More about the peace celebration can be found in Frisse, *Berlin, Ontario,* 127–36.
13 See McKegney, *Kaiser's Bust.*
14 English and McLaughlin, *Kitchener,* 128. On Berlin during World War I and the standing of the Germans, see also Frisse, *Berlin, Ontario.*
15 *Berliner Journal,* 12 August 1914.
16 *Berliner Journal,* 20 January 1915.
17 *Berliner Journal,* 9 September 1914.
18 *Berliner Journal,* 9 September 1914.
19 *Berliner Journal,* 28 July 1915.
20 *Berliner Journal,* 28 July 1915. The reason behind this pronouncement was an article in the *Journal* that stated that the German citizens who had been interned by the Canadian government were "on the whole satisfied with their situation."
21 *Berliner Journal,* 23 September 1914. See also in the same issue "An den Leser der 'Glocke' in Neustadt auf sein Schreiben" as well as *Berliner Journal,* 7 October 1914.
22 *Berliner Journal,* 23 February 1916.
23 *Berliner Journal,* 25 March 1916.
24 *Berliner Journal,* 19 May 1915.
25 Articles in the *Ontario Journal* on 25 April 1917, 25 July 1917, 1 August 1917, 8 August 1917.
26 *Ontario Journal,* 6 March 1918: "Will deutsche Sprache verbieten."
27 *Ontario Journal,* 13 March 1918. See also *Ontario Journal,* 12 June 1918.
28 *Ontario Journal,* 20 November 1918.

Archival Material

Berliner Journal, 1859–1918, University of Waterloo, Dana Porter Library, Doris Lewis Rare Book Room.

Works Cited

English, John, and Kenneth McLaughlin. *Kitchener: An Illustrated History.* Waterloo, ON: Wilfrid Laurier University Press, 1983.

Frisse, Ulrich. *Berlin, Ontario (1800–1916). Historische Identitäten von "Kanadas deutscher Hauptstadt." Ein Beitrag zur deutsch-kanadischen Migrations-, Akkulturations- und Perzeptionsgeschichte des 19. und frühen 20. Jahrhunderts.* New Dundee, ON: Trans-Atlantic Publishing, 2003.

Löchte, Anne. *Das "Berliner Journal" (1859–1918). Eine deutschsprachige Zeitung in Kanada.* Göttingen: V&R unipress, 2007.

McKegney, Patricia. *The Kaiser's Bust: A Study of War-Time Propaganda in Berlin, Ontario 1914–1918.* Wellesley, ON: New Bamberg Press, 1991.

Trefousse, Hans L. "Die deutschamerikanischen Einwanderer und das neugegründete Reich." In *Amerika und die Deutschen. Bestandsaufnahme einer 300 jährigen Geschichte,* edited by Frank Trommler, 177–91. Opladen: Westdeutscher Verlag, 1986.

ELEVEN

The Politics of Diaspora

*Russian German Émigré Activists
in Interwar Germany*

James Casteel

This chapter explores the essential role that Russian German émigrés to Germany played in shaping the politics of German diasporas in the interwar period. Together with *völkisch* activists in Germany, they generated new narratives of common German identity between Russian Germans and Germans in the Reich, thus expanding the boundaries of Germanness to include Germans from Russia as German. In these narratives, war and revolution figured as shared moments of victimization and betrayal by internal and external enemies of Germanness. While Bolshevism was the main focus of their hostility, increasingly they came to imagine one source behind the enemies of Germanness: the Jew. The Germanocentric lens through which Russian German émigrés interpreted their situation as well as their staunch anti-Bolshevism made the Nazi project of revitalizing the *Volksgemeinschaft* an attractive one to them. Thus behind their narratives of victimization was a more complex history in which, in many cases, victims also became victimizers.

Theorizing Diaspora

THE EXPERIENCE OF GERMANS IN RUSSIA in the twentieth century offers a striking example of the nationalization of diasporic populations. What we witness in this case is not so much the unmaking of a diaspora or the creation of a diaspora, but rather a transformation of the social, cultural, and political field in which diaspora politics was articulated. This transformation began with the creation of a German nation-state in the late nineteenth century but reached its pinnacle after World War I with the recasting of international politics in terms of the self-determination of nations that attempted to make nationhood and territorial boundaries coincide throughout multi-ethnic central and eastern Europe. In the case of the Russian Germans, influential segments of the diaspora—especially among émigrés active in Germany during the interwar period—began to identify with Reich German nationhood and tried to influence both German and Soviet state policies. They also attempted to awaken the national consciousness among members of the diasporic population in the Soviet Union and North America.[1] In Rogers Brubaker's terms, this was very much a "reframing" of the politics of diaspora, one that was shaped by three factors: the identification of members of the Russian German diaspora with Germany, the German state's and society's recognition of Germans from Russia as "German," and the policies of the Soviet state toward the German diaspora populations.[2]

In interwar Germany, Russian German émigrés along with other Reich German *völkisch* activists played a key role in motivating state and societal actors to assist Germans in the Soviet Union. In the process, they expanded the scope of German nationhood to include Germans from Russia (as well as other *Auslandsdeutsche*) as Germans, thereby suggesting that they should be entitled to some (but not all) of the rights and social privileges of the German nation-state. Their actions also implied that the German government and public had a moral obligation and responsibility for Germans from Russia precisely because of their Germanness—an attribute that was defined increasingly in racial rather than cultural terms.[3]

In addition, the policies of the foreign homeland also shaped the nationalization of the Russian Germans, both through positive attempts to promote ethnic German national identities in the Soviet states and negatively through a variety of assimilatory and persecutory measures. Already under the tsar, policies of Russification contributed to the crystallization of a German identity among the Baltic German elites that explicitly made connections to the German nation-state. With World War I, the Bolshevik Revolution, and civil wars, efforts to mobilize all Germans of Russia on the basis of their German identity spread to the other German communities in the Soviet Union, including the rural colonists. Under the Soviet state, German identification as a national group was institutionalized with the founding of the autonomous Volga German Republic. In addition, Soviet policies that were often detrimental to some segments of the German population reinforced the desire to identify as German and to view the German nation-state as a potential external source of support.

Such attempts at the politicization and nationalization of the Russian German diaspora resemble efforts directed at Germans in the successor states to the Habsburg Empire after World War I. In a seminal article on the topic, Pieter Judson discusses the usefulness of applying the term "diaspora" to the Germans in Habsburg lands.[4] He argues that before World War I, Germans in the Habsburg Empire did not see themselves as a diasporic people and certainly did not identify with the Prussian-centred German nation-state. Only the dissolution of the Habsburg Empire and the redrawing of the political map of central and eastern Europe after World War I made such an identification possible. German minorities suddenly found themselves in nationalizing states in which they could either assimilate to the dominant nationality or be expelled. For Judson, it was the very attempt by the Nazis and *völkisch* activists to politicize ethnic Germans in central and eastern Europe that resulted in their identification with the German nation-state and the creation of a diasporic consciousness. While nationalist publicists in Germany saw them as a "lost diaspora," the communities did not identify as such until the 1930s, when "Nazi propaganda and offers of support (cultural, political and financial) ... succeed[ed] in creating a new self-understanding among them as diasporas of the German nation-state."

Judson's approach allows an understanding of the process of the nationalization of central European political space in a more complex manner that takes into account its contingencies. It is also useful for elucidating the case of the Russian Germans, which followed a related but different trajectory. Unlike the Habsburg case or *Grenzdeutsche* in Poland, Russian Germans did possess an existing consciousness as a diaspora, but one in which Germanness was understood in cultural and religious terms, and not in national ones. Most Germans had migrated to Russia before a German nation-state came into existence. While the *"alte Heimat"* of Germany shaped Russian German identity before World War I, it was a vague and idealized landscape of memory, with little connection to the existing social and political issues of Germany. Their identification was predominantly confessional, regional, and parochial, with *Heimat* being understood as the locality in Russia where they lived.[5] This began to change in the late nineteenth century. The formation of the German nation-state gave Germans from Russia a new reference point. Russification also led Baltic Germans to define themselves in national terms and to identify with Germany. Many Russian Germans studied in Germany and forged contacts with German nationalists. Still, until World War I and the Russian Revolution, attempts to organize the disparate ethnic German populations across the Russian Empire, represent their common interests, and build ties to Germany remained largely ineffective.

It was only in the interwar period, with the ruptures of war, revolution, and civil war in Russia, that connections with their brethren in Germany took on a new significance. The emergence of nationhood and nation-states as a dominant framework for identity did not mean that local, confessional, and dynastic loyalties ceased to exist. Rather, such identities coexisted with national ones. What did occur was a reframing of the space for social, cultural, and political action such that claims could be made on the German nation-state with the expectation that the state would have to respond in some manner to the demands of the diaspora. It was in this context that Russian German émigrés in Germany redefined themselves as a modern diaspora of the German nation-state. While émigrés were nostalgic and lamented the loss of their homeland in pre-revolutionary Russia, they also engaged in an effort to connect Germans in Russia to the Germans in the Reich making them useful for Germany. The effects of their attempts to nationalize and politicize the diaspora remained limited during the 1920s and '30s, but with the outbreak of World War II the Russian Germans increasingly came to identify or be perceived by others in national terms.

Russian German Émigrés in Germany and the Nationalization of the Diaspora

Russian German émigrés in Germany played a key role in this process of imagining a nationalized diaspora. Approximately one hundred thousand Germans from Russia emigrated during the war, revolution, and civil war. Over half of that group remained in Germany: approximately 58,000, according to the German census of 1925.[6] Émigrés became very active in interwar politics and played a significant role in publicizing the plight of Germans in Russia in Germany. They formed a variety of *Landsmannschaften* representing Russian German émigrés from the Black Sea, Volga, Siberia, St. Petersburg, the Caucasus, Congress Poland, and the Baltic as well as Mennonites. These émigré groups were able to build on the pre-existing ties to Baltic Germans who had settled in Germany before the war. The Baltic Germans were highly assimilated into German intellectual and cultural life and had created a receptive audience in Germany for the newer migrants through their advocacy for Germans in Russia during World War I and their support for plans to resettle them in Germany and its expanded territory in eastern Europe. Émigrés worked together with a variety of German *völkisch* activists in organizations such as the Verein für das Deutschtum im Ausland and the German Protective League for Border and Foreign Germans. They also received support from academic institutions interested in the question of Germans outside the Reich, especially the Deutsches Auslands-Institut in Stuttgart.[7]

It was in this context of a broader Reich German consciousness of ethnic Germans abroad, and in Russia in particular, that Germans from Russia were able for the first time to create organizations representing all of the German communities of Russia, thereby positing a common Russian German identity and one that entailed identification with Germans in the Reich. The Ausschuß der deutschen Gruppen Altrußlands, founded in 1919, was the first attempt to create an umbrella association, but soon dissolved over internal rivalries, especially between the Baltic German leadership and Johannes Schleuning, a Volga German pastor and activist.[8] These tensions led to the establishment of two rival umbrella organizations, the Zentralkomittee der Deutschen aus Rußland and the Arbeitsgemeinschaft der Deutschen aus Rußland und Polen, the former receiving support from the German Foreign Office and the latter from the Ministry of the Interior. Both actively publicized the plight of Germans in Russia and lobbied the German government to provide financial support for German communities in Russia as well as for immigrants in Germany. The Zentralkomittee published the periodical *Deutsches Leben in Rußland*, edited by Schleuning, whereas the Arbeitsgemeinschaft produced *Deutsche Post aus dem Osten* (*DPO*), edited by Carlo von Kügelgen. In 1935, after the Nazis had come to power, all the organizations representing Germans from Russia were merged into the Verband der Deutschen aus Russland, later Verband der Russlanddeutschen, and the *DPO* became its main publication with many of the same authors continuing to write for it.[9]

The *DPO* and the writings of individuals associated with it demonstrate the ways in which these Russian German émigrés were able to construct a pan-German identity that included the Russian Germans as members of the German national community. Published monthly from 1926 to 1943, the *DPO* was intended to maintain connections between the dispersed Russian German populations in Germany and the Soviet Union as well as in the Americas. It provided articles from Russian German émigrés in Germany, reports on the conditions from various parts of the diaspora, and relevant news from Germany. The discussion of authors in this journal should be contextualized in the broader climate of what one might term the *völkisch* turn in German intellectual, cultural, and political life in the interwar period. The resentment felt by many Reich German activists against the outcome of the war and the perceived injustice of the Peace Treaty of Versailles as well as their dissatisfaction with the institutions of the Weimar Republic led many to view not the state but the *Volk* as the source of German hope for the future—a *Volk* that extended beyond the narrow borders of the German nation-state.

Russian German émigré writing tended to interpret tsarist and Soviet policies through an ethnocentric lens. While policies such as Soviet grain requisitions, collectivization, discrimination against kulaks, and the Great Terror were brutal and had substantial material and human cost for German communities in Russia, they were not anti-German in their intent. It was only during wartime (or when the threat of war seemed imminent) that tsarist and Soviet state policies specifically targeted groups of Germans as supposed "internal enemies," with the dispossession of land among German communities in the western borderlands during World War I and most famously with the deportations of the Volga Germans after the German invasion of the Soviet Union during World War II.[10] Accounts of contemporaries as well as some of the historiography have internalized this image of the Russian Germans as victims of tsarist, Soviet, and even Nazi persecution and crimes, but have tended to neglect the other roles that Germans from Russia played as supporters or beneficiaries of both regimes. In other words, while victimization was a factor in their experiences, it does not capture the full nuance of their history.[11]

Memories of War and Revolution, Narratives of Victimization and Betrayal

A key motif in how this common German identity was constructed between the Germans from Russia and Reich Germans was the reference to the common fate of World War I and the revolutions in Germany and Russia. An imagined national community was formed that was held together by a narrative of their experiences of struggle against internal and external enemies of Germanness. The war, revolution, and civil wars that followed provided the context for massive migration of peoples in both directions. German (as well as Austrian) soldiers and civilians found themselves for the first time in Russia on the front or as prisoners of war. To their surprise, they discovered that there were Germans living in Russian lands. In addition, Germans from Russia travelled westward with Russian armies and there were a number of civilian refugees after the revolution and civil wars. This "rediscovery" of Germans from Russia by Reich Germans was the product of wartime transnational (or perhaps trans-imperial) interactions, in the context of a German bid to expand the territory and resources under its control in order to retain the capacity to remain a power with global influence.[12]

While this "rediscovery" of the Russian Germans was born of a history of transnational interactions and movements of people between Germany and Russia, the collective memory of the experience of the war and revolution among Russian German émigrés (and increasingly also shared among *völkisch* activists in the Reich) framed this encounter somewhat differently. The dominant narrative was that of the "stab in the back," which played such a prevalent role in German politics and culture between the wars. The stab-in-the-back myth was premised on the presumption that Germany had in fact won the war. The public was never informed about the reality of defeat, and blame was placed on the civilian government and revolutionaries for having betrayed the German military, despite the fact that it was the military leadership itself that urged a reluctant civilian government to begin negotiating an armistice. As recent literature has demonstrated, Germany's loss of territory in eastern Europe that had been secured with the Treaty of Brest-Litovsk in March 1918 was an important aspect of this myth. The dissolution of the short-lived German empire in eastern Europe produced new fears of dangers emanating from the wild east, represented by the figures of the Bolshevik and of the Jew.[13]

Russian German émigrés along with *völkisch* activists in Germany connected the stab-in-the-back myth to the Weimar Republic's policies toward the Russian Germans. The revocation of the Treaty of Brest-Litovsk served as a symbolic reminder of the German state having turned its back on its promises and obligations to the Russian Germans. As one Russian German author described it, the Russian Revolution and German victories in eastern Europe during World War I had brought the hope to many Russian Germans of "the final liberation" from tsarist oppression with the granting of a ten-year window for Germans from Russia to emigrate to Germany and become German citizens. However, German defeat meant that the treaty was no longer binding, and the opportunity was not granted for mass emigration to Germany.[14]

In addition to ending the possibility of the resettlement of Russian Germans in Germany, the revolution and revocation of the Treaty of Brest-Litovsk were also viewed as having left Russian German communities at the mercy of the Bolsheviks. Russian German activist Schleuning argued that the German Revolution ended the possibilities of living in Russia or returning to the motherland, leaving only the option of self-defence: "They wanted to fight as Germans, and if necessary, go down fighting."[15] For Schleuning, Bolshevism was a new incarnation of the "Asiatic wilderness" that German settlers had been trying to civilize for generations. Now in a more dangerous form, it sought "revenge" on its former "conquerors" through the "annihilation of the German invaders," reversing years of German cultural and civilizing work in Russia.[16] Such depictions presented the plight of the Russian Germans as part of a universal struggle between European civilization and Asiatic barbarism and contributed to the reimagining of the histories of the German diasporas as part of an expansive German effort to colonize the eastern European landmass. The Russian German experiences of suffering and persecution at the hands of Germany's enemies were used to mark the Germanness of the territories they inhabited and thus reclaimed these spaces for the German *Volk* in general.

Although Russian German émigrés were generally speaking staunch anti-Bolsheviks, this did not mean that they were forever without hope that the Soviet regime could be tamed and that conditions for Germans in Russia would improve. In particular, in the mid 1920s with German Soviet rapprochement, the recovery from the Volga famine, and the establishment of the Volga German Soviet Republic, some could entertain the possibility that the Germans of Russia could flourish once again and become politically and economically useful to Germany. For example, Georg Löbsack wrote in the summer of 1929 that the Volga German settlements offered a chance for Germany to continue its world-historical task of mediating between the technology-oriented western civilization and the spiritual soul of the east.[17] Such optimism evaporated after the beginnings of collectivization and the campaign against kulaks in the Soviet Union. In the fall of 1929, outside Moscow, the gathering of Russian Germans fleeing collectivization and demanding to emigrate from the Soviet Union was a watershed event in this regard and was covered widely in the German press.[18] After receiving news of this event, Löbsack's optimism was dashed. Subsequently he described the recent history of German Russian relations as "tragic," having been "so disastrously mutilated" at Brest-Litovsk, and he blamed the dual revolutions in Germany and in Russia for the abandonment of the Russian Germans.[19] For him, the suffering of Germans in Russia was not without meaning since it had strengthened the "*völkisch*-biological" substance of the German people.

In 1936, shortly before his death, Löbsack published a memoir of his experience of seven years of war, revolution, and civil war in Russia. The book was praised for his detailed rendering of the travails of the Russian Germans at the hands of the Bolsheviks. In particular, Löbsack interpreted the tragedy of the Volga Germans as part of a global German struggle, arguing that the experiences of the Volga Germans had lessons for all Germans in their struggle for "self-determination."[20] Löbsack escaped Bolshevik Russia accompanied by an elderly woman by traversing the western borderlands and illegally crossing the border into Poland. His narrative of his escape lays claim to the territory as a site of remembrance of shared German experiences: the battle of Germans from Germany against Russian Germans serving in the tsar's army, the deportation of the Volhynia Germans, the reuniting of German prisoners of war (POWs) with their Russian German brethren about whose existence they had known nothing, and the eastward treks of the Russian Germans as they "returned" to Germany. In Löbsack's view, the war was not just a conflict between states, but rather one in which the very existence of the German people was at stake.[21]

Löbsack's narrative also had an anti-Semitic undertone. When he arrived in Minsk on his way to the Polish border, Löbsack became aware of the presence of Jews who, he claimed, no longer hid in their ghettos since the Bolsheviks had come to power.[22] This passage begins a convoluted discussion of the "secret connection" between Jews and Bolshevism that seems to have plagued Russia since 1917. Löbsack also depicted Germany as having been subjected to "Jewish-Bolshevik" influence. Upon his return to the old homeland, Löbsack speculated about the cause of the war and why the victorious Treaty of Brest-Litovsk was overturned: "Was [Germany] already even then so much under the control of Bolshevism?" He viewed the separate struggles of diverse German communities in Russia as part of the "same struggle … a struggle of the German *Volk* in Eurasia" and one that contributed to the struggles of Germans throughout the world. For Löbsack, the main enemy of the Germans in Germany and in Russia was Bolshevism, but behind Bolshevism stood the figure of the Jew.[23]

Heinrich Schröder, a Russian German activist from the Black Sea region, echoed Löbsack's narrative of the war and revolution as having contributed to the crystallization of a common German identity among Reich Germans and the Germans of Russia. Of a younger generation than Löbsack that came of age during the war and civil war, Schröder was far more radical in his anti-Semitic rhetoric and devotion to National Socialism. Schröder viewed Germans from Russia as having been victimized by a continuing anti-German movement: they too had been stabbed in the back by the "November betrayal" of the German Revolution and abandoned to their fate.[24] Schröder urged Russian German émigrés to tell of their first-hand knowledge of the "Soviet-Jewish campaign of annihilation"[25] against the Russian Germans. Such sentiments and the deep inversion of reality that informed them were echoed in numerous articles that portrayed Germans from Russia as innocent victims of a Jewish-Bolshevik conspiracy. While real experiences of victimization under Soviet rule informed the rhetoric and actions of Russian German émigrés, in their attempts to interpret and make sense of their experiences, they increasingly came to imagine that at the root of their victimization—and indeed the victimization of all Germans—lay the figure of the Jew.

Conclusion

Like many of their Reich German counterparts, Russian German émigrés considered World War I and the revolutions that followed as traumatic ruptures, which were followed by civil war and the profound transformation of their way of life under Soviet rule. In assigning meaning to their individual and collective suffering, they viewed their efforts as contributions to Germanness, a quality that was possessed not by the state (or at least not by the Weimar Republic), but rather one that was located in the *Volk* itself. This nationalization of the diaspora also invoked a discourse of victimization and betrayal by internal and external enemies who threatened Germanness. Although Bolshevism was the main focus of their hostility (to a greater extent than for their Reich German counterparts for whom anti-Versailles sentiments was more prevalent), increasingly they came to imagine one source behind the enemies of Germanness: the Jew. The Germanocentric lens through which Russian German émigrés viewed their past and their prospects for the future, as well as their staunch anti-Bolshevism, allowed these émigrés to meld with *völkisch* activists in the Weimar Republic and made the Nazi project of revitalizing the *Volksgemeinschaft* attractive. As experts on "the east," Russian German émigrés provided academic, ideological, and administrative support for Nazi resettlement and ethnic cleansing in eastern Europe, including the Holocaust. While the levels of complicity varied from support of Nazi policies to active perpetration, the line between liberating ethnic Germans from Bolshevism and annihilating Jews, Gypsies, and communists was often a very thin one—one that built on the dominant narratives of Russian German identity discussed above.[26]

The Nazi project of Germanization, ethnic cleansing, and genocide in eastern Europe during World War II transformed the circumstances of the Germans of Russia, as it did those of all ethnic Germans in eastern Europe, and contributed both directly and indirectly to the further nationalization of the diaspora.[27] As Doris Bergen has persuasively demonstrated, Nazi policies made the *Volksdeutsche* of eastern Europe into the "official beneficiaries" of ethnic cleansing and genocide, as *Volksdeutsche* who were resettled or those who already lived in the area profited from the deportations of their non-German neighbours and the murder of their Jewish ones.[28] In response to the Nazi invasion and motivated by fears of their own "internal enemies," the Soviets deported Germans from the Volga region in 1941 before the arrival of the German army. Thus Nazi rule solidified ethnic categories throughout the multiethnic space of central and eastern Europe, constructing a rigid dichotomy between German and non-German that would outlast the war, informing the postwar period of expulsions and ethnic reorganization of central and eastern Europe as well as state policies toward ethnic Germans in the Soviet Union. Russian German émigrés in Germany and those who had fled or had been expelled at the war's end were able to connect their recent experiences of flight, expulsion, or incarceration in the Soviet Union with longer-term narratives of victimization by the Bolsheviks in the emerging Cold War.[29] As shown here, however, behind this narrative of victimhood is a more complex history in which, in many cases, victims also became victimizers.

Notes

1   See Bridenthal, "Germans from Russia."
2   Brubaker, *Nationalism Reframed*, especially 4–6, 107–47.

3   See Casteel, "The Russian Germans."
4   Judson, "When Is a Diaspora Not a Diaspora?," 219.
5   Bridenthal, "Germans from Russia," 189.
6   Williams, *Culture in Exile*, 354.
7   Fleischhauer, *Das Dritte Reich*, 14–23; Oltmer, *Migration und Politik*, 151–82; Grundmann, *Deutschtumspolitik*, 123–30.
8   Deutsches Ausland-Institut (BArch); von Stackelberg, "Der erste Zusammenschluß"; Ehrt, "Die Anfänge."
9   Buchsweiler, Volksdeutsche in der Ukraine, 54–57.
10 See Martin, *Affirmative Action Empire*, 35–36, 273–308, 328–43.
11 For an exception, see Neufeldt, *Fate of Mennonites*.
12 See Sanborn, "Unsettling the Empire."
13 Geyer, "Insurrectionary Warfare"; Liulevicius, *War Lands on the Eastern Front*, 249–51.
14 Niedermayer, "Der Brester Friedensvertrag," 97.
15 Schleuning, *In Kampf und Todesnot*, 42–65, cit. 65. Translations here and elsewhere are by the author.
16 Schleuning, *Die Wolgadeutschen*, 35.
17 Löbsack, "Briefe an die Steppe," Parts 2 and 3.
18 The *DPO* provided articles from major German dailies and commentary on the situation. See *DPO* 5 issues 11 and 12 (November and December 1929).
19 Löbsack, "Steppendeutscher," 146; "Weltdeutsche Volkssoziologie."
20 Löbsack, *Einsam kämpft*, 10. For praise, see the review in *DPO* 8, 2 (April 1936), 8–9, and Löbsack's obituary, the lead article of *DPO* 8, 9 (November 1936), 1–2.
21 Löbsack, *Einsam kämpft*, 381–84.
22 Löbsack, *Einsam kämpft*, 379–80, cit. 379. There were of course no ghettos in eastern Europe until the Nazis created them.
23 Löbsack, *Einsam kämpft*, 395, 396.
24 Schröder, *Die systematische Vernichtung*, 9–13.
25 Schröder, "Russlanddeutsche."
26 See Schmaltz and Sinner, "Nazi Ethnographic Research." Many interwar émigrés from Russia were recruited for the *Einsatzgruppen*. See Fleischhauer, *Das Dritte Reich*, 101–02.
27 See also Chapter 31.
28 Bergen, "Tenuousness and Tenacity," 272.
29 About 350,000 Germans from Russia found themselves in Greater Germany at the end of the war. Most were repatriated to the Soviet Union leaving 70,000–80,000 in West Germany. Fleischhauer, *Das Dritte Reich*, 237–43. The situation of Germans in the Soviet Union who never experienced Nazi occupation was very different.

Archival Materials

Deutsches Ausland-Institut, R 57 (neu), Bundesarchiv Koblenz (BArch Koblenz).

Works Cited

Bergen, Doris L. "Tenuousness and Tenacity: The *Volksdeutsche* of Eastern Europe, World War II, and the Holocaust." In *The Heimat Abroad: The Boundaries of Germanness*, edited by Krista O'Donnell, Renate Bridenthal, and Nancy Reagin, 267–86. Ann Arbor: University of Michigan Press, 2005.

Bridenthal, Renate. "Germans from Russia: The Political Network of a Double Diaspora." In *The Heimat Abroad*, edited by Krista O'Donnell, Renate Bridenthal, and Nancy Reagin, 187–218. Ann Arbor: University of Michigan Press, 2005.

Brubaker, Rogers. *Nationalism Reframed: Nationhood and the National Question in the New Europe.* Cambridge: Cambridge University Press, 1996.

Buchsweiler, Meir. *Volksdeutsche in der Ukraine am Vorabend und Beginn des Zweiten Weltkriegs: ein Fall doppelter Loyalität?* Tel Aviv: Bleicher Verlag, 1984.

Casteel, James. "The Russian Germans in the Interwar German National Imaginary." *Central European History* 40, no. 3 (2007).

Ehrt, Adolf. "Die Anfänge rußlanddeutschen Organisationswesens in Deutschland." *Deutsche Post aus dem Osten* 4, 3 (March 1929), 51–53.

Fleischhauer, Ingeborg. *Das Dritte Reich und die Deutschen in der Sowjetunion. Schriftenreihe der Vierteljahrshefte für Zeitgeschichte* 46. Stuttgart: Deutscher Verlags-Anstalt, 1983.

Geyer, Michael. "Insurrectionary Warfare: The German Debate about a Levée en Masse in October 1918." *Journal of Modern History* 73, no. 3 (2001): 459–527.

Grundmann, Karl-Heinz. *Deutschtumspolitik zur Zeit der Weimarer Republik.* Hannover-Döhren: Harro v. Hirschheydt, 1977.

Judson, Pieter. "When Is a Diaspora Not a Diaspora? Rethinking Nation-Centred Narratives about Germans in Habsburg East Central Europe." In *The Heimat Abroad*, edited by Krista O'Donnell, Renate Bridenthal, and Nancy Reagin, 219–47. Ann Arbor: University of Michigan Press, 2005.

Liulevicius, Vejas Gabriel. *War Lands on the Eastern Front: Culture, National Identity, and German Occupation in World War I.* Cambridge: Cambridge University Press, 2000.

Löbsack, Georg. "Briefe an die Steppe. Wolgadeutsche Studien," Part 2, *Deutsche Post aus dem Osten* 4, 5 (May 1929), 98–99.

Löbsack, Georg. "Briefe an die Steppe. Wolgadeutsche Studien," Part 3, *Deutsche Post aus dem Osten* 4, 6 (June 1929), 122–24.

Löbsack, Georg. "Steppendeutscher Volksgeist und Sowjetstaatsrecht," *Deutsche Post aus dem Osten* 5, 8 (August 1930), 145–46.

Löbsack, George. "Weltdeutsche Volkssoziologie," *Deutsche Post aus dem Osten* 5, 11 (November 1930), 201–04.

Löbsack, Georg. *Einsam kämpft das Wolgaland. Ein Bericht aus 7 Jahren Krieg und Revolution.* Leipzig: R. Voigtländer, 1936.

Martin, Terry. *The Affirmative Action Empire: Nations and Nationalism in the Soviet Union, 1923–1939.* Ithaca, NY: Cornell University Press, 2001.

Niedermayer, Ferdinand. "Der Brester Friedensvertrag und die Rußlanddeutschen," *Deutsche Post aus dem Osten* 4, no. 5 (May 1929), 97–98.

Neufeldt, Colin Peter. *The Fate of Mennonites in Ukraine and Crimea during Soviet Collectivization and Famine (1930–1933).* PhD diss., University of Alberta, 1998.

Oltmer, Jochen. *Migration und Politik in der Weimarer Republik.* Göttingen: Vandenhoeck & Ruprecht, 2005.

Sanborn, Joshua A. "Unsettling the Empire: Violent Migrations and Social Disaster in Russia during World War I." *Journal of Modern History* 77, no. 2 (2005): 290–324.

Schleuning, Johannes. *In Kampf und Todesnot. Die Tragödie des Russlanddeutschtums*. Berlin: Bernard & Graefe, 1930.

———. *Die Wolgadeutschen. Ihr Werden und ihr Todesweg*. Berlin: Kranzverlag, 1932.

Schmaltz, Eric J., and Samuel D. Sinner. "The Nazi Ethnographic Research of Georg Leibbrandt and Karl Stumpp in Ukraine, and Its North American Legacy." In *German Scholars and Ethnic Cleansing*, edited by Ingo Haar and Michael Fahlbusch, 51–85. New York: Berghahn Books, 2005.

Schröder, Heinrich. *Die systematische Vernichtung der Rußland-Deutschen*. Langensalza: Julius Beltz, 1934.

Schröder, Heinrich. "Russlanddeutsche—an die Front." *Deutsche Post aus dem Osten* 8, 10 (December 1936): 24.

von Stackelberg, Eduard Freiherr. "Der erste Zusammenschluß der Rußlanddeutschen." *Deutsche Post aus dem Osten* 4, 3 (March 1929), 49–50.

Williams, Robert C. *Culture in Exile: Russian Émigrés in Germany, 1881–1941*. Ithaca, NY: Cornell University Press, 1972.

TWELVE

Creating Transcultural Space

Ethnicity, Gender, and the Arts in Chicago, from the 1890s to the 1950s

Christiane Harzig

In this essay, I introduce the Columbia Damen Club (CDC), a group of women who inserted themselves into the urban landscape of Chicago with a determined interest in "high cultural" issues. These women, ensconced in a bourgeois culture, were fluent in both English and German and educated in both cultures. They were well situated in one culture and ardently committed to the other; they related to the German American community as much as they networked among Chicago's club women. They created a space that may best be understood as transcultural. While the more commonly used concepts of inter-nationalism and interculturalism often imply a set of distinct and fixed entities indicated by lines of demarcation, the concepts of transnationalism and transculturalism refer to processes and developments, suggesting emergence rather than being, life experiences rather than moments in time, or negotiations between nation-state–related entities. The women created a space where the arts were pursued, performed and appreciated, and communications across cultures were ongoing, despite political and at times cultural hostilities. Their class and ethnic position challenge our dichotomous understanding of centre and margin, of "anglos" and "others," of "natives" and "newcomers"; and they add another dimension to the face of progressive urbanism.

CHICAGO, AT THE TURN TOWARD THE TWENTIETH CENTURY, hosted one of the longest-standing, vibrant albeit divergent, German diaspora cultures in North America. With one third of its population claiming German heritage, the city was the site of a vital working class culture from the 1860s to the 1980s. It supported burgeoning Protestant, Catholic, and Jewish communities, sported hundreds of singing, sports, and charity organizations and German theatres and publications. However, Chicago is better known for its role in shaping a modern urban culture combining rugged individualism and an emerging gendered social consciousness. Reform-minded, modern women and men, fighting an uphill battle against social Darwinism and rampant corruption, inserted themselves into the narrative of this urban development.[1] In a dichotomously constructed narrative, with an anglo middle class and a lower class "other" (including African Americans and immigrants), was there a place for diverging patterns, different visions, and variant interests? The Columbia Damen Club (CDC), a group of women who inserted placed themselves in the urban landscape with a different agenda. Due to their determined interest in high cultural issues, with social problems and solutions taking the backstage, they created a space where ideas could flow freely, where the arts were pursued, performed, and appreciated, and where communications across cultures were ongoing, despite political and at times cultural hostilities. Their class and ethnic position challenge our understanding of centre and margin, of anglos and others, of natives and newcomers; their presence added another dimension to the face of progressive urbanism.

The women, ensconced in a bourgeois culture, were fluent in both English and German. They were well situated in one culture and ardently committed to the other; they related to the German American community as much as they networked among Chicago's club women, and, at the same time, they offered a slice of German high for Chicagoans to taste. They created a space that may best be understood as transcultural. While the more commonly used concepts of inter-nationalism and interculturalism often imply a set of distinct and fixed entities indicated by lines of demarcation, the concepts of transnationalism and transculturalism refer to processes and developments, suggesting emergence rather than being, life experiences rather than moments in time, or negotiations between nation-state–related entities. "Transnationalism denotes," as Dirk Hoerder writes, "the competence to live in two or more differing cultures and, in the process, create a transcultural space."[2] The space created by the activities of the CDC members came into existence by triangular negotiations, with the Chicago cityscape, women acculturated in the German American community, and cultural expressions and developments from Germany. None of the players entered the process in a "pure" form, nor did participants remain unchanged. The activities of the clubwomen show the historical workings of transculturalism in Chicago during the first half of the twentieth century.

The Beginnings

The CDC's very existence was the result of transcultural exchanges. On 4 April 1893, a number of German women assembled in the Orpheus Halle in the Schiller Building.[3] They had come together to consult and decide upon whom to invite from Germany to participate in the Congress of Education, which was to take place in conjunction with the Columbian World's Fair. Dorothea Boettcher, a well-known poetess, journalist, and feminist in the German American community, greeted the gathering and introduced Harriet C. Brainard, president of the World's Congress Auxiliary for higher educational affairs. Brainard, an English teacher, presented her case: American women, she outlined, had already accomplished many and great things while organizing the World's Fair. It was now the duty of the German women to contribute their share, that is, to make sure that "Germany, the land of poets and thinkers[4] be represented by a spokeswoman of the most advanced ideas in the realm of higher education."[5]

This meeting had three major consequences: it gave birth to a flourishing German American women's club; it brought Käthe Schirmacher, one of the most prominent activists of the German women's movement, to address the congress; and it initiated an ongoing, although cautious, relationship with the University of Chicago.[6] The association, the club members agreed, should strive to become the intellectual and spiritual centre of women's lives in the city. It should participate in all efforts of American women and learn from them, and it should introduce German ideas into English-speaking circles. It would be a great blessing if prejudices on both sides could be overcome and the well educated from both "nations" could learn to love and respect each other and work toward common goals. The women then agreed on the name Columbia Damen Club in honour of the Columbian Exhibition.[7] A committee was to draft statutes for the club, which had now grown to forty members. Schirmacher responded positively to the invitation since she was already attending the women's conference during the World's Fair in Chicago, and agreed to address the congress in English, choosing the topic "Why Are German Universities the Last to Open Up for Women?" With proceeds from the Helene Lange Fond, named after a prominent European feminist, the club agreed to support Schirmacher financially during her extended stay in Chicago and also to establish an endowment to support a deserving student at the University of Chicago. In transcultural fashion, the endowment would serve as a model of unprejudiced behaviour for future scholarships, and thus the main purpose of the club: to work together with well-educated American women.[8]

These events established a pattern. From the turn of the century on, the club settled into a routine of meeting once a month, sometimes to organize special events in the community, but mainly to listen to musical performances, engage in intellectual debate, and enjoy literary entertainment. Often it provided a venue for visitors from Germany to perform but it relied mostly on local talent. Guests were welcomed to an annual "English Afternoon," albeit by invitation of club members and for an entrance fee.[9] The content of their activities evolved over time, quite divorced from local, national, and international events.

Impact of Changing Times

The CDC's development saw three phases: 1893–1917, 1917 to the late 1940s, and the 1950s to the present. This section describes the first two. Each was marked by international events and reflected the women's efforts to shape the transcultural space they intended to create. From 1893 to 1917 the club struggled to find its direction and define its purpose, with conflicting forces at work: those seeking either to increase or to decrease contact with the American women's movement, the discussion of feminist issues and ideas, social involvement, and acts of charity, and the club's preoccupation with high culture. The programs, minutes, and correspondence reflected these diverging positions.

While during the early years the club invited others to participate and learn about the German arts and directed their activities mainly at the German American community, the war years—starting the second phase—changed the thrust of their initiatives. The club became more involved in the city's female public sphere. In addition to regular visits to the Art Institute of Chicago and celebrating the memory of its own history at jubilees (1918, 1933), CDC members were busy with support work connected the two world wars, fundraising for charity during the Depression and projects to boost the waning German community, and hosting events for the Illinois Federation of Women's Clubs (IFWC), which the club had joined in 1917. Especially in the early 1920s they mounted fundraising drives to support orphans and widows in Germany and Austria, activities initiated and organized by Jane Addams and her fellow international feminists.[10] For the CDC women, who were asked for generous support, this was an ideal opportunity. They could build on former German Austrian Hungarian cooperation, cooperate with their American kindred spirits, and draw upon their cultural resources.[11]

The fundraising efforts in the 1920s and early '30s were much related to the needs and demands of the German community. A number of institutions based in Germany, for example a social organization running a soup kitchen in Karlsruhe, the German Red Cross in Berlin, and a student fraternity in Munich, asked for help from Cora Holinger, the socially inclined president.[12] The club also took up sponsorship of the German Theatre, donated needlework and baking to Christmas bazaars, and staged card parties to replenish the Chicago scholarship fund. The idea of the scholarship was rejuvenated in 1919, this time to counterbalance the "prevailing war-hysteria throughout the country [which] has precipitated much hasty and foolish opposition to German as a subject in high school and college."[13] An annual award was given to one particularly deserving student, who, unlike in earlier days, sometimes was female.[14] In the same spirit, in 1925 department store owner William A. Wieboldt and his wife, a long time member of the CDC, were reported to have donated half a million dollars in support of a new building for modern languages at the University of Chicago. At the time, Wieboldt Hall housed the departments of German, English, and Romance languages and is still part of the campus today.[15]

World War II changed this pattern in that it again appealed to the women's American identity in support of the war. In October 1941 the executive board addressed its members:

> Since all the women's clubs in the country are preparing to participate in relief work, the Columbia Damen Club should not avoid the activities of the Red Cross intended as entertainment and diversion for our recruits, or any relief program of our government. Our work may soon be required by law. We ask all those members who understand the necessity of this request to be prepared. The task at hand is: surgical dressings for the army.[16]

Throughout the war years, the club members continued to contribute their services to the Red Cross. A Christmas charity collection was "so successful" that the club was able to send CARE packages to Germany. The executive board members were pleased with themselves, and the recipients most likely were, too.[17]

A census check of the women who took up office with the club showed that their motivation did not stem from a cultural legacy from Germany, but rather from their living in an American urban environment. Most of the officers either were born in the U.S., many of them in Illinois, or had come as young children with their parents or had lived at least ten years in the U.S. before becoming active members.[18] Being a club member was also a matter of social standing. The women's husbands were

either self-employed store owners or merchants, such as Wieboldt, a gro-
cer in 1900 and a department store owner in 1920, or Max Stern, a sales-
man in 1900 and later a print-shop owner doing business for the CDC; or
their husbands belonged to the intellectual class (doctors, artists) or political elite (consul to Spain and various Latin American countries). Most of
them lived in extended households with immediate family and other relatives, often with more than one maid. Very few were single women or
self-employed. They usually addressed each other by their husband's first
and last name and their relationships seemed more formal than intimate.
In the 1920s and '30s it had become a matter of social prestige to be a member of the club.

It is often argued that anti-German hysteria during World War I brought
an end to the visible public presence of Germans in the American Midwest and elsewhere, but from the CDC's activities during the years 1914–45,
the war does not seem to have put an end to German American cultural
activities. On the contrary, war-related activities drew German American
women, more than ever before, into the female-dominated fold of their
new fatherland; and as Russel Kazal has noted for Philadelphia, their club
did not experience an overall decline in membership.[19] Membership
remained stable. In 1917, seventeen new members joined, including a
growing number of women with names that did not sound German.[20] Up
to the end of the 1930s they also successfully recruited new members
from among their daughters, so the club did not yet suffer from the generational transition that was so clearly felt by many "old immigration"
associations.[21]

The Program

Emerging from the 1910s to the '50s is a transcultural space,
one not marked by cultural frontiers, discarding or preserving some cultural baggage; rather, a space filled with ongoing intellectual political and
cultural intercourse, with neither the "typical" American nor the "typical" German taking precedence. The CDC presented the interesting, the
challenging, and the exotic, as well as the tried and tested, the classical and
the traditional. Throughout the years, the women were able to attract and
engage an assortment of speakers representing an astounding array of
political ideas, social concepts, artistic talent, and sophisticated entertainment. Many represented the contemporary elite in their respective genres or fields, or achieved fame in posterity.

The club asked professors and lecturers from the German departments of the University of Chicago, the universities of Illinois and Wisconsin, and Northwestern University to lecture in German on topics of high
culture. In the 1920s Martin Schütze, Hans Gronow, and Julius Goebel

were regular speakers. Authors, travel writers, (female) journalists, artists, and scientists from Germany travelling through Chicago were invited as well. For musical performances, they engaged both local and internationally known celebrities, and also often featured the talents of their own members or their daughters. Obviously, the club could rely on a vast array of artistic talent, but for special occasions they relied on celebrities. In 1930, for example, the new club year was opened with a performance by the internationally famous cello virtuoso Bruno Steindel.

Over the years, lecture topics focused on a number of themes. By far, most meetings were devoted to literature and the arts, either performed or addressed and discussed. Sometimes topics were of current interest, or they ventured into avant-garde topics such as modern German and Austrian drama.[22] Some lectures reflected the canon and its contemporary implications; sometimes authors read from their works.[23] There were lectures related to the female experience, sometimes even venturing into gender studies. Amalie von Ende, a feminist journalist working for the Women's Paper at the *Illinois Staats-Zeitung*, talked about the "Modern German Woman,"[24] and Dr. Gunther Jacoby (University of Greifswald) pondered over the "English, American, and German Concepts of Manhood."[25] The clubwomen honoured the 1931 Nobel Prize winner Jane Addams with an address by her nephew and biographer, James Weber Linn. Topics that addressed the German American experience either looked into its history (Baron von Steuben, pioneer life) or picked up controversial issues of the time. In 1915, the relationship between American Germanness and the new Americanism was addresse;[26] in 1922, the question of whether to remain German or become American was asked;[27] and in 1925, Dr. Eduard Baumgarten from the University of Chicago compared German with American universities.[28] Sometimes the feminist and ethnic interests came together, for example in March 1932 when Cecilie Hammerstein-Illing, a journalist writing for *Die Neue Zeit*, reflected on "German-American Women as Bearers of Culture in Chicago's History."[29]

Political issues were not avoided. In 1909, the women greatly enjoyed instruction in "Parliamentarism" and decided to hold their elections accordingly.[30] The relationship between Germany and America in war and peace and political trends in Germany were discussed regularly. However, topics related to family and household affairs, to youth and the relationship between the generations were more prominent. Sometimes Chicago politics related to social issues were discussed. Finally, yet importantly, travel accounts, anthropological insights into foreign cultures, and anything catering to the "exotic" were enduring favourite topics.

In May 1928, Alfred Adler (1870–1937)—a Jewish physician, educator, and psychologist from Vienna who later relocated to Long Island—gave a lecture at the club on "Individual Psychology," presenting an approach to psychology that he was reputed to have founded.[31] Joseph Dommers Vehling lectured on "The Influence and Future of Germanness" in November 1934.[32] His claim to fame was a translation of Apicius's *De re coquinaria*, an ancient Roman cookbook. Vehling's book was later translated into English and has been reprinted many times. Although it apparently contained errors, it became a primary reference work on the history of cooking today.

With guests Mimi Jehlen, Mary Hastings Bradley, and Minna Schmidt, the club invited women who not only had something interesting to say but also were outstanding (female) personalities. Jehlen was a professor in the German department at the University of Illinois, Urbana. In May 1936 she lectured on German fairy tales. Bradley had gone on various sporting trips to Africa in the 1920s, capturing animals, observing local customs, and later providing vivid accounts of her observations. She was widely published and recognized in the 1930s and again in the 1950s; her book *The Road to Desperation* appeared in 1932. When she came to give an illustrated lecture on "A Vanishing Africa" in November 1936, Bradley clearly satisfied the longing for the exotic "other" so prominent among CDC members.

Schmidt addressed another topic of interest to the clubwomen: fashion, albeit steeped in cultural history. A regular on the CDC lecture circuit and most likely also a member, she was introduced as a PhD in law and the science of costume. In September 1927 she lectured on "Three Thousand Years of Costumes of Famous Women, Their History, and Literature." Clubwomen were invited to perform a minuet to round out the cultural experience and fun. In December 1940 Schmidt turned to more serious matters, lecturing on "Women-Philanthropists Who Became Famous in Art, Literature, Science, and Education." She also ran a costume and wig shop on North Clark Avenue.

Colin Ross and Friedrich Schönemann were among the more controversial CDC lecturers. Ross, despite his English-sounding name, was an ardent German nationalist and the author of numerous travel accounts. Travelling the world between 1910 and 1950, he wrote from a white/German supremacist and racist point of view. He was an ardent supporter of the Third Reich and a friend to many prominent Nazi families, although not as an anti-Semitic as official ideology demanded. Having lived in Chicago for several years, he claimed the right to be critical of the American way of life, which he saw as dominated by democracy and capitalism, both of which he rejected. He killed his wife and himself in April 1945. Schönemann was the most visible of the academic experts on America during the Nazi period. In 1936, he was named chair in the literary and cultural history of North America at the University of Berlin. Today he is considered one of the most controversial predecessors of American studies in Germany.[33] When he lectured on "The Cultural Face of the New Germany" in November 1933, just months after Hitler's takeover, he pursued the mission of spreading Nazi ideology. However, the club's program of the 1930s was by no means dominated by Nazi ideologues. The women, a number of them Jewish, were not taken by the myth of racial superiority. They afforded the speakers an opportunity to present their case, but the program showed no indication that they were particularly interested in it.[34]

What do literati such as Hastings, Bradley, and Ross, academics such as Jehlen, Adler, and Schönemann, or journalists such as von Ende and Hammerstein-Illing have in common? Is there a current theme in the CDC's cultural program during the fifty years under consideration here? What seems like an assortment of individuals upon closer scrutiny is an ensemble of transculturalists. Not only were they travelling abroad, venturing into foreign spaces, and exposing themselves to various cultural experiences, but in their artistic and intellectual articulations they were also extending beyond the boundaries of their national cultures. They reached out and crossed localized confines, either by addressing issues of transcultural interest, by living transcultural lives, or by reflecting and discussing issues beyond national concerns. Although the club's standard repertoire of musical and literary performances came from Germany's classical and romantic period, it is the validity of the artist in a transcultural trajectory, his or her presence in a universal canon, albeit a Eurocentric one, that made that individual of interest to the clubwomen. The CDC provided a way station for transcultural experiences.

Conclusion

When German American women came together in the early 1890s to create the CDC, they situated themselves between the women's movement, which they perceived as anglo-American, and the highly cultured upper echelon of the German American community. They wanted to construct a bridge between these two societal representations. However, it soon became clear that, unlike many politically and socially active women in Chicago, they did not want to make the city a better place—at least not through social activism. Rather, they wanted to create a new space, a space filled with art, intellectual exchange, and knowledge. As it turned out, this space also became filled with transcultural negotiations and understandings. In doing so, the women drew upon their own resources, which were shaped by a transcultural upbringing in a German family context situated in an American urban environment, by cultural and political developments in Germany and the United States, and by the opportunities presented by the city of Chicago.

To accomplish their aim the women adjusted to the format of an American women's club. They held regular elections, collected dues, accepted new members through recommendations, installed subcommittees as necessary, regularly visited the Art Institute, and, anti-German feelings notwithstanding, became part of an umbrella organization that until then had not demonstrated a great deal of interest in the multiethnic polity of Chicago and Illinois. The clubwomen may have discussed the IFWC's affairs during their general annual meetings, but from the 1920s onward, the Chicago women's movement had only a fleeting presence in the routine and program of the CDC. The club members preferred to direct their charitable attention to the needs of the German American community, which from their perspective had a central European outlook, including the Austrian and Hungarian elements. German Jewish women were found among its members and anti-Semitism had no discursive presence in the club's representations, but neither had the African American or any other ethnic presence found in Chicago. Their interest in the "foreign" or "other" did not reach out to the multicultural environment of the city but was directed further afield.

Literature and the arts clearly occupied the centre of the transcultural space they had created. It was also an area in which they did not have to compete with their fellow male German Americans. It did not interfere with any male-dominated activities; in fact, it must have been much in the interest of German American community gatekeepers. Their activities aided them in keeping alive the concept of a German influence in America, cultural or otherwise.[35] Since their space was not exclusively female, there was enough room for gendered encounters and the occasional venturing into American-dominated feminist activities could be tolerated.

The transcultural space created by the members of the Columbia Damen Club with their programs was marked by current events, by explorations into aspects of identity and positioning, and by promoting an informed understanding of Germany, America, and the "other." Although German literature had a strong presence, the program did not replicate the agenda of German departments in universities across the country, nor did it follow the lead of nationally published reviews of German books. The club never paid particular attention to the emerging new literature of the 1920s,[36] not even to Thomas Mann, although it did invite his children, Klaus and Erika, to appear.[37] By the end of the 1920s, Germany had become an externalized space, a space they felt an affinity to but they also had to study with the help of lectures. Together with the rest of Chicago, they wanted to be informed about new developments. If there was a cultural blockade after World War I, the CDC neither made a point of it nor chose to ignore it. Although their social citizenship may have been German, their political citizenship was clearly American. Their cultural citizenship was a transcultural and transnational one.

The author thanks the Faculty of Philosophy at the University of Erfurt for its financial support, Kathy and Michael Conzen for their hospitality in Chicago, and Thomas Kozak for assisting with his superior language skills.

Notes

1   See Flanagan, *Seeing with Their Hearts.*
2   Hoerder, "Transculturalism(s)," 8.
3   The minutes of their society refer to *"deutsche Damen,"* i.e., German ladies. This indicates self-identification as German. Unless noted otherwise, in this chapter the term "German" is used as a self-identifying category. "Protokollbuch," entry 4 April 1893. Chicago Historical Society (CHS), Chicago Columbia Club Collection (CCC), Box 1.
4   In the minutes, this was labelled with the trope *"Dichter und Denker."* All translations from German are by the author.
5   Minutes, 4 April 1893.
6   For more on Schirmacher see Walzer, *Käthe Schirmacher.*
7   Minutes, 13 April 1893. The World's Columbian Exposition took place in Chicago in 1893; it was to demonstrate United States' achievement in the previous four hundred years.
8   Minutes, 13 April 1893.
9   Invitation, 6 March 1913. CCC, Box 3.
10 See Sklar, Schüler, and Strasser, *Social Justice Feminists.*
11 Invitation, 6 November 1919.
12 Correspondence, 12 December 1921, 15 January 1924, 12 January 1924. CCC, Box 6, Folder 1920–1929.
13 Correspondence, Stan William Tutting (Department of Germanic Languages and Literatures) to Mrs. Holinger, 13 March 1919. CCC, Box 6, Folder 1916–1919.
14 Correspondence, 14 April 1919.
15 *Abendpost,* 17 April 1925, 3.
16 Invitation, 5 February 1942.
17 Invitation, 2 January 1947.
18 The census year closest to their being mentioned in the minutes or the programs was checked.
19 See Kazal, *Becoming Old Stock.*
20 Jahresbericht der Präsidentin des Columbia Damenclub 1916/1917 (annual report of the president). CCC, Box 5.
21 See *Hundert Jahre Chicago Columbia Club, 1893–1993,* 18: *"Zwölf junge Damen aus der Jugendgruppe (Töchter von Mitgliedern) des Chicago Columbia Clubs,"* 1939–1940, unpublished manuscript. In possession of the author.
22 Invitation, 1 March 1923.
23 For example, on 5 March 1931 there was a lecture entitled "The Faustian Man Today." Authors who read from their works included Paul Rohrbach (3 November 1921) and Adele Gerhard (2 February 1939).

24 2 February 1914. On von Ende see Harzig, *Familie,* 221–24.
25 Invitation, 1 February 1912.
26 Invitation, 4 November 1915.
27 Invitation, 7 December 1922.
28 Invitation, 3 December 1925.
29 Invitation, 3 March 1932.
30 Invitation, 4 March 1909.
31 See Alfred Adler Institutes, "Biographical Sketch."
32 Vehling was introduced as a member of the German Writers' Association, so he clearly was not in open opposition to the Nazi regime.
33 See Gassert, "Political Reconnaissance Work," 35.
34 Mrs. Max Stern was among the founding members. Minutes 13 April 1893. Alfred Adler and Amalie von Ende, lecturers at the club, were prominent Jews of their time.
35 See Conzen, "Phantom Landscapes."
36 See Koepke, "Lifting the Cultural Blockade."
37 Program, 1 March 1928.

Archival Material

Chicago Historical Society (CHS), Chicago Columbia Club Collection (CCC).

Works Cited

Alfred Adler Institutes of San Francisco and Northwestern Washington. "Biographical Sketch of Alfred Adler." <ourworld.compuserve.com/homepages/hstein/adler.htm> (March 2008).

Conzen, Kathleen N. "Phantom Landscapes of Colonization: Germans in the Making of a Pluralist America." In *The German-American Encounter: Conflict and Cooperation between Two Cultures, 1800–2000,* edited by Frank Trommler and Elliott Shore, 37–48. New York: Berghahn, 2001.

Flanagan, Maureen A. *Seeing with Their Hearts: Chicago Women and the Vision of the Good City, 1871–1933.* Princeton: Princeton University Press, 2002.

Gassert, Philipp. "Between Political Reconnaissance Work and Democratizing Science: American Studies in Germany, 1917–1953." *Bulletin of the German Historical Institute* 32 (Spring 2003): 33–51.

Harzig, Christiane. *Familie, Arbeit und weibliche Öffentlichkeit in einer Einwanderungsstadt. Deutschamerikanerinnen in Chicago um die Jahrhundertwende.* St. Katharinen: Scripta Mercaturae, 1991.

Hoerder, Dirk. "Transculturalism(s): From Nation-State to Human Agency in Social Spaces and Cultural Regions." *Zeitschrift für Kanadastudien* 45, no. 2 (2004): 7–20.

Kazal, Russel A. *Becoming Old Stock: The Paradox of German-American Identity.* Princeton: Princeton University Press, 2004.

Koepke, Wulf. "Lifting the Cultural Blockade: The American Discovery of a New German Literature after World War I: Ten Years of Critical Commentary in the *Nation* and the *New Republic*." In *The Fortunes of German Writers in America: Studies in Literary Reception,* edited by Wolfgang Elfe, James Harding, and

Gunther Holst, 81–98. Columbia, SC: University of South Carolina Press, 1992.

Sklar, Kathryn Kish, Anja Schüler, and Susan Strasser, eds. *Social Justice Feminists in the United States and Germany: A Dialogue in Documents, 1885–1933.* Ithaca, NY: Cornell University Press, 1997.

Walzer, Anke. *Käthe Schirmacher. Eine deutsche Frauenrechtlerin auf dem Wege vom Liberalismus zum konservativen Nationalismus.* Pfaffenweiler; Centaurus Verlagsgesellschaft, 1991.

THIRTEEN

The German Democratic Republic and the Citizens of German Origin in Canada:

The Role of the Gesellschaft Neue Heimat, 1980–1990

Manuel Meune

Since 1964 in the German Democratic Republic (GDR), the Gesellschaft Neue Heimat (GNH) endeavoured to maintain cultural contacts with citizens of German origin abroad by offering these individuals informational material and "information tours." This society was subordinate to the Liga für Völkerfreundschaft, which aimed to strengthen relationships with all GDR-interested persons abroad. Some of the GNH correspondents were sympathetic toward the GDR, and would provide the country with information about the ideological disposition of German Canadians. It is documented in the letters between the GNH in Berlin and German Canadian club directors, German teachers, and pastors, however, that many who harboured little sympathy for communism would actively engage the GNH leadership in political debate. This correspondence demonstrates how Germans living abroad took part in the German German dialogue, and how they managed to save the "human substance" during even the most heated arguments. The role of the GNH should not be exaggerated, but given that their discussion partners were often important individuals in influential positions, it is evident that this organization did in fact achieve considerable success.

THE VEREIN FÜR DAS DEUTSCHTUM IM AUSLAND (VDA), which was formed during the Weimar Republic and later fully developed during the Nazi period, was banned in 1945. Founded anew in the Federal Republic of Germany in 1955, it was once again able to represent the cultural interests of German speakers abroad, although it was often reputed to be associated with ultra-conservative goals, due to its relationship with the problematic conception of *Deutschtum*. Less well known is the fact that in 1964, as a type of socialist counterpart to the VDA, the GNH was founded in the GDR. The goal of this organization was to maintain contact with *Bürgern deutscher Herkunft im Ausland* (BdHA)—as they were called in the GDR—and to acquaint them with the other German reality.

The GNH was subordinate to the Liga für Völkerfreundschaft.[1] In order to promote the international recognition of the GDR, this para-diplomatic entity strived to cultivate relations with GDR-interested individuals abroad, and this was especially done through "national friendship societies." Such friendship committees were also created in Canada, for example the Canada-GDR Committee in Toronto.[2] Although the directors of the groups were often German-speaking communists, these organizations were intended to remain open to all "progressive" people from the general public. But the GNH exclusively supported Germans living abroad—and actually only those living overseas, since the presence of German-speaking minorities in eastern Europe was a taboo subject. Due to the sensitive nature of the theme of emigration, the "BdHA issue" remained the preoccupation of a few select party and cultural functionaries.

It is difficult to determine when the first contacts were made between the GNH and Canadian institutions. The first letters to which the author had access go back to 1975, shortly after the recognition of the GDR by Pierre Trudeau's Canada.[3] This chapter will deal predominantly with the 1980s, examining the correspondence between the GNH's main contact in Berlin, Erich Wischnewski, and three categories of correspondents who were seen as important in exercising influence over German Canadians and even over the entire Canadian population: club representatives, German teachers, and pastors.

The GNH was considered much less political than the Liga für Völkerfreundschaft.[4] Accordingly, the tone of the correspondence with the GNH was different than that of the correspondence between the "League" and the directors of the Canada-GDR Committee. The GNH was by no means ideologically neutral, but the discourse would change, depending on the level of sympathy shown by the correspondents toward the GDR regime. It may be the case that particularly negative reactions do not exist in the archive, but when one considers how critically the GDR theme was handled in letters by many readers in the German-Canadian press of the period, it is remarkable that so many correspondents actually used rather pleasant words when writing to the GNH.

Contacts with German Canadian Clubs

People often turned to the GNH as representatives of an organization because they had discovered *Neue Heimat*, the GNH periodical published for Germans living abroad, and saw it as the only contact to the GDR prior to the opening of a GDR embassy in Ottawa in 1988. In some instances, it provided people with a kind of individual psychological relief. For example, commenting on a photograph in the *Neue Heimat*, in which a Soviet soldier is handing out bread to children, a woman writes that the only thing she associates with Russians and the end of the war is rape.[5] Wischnewski answers diplomatically that war bestializes individuals "on both sides."[6] Although he makes use of the opportunity to offer the woman GDR material for her club, he does not attempt to demonstrate—as he does in other letters—the superiority of the Soviet system.

According to the documents available, contact with the German-Canadian Congress, which was founded in 1984, was first taken up in 1987, but the tone was friendly. Reference is made to the "interested recipients" of the *Neue Heimat*, who are finding "a part of their 'old homeland.'"[7] Nothing seems to stand in the way of a complete normalization of relations with the GDR.[8] Letters arrived from all parts of Canada. Items were requested, offered, and sent off; examples include calendars, dictionaries, postage stamps, vinyl records, presentation slides, and posters. People often had specific requests for items that the GNH did not have on hand, and in such instances the GNH contacted places that could help support it in its "overseas information service." For example, it contacted district councils or museums to acquire a city's coat of arms, sewing patterns for traditional Thuringian costumes, or information about Brunswick uniforms used by the British auxiliary troops in Canada.[9] When the interest pertained to the Napoleonic Wars of Liberation, the reference toward "maintaining the progressive traditions of German history" was not absent.[10] Indeed, regardless of their political convictions, it was hoped of the "citizens of German origin" that they would become more sympathetic toward the GDR, as embodied in the standard phrase: "We have included some additional information for you about our country."[11]

At times, the correspondents appear to be flattering the GNH in order to gain advantages for their acquaintances still living in the GDR. B.P. from Ontario, for example, wanted to "disseminate the real picture about the GDR"[12] to Canadians, and hoped that his friends in Jena would be able to participate in a German-Canadian event in the West German city of Wolfenbüttel.[13] But the GNH was not responsible for that, and the organization was more likely to stimulate sympathy for the regime by offering "information trips," for example to media workers and club directors (twelve days with lodging, airfare not included). Moderators of German-language programs received records—on the condition that the origin of the music was mentioned—and when the GNH felt that the interest was genuine, an invitation was issued. Regarding club directors, the standard phrase was: "It would please us if you or another representative of your club would take part in a trip like this, since until now we have only been able to maintain written contact with your club."[14] In addition, the GNH would turn to associations on certain occasions, such as on the 750th anniversary of Berlin in 1987, in order to offer them photographs and literature.[15]

German Teachers and Book Dealers as Partners and Informants

Owing to their work-related interest in contemporary politics, and to their status as role models, German teachers were also important, highly sought-after partners whom the GNH supported in promoting the German language abroad. Ronald Rhodes of Kitchener was one of those who went on a study trip. His report for the *Neue Heimat* emphasized the "contrasts" between the "colourful" and the "grey," mentioning that "unbelievable things" had been accomplished, and yet that "so much remains to be done"; but the report was published in its entirety.[16] For H.R. of Alberta, the trip seems to have had a deeper impact. She wrote afterward: "Our picture of the country changed appreciably. Early on, we greeted all of our impressions with scepticism, but by the end of the trip we had revised our opinions."[17] While she had earlier emphasized that teachers should receive information "about the other side"—since otherwise the Goethe Institute would be the sole source of informatio[18]—she stated that the importance of "personally getting to know" the country and its people first became clear to her after the trip.[19] She now wished to fight prejudices and to contribute to changing the image of the GDR, for example at teacher conferences.[20] She informed the GNH about which films were and were not well liked among teachers, and about how those teachers reacted when offered informational trips.[21] She did not shy away from unpleasant questions and expressed constructive criticism about the content of GDR brochures.[22] Ronald Rhodes had also mentioned the counter-productivity of propagandistic acts, such as the books donated for the "German language competition"; in his opinion, the *Jugendlexikon* contained "too many political entries," and a book about crafts would "probably be better."[23]

But this was by no means only about teachers being misused as informants. Rather, these components of the correspondence show how little the GDR authorities actually knew about the German-Canadian school system and about German-Canadian clubs. In addition to teachers, another reliable source for information was the bookseller and long-time GDR sympathizer Hans Grunsky, who settled in Toronto in the 1930s. Besides his contact with the Canada-GDR Committee, he had insight into the world of German-Canadian clubs and societies. He organized a GDR table at the yearly German book exhibition and provided the GNH with information about how it was received. He reported the relief that some people felt upon learning that for the first time, the 1981 exhibition would not be held in the Goethe Institute.[24] He informed on academics as potential "study-trip participants,"[25] and on club directors who had an "anti-left attitude."[26] He helped the GNH in updating its obsolete list of German-language schools, lamenting how the Herder Institute in Leipzig was suffering from a lack of legitimacy since, by contrast, the schools apparently received "all of the teaching materials" from the Goethe Institute via the Trans-Canada Alliance.[27] He also informed on the *Kanada Kurier*, a weekly newspaper that was often considered reactionary, stating that its reporting had become "more frequent and more positive" since Bernd Längin, the editor-in-chief, had taken part in a study trip to the GDR in 1982. If this change were to be "permanent," Grunsky writes, it would "be a big step forward."[28]

Thankful and Mistrustful: The Pastors' Balancing Act

In 1983, the year in which Luther's 500th birthday was cele-brated, the GDR launched one of its largest charm offensives, directed at the international community. The somewhat less ideologically charged references to "great figures" such as Frederick the Great or Luther were intended to generate more sympathy for the GDR state. In this sense, the GNH was anticipating a breakthrough by offering promotional material to pastors and by organizing trips to Luther memorial sites for them. The pastors received letters emphasizing the role of churches in the GDR, quali-fying this slightly, as in this letter, where the expression "citizens of German heritage abroad" is, by way of exception, not used:

> We support the efforts of Germans residing overseas in maintaining a connection to their former homeland, and in cultivating German lan-guage, customs and culture.... In the context of these support efforts abroad, numerous relationships with church communities are in exis-tence in Canada as well, and it is understandable that the celebration of the 500th birthday of Dr. Martin Luther ... is the central focus of the in-terest.[29]

In cases where pastors sought to use the occasion of official trips to con-tinue the dialogue—and could thereby potentially contribute to the legit-imacy of GDR politics—the pressure placed on them by certain authorities was particularly intense. Pastor F. was one such individual who lobbied for a fair relationship with the GDR and experienced problems because of it.[30] He was referred to by Grunsky as a "completely unpartisan and there-fore much more influential contributor toward the greater goals," and was successful in 1983 in bringing a small group of young people with him to the GDR. His efforts to find more interested individuals in Toronto and Montreal remained unsuccessful, however,[31] and Wischnewski bemoaned the "difficulties that people are creating for him," because "now no one really has the heart to accept an invitation."[32]

At least eight pastors were in contact with the GNH (from Manitoba, Quebec, and Ontario) and reacted to these offers in different ways. Pas-tor E. from Winnipeg, who was considering a "pilgrimage to the land of Luther," appeared to be impressed by the films and books sent by the GNH on the occasion of the "anniversary of the great German reformer"[33] when he wrote: "we can only loudly ... answer: 'yes and amen.'"[34] Some trips were declined for personal reasons, but some people declined for polit-ical reasons, not wanting to serve as a token Lutheran for the regime. Pas-tor R., for instance, felt an uncomfortable pressure, which continued to grow with the accumulation of gifts: he declined the trip "after serious consideration." Despite his gratitude for the gratis presentation slides, he wanted to "practice more self-restraint in accepting such things," and this pertained equally to the trip he was offered.[35] Reacting to the subtle alle-gation of absent altruism, Wischnewski appeared to be piqued, but answered diplomatically that "no obligations" were expected to emanate from the Luther material, which had been "sent with pleasure." He fur-ther stated that the GNH, "as a society in the land where Dr. Martin Luther was born and had his major influence," only wished to support "the Lutheran church abroad," and asked whether the role of the church was not "to reunite through benevolent deeds that which certain malicious pol-itics divides."[36]

Also illuminating is the correspondence, which dates back to 1975, between Pastor P. from Ontario and Wischnewski's predecessor, Heinz Zantopf. With reference to freedom of travel, Zantopf relativized the "purely human standpoint" of the pastor by pointing to the recognition of "real historical and social processes."[37] The "debate about the truth" was continued with Wischnewski when Pastor P. declined the Luther tour in 1982. The pastor reported being horrified by the attempt "to present Luther as a social and civil reformer":

> Luther was the man he was because he was a staunch Christian, a per-son who in all respects placed God in Jesus Christ before everything else ... Even an atheistic state must give an accurate depiction of CAUSE and EFFECT. In the same sense, as a Christian, I cannot address the top-ics of socialism and communism without focusing on the authors of those philosophies, such as Lenin, Marx, Engels, etc. For that reason,

since the Luther committee is only presenting half—and not the WHOLE—truth about Luther, I would ask you to refrain from sending me any further publications from that committee.[38]

Pastor P. added one more sentence, however, which was typical of the longstanding relationship of some German Canadians with the GNH authorities: "Nothing personal. My criticism concerns the issue at hand and is not aimed at you personally."[39]

Provocative Words and Political Debates

As has been mentioned, the political dimension was not as pronounced in the GNH as it was in the Liga für Völkerfreundschaft. Words such as *Volkstumsarbeit* or *Deutschtum* were often seen as anachronistic or subversive in East and West Germany. But they remained largely unproblematic in German Canadian circles and were therefore not dismissed as irrelevant by the GNH. If a correspondent expressed thanks for the help received regarding *Volkstumsarbeit* or in "maintaining Germanness in Canada," there was no trace of a patronizing tone in correspondence from the GNH—unlike in letters from the Liga—according to Horst Döhler, the president of the Canada-GDR Committee.[40] Döhler lamented that the Liga brushed off his work as being *deutschtümelnd*, without having even the faintest idea about life in Canada. Another point was that instead of using the phrase "citizens of German origin," the GNH would sometimes use the hyphenated "*Deutsch-Canadier*," with the letter C, though, as if using a K were too germanophile. When a professor wrote from Ontario requesting materials for an exhibition, Wischnewski responded that the GNH would gladly support his "endeavour to maintain German language and culture among the *Deutsch-Canadier*."[41] And in 1987, when the task was to generate interest for the Berlin anniversary festivities, the term "countrymen abroad" was employed in a very ambiguous fashion, as if the situation of the two separate German states were already somehow passé.[42]

The situation became somewhat complicated when it came to using the awkward terms "*Deutsch*" and "*Deutschland*," for example when K.M. from Alberta, who at least used the GDR-specific abbreviation BRD [*Bundesrepublik Deutschland*] for the Federal Republic of Germany—the German equivalent of FRG being frowned upon in West Germany—requested some photographs in anticipation of a multicultural event:

It must unfortunately be said that the German offering is presently inadequate. One of the reasons for this is the exclusion of the GDR, since most of the post-war immigrants hail from the territory of the FRG, or from areas east of the present German states, whose eastern cultural boundary ... is delineated by the rivers Elbe and Werra. I am a native Berliner whose notion of German culture lies within the boundaries of the entire German-speaking territory, be it in Cottbus, Vienna, Zurich, or Kiel. For the 1987 Edmonton Heritage Days I intend to put together a presentation panel with maps and pictures ... which also incorporates the territory of the GDR. The <u>central focus of the panel will be a map of Germany</u> [underlined in red by the GNH].[43]

As expected, the word "Germany" and the term "German culture" were perceived as a source of irritation. The GNH, however, did not want to create the impression that it was fixated on German German relations. Thus, it initially used the neighbouring German-speaking countries in order to denounce the cultural-ethnic definition of "German." In answer to this, K.M. reassured the GNH that the Swiss and Austrians would not be part of his project. Indeed, he again underscored the extent to which the identity formation of German speakers in Canada was a particular phenomenon, and why the ethnic definition of the German nation often took precedence over the political one:

> [Many] come from Eastern Prussia, Western Prussia, Poznan, Silesia and Pomerania ... and often know Germany only in its borders from 1914 or 1937 ... The Potsdam Agreement and its consequences usually only have significance for Canadians who immigrated after World War II. In the context of German Studies in Canada, all three German cultures are normally included, <u>since in most cases cultural identity on the basis of language has blurred the idea of identity based on nationality</u> ... I do not only concern myself with "German" affairs, but also with German-speaking affairs. In the case of the exhibition, though, I am dealing with "Germans" only in the sense of "from Germany."[44]

Someone in the GNH had underlined the sentence about language affiliation and had placed an exclamation mark in the margin. Nevertheless, Wischnewski was satisfied with this explanation and was prepared to send the exhibition material, as long as the result would "not be a pan-German representation, but rather information about both existing German states."[45]

There were also other provocative themes. G.R. from Ontario, for example, complained about the word *Frieden* [peace], which was apparently "mentioned thousands of times" in the periodical *Neue Heimat*. The Soviet Union had already become so strong, he wrote, that "even the USA would not dare to attack it," not even, he adds with innuendo, "if another 1000 Afghanistans were annexed."[46] In its answer, the self-criticism of the GNH is only undertaken for the sake of appearances, and its insistence on the "truth" is in no way diminished:

> To what extent the editorial staff of our periodical treats this problem, in order that the readers will be able to understand it, is something that I do not want to judge here, but we would not call it "drivel" ... It is baf-

fling that you only mention Honecker and Andropov—in your eyes, is Reagan an angel of peace? Important components of trust are openness, honesty, and truth, especially with regards to information. We take this opportunity to enclose a small informational magazine for your perusal.[47]

G.R. answered that he would like to "lock Reagan and Andropov up in a room" until they came to a "sensible result," and the reply to this was that war and peace were "not only in the hands of two men" and that politics in the United States were "determined by the strength of its military and its industry."[48] As a NATO member state, Canada was "also responsible" for the stationing of new missiles.[49] Faced with the unwillingness of his counterpart to appreciate that both the Soviets and the Americans were to blame for the arms race, that both were "immoral," G.R. exclaimed: "We grew up in two different worlds ... and therefore you [will] never understand me."[50] Nevertheless, the correspondence continued. Despite his criticism, G.R. was invited to the GDR and found himself engaging in a delicate balancing act. On the one hand, he did not want to endanger the trip by criticizing the GDR bureaucracy; on the other, however, he felt the need to expose the contradictions of the regime: "We have corresponded for quite a while, and you know that I'm not a murderer ... I admit that I have been critical in some places, but really, how can I see the good in it all, when the trip is being complicated for me in this fashion?"[51] The reply to this sounded unintentionally ironic, as if GDR citizens were regularly allowed to travel freely to the West: "When we apply for an entry permit to Canada, we do not get it in 14 days either. In each country, and in each consulate, there is a specified processing time for such things."[52] G.R. replied to this—referencing Honecker's failed trip to West Germany—with a humour reminiscent of GDR jokes:

> [I beg] your pardon.... [A person] will sometimes not want to accept the fact that it takes weeks or even months of waiting until one finally receives permission to travel from Germany to Germany. (Even Mr. Honecker did not receive it.) Please understand that last bit in a humorous sense! Our newspapers wrote a considerable amount about how Honecker's visit was denied. It's all quite regrettable, actually. An excerpt from the Guelph newspaper: Erich Honecker has become the latest East German to try, and fail, to cross the Berlin Wall.[53]

In an earlier letter G.R. had presupposed that it was a matter of course for a GDR functionary to travel to Canada: "A more personal impression would naturally be the best—why don't you come over?"[54] This humour may sound tasteless, but it appears to be typical for a number of letters in which a benevolent yet provocative tone is consciously employed. Ultimately, the entire correspondence serves as an example of how German

Canadians participated in the German German dialogue in their own way from afar, and of how the "human substance" was preserved even during the seemingly hopeless exchange of arguments. Also, the "neutral" GNH, which represented a niche within the Liga für Völkerfreundschaft was far superior to the latter in demonstrating how a respectful relationship can be developed among "class enemies."

The *Wende* Correspondence: What Conclusions Can Be Drawn?

On the basis of official letters, it is difficult to find evidence indicating the depth of the human relations that were forged. In some cases, the *Wende* letters show conclusively how amicable those relations had become—often after meetings in the GDR. However, most individuals received standard phrases about the fact that in the meantime "a lot of positive things have happened," but also that "some negative things" had occurred. In 1990, as the GDR was on its way out, German Canadian supporters began to speak up, giving their interpretation of past events. They wrote encouraging accounts, or suggested solutions for saving the GNH. One teacher requested that books be sent to him even if they were no longer contemporary: "Everything can be adapted,"[55] he wrote, almost ostalgically.[56] The fatalistic response reads: "We will send them to you soon because no one knows how the world will look by year's end!"[57] This was because, by 1990, the GNH was merging with the VDA and had lost its autonomy. In the context of the reorientation, the "westernization" of the dealings with "citizens of German heritage abroad" transpired in lockstep with a shift of the organization's priorities toward eastern Europe. Wischnewski was caught indecisively between a commitment to the new developments and a need to hold onto old principles:

> The situation with German unity has reached an advanced stage. Although that is good and desirable, it has its consequences; some new issues have surfaced that are not necessarily advantageous for the people living here. For the moment, the free market has only stood for competition, and above all unemployment ... The work of the Gesellschaft Neue Heimat will continue—and even stronger than before. The difference is that we will now dedicate ourselves primarily to addressing the problems of the Germans in Eastern Europe; they are in dire need of our support. You have doubtlessly read already in our periodical *Neue Heimat* that we have agreed to work closely with the VDA of the Federal Republic...a logical development.[58]

The best evidence of the mental processes many people went through can be seen in their choice of words: the BRD became the *Bundesrepublik*, and the "German speakers" had become "Germans." This swift adjustment was criticized by many employees of the "more political" Liga für Völker-freundschaft,[59] which found it regrettable that GNH members were so quick to offer their files to the infamous VDA. An explanation for why the employees of GNH were able to adapt to the new system so rapidly may be found in the fact that they had previously held the party line while not shying away from dialogues in which Germans living abroad were allowed to express conservative ideas.

It is not easy to estimate the actual role of the GNH. To gain a more accurate portrait than is possible here, its activity in the United States would also need to be analyzed. One should not overestimate its influence, especially when one considers that it employed fewer than ten individuals (the Liga employed about a hundred) and that in the 1980s it was only in constant contact with twenty-five people from Canada at most—or when one observes that the VDA did not even mention the existence of the GNH, nor the fusion of the two authorities, anywhere on its website. But when one takes into account that the correspondents were often influential individuals who played a central role in German Canadian circles, it becomes evident that the GNH did in fact enjoy a certain degree of modest success—when compared with those of West German institutions—but nonetheless achievements that contributed to the normalization of the GDR among German Canadians, even when for many it was outweighed by antipathy or indifference.

Translated from the German original by Mark Wilkinson and Mathias Schulze.

Notes

1 See Kasper and Köcher, Die Liga für Völkerfreundschaft.
2 See Meune, "Engels."
3 All letters quoted are unpublished and come from the Stiftung Archiv der Parteien und Massenorganisationen der DDR im Bundesarchiv (SAPMO-DDR) in Berlin. They were translated into English.
4 Peter Lorf, interview: "To the GNH employees it did not matter who was left and who was right. Their objectives were different—and they had fewer resources."
5 G.S., 17 July 1985. For letters to the GNH, unless otherwise indicated the recipient is Erich Wischnewski. Only the names of the senders are given, except for some letters whose authorship is concealed by random initials.
6 Wischnewski to G.S., 25 July 1985.
7 Mathias Küster, 20 July 1988.
8 Küster, 4 February 1988.
9 Wischnewski to A.G., 5 July 1982; B.P., 12 February 1985, 26 April 1988.
10 B.P., 13 April 1988.
11 This phrase is found in several letters.
12 B.P., 29 April 1985; 22 October 1987; 1 July 1988.
13 B.P., 19 May 1989.

14 Wischnewski to H.A., 10 July 1987.
15 Wischnewski to Germania Club in Hamilton, 29 April 1986.
16 Rhodes, "Stationen."
17 H.R. to Peter Schreiber, GDR Embassy, Ottawa, 7 June 1988.
18 H.R., 16 February 1987.
19 H.R., 27 December 1988.
20 H.R., 24 May 1988.
21 H.R., 13 October 1988.
22 H.R., 18 November 1988.
23 Rhodes, 14 April 1987.
24 The 1981 exhibition took place in the *Donauschwaben-Klub*; Hans Grunsky, 6 January 1981.
25 Grunsky, 6 December 1981.
26 Grunsky, 2 May 1983, 7 November 1981.
27 Grunsky, 9 August 1983.
28 Grunsky, 2 July 1982.
29 Wischnewski to Pastor E., 25 August 1982.
30 Grunsky, 25 November 1981.
31 Grunsky, 23 May 1983.
32 Wischnewski to Grunsky, 30 June 1983.
33 Wischnewski to Pastor E., 25 August 1982.
34 Pastor E., 26 June 1982, 12 April 1983.
35 Pastor R., 10 March 1984.
36 Wischnewski to Pastor R., 7 May 1984.
37 Zantopf to Pastor P., 20 May 1975.
38 Pastor P., 8 November 1982.
39 Pastor P., 8 November 1982.
40 J.L., 20 July 1988; R.F., 22 November 1982.
41 Wischnewski to Hartmut Fröschle, 11 June 1985.
42 Wischnewski to Germania Club Hamilton, 29 April 1986.
43 K.M. to the Ministry of Culture (forwarded to the GNH), 1 September 1986.
44 K.M., 9 November 1986.
45 Wischnewski to K.M., 3 December 1986.
46 G.R., 25 May 1981.
47 Wischnewski to G.R., 27 December 1982.
48 Wischnewski to G.R., 13 December 1983.
49 Wischnewski to G.R., 10 January 1984.
50 G.R., 2 February 1984.
51 G.R., 16 August 1984.
52 Wischnewski to G.R., 6 September 1984.
53 G.R., 14 September 1984.
54 G.R., 2 February 1984.
55 Rhodes, 3 April 1990.
56 This is the adjective corresponding to *Ostalgie*, a blend of *Osten* and *Nostalgie*, meaning nostalgia for the East.
57 Wischnewski to Rhodes, 13 June 1990.
58 Wischnewski to H.R., 18 June 1990.
59 Ginga Eichler, interview.

Interview Sources

All interviews conducted by the author. Ginga Eichler, former delegate for North America, Liga für Völkerfreundschaft, Berlin, August 2004.

Peter Lorf, former acting culture minister for international relations, German Democratic Republic, August 2004.

Archival Material

Stiftung Archiv der Parteien und Massenorganisationen der DDR im Bundesarchiv (SAPMO-DDR) in Berlin. Letters. DY13, 2950–2951.

Works Cited

Kasper, Gerhard, and Bernhard Köcher. *Die Liga für Völkerfreundschaft der DDR 1961–1990*. Berlin: AGEF, 2003.

Meune, Manuel. "'Engels war der grösste marxistische Deutschtümler': Horst Döhler and the Canada-GDR Committee Facing the Liga für Völkerfreundschaft." *German-Canadian Yearbook* 18 (2004): 197–217.

Rhodes, Ronald. "Stationen einer Reise." *Neue Heimat* 6 (1986): Rubrik "Aus der Sicht der Gäste."

PART TWO

MIGRATION

FOURTEEN

Moving beyond Hyphenated German Culture

Establishing a Research Agenda for Expatriate and Heritage German Literary Studies

James M. Skidmore

This chapter examines the history of the study of German literature outside of Germany and central Europe. Using examples drawn from German Canadian and German American literary scholarship, it explores the research agendas of these disciplines in the twentieth century. By describing the cultural politics that informed the discipline during this period, it is possible to establish that the model of historical preservation governing the discipline has outlived its usefulness. More recent research indicates that a change in the nature of the discipline is under way, and examples are offered of interpretive strategies that would enable the discipline to become less entwined with cultural politics and more closely connected to recent advances in literary scholarship.

Introduction

EVEN THOUGH THE DIASPORA EXPERIENCES conference attracted a great deal of interest in August 2006—more than fifty papers were given on all manner of research relating to the dispersal of German speakers throughout the world—the number of presentations on immigrant German literary studies was really quite small. The most obvious reason for this might well be that the body of literature that is the focus of such studies is itself relatively limited. But *Germanistik* is actually quite tolerant of subdisciplines that focus on particular eras, authors, or even motifs, and so there is no reason why this should not be so for the topic under discussion here.

As with any discipline, it is necessary to pause from time to time and examine the lie of the land in order to ascertain which way we are headed and which way we wish to head, two directions that quite often are not the same. Academic scholarship is all about renewal and reconfiguration, after all: energetic, interesting scholarship only thrives when debates and contributions are numerous and lively. This chapter is based on the contention that lethargy has infected this discipline; as such, the present discussion takes on a polemical tone that is perhaps necessary in order to spur reflection and debate. These polemics can hardly be avoided; a research agenda is being proposed that contains a provocative vision of a new way for studying the literature of German-speaking peoples living outside central Europe.

Before a research agenda can be proposed, the current state of the discipline must be established; in order to do that, some investigation of past research agendas is in order. To keep this task to a manageable size, the scope of this investigation will be largely limited to the fields of German Canadian and German American literary studies. Those familiar with other hyphenated literatures will recognize developments or debates that are similar to the progress of this discipline in other corners of the world, and while the development of the field will be outlined in a roughly chronological order—we want to see, after all, where we have come from and where we have arrived—no claims for completeness are being made. Instead, both the agendas that govern the exercise of this discipline and the debates that have given the discipline its critical edge will be examined. This discipline is in the process of renewing itself—we might even call it a *Generationswechsel*—and as a result the foundations upon which the discipline rests are in a state of flux. We are experiencing a tectonic—or is it a Teutonic?—shift.

Research Agendas Past

Why have we studied these strange hybrid, hyphenated German literatures? Is it simply natural curiosity? We would be living in a dream world if we believed that the impetus behind the development of German Canadian literary studies, for example, was scientific in nature. Cultural politics have always played a role, at times influencing scholars to forego objective critical judgement and analysis in favour of perpetuating political agendas.

An early example of ideology influencing German Canadian literary studies is Karl Kurt Klein's 1939 monograph *Literaturgeschichte des Deutschtums im Ausland*, one of the first detailed descriptions of German Canadian literature. While many scholars refer to Klein's success in breaking new ground in the field of German Canadian studies (not to mention countless other German hybrid literatures), no reference is made to the fact that Klein's book must be read within the context of the Third Reich, the belief in the unity of the German people, and the necessity to reunify all German peoples, concepts that informed the political beliefs of the National Socialist party. Klein's work cannot be directly connected to Nazism, even though the language of the time does surface in his book, as for example in his opening sentence when he refers to the " *100 Millionen Menschen deutschen Blutes.*"[1] Rather, Klein's contributions are set against the background of his belief in a quasi-mystical identity for Germans throughout the world. In his words,

> [*außendeutsche Stammesdichtung*] *ist die Quelle, aus der der Geist emporsteigt und Kräfte auslöst. Sie gibt den Außendeutschen in ihrem Inseldasein den Glauben an sich selbst und macht sie geistig wehrfähig. Sie stellt den Zusammenhang her mit dem Geistesstrom des Mutterlandes, leitet seine Fluten in dürstende Seelen und überbrückt Spannungen zwischen Heimat- und Volksliebe, der Treue zum Vater- und Mutterland.*[2]

It may be small wonder, then, that Klein's assessment of Canadian German literature (note the order of the national adjectives) focuses mainly on confessional influences, namely Protestant, Catholic, and especially Mennonite writings. Klein's masterpiece, reprinted in 1979 with a new foreword and updated bibliography by Alexander Ritter, contains a wealth of useful information for the history of German-language literature outside of German-language culture's traditional central European base.[3] Nevertheless, Klein's motivation for doing this ground-breaking work goes beyond the purely scientific.

Nor was Klein the only scholar to follow such a path. Heinz Lehmann, also writing in the 1930s, but conducting broader historical studies of German settlement in Canada before World War II, saw it as his duty to help Germans abroad to remain in contact with Germany. As Angelika Sauer points out, Lehmann's definition of German Canadian identity was based on four characteristics: "language; historical tradition; a special, romantic relationship with nature; and a mystical, spiritual bond with the German Fatherland."[4] Lehmann shares Klein's belief in a German culture that is unique and invested with special qualities.

Even in the 1970s and '80s, when there was a noticeable increase in professional academic interest in things German Canadian, it can be said that the motivation was in part non-scholarly. The creation in 1973 of the *German-Canadian Yearbook* by Hartmut Froeschle at the University of Toronto marks the point at which German Canadian studies truly came into their own as an academic discipline. An additional publication, the *Annalen*, centred at McGill University, started publishing papers in 1976 from the approximately eight symposia in German Canadian studies held in the 1970s and 1980s. Prior to the appearance of the *German-Canadian Yearbook*, some preliminary bibliographies had been published in the journal *Canadian Ethnic Studies* by Clive H. Cardinal and others,[5] and a collection of German Canadian literature, entitled *Ahornblätter,* edited by Heinz Kloss had appeared in Germany in 1961.[6] But it was the *German-Canadian Yearbook*, with its broad mandate to publish articles, reviews, original texts, biographies, and bibliographies that set the tone of German Canadian studies for the 1970s and '80s.

The yearbook has never understood itself as a purely academic enterprise; as Froeschle has explained elsewhere, it existed to provide a forum for the publication of German-language texts that might not otherwise have seen the light of day.[7] By publishing original literature as well as excerpts from the works of German Canadian writers both dead and alive in addition to articles on the history and lives of German Canadians, bibliographies of texts related to German Canadiana, and letters of greeting from Canadian and German politicians, the yearbook attempted to collect in one spot all manner of materials related to German Canadian culture. It succeeded in becoming the pre-eminent publication of German Canadian studies, and as such saw itself strengthened in its role as mediator between Germans and Canadians, between academics and the general population, between Mennonites and recent German immigrants.[8]

In retrospect it was to be expected that a publication such as the *German-Canadian Yearbook* would establish itself in the 1970s. Canadian universities had expanded both in number and size in the 1960s, and German programs expanded along with them. Many of the academics hired into German programs were immigrants who had a personal interest in the immigrant experience or who themselves had literary ambitions modest and otherwise. These academics—Hartmut Froeschle, Walter E. Riedel, Hermann Boeschenstein, and Karin Gürttler, to name the most prominent—have rendered an invaluable service in the establishment of German Canadian literary studies.[9]

It should also not be forgotten that in 1971 the Canadian government established the Multiculturalism Policy of Canada. This policy sought to avoid the "melting pot" strategy that had come to symbolize the American approach to immigration by encouraging ethnic groups in Canada to preserve and celebrate their cultural heritages within the framework of an officially bilingual nation. Students of German Canadian literature felt that their enterprise fit together nicely with official Canadian policy; in the words of Walter Riedel, "the German-Canadian contribution to the multicultural mosaic of Canada forms a part of such an endeavour."[10] German Canadian literature as the servant of a political ideology is nothing new, as the Klein example from 1939 has taught us, and in any event few can find anything reprehensible about the Canadian policy on multiculturalism; one need not be overly concerned about this development. The important fact to take note of, however, is that once again we have an attempt to integrate literary study into larger ideological frameworks. Although far less chauvinistic than Klein's attempts to envelop German-language literature in a spiritual aura that meshed so well with Nazi ideology, the work by Froeschle, Riedel, and others was at least partially motivated by the desire to establish within Canada's multicultural framework a place for German-language literature and culture.[11]

Not surprisingly, one of the first preoccupations for these scholars in the field of German Canadian literary study had to be the establishment of the literary corpus itself, hence the strong archaeological nature of the enterprise. The publication divided its interests in a roughly even fashion among history, literary studies, bibliographies, and original texts. One notices, however, that the yearbook is largely concerned with preserving German cultural heritage in Canada, either by publishing original texts or by presenting positivistic accounts of the lives and times of German settlers. The successful assimilation of successive waves of German immigrants meant that German-language texts written in Canada were never numerous and on the decline, and it was this fear of a disappearance of German Canadian culture from the Canadian mosaic that kindled a devotion to preservation.

When the preservation impulse becomes the guiding principle for a field of study, there is always the danger that the discipline can stagnate. Friedrich Nietzsche, in his 1873 essay "Vom Nutzen und Nachtheil der Historie für das Leben," speaks of three modes of history: monumental, antiquarian, and critical. Antiquarian history receives the least amount of attention from Nietzsche. Although he recognizes that it is at times necessary, he dismisses antiquarian history because its impulse is to preserve and revere, and the emerging modern world requires a forward-looking historiography, as paradoxical as that may sound, not a backward-looking one.[12] Nietzsche rightly points out that antiquarian history is ill suited to any kind of process that calls for reform or change; concerned as he was about the stagnation of modern European culture, Nietzsche could only lash out at any historiography that sought to preserve that corrupted society. While Nietzsche's own reservations vis-à-vis historical conservation may be too extreme for our purposes, his understanding of the pitfalls surrounding a historical enterprise that is, in a sense, defensive by nature applies to this analysis of German heritage literary studies. Nietzsche is in effect warning us to avoid being caught in the trap of preservation. It is a trap because while we think that by conserving a literature we are saving it, we are at the same time undermining its very sustainability by preventing it from functioning and competing in the free market of ideas. Conservation elevates the text, making it an object of reverence, and that which is revered resists analysis and interpretation. It may comfort members of the heritage community to know that a text has been preserved, but without deeper scrutiny and investigation, the text actually remains in danger of eventually being forgotten.

The contributions of the *German-Canadian Yearbook* and, by extension, the field of German Canadian studies in the 1970s and '80s, have been largely antiquarian in nature. In general, these preservation efforts, motivated partially as a result of the political climate at the time that was embracing a new multicultural identity for Canada, and partially by the desire of German Canadians to be seen as an important culture within the Canadian mosaic, are to be applauded since they continue to provide scholars with a wealth of information regarding German Canadian literature. The impulse to preserve was also motivated by other factors, not the least of which was the simple need to establish a canon that could serve as the central object of study.

As the terrain of German Canadian literary studies was mapped out in the 1970s and '80s, and the efforts at systematically preserving German Canadian literature began in earnest, a number of questions arose. One of the central issues was what, exactly, constituted German Canadian literature? For his part, Helmut Froeschle was quite expansive in his definition. Realizing that the number of creative fictional works was limited, he advocated the collection and sorting of all kinds of texts, including letters, diaries, travel accounts, and translations into German; only once the assembling of the texts was complete, he argued, could the work of interpretation begin. Strangely, however, at the same time he undercut the literary value of this work: "*Die Beschäftigung mit der deutschkanadischen Literatur— Literatur im weitesten Sinn—ist natürlich ergiebiger für Historiker, Soziologen, Völkerkundler, Kulturhistoriker und Linguisten als für Literarhistoriker; aber auch auf deren Feld gibt es einiges zu entdecken und zu klären.*"[13] Froeschle, an advocate of the conservational approach, recognizes that these materials will not necessarily meet the criteria of the literary scholar, a contention verified by Hermann Boeschenstein's remark that "care must be taken not to overestimate the literary value of the material."[14] Boeschenstein is much more concerned with separating the wheat from the chaff in German Canadian literature; while recognizing that some fiction merits closer analysis, he argues that German Canadian autobiography has much more to offer the literary scholar.[15]

The Froeschle and Boeschenstein positions reflect the difference between positivist and normative approaches to literature. Another issue was the proper categorization of the various works. Should one classify them by simple chronology of appearance, by the geographical origins of the writer, or by themes such as the Canadian landscape, the immigrant experience, or the relationship of the author's writings to an older German tradition?[16] The topic becomes murkier when one poses questions about length of the author's stay in Canada, where the work has been written, and where it appears.[17] The language of the text, at least at this point in the discipline's history, is less of an issue, although translations of English works into German by German Canadian authors become for some a valid area of inquiry.[18]

One remarkable aspect about the beginnings of a coherent discipline of German Canadian literary studies is the reaffirmation of the antiquarian approach: the discussion is not so much about the establishment of a literary tradition or an agenda for scholarship, but rather a debate about how best to organize the materials. The more fundamental question of whether a German Canadian literature even exists is answered in a similar manner: not with arguments supporting the development of a literary tradition, but with a chronology of the various waves of German settlement in Canada since the 1700s and the types of writing associated with each epoch. In establishing their field and its realm of responsibilities, the early scholars of German Canadian literature approached the object of their inquiry by demonstrating that German Canadian literature existed, that it formed part of the Canadian cultural mosaic, and that it was a valid area for academic research. To assist the promotion of this agenda, an antiquarian historical approach was adopted that forewent advanced critical analysis in favour of the collection and categorization of texts.

The field of German Canadian studies was not the only academic enterprise where archival work was placed ahead of analysis and interpretation. The story of the *Yearbook of German-American Studies* is not all that different from its Canadian counterpart. Published since the late 1960s, the journal established early on a focus on cataloguing German-language writing that might otherwise not be preserved. Later volumes have been marked by a bias toward historical topics touching German American contributions to regional and national development in the United States prior to World War I.

Research Agendas Recent

When we turn to more recent research into these hyphenated German literary studies, we see almost immediately that while the landscape has changed to some degree, familiar landmarks still exist. The *German-Canadian Yearbook* published its eighteenth volume in 2004, including original literature in addition to brief biographical sketches and articles on German Canadian history and literature. But that would be the last volume of the yearbook; it ceased production, although efforts have been made to save it. At the same time, a new generation of scholars has started taking German Canadian studies in directions that run counter to the politically motivated antiquarian approach of years past.

One question raised in recent years is the validity of the notion German Canadian distinctiveness. Is there really such a thing as a German Canadian identity? Myka Burke answers in the affirmative, claiming simply that "German Canadians are a distinct entity. They certainly could not be held for German Americans nor could they be held for Italian Canadians. They are German Canadian and they are distinct!"[19] Burke's prima facie acceptance of a hybrid multicultural identity for German Canadians resists probing to any extent the limits of that category's usefulness or reflection of reality. Other scholars have not been so quick to accept the suitability of the German Canadian moniker. *A Chorus of Different Voices,* edited by Angelika Sauer and Mathias Zimmer, the result of a workshop in Edmonton that addressed the notion of German Canadian identity, questions received wisdom. Mathias Zimmer, writing about German Canadian identity as developed by different groups of German immigrants to Canada, argues that German Canadian identity may have existed historically, but that modern industrial society prohibits its existence.[20] Zimmer's skepticism actually extends to the concept of multiculturalism, which he views as having degenerated into bland ideology.[21] More importantly, Zimmer, quoting Roman Onufrijchuk, argues effectively that the politics of multiculturalism produces "an ethnicity that does not develop, an ethnicity trapped in a repetitive loop" by putting "a premium on the preservation of certain stereotypes of ethnicity, thus ossifying a historical or idealized status quo and trapping ethnic groups in ascribed stereotypes which in turn widens the gap between the cultural dynamics 'at home' and abroad."[22] Zimmer is, in effect, rejecting the antiquarian mode of history on the basis of its servitude in the ideology of multiculturalism. Preserving culture only serves to make it lifeless and to restrict connections to the ever-progressing originating culture.

Unlike Burke, whose approach is to wrap German Canadian identity in the protective cloak of multiculturalism, Zimmer, at the opposite end of the spectrum, subverts the notion of German Canadian identity, not in order to reject the study of the German immigration to Canada, but in order to prevent the use of cultural identity "to legitimize an artificial segmentation of society."[23] Frank Trommler, writing from the perspective of German American literary studies, also argues for a new understanding of ethnic studies:

Reevaluating the relationship of literary scholarship and ethnic studies means, at this moment, two things: catching up with the advances in the social sciences without losing sight of the framework of literary criticism; and producing accessible knowledge about texts and artefacts as cultural achievements, educational tools, and popular possessions which function as catalysts—not just reflections—of ethnic identities.[24]

In the second part of this quotation, Trommler reiterates the point made by Zimmer: the antiquarian approach to ethnic history will only result in the ossification of that ethnic group's cultural creative productivity. Culture will be preserved, but as an exhibit in a jar of formaldehyde, not as a generator of ethnic identity.

Writing about the academic discipline of German Canadian historical studies, and not German Canadian identity per se, Angelika Sauer laments the selective, "almost normative" approach to German Canadian studies that has resulted in a field that is "closely entangled—too closely perhaps—with politics";[25] as a result, studies of the German Canadian community have downplayed differences and conflicts and ignored "individuals or groups who did not fit a certain mold."[26] What Sauer is calling for is nothing less than the disengagement of German Canadian studies from German Canadian heritage politics. When she points out that "it could be argued that at the center of German Canadian identity today lies the perception of victimization, stigmatization and discrimination" and that "this is the meaning given to the group's history by its members and used by them as an explanation of the group's invisibility in Canadian society,"[27] she underscores the importance for academic scholarship to maintain an agenda independent of the German Canadian desire to place a tile on the Canadian cultural mosaic. To put it more simply: German Canadian studies must remain separate and disconnected from German Canadian cultural politics, or the discipline will suffer as a result.

In a related development in the United States, a volume of essays entitled *German? American? Literature?* questions the received wisdom that a unified German American tradition ever existed.[28] The title of that collection alone speaks volumes, questioning as it does every basic notion of the discipline it is investigating, although many of the essays themselves fall into the familiar habit of describing unknown German American connections or lamenting German American literature's lack of profile in the American literary market. Frank Trommler and Sander Gilman's essays are notable exceptions in this regard. Trommler's reformulation of ethnic studies was mentioned above; Gilman's chapter attempts to explain the fascination of early scholars of German American literature for the antiquarian approach. He sees it as a natural result faced by many ethnic literary traditions as they "decline into *Heimatliteratur* and parochialism."[29] He continues: "the more antiquarian the exponents of German American writing became, the less scholarship on the wider level took note or interest in them."[30] Gilman pulls no punches when he criticizes the German American studies, and sees only a small glimmer of sunlight in studies that provided feminist or progressive readings of traditional German American themes, or explored the notion of exile and the German Jewish diaspora.

Gilman's disjointed polemic raises indirectly an issue that deserves far more direct analysis. Many nations hosted German exiles during the Third Reich. Among these refugees were more than two thousand writers, and many of the best known ended up in the United States: Bertolt Brecht, Hermann Broch, Lion Feuchtwanger, Franz Werfel, and more Manns than you could shake a stick at. This was a concentrated immigration of intellectual and artistic talent on a scale like no other in American history. Despite this fact, German American studies has yet to embrace the study of these exiled writers. The *Yearbook of German-American Studies* is a reliable barometer of this disciplinary divide: while the yearbook has numerous articles on German immigrants and their influence in nineteenth-century America, and articles on the treatment of German Americans in the twentieth century, few if any articles discuss exile writing. German American studies and exile studies are, to borrow a Canadian expression, two solitudes, two completely independent spheres of inquiry. German American studies seem unable to define the exiled writers as German Americans, even though, as Wolfgang Hochbruck points out, Thomas Mann lived in the United States longer than two authors (Otto Ruppius and Friedrich Gerstäcker) whose German Americanness is rarely questioned.[31] The inability of the discipline to examine one of the most important examples of German American interaction contributes to the marginalization of German American literary studies within the academy. At the same time, exile literature studies have tended to focus on the authors' relationship to, criticism of, and yearning for the country from which they were exiled, and not the countries where they found safe harbour.

Research Agendas Future

Reviewing some key moments in the development of immigrant German literary studies, we see criticism in recent years of the entwining of scholarship and politics in addition to skepticism with regard to how well multicultural ideology serves to maintain and strengthen national minority ethnic groups. The example from the United States shows that the discipline under discussion lacks an ability to study a major aspect of its own field. In the Canadian example, the participation of German Canadian studies in larger German Canadian cultural-political initiatives has come under attack. The stability, if not the validity, of German Canadian and German American identity has been problematized and questioned. How should German Canadian and German American literary studies adapt to this changed climate? What kind of research agenda will enable the studies of any expatriate German or hyphenated German literature to weather this storm? Does the notion of identity serve us well anymore? Should we really be trying to "identify" German Canadianness, German Americanness, German "Xness," or should we be more interested in the interactions of the two sides of the equation?

For a fresh perspective on the discussion of future research agendas, one can point to the two "Refractions" conferences held in Banff and Düsseldorf in 2002 and 2003.[32] The first conference dealt with "Refractions of Germany in Canadian Literature and Culture," whereas the second was a mirror image of the first entitled "Refractions of Canada in European Literature and Culture." These conferences attracted European and Canadian scholars of German literature, English literature, history, and other disciplines who reflected on the notions of interaction and interchange between Canadian and German culture on a variety of disciplinary and theoretical levels. A feature of the conference was the situating of cultural artefacts within discursive spaces that enabled interdisciplinary inquiry unfettered by normative disciplinary practices. The conferences pointed the way to obviating the need for disciplinary borders. In order to avoid the political pitfalls described earlier in this essay it is necessary to develop a discipline that remains porous and fluid enough to take in the breadth of thought seen in the Refractions conferences. In the specific Canadian context, for example, this would entail replacing the debates regarding whether English-language texts by authors of greater or lesser German heritage should be considered part of the "German Canadian" tradition with studies that examine the aesthetic, social, or numerous other contexts of the work. Such an approach, if pushed to its logical extreme, would see the dissolution of a discipline named "German-Canadian literary studies," but that loss would be compensated by the improved intellectual rigour and vigour of the literary studies undertaken.

To lay the groundwork of this new agenda, we need to return to our discipline as a whole after our lengthy journey through the territory of German Canadian and German American studies. Perhaps our first order of business should be to name the discipline. What name can be given to the study of German-language literature produced outside of Germany, Austria, and Switzerland? What about second- and third-generation expatriate Germans who write in the language of their new country? Or writers of no discernible German heritage who write about topics connected to the German-speaking world? The Diaspora conference organizers wrestled with this categorization problem when naming the conference and settled on "Diaspora Experiences: German-Speaking Immigrants and their Experiences." But to extend that concept by naming this subdiscipline "German Diaspora literary studies" is an unsatisfactory solution. There is of course the sensitive issue of Germans or German speakers using a term so closely associated with the victims of the German Nazi government, for in the narrowest of definitions this word refers exclusively to the Jews living among Gentiles after the Captivity, and the history of central Europe in the nineteenth and twentieth centuries has shown us how precarious an existence that was for Jews, although more recently the notion of diaspora has been applied to other contexts (e.g., the African American diaspora). In either case, there is an implication that this emigration was forced upon the immigrants, and that those immigrants have a desire to return to and resettle the land from which they or their ancestors came. Do those conditions apply to German emigration? In some instances, yes, for example the exile occasioned by the creation of the Third Reich in 1933, but not in all instances. This is the main problem with using the term "diaspora": it imposes a thematic straitjacket on the literature that may well not describe the content of that literature. Diaspora reinforces the idea of a dominating culture; perhaps we must start thinking of interweaving cultures.

Other terms, though more neutral than diaspora, are also less eloquent. "German-speaking immigrant" literature is as clumsy a term as expatriate or heritage German literary studies. They do not cover the range of literature that should be included in this agenda, and the terms themselves are also less impartial than one might think. To speak of "heritage" literature, for example, implies a literature of special importance to those who share the same cultural origins while at the same time presupposing that outsiders to that cultural group will not have any interest in that literature. Referring to "expatriate literature" implies a closer connection to the "home land" than might really be the case for second- or third-generation immigrants. And "immigrant literature" is tricky, too, since it can unintentionally encourage scholars to concentrate only on the texts' connections to and participation in the immigrant experience, thereby resulting in a focus that is blind to other interpretive strategies.

We should perhaps speak of intercultural or transcultural German literary studies. As Christiane Harzig points out in Chapter 12, interculturalism implies borders (even though they may well be borders in name only), and transculturalism focuses on processes and developments—change as opposed to ossification. It is this latter solution that leaves open the most possibilities. Its limits are fewer, and that would prevent us from being confined by any disciplinary boundaries. In Chapter 7 Grit Liebscher and Jennifer Dailey-O'Cain call attention to the fact that social categories of German Canadians and their language are constructed in the interaction itself between German and Canadian, and it is the movement, and the resulting instability of the interaction, that we must also focus on in literary studies. Or, as Janet Fuller states in Chapter 2, German identity is no one thing; in the so-called diaspora, hybridity—and the ebb and flow of this hybridity—is key. Retaining these hybrid terms (such as "German-Canadian literary studies") works if the hybrid is viewed not as a stable identity, but rather as an identification that is in flux. Scholars are beginning to recognize this fluidity. Wolfgang Hochbruck takes an icon of German American studies, Friedrich Gerstäcker, and rereads him from within the theoretical discourse of transnational (as opposed to hyphenated) literature: "Gerstäcker was a German-American writer in more senses than one: immigrant, re-migrant, cosmopolitan as well as a German national, trans-nationally read as well as respected, his cultural practice preceded the current theoretical mode by a century and a half."[33] But even authors whose biographies do not immediately lend themselves as easily as Gerstäcker's to this borderless and hyphenless investigative framework could benefit from such an approach.

The dissolution of borders is but the first cornerstone in establishing a research agenda that is quite broad and open to texts that participate in a variety of genres and traditions. To make this possible, however, we will need to lay a second cornerstone: in order to realize a new strategy for this now nameless discipline, we will have to remove the discipline as much as possible from the cultural politics of the ethnic groups it is studying. A future agenda for our discipline must be one that eschews cultural and multicultural politics in favour of a broader approach grounded in current practices governing the disciplinary study of literature. Instead of ghettoizing the study of minority German literatures in the kinds of antiquarian projects described earlier in this presentation, it should be the objective of scholars to embed these literatures into the disciplinary discourses that dominate the study of literature in general by using the same standards of practice, methodology, and theory that govern the study of standard literatures. In the case of *Germanistik* writ large, there is certainly enough ideological and theoretical space available to entertain a variety of approaches.

In practical terms there are a number of investigative avenues that our discipline could explore. These analytical frameworks could give the discipline methodological forms that would facilitate the analysis of a variety of themes and topics. One approach would be to consider the texts we study within the framework of cultural imaginaries. The "imaginary" is a term most often linked to Jacques Lacan and his study of the childhood subject in psychoanalysis. Leaning on Lacan, Graham Dawson defines the "cultural imaginary" as "those vast networks of interlinking discursive themes, images, motifs and narrative forms that are publicly available within a culture at any one time, and articulate its psychic and social dimensions."[34] Whereas in the past literary studies have often been content to discuss the "image" of something (e.g., the image of Canada in German literature), an approach that adopts an analysis of the cultural imaginary attempts to arrive at a farther reaching, more complex understanding of the interrelationships among art, culture, and society that plays out in literary texts. Although not a method as such, the study of the cultural imaginary in texts associated with German-language culture outside of German-speaking Europe has the potential of elucidating aspects of the complex nature of the hybrid German culture. In the Refractions conferences, for example, studies of Henry Kreissel, Mavis Gallant, and Jane Urquhart, among others, were able to coexist peacefully because the overriding interest in understanding the interaction of German and Canadian culture erased the borders that are put up when one tries to categorize texts on the basis of a German Canadian taxonomy. Doris Wolf has engaged in this kind of interpretation with Canadian authors such as Suzette Mayr, and her contribution in Chapter 36 continues this process.

A related concept useful to our discipline, and one that has already gained a small foothold, is the idea of cultural mediation. Often used to describe the effects of translation on mediating the transfer of a text from one culture to another, mediation has expanded in scope to mean the "cultural contact zones" that can exist when individual artists move between different national or social cultures.[35] In our disciplinary context this interpretive framework has been used successfully to analyse the nature of Felix Paul Greve/Frederick Philip Grove's mediating role between German and Canadian literary and national cultures.[36] The above-mentioned study of Gerstäcker by Hochbruck would also fit into this category, as would even some newer work in exile studies that explores the interaction between exiles and Americans or Britons.[37]

Greater use of comparative analysis could also be made. Hugo Hamilton stated in his reading from *The Speckled People* and lecture at the Diaspora conference that the kind of memoir he writes does not exist in Germany. Is that true? Can Hamilton not be read comparatively with works such as *Die Geschichte Meines Bruders* by Uwe Timm? Or with the memoirs that Doris Wolf mentions in her chapter in this book?

The interdisciplinarity that has informed so many of the chapters in this book must be incorporated into these literary studies as well. Does the work on German immigrants—the loss or change of their language as

examined therein by Monika Schmid or Grit Liebscher and Jennifer Dailey-O'Cain, the silences attending their construction of the past as discussed by Alexander Freund—offer literary historians new opportunities
to re-examine texts from new perspectives? The social scientists have also
taught us that it is the process of interaction of German and host cultures
that has occasioned change. Should we not be rereading Walter Bauer,
Grove/Greve, Else Seel, and others with an eye to finding connections
between the data collected by social scientists and the literature produced
by the same culture?

A focus on reception analysis might make us more aware of the role
of German literature outside of central Europe. When Anne Löchte presented the paper that is included in Chapter 10, Hartmut Froeschle
inquired about the creative literature published in the *Berliner Journal*,
and Löchte pointed out that only the dialect letters of Joe Klotzkopf were
of any importance in this regard; otherwise the paper's *Belletristik* was limited to serialized popular novels from Germany. But is that not of interest to us? What would we find out about the role of literature in identity
formation if we examined these serializations: how they came to be in the
paper, if they were popular among the readership, if they had any influence on the discourses of the day?

These various strategies, along with others not named here, would
surely assist our discipline in becoming more aware of the sociocultural
context in which the literature it studies is produced and received. The
integrating, comparative aspects of these strategies would also push our
discipline into greater contact with other ethnic literary studies and with
the growing field of minority literature study in Germany. More can be done
to integrate the work of others in related fields such as immigration history or sociolinguistics into the study of literature if enough care is taken
to address the specific issues surrounding interdisciplinary inquiry. A great
deal can also be undertaken to reclaim older texts for a new audience of
scholars, to speak to the decline of German-language literature outside of
central Europe by examining the social milieu of that literature and the
interaction of German-language or heritage authors with new language
cultures.

It should come as no surprise that, if there is an underlying theme or
a subtext to this volume of essays, it is the question of identity. Do these
people living outside of Germany, yet with some sort of connection or
attachment to Germany, construct their own identity? Is it formed for
them? What impact do mother tongues, host languages, family history,
government policies, economic conditions, and who knows what else have
on the formation of this identity? The agenda of literary studies should
and must be to show how texts—be they fictional or not or a mixture

thereof—speak to, undermine, or problematize the issues of identity formation. There is quite simply no shortage of work to be done in this nameless discipline. Not labelling the discipline actually works to our advantage: since these labels can act as disciplinary blinders, eschewing them will enable us to see the innovative avenues of interpretation that are waiting to be explored. Just as hyphenated German authors mediate multiple cultural imaginaries, so, too, must the discipline that studies them.

Notes

1 Klein, *Literaturgeschichte des Deutschtums im Ausland* (1939), vii.
2 Klein, *Literaturgeschichte des Deutschtums im Ausland* (1939), 444.
3 Klein, *Literaturgeschichte des Deutschtums im Ausland* (1979).
4 Sauer, "'Ideal German Canadian,'" 229.
5 See Cardinal, "Preliminary Check List, Part 1," "Preliminary Check List, Part 2"; Cardinal and Malycky, "German-Canadian Creative Literature"; Windthorst, "German-Canadian Creative Literature."
6 Kloss, *Ahornblätter.*
7 Froeschle, "Literaturkritik," 10.
8 Froeschle, "Einleitung," ix.
9 Some view this contribution as the cynical self-interest of a group of academics who needed to maintain German-language learning in order to keep their jobs. See Sauer, "'Ideal German Canadian,'" 232.
10 Riedel, "Introduction," 4.
11 This was thought to be an uphill battle since some believed that Canadian literary history, dominated by a centralized hierarchical Anglo-Saxon tradition, could make no room for a German Canadian literary tradition. For a fuller explanation of this theory see Gürttler, "Introduction," iii.
12 Nietzsche, "Vom Nutzen und Nachtheil," 264.
13 Froeschle, "Literaturkritik," 12.
14 Boeschenstein, "Is There a Canadian Image," 15. Boeschenstein writes on the previous page that "the season for shooting down some of these reputations is open."
15 Boeschenstein, "Is There a Canadian Image," 16.
16 Froeschle, "Literaturkritik," 8.
17 Kloss, *Ahornblätter,* 38.
18 German-language German Canadian literature was the preference, however, since only it could help preserve German language and culture in largely non-German environments. See Ritter, "Literaturwissenschaft," 217.
19 Burke, "Canadian Content, Anyone?," 45.
20 Zimmer, "Deconstructing," 21.
21 Zimmer, "Deconstructing," 31.
22 Zimmer, "Deconstructing," 32.
23 Zimmer, "Deconstructing," 33.
24 Trommler, "Literary Scholarship," 39–40.
25 Sauer, " 'Ideal German Canadian,'" 228.
26 Sauer, " 'Ideal German Canadian,'" 232.
27 Sauer, "'Ideal German Canadian,'" 236.
28 Sollors, "German American Tradition," 5.
29 Gilman, "German? American? Literature?," 8.
30 Gilman, "German? American? Literature?," 10.

31 Hochbruck, "'Re-cognition,'" 270.
32 The proceedings of both conferences have been published. See Antor et al., *Refractions of Canada;* Antor et al., *Refractions of Germany.*
33 Hochbruck, "'Re-cognition,'" 278.
34 Dawson, *Soldier Heroes,* 48.
35 Hjartarson and Kulba, "'Borne Across the World,'" xix.
36 See Martens, *Pioneering North America*; Hjartarson and Kulba, *Politics of Cultural Mediation.*
37 For preliminary efforts in this regard see Brunnhuber, *Faces of Janus;* de Jonge, "Gebrochene Welt"; Riesthuis, "Blacks and Exiles."

Works Cited

Antor, Heinz, Gordon Bölling, Annette Kern-Stähler, and Klaus Stierstorfer, eds. *Refractions of Canada in European Literature and Culture.* Berlin: de Gruyter, 2005.

Antor, Heinz, Sylvia Brown, John Considine, and Klaus Stierstorfer, eds. *Refractions of Germany in Canadian Literature and Culture.* Berlin: de Gruyter, 2003.

Boeschenstein, Hermann. "Is There a Canadian Image in German Literature?" *Seminar* 3, no. 1 (1967): 1–20.

Brunnhuber, Nicole. *The Faces of Janus: English-Language Fiction by German-Speaking Exiles in Great Britain, 1933–45.* Oxford: Peter Lang, 2005.

Burke, Myka. "Canadian Content, Anyone? German-Canadian Cultural and Literary Identity." *German-Canadian Yearbook* 17 (2002): 37–45.

Cardinal, Clive H. "A Preliminary Check List of Studies on German-Canadian Creative Literature, Part 1: General Studies." *Canadian Ethnic Studies* 1 (1969): 38–62.

———. "A Preliminary Check List of Studies on German-Canadian Creative Literature, Part 2: Specific Studies." *Canadian Ethnic Studies* 2 (1970): 63–69.

Cardinal, Clive H., and Alexander Malycky. "German-Canadian Creative Literature: a Preliminary Check List of Authors and Pseudonyms." *Canadian Ethnic Studies* 1 (1969): 31–37.

Dawson, Graham. *Soldier Heroes: British Adventure, Empire, and the Imagining of Masculinities.* London: Routledge, 1994.

de Jonge, Carina. "Gebrochene Welt, Gebrochenes Deutsch? Der Einfluss der Sprache des Gastlandes auf das Deutsch von Exilschriftstellern Anhand des Beispiels Konrad Merz." *Neophilologus* 88, no. 1 (2004): 81–101.

Fluck, Winfried, and Werner Sollors, eds. *German? American? Literature? New Directions in German-American Studies.* New York: Peter Lang, 2002.

Froeschle, Hartmut. "Einleitung." In *Nachrichten aus Ontario. Deutschsprachige Literatur in Kanada,* edited by Hartmut Froeschle, vii–xiv. Hildesheim: Olms, 1981.

———. "Literaturkritik. Die Deutschkanadische Literatur: Umfang und Problemdarstellungen." In *Nachrichten aus Ontario. Deutschsprachige Literatur in Kanada,* edited by Hartmut Froeschle, 1–12. Hildesheim: Olms, 1981.

Gilman, Sander L. "German? American? Literature? Some Thoughts on the Problem of Question Marks and Hyphens." In *German? American? Literature? New*

Directions in German-American Studies, edited by Winfried Fluck and Werner Sollors, 7–23. New York: Peter Lang, 2002.

Gürttler, Karin. "Introduction." In *Annalen 6: Interrelations and Interactions. Sixth Symposium German-Canadian Studies*, edited by Karin Gürttler and Edward Mornin, i–vi. N.p., 1988.

Hamilton, Hugo. *The Speckled People*. London: Fourth Estate, 2003.

Hjartarson, Paul, and Tracy Kulba. "'Borne Across the World': Else Plötz (Baroness Elsa Von Freytag-Loringhoven), Felix Paul Greve (Frederick Philip Grove), and the Politics of Cultural Mediation." In *The Politics of Cultural Mediation: Baroness Elsa von Freytag-Loringhoven and Felix Paul Greve*, edited by Paul Hjartarson and Tracy Kulba, xix–xxxv. Edmonton: University of Alberta Press, 2003.

———, eds. *The Politics of Cultural Mediation: Baroness Elsa von Freytag-Loringhoven and Felix Paul Greve*. Edmonton: University of Alberta Press, 2003.

Hochbruck, Wolfgang. "'Re-cognition' of the Borders of German-American Authorship: The Case of Friedrich Gerstäcker." *Comparative American Studies* 4, no. 3 (2006): 269–84.

Klein, Karl Kurt. *Literaturgeschichte des Deutschtums im Ausland. Schriftum und Geistesleben der deutschen Volksgruppen im Ausland vom Mittelalter bis zur Gegenwart*. Leipzig: Bibliographisches Institut, 1939.

———. *Literaturgeschichte des Deutschtums im Ausland. Neu herausgeben mit einer Bibliographie (1945–1978) von Alexander Ritter*. Hildesheim: Olms, 1979.

Kloss, Heinz, ed. *Ahornblätter: Anthologie deutschkanadischer Dichtung*. Würzburg: Holzner Verlag, 1961.

Martens, Klaus, ed. *Pioneering North America: Mediators of European Culture and Literature*. Würzburg: Königshausen and Neumann, 2000.

Nietzsche, Friedrich. "Vom Nutzen und Nachtheil der Historie für das Leben." In *Werke. Kritische Gesamtausgabe*, edited by Giorgio Colli and Mazzino Montinari. Section 3, Vol. 1, *Die Geburt der Tragödie. Unzeitgemäße Zeitbetrachtungen I–III (1872–1874)*, 239–330. Berlin: de Gruyter, 1972.

Riedel, Walter E. "Introduction: Canada's Cultural Mosaic and the Literature of the German-Speaking Canadians." In *The Old World and the New: Literary Perspectives of German-Speaking Canadians*, edited by Walter E. Riedel, 3–13. Toronto: University of Toronto Press, 1984.

Riesthuis, Joachim Gerhard Ludovicus Anton. "Blacks and Exiles: African American and German Exiled Authors." PhD diss., University of Chicago, 2004.

Ritter, Alexander. "Literaturwissenschaft und deutschsprachige Literatur des Auslands: Eine Tour d'Horizon zum Forschungsstand." *German-Canadian Yearbook* 4 (1978): 215–24.

Sauer, Angelika. "The 'Ideal German Canadian': Politics, Academics, and the Historiographical Construction of German-Canadian Identity." In *A Chorus of Different Voices: German-Canadian Identities*, edited by Angelika E. Sauer and Matthias Zimmer, 227–38. New York: Peter Lang, 1998.

Sollors, Werner. "The German American Tradition Reconsidered." In *German? American? Literature? New Directions in German-American Studies*, edited by Winfried Fluck and Werner Sollors, 3–5. New York: Peter Lang, 2002.

Trommler, Frank. "Literary Scholarship and Ethnic Studies: A Reevaluation." In *German? American? Literature? New Directions in German-American Studies,* edited by Winfried Fluck and Werner Sollors, 25–40. New Directions in German-American Studies 2. New York: Peter Lang, 2002.

Windthorst, Rolf E. "German-Canadian Creative Literature: A Preliminary Check List of Imprints." *Canadian Ethnic Studies* 2 (1970): 55–62.

Zimmer, Matthias. "Deconstructing German-Canadian Identity." In *A Chorus of Different Voices: German-Canadian Identities,* edited by Angelika E. Sauer and Matthias Zimmer, 21–39. New York: Peter Lang, 1998.

FIFTEEN

Some Facts and Figures on German-speaking Exiles in Ireland, 1933–1945

Gisela Holfter

This chapter presents a brief introduction to Ireland in the early 1930s, Irish policy toward refugees, and the question of anti-Semitism in Ireland. Research into German-speaking refugees in Ireland has started only recently. For the first time some indications on who came, and on when and where, are presented. This is followed up with four case studies to illustrate the different fates of the refugees: Elsa Höfler, who committed suicide in Limerick; George Clare, author of *Last Waltz in Vienna*; Nobel Prize winner for physics Erwin Schrödinger; and John Hennig, the foremost researcher in Irish German studies.

Introduction

IRELAND HAS NOT SO FAR BEEN A SUBJECT of international exile studies.[1] In Ireland there has been a far stronger focus on emigration and recording the Irish experience. But with its economic success since the mid 1990s Ireland has increasingly become a country of immigration. And there is—at least in the media—interest in the question whether Ireland let anyone in at all in the 1930s, and, if so, how many. Estimates vary considerably but tend to be on the low side,[2] at times even giving the impression that there were no refugees allowed in at all, as in the following *Irish Times* extract from 2006:

> Shame, too, for those countries which failed to respond to the pleas of German and Austrian Jews—most of them children—seeking refuge from persecution. Without making great play of it, the author duly

chronicles the fact that Ireland's door was firmly shut in their faces. It's one of the most shameful chapters in our history.[3]

After a glance at Irish policy toward refugees and the question of anti-Semitism in Ireland, this chapter presents some preliminary findings about who came to Ireland and when. This is followed up with a number of case studies to illustrate a spectrum of experiences of the refugees: Elsa Höfler, a Jewish woman from Vienna who committed suicide in Limerick; Georg Klaar (George Clare), author of the well-known *Last Waltz in Vienna;* Erwin Schrödinger, being in a very privileged position as Nobel Prize winner, director of the newly founded Dublin Institute of Advanced Studies, and a friend of Irish Taoiseach Eamon de Valera; and John Hennig, who became the "father of Irish-German studies."

Ireland at the Time

Ireland saw its first change of government in 1932 after the hard-won peace following the civil war in 1922–23. In 1937, a constitution was adopted, allowing for a special position for the Catholic church but recognizing the other religions, explicitly among them the Jewish congregation. The economic situation in the 1930s was dire. In 1936 alone, 22,000 people left to seek employment abroad, mainly in Britain,[4] and in 1937 emigration numbers reached 26,000[5]—this in a population of under 3 million. In this context the Irish position of not being able to accommodate any refugees at the international refugee conference in Evian-les-Bains in 1938 does not sound quite as hollow as it would from today's perspective and the knowledge of the Holocaust. On 1 September 1939, a state of emergency was declared and a day later de Valera announced that Ireland would remain neutral. The time of the Second World War continues to be called the "Emergency" in Ireland.

The main legislation implemented to deal with the "refugee problem" was the Aliens Act of 1935, which stated that all aliens needed permission to land. Overall, Dermot Keogh's statement in his study on *Jews in Twentieth-Century Ireland* applies: "Ireland did not prove to be a safe haven of hope for many fleeing persecution on the continent." [6] And there was certainly evidence of official anti-Semitism from 1933 onward as the correspondence between Leo McAuley at the Irish Legation in Berlin and J.V. Fahy, the secretary of the Department of External Affairs, in April 1933 shows: "As far as possible the Legation has discouraged such persons from going to Ireland, as they are really only refugees."[7] McAuley received the following as an answer from the Dublin headquarters:

I am directed by the Minister to inform you that he approves of the action which you are taking as regards Jewish refugees desiring to come from Germany to the Irish Free State. As far as possible such persons should be discouraged from coming here.

One can therefore from early on find proof for Bryan Fanning's assessment:

> Anti-Jewish discrimination which resulted in the rejection of visa applications emerged at a political level, in the voluntary sector apparatus of refugee aid, in the actions of at least one importantly placed official as well as in the administrative criteria.[8]

An Irish Military Intelligence file in the National Archives of Ireland in Dublin provides excellent documentation on the refugees who did obtain approval. Dated February 1943, it contains all Germans, Austrians, and Czechs (344 in all) registered in Ireland at the time. They were sorted in the following categories:

A = Conforming to the Nazi regime, taking part in German Colony's activities or believed to be pro-Nazi.

A1 = As above, but particularly prominent.

B = Refugees. This term is reserved for aliens who have come here as the result of loss of employment or in a more or less destitute condition, or under the auspices of philanthropic persons or institutions, and is not applied to those who simply transferred themselves to this country owing to the more favourable conditions obtaining here, without undergoing special hardship other than of removal, and who have usually come to take up employment already prepared for them. This distinction is difficult to draw and may leave room for disagreement in a few borderline cases, but it has been attempted as it seems of practical value in determining the probable attitude of those concerned in various situations which may arise.

C = Jews or of Jewish descent. Both are placed in the same category, as the distinction would in many cases be very difficult, and because the presence of both in this country is due to the same cause. Categories B and C coincide to a great extent.

D = Aliens who have given no indication of active political sympathies and who do not to our knowledge fall under B and C.

E = Anti-Nazi, other than B and C (mainly Czechs).

F = Not in A or A1, but regarded with distrust owing to special circumstances or undesirable character.[9]

These categories are clearly an attempt to come to terms with a—from the Irish perspective—bewildering assortment of German-speaking aliens within their territory. There were ambiguities regarding this classification. To mention just a few limitations: First, not everyone in category A conformed to the Nazi regime. There was at least one case where this was definitely not so. But for present purposes, the ninety-nine people in category A are not included in this discussion, as the vast majority would not count as refugees and many had come to Ireland before 1933. On the other hand, all twenty D's—who showed no indication of political sympathies—are included, as some of them are known to have been refugees. Most, however, were part of a religious order. Additionally, a number of people listed under B or C had already migrated to Ireland in the 1920s and therefore are not considered in this analysis. This gives the resulting figure of 193 people. Moreover, probably the most important limitation of this analysis is that not all refugees are listed here, so the numbers assessed are significantly lower than the actual number.

Who is not on the list? First of all, anyone who had come to Ireland as a refugee since 1933 but left—most often for Great Britain—before the time the list was created in 1943. It is not yet known how many people are in this group.[10] Also, most children are missing, as is anyone who arrived in Ireland but did not register.

The Military Intelligence list gives the following information: category, name, address, present occupation, and date of arrival. It is sorted geographically, by the different Irish counties. The overwhelming majority of the refugees, nearly two thirds, stayed in or around Dublin. The number of exiles in all the other counties—even if taken all together—does not even total half of the number staying around Dublin. In some ways, a clear preference for Dublin was to be expected as Ireland is very centralized and most opportunities for work and all support organizations were to be found there. In addition, Dublin (or, more accurately, Dún Laoghaire) was often the port of entry.

The chronological pattern of arrivals also gives a very clear predominance. Far more than half of all refugees looked at here arrived in 1939 (see Figure 1). Two things are striking. First, there seems to have been no immigration of anyone who was classified by the Military Intelligence other than category A in 1933, and second, the majority of immigrants arrived just before the war. Taken together, in 1938 and 1939 of the 193 people in this analysis, 160 arrived (83 percent), and of these, 155 arrived between June 1938 and October 1939. However, the relatively large numbers of refugees for 1939 decreased dramatically at the end of that year, a reflection of the change in circumstances following the outbreak of war and the consequent decrease in travel opportunities. If one looks at emigrants leaving Germany in 1938 and 1939 it was only 42 percent of total emigration between 1933 and 1945, which is estimated around 278,500.[11] This is only part of the picture as emigration from Austria started to soar in spring 1938 after the Anschluss. However, in that period, more people

FIGURE 1   Chronology of German Immigration in Ireland, 1934-1942

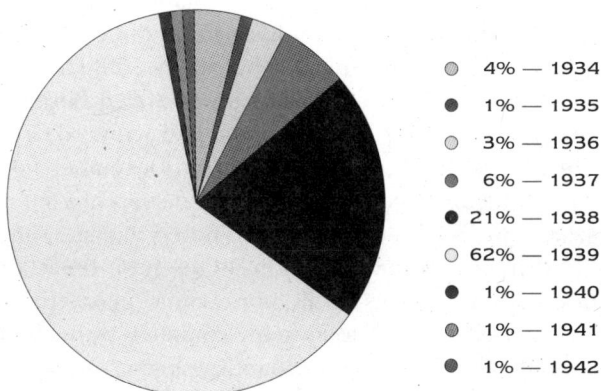

- 4% — 1934
- 1% — 1935
- 3% — 1936
- 6% — 1937
- 21% — 1938
- 62% — 1939
- 1% — 1940
- 1% — 1941
- 1% — 1942

left Germany in 1933 and in 1939, seemingly without having major impact on Ireland. The comparatively high number of immigrants in this analysis who arrived in 1937 (thirteen) again contrasts with the overall number of German emigrants, as it was one of the years with lower emigration.

Experiences of Individuals

So who came? The numbers presented cannot give any real information on the actual situation of the emigrants. In order to gain insights we need to look at individuals. In the following discussion, four migration biographies reflect the above-mentioned trends to some extent: two immigrants arrived in 1939 and stayed in Dublin like the vast majority; two came in 1938, one to Galway, one to Limerick, and neither is on the list on which the above analysis was based, because one had become a British soldier and the other one was dead by the time the list was drawn up.

Elsa Höfler

Not much is known about Elsa Höfler, despite the fact that her suicide in Limerick in October 1938 received a lot of public attention. Because of this, she has captured the imagination of a number of people from Limerick. Several newspaper articles have been written about her,[12] and her fate inspired the character Elsa in Mike Finn's play *Pigtown*.[13] In 1971, Frank McCourt wrote about her in his essay "On the Trail of a Jewish Princess," about a woman who arrived in Ireland as a refugee before the war and committed suicide.[14] However, the narrator encounters so many different versions of her origin and fate that he seems to feel justified in the end in clinging to the myth, rather than the facts, of a Jewish princess from either Germany, Russia, Rumania, or Poland—who in all probability never existed in the first place. But Elsa Höfler did exist. She was born on 27 April 1881 as Elsa Reininger in Neubistritz (Nová Bystřice), Bohemia, and lived in Vienna for most of her life. She married Berisch Höfler— born on 3 August 1874, a Polish national who had acquired Greek nationality—and they had a daughter, Margaret. From December 1935 to early September 1938 she was registered in the first district in Vienna with the address Salzgries 14/8A; however, it is also noted that she signed out in August 1938 with an unknown location.[15] One month earlier she had filled out the compulsory forms for all "non-Aryans" in Austria who owned more than 5,000 Reichmarks (today approximately 75,000 euros). This included not only savings, shares, outstanding loans, property, and valuables but also income and pension expectations. It seems that both Elsa and her husband were fairly well off. Elsa also listed 223 Reichmarks' worth of foreign currency.[16]

The Höflers' link to Limerick seems to have been their daughter, Margaret, who was married to Gaskel Kaitcher and is said to have played violin at the Limerick cinema. Elsa arrived in September 1938 and rented a room for nearly four weeks at 18 Newenham Street, Limerick, following her husband, who had arrived a few weeks earlier. At the inquest after Elsa's death, her husband stated that she had been ill for nine years and was very depressed about the situation with Hitler. Her daughter mentioned that she was suffering from "nerve trouble"[17] and was unable to sleep, and also that she had seen a revolver in her mother's possession some ten years earlier when Elsa had suffered a breakdown and spent a year in hospital. Elsa Höfler's passport (in the name of Elsa Reininger) was issued by the Czechoslovakian consul in Vienna and bore an endorsement of the British immigration officer, dated 22 October, giving her permission to land in Newhaven in England. It stipulated that she was not to remain longer than forty-eight hours in the United Kingdom.[18] She committed suicide on 27 October in the Crescent Hotel in Limerick, having spent her last hours writing letters.[19] Elsa Höfler is buried in an unmarked grave in the Jewish cemetery in Kilmurry, close to the University of Limerick. It is not known what happened to her daughter, son-in-law, or husband and there is no photograph of her.

George Clare

George Clare spent three years in Ireland, from 1938 to 1941. His experiences are arguably the best known of all the refugees to Ireland, thanks to his memoir *Last Waltz in Vienna* (originally *Das waren die Klaars*), praised by Graham Greene, John le Carré, Arthur Koestler, and Lord Longford, among others. He is also often referred to by historians, as his family's experiences with the Irish envoy in Berlin, Charles Bewley, clearly showed the official's reluctance to help Jewish refugees. In Clare's case it seems to have been only with the help of the German secretary of the legation, with whom his mother had established friendly relations, that the family was issued visas the day after Kristallnacht.[20] George Clare, born on 20 December 1920 in Vienna as Georg Klaar, was the only son of Ernestine (called Stella) and Ernst Klaar, a successful banker, who contributed financially to the ribbon factory that was one of the successful businesses set up · by Jewish refugees in Ireland at the time.

Clare arrived in Ireland with his mother on 12 November 1938 and went to Galway in connection with the ribbon factory there. On 27 March 1939, Stella and George left Galway for London and were reunited with Ernst.[21] The father had decided to take up a position with his bank in Paris rather than make use of his visa to Ireland, but George stayed behind. This later turned out to be a terrible miscalculation—both George's mother and father eventually perished in a concentration camp. After three years George could not bear to be in Ireland any longer. He saw no future for himself and wrote to his parents that they did not understand the limitations of living in a small town. On 24 March 1941, he left to join a non-combatant unit in Northern Ireland. A month later, on 29 April 1941, he left for England and joined the Royal Air Force. After the war he was stationed in Germany. He then had a career in journalism and publishing and became head of the Axel Springer publishing house in London, where he still lives today.

Erwin Schrödinger

Erwin Schrödinger, born in 1887 in Vienna, had none of the usual difficulties other exiles experienced. Being recognized as one of the leading physicists of his time and having received the Nobel Prize for physics in 1933 certainly helped him, as did Eamon de Valera's intention of setting up an international research institute of high calibre following the example of the Institute of Advanced Studies in Princeton. To turn it into a success one needed internationally acclaimed academics who would have a strong interest to come to Ireland. Erwin Schrödinger fitted that bill beautifully, given his international standing on one hand and, on the other, his situation in Austria after the Anschluss, having resigned his prestigious chair in Berlin in 1933 in disgust with the new regime. His decision to return from Oxford to Graz in 1936 meant therefore that in 1938 he was in a precarious situation. De Valera accordingly made sure that Schrödinger and the people close to him were issued visas to enter

Ireland after a hiatus in Belgium. Schrödinger arrived in Dublin in October 1939 and became a senior professor in the newly established Dublin Institute of Advanced Studies in October 1940. In November he was made director of the institute. Schrödinger certainly fulfilled all hopes that de Valera had set in him. He created a highly acclaimed international centre for theoretical physics and attracted other renowned scholars in the field as he gathered a staff of distinguished academics from all over the world around him. From 1942 onward he also organized annual colloquia attended, over the years, by nearly all physicists of distinction. However, as his daughter, Ruth Braunizer, pointed out, at the same time his diaries indicated a growing sense of isolation in Ireland.[22] Already in October 1940 he had written:

> I have now been away from "home" for a little more than two years. There has been a cut through everything. Written accounts had to be left behind. I am even left without the offprints of my papers and of the few published books. Every now and then the situation becomes such as to make me fear to preserve any kind of diary. Are we to turn into ants after all?[23]

His situation, despite being a privileged one, would still have been a far cry from the surroundings—not least in terms of academic support—that he had known in Zürich, Berlin, Oxford, and Graz, and therefore this rather dejected view is understandable. It was offset, in any case, by a growing fondness and strong thankfulness to Ireland. In 1956, a personal chair was established for him in Vienna and he left Dublin. Looking back, Schrödinger viewed his Irish time as "very, very nice … Otherwise I would have never learnt to know and love this beautiful island Ireland. Quite inconceivable that I could have spent those 17 years in Graz instead."[24] He died in Vienna in January 1961 and is buried in the Tyrolean village of Alpbach, coincidentally in the shadow of a church with close links to Irish monks.

John Hennig

Paul Gottfried Johannes Hennig was born in Leipzig, on 3 March 1911 into a family with strong Protestant beliefs. As a young man he attended the famous Thomas School where Bach had been a cantor. He got into Ireland as a twenty-eight-year-old German doctor of philosophy. John Hennig had given up on his academic career as he had made up his mind to marry his Jewish fiancée in 1933, despite knowing that this was not the thing to do in Hitler's Germany. He therefore took up a position in the firm of his father-in-law, a gifted entrepreneur and inventor in Aachen. Hennig converted from Protestantism to Catholicism in 1936. Two years later, with the birth of their second daughter, his wife became Catholic as well.

Hennig's conversion was to have a deciding influence on their lives: he met an Irish Jesuit who considered Hennig's English good enough that he might be considered for a teaching post in Belvedere College, Dublin. His application for a visa, made after a visit to Dublin, was eventually granted after a long wait, during which the family moved to Belgium for safety.

During his first six years in Ireland Hennig taught German at Belvedere College and also part time in Maynooth, and privately as often as possible. After the war he made a living as records officer in the Library and Records Section of Bord na Móna, the Irish Peat Board, and carried out a comprehensive study of world literature on peat production and utilization techniques and the latest advances in machine design. After three years with the peat board he became an archivist for the Electricity Supply Board.

Hennig was an exceptionally prolific author, writing and publishing widely in various areas, particularly theology (liturgical studies), philosophy, history, medieval studies, and the history of the church. His articles appeared in more than thirty journals and magazines plus numerous newspapers. Indeed, he can be regarded as the founding father of Irish German studies. In 1947, he was elected a member of the Royal Irish Academy.

In 1956, Hennig and his family finally decided to leave Ireland and live in Basel, Switzerland. In 1967, Hennig was voted an extraordinary member of the Institute of Liturgical and Monastic Research at the monastery of Maria Laach. He was awarded an honorary doctorate by the Faculty of Philosophy and History of the University of Basel in 1970. But despite all honours, Hennig shared the trauma of many refugees—he describes it at the end of his autobiography: "But that doesn't change the fact that I have lost my roots not only from a social, professional, political, and linguistic point of view, but also in terms of religion."[25] Hennig did not return to Ireland and died in Basel on 11 December 1986.

Conclusion

The privileged, the hindered academic, the young factory worker who became a soldier, and the suicide—four very different fates, but all of them deeply affected by the interruption of their expected lives and by their time in Ireland. If one compares the situation in Ireland with that in other European countries one becomes aware how relatively few refugees were let in. Only a few hundred entered Ireland, in comparison with 60,000 to 80,000 who arrived in the United Kingdom. Other small countries such as Portugal took in far more refugees and provided at least temporary refuge or the passage way, for example, for Heinrich Mann, Lion Feuchtwanger, Stefan Zweig, Alfred Döblin, Franz Werfel, Erich

Ollenhauer, Otto von Habsburg, and Hannah Arendt, among many others. The small number of refugees admitted to Ireland explains, to some extent, the general lack of research in this area so far—and also, of course, that among the refugees there were hardly any famous names and no writers. However, the refugees who did go to Ireland made a significant impact. Several dozen of them stayed on in Ireland and became naturalized citizens. Many, such as John Hennig and Erwin Schrödinger, stayed for a long time after the war before they moved on or back. And even the ones who left after the war have given much back over the years.

It is time to write down their story—and at the same time to be aware that each of them had their own complex situation in exile that we will never be able to fully understand. That understanding is made more difficult by the long delay in research; indeed, not many of the people who found refuge in Ireland are alive anymore. But at least the work has begun on appreciating their experience, their difficulties, and also their contributions, and its importance at the time and in the present.

The author is grateful for to the Royal Irish Academy and the Austrian Academy of Science for making research trip to Vienna possible and to the Irish Research Council for the Humanities and Social Sciences for a research fellowship in 2006– 07.

Notes

1   Important reference works such as Krohn et al., *Handbuch der deutschsprachigen Emigration*, hardly mention Ireland. In another standard work, Röder and Strauss, *Biographisches Handbuch der deutschsprachigen Emigration nach 1933*, 1–3, there are twenty entries under Ireland, but only fifteen of them name refugees who were in Ireland between 1933 and 1945. For an overview see Holfter, "Introduction and Overview," 5f.

2   Tom Farrell for example maintained that "only 25 Jewish refugees entered Ireland, many of them converts to Christianity" (Farrell, *Irish Times*, 24 June 1997), whereas Brian Fallon stated that "no reliable figures are available, but it seems that fewer than a hundred were admitted, a miserably inadequate number." See Fallon, *Age of Innocence*, 222.

3   Bréadún, "Chronicle of Shame and Pride," 12.

4   Lee, *Ireland*, 201.

5   Lee, *Ireland*, 187.

6   Keogh, *Jews in Twentieth-Century Ireland*, 116.

7   Keogh, *Jews in Twentieth-Century Ireland*, 116.

8   Fanning, *Racism and Social Change*, 72; see also Goldstone, "Benevolent Helpfulness?"

9   National Archives of Ireland, Dublin, P 11.

10 This is an ongoing research project by Horst Dickel and Gisela Holfter.

11 Wolfgang Benz estimates the following: 1933: 37,000–38,000; 1934: 22,000–23,000; 1935: 20,000–21,000; 1936: 24,000–25,000; 1937: 23,000; 1938: 33,000–40,000; 1939: 75,000–80,000; 1940: 15,000; 1941: 8,000; 1942–1945: 8,500. Benz, *Flucht aus Deutschland*, 64–65.

12 See, for example, Ryan, "Remembering Elsa Reininger"; Halligan, "Heartbreak in City Hotel"; O'Shaughnessy, "Holocaust Portents."

13 Mike Finn's *Pigtown* was first produced in 1999 in Limerick.

14 McCourt, "On the Trail of a Jewish Princess," 2.

15 Email correspondence with the Magistrate of the City of Vienna, Wiener Stadt- und Landesarchiv, MA 8—ME-3437/06, 11 July 2006.

16 Österreichisches Staatsarchiv, Archiv der Republik, Vienna, VA 29683, Elsa Höfler.

17 "City Hotel Tragedy."

18 "City Hotel Tragedy."

19 Receipts for three letters were found, with one to the police in Limerick. Two other letters, one of them in German, one in English, were in her handbag. Ibid.

20 See Bourke, "Irland, George Clare, und die Kagran Gruppe"; O'Connor, "Obliviousness"; Keogh, *Jews in Twentieth-Century Ireland*, 136–38.

21 Military Archives, Dublin, G2/252, file on Ernest Klaar, Ernestine Klaar, and Georg Klaar.

22 Braunizer, "Memories of Dublin," 266.

23 Braunizer, "Memories of Dublin," 266.

24 Hoffmann, *Erwin Schrödinger*, 77.

25 Hennig, *Die bleibende Statt*, 211.

Archival Material

National Archives of Ireland, Dublin.

Military Archives, Dublin.

Wiener Stadt- und Landesarchiv, Vienna.

Österreichisches Staatsarchive, Archiv der Republik, Vienna.

Works Cited

Benz, Wolfgang. *Flucht aus Deutschland*. Munich: dtv, 2001.

Bourke, Eoin. "Irland, George Clare und die Kagran Gruppe." In *Vom Weggehen— Zum Exil von Kunst und Wissenschaft*, edited by Sandra Wiesinger-Stock, Erika Weinzierl, and Konstantin Kaiser, 102–12. Vienna: Mandelbaum, 2006.

Braunizer, Ruth. "Memories of Dublin: Excerpts from Erwin Schrödinger's Diaries." In *German-Speaking Exiles in Ireland 1933–1945*, edited by Gisela Holfter, 265–74. Amsterdam: Rodopi, 2006.

Bréadún, Deaglán de. "A Chronicle of Shame and Pride." *Irish Times* Weekend Review (29 April 2006): 12.

"City Hotel Tragedy—Death of Alien Jewess: Evidence at the Inquest. Verdict of the Jury," *Limerick Leader* (31 October 1938).

Fallon, Brian. *An Age of Innocence: Irish Culture 1930–1960*. Dublin: Gill & Macmillan, 1999.

Fanning, Bryan. *Racism and Social Change in the Republic of Ireland*. Manchester: Manchester University Press, 2002.

Farrell, Tom. "An Irishman's Diary." *Irish Times*, 24 June 1997.

Goldstone, Katrina. "Benevolent Helpfulness? Ireland and the International Reaction to Jewish Refugees, 1933–39." In *Irish Foreign Policy 1919–1966*, edited by Michael Kennedy and Joseph Morrison Skelly, 116–36. Dublin: Four Courts, 2000.

Halligan, Brendan. "Heartbreak in City Hotel." *Limerick Leader*, 25 March 2000.

Hennig, John. *Die bleibende Statt*. Bremen: privately published, 1987.

Hoffmann, Dieter. *Erwin Schrödinger*. Leipzig: Teubner Verlagsgesellschaft, 1984.

Holfter, Gisela. "An Introduction and Overview." In *German-Speaking Exiles in Ireland 1933–1945*, edited by Gisela Holfter, 1–19. Amsterdam: Rodopi, 2006.

Keogh, Dermot. *Jews in Twentieth-Century Ireland*. Cork: Cork University Press, 1998.

Krohn, Claus-Dieter, Patrik von zur Mühlen, Gerhard Paul, and Lutz Winckler. *Handbuch der deutschsprachigen Emigration 1933–1945*. Darmstadt: Primus, 1998.

Lee, Joseph. *Ireland 1912–1985*. Cambridge: Cambridge University Press, 1989.

McCourt, Frank. "On the Trail of a Jewish Princess." *Voice* (September 1971): 2.

O'Shaughnessy, Denis. "Holocaust Portents in Tragic Suicide." In *Limerick: 100 Stories of the Century*. Limerick: Leader Print, 2000: 199–200.

Röder, Werner, and Herbert A. Strauss. *Biographisches Handbuch der deutschsprachigen Emigration nach 1933*. Munich: K.G. Saur, 1980–1983.

Ryan, Des. "Remembering Elsa Reininger." *Limerick Leader*, 16 July 1997.

SIXTEEN

Conversion as a "Two-edged Sword": Evangelicalism among Pittsburgh's German Immigrants

Nora Faires

As evangelical Protestantism swept the United States in the nineteenth century, some Methodist leaders turned their eyes to would-be converts emigrating from the German states. Pittsburgh, growing rapidly at mid-century, numbered among the cities where Methodism established an outpost for immigrant evangelism. This essay discusses the very limited success of Methodism in attracting German converts in the Pittsburgh region, while arguing for a greater understanding of the overall impact of this Americanizing project. Most German newcomers firmly rejected American evangelicalism and opposed the social prohibitions, such as temperance, that its advocates championed. But for those few German immigrants who embraced it, conversion not only wrought wrenching personal transformations but it also allied them with cultural trends ascendant in an expansive Protestant America. More generally, Methodist proselytizing among German immigrants furthered the splintering of an already diverse and fractious enclave.

IN 1838, TWENTY-THREE-YEAR-OLD TAILOR Engelhardt Riemenschneider resolved to leave the United States and return to Hesse, where he hoped to claim an inheritance. Disappointed with his prospects in America, then in the grips of a financial panic, Riemenschneider also chafed at American Sabbatarian restrictions. "The greatest difficulty," he later recounted, "was that I was not allowed to violate the Sabbath here as I had been accustomed to in Germany, in playing, dancing, and frolicking."[1] On his way from Wheeling to Baltimore, he stopped in Pittsburgh to visit an uncle and earn more money for his transatlantic passage. At a schoolhouse near his workplace he heard preaching in German. Enticed by the sound of his native tongue, he soon found himself overcome by the preacher's message, the sermon cutting "like a two-edged sword through [his] soul."[2] After three weeks of spiritual turmoil, Riemenschneider experienced a profound conversion. He joined the fledgling congregation, becoming its pastor in 1846. In embracing evangelical religion he severed ties with the countrymen with whom he had enjoyed card playing, drinking, and "frolicking." In 1850 he at last departed for Hesse, as a missionary for that distinctive antebellum American religious creation, German Methodism.[3]

An account of Riemenschneider's conversion appeared, along with that of a score of other German immigrants, in a book compiled in 1859 by physician and preacher Adam Miller, a former Mennonite who had become a champion of Methodism. The compilation partakes of the vigorous optimism that characterized the Methodist church, which had grown from a minor religious body after the American Revolution to the nation's largest denomination by 1850.

The roots of the Methodist denomination in the United States lie in a movement within the Church of England that began during the eighteenth century and was led principally by two Oxford-trained brothers, John Wesley, a powerful orator, and Charles, a great writer of hymns. John Wesley experienced a religious conversion in 1738, while worshipping in London at a congregation of Moravians, a German pietist group. Thereafter he began formulating the doctrine that became the basis of a reform movement within the Church of England and, by the end of the century, its own denomination in Britain and its North American colonies. Following the American Revolution, Methodism spread quickly in the new republic.

According to noted religious historian David Hempton, Methodism constituted an "empire of the spirit" that thrived on the "energy unleashed by dialectical friction."[4] Accordingly, Methodism embodied "discipline and sobriety" along with "ecstasy and enthusiasm"; a "voluntary association" of believers, its adherents followed strict "rules, regulations, and books of discipline." Most saliently, it was a religion of evangelicalism, promising converts everlasting salvation through asking God's forgiveness and thereafter living a life in accord with biblical teachings, as understood by the denomination. The Methodist doctrine of "justification by faith" set the church apart from many Protestant bodies of the day, which emphasized "predestination," the fate of sinners having been preordained by God. Methodists' conviction of their grace and their zeal to bring others to salvation led many to undertake energetic missionizing, to scrutinize their own and other adherents' conduct for behaviour that failed to measure up to their rigorous discipline, and to seek to create social conditions they believed accorded with God's will and were conducive to conversion.

In examining the denomination's meteoric rise, scholars have pondered the struggle that becoming Methodist entailed: a personal wrestling with God, an often prolonged spiritual torment that resulted in transcendent joy in the conviction of heavenly grace, and the onset of a life of strict discipline within the church. The arduous process of conversion embedded the believer in the community; meanwhile, the scorn of kin and neighbours further cemented the congregational bond.[5] The change was even more profound for German immigrants who embraced Methodism, for it required adopting unaccustomed behaviour.

Methodism began its mission to German immigrants in the 1830s, as the ranks of these immigrants multiplied in the industrializing Pittsburgh region. The combined population of Pittsburgh and the contiguous city of Allegheny, located along the Ohio River's northern bank, quadrupled between 1830 and 1850, and of these cities' 68,000 inhabitants at mid-century, more than 10,000 hailed from a German state. In 1846 the traveller Franz von Löher remarked on this large immigrant presence.[6] Here "Sunday looked like Sunday in Germany. The streets were alive with people crowding outdoors. No dance music ... true, but great merrymaking nevertheless." It was these immigrants, many of whom spent their Sabbaths gathered on Pittsburgh's hillsides picnicking and quaffing beer, that German Methodism sought to convert.

"A Favourable Crisis"

The story of German Methodism begins with its "patriarch," Wilhelm Nast, who used as his first name both Wilhelm and the anglicized William. Born in Stuttgart and descended from scholars and Lutheran clergy, he immigrated in 1828 at the age of twenty-one and quickly gained a faculty post at Kenyon College in central Ohio. In 1835 he converted to Methodism, later recalling that at the revival he "gave himself to the Lord without reserve," filled with "joy unspeakable" and determined to "become a witness ... of our great Shepherd, in seeking that which was lost."[7] Possessed of great commitment and organizational prowess, Nast nonetheless set himself a daunting task in seeking to become Methodism's shepherd to the vast flock of America's German immigrants.

The first years of Nast's ministry resulted in few converts, despite his founding of *Der Christliche Apologete*, a newspaper that served as the Methodist voice to German Americans throughout the nineteenth century.[8] But by 1843 Nast had secured a beachhead for German Methodism, with twenty German-speaking Methodist missionaries and twelve houses of worship, most in midwestern river and lake ports. That year denominational leaders formed a committee to evaluate the mission's prospects. Filed at the Methodist annual conference in 1844, the committee's report provides fascinating testimony regarding the criteria used by denominational leaders to gauge Methodism's possible success among German immigrants, their ideas regarding a German national religious character, and their understanding that entry into American society proved deeply unsettling for these immigrants.[9] Mingling zeal with calculation, the report reflects a deepening awareness of the changing demographic landscape of America.

The report begins by pronouncing the state of religion among the Germans in America deplorable.[10] "The great majority of German emigrants," the committee declared, "are not only ignorant of experimental godliness, but have many positive errors existing among them." The report dutifully enumerated the most flagrant mistakes: "With few exceptions, [they] have no distinct view of the gospel as a system of salvation *by faith*, and relying on the efficacy of sacraments appear almost entirely satisfied with the outward *forms* of religion. Rationalism, and other forms of infidelity, prevail to an alarming extent." The German clergy were criticized "as a whole scarcely worthy of the name" because they "throw the whole weight of their influences in opposition to evangelical truth and piety" thus "producing a vast amount of prejudice." Most dire for the cause of evangelicalism, "a large proportion of [Germans] are under the dominion of popery."[11]

After painting this grim portrait, the committee abruptly shifted its tone, contending that the group's affinity for religious "errors" demonstrated that Germans had "strong predisposition to religion of some kind."[12] In the German states, absent the beneficent influence of Methodism, such inclinations had left these men and women prey to all manner of improper teachings. Consequently, the task for American Methodism was to revivify and reshape the Germans' underlying spiritual predispositions. The time was ripe because the "great mass of mind found in the German emigrant" was "in a state of transition, ready to assume any shape that may be given to it, or to receive the likeness of anything that can be impressed upon it." The present hour constituted a "favourable crisis in which to bring the pure gospel system to bear upon [the immigrant soul]."[13]

While all immigrant groups would face a period of transition, the report maintained that few would prove as susceptible to the Methodist message as the Germans. "Twenty German Romanists will embrace Protestantism sooner than one from Ireland," it declared, adding that "the success of the immortal Luther, under God, we believe, is attributable in a good degree to the character of the people in whom the doctrines of the Reformation were preached." The report claimed that "Germans are naturally serious and ardent in their constitutional make, and whenever set right in principle and practice they generally adhere thereto."[14] Given the opportunity to hear the Methodist message, German immigrants would accept it and, having done so, would prove fervent and steadfast converts. The committee urged a concerted and immediate denominational missionary effort to German immigrants, predicting a great harvest of believers, and thereby endorsed Wilhelm Nast's mission, affording it rhetorical support if not sustained financial and organizational backing.

German Methodism in the Pittsburgh Region

Nast had succeeded in Pittsburgh five years before the denomination placed its imprimatur on his work. He led a two-week revival in the city in October 1838, awakening 35 immigrants, including young Engelhardt Riemenschneider.[15] Congregants walked miles to come to church, where services at times became very emotional, prayers and sermons interrupted by sobbing and moans of anguish as those who recognized their sins sought release through God's blessing. Within months the First German Methodist Episcopal Church of Pittsburgh numbered more than one hundred members.[16]

Two events occurring the next year provided touchstones of faith for the church. In the summer of 1839 John Hartmann, a Nast convert and the congregation's leader, held a week-long *Lagerversammlung*, as the German Methodists called their camp meetings. A parish history recounts that a skeptical young man came to heckle the believers and poison their well. Instead he became overwhelmed by Hartmann's fervent preaching and confessed his evil design, calling upon God and the assembly to forgive him.[17] A second trope in the congregation's narrative of spiritual blessing also involved German opponents of Methodism, although those were less easily won over. Crowds sometimes threw rocks at the homes of German Methodists and jeered the converts on the streets, taunting them for opposing alcohol. One Sunday morning an immigrant innkeeper and a throng of his patrons stormed the schoolhouse where the congregation met, smashing windows and knocking down the door. The preacher reputedly raised his bible and proclaimed that he would cast forth the innkeeper and the rabble from the house of God. Shaken by the preacher's conviction, the mob fled the schoolhouse.[18]

A third episode in 1839 unsurprisingly gets short shrift in congregational accounts, yet speaks eloquently to the wrenching nature of Methodist conversion for German immigrants and the potentially unstable realm such converts inhabited. Wilhelm Keil, a Prussian immigrant, was one of Nast's converts; like Riemenschneider, he was a tailor who soon became a prominent member of the congregation. Here the similarities end. Keil's religious metamorphoses were the stuff of Second Great Awakening melodrama—an extreme example of what might ensue during the "favourable crisis" that the 1844 Methodist denominational report had observed.[19] Arriving in the United States in 1835, by the time he attended the Pittsburgh revival he had already engaged in fringe practices including what he later deemed "sorcery." Upon joining the German Methodist congregation he publicly burned his book of witchcraft, renouncing words he claimed to have written in blood.[20] Yet the chimerical Keil did not stay long in the Methodist fold, even after private instruction by Nast. Keil denounced Methodism's paid ministry as antithetical to true evangelism, espoused Native American medical practices, and dabbled in what the Methodist clergy deemed the "black arts." Gathering some of Hartmann's hard-won souls into a new society, Keil fractured the region's small German Methodist community. He then travelled twenty-four kilometres down the Ohio River to Economy, home of the Harmony Society (or "Rappites"), a noted German pietist colony, where he garnered even more converts for his own communal society.

Weakened in numbers and vitality by the departure of Keil and his followers, Pittsburgh's First German Methodist congregation struggled on. Even as the numbers of German immigrants in Pittsburgh mushroomed in the 1840s and '50s, church membership grew slowly, rising to only one hundred and fifty in the Civil War years, and falling to fifty by 1881.[21] Still, several of the mission churches established by the congregation fared better, especially across the river in Allegheny City. Here, as at Pittsburgh's German Methodist church, dramatic moments galvanized inaugural members into a community of believers and demonstrated spiritual grace to some in the immigrant enclave. During the cholera epidemic that swept through Allegheny City in 1853, the congregation's newly arrived preacher and several church members ministered tirelessly to those struck by the fever. In the wake of this demonstration of courage, dedication, and immunity from contagion, the church gained forty converts. Membership then expanded slowly, edging past that of the Pittsburgh congregation and peaking at fewer than two hundred in the decades after the Civil War.[22]

By 1888 the Pittsburgh region was home to three German Methodist churches and four missions, which together numbered six hundred congregants. The congregations employed six ministers and two missionaries, and enrolled seven hundred Sunday school pupils. Pittsburgh's central German Sunday school library housed one thousand volumes and

each week volunteers distributed four thousand copies of the locally published *Hausbesucher*. Surveying these developments, the minister of the
Pittsburgh congregation,.Pastor C.C. Golder, expressed pride in German
Methodist accomplishments and optimism about its prospects. He deemed
the region an especially appropriate location for the mission that the
overall Methodist denomination had launched in American manufacturing centres. Pittsburgh's immigrants, living in "thickly populated city quarters" and exposed to the "moral neglect rife here," he maintained, "demand
energetic and self-denying work in this territory."[23] But it is fair to ask
whether his faith in the efficacy of this new industrial proselytizing was warranted, and whether his pride in German Methodist attainments was justified. By 1880 more than 40,000 German immigrants lived in the cities
of Pittsburgh and Allegheny, yet German Methodism claimed only six
hundred souls in the region. From this perspective, Golder's conviction
that Pittsburgh was a likely site for successful German Methodist work
sounds suspiciously reminiscent of the 1844 report predicting that a
"favourable state" for evangelizing the mass of German immigrants was at
hand.

Reconsidering German Methodism

The Pittsburgh region did not constitute an unusually inhospitable climate for German Methodist missionizing; rates of membership
here mirrored national patterns. In all, German Methodists numbered
only some 26,000 during the Civil War era, doubling in the subsequent
quarter century to 54,000, and peaking at 60,000 in 1917, after large-
scale immigration from Germany had long since ended and as America
entered a war against these immigrants' homeland.[24] The German
Methodist mission did succeed in drawing in more converts nationally
than did the overall denominational outreach to Scandinavian immigrants during the nineteenth century.[25] Nevertheless, judged solely in
terms of converts, German Methodism remained a minor American religious tendency from its founding in the 1830s until its demise in the
1920s, when its separate identity was subsumed within the Methodist Episcopal denomination. Yet reading scholarly accounts of German Methodism produces a very different impression, one more in line with Golder's
congratulatory reflections and sanguine predictions and with Adam Miller's
question of 1859, "Where did the Methodist Church get all these German preachers?" Paul F. Douglass outlines the rapid "advance" of the mission in his 1939 survey, *The Story of German Methodism*. In the introduction
to the book, Methodist bishop John L. Nuelsen contends that "the progress
of Methodism among the Germans in the United States" nearly amounts
to "a miracle in religious history."[26] Similarly, Carl Wittke, writing in 1959,

discusses German Methodism's "phenomenal spread" in the 1850s and '60s.[27] In general, such language reflects the denominational boosterism prevalent in older religious history. This high-blown rhetoric, so at odds with the net gains achieved in numbers of congregational members, raises a question: beyond mere souls saved, how should we understand the impact and import of German Methodism?

As historians of German Methodism rightly claim, the church excelled at institution building, creating sanctuaries, hospitals, and homes for the aged and for children and, intriguingly, for students of gender, establishing deaconess associations.[28] This network of institutions presumably provided church members with the opportunity to live and die among fellow believers, further insulating them from the influences of other German religious and secular organizations and binding them more closely to Methodism as creed and denomination. Similarly, denominational scholars from Miller onward stress the mission to Germany as a hallmark of German Methodism's accomplishments.

More generally, the core of this literature celebrates the transformation that German Methodism achieved convert by convert, underscores the extent of change necessary to wrest each German immigrant soul from a welter of false beliefs, irreligion, and immorality, and tacitly acknowledges that the campaign to bring these immigrants to Methodism was especially hard fought. Each awakening seems to have constituted a more than usually arduous spiritual victory over the forces arrayed against it. While the narrative line of this literature follows the customary upward trajectory, seeing Methodist progress in winning German souls as a working out of a blessed design, read against the grain this literature seems suffused with wonder: the writers of these denominational accounts appear awed that German Methodism prevailed at all.

As these writers well understood, adopting Methodism demanded of German immigrants a formidable cultural as well religious remaking. Conversion meant relinquishing familiar liturgies, dispensing with catechisms and confirmation robes in favour of emotional outpourings of faith and the singing of Wesleyan hymns. German Methodists also were to forego educating their children in German-language parochial schools in favour of sending the second generation to the "people's college," as one nineteenth-century denominational leader referred to the American public school.[29] Here they would learn English and mix with those outside the ethnic group. Of course, the most visible changes mandated by taking up Methodism came in the realm of social behaviour: following Sabbatarian restrictions, forswearing customary leisure activities such as attending the theatre and gambling, and pledging abstinence since intemperance constituted "one of the strongholds of Satan."[30]

Above all, German Methodism was an enterprise in acculturation, an Americanization campaign that permitted language retention, at least for the first generation, while promoting intense assimilation to an appropriately evangelical Protestant America. As Reverend W.H. Daniels, an advocate of the immigrant mission, declared in 1880, "German Methodism is not instrumental in saving souls alone" but also "assists in establishing American institutions, and making them effective."[31] Its "special work," he contended, was to propagate "genuine Protestant principles in circles to which it alone can gain access." Conversion was intended to turn the eyes of Germans away from the immigrant enclave, except that small portion already awakened, and toward Methodism and America.

Hence German Methodism was an ambitious cultural project. The tiny percentage of immigrants who became members travelled far from their Old World beliefs and into the main current of American religious life. To the mass of unconverted immigrants German Methodism embodied the triple horrors of ascendant American religiosity: emotional uproar, social prohibition, and relentless proselytizing. While most immigrants probably paid little attention to the converts' entreaties, the situation in Pittsburgh demonstrates that some targets of missionizing resisted, harassing their hymn-singing, bible-toting, beer-banning brethren.

Moreover, the emergence of German Methodism escalated the sometimes vitriolic debates that raged within the ethnic group regarding right belief and right behaviour, debates that spilled over into the political landscape. The ethnocultural politics of the 1850s and beyond demonstrated just how firmly entrenched among German immigrants was what a prominent Methodist bishop termed the "ostentatious display of the lesser morals"—enjoying the Sabbath in traditional German style and drinking lager beer on all days of the week—and how little these practices had given "place to evangelical piety."[32] The high stakes of these political fights and the fact that they pitted evangelical Germans against others in the immigrant enclave further testify to the effects of the Methodist mission. The direct emissary of an aggressively evangelical Protestant American culture, German Methodism helped to splinter an already religiously diverse ethnic group, heightening a sectarianism that both cut across and reinforced other lines of division within the group.

In a provocative article, historian James Bratt has argued that by the mid-1830s the evangelical tide had turned, ushering in a sea change in American religiosity.[33] In part Bratt's argument rests on an appreciation that the massive immigration that began in the 1830s and '40s must be taken into account in understanding the development of American Protestantism. The study of nineteenth-century America can benefit from an examination of the movement of immigrant faiths, including the varied

beliefs of German newcomers, from the margins to the narrative mainstream, paralleling the greater attention to the life of other outsiders,
such as African Americans, Native Americans, and women, that has so
revised and revitalized our understanding of the national story—further
justification to connect more closely the study of ethnicity and religion.[34]
In the case of Germans and Methodism we need to chart with whom the
evangelical, Americanizing project succeeded and with what consequences,
and how evangelicalism fit into the panorama of religious beliefs and
behaviour that characterized the immigrant group in the nineteenth century. We might then better assess important aspects of the transformation of American culture that accompanied mass immigration and more
fully understand the evolution of a diverse, often contentious German
America.

This work was supported by funds from the Faculty Research and Creative Activities Support Fund, Western Michigan University. The author is grateful to Linda K.
Pritchard, Michael J. Schroeder, and Jewel L. Spangler for their thoughtful comments on this essay.

Notes

1 Miller, *German Methodist Preachers*, 120–21.
2 On the formation of the congregation see Golder, *Geschichte der Gemeinden*.
3 A brief notice of Riemenschneider's missionary work in Germany appears in the
   column "Germany: A Minister Awake," *Pittsburgh Christian Advocate*, 3 February
   1852. On the German Methodist mission to the German states, see Wittke, *Nast*,
   46; Douglass, *Story of German Methodism*, 37–39, 55, 118.
4 Hempton, *Methodism*, 7.
5 See, for example, Schneider, *Way of the Cross*; Heyrman, *Southern Cross*; Wigger,
   Taking Heaven by Storm; and Andrews, *Methodists*.
6 Trautmann, "Western Pennsylvania," 230. Trautmann introduced and translated
   three chapters of Löher's two-volume *Land und Leute*.
7 Wittke, *Nast*, 3–11; 37–39; Douglass, *Story of German Methodism*, 9–21; Miller, *German
   Methodist Preachers*, 59–66.
8 Daniels, Illustrated History of Methodism, 660–61.
9 *Journal of the General Conference*, 183.
10 *Journal of the General Conference*, 183.
11 *Journal of the General Conference*, 183.
12 *Journal of the General Conference*, 183.
13 *Journal of the General Conference*, 183.
14 *Journal of the General Conference*, 184.
15 Golder, *Geschichte der Gemeinden*, 4. On Methodism and German Methodism, especially in the Pittsburgh region, see Sturm, "Social Gospel"; Smeltzer, *Methodism
   on the Headwaters*; Smeltzer, "Place of Methodism"; Daniels, *Illustrated History of
   Methodism*, 660–69; Finley, "Dutchman's Experience"; Frantz, "Early German Methodism"; and Harrison, "Wilhelm Nast."
16 Golder, *Geschichte der Gemeinden*, 6, 10.

17   Golder, *Geschichte der Gemeinden*, 13.
18   Golder, *Geschichte der Gemeinden*, 13.
19   On Keil see Gooch, "William Keil"; Heming, "'Temples Stand, Temples Fall'";
     Duke, "Profile of Religion"; and Wittke, *Nast*, 46–47.
20   Golder, *Geschichte der Gemeinden*, 10–11.
21   Golder, *Geschichte der Gemeinden*, 18.
22   Golder, *Geschichte der Gemeinden*, 20–21.
23   Golder, *Geschichte der Gemeinden*, 35–36.
24   Douglass, *Story of German Methodism*, 221–24; Wittke, *Nast*, 48–49.
25   *Minutes of the Pittsburgh Annual Conference* (1886), 40.
26   J. Alfred Faulkner, as quoted in John L. Nuelsen's "Introduction" to Douglass, *Story of German Methodism*, xii. See also Sinnema, *German Methodism in Ohio*.
27   Wittke, *Nast*, 75, 77.
28   See especially the tables on organizational development included in Douglass, *Story of German Methodism*, 282–85.
29   Wood, *Methodism and the Centennial*, 82; Wittke, *Nast*, 98.
30   *Minutes of the Pittsburgh Annual Conference* (1857), 26; *Minutes of the Pittsburgh Annual Conference* (1886), 41.
31   Daniels, *Illustrated History of Methodism*, 669.
32   Bishop Francis Asbury, as quoted in Eller, *These Evangelical United Brethren*, 38.
33   Bratt, "The Reorientation of American Protestantism."
34   On the historiographical background of this issue see Higham, "Ethnicity and American Protestantism."

Works Cited

Andrews, Dee E. *The Methodists and Revolutionary America, 1760–1800*. Princeton: Princeton University Press, 2000.

Bratt, James D. "The Reorientation of American Protestantism, 1835–1845." *Church History* 67 (March 1998): 52–82.

Daniels, W.H. *The Illustrated History of Methodism*. New York: Methodist Book Concern, 1880.

Douglass, Paul F. *The Story of German Methodism: Biography of an Immigrant Soul*. New York: Methodist Book Concern, 1939.

Duke, David Nelson. "A Profile of Religion in the Bethel-Aurora Colonies." *Oregon Historical Quarterly* 92 (1991–92): 346–59.

Eller, Paul H. *These Evangelical United Brethren*. Dayton, OH: Otterbein Press, 1957.

Finley, James B. "The Dutchman's Experience." In *Sketches of Western Methodism: Biographical, Historical, and Miscellaneous, Illustrative of Pioneer Life*, edited by W.P. Strickland, 359–98. Cincinnati: Methodist Book Concern, 1854.

Frantz, John B. "Early German Methodism in America." *Yearbook of German-American Studies* 26 (1991): 171–84.

Golder, Christian C. *Geschichte der deutschen Methodistengemeinden in Pittsburgh und Allegheny City, PA*. Pittsburgh: City Mission Publishing, 1888.

Gooch, John O. "William Keil, A Strange Communal Leader." *Methodist History* 4 (1967): 36–41.

Harrison, Daniel W. "Wilhelm Nast (1807–1899): Founder of German-Speaking Methodism in America and Architect of the Methodist Episcopal Church Mission in Europe." *Methodist History* 39 (2001): 154–66.

Heming, Carol Piper. "'Temples Stand, Temples Fall': The Utopian Vision of Wilhelm Keil." *Missouri Historical Review* 85 (1990): 21–39.

Hempton, David. *Methodism: The Empire of the Spirit.* New Haven, CT: Yale University Press, 2005.

Heyrman, Christine Leigh. *Southern Cross: The Beginnings of the Bible Belt.* New York: Knopf, 1997.

Higham, John. "Ethnicity and American Protestantism: Collective Identity in the Mainstream." In *New Directions in American Religious History,* edited by Harry S. Stout and D.G. Hart, 239–59. New York: Oxford University Press, 1997.

Journal of the General Conference of the Methodist Episcopal Church. Volume II, 1840, 1844. Together with the Debates of 1844. Published by Order of the Conference. New York: Carlton Phillips, 1856.

Löher, Franz. *Land und Leute in der alten and neuen Welt: Reiseskizzen.* Göttingen and New York, 1855.

Miller, Adam. *Experience of German Methodist Preachers.* Cincinnati: Methodist Book Concern, 1859.

Minutes of the Pittsburgh Annual Conference of the Methodist Episcopal Church, 1857. Pittsburgh: W.S. Haven, 1857.

Minutes of the Pittsburgh Annual Conference of the Methodist Episcopal Church, 1886. Pittsburgh: Myers, Shinkle, 1886.

Pittsburgh Christian Advocate (periodical), 1852.

Schneider, A. Gregory. *The Way of the Cross Leads Home: The Domestication of American Methodism.* Bloomington: Indiana University Press, 1993.

Sinnema, John R. *German Methodism in Ohio: Its Leaders and Institutions.* Berea, OH: American-German Institute, Baldwin Wallace College, 1983.

Smeltzer, Wallace Guy. *Methodism on the Headwaters of the Ohio.* Nashville, TN: Pantheon Press, 1957.

———. "The Place of Methodism in the Religious Life of the Pittsburgh Region." *Western Pennsylvania Historical Magazine* 23 (September 1940): 147–57.

Sturm, Theodore Paul. "The Social Gospel in the Methodist Churches in Pittsburgh, 1865–1920." PhD diss., West Virginia University, 1971.

Trautmann, Frederic, trans. "Western Pennsylvania through a German's Eyes: The Travels of Franz von Löher, 1846." *Western Pennsylvania Historical Magazine* 62 (July 1982): 221–37.

Wigger, John H. *Taking Heaven by Storm: Methodism and the Rise of Popular Christianity in America.* New York: Oxford University Press, 1998.

Wittke, Carl. *William Nast: Patriarch of German Methodism.* Detroit: Wayne State University Press, 1959.

Wood, Ezra Morgan. *Methodism and the Centennial of American Independence.* New York: Nelson and Phillips, 1876.

SEVENTEEN

The Diasporic Moment

Elise von Koerber, Dr. Otto Hahn, and the Attempt to Create a German Diaspora in Canada

Angelika E. Sauer

In the two decades of the 1870s and '80s, a confluence of factors created the ideal political conditions for the creation of German-speaking settlements in Canada that could provide a permanent connection to the homeland. During this time, German Canadian immigration agents Elise von Koerber and Dr. Otto Hahn acted as transnational cultural brokers and facilitators, attempting to promote their ideas with both Canadian and European governments. While both seemed aware of the potential of diasporic connections, their efforts resulted in limited success. Their cooperation is most visible in a Swiss and German settlement area in the Nipissing district of northern Ontario. Beyond this, however, the competition by the United States and the effect of existing commercial patterns proved to be too strong to overcome, and the migrants themselves were too diverse to fit into a national diaspora pattern.

THE 1870S AND '80S ARE A SPECIAL PERIOD in German Canadian history because they brought together the overlapping interests of two emerging modern nation-states. Canada was involved in an enormous effort of conquest and settlement, incorporating territories in northwestern Ontario, Manitoba, and further west into the new country and trying to build and finance the physical and ideological infrastructure of incorporation. In the newly formed German Empire, where the social consequences of rapid industrialization fuelled class divisions and a socialist movement, many intellectuals strove to devise policies that would lessen class tensions without touching the capitalist structure of the new Reich. They increasingly targeted emigration as an ideal solution to the prole-tarization of a large part of the German population, with the added bonus of creating overseas markets and cultural links to the world. In this con-fluence of push and pull factors, successive Canadian governments briefly looked to German-speaking Europeans as a source of nation building, and employed the services of Canadian and German government agents to actively recruit German-speaking settlers. The decade between the mid 1870s and mid 1880s thus provided a sort of "perfect storm" scenario, a rare diasporic moment in German Canadian history.

The concept of diaspora to explain the transnational nature of migrants' identities, social fields, and relations was introduced into the mainstream of migration scholarship by social scientists more than a hundred years later, in the 1990s. In its basic form, the concept suggests that the nationals of one country maintain their sense of national identity after migration or dispersal and stay connected to the homeland, and that the homeland remains interested in them as continuing parts of a dispersed nation. In this analytical framework, migrants become an unbounded nation or a global network of nationals in different locations, all aware of each oth-ers' existence and feeling connected in a common national cause.[1]

Historians of migration continue to be somewhat skeptical about the usefulness of the concept, preferring to focus their attention on the social processes that linked specific local places of origin to places of settle-ment.[2] They have endorsed the general usefulness of the transnational the-oretical framework,[3] but have found that transnational studies only suc-ceed in connecting the local to the global, without being able to deal with the national.[4] Historians of immigration policies, who do write from the national perspective of the receiving countries, may touch upon what con-nects certain countries or regions that provide emigrants with specific regions in the receiving country. However, since their starting point and analytical framework is the nation-state, they do not consciously reflect upon the creation of transnational communities or diasporas.[5]

How do we bridge the gap between national governments and transna-tional processes? This chapter argues that government immigration agents played an important role as transnational cultural brokers and diasporic facilitators. They used their own transcultural competencies to tap into exist-ing transnational networks, and where these networks did not exist due to a lack of prior settlement, they tried to simulate the mechanism of other, self-regulating immigration flows. The chapter focuses on two agents hired by the Canadian government for recruitment in Germany: a Ger-man-born immigrant woman who became an immigration agent in 1872 and a German lawyer who became interested in Canada in the mid 1870s and was employed by the Canadian government to work in Germany for nearly a decade. Elise von Koerber and Dr. Otto Hahn cooperated in the task of finding German immigrants for Canada. While their success was limited in terms of overall numbers, they did create both the conceptual framework and a fleeting reality of a regional German-speaking diaspora in Canada.

In the early 1870s, the government of Sir John A. Macdonald applied itself to the task of settling the newly incorporated territories to the north and west of the old province of Canada with Euro-Canadian and European agriculturalists. The new government reverted to the pre-Confederation tradition of looking beyond Great Britain to especially German-speaking Europe for hard-working peasant families.[6] In January 1872, minister of agriculture J.H. Pope appointed two German Ontarians, Jacob Klotz[7] and William Hespeler,[8] to coordinate recruitment efforts in German territories. Both found out very quickly that most Germans had never heard of Canada[9] and that the new country could not compete with the pervasive lure of the United States "where nearly every family here has relatives or friends."[10] As far as settlers from the German Empire were concerned, Canada did not have the critical mass of prior German settlers required to start a chain reaction.

The simulation of the mechanisms of chain migration for successful government recruitment was at the heart of the efforts of an extraordinary lady who emerged in the 1870s as an advocate and promoter of German migration to Canada. Elise von Koerber had been born in the German Duchy of Baden in 1839. She and her Austrian husband immigrated to the Province of Canada in the late 1850s, where they had four children. Koerber's husband worked as civil servant in the Crown Lands Department until his untimely death. At that point Koerber herself sought employment with the federal government in the field of migration management. She worked in Europe from late 1872 until her position was discontinued at the end of 1878. She then acted as a consultant to the government in Ottawa on European migration matters and later resumed her migration work under the auspices of philanthropic societies. She died in 1884.

Koerber had a firm concept as to how the Canadian government should approach the task at hand. With great consistency, she advocated a system of migration management that would curtail the activities of commercial interests in the process but involve trustworthy, government-appointed parties on both sides of the Atlantic in the recruitment, conveyance, and protection of migrants from point of origin to point of settlement. At the heart of her system were government agents appointed by the government of the receiving country. These agents would be disinterested modern civil servants with a firm knowledge of the sending country, its language, conditions, and laws. The Canadian agent would employ the help of local middlemen to make Canada more familiar to continental Europeans and their governments. Koerber recommended that the Canadian government invite fact-finding delegations of men who represented different interests, such as agriculture and manufacturing, and who enjoyed the confidence of their respective governments. Their reports would be the official information about Canada that could be circulated without local governments objecting.[11]

Koerber envisioned migration as a means to tie two countries together in a more intimate relationship, with the Canadian agent taking on consular functions, combining "with their emigration work the fostering abroad of Canadian commercial, manufacturing and mining interests." She saw great potential for Canada to establish close ties with continental governments, especially the Swiss and the German. The German government in particular, she argued, preferred Germans to go to Canada over the United States because they were able to maintain their language and culture in closely knit group settlements that would also serve to attract other compatriots. Emigration would lead to trade. In fact, she told politicians, Canadians should "look upon emigration as a wider subject than the mere bringing of emigrants here. They should look upon it in its commercial relation." If the German shipping line Hapag Lloyd could be convinced to run a connection between Hamburg and Montreal, Quebec City, or Halifax, then German migrants would have an easier time coming to Canada and Canadian products would have an easier time reaching the German market. This argument was the mirror image of the one made by German liberal emigration promoters with respect to creating new markets for German products.[12]

Despite her confidence, Koerber, like Klotz and Hespeler before her, found her work in German territory to be an uphill battle. After several disastrous, privately organized settlement initiatives in Central and South America, Bismarck's Reich government was openly hostile toward emigration, and most state governments followed the lead established by Prussia in strictly curtailing and regulating foreign activities deemed incitement of emigration. In fact, Koerber's own birthplace, the state of Baden, expelled her from its territory and threatened imprisonment. Germany, it seemed, was an "impregnable fortress."[13] Stymied in her efforts to recruit among the people she knew best—the people of Baden and Alsace—Koerber devoted her initial efforts to Switzerland. In 1873, she made a trip back to Canada to choose a location for a Swiss colony. She negotiated with the Ontario government a reserve of free grant lands in the Nipissing district of Ontario, where they could farm but also establish mills and manufacturing, such as paper and watch making. After picking the location, she returned to Europe to pick local middlemen, and then accompanied a Swiss delegation back to Canada. By the following winter the first of her recruits started to arrive in unorganized trickles: altogether about one hundred and fifty of them from several different cantons. This was the nucleus she needed. After Koerber published an official report on Canadian conditions, a steady stream of Swiss settlers went to northern Ontario, including some orphaned youths. Altogether, the Department of Agriculture credited her with "inducing between 2,000 and 3,000 Swiss and German emigrants to make their homes in Canada" mostly by creating "national colonies" and finding land that was suited to the settlers' habits and occupations.[14]

Despite her success in Switzerland, Koerber's prime personal interest lay in developing a network of non-commercial interests for the protection and management of female emigrants from Germany. Women seemed in particular need of more opportunities for employment, and Koerber envisioned a network of women's organizations to act as an "Inter-Oceanic Employment Bureau" that would match so-called surplus women with overseas jobs.[15] Her concern for the female migrant was shared by a number of German women's organizations and male politicians, especially in southwest Germany. In the late fall of 1875, Koerber travelled to Stuttgart for a meeting with a former premier. Württemberg was a steady source of emigrants: in the three decades since 1840, nearly 270,000 people had left their homes mostly for North America.[16] Many intellectuals in Württemberg considered emigration as necessary in light of Malthusian fears of a surplus population and equally strong fears of socialist rumblings.[17] Koerber was given "the name of a gentleman who, some years ago, exerted himself to help emigration": Dr. Otto Hahn of Reutlingen. Their first meeting, which went on for hours, was the beginning of several years of cooperation on behalf of Canada.[18]

Hahn, born in July of 1828, had studied law and worked successfully as a civil servant when, in 1861, he followed his religious convictions of the Swedenborgian New Church and joined Gustav Werner's Bruderhaus in Reutlingen. During the three years he spent in this religious community, he developed the idea of an agrarian colony of Württemberg Christian freethinkers in Costa Rica.[19] The plan was dropped for reasons unknown, but in 1864 Hahn, no longer a member of the commune and on his way to becoming a wealthy lawyer, continued to think about emigration of people from Wurttemberg to the New World and "did of his ownself a great deal—traveled to North and Central America [specifically Venezuela], published at his own expenses, spoke publicly and really succeeded in sending a large number of people to the States."[20] In his 1866 pamphlet

Amerika: Der Bauer und Arbeiter in Schwaben und in Amerika, he gave a some-what naive and sketchy overview of the opportunities that the American Homestead Law offered to the Swabian smallholder if organized by an emigration association.[21] He grew increasingly discouraged by his inabil-ity to raise money and dropped his emigration project in 1873, devoting himself to geological studies instead.[22]

The meeting with the energetic and enthusiastic Koerber in late 1875 revitalized Otto Hahn and rekindled his interests in the issue of emigra-tion, especially since she indicated that Canada encouraged the kind of close-knit settlements that would allow a group of settlers to stay together as a colony, the way he had envisioned it in his publication on the United States. He proposed to head a delegation of experts to investigate Cana-dian settlement conditions, report to the Württemberg government, and recruit a group of emigrants. Koerber supported his ideas with her supe-riors, asking them repeatedly to appoint him as a government agent and to issue an official invitation.[23] She trusted Hahn's judgment "that the desire to emigrate is latent in the hearts of many ... and might ... be directed to Canada."[24] Both Koerber and Hahn assumed that only a proactive atti-tude by Ottawa would succeed in securing a share of Germans for the new country.

Dr. Hahn finally received his invitation from Ottawa for an expenses-paid visit in May 1878.[25] He decided to sacrifice his personal comfort and his family life (he was the father of seventeen children, ten of whom man-aged to survive past infancy) and make the trip to study Canada as a des-tination for Germans. He left in July, travelling via Paris and London to Liverpool, hence by Allan Line to Quebec and on to Montreal. Once in Toronto, after an eleven-hour trip from Ottawa he made an excursion to Berlin, Ontario, where he visited the minister of the local Swedenborgian congregation.[26] Then he embarked on a trip to "the wilderness," to Mag-netawan and Koerber's Swiss colony. He noted the potential of Lake Nipiss-ing to become Ontario's Lake Constance (*Bodensee*) and concluded: "*Dieses Land halte ich für württembergische Einwanderung für sehr gut.*" It seems that Otto Hahn had finally found his New World utopia. He wrote full of gen-uine enthusiasm that this part of Canada could be a place "*für uns Schwa-ben ... welches alle Vortheile des Heimathlandes bietet, ohne irgend erhebliche Nachtheile gegenüber der alten Heimat*" Before he left, Hahn purchased land in Magnetawan previously owned by Elisabeth Annie Blaser, who worked on a Swiss orphan project, and began to plan "to build a house which could serve as home for poor children and poor lads."[27]

After his return to Reutlingen in the fall of 1878, Hahn and Koerber approached philanthropist Gustav Werner, Hahn's old friend from his time in the commune, with their plan of building a new agriculturally oriented Bruderhaus in northern Ontario.[28] After some hesitation Werner agreed to support the venture and helped organize the first group, which left for Canada in the spring of 1879. They soon sent favourable reports and Koerber was optimistic: "In this gentleman's hand this emigration will soon become a matter of satisfaction to this country."[29] The re-elected Macdonald government followed Koerber's urging to appoint Hahn as agent in May 1879.[30]

Ironically, Koerber's own career took an unexpected turn for the worse. By 1878, she had noticed increasing German interest in her plans to organize transnational networks for the management of female emigration from Germany to Canada and associations were formed to help recruit suitable German women for a new life in Canada. At this very moment of triumph, while she was chairing an organizational meeting in Berlin, her appointment was terminated and she was recalled to Canada.[31]

What makes the Koerber-Hahn cooperation particularly interesting in the history of German diaspora building is that both became directly connected to the very circles in Germany that discussed the promotion of enduring links and interactions between homeland and emigrants as a tool to promote Germany's commercial, cultural, and political interests abroad. In November 1878 in Berlin, a number of intellectuals and businesspeople along with a sprinkling of German officials formed the Centralverein für Handelsgeographie und Förderung deutscher Interessen im Ausland. According to its constitution, the association's purpose was to build and maintain lively ties between Germans living abroad and their mother country, to explore geographic and socioeconomic conditions in potential areas of German settlement overseas, and to promote emigration to countries where Germans could keep their sense of connectedness to the larger German community. Various branches of this association formed over the next several years, including the Württemberg branch in Stuttgart.[32]

Elise von Koerber's successful visit to Berlin in late 1878 coincided with the founding of the association, and this was no mere coincidence. Koerber herself sent a newspaper article reporting the founding of the Centralverein to Ottawa. Her meeting to set up a network for the protection of German emigrant women was chaired by Legationsrat Theodor von Bunsen, a prominent member of the Centralverein, who lent his support because her plans fitted well into the ideas of the new organization.[33] Her acquaintance with Otto Hahn further enhanced her credentials in Berlin. In his 1866 and 1878 publications, Hahn had demonstrated that his thinking about emigration moved in the same direction as that of the Centralverein, especially when he defended emigration as a way to establish lasting commercial and cultural connections with overseas territory.[34] With the founding of a Württemberg branch of the Verein für

Handelsgeographie, Hahn quickly became the Centralverein's most important source of information about Canada.[35]

Hahn managed to craft an ingenious argument for the promotion of German emigration to Canada and against the acquisition of German formal colonies.[36] His ideas probably met with quite a bit of disapproval in conservative circles but he couched them in such nationalistic terms that even the Deutsche Kolonialverein under the leadership of Count Hohenlohe-Langenburg took notice of his work.[37] In 1883, the prince travelled to Canada and afterward confessed that "when I am asked by Germans who want to emigrate ... where they are to go, I advise them to turn their steps to Canada, as I am convinced that nowhere in America, except when Germany is lucky enough to possess colonies, will our peasants and working men feel more comfortable."[38] Count Hohenlohe and Otto Hahn remained in contact after this visit. As Canada's official link with prospective German emigrants, Hahn's initial work remained focused on Ontario. From 1879 to 1881 he sent annual contingents of Württemberg settlers to the German settlements in the Lake Nipissing area, which had, in effect, become a diaspora of settlers from the Swiss and German sides of the Lake Constance region. Being quite aware of the powerful attraction provided by chain migration to the western United States,[39] he was hoping to create his own Canadian magnet in form of successful nuclei at "such points where the difficulties are not too great, and where friends can easily follow." He had no time and interest in Manitoba and areas further west: "I have not been able to induce emigrants from here to settle in that province; the journey is rather expensive and there is as yet no nucleus for settlements there. The climate moreover is very different from that of Germany."[40] Unfortunately for Hahn, the Macdonald government was now intent on settling the Prairies, and he was informed that the "climate is very well spoken of, and if it suits Englishmen and Italians, it should not be disagreeable to Germans."[41] Dr. Hahn got the message and began to distribute favourable information about Manitoba and the Northwest, despite some obvious misgivings.

Being a prolific and self-confident writer, Otto Hahn produced a number of publications and organized a delegation of four experts in 1881. To his thinking, parts of Canada fulfilled the conditions he had set out as a young man for the founding of "Ackerbaukolonien": a suitable non-tropical climate and a population inferior in civilization and work habits to the Germans. He staked the future and prosperity of the German Empire on land and agriculture and the continuing allegiance of German migrants to their fatherland. Migration, he explained, did not have to mean emigration: "Wanderung ist Wechsel im Ort der Arbeit." Rather than emigration and a change in citizenship, there could be transmigration, facilitated by the German government, that would allow Germans to work and prosper abroad, provide important links between Germany and the world and finally return with capital to invest in the German economy. The country that had released them to be productive would remain in their hearts and they would continue to feel German through the "geistige Verbindung mit ihren Stammes- und Glaubensgenossen in Deutschland." Germany was the permanent spiritual Heimat for the German diaspora in Canada for him and trans-migration was the alternative not just to a German colonial empire but also to German emigration.[42]

None of Hahn's arguments and efforts seemed to bear the fruit that he and the Canadian government had hoped for.[43] He finally gave up on the business of promoting Canada in Germany and decided to move his entire family to Canada, and "to erect a sort of station in the shape of a large farm" to attract and train German settlers and direct them to their eventual place of settlement.[44] Unfortunately, at the very moment that Hahn, his wife, and ten children crossed the Atlantic, a letter arrived in Reutlingen announcing that the Canadian government no longer required his services. The Hahns never got their large farm but settled in Toronto, where Otto resumed his other passion, the pursuit of geological and other scientific studies.

The Koerber-Hahn chapter in German Canadian history did not leave a lasting mark on Canada. The Lake Constance diaspora in Northern Ontario eventually dispersed and is no longer part of local historical consciousness. German emigrants continued to choose the United States over Canada, not the least because the United States was easier and cheaper to reach. In the end, there never was one German diaspora but at best many regional diasporas with limited lifespan. The work of the agents shows their awareness of patterns that were both local and global but not national, although they participated in nation-centred discourses about migration. This suggests the usefulness of studying village or region-based diasporic networks and abandoning the construct of a national diaspora.

Notes

1 Cohen, *Global Diasporas.*
2 Hoerder, "German-Language Diasporas."
3 Gerber, "Theories and Lives." For a good definition of the transnational life, see page 35.
4 Gabaccia, "Is Everywhere Nowhere?"
5 Macdonald, *Canada: Immigration and Colonization*; Wagner, *History of Migration.*
6 Walsh, "Landscapes of Longing."
7 Minister's report, 13 January 1872, and Order-in-Council, 16 January 1872, Library and Archives Canada, Records of the Department of Agriculture, RG17 vol. 56, file 5343. Mack to Minister, 29 January 1872, RG17 vol. 56, file 5398.
8 Order-in-Council, 28 February 1872, RG17 vol. 58, file 5533.

9 Hespeler to Pope, 20 May 1872, RG17 vol. 65, file 6246. Klotz met up with Hespeler in Alsace in late April and told him "that as yet a very limited portion of Emigrants from these parts have left for Canada as 7/8 of people have never heard of the Dominion."

10 Hespeler to Pope, 20 May 1872, RG17 vol. 65, file 6246, and Hespeler to Pope, 17 June 1872, RG17 vol. 66, file 6364.

11 This system is laid out in three public appearances in 1879 and 1880: address on Continental Immigration, delivered before the City Council of Toronto, September 1879 (hereafter: City Council Speech) available at <www.canadiana.org/ ECO/ItemRecord/63090?id=e471e5d3e77c2e6a>; testimony of John Lowe before House of Commons Committee, *Sessional Papers* 1879, appendix 1; and Koerber testimony before the House of Commons Committee, April 1880, *Sessional Papers* 1880, appendix 3.

12 Koerber testimony before the House of Commons Committee, April 1880, *Sessional Papers* 1880, appendix 3, especially 18–19.

13 City Council Speech, 9.

14 *Sessional Papers* 1879, Appendix 1. A historical plaque in Magnetawan, the site of Koerber's Swiss colony, gives her credit for several hundred Swiss settlers. See West, "Canadian Immigration Agents."

15 Colonial Office to Governor General, 9 July 1883, Records of the Department of External Affairs, RG25 B-1-a, vol. 31.

16 Philippovich, *Auswanderung und Auswanderungspolitik*, 236–37.

17 Bretting and Bickelmann, Auswanderungsagenturen, 220.

18 Koerber to Jenkins, 4 December 1875, *Sessional Papers* 1876, 153.

19 Zwink, "Otto Hahn." (Quoted from a prepublication manuscript.)

20 Koerber to Jenkins, 4 December 1875, *Sessional Papers* A 1876, 153.

21 Hahn, *Amerika*, 20–24.

22 Koerber to Jenkins, 4 December 1875, *Sessional Papers* A 1876, 153.

23 Koerber to Minister, 11 December 1876, RG17 vol. 17418096.

24 Koerber to Jenkins, 4 December 1875, *Sessional Papers* A 1876, 153.

25 The following is based on Hahn's publication *Canada: Meine Reise.*

26 Frisse, *Berlin, Ontario*, 179–80.

27 Koerber to Lowe 23 November 1877, RG17 vol. 236, file 24267. In 1880, payments from Hahn's expense account went to Elisabeth Blaser in Muskoka. The census identifies Elisabeth Annie Blaser as a member of the Free Church.

28 Koerber, April 1880 testimony before the House of Commons Committee, *Sessional Papers* 1880.

29 City Council speech, 6ff. Koerber to London, 17 October 1878 RG17 vol. 234, file 24032, and Koerber to Minister, 3 November 1878: "Dr. Hahn has taken it into his energetic hands to bring you the Württemberg emigration which is most important for Canada and will adopt considerable proportions." Koerber to London, 17 October 1878 RG17 vol. 234, file 24032.

30 Hahn to Minister, 18 June 1879, RG17 vol. 252, file 26000. Koerber maintained in her speech to the Toronto City Council and in her parliamentary testimony in 1879 and 1880 that Hahn had declined a salary and received reimbursement for expenses only. Appropriations throughout the later 1880s show, however, that he did indeed receive a not unsubstantial salary until the fall of 1889.

31 Elise von Koerber, "Reception and Protection of Female Immigrants in Canada," delivered in Ottawa, spring 1879, available at <www.canadiana.org/ECO/Item Record/63090?id=e471e5d3e77c2e6a>.

32 Bade, *Friedrich Fabri*, 202.

33 Article from *Deutsches Morgenblatt*, November 1878, RG17 vol. 238 docket 24423.

34 Hahn called emigration a momentary loss to Württemberg *"aber durch Anknüpfung von Verbindungen, Eröffnung eines Weges an einen bestimmten Ort, fließt auch etwas zurück."* Hahn, in *Amerika*, 23. He made a similar argument about trade and commercial links in Hahn, *Canada: Meine Reise*, 26.

35 Hahn, "Canada: Vortrag."

36 Hahn, "Wanderung, Auswanderung, Kolonien."

37 Hahn, "Fortschritt von Kanada."

38 Hohenlohe letter, 31 October 1884, printed in *Sessional Papers* 1885, 160–61.

39 "Families go to the West of the United States on the invitation of friends and relatives, and their assurance of success." Hahn to department, May 1881, RG17 vol. 314, file 32301.

40 Hahn to high commissioner, London, 16 March 1881, RG17 vol. 307, file 31668.

41 High commissioner to Hahn, 22 March 1881, RG17 vol. 307, file 31668.

42 Hahn, "Wanderung, Auswanderung, Kolonien," 9 and 14. See also a draft for a new publication of Hahn's "Nachrichten aus Canada" dated 1888, in Hahn to Colmer, 1 May 1888, RG17 vol. 579, file 65380.

43 In his short autobiography written in 1890, Hahn maintained that as a result of his work *"eine ziemlich große Anzahl Deutscher"* settled in Canada. Hahn, "Hahn, Dr. Otto." The contemporary sympathetic publication by Philippovich, *Auswanderung und Auswanderungspolitik*, 282, claims that his efforts did not meet with much success.

44 Hahn to Colmer, 1 May 1888, RG17 vol. 579, file 65380. The timing of his departure for Canada was probably prompted by the fact that he had several sons who were nearing military age.

Archival Materials

Canada, Parliament, *Sessional Papers*, 1872–1880.

Library and Archives Canada, Records of the Department of External Affairs (RG25); Records of the Department of Agriculture (RG17).

Works Cited

Bade, Klaus. *Friedrich Fabri und der Imperialismus in der Bismarckzeit. Revolution-Depression-Expansion.* Internet edition with a new preface. Osnabrück: 2005. <www.imis.uni-osnabrueck.de/BadeFabri.pdf> (March 2008).

Bretting, Agnes, and Hartmut Bickelmann. *Auswanderungsagenturen und Auswanderervereine im 19. und 20. Jahrhundert.* Stuttgart: Franz Steiner Verlag, 1991.

Cohen, Robin. *Global Diasporas: An Introduction.* Seattle: University of Washington Press, 1997.

Frisse, Ulrich. *Berlin, Ontario (1800–1916). Historische Identitäten von "Kanadas deutscher Hauptstadt." Ein Beitrag zur deutsch-kanadischen Migrations-, Akkulturations- und Perzeptionsgeschichte des 19. und frühen 20. Jahrhunderts.* New Dundee, ON: Trans-Atlantic Publishing, 2003.

Gabaccia, Donna. "Is Everywhere Nowhere? Nomads, Nations, and the Immigrant Paradigm of United States History." *Journal of American History* 86, no. 3 (1999): 1115–34.

Gerber, David. "Theories and Lives: Transnationalism and the Conceptualization of International Migrations to the United States." *IMIS Beiträge* 15 (2000): 31–53.

Hahn, Otto. *Amerika: Der Bauer und Arbeiter in Schwaben und in Amerika.* Tübingen: Osiandersche Buchhandlung, 1866.

———. *Canada: Meine Reise an den Nipissing (Ontario) und die Schweizerkolonie.* Reutlingen: Carl Rupp, 1878.

———. "Canada: Vortrag gehalten in Reutlingen June 1, 1882." *Jahresbericht des Württembergischen Vereins für Handelsgeographie und Förderung Deutscher Interessen im Ausland* 1 and 2 (1882–1884): 10–14.

———. "Der Fortschritt von Kanada." *Deutsche Kolonialzeitung.* 24 March 1888: 94.

———. "Hahn, Dr. Otto." In *Württembergische Forschungsreisende und Geographen des 19. Jahrhunderts: Festschrift zur Feier des 25 jährigen Regierungsjubiläums Sr. Majestät des Königs Karl/im Auftrag des Württ. Vereins für Handelsgeographie* edited by Emil Metzger. 106–09. Stuttgart: W. Kohlhammer, 1889.

———. "Wanderung, Auswanderung, Kolonien." *Jahresbericht des Württembergischen Vereins für Handelsgeographie und Förderung Deutscher Interessen im Auslande* 5/6 (1888): 1–21.

Hoerder, Dirk. "The German-Language Diasporas: A Survey, Critique, and Interpretation." *Diaspora* 11, no. 1 (2002): 7–44.

Macdonald, Norman. *Canada: Immigration and Colonization 1841 to 1903.* Toronto: Macmillan, 1966.

Philippovich, E. von., ed. *Auswanderung und Auswanderungspolitik in Deutschland.* Leipzig: Verein für Socialpolitik, 1892.

Wagner, Jonathan. *A History of Migration from Germany to Canada, 1850–1939.* Vancouver: University of British Columbia Press, 2006.

Walsh, John C. "Landscapes of Longing: Colonization and the Problem of State Formation in Canada West." PhD diss., University of Guelph, 2001.

West, Roxroy. "Canadian Immigration Agents and Swiss Immigration, 1870–1930." MA thesis, University of Ottawa, 1978.

Zwink, Eberhard. "Otto Hahn (1828–1904): Stationen auf dem Lebensweg eines Hahn-/Paulus-Nachkommen." *Pietismus und Neuzeit* 24 (1998): 328–53.

EIGHTEEN

German Migrants in Postwar Britain

Immigration Policy, Recruitment, and Reception

Johannes-Dieter Steinert

Inge Weber-Newth

The reception of Germans in Britain in the immediate postwar period must be seen in the broader context of a labour shortage that could not be satisfied by the domestic workforce. Germans were targeted as part of a comprehensive recruitment initiative that was aimed primarily at eastern European refugees and former forced labourers. This chapter gives insight into the thinking behind the British government's decision to favour some selected ethnic groups whilst excluding others. It will first focus on the general political framework of British postwar immigration policy, which enabled the recruitment and reception of foreign nationals. An overview is then given of the experiences of those Germans who arrived in Britain as a result of this policy. It highlights the migrants' perception of life during the early stages of their migration and shows how the circumstances of their arrival affected their reception in Britain. This contribution draws on the results of a research project that was carried out in the late 1990s.[1]

AMONG THE ONE MILLION MIGRANTS Britain received between 1945 and 1951[2] there were almost 60,000 German nationals. The reception of Germans in Britain was by no means a new phenomenon, since Britain had welcomed and integrated Germans at different times in history. But their admission shortly after the end of World War II against the background of war crimes and mass murder is significant. It must be seen in the broader context of a recruitment initiative for foreign labour led by the British government, which targeted mainly East Europeans: 80,000

Ukrainians, Poles, and Balts, former forced labourers and refugees from camps in Germany and Austria who were allowed entry under the "Westward Ho" scheme. In addition, 8,000 Ukrainian prisoners of war who had fought in the SS (and had been brought to Britain from Italy in 1947) settled in Britain side by side with their East European compatriots. At the same time, the British government restricted the immigration of Jewish survivors of the Holocaust and was anxious not to encourage non-white British subjects to enter the country and to settle permanently.

As different policies guided the recruitment process, for the purposes of this chapter the total number of about 60,000 German migrants are broken down into different groups:

- some 15,000 former prisoners of war, who were allowed to remain in Britain;
- about 10,000 women recruited in Germany under the government's "North Sea" scheme for work in the public health systems and in hardship households;
- more than 20,000 German female work permit holders, committed by contract to private domestic work;
- approximately 10,000 war brides, married to British soldiers or members of the Control Commission for Germany;
- some 1,300 male and female ethnic Germans (born in East European countries) included in the official Westward Ho scheme; and
- more than 1,300 German women from the Sudeten area of Czechoslovakia, recruited for work in the cotton mills of Lancashire, also under the Westward Ho scheme.

British Immigration Policy

The British decision to recruit foreign labour was the result of great external debts and an acute need for labour immediately after the war.[3] In order to raise its exports quickly, the government decided to strengthen the old industries: coal mining and the textile, iron, and steel industries. However, foreign workers were also required in the newly founded national health system and in agriculture, as well as for construction work and in the domestic sector.

In general, the employment of foreign labour was not a new occurrence, but for the first time, government officials were involved in the development and application of this process. In making this decision, the British government took into consideration its own foreign policy (especially its relations with the USSR at the start of the Cold War), public opinion at home, and the interests of trade unions and employers. Recruitment was not influenced by humanitarian considerations but by job skills, age, sex, and personal independence, the latter being important because of the shortage of accommodation in postwar Britain.[4]

Although the state of the labour market was a major consideration, it would be misleading to explain British policy purely as a response to its needs. The demand for labour could have easily been met by workers from the local populations in the dominions or colonies, who were British subjects. The decision to recruit displaced persons (DPs) in Europe was, however, a decision against non-white British subjects and against encouraging them to come to Britain.[5] In 1949 the report of the Royal Commission on Population declared: "Immigration on a large scale into a fully established society like ours could only be welcomed without reserve if the immigrants were of good human stock and were not prevented by their religion or race from intermarrying with the host population and becoming merged in it.[6]

By giving preference to Europeans and assuming that they would be more skilled and easier to assimilate than non-Europeans, British policy racialized potential migrants.[7] Furthermore, Europeans could be tied to their work by contract for a period of time and be deported, if necessary. It was also feared that non-white migrants might be more interested in social benefits than work.[8] Such ethno-political criteria played a role in the immigration policies of most overseas and European countries.[9]

It is significant that for Britain race ranked higher than nationality, clearly demonstrating the contradiction between "formal nationality policy" and "informally constructed national identity."[10] Regardless of any legal definition, only a white person was considered to have the necessary qualities and abilities to become "really British."

The Westward Ho scheme began in 1947, and was almost immediately followed by a political debate about the employment of German male and female workers. Initially this discussion focused on the question of the continued employment of German prisoners of war, mainly working in agriculture since 1945. The peak was reached in August 1946, when more than 360,000 men were employed. The start of repatriation was accompanied by heated public discussion about "slaves" and "forced labour" in Britain with a degree of sympathy for the German "underdogs," especially in small villages where German prisoners of war (POWs) were billeted on farms and were well known by the locals.

Finally, after extensive negotiations, even the British trade unions agreed that all German POWs who signed an individual contract with a farmer could remain in Britain. They had to stay on the farms and were bound to agricultural work for a number of years. The conditions guaranteed that the Germans were unable to compete with British farm workers and they worked and lived on farms rejected by British workers.[11]

The recruitment of German women under the Westward Ho or the North Sea scheme was also linked to the migration of DPs.[12] In view of the great demand for accommodation during the postwar years, only single men and women were recruited—it was only at the initial stage that some families were incorporated and family hostels built.[13] Because female DPs in Europe were increasingly unwilling to come to Britain without their dependants and the possibility of satisfying demand by recruitment of women from Italy appeared unlikely,[14] the British government favoured a plan to recruit German women and ethnic German women for the textile industries. Again, it was up to the unions to decide. In Lancashire and West Riding the unions opposed the idea of employing German women in the mills but agreed to the employment of ethnic Germans. There was also consent from Lancashire's cotton industry unions regarding the entry of German women from the Sudetenland. In view of the traditional textile industry in this area, these German refugees seemed a useful source of labour. Since most of them had been expelled from Czechoslovakia to the American zone of occupation in Germany, a bilateral British-American agreement had to be negotiated. The original British idea not to treat these women as German nationals irrespective of their former naturalization (from Czech to German) had to be abandoned because of American intransigence, and the Sudeten women entered Britain bearing German passports. The unions refrained from opposition and the government avoided publicity.[15] However, the expectations of filling the "manpower" gap in the export-oriented cotton industry with young, unattached, and skilled female Sudeten German migrants were too optimistic. "Britain's Bread Hangs by Lancashire's Thread" was a popular slogan, reflecting the critical situation of the British economy.[16] The scheme was introduced in 1949, but all hopes were dashed when only 1,304 women were prepared to go to Lancashire—the economic situation in Germany had changed and for many young women the prospect of leaving their family, fiancés, and friends was not at all tempting.

The ethnic Germans, including the Sudeten women, and the former German POWs received unlimited residence rights. In contrast, the German women recruited under the North Sea scheme for work in British hospitals and hardship households were given work permits allowing them to stay for only two or three years, with the possibility of extension. The scheme operated between January 1949 and December 1950 and enabled 9,713 German women to go to Britain, selected and supported by British government officials[17] Their introduction to the British public was unspectacular, but not free from risk to the government. A test of public opinion took place in July 1948 when British newspapers reported the impressions of a British delegation of female members of Parliament and the chief woman officer of the Trades Union Congress during their visits and discussions in Germany. The *Yorkshire Observer*, for example, headlined its front-page article "To Aid Industry. Britain May Get German Women."[18]

The absence of negative public reaction encouraged the Ministry of Labour to inform the British press a month later about the recruitment of a limited number of German women for "domestic work in hospitals and institutions and for farmers' households in urgent need of domestic help." The statement continued:

> There are many thousands of women in the British zone of Germany who have been wanting to work in England [sic] for the past two years, but the British Government has feared the effect on public opinion and has moved slowly and cautiously.... The future for large numbers of young women in Germany today is bleak, many have little prospect of marriage in Germany. Obviously, there will be hopes of finding homes and husbands in this country, and it is over this that the Government fears that British women will resent their coming. But if this country needs German women to work here, it cannot deny to those who volunteer the ordinary human chances of a happy personal life.[19]

Like all other European migrants, the German women filled a gap in the British labour market. Their jobs were often physically strenuous, sometimes dangerous, and always unpopular for British workers. These factors together with their restricted work permits made it easier for the unions to agree.

While the various steps of political decision making can be construed in light of the governmental files kept in the Public Record Office (PRO), the question of why British officials preferred German migrants to other Europeans and praised them highly remains inexplicable. This allows for much speculation, but there is no clear answer. In 1948 an immigration officers' report recorded: "Speaking generally the [German] girls seem to be of a much better type than the average DP."[20] A similar statement was made by a Foreign Office official who traced the ability of German POWs to assimilate in September 1947: "They are of good stock and more easily assimilated to the British economy than other foreign immigrants."[21] And in April 1949 a Ministry of Labour official noted: "It is thought that the rather better knowledge of English possessed by German and Austrian women had made it easier for them to settle down. Both groups have more in common with the British people than the EVWs [European Volunteer Workers] and can therefore more easily acclimatise themselves to life in this country."[22]

Reception and Experience in Britain

The migrants' first experiences and the chance to meet and mix socially with British people were largely determined by the type of work they took up. The POWs gradually started to grow into their local communities after the strict ban on fraternization was lifted.[23] This was particularly the case once they had left the POW camps and were billeted in farms. Often separated from their German compatriots on isolated farms, they made friends with British people, who admired their hard work and showed some understanding for their fate. Many POWs married British women and initially remained in the rural areas. A return to Germany was not considered since many of them had lost their social ties during the years in the army and in captivity. Many also originated from the eastern territories to which they were unable to return, or from the eastern part of Germany—now under communist rule—to which they did not wish to return. Generally, the settling-in process developed relatively smoothly as the POWs were not regarded as competitors for jobs or accommodation. Thus possible conflicts were limited, but this changed when work restrictions ceased.

The 10,000 war brides experienced a different start. They had met their future husbands as soldiers or members of the British Control Commission and were conscious that their decision to follow their boyfriends or fiancés to Britain was not of a temporary nature. In general, war brides were able to rely on support from their partners; sometimes their in-laws provided accommodation and helped them to find their way into society. However, marital problems were recorded by church officials and occasionally mentioned in interviews.[24] The interviews suggest that, apart from personal problems, this was particularly the case for women who had come to Britain with high expectations for their new lives. Many did not anticipate the austere economic situation of postwar Britain. Disappointed by a life with material shortages and a husband's modest civilian status or unable to cope with a demobbed, unemployed husband, many women separated from their husbands and returned to Germany.[25]

This is in contrast to the women who migrated to Britain for employment reasons. Only women who opted for the health sector had a real chance of meeting British partners. Due to the location of their workplace, the majority of women recruited as domestics in households and those in the textile industry met foreign partners, predominantly from East European countries. Whereas most women married to British husbands followed the national agenda of giving up full-time work during the 1950s, women married to East Europeans had set high material goals, which were only achievable when both partners worked full time.

The recruited women also experienced different work environments. Although work in a hospital or sanatorium was sometimes linked to health risks (particularly in a tuberculosis ward or sanatorium) and was described as physically strenuous, overall they viewed their work experience as positive. Patients depended on their care and they were gradually given varied jobs and responsibility on the wards, which improved their status. They enjoyed being needed and respected by patients and staff alike. In their interviews they often remembered fondly the work environment with staff from other nationalities and their independence as young professional women.

Women who were employed in hardship households had a different experience; they complained about loneliness, isolation, homesickness, and their dependence on one employer.[26] But the work and living conditions of the Sudeten women in Lancashire's cotton industry were also described as difficult. Hostels and mills made a grim impression, particularly the noisy and dirty work environment with old-fashioned machinery. Additionally, the women in this environment felt much more that they were the targets of discriminatory harassment from other workers than women in the health sector, who felt protected by their institutions. Not surprisingly, a significant number of the women left the mills before their contracts expired; others used the textile crisis in 1952 to leave the industry or the area altogether. In the meantime, many Sudeten women had met and married partners from eastern Europe. One of the attractions to them was the ability of the men to speak German and to share a preference for continental food. In the short term this was comforting and eased the feeling of exclusion. In the longer run, marriages with other migrants had a slowing effect on their English-language acquisition and a full immersion into British life.

For those Germans who remained and settled in Britain after their contracts expired, the reason for their settlement in Britain was personal: most of the recruited women and POWs had already married or were in serious relationships after their work contracts had terminated. Single or unattached migrants returned to Germany or migrated further, for example to the United States or Canada.

Life for the ex-POWs and recruited women in Britain started with nothing materially but most managed to adapt quickly and achieved a modest living standard without much outside support. This is particularly true of the recruited women in the textile industry, whose motivation to leave their communal accommodation typically led to the purchase of a small house within a few years of their arrival. They managed this financially through hard work, sometimes taking multiple jobs, and a complete absence of any holidays or extravagances.[27] The theme of hard work runs also through the interviews with most ex-POWs, who defined themselves through a lifetime of hard work. Many left industrial work after several years to become self-employed, mainly in the service sector. However, hardly any ex-POWs reached high or influential social positions in their jobs. The majority felt that their German background had prevented them from achieving more.

In general gender roles were clearly defined: women bore sole responsibility for upbringing their children and organizing their households. Experiences of wartime frugality and sacrifice helped them to manage during the difficult postwar years in Britain. It is to the credit of the women that they successfully transmitted German to their children, who spoke it usually until they started school; thereafter, the children wanted to conform to the dominant culture. German mothers were very ambitious for their children to perform well at school, to attend grammar school, and, if possible, to obtain a higher education. In many cases the second generation achieved what was impossible for the first generation: ascent to the middle classes.

According to most of the recruited women interviewed, they had married quickly and without a long courting time, often for pragmatic reasons. Based on the desire to secure a safe home for their children, the marriages lasted a lifetime. German churches—both Catholic and Protestant—played a crucial role in the pastoral care of the German migrants; they also fulfilled an important social function by providing the much-needed space for cultural gatherings.

The reception of the Germans in the late 1940s and early '50s took place in a cultural climate that was still affected by the experiences of war and the revelations of war crimes. Large parts of the British population held negative attitudes toward Germans as shown by the results of a Mass Observation Study carried out in 1946, in which about half of the group sampled expressed antagonism or an entire lack of sympathy for Germans.[28] Later studies showed slight improvements but negative attitudes toward Germans prevailed well into the 1950s.[29] Examples of this can be found in contemporary radio plays or films.[30]

The interviews show that migrants were aware of an anti-German climate, although regional differences were noticed.[31] Some felt they had to make a conscious effort to hide their nationality and had developed particular mechanisms and strategies, part of which was avoiding the use of German in public. Some consciously tried to avoid negative attention and led an unassuming and inconspicuous lifestyle; others mentioned that they felt the adaptation to British cultural norms and to appear British was important: "to avoid trouble; it was necessary to be quiet."[32] The wish not to appear German in public also led them to anglicize names and to hide their country of origin. The latter was widely practised, particularly among the ethnic Germans, who often preferred to be identified as Czechs or Poles. One of those interviewed characterized the strategy of migrants of his generation: "All Germans who live here [in Britain] aim at submerging because they have this inferiority complex which stems from the war."[33] Their spatially dispersed settlement helped them to establish their lives in relative ethnic anonymity.

Images of the Germans as Nazis and their portrayal as enemies in the media existed over years and—for some combined with the occasional experience of direct hostility—had a powerful impact on the way the migrants and their families perceived their reception in Britain. Many Germans felt nationally stigmatized and judged the first decade after their arrival in Britain as uncomfortable. Although most migrants accepted Germany as the perpetrator of war, the interviews reveal a forceful dimension of their own war memories, which were shaped by the experiences of flight, bombing, expulsion, or rape. In their view Germans had also suffered greatly as victims of the war. They personally felt unjustly identified as perpetrators purely on grounds of their nationality and wished that a broader, more differentiated perspective would prevail.

The conditions of their migration as single persons and their dispersed settlement all over Britain allowed relatively little contact or cohesion among the migrants. As a consequence of Germany's role during the two world wars, German communities that could have provided a German infrastructure or space for cultural exchange no longer existed.[34] The only form of community life that existed on a very small scale was offered by the few Catholic and Protestant churches in some areas of Britain. Although these churches provided a very important focal point for some individuals, they were hardly seen as a substitute for the missing community life that other ethnic minorities could turn to. Thus many experienced the early years in Britain as outsider. Even after having lived in Britain for more than fifty years some Germans expressed the feeling that they still do not really belong to British society. Not surprisingly, then, most Germans (except the war brides) kept their original citizenship. Their passport embodied their strong relationship with Germany. Most saw citizenship as an expression of national belonging that is unchangeable. Comments such as "I was born German and I will die German" were no exception.[35]

These individuals' relationship with Germany is mainly based on memories of their original *Heimat*, and the childhood and youth left behind. Their relationship to the Federal Republic of Germany, however, was ambivalent: on the one hand, many continued to follow the development of modern Germany with great interest (via satellite television, for example) and to identify proudly with Germany's achievements after the war; on the other hand, they felt alienated from the country they had left more than fifty years earlier. Despite the strong bonds with their country of origin, most felt ambiguous about their belonging. A commonly expressed feeling of identity is that they felt German when in Britain, but British when in Germany. In old age, several were toying with the idea of returning to Germany, particularly if they no longer had any family ties in Britain and lived in poor circumstances on modest pensions and with few social contacts. Nonetheless, despite having faced severe problems initially, most interviewees did not consider returning to Germany, and only a few said they had missed the chance of return. Having set up home in Britain, mostly in their own properties, having raised families and lived there for more than fifty years, they had come to regard Britain as their home.

Conclusion

The Germans who chose to stay in Britain after their work contracts expired assimilated well into British society, as the government had expected in their original prognosis. The provision of work, the closeness of a West European culture, a relatively dispersed settlement, and the absence of a German community provided ideal conditions for this process. The migrants themselves wanted to be accepted by their British communities; they were prepared to adapt quickly to the English language and to conform to British cultural norms. The analysis of the life stories also reveals that assimilation into the new culture often only occurred superficially or remained partial. No migrant interviewed identified himself or herself as British and most preferred to keep their German citizenship. This expression of identity and loyalty to their country of origin is linked to the circumstances that led to their arrival in Britain. In retrospect most of the Germans in this study see their migration as an inevitable result of war and as their only possible choice at the time. Thus the immigration policy of the British government created a framework for settlement but did not anticipate that the general cultural environment was not yet ready to fully welcome the former enemy so soon after the end of war.

Notes

1 Steinert and Weber-Newth, *Labour & Love*; Weber-Newth and Steinert, *Germans in Postwar Britain*.
2 Isaac, *British Post-War Migration*, 170.
3 See, for example, Cairncross, *Years of Recovery*.
4 For a comprehensive account of British postwar recruitment of foreign labour in Europe, see Kay and Miles, *Refugees or Migrant Workers?*

5 *Population Policy*, 114.
6 *Royal Commission*, 124.
7 See, for example, Holmes, *A Tolerant Country*, 51.
8 Layton-Henry, *The Politics of Immigration*, 27–28.
9 See Steinert, *Migration und Politik*.
10 Paul, "The Politics of Citizenship," 462.
11 Public Record Office (PRO), London, Foreign Office [FO] 371/70541, Ministry of Agriculture and Fisheries [MAF] to FO, 3 August 1948; FO to MAF, 8 August 1948; Home Office [HO] to MAF, 12 August 1948.
12 For the historical context see Steinert and Weber-Newth, *Beyond Camps and Forced Labour*.
13 Kay, "Westward Ho."
14 PRO FO 371/66714, George Isaacs to Ernest Bevin, 4 November 1947.
15 PRO LAB 13/44.
16 Singleton, "Decline," 301.
17 PRO HO 213/596.
18 "To aid industry."
19 "German Women for Britain."
20 PRO HO 213/1794, Immigration Officers' Report Munster DP Transit Camp: Operation Westward Ho, 1 October 1948.
21 PRO FO 371/64379, Note FO, 25 September 1947.
22 PRO Ministry of Labour [LAB] 26/261, précis of reports received from Regional Office, April 1949.
23 PRO War Office [WO] 32/11686, memorandum, 12 December 1946.
24 See Steinert and Weber-Newth, *Labour & Love*.
25 Deutscher Caritasverband, Freiburg, 372.16, Übersicht über das Problem der seelsorgerischen Betreuung der deutschen Zivilarbeiter, May 1949; Evangelisches Zentralarchiv, Berlin, 6/85/185, Hans Bolewski, Bericht über meine Tätigkeit als Auslandspfarrer in Schottland, 20 October 1950.
26 PRO FO 105/249, Else S. (Easingwood) to Margarete Fuhrmann, 17 July 1949.
27 "Interview Elly G.," Steinert and Weber-Newth, *Labour & Love*, 241.
28 IWM Harvester Mass-Observation Archive, February 1948, File Report (No. 2565): Attitudes to the German People: A Review of Attitude Changes among British Public during the War.
29 Gallup, *Gallup International Public Opinion Polls*.
30 Falcon, "Images of Germany."
31 Steinert and Weber-Newth, *Labour & Love*.
32 "Interview Kurt N.," Steinert and Weber-Newth, *Labour & Love*, 267.
33 "Interview Harry L." Steinert and Weber-Newth, *Labour & Love*, 267.
34 See Panayi, *Germans in Britain*.
35 "Interviews Günther S.," Steinert and Weber-Newth, *Labour & Love*, 279.

Archival Material

Deutscher Caritasverband, Freiburg.
Evangelisches Zentralarchiv, Berlin.
Imperial War Museum (IWM), London. Harvester Mass-Observation Archive.
Public Record Office (PRO), London.

Interview Sources

All interviews are published in Johannes-Dieter Steinert and Inge Weber-Newth, *Labour & Love. Deutsche in Großbritannien nach dem Zweiten Weltkrieg* (Osnabrück: Secolo, 2000).

Works Cited

Cairncross, Alec. *Years of Recovery: British Economic Policy 1945–51.* London and New York: Methuen, 1985.

Falcon, Richard. "Images of Germany and the Germans in British Film and Television Fictions: A Brief Chronological Overview." In *As Others See Us: Anglo-German Perceptions*, edited by Harald Husemann, 7–27. Frankfurt: Peter Lang, 1994.

Gallup, George H. *The Gallup International Public Opinion Polls. Great Britain 1937–1975.* New York: Random House, 1976.

"German Women for Britain. Hospitals and Farms." *Manchester Guardian*, 5 August 1948.

Holmes, Colin. *A Tolerant Country? Immigrants, Refugees, and Minorities in Britain.* London: Faber and Faber, 1991.

Isaac, Julius. *British Post-War Migration.* Cambridge: Cambridge University Press, 1954.

Kay, Diana. "Westward Ho! The Recruitment of Displaced Persons for British Industry." In *European Immigrants in Britain 1933–1950*, edited by Johannes-Dieter Steinert and Inge Weber-Newth, 151–71. Munich: Saur, 2003.

Kay, Diana, and Robert Miles. *Refugees or Migrant Workers? European Volunteer Workers in Britain 1946–1951.* London and New York: Routledge, 1992.

Layton-Henry, Zig. *The Politics of Immigration: Immigration, "Race," and "Race" Relations in Post-War Britain.* Oxford: Blackwell Publishing, 1992.

Panayi, Panikos, ed. *Germans in Britain since 1500.* London: Hambledon Press, 1996.

Paul, Kathleen. "The Politics of Citizenship in Post-War Britain." *Contemporary Record* (1992): 452–73.

Population Policy in Great Britain. A Report by PEP. London: Political and Economic Planning, 1948.

Royal Commission on Population. Report. London: His Majesty's Stationery Office, 1949.

Singleton, John. "The Decline of the British Cotton Industry Since 1940." In *The Lancashire Cotton Industry: A History Since 1700*, edited by Mary B. Rose, 296–324. Preston: Lancashire County Books, 1996.

Steinert, Johannes-Dieter. *Migration und Politik. Westdeutschland—Europa—Übersee 1945–1961.* Osnabrück: Secolo, 1995.

Steinert, Johannes-Dieter, and Inge Weber-Newth, eds., *Beyond Camps and Forced Labour: Current International Research on Survivors of Nazi Persecution.* Proceedings of the first international multidisciplinary conference on "Beyond Camps and Forced Labour," London, 29–31 January 2003 (Osnabrück: Secolo, 2005).

Steinert, Johannes-Dieter, and Inge Weber-Newth. *Labour & Love. Deutsche in Großbritannien nach dem Zweiten Weltkrieg.* Osnabrück: Secolo, 2000.

"To Aid Industry. Britain May Get German Women." *Yorkshire Observer,* 9 July 1948.

Weber-Newth, Inge, and Johannes-Dieter Steinert. *Germans in Postwar Britain: An Enemy Embrace.* London: Routledge, 2005.

NINETEEN

Immigration of German-speaking People to the Territory of Modern-day Turkey (1850–1918)

Christin Pschichholz

German migration to the Ottoman Empire in the nineteenth century and prior to World War I was a phenomenon altogether different from the waves of German emigrants to North and South America. The number of German people in Istanbul was around three thousand by World War I. This chapter argues, however, that between 1850 and 1918 German immigrants in modern-day Turkey faced an experience distinct from that of other expatriated Germans as a result of several factors, notably Ottoman societal practices of defining minorities on the basis of religion. Focusing mainly on Izmir and Istanbul, this chapter shows that the German-speaking migrants were not a self-contained group. They were primarily merchants and artisans who developed different patterns of assimilation in the cosmopolitan environment. The activities of the Deutsche Evangelische Gemeinde in Istanbul offers insight into different tendencies of assimilation of this very diverse group in terms of ancestry, family status, duration of stay, social background, therewith religion and mentality.

OTTOMAN GERMAN AND TURKISH GERMAN MIGRATION patterns merit attention, if for no other reason than the sheer number of Turkish immigrants currently residing in Germany. For most scholars, however, German migration to the Ottoman and Turkish territories is still largely considered an exotic field of research.[1] This is probably due to the comparatively small number of German-speaking migrants in the

Ottoman Empire, as well as the long-lasting lack of interest of German historians in subjects related to the Ottoman Empire other than issues of
diplomacy and political relations.[2] German migration to the Ottoman
Empire in the nineteenth century and prior to World War I was a phenomenon altogether different from the waves of German emigration to
North and South America. Because the small settlements in today's Turkey
existed in a specific political and cultural environment, however, this subject is valuable for studies on the commonalities and differences experienced by German-speaking immigrants in general. Various domestic
changes, including reforms and conflicts in the multi-ethnic Ottoman
Empire, the political imperialistic influence of European powers, and the
heterogeneous Ottoman society, offer an extraordinary perspective on
German-speaking immigration.[3]

The period under consideration starts with the noticeable growth of
German-speaking migration in the middle of the nineteenth century to
cities such as Istanbul and Izmir, and ends after World War I with the
expulsion of Germans due to the occupation of the French and English
armies.[4] Although there were small German-speaking settlements along
railway lines and in the Black Sea region, the main focus of this chapter
will be restricted to the larger settlements in Istanbul and Izmir. It discusses the migration process and questions the contemporary characterization of German-speaking migrants as a "German colony." After a brief
and general overview of European migration to the Ottoman Empire,
there follows an analysis of the communities in terms of their migration
background and characteristic stages of development, as well as their coexistence with Ottoman society and the role of the Deutsche Evangelische
Gemeinde in fostering intra-group cohesion, religion, and nationalism. The
records of the Gemeinde, a group that settled in areas that are in the territory of Turkey today, provide the main sources. These include the correspondence between the Gemeinden and different German ministries
and authorities, detailed annual reports, and the church register. They
provide statistical background and address topics important to German-
speaking immigration.

European Migration to the Ottoman Empire

To understand immigration processes, it is important to be
aware of specific characteristics of the host country. Although the following general remarks cannot give a complete overview of the complex issue
of migration into and within the Ottoman Empire, they can help put the
German-speaking immigration into an appropriate context. In the introduction to their survey of the sociohistorical phenomenon of migration
in the Ottoman Empire, Fikret Adanir and Hilmar Kaiser state that "the

geographic space in which the Ottoman Empire was located has, throughout history, been a typical zone of human migration, if we take the term in its broadest meaning, that is, moving and passing from one country, place, or locality to another, permanently or periodically."[5] Migration occurred for economic and political reasons and it affected the demographic structure of the population in the Ottoman Empire.[6] One aspect of the complex migration processes in the nineteenth century is the migration from European countries to the commercial centres of the Empire such as Aleppo, Beirut, Istanbul, Izmir, and Salonika. Besides the demographic growth resulting from internal migration from Anatolia and European countries, the development in these cities included the fusion of traditional aspects with processes of modernization. The embassies, numerous shops, and long-time inhabitants of European origin, who were engaged in trade mostly with Ottoman Greeks and Armenians, indicate the presence of European communities in the Istanbul districts of Galata and Pera (Beyoğlu). The new commercial and financial centres outside the old "economic heart," between Eminönü and Beyazid, became attractive alternatives. As a result, a complex interplay of domestic developments and transformation processes emerged in these multi-ethnic Ottoman cities.[7]

The lenient nature of the Ottoman policy toward foreigners enabled the effortless entry of migrants. For centuries, outsiders had easy access to Ottoman lands. Merchants, for example, were allowed not only to cross the borders, but also to reside within the empire without becoming subjects of the Ottoman sultan.[8] The so-called capitulations—amnesties that guaranteed residence, travel, and trade in the Ottoman territories—formed the basis of foreign trade. Documents known as *ahdnames* were formally granted by the head of the Islamic community in return for a pledge of friendship from the non-Muslims. These also guaranteed juridical, political, and religious rights. First rights were given to France and England, but even western nations lacking capitulations before the second half of the sixteenth century could be active in Levant trade—trade with a large area of today's Middle East—by travelling under the flag of nations holding capitulations, or through the intervention of the Genoese, Venetians, or Ragusans. Against this background, European migration mainly took place within centres of commerce.[9] From a European perspective, therefore, the Ottoman Empire was already a destination for migrants long before the nineteenth century. German-speaking migrants before then were an infrequent part of this process. As Ralf C. Müller mentioned in his analysis of immigration from western and central Europe to the Ottoman Empire in the fifteenth and sixteenth centuries, long-term residence of German-speaking merchants occurred along commercial routes. Moreover, German handicrafts in the sixteenth century were distributed not only regionally but also further afield through migration. German-speaking artisans did not confine themselves to migrating within German-speaking territories, or to the often assumed radius of the Netherlands, Paris, Rome, Croatia, Siebenbürgen (Transylvania), the Baltic provinces, southern Sweden, and Denmark; they also crossed the borders of the Ottoman Empire.[10] These initiatives led to an increase in the number of German-speaking migrants in the nineteenth century.

German-Speaking Communities in Istanbul and Izmir

This increased number of German merchants in the Levantine in the 1830s and '40s were involved mostly in commissioned business.[11] Unlike the financial distress that led many artisans to migrate and take up residence in the Ottoman Empire in increasing numbers, it was the commercial attractiveness of the Ottoman port cities that motivated the migration of merchants. The church registries show that a variety of craftspersons were represented among German-speaking migrants. A limited number of small salespeople, coachmen, and medical professionals also complemented the German-speaking settlement in the middle of the nineteenth century.

But where did the German-speaking people come from? Reports of church organizations and pastors make clear that German artisans wandered in search of employment across the Balkans and areas of Russia until they came to Ottoman port cities such as Istanbul and Izmir. While some stayed for long periods or their whole lives, others chose to continue their journey after a short sojourn. Focusing on this aspect, the annual report of the Deutsche Evangelische Gemeinde indicated that migrants had come to Istanbul after temporarily settling or travelling in areas of Hungary, Moldova, Wallachia, Greece, Russia, or the European parts of the Ottoman Empire.[12] Thus, the migration to Istanbul and Izmir was linked, at least in part, to the migration of individuals in the first half of the nineteenth century across the eastern borders of what was later the German Empire.

The birthplaces of the German-speaking migrants included the territories of the later German Empire, Bohemia, Moravia, and Austria, as well as Russia, the Black Sea region, Romania, Hungary, and the Balkans. These had all been destinations of waves of migration from Hessen, West Prussia, southwest Germany, and Poland in the eighteenth and nineteenth centuries. Even a small number of birthplaces in Italy and Greece are mentioned, as are the descendants of German-speaking migrants who were born in Ottoman cities.

Because of the fact that primarily unmarried artisans and merchants came to Istanbul, men dominated the migration process. Women, however, constituted a substantial minority as wives or daughters. The presence of deaconesses and nurses, who belonged to the category of temporary migrants, makes it impossible to define female migrants solely as fellow passengers.

In 1850, the number of German-speaking people in Istanbul was around one thousand, which increased to three thousand by World War I. In Izmir, by contrast, the number of artisans, workers, and merchants was considerably lower. In the same period, from around the middle of the nineteenth century until 1914, this number increased from approximately 150 to 350 people. Other cities in the territory of modern Turkey accommodated groups of up to a hundred migrants. Small groups of artisans and people involved in the production and trade of silk lived in Bursa, Amasya, and Trabzon. The church registries of the Gemeinde mention German families in Zonguldak, Ereğli, Kütahya, Akşehir, Beyşehir, and Kastamonu. As a result of permission being granted for the construction of a railway at the end of nineteenth century, workers, engineers, engine drivers, and railway officials came to Anatolian cities alongside artisans and workers. Following the expansion of the railway system, communities of German-speaking people settled mainly in Edirne, Konya, and Eskişehir as well as many other cities along the railway.

As previously mentioned, the communities also included people who were connected with German institutions, such as ambassadors, missionaries, deaconesses, and Prussian officers.[13] In Istanbul, the growth of the German community resulted in the establishment of a school, a kindergarten, and a hospital, thus providing employment for teachers, nurses, and doctors. Moreover, the gain in economic influence before World War I resulted in higher exports and an increasing presence of German companies involved mostly in the railway construction and the arms trade.[14] In line with Leslie Page Moch's definition, which states that migration can also include semi-permanent changes in residence,[15] it is useful to divide German migrants into two groups, although these categories are flexible. Migrant labourers, mostly artisans and merchants, formed one group of German-speaking migrants. The other comprised persons sent by German institutions with a specific function, including many railway employees. This categorization does not exclude the fact that temporary migrants often spent much of their life, or even all of it, living in the Ottoman capital. Establishing a business or starting a family reduced the importance of returning home. The process of individual migration to the Ottoman port cities resulted in a heterogeneous group of German-speaking immigrants in terms of ancestry, family status, duration of stay, social background, as well as religious confession, and mentality.

Legal Status and the Deutsche Evangelische Gemeinde

The heterogenic community of German-speaking people, excluding subjects of Austria, were under the administrative charge of the Prussian, and later German, embassy. The capitulations legitimized the German communities—whatever their members' religious confession—as autonomous groups under a deputy or consul.[16] The German immigrants' privileges linked them specifically to the embassy and thereby to German legislation, foreign policy, and German Ottoman relations until the abrogation of the capitulations in 1914. They were thus in a different situation than the Greek Orthodox, Armenian, and Jewish communities, which held semi-autonomous status as millet. These non-Muslim communities had privileges of self-administration and their own religious leaders, but were subject to the Ottoman sultan.

The legal status, language, religion, and cultural background of German immigrants under German jurisdiction around the middle of the nineteenth century created a foundation for social meeting points. The records of the officially recognized Deutsche Evangelische Gemeinde in Istanbul, one such meeting point, provide insight into the developments in the German community. German-speaking Jewish, Catholic, and Protestant migrants first joined other established communities for religious life and services. In the 1820s and '30s, Protestant migrants attended the services of the Swedish and Dutch communities. Thereafter, a German missionary organized services until 1843. Thus, an informal Protestant community was formed. Together with this missionary, some German-speaking Protestants petitioned the Prussian church and king requesting a rectorate that would ensure regular services, religious services in the German language, and a more formally organized Gemeinde. In the same year, Friedrich Wilhelm IV and the Prussian government decided to set up a *Gesandtschaftspredigerstelle*, as they had previously done at other embassies. The delegated pastor and the Gemeinde were integrated into the Prussian church and put under the protection of the Prussian king. With the presence of the pastor and a more unified Gemeinde, German-speaking Protestants could maintain their religion and traditions. Moreover, a pastorate could represent their interests in founding their own school and a welfare association. The Gemeinde grew, in keeping with the overall immigrant flow. In the 1850s, the annual reports mentioned a number of approximately four hundred members, which increased to one thousand at the turn of the century.[17]

Another organization, the Teutonia, which did not have a religious connection, had approximately one hundred members (between 1849 and 1855).[18] It grew out of a *Stammtisch* of artisans and merchants, and was established in Istanbul in 1847. It developed into a centre for German culture and *savoir vivre*, offering performances, lectures, and song festivals. Its clubhouse maintained a library, a bowling alley, and a fencing hall. Besides Teutonia, smaller organizations were formed, such as a gymnastics club, a choral society, and an excursion club.

Increasing economic and political relations during the Wilhelmine era caused the number of engineers, managers of German companies, officials, officers, teachers, and doctors to grow. The formation and development of the Gemeinde and the Teutonia association were similar. Their early organizers in the 1840s were artisans and merchants, but these were gradually replaced by primarily temporary middle-class migrants.

Coexistence within Ottoman Society

The existence of several German institutions such as clubs, schools, and welfare associations, as well as the increasing presence of German companies, might indicate a self-contained German colony. Reports of the Teutonia—mostly given by persons with leading positions in the community or newspaper articles in Germany—give the impression of a German-speaking community as a self-contained group with scant contact with the surrounding population and a low rate of assimilation. This description has even been adopted by recent dissertations and forms a paradigm about non-Muslim minorities that suggests national and monocultural identities.[19] However, these reports should be read in the context of the broad discussion about German emigration in the nineteenth century, including the concept of maintaining the *Volkstum*, informal colonization, and economic influence. Even in the middle of the nineteenth century, the combination of migration and economic influence of non-assimilated groups, as a starting point for informal colonization was popular in publications.[20] This Zeitgeist is reflected in these reports. The characterization, moreover, only applies to a small group of temporary migrants most of whom held positions at German institutions and companies. Indeed, closer inspection shows that the characterization does not reflect the larger group of German-speaking migrants. The records of the Deutsche Evangelische Gemeinde, which were not intended as a public record, reveal that the image of a self-contained group is false. With different points of interaction in the multilayered Ottoman society of the port cities, the German-speaking community was a small minority among many within an Islamic majority. Consequently, there is no discernible pattern of assimilation or non-assimilation, only one of different tendencies.

The German-speaking migrants in Istanbul did not reside in homogenous neighbourhoods like those of long-established groups of Jews, Greek Orthodox, or Armenians. They lived, instead, in districts that were generally preferred by Europeans such as Pera (Beyoğlu), Moda, and

Kadıköy. They also settled in Stambul, Maltepe, Makriköy (Bakırköy), Yedikule, Ortaköy, Erenköy, Yeniköy, and San Stefano (Yeşilköy), as well as in outlying districts along the Bosporus. Accordingly, the German-speaking migrants were scattered in several different districts in a multi-ethnic, multi-religious, and international environment. Interaction between the Ottoman and European communities arose from this multi-ethnic environment. Artisans, for example, were often employees of smaller Turkish companies or conducted business with them. Remarkably, some gardeners, watchmakers, and carpenters worked directly for the sultan.[21] German-speaking merchants who were mostly involved in business with Greeks, Armenians, Turks, and long-time residents or newly arrived Europeans, had to learn Greek, French, Italian, and Turkish, depending on their jobs. The German railway workers with mid-level positions had European as well as Ottoman Christian colleagues.[22] Furthermore, social gatherings in pubs, bars, and coffeehouses were not subject to religious or ethnic segregation, but rather to social status. Intermarriage between different nationalities and Christian confessions was quite common. Sources often highlight marriages of artisans or merchants to Greek, Armenian, and (infrequently) Jewish women as well as members of long-established families with European roots. Yet despite the fact that employment of Germans in Turkish businesses and trade between western merchants and Muslim communities were common, marriages between Europeans and Ottoman Christians were understandably more common than those between Europeans and Ottoman Muslims because they did not require conversion.[23]

Business contacts and social interaction, as well as the integration of ethno-confessional heterogeneous neighbourhoods, reveal that a linguistic demarcation was hardly possible. The oft-mentioned concern of pastors about the disregard of the German language in migrant families shows the linguistic assimilation, especially among second-generation German-speaking migrants. Pastors in Istanbul reported complaints that children of immigrants at the age of six already spoke four or five different languages, yet had no solid knowledge of German. According to the yearly reports, migrant children in Bursa spoke better Turkish than German. In Izmir, the widely spread Greek language was spoken. Families with German parents who spoke mainly German were in the minority.[24] Similarly, pastors complained about the "indifference" of many German Protestants who adopted other religious traditions and did not differentiate strictly between Protestantism and the wide range of other Christian confessions. Such was the case when a German Protestant mother of an ill child said the Lord's Prayer and borrowed the neighbours' Greek Orthodox icons in the hopes of recovery.[25] For the pastor, this anecdote represented a fall from the Protestant faith. At the same time, it illustrates religious-cultural assimilation by integrating other Christian confessions into a migrant's religious life. In general, the intensity of church life among the German-speaking migrants, even apart from those who did not attach importance to it, varied greatly. For a small group, the Gemeinde symbolized the combination of nationalism and religion. Many more migrants, however, saw the Gemeinde as an opportunity to preserve their religious background and mother tongue. Attending a church service in German meant fostering religion and language. The ceremonies of christening, confirmation, and funerals, in particular, connected families over generations with this religious community, thus providing a framework for social contacts.

German migrants in the Ottoman Empire experienced a broad range of encounters in a different cultural, religious, and multilingual environment. Most migrants' experiences fit the concept of accommodation.[26] Through employment, migrants were involved in the host society. Their status can be described as a partial integration that allowed them to keep their own identity. They were more or less active members of the clubs and institutions of the German-speaking community. At the same time they did not live and work in a solely German-speaking environment. Many German-speaking migrants participated in ethnic-cultural pluralism. In Istanbul, for example, primarily merchants, but also other professionals from the middle class, were part of what was referred to in contemporary travelogues as the *Pera-Gesellschaft* or *société de Péra*,[27] European migrant families residing mostly in Pera and bordering districts, who had lived for generations in Istanbul and developed into a bourgeoisie with deep economic and social contacts to the Christian community. A long tradition of the assimilation of migrants among multi-ethnic communities led to a multilingual and cosmopolitan population. Some segregation was also part of the German migrant scene in the host society. Several European migrant groups avoided deeper integration. Temporary migrants working for German companies or institutions were only marginally involved in the cosmopolitan society and thus had very little contact with the Ottoman environment. The Deutsche Evangelische Gemeinde consequently needed to attract a heterogeneous group of immigrants with different social and cultural backgrounds and the capacity to integrate. Prussia sent pastors to the Gemeinde and the archival records of the *Auslandsgemeinden* offer insight into the meaning of the expression "German colony" and the complex network of German institutions and German-speaking migrants it represents. Despite the various national and religious traditions among the Prussian clergy, it is generally true that they felt beholden to church and state because of their closeness to Prussian officialdom. Moreover, the context of migration and increased number of *Auslandsgemeinden*, combined with a national consciousness, formed the foundation for a newly defined theological orientation that combined the interest of the religious diaspora with nationalism and German *Volk* ideology.[28] Two main themes, apart from pastoral care, emerged in the clergymen's reports that reflected the multi-religious environment and the political tensions arising from the imperialistic interest of the European powers in the Ottoman Empire. Pastors were to foster an intra-group cohesion in order to avoid other confessional influence while at the same time aiming to keep members in the Protestant church. Against the background of the polemics between Catholics and Protestants in Germany in the nineteenth and twentieth centuries, it is not surprising that the coexistence of the Greek Orthodox, Russian Orthodox, Syrian Orthodox, Catholic, Armenian Gregorian, and Assyrian faiths was perceived as a challenge.

Pastors also aspired to increase the presence of Protestantism and the German nation through the stability of the Gemeinde. This idea was linked to the aspiration to enlarge the impact of Protestantism and German economic influence. These aspirations, however, were out of touch with the reality of the immigrant community and incompatible with migrant involvement in Ottoman urban society.

The existence of several German institutions, such as clubs, schools, welfare associations, and the increasing presence of German companies, should not overshadow the importance of the many merchants and artisans who were assimilated into multi-ethnic urban Ottoman society. The migrants, who came individually, with different ancestries, family status, and social backgrounds, and who remained for various lengths of time, formed a heterogeneous group and assimilated into a heterogeneous society. As the result of religious, ethnic, and national pluralism, they defined their relationship to religion, language, and nationality in many different ways.

Notes

1 Even the exile of German academics and artists between 1933 and 1945 has not raised much interest in this aspect of German Turkish relations. See Bozay, *Exil Türkei.*

2 For exceptions see Gencer, *Bildungspolitik*; Fuhrmann, *Traum vom deutschen Orient.*

3 For further information see Faroqhi, *Geschichte des Osmanischen Reichs*; Quataert, *Ottoman Empire,* 110–91.

4 After the establishment of the sovereignty of the Turkish Republic in 1923, however, migrants returned, but under modified circumstances.

5 Adanir and Kaiser, "Migration, Deportation, and Nation-Building," 273.

6 Quataert, *Ottoman Empire,* 114. For more information see Karpat, *Ottoman Population.*

7 Eldem, "Istanbul," 202.

8 Faroqhi, *Ottoman Empire,* 213.

9 İnalcık, "Ottoman State," 189.

10 Müller, *Franken im Osten,* 292–352.

11 Annual report 1863/64, Evangelisches Zentralarchiv (EZA) 5/1937, 129.
12 Annual Report 1863/64, EZA 1937, 129.
13 For more information on the delegation of Prussian officers to Ottoman Empire see Wallach, *Anatomie einer Militärhilfe*, 15–18, 42, 61–63.
14 Trumpener, "Germany," 119.
15 Moch, *Moving Europeans*, 8.
16 This occurred with the cooperation of the Ottoman authorities. See İnalcık, "Ottoman State," 190.
17 This number is considerably greater than that of the official registered paying members, since these included only men.
18 Radt, *Geschichte der Teutonia*, 136.
19 Radt, *Geschichte der Teutonia*; Dietrich, *Deutschsein*; Gencer, *Bildungspolitik*, 128.
20 See Fenske, "Ungeduldige Zuschauer," 43.
21 Church register of marriages, 132; church register of deaths, 115, 107.
22 Quataert, *Social Disintegration*, 79.
23 The correspondence of the German embassy indicates that marriage between Germans and Ottoman Muslims occurred but was exceptional. Politisches Archiv (PA), Bestand Konstantinopel, 342.
24 12th Report "Diakonissen-Stationen" 1874–1876, 27; 15th Report "Diakonissen-Stationen" 1880–82, 24; 22nd Report "Diakonissen-Stationen" 1894–96, 20; "Dank- und Denkblätter," VIII. Jg., 1H., 1908, 1; all in Archiv der Fliedner Kulturstiftung (FKSK).
25 3rd Report "Diakonissen-Stationen" 1856–57, 77–78, FKSK.
26 Jürgen Osterhammel describes group strategies of host and foreigners in "Kulturelle Grenzen," 120–22. He bases his discussion on a concept by Christoph Marx.
27 See Tischler, "Interkulturalität," 363; Schmitt, *Levantiner*.
28 Wellnitz, *Deutsche evangelische Gemeinden*, 6. Röhrig, *Diaspora-Kirche in der Minderheit*, 39.

Archival Material

Evangelisches Zentralarchiv (EZA), Berlin.
Politisches Archiv (PA), Berlin.
Archiv der Fliedner Kulturstiftung (FKSK), Düsseldorf.
Evangelische Gemeinde deutscher Sprache, registers, Istanbul.

Works Cited

Adanir, Fikret, and Kaiser, Hilmar. "Migration, Deportation, and Nation-Building: The Case of the Ottoman Empire." In *Migration and Migrants in Historical Perspective. Permanencies and Innovations*, edited by René Leboutte, 273–91. Brussels: Peter Lang, 2000.
Bozay, Kemal. *Exil Türkei. Ein Forschungsbeitrag zur deutschsprachigen Emigration in der Türkei (1933–1945)*. Münster: LIT Verlag, 2001.
Dietrich, Anne. *Deutschsein in Istanbul: Nationalisierung und Orientierung in der deutschsprachigen Community von 1843 bis 1956*. Opladen: Leske + Budrich, 1998.
Eldem, Edhem. "Istanbul: From Imperial to Peripheralized Capital." In *The Ottoman City between East and West: Aleppo, Izmir, and Istanbul*, edited by

Edhem Eldem, Daniel Goffmann, and Bruce Alan Masters, 135–214. Cambridge: Cambridge University Press, 1999.

Faroqhi, Suraiya. *Geschichte des Osmanischen Reiches.* 2nd edition. Munich: Beck, 2001.

Fenske, Hans. "Ungeduldige Zuschauer. Die Deutschen und die europäische Expansion 1815–1880." In *Imperialistische Kontinuität und nationale Ungeduld im 19. Jahrhundert*, edited by Wolfgang Reinhard, 87–140. Frankfurt: Fischer, 1991.

Fuhrmann, Malte. *Der Traum vom deutschen Orient. Zwei deutsche Kolonien im Osmanischen Reich 1851–1918.* Frankfurt: Campus, 2006.

Gencer, Mustafa. *Bildungspolitik, Modernisierung und kulturelle Interaktion. Deutschtürkische Beziehungen (1908–1918).* Münster: LIT Verlag, 2002.

İnalcık, Halil. "The Ottoman State: Economy and Society, 1300–1600." In *An Economic and Social History of the Ottoman Empire*, Volume 1, *1300–1600*, edited by Halil İnalcık, with Donald Quataert, 9–409. Cambridge: Cambridge University Press, 1994.

Karpat, Kemal H. *Ottoman Population 1830–1914: Demographic and Social Characteristics.* Madison: University of Wisconsin Press, 1985.

Moch, Leslie Page. *Moving Europeans. Migration in Western Europe since 1650.* Bloomington: Indiana University Press, 1992.

Müller, Ralf C. *Franken im Osten. Art, Umfang, Struktur und Dynamik der Migration aus dem lateinischen Westen in das osmanische Reich des 15./16. Jahrhunderts auf der Grundlage von Reiseberichten.* Leipzig: Eudora, 2005.

Osterhammel, Jürgen. "Kulturelle Grenzen in der Expansion Europas." *Saeculum* 46 (1995): 101–38.

Quataert, Donald. *The Ottoman Empire 1700–1922.* 3rd edition. Cambridge: Cambridge University Press, 2003.

———. *Social Disintegration and Popular Resistance in the Ottoman Empire, 1881–1908. Reactions to European Economic Penetration.* New York: New York University Press, 1983.

Radt, Barbara. *Geschichte der Teutonia.* Istanbul: Ergon, 2001.

Röhrig, Hermann-Josef. *Diaspora—Kirche in der Minderheit. Eine Untersuchung zum Wandel des Diasporaproblems in der evangelischen Theologie unter besonderer Berücksichtigung der Zeitschrift "Die evangelische Diaspora."* Erfurt: Universität Erfurt, 1992.

Schmitt, Oliver Jens. *Levantiner. Lebenswelten und Identitäten einer ethnokonfessionellen Gruppe im Osmanischen Reich im "langen 19. Jahrhundert."* Munich: Oldenbourg Wissenschaftsverlag, 2005.

Tischler, Ulrike. "Interkulturalität am Schnittpunkt zweier Kontinente. Zur Istanbuler Pera-Gesellschaft im 20. Jahrhundert." In *Übergänge und Verflechtungen. Kultureller Transfer Europa*, edited by Gregor Kokorz and Helga Mitterbauer, 361–76. Bern: Peter Lang, 2004.

Trumpener, Ulrich. "Germany and the End of the Ottoman Empire." In *The Great Powers and the End of the Ottoman Empire*, edited by Marian Kent, 111–40. London: Allen & Unwin, 1996.

Wallach, Jehuda L. *Anatomie einer Militärhilfe. Die preußisch-deutschen. Militärmissionen in der Türkei 1835–1919*. Düsseldorf: Droste, 1976.

Wellnitz, Britta. *Deutsche evangelische Gemeinden im Ausland: ihre Entstehungsgeschichte und die Entwicklung ihrer Rechtsbeziehungen zur Evangelischen Kirche in Deutschland*. Tübingen: Mohr-Siebeck, 2003.

TWENTY

Associating or Quarrelling?

Migration, Acculturation, and Transmission among Social-democratic Sudeten Germans in Canada

Patrick Farges

Sudeten Germans, who immigrated to Canada after World War II due to the loss of their homeland, have become a diaspora within the German Canadian mosaic. However, approximately one thousand of them, refugees from Nazism, settled in Canada prior to that postwar immigration. They came to Canada in 1939 after the Munich Agreement, through which Germany took over the Sudetenland. These refugees first settled as farmers in Saskatchewan and British Columbia, but most of them moved to urban centres in order to find more appropriate jobs. They took an active part in the Canadian left, joining trade unions and the Co-operative Commonwealth Federation (CCF), which later became New Democratic Party (NDP). The "1939ers" also developed an intense network of associations and newspapers, some of which still exist to this day. How did their social democratic values evolve on Canadian soil? To what extent did they take part in bringing about a German Canadian identity? How did they transmit their anti-Nazi and leftist heritage? What was the function of the numerous internal conflicts that existed among them?

THIS CHAPTER, WHICH IS PART OF A RESEARCH PROJECT on the acculturation of migrants, is based on the analysis of "ego documents" (testimonies, autobiographical texts, correspondence, interviews) gathered in archival collections in Canada and elsewhere. It aims at giving a micro-historical, "bottom up" insight into the processes of the formation and transmission of political and memorial patterns within a diasporic community. These primary sources are the "records of many lives" and they "permit a composite view of societies in the process of being created."[1] Exile studies, the field of research that, in the context of this chapter, focuses on German-speaking refugees who fled the rise of Nazism in Europe after 1933, concentrated for a long time solely on the grandiose lives of famous émigrés, neglecting those of "ordinary people."[2] As Waltraud Strickhausen, Annette Puckhaber, and Patrick Farges[3] have shown, the refugees from Nazism who were able to reach Canada in the 1930s were, apart from few exceptions, ordinary people. By allowing fewer than 6,000 refugees to enter the country, Canada demonstrated its narrow-mindedness toward the refugee issue at the time. Approximately 1,000 of those 6,000 were political refugees: anti-Nazi, social-democratic German speakers from the Sudetenland (Czechoslovakia).[4] They became the largest group of German-speaking immigrants at the time and were, in fact, among the very few refugees allowed to enter Canada on a group scheme. They were forced to settle in two remote areas of Northern Saskatchewan and British Columbia, with no regard for their qualifications or professional skills.

Migration as Dense Transition

Migration studies have become an increasingly transnational and interdisciplinary field. Newer approaches to migrant cultures focus on acculturation mechanisms, migration networks, group dynamics, and chain solidarities, i.e., on the meso level between micro-historical analysis and macro-social processes.[5] As with the example of Sudeten German refugees in Canada, the phases of departure, arrival, and memory transmission are shaped by this meso sphere. For them, participating in familial, professional, and political networks formed the basis for their social integration.

The Munich Agreement in September 1938 abruptly changed the fate of the Sudetenland, because it was annexed by Nazi Germany. For the anti-Nazis in the region, among whom were numerous refugees who had left Germany between 1933 and 1938, the situation soon became critical. Hence, approximately 30,000 people fled the Sudetenland toward inner Czechoslovakia.[6] But this refuge did not hold for very long, as Hitler occupied the rest of Bohemia and Moravia in March 1939. Czechoslovakia thus became a gigantic trap for refugees and regime opponents. For one group, safety came from abroad, as the social-democratic leader Wenzel Jaksch[7] had prophesized in an address to the party executive in September 1938: "And if there should be no room left in Europe for freedom-loving Sudeten German social democrats, then perhaps there might be room for them on the plains and in the forests of Canada."[8] Early in 1939, Canadian authorities agreed to let in up to 1,200 families. In the end, however, only 307 families and 72 bachelors (1,053 persons in total) managed to enter Canada before the beginning of the war.

This particular in-migration scheme was the consequence of a specific international context. In 1938, the Evian Conference on refugees had increased international pressure to take in refugees from Europe. By accepting Sudeten Germans, Canada, which had participated in the conference, was somewhat relieved of this pressure. Moreover, in doing so, Ottawa was hoping to please London. With regard to Canadian public opinion, however, this scheme had to remain a secret, and under no circumstance should the Sudeten Germans be considered "landed refugees." Officially, they were agricultural, and hence "preferred," immigrants. In addition, Canada would now be able to refuse "non-preferred" Jewish immigrants, by far the more numerous category among European refugees in the 1930s.[9] The group of Sudeten Germans then travelled from the Polish port of Gdynia (Gedingen) via Sweden to the United Kingdom and finally Canada.[10] They landed in the Maritime provinces during the summer of 1939 and were divided in two groups: 155 families and 37 bachelors travelled by train to the St. Walburg area in northern Saskatchewan to settle on lots belonging to the Canadian National Railway, while the others settled on Canadian Pacific Railway's lots in the Peace River district of British Columbia.[11]

For the Sudeten Germans, who had not been prepared to act as pioneers in the Canadian West, a whole new story began. Group dynamics and group solidarity became core values on which individuals increasingly and crucially depended. The feeling of belonging was partly grounded in a common experience of uprooting and exile, in the transatlantic as well as trans-Canadian adventurous journey, and in the collective survival in the settlements under extreme conditions. In their life stories, the 1939ers recalled how dense this transition between "there" and "here," "then" and "now," the old and the new home really was.[12]

In addition, the group's original socialization as Sudeten Germans and social democrats should not be underestimated. In 1919 under the Treaty of Saint Germain, Sudeten Germans had become German-speaking citizens of the newly founded Czechoslovak Republic. Before that date, they had been subjects of the Austro-Hungarian Empire. Sudeten German social democracy was thus the heir of vehement debates among Austro-Hungarian socialists: the Nationalitätenfrage, Austro-Marxism, etc. A specifically Sudeten German social democracy only emerged at the Congress of Teplitz-Schönau (30 August to 3 September 1919), when Josef Seliger became the leader of an autonomous Deutsche Sozialdemokratische Arbeiterpartei in der Tschechoslowakischen Republik (DSAP). Territorial shifts after 1919 only reinforced the problem of national identities in this multi-ethnic region. In 1931, a Sudeten German social democrat wrote: "No doubt, the political system of parties in Czechoslovakia is the most complex in Central Europe and even in the world ... Each social movement or class party appears under at least two forms in this State with multiple nationalities: as a Czech, a German, a Hungarian and a Slovak movement."[13] The ideal of internationalism was progressively receding and giving way to the idea of national variations of socialism. The Sudeten German refugees thus brought to Canada a complex political culture that had already gone through deep transformations since the end of World War I.

A further element of group cohesion is to be found in the social democrats' network of political and cultural organizations. In 1963, an inquiry among the 1939ers showed how involved they had been, and still were, in associations, in the old country as well as in the new. Before emigrating, all respondents had been members of at least one social-democratic organization: the party itself (24 percent), a trade union (23 percent), the Sports Union (19 percent), the paramilitary Reichswehr (15 percent), the Youth Organization (12 percent), or the Women's Movement (5 percent).[14] This tradition was continued in Canada. As early as 1941, Sudeten German refugees founded the first Sudeten Club in Hamilton (Ontario), and, in the midst of war, the club would hold its meetings in German, the language of the enemy! Moreover, the name of the monthly newspaper published between 1947 and 1995, *Vorwärts/Forward*—which described itself as the "only German social-democratic newspaper in North America"[15]— refers directly to that political tradition. The Club Forward in Toronto, which published the *Vorwärts/Forward*, was created to "unite all German-speaking individuals with socialist and democratic values, of both sexes, to introduce them to the Canadian workers' movement and to collaborate actively with it."[16] The original settlement as a group certainly contributed to furthering a collective cohesion that was maintained over decades, and well into the second generation, despite geographical dispersion.

In contrast, strong conflicts soon emerged among Sudeten Germans in Canada, both of a political and personal nature. In 1961, Steffi Andersch wrote to Wilhelm Wanka: "How can you expect whole nations to live in peace, when even a handful of Sudeten Germans in Canada are not able to get on together?"[17] As early as the end of the 1940s, strong dissensions surfaced among the settlers in Tomslake (British Columbia). Some had long been opposed to the party line defended by Jaksch and other exiled party leaders in London; others were challenging Wanka's legitimacy as the "natural" leader in Canada. A climax was reached in 1949 when a group of fifty-four settlers collectively signed an "Open Letter to Wenzel

Jaksch" that publicly criticized Wanka.[18] This event had a sequel on the level of local as well as provincial politics, for Wanka openly supported the Liberal Party candidate during the 1949 provincial election campaign in British Columbia, while his opponents supported the social-democratic candidate of the "brother party" CCF. As Wanka would explain later, his primary goal had been to show some gratitude toward the party that had enabled the group's migration in 1939. At the same time, as a "rightist," he had strongly been opposed to certain aspects of the CCF platform, such as the rejection of the European Recovery Program for Western Europe (a.k.a. the Marshall Plan) or that of the North Atlantic Treaty. Henry Weisbach, the "leftist" who soon became Wanka's strongest opponent among the 1939ers, was a member of the CCF (and, after 1961, of its successor, the NDP). He legitimized his involvement in the Socialist International as follows: "Our opinions differ substantially from those of the so-called 'Sudeten emigration.' As newcomers to this land, we have always defended the idea that we could best fight for better living conditions by joining the local official social democratic party—in our case the CCF."[19] The 1949 election caused a great cleavage among Sudeten Germans in Canada and led to reciprocal accusations of ideological treason. The raison d'être of such intense quarrels is examined further below.

Lobbying for a Chain Migration after the War

In the first years after the war, the 1939ers were confronted with the double issue of returning to their homeland and worrying about their relatives who had stayed in Europe. But soon the new international context and the geopolitical configuration of the Cold War made remigration impossible, especially after the Beneš decree had ordered the "de-Germanization" of Czechoslovakia. Consequently, up to 3.5 million people were expelled and forced into migration—an often forgotten trauma. According to more recent statistics, between 15,000 and 30,000 expellees were killed during these expulsions.[20]

Because of their particular concerns about the new context in Europe, Sudeten Germans were among the first German Canadians to send care parcels to Europe. Here their networks and group solidarities came to a good use in handling the situation. They were involved in the Canadian Society for German Relief, founded in 1946 in Kitchener.[21] Their efforts were central in mobilizing German Canadians, as the society brought together for the first time different currents within the community. The Hamilton branch, dominated by the president of the local Sudeten Club, Emil Kutscha, was particularly effective in raising funds. In accordance with the sociability that Sudeten Germans had brought with them from the old country, sending care parcels was made possible by the organization of social events such as balls, concerts, bingo nights, picnics, garden parties, film screenings, and conferences.

The first years after the war (1945–50) were also a pivotal period in redefining Canada's immigration policy.[22] In the immediate aftermath of the war, Canada showed no particular interest in immigration issues. Looking back at the economic situation after World War I, government officials feared that a wave of homecoming soldiers would flood the job market. Hence immigration should not be furthered. In addition, the Order-in-Council excluding all enemy aliens from immigration was still in force. Until the end of 1950, German nationals or ethnic Germans could not officially enter Canada. Since 1947, however, Canada had been making exceptions, even in the case of Germans, as the country was trying to attract immigrants with specific scientific or technical skills.[23] But the 1939ers were able to use a second loophole to bring over their relatives. In May 1947, the Canadian government declared that Sudeten Germans had not become German citizens as a result of the Munich Agreement in September 1938, because Canada had never recognized its validity. Consequently, Sudeten Germans could migrate to Canada as Czechoslovak citizens. Finally, the 1939ers also benefited from Prime Minister Mackenzie King's "Close Relative Scheme," which allowed Canadian citizens to sponsor first-degree relatives.

From an international point of view, as of July 1947 the relocation of displaced persons (refugees, expellees, and Holocaust survivors) was in the hands of the International Refugee Organization (IRO). For instance, the IRO was in charge of controlling the number of migrants bound for Canada, Australia, and the United States. According to the instructions of the UN General Assembly on 13 December 1946, the IRO's mandate expressly excluded Germans and ethnic Germans. In order to overcome this obstacle, German Canadians founded the Canadian Christian Council for the Resettlement of Refugees (CCCRR)—outside the mandate of the IRO, at the initiative of CPR official T.O.F. Herzer.[24] The CCCRR received active support from several, mainly religious organizations. But among them were the Sudeten German social democrats who, as "model immigrants," could favourably impress Canadian authorities and recruit those "preferred" immigrants who would meet Canada's selective immigration criteria. Willi Wanka, who had led the 1939 group immigration scheme and who chaired the Committee for the Relief of Democratic Sudeten Refugees, was actively involved in the CCCRR, and he was sent to Europe in 1947 to speed up the screening process for potential immigrants.[25] Under CCCRR supervision, close to 35,000 ethnic Germans reached Canadian shores, most of whom came under the Close Relative Scheme. This is one example of chain migration. Due to their network of associations, their strong group solidarity, and their experience of political struggles, the Sudeten German social democrats also contributed to bringing about institutional changes within Canada's immigration regulations. On 28 March 1950, all remaining obstacles to the immigration of Germans were finally lifted, which led to an extraordinary migration wave in the 1950s.[26]

Multiculturalism or How to Become a German Canadian

The transformations that Canada underwent between 1945 and the 1970s are unique in more ways than one. Because it took part in the war effort, Canada—with little international profile—slowly rose to become a middle power in international relations whose voice grew to be heard. This new visibility had consequences for Canadian modes of representing itself as a nation. But again, the 1939ers adopted a somewhat different posture than other "new Canadians." Unlike other German-speaking refugees, for instance, who had not been allowed to join Canadian armed forces, there had been Sudeten Germans among V-Day troops in Europe.[27] In addition, the eminent role some individuals had played in various political domains (such as the immigration policy) gave the whole group an increased cultural as well as political visibility. For example, on 12 November 1958, Henry Weisbach, the president of the Toronto Sudeten Club Forward, met Nobel Prize winner and leader of the Liberal Party Lester B. Pearson.

All along, the Sudeten Germans seemed to confirm their status as preferred immigrants who had conquered uncivilized lands in the Canadian wilderness. Their life stories retain this quintessential Canadian experience of domesticating nature. Otto Sulek's foreword to Margarete Rabas's autobiography reads as follows: "The Sudeten Germans were certainly one of the last groups of migrants who can be considered pioneers. They fought the wilderness in order to build a new existence."[28] In his autobiography, Willi Wanka is even more emphatic: "With our sweat, sometimes our tears, we conquered new farming lands and expanded the 'frontier,' this border of civilization in the northern parts of British Columbia and Saskatchewan."[29] The former craftspeople, employees, and party officials from Central Europe managed to become Canadian farmers and thus followed the—imaginary—footsteps of their German(-Canadian) "ancestors," whose cultural heritage was just being rediscovered and recuperated in the 1960s and '70s. The German Canadians, however, were an extraordinarily diverse group: new versus old immigrants, ethnic Germans versus German nationals, Austrians versus Germans, etc. Bringing together a majority of German

Canadians seemed an impossible task at the time. But the 1939ers were interested in just that task, as they became precursors of a German Canadian cause commune.

As mentioned previously, the foundation of Sudeten Clubs dates back to the 1940s. After the war, the 1939ers kept alive the dynamics surrounding the common lobbying effort to change Canadian immigration regulations. The first umbrella organization, the Trans-Canada Alliance of German Canadians (TCA), was founded in Kitchener.[30] Initially, the Sudeten Germans Henry Weisbach and Emil Kutscha were actively involved in the TCA, despite their long-lasting disagreements with some more traditional and conservative German Canadian organizations of "old immigrants." In 1952, however, the leftist Sudeten Germans decided that "in the interest of [their Sudeten-]Club's survival and of [their] action as social democrats within the CCF, ... any further cooperation with the Canadian German Alliance [was] to cease immediately."[31]

But this ideologically motivated reaction soon gave way to more pragmatic considerations. The proportion of 1939ers in the Sudeten Clubs was receding dangerously and a generational change was bringing obvious modifications to the migrant culture. As Margarete Rabas synthetically declared in 1962: "We have to try and attract the newer post-war immigrants, even those who are not social democrats. We should privilege ethnic origin [*Landsmannschaft*] over political ideas [*Gesinnungsgemeinschaft*]."[32] In 1970, Henry Weisbach could only agree with her analysis: "At times, our extremely polarized and ideological political debates as well as our general attitude chased away the younger generation."[33] For the Sudeten Germans, a new task was found in adopting and promoting an inclusive German Canadian identity and in celebrating the nostalgia for a twice-lost homeland.[34] In addition to the old ideological solidarity, they developed a new ethnic awareness. Thus in 1957, the Ontario group led by Henry Weisbach founded the Central Federation of Sudeten German Organizations in North America (CFSGO), an institution meant to "represent the interests ... of all Sudeten Germans, regardless of their political or religious beliefs."[35] One of the CFSGO's objectives was to lobby Bonn on matters of compensation. The CFSGO sought (and found) support among German Canadian organizations, especially on a local level. The CFSGO soon became the instrument to increase Sudeten German visibility within the German Canadian community. Old political wounds healed: Emil Kutscha, who had left the TCA a few years before, now became a representative of TCA in charge of seniors' interests, and Henry Weisbach was even TCA president (1967–74).

At the same time, ethnic identities in Canada slowly surfaced in the 1960s and soon crystallized. The discovery of the German Canadian element as the third founding nation is closely related to the definition and diffusion of multiculturalism, a process that started long before it became an official policy under Prime Minister Pierre Elliott Trudeau in 1971. In reality, Canadian multiculturalism covers three dimensions. It is a demographic reality in postwar Canada, a symbolic representation of the Canada as a "mosaic" culture, and a body of institutions allied with provincial as well as federal programs. In this context, ethnic visibility became a means to attract budgets in order to finance research, museums, schools, and cultural events that aimed at demonstrating the special historical contribution of groups to the making of the mosaic. Due to these "politics of recognition,"[36] Canada became a battlefield of identities. And more and more German Canadian voices wanted to be heard in order to oppose the fiction of a "silent ethnic group" and the myth of the "untroublesome Canadians."[37] In the 1960s and '70s, no other group, with the exception perhaps of Ukrainian Canadians, put so much effort into making itself visible on the multicultural quilt.

To some extent, the Sudeten Germans within the emerging German Canadian community were successful in promoting their interests, in adapting to changing contexts, and in transmitting their heritage. Some Sudeten German clubs exist to this day; others continued well into the 1990s. The monthly *Vorwärts/Forward* was published continuously from 1947 to 1995, and then changed its name to *Freundschaft*. In retrospect, the leftist 1939ers contributed to bringing about a complex German Canadian identity by making use of their ethnic awareness and their love for the *Heimat*, which they shared with other German Canadians.

Between Cooperation and Conflict: *"Vereinsmeier"* and *"Querulanten"*

After twenty-five years in Canada, here is what Emil Kutscha had to say: "Among German organizations [in Canada], we have always been in the first row—by founding the 'Canadian Society for German Relief' and the 'Trans-Canada Alliance,' or by defending old-age issues. Our organizations have always been there to further German-Canadian interests … Of course, our activities in the old homeland helped us a lot. But we were also able to use our experience in public matters in this our new home. Here lies our historical merit."[38] The acculturation of this group of "model immigrants" is marked by strong group solidarities as well as vehement conflicts. The 1939ers sometimes called themselves *Vereinsmeier* and *Querlanten*. Micro-historically, their acculturation shows that in spite of a restrictive institutional framework, these refugees were able to carve out for themselves a space for free decision making. Their migration from Europe had been decided by external circumstances. They felt, however, that they were collectively and individually in charge of their adaptation to the new country. In doing so, they even sometimes contributed to the modification of the institutional framework surrounding them, as in the case of immigration regulations and the recognition of a German Canadian identity.

In this context, the group's internal conflicts, either of political or personal nature, should not be viewed as insignificant quarrels, even if they might appear as such to bystanders: Städter versus Siedler, chaff people versus wheat people, members of the Liberal Party versus members of the Socialist Party, leftists versus rightists, Czechoslovakists versus internationalists, *Gesinnungsgenossen* versus *Landsmänner*. On the contrary, these conflicts were absolutely central: they were existential and identity-building elements within a specific milieu—that of political refugees. Among themselves, hierarchical positions and power structures were always connected and relational, co-constructed and interdependent. Ideologically as well as ethnically, this group of refugees was strongly endocentric. There is no point in asking if these conflicts were macro-socially efficient, because they made sense within the group's boundaries. The main protagonists— Emil Kutscha, Margarete Rabas, Willi Wanka, Henry Weisbach—*knew* that despite the conflicts they crucially depended on each other. This is probably in part why they did not permanently return to Europe, not even Willi Wanka, who certainly would have had the opportunity to start afresh in Germany. For some time, in fact, he might even have thought about joining Wenzel Jaksch's team in the Federal Republic of Germany. In October 1961, when he was asked by another 1939er if he was considering going back, he answered negatively, adding: "I do agree with you: we belong to the forgotten over there."[39] On the Canadian Sudeten German scene, however, Wanka belonged to the very famous, and he certainly did not want to jeopardize that position.

Notes

1   Hoerder, *Creating Societies*, ix.
2   Benz, *Das Exil der kleinen Leute*.
3   Strickhausen, "Kanada"; Puckhaber, *Ein Privileg für wenige*; Patrick Farges, "Le trait d'union."
4   The sense of national belonging among Sudeten Germans is historically and culturally problematic. Sudeten Germans often emphasized their attachment to the German language and hence to a German *Kulturnation*. Over time, "Sudetenland" became the generic term for all border regions of Bohemia, Moravia, and Silesia in which ethnic Germans lived in majority.
5   Faist, "Crucial Meso-Level."
6   Hahn, "Gegner und Opfer."
7   Wenzel Jaksch was elected a member of the party executive in 1935 and defended a "German," "national" social democracy, i.e., independent from the Czechoslovak social democratic party.

8 Quoted in Wieden, *Sudeten Canadians*, 97.

9 Abella and Troper, *None Is Too Many*, 48–49.

10 Some refugees remained in Sweden. See Tempsch, "Från Centraleuropa till folkhemmet." The author thanks Klaus Schulte and Hélène Roussel for this reference.

11 These "block settlements" were numerous at the time and often managed by railway companies.

12 On transition phases in life stories, see Heinz, *Theoretical Advances*; Linde, *Life Stories*.

13 Emil Franzel, quoted in Jacques, "*Witiko*," 53. All translations from French and German sources are by the author.

14 National Archives of Canada (NAC), MG28-V6, Sudeten Club Forward, questionnaires, Special issue of *Vorwärts/Forward*, 1963.

15 *Vorwärts/Forward* 2.9 (February 1950), 6.

16 NAC, MG28-V6, Sudeten-Club Forward, Statutes, 6 June 1947.

17 NAC, MG30-C232, Wilhelm Wanka Papers, Letter from Steffi Andersch to Willi Wanka, 21 March, 1961.

18 Open Letter to Wenzel Jaksch, in *Vorwärts/Forward* 2.1–2 (June–July 1949), 10–12.

19 NAC, MG28-V6, Sudeten-Club Forward, Letter from Henry Weisbach to the Socialist International in London, 20 August 1953.

20 For a long time, historians, including Steininger, *Deutsche Geschichte*, 359, thought—and wrote—that the death toll amounted to 220,000–270,000. A revised statistic was made public in 1996 by the "German-Czech Historical Commission" (Gemeinsame Deutsch-Tschechische Historikerkommission, "Stellungnahme der Deutsch-Tschechischen Historikerkommission zu den Vertreibungsverlusten," 17 December 1996). The author is grateful to Hans Lemberg for this reference.

21 Leibbrandt, "Canadian-German Society."

22 Sauer, "A Matter of Domestic Policy?"

23 Koch-Kraft, *Deutsche in Kanada*, 41–42, 66.

24 NAC, MG30-C232, "Wilhelm Wanka Papers," Box 2, File 2, T.O.F. Herzer, "A Brief History of the CCCRR;" 3 March 1951; Sturhahn, "Canadian Christian Council."

25 Wanka, "Auftakt zur deutschen Nachkriegseinwanderung."

26 Freund, *Aufbrüche nach dem Zusammenbruch*.

27 Amstatter, *Tomslake*, 20.

28 Sulek, "Vorwort."

29 Wanka, *Opfer des Friedens*, 19.

30 Wieden, *Trans-Canada Alliance*.

31 Seliger-Archiv (SelA), "Treuegemeinschaft Kanada," Box 1, Minutes of the General Assembly of the Sudeten Club Forward, 6 April 1952.

32 NAC, MG30-C232, "Emil Kutscha Papers," Letter from Margarete Rabas to Willi Wanka, 7 October 1962.

33 SelA, "Treuegemeinschaft Kanada," Box 1, Minutes of the General Assembly of the Central Federation of Sudeten German Organisations in North America (CFSGO), 29 August 1970.

34 In 1946, Willi Wanka wrote a pamphlet entitled *Twice Victims of Munich: The Tragedy of the Democratic Sudeten Germans*. See also Drysdale, "Three Times Betrayed." The author thanks Christian Lieb for this reference.

35 NAC, MG30-C232, CFSGO Statutes, 31 August 1957.

36 Taylor, "Politics of Recognition."

37   Allen, "The Untroublesome Canadians."
38   Emil Kutscha, "25 Jahre Sudetenklub Vorwärts," *Vorwärts / Forward* 24 (Special Issue 1972): 1.
39   NAC, MG30-C232, Letter from Willi Wanka to Frank Rehwald, 21 October 1961.

Archival Materials

National Archives of Canada, Ottawa (NAC). MG28-V5, "Central Federation of Sudeten-German Organizations in Canada"; MG28-V6, "Sudeten Club Forward"; MG30-C132, "Emil Kutscha Papers"; MG30-C232, "Wilhelm Wanka Papers."
Seliger-Archiv Bonn (SelA). "Treuegemeinschaft Kanada"; *Freundschaft*, 1995–; *Vorwärts/Forward*, 1947–95.

Works Cited

Abella, Irving and Harold Troper. *None Is Too Many: Canada and the Jews of Europe 1933–1948*. 1983. Toronto: Key Porter Books, 2000.
Allen, Ralph. "The Untroublesome Canadians." *Maclean's* (7 March 1964): 19–21, 51–52.
Amstatter, Andrew. *Tomslake: The History of the Sudeten Germans in Canada*. Saanichton: Hancock, 1978.
Benz, Wolfgang, ed. *Das Exil der kleinen Leute. Alltagserfahrung deutscher Juden in der Emigration*. Munich: Beck, 1991.
Drysdale, Marg. "Three Times Betrayed: The Sudeten Germans of Tomslake, BC." MA thesis, University of Victoria, 2006.
Faist, Thomas. "The Crucial Meso-Level." In *International Migration, Immobility, and Development—Multidisciplinary Perspectives*, edited by Tomas Hammar, Grete Brochmann, Kristof Tamas, and Thomas Faist, 187–217. Oxford: Berg, 1997.
Farges, Patrick. *Le trait d'union ou l'intégration sans l'oubli. Itinéraires d'exilés germanophones au Canada (1933 à nos jours)*. Paris: Editions de la MSH, 2008.
Freund, Alexander. *Aufbrüche nach dem Zusammenbruch. Die deutsche Nordamerika-Auswanderung nach dem Zweiten Weltkrieg*. Göttingen: V&R unipress, 2004.
Gemeinsame Deutsch-Tschechische Historikerkommission. "Stellungnahme der Deutsch-Tschechischen Historikerkommission zu den Vertreibungsverlusten." Press Release, 17 December 1996. *sehepunkte* 9 (2002): 245–48.
Hahn, Fred. "Gegner und Opfer des Nationalsozialismus als Emigranten aus den böhmischen Ländern nach Amerika." In *Drehscheibe Prag—Zur deutschen Emigration in der Tschechoslowakei 1933–1939*, edited by Peter Becher and Peter Heumos, 151–64. Munich: Oldenbourg, 1992.
Heinz, Walter R., ed. *Theoretical Advances in Life Course Research*. Weinheim: Deutscher Studien Verlag, 1991.
Hoerder, Dirk. *Creating Societies: Immigrant Lives in Canada*. Montreal and Kingston: McGill-Queen's University Press, 1999.
Jacques, Christian. "De l'invention de la 'germanité sudète': la revue *Witiko* (1928–1931)." PhD diss., University of Strasbourg 2—Marc Bloch, 2004.

Koch-Kraft, Andrea. *Deutsche in Kanada—Einwanderung und Adaption. Mit einer Untersuchung zur Situation der Nachkriegsimmigration in Edmonton, Alberta.* Bochum: Universitäts-Verlag Brockmeyer, 1990.

Leibbrandt, Gottlieb. "Canadian-German Society." *German-Canadian Yearbook* 1 (1973): 255–62.

Linde, Charlotte. *Life Stories: The Creation of Coherence.* New York: Oxford University Press, 1993.

Puckhaber, Annette. *Ein Privileg für wenige—Die deutschsprachige Migration nach Kanada im Schatten des Nationalsozialismus.* Münster: LIT Verlag, 2002.

Sauer, Angelika E. "A Matter of Domestic Policy? Canadian Immigration Policy and the Admission of Germans (1945–50)." *Canadian Historical Review* 74, no. 2 (June 1993): 226–63.

Steininger, Rolf. *Deutsche Geschichte.* Volume 3. Frankfurt: Fischer Taschenbuch Verlag, 2002.

Strickhausen, Waltraud. "Kanada." In *Handbuch der deutschsprachigen Emigration 1933–1945,* edited by Claus-Dieter Krohn, Patrik von zur Mühlen, Gerhard Paul, and Lutz Winckler, 284–96. Darmstadt: Primus, 1998.

Sturhahn William. "The Canadian Christian Council for the Resettlement of Refugees. Its Contribution to German Post-War Immigration to Canada." In *Kontakte—Konflikte—Konzepte. Annalen Deutschkanadische Studien* 3, edited by Karin R. Gürttler and Herfried Scheer, 45–52. Montreal: Université de Montréal, 1980.

Sulek, Otto. "Vorwort." In *Leben und Schaffen der Sudetendeutschen in Kanada,* by Margarete Rabas, 1. Winnipeg: Wolf Verlag, 1993.

Taylor, Charles. "The Politics of Recognition." In *Multiculturalism: Examining the Politics of Recognition,* edited by Amy Gutmann, 25–73. Princeton: Princeton University Press, 1994.

Tempsch, Rudolf. "Från Centraleuropa till folkhemmet: Den sudettyska invandringen till Sverige 1938–1955." PhD diss., University of Göteborg, 1997.

Wanka, Wilhelm. "Auftakt zur deutschen Nachkriegseinwanderung nach Kanada." *German-Canadian Yearbook* 9 (1986): 125–40.

———. *Opfer des Friedens—Die Sudetensiedlungen in Kanada.* Munich: Langen Müller Verlag, 1988.

———. *Twice Victims of Munich: The Tragedy of the Democratic Sudeten Germans.* Tupper Creek, BC: 1946.

Wieden Fritz. *Sudeten Canadians.* 2nd ed. Toronto: Sudeten Club Forward, 1982.

———. *The Trans-Canada Alliance of German Canadians: A Study in Culture.* Windsor, ON: Tolle Lege Enterprises, 1985.

TWENTY-ONE

Sudeten German Refugees in Canada and the Forced Migration of Germans in Postwar Central and Eastern Europe

Pascal Maeder

Virtually all works on the Sudeten German refugees in Canada focus on aspects of their immigration. This chapter, by contrast, sheds light on the way these refugees reacted to the Allied-approved expulsion of Germans from central and eastern Europe in the aftermath of World War II. Having fled from Nazi persecution in 1938–39, the expulsion left many Sudeten German refugees stranded in Canada. There, the Sudeten German refugees very much identified themselves as expellees, organized protests, called for the "right to a homeland," and established associations allied to powerful West German groups that lobbied for expellees. In the context of the Cold War, Sudeten Germans were presumed victims of communism and were thus in effect included in the expellee diaspora scattered across West Germany and the capitalist West. In Canada they developed their own strategies, based by and large on their experiences in the "Old" and "New" worlds.

Introduction

IN 1939, WHEN JUST OVER A THOUSAND MEMBERS of the German Socialist Workers' Party of Czechoslovakia (GSWP) escaped Nazi persecution and arrived in Canada, they generally assumed that their stay in North America would be temporary. Six years later, however, the demise of Nazi Germany and the ensuing Allied-sanctioned expulsion of Germans from central and eastern Europe wiped out their last hopes of return. Most of the expelled Germans were forcibly resettled in war-torn and occupied Germany; however, several hundred thousand expellees also resettled throughout western Europe and Austria, Africa, East Asia, and the Americas, including the thousand Sudeten German refugees in Canada.

This chapter sheds light on the way these Sudeten German refugees lived through the forced migration in the aftermath of World War II. Historians have thus far overlooked the Sudeten Germans' expellee identity and instead have focused on the circumstances of their immigration. Given Canada's restrictive immigration rules between 1931 and 1947, in particular toward refugees from Nazi Germany, the admission of the Sudeten German refugees has certainly warranted detailed investigations.[1] The same holds true for their settlement in two remote areas of British Columbia and Saskatchewan. As former party activists and trade union leaders, they predictably struggled to adjust and soon left *en masse* for urban centres, notably Hamilton, Toronto, and Montreal.[2] However, the Sudeten German refugees felt affected by the forced migration and so, effectively, felt expelled too. Similar to other Germans from central and eastern Europe, who were in exile or captured by the Allies, they experienced the forced migration *in absentia* and held, as one historian put it, "fictional expulsion experiences."[3] The first section of this chapter therefore extends the standard expellee narrative, which generally divides the forced migration into three distinctive phases: the flight ahead of the Soviet armies in 1944–45, the ad hoc vigilante expulsions in the heat of Allied victory, and the organized and Allied-sanctioned mass transports from central and eastern Europe to occupied Germany.[4] The second section considers the way the Sudeten Germans organized and framed their protest against the expulsions and allied with like-minded groups both inside and outside of Canada. Their clubs and associations certainly never reached the size and power of Sudeten German organizations in the Federal Republic of Germany (FRG).[5] Nevertheless, as they founded a series of clubs, a bitter rivalry between two groups ensued, which eventually forced West German expellee leaders to intervene. In fact, in Canada the Sudeten Germans set off a dynamic distinct from the expellee powerhouse in West Germany.

Stranded Refugees

In 1941 the Sudeten German refugees in Canada were made aware of the forced migration that the Czechoslovak government-in-exile planned in the event of an Allied victory.[6] One year later, following the massacre of Lidice, a Czech village destroyed in retaliation for the murder of the Nazi governor of the occupied Czech rump state, Czech émigrés in North America openly called for the expulsion of the Sudeten German minority from liberated Czechoslovakia. Apparently, at one public rally in Saskatchewan, attending Sudeten German refugees protested and a turbulent row broke out.[7] Thus, in marked contrast to the residents of central and eastern Europe, the Sudeten German refugees knew what to expect after Nazi Germany's demise. By July/August 1945, when the first personal letters from Czechoslovakia arrived in Canada, the news confirmed, by and large, their worst fears. The Skoutajan family, for example, received the first letter from their relatives in Aussig (Ústí nad Labem) in early August 1945 and learned about the way relatives and friends were disenfranchised, rounded up, and deported even though as social democrats they had actively opposed the takeover of the Sudeten areas by Nazi Germany.[8]

Meanwhile, an ocean apart, the Sudeten German refugees realized that the forced migration in Czechoslovakia inevitably left them stranded. At the outset, most refugees had assumed that their stay in Canada would be temporary. When, for example, in 1941 the first refugees left the isolated farms in the western provinces, they apparently still regarded Hamilton, Montreal, or Toronto as "halfway station[s]" to home.[9] As the war progressed and Czechoslovakia's liberation neared, the refugees increasingly realized that they would be unable to return to the homeland. By the end of 1944, more than a third of the settlers in Tupper Creek, British Columbia, had filed an application for Canadian citizenship and so gave a clear indication as to where they expected to live in the postwar era.[10] According to Czechoslovak law of August 1945 the refugees were theoretically still able to reconfirm their Czechoslovak citizenship (and therefore return to Czechoslovakia) as long as they were not guilty of treacherous activity and had actively fought against the Nazis.[11] However, none of the refugees are known to have used this law.[12]

Instead, within weeks of Nazi Germany's surrender, the Sudeten German refugees set out to provide assistance to expellees in war-torn Europe. They sent remittances to friends and relatives who landed in occupied Germany deprived of their belongings and assets. Through the normal postal route they sent packages filled with food, clothing, or any other goods that were desperately needed in the face of rampant shortages.[13] Beyond the individual assistance of friends and relatives donations to a series of organizations offered another way to help expellees in Europe. The Sudeten Germans made donations to the New York branch of the *Arbeiterwohlfahrt*, which provided relief to Nazi victims in occupied Germany and, in particular, to persecuted trade unionists and social democrats. Second, on behalf of the left-wing Co-operative Commonwealth Federation (CCF), which was the only Canadian party that openly called for humanitarian aid in occupied Germany, the Sudeten Germans in Toronto and Hamilton went out into the community and collected money.[14] Third, and most important, Ontario's Sudeten Germans also actively participated in the building of postwar Canada's only secular aid agency for needy Germans, the Canadian Society for German Relief (CSGR). Together with a group of Mennonites in Kitchener, several Sudeten Germans from Hamilton kickstarted the CSGR and drafted a charter that expressed the organization's aim to "alleviate human suffering among the German people, especially among the sick, the aged, the children and expelled persons."[15]

The Sudeten Germans also campaigned for the immigration of expellees to Canada. Although both aid and immigration rapidly became two parts of the same relief effort, especially once the international resettlement of roughly 1.2 million displaced persons (DPS) from occupied Germany got underway, the Sudeten Germans in Canada had already hatched plans for the postwar immigration of comrades and co-ethnics as early as April 1945.[16] Months later, the Sudeten Germans gained the support of top railway officials and published a pamphlet that called for the immigration of, as it claimed, "democratically minded Sudeten Germans."[17] In Europe, these first forays were taken seriously as one group of Sudeten Germans apparently prepared to move to Canada. However, until the first Sudeten Germans arrived in Canada, another year had passed. First of all, for lack of staff and facilities, Canadian authorities were unable to process immigrants from occupied Germany. Second, once facilities were in place, Canadian authorities were unable to use the International Refugee Organization (IRO) for the processing of expellees such as the Sudeten Germans. Only once the Sudeten Germans joined forces with denominational German Canadian relief groups were they able to sponsor the immigration of relatives through the newly founded Canadian Christian Council for the Resettlement of Refugees (outside the mandate of the IRO) (CCCRR). Within three years of its foundation, the CCCRR, which benefited from government support, moved over 15,000 ethnic German expellees across the Atlantic, including several hundred Sudeten Germans.[18]

Diaspora Politics

Once in exile, Wenzel Jaksch, the leader of the once strongest German party in Czechoslovakia, dissolved the German Socialist Workers' Party of Czechoslovakia (GSWP) and formed the Loyal Group of Sudeten German Social Democrats (LG) with headquarters in London, England. Wilhelm Wanka, as Jaksch's former personal secretary and member of the party's executive, was nominally the head of the Canadian branch of the LG, which included a third of all the Sudeten German social democrats in exile. During the first decade in Canada Wanka and his supporters dominated Canada's Sudeten German community politically. In October 1940, when a dissident group among the Sudeten German refugees in England founded the International Group of GSWP, Wanka vigorously repressed dissent and supported Jaksch's contested ethno-nationalist party line, notably his call for Sudeten German autonomy and, more specifically, his seemingly fascist "*Volkssozialismus.*"[19] The repression was such that apparently some of the residents of Tupper Creek felt as though they were residing in a "concentration camp without barbed wire."[20] In the aftermath of the war, Jaksch relocated to West Germany and founded the Seliger community in order to pull together the former social democrats from Czechoslovakia and join, as a group, the Sudeten German Homeland Society.[21] Wanka dissolved the LG and in 1947 founded the Canadian German Association. In the early postwar period it was also Wanka's group that successfully lobbied for the immigration of Sudeten German relatives. Wanka, for one, used his good relations with government and railways officials, whereas his fellow Sudeten German Franz Rehwald used his position as the editor-in-chief of Winnipeg's German Canadian weekly, the *Nordwesten*, to drum up support for the relief and immigration of expelled Germans. Rehwald widely criticized communists as the main culprits of the forced migration in central and eastern Europe and pressed for extensive coverage that showcased atrocities committed by Soviet troops or Polish or Czech militias. Rehwald also formed close ties with Winnipeg's vibrant German Canadian communities and, among them, key figures involved in immigration such as Herbert Klassen from the Mennonite Board of Colonization and, in particular, T.O.F. Herzer, the head of the Canadian Pacific Railway's Canadian Colonization Association. In conjunction with Herzer, Klassen, and others, Rehwald ultimately succeeded in gaining the government's support for the admission of ethnic German expellees and the foundation of the CCCRR.[22]

From the 1950s, however, the rising star among the Sudeten German refugees was Henry Weisbach. In the early 1940s he had briefly lent his support to the dissident International Group. Like others who opposed Jaksch's ethno-nationalist party line, he adhered to a more traditional Marxist interpretation of socialism and until the mid 1940s believed in the future of a multi-ethnic Czechoslovak state. By 1945, Weisbach had written off his support for the International Group and joined the chorus of protest against the expulsion of Germans from central and eastern Europe led by Jaksch and the Wanka group. However, characteristic of Jaksch opponents, Weisbach dissociated himself from the protest strategy used by the Wanka group and judged it a concert with "the refined version of National Socialists in Canada."[23] Instead, he voiced his disapproval of the forced migration in the small German Canadian socialist press reminding readers, as he wrote, that not all Sudeten Germans were guilty of treason, especially not those who, like him and his fellow comrades, had actively fought against the Nazis.[24] In the first postwar decade Weisbach then built up the Sudeten German Club Forward, which joined, not surprisingly, Canada's left-wing party, the CCF.[25] In 1956, Weisbach co-founded the Central Association of Sudeten German Organizations in Canada, which devoted itself largely to questions arising from West Germany's compensation of expellees. Its member associations were all CCF-affiliated Sudeten German clubs.[26]

Relations among the rivalling Sudeten German groups were extremely hostile. The federal and provincial elections in British Columbia of June 1949 sparked the first major crisis when Wanka's group canvassed the support for the governing Liberal Party and thus infuriated Sudeten Germans organized within the CCF. Jaksch was eventually forced to intervene in an attempt to mend fences. Justifying Wanka's political move as a strategic measure to help further the admission of German immigrants to Canada, he gave his backing to Wanka and called on all Sudeten German henceforth to join the CCF.[27] However, Wanka defied Jaksch's verdict and continued to canvass support for the Liberal Party. In his eyes expellee interests in Canada could simply not be furthered through the CCF. To some degree Wanka was right. In terms of aid from and immigration to Canada, support for the governing Liberal Party was the way to go and, ultimately, bore fruit with the establishment of the CCCRR and the removal in 1950 of the ban against the immigration of German nationals. That said, after 1950 Wanka's unorthodox political strategy was bound to fail. First, the Canadian public and government by and large condoned the expulsion of Germans from central and eastern Europe.[28] In the face of Nazi Germany's legacy the Sudeten Germans' campaign against the forced migration met with little sympathy outside the German Canadian community. As one Sudeten German wrote, "we handed out the leaflets for free ... yet the end result was 'I am sorry' but you are Germans too. They [Canadians] care for Sacco, Vancetti, and Hottentots [*sic*], but not for the German social democrats from the CSR."[29]

Second, despite the fact that their number significantly grew in the postwar period, Canada's Sudeten Germans and expellees received scant political and financial support from the FRG. Roughly one third of the 240,000 German postwar immigrants to Canada were of expellee background and, among them, around 16 percent and 33 percent respectively were from Czechoslovakia and the former German territories east of the Oder and Neiße rivers.[30] However, with the exception of the Sudeten Germans none of West Germany's major expellee groups, such as the Silesians or East Prussians, attempted to form or sponsor an allied organization in Canada. Moreover, West German officials in Canada refrained from explicitly backing expellee interests. In fact, whereas in West Germany government authorities widely backed expellee organizations and provided vitally important funds,[31] in Canada West German officials discouraged the formation of local expellee groups. As one West German official in Toronto put it, in Canada there was no point in forming expellee organizations and calling for reparations and justice as long as German assets confiscated during World War II remained frozen in Canadian hands.[32]

Third, in the long run, Wanka's strategy was doomed to fail in view of the scant and fragmented expellee organizations established in postwar Canada. Between the local expellee groups no union emerged as in the Bund der Vertriebenen in West Germany. Besides the Sudeten German organizations, only three ethnic German homeland societies were founded, namely the German Baltic, the Danube-Swabian, and the Transylvanian homeland societies. Like the Sudeten German clubs these organizations were small and counted at best several thousand members. All three homeland societies also only half-heartedly embraced the expellees' call for the *Heimatrecht* and, with it, the return to the homeland. In accordance with the West German ethnic German homeland societies, which had concluded that a return was neither possible nor desirable in the context of the Cold War, and the relative backwardness of their country of origin,[33] the three ethnic German homeland societies outside the Sudeten German organizations similarly kept a very low profile on key expellee demands.[34]

Weisbach's foundation of the Central Association of the Sudeten Germans in 1956 sparked the second major crisis within the organized Sudeten German community. As Wanka saw his leadership eroding, he attempted a counterattack and in 1960 founded the Western Canadian Working Community of the Sudeten Germans. In doing so, he followed the advice of Jaksch's deputy, Richard Reitzner, who in 1958 had travelled to Canada to negotiate between the two rival groups.[35] In addition, Wanka also received further backing from West Germany in the shape of the Sudeten German Homeland Society, which considered Weisbach's person "*nicht einwandfrei*" as the leading representative of Canada's organized Sudeten German community.[36] However, in the end Wanka's counterattack failed. Compared to Weisbach, whose power base stretched from British Columbia to Quebec, Wanka's influence remained largely confined to sections of the diminished Sudeten German settlements in British Columbia and Saskatchewan. By the early 1960s Weisbach gained Jaksch's full and undivided support because Canada's rapid industrialization eroded Wanka's power base. From the more than two hundred Sudeten German households that in 1939 settled in Tupper Creek, only seventy-two were left by 1954.[37] In accord with the majority of Canada's postwar immigrants, the Sudeten German refugees moved to urban centres, especially in southern Ontario. Furthermore, and as a result of Canada's rapid industrialization, the triangle Toronto/Hamilton/Kitchener replaced Winnipeg/Saskatoon as the leading German Canadian hub. Weisbach had links with the Danube-Swabian homeland society, the largest and most active local expellee organization, and, most importantly, had risen to prominence as the president in the German Canadian umbrella organization, the Trans-Canada Alliance of German Canadians (TCA). Both organizations had their power base in southwestern Ontario.[38] Thus, all in all, by the early 1960s Weisbach's leading position had become indispensable to Jaksch despite the previous, chiefly ideological, disagreements between them. As newly elected president of West Germany's all-powerful Vertriebenenverband, Jaksch could ill afford to back the marginalized Wanka group and lent his undivided support to the group around Weisbach. As Jaksch noted after his visit to Canada in 1962, Weisbach was "at the centre of 'Deutsch-Kanadiertums'" and, as such, had introduced him to the country's main German Canadian organizations.[39]

Conclusion

Over the course of their settlement in Canada the Sudeten German refugees adopted a distinct expellee identity born out of their background as social democrats from Czechoslovakia and their flight from Nazi Germany. Immediately after the end of World War II, as the forced migration dashed their hopes of return, they stayed in Canada and attempted to assist expellees in war-torn Europe. Moreover, in Canada the Sudeten German refugees fully participated in the political fights led by expellee organizations in West Germany. In doing so, the Sudeten German refugees effectively became members of a transnational expellee diaspora.

Despite their marginal position in Canadian society the head organization of the former social democrats from Czechoslovakia (Seliger community), based in West Germany, kept close links with the Sudeten German refugees in Canada. Jaksch was acutely aware of the power dynamics in the Canadian diaspora.

From Toronto, Weisbach built up a national network of like-minded Sudeten German associations and in 1956 founded the Central Association of Sudeten German Organizations in Canada. In addition, he became a leading member of the national German Canadian umbrella organization, the TCA. Over the course of the postwar years Wanka, by contrast, became increasingly isolated. From his home in northeastern British Columbia, he was neither able to reach out to the Sudeten German refugees scattered across the country nor able to sustain contacts that he had made with Canadian officials and German Canadian community leaders during the 1940s. Thus these developments ultimately forced the West German leadership to adjust and change partners in Canada.

Notes

1   Puckhaber, *Ein Privileg.*
2   Wanka, *Opfer des Friedens.*
3   Niethammer, "Flucht ins Konventionelle," 320.
4   *Dokumentation der Vertreibung,* vol. 1, 61E–62E, 140E–150E.
5   Ahonen, *After the Expulsion,* 15–54; Stickler, *Ostdeutsch,* 155–171.
6   Maiwald, Letter to Sweden, 2 May 1942, quoted in *Vorwärts/Forward* 16: 10 (April 1964), 13.
7   Note enclosed with "The Story of Two Peoples or Czechoslovak and German Morality," released by the Czechoslovak National Council of America, October 1942, National Archives of Canada (NAC), Immigration Branch Records, RG 76, vol. 617, file 916207, pt. 10, reel C-10436.
8   Skoutajan, *Uprooted and Transplanted,* 191–212.
9   Scharing, "Montreal," *Vorwärts/Forward* 16: 4 (September 1964), 7; Interview Henry and Hermine Weisbach, 2 and 13 April 1984, Multicultural History Society of Ontario (MHSO), German Collection.
10 Wanka, The Sudeten Settlement of Tupper Creek, BC, in 1944: Complete Report, n.d., 21, NAC, "Willi Wanka Papers," MG 30 C 232, vol. 3, file 1.
11 *Deutschen und Magyaren.*
12 Interview Henry and Hermine Weisbach, 2 and 13 April 1984, MHSO, German Collection.
13 For example, Else Reilich to Augsten, 29 June 1947, Archiv der Seliger-Gemeinde im Archiv der Sozialen Demokratie (ASG), Nachlass Frank J. Reilich, file 471.
14 Weisbach to CFF, n.d. [ca 1947], NAC, Sudetenklub Vorwärts Papers, MG 28 V 6, vol. 2, file CCF; "Sudetenklub Hamilton."
15 *Vorwärts/Forward* (September/October 1970), 23; Constitution of the Canadian Society for German Relief, n.d., Archives of Ontario (AO), MHSO Papers (F 1405), Klaus Bongart Papers, MFN 295, A 1, reel 1.
16 Wanka to Jaksch, 15 April 1945, NAC, Willi Wanka Papers, MG30 C 232, vol. 1, file 18.
17 Wanka, *Twice Victim of Munich.* For the pamphlet's funding by the CPR, see Wanka to Jaksch, 6 July 1945, NAC, Willi Wanka Papers, MG 30 C 232, vol. 1, file 18.
18 Sauer, "A Matter," 240–244.
19 Bachstein, *Wenzel Jaksch,* 67–114.
20 Weisbach to Kögler, 29 August 1941, ASG, Korrespondenz Kögler, file 952.
21 Ahonen, *After the Expulsion,* 35.
22 Sauer, "Matter," 250–63; Wanka, "Begegnungen," 106–110.
23 Weisbach to Kern, 6 February 1946, Sudetendeutsches Archiv (SudAr), Nachlass Karl Kern, file 22.
24 *Volksstimme,* February 1948, 6, Archives of Ontario.
25 *Die Brücke,* 16 December 1948, Archives of Ontario.
26 *Vorwärts/Forward* 8: 10 (March 1957), 2; Henry Weisbach, Why the Sudeten German Central Organization, n.d. [*ca.* 1957], NAC, External Affairs Records, vol. 8382, File 10935-H-1-40.
27 "Open Letter to Jaksch," *Vorwärts/Forward* 2: 1–2 (July 1949), 10–12; Weisbach to Kern, 6 February 1949, SudAr, Nachlass Karl Kern, file 22; Jaksch, Zu den Differenzen in der Siedlergruppe Tomslake-Tupper Creek, 5 October 1949, ASG,

Emigration Kanada, file 818, also contained in NAC, Willi Wanka Papers, MG 30 C
232, vol. 3, file 12.

28 Sauer, "Future Orders."

29 Kutscha to Jaksch, 23 August 1945, NAC, Emil Kutscha Papers, MG 30 C 132, vol. 3,
file Correspondence Treuegemeinschaft Sudetendeutscher Sozialdemokraten,
1942–1948.

30 Maeder, "Forging," 354–359.

31 Ahonen, *After the Expulsion*, 53; Stickler, *Ostdeutsch*, 148–54.

32 Von Waldheim to Stopp, 13 February 1959, NAC, Trans-Canada Alliance of German
Canadians Papers, MG 28 V 4, vol. 15, file 9.

33 Ahonen, *After the Expulsion*, 41.

34 Maeder, "Forging," 248–71.

35 Wanka to Jaksch, 9 January 1961; Wanka to Jaksch, 15 June 1961, NAC, Willi Wanka
Papers, MG 30 C 232, vol. 2, file 10.

36 Rückel to Lodgman von Auen, 6 March 1956; Rückel to Eichler, 18 April 1956;
Eichler to Rückel, 6 June 1956; and Bundesverband der Sudetendeutschen Lands-
mannschaft to Peckert, 23 October 1957, SudAr, Nachlass Rudolph Lodgman von
Auen, CV/1a IX 20.

37 *Vorwärts/Forward* 7: 11 (April 1954), 5; Schoen, *The Tupper Boys*, 83–134.

38 Wieden, *Sudeten Canadians*, 214–20.

39 Jaksch to Wanka, 31 October 1962, NAC, Willi Wanka Papers, MG 30 C 232, vol. 2,
file 10.

Archival Material

Archiv der Seliger-Gemeinde im Archiv der Sozialen Demokratie: Emigration
Kanada (ASG), Korrespondenz Kögler, Nachlass Frank J. Reilich, *Vorwärts/
Forward* 1947–95.

Multicultural History Society of Ontario (MHSO), German Collection.

Archives of Ontario: *Die Brücke*, Klaus Bongart Papers, MHSO Papers, *Volksstimme*.

National Archives of Canada (NAC), External Affairs Records, Immigration Branch
Records, Emil Kutscha Papers, Sudetenclub Vorwärts Papers, Trans-Canada
Alliance of German Canadians Papers, Wilhelm Wanka Papers.

Sudetendeutsches Archiv (SudAr). Nachlass Rudolph Lodgman von Auen; Nachlass Karl Kern.

Works Cited

Ahonen, Pertti. *After the Expulsion: West Germany and Eastern Europe*. Oxford: Oxford University Press, 2003.

Bachstein, Martin K. *Wenzel Jaksch und die Sudetendeutsche Sozialdemokratie*. Munich:
Oldenburg, 1974.

*Die Deutschen und Magyaren in den Dekreten des Präsidenten der Republik: Studien
und Dokumente*, edited by Karel Jech. Brno: USD, 2003.

Dokumentation der Vertreibung der Deutschen aus Ost-Mitteleuropa, edited by Theodor
Schieder et al. 5 volumes. Bonn: Bundesministerium für Vertriebene, Flüchtlinge und Kriegsgeschädigte, 1953–1961.

Maeder, Pascal. "Forging a New Heimat: Expellees in Post-War West Germany
and Canada." PhD thesis, York University, 2007.

Niethammer, Lutz. "Flucht ins Konventionelle? Einige Randglossen zu Forschungs-
problemen der deutschen Nachkriegsmigration." In *Flüchtlinge und Vertri-
ebene in der westdeutschen Nachkriegsgeschichte: Bilanzierung der Forschung und
Perspektiven für die künftige Forschungsarbeit,* edited by Doris von der Brelie-
Lewien, Helga Grebing, and Rainer Schulze, 316–23. Hildesheim: A. Lax,
1987.
Puckhaber, Annette. *Ein Privileg für wenige—Die deutschsprachige Migration nach
Kanada im Schatten des Nationalsozialismus.* Münster: LIT Verlag, 2002.
Sauer, Angelika E. "A Matter of Domestic Policy? Canadian Immigration Policy and
the Admission of Germans, 1945–1950." *Canadian Historical Review* 84 (June
1993): 226–63.
Sauer, Angelika E. "Future Orders: Canada and Post-Hostilities Germany." In *1945
in Canada and Germany: Viewing the Past through the Present,* edited by Hans
Braun and Wolfgang Kloos, 37–50. Kiel: L&F, 1996.
Schoen, Walter. *The Tupper Boys: A History of the Sudeten Settlement at Tomslake, BC.*
Victoria: Trafford, 2004.
Skoutajan, Hanns. *Uprooted and Transplanted: A Sudeten Odyssey from Tragedy to Free-
dom, 1938–1958.* Owen Sound: Ginger Press, 2000.
Stickler, Matthias. *"Ostdeutsch heisst Gesamtdeutsch": Organisation, Selbstverständnis
und heimatpolitische Zielsetzungen der deutschen Vertriebenenverbände 1949–1972.*
Düsseldorf: Droste, 2004.
Wanka, Willi. "Begegnungen und Episoden aus meiner Flüchtlingsarbeit," *Sude-
tenjahrbuch* 18 (1969): 102–11.
Wanka, Wilhelm. *Opfer des Friedens—Die Sudetensiedlungen in Kanada.* Munich:
Langen Müller Verlag, 1988.
Wanka, Willi. *Twice Victim of Munich: The Tragedy of the Democratic Sudeten Germans.*
Tupper Creek, BC: private publication, 1946.
Wieden, Fritz. *Sudeten Canadians.* 2nd edition. Toronto: Sudeten Club Forward,
1982.

TWENTY-TWO

Language Attrition among Germans Living in the Netherlands

Anne Ribbert

This chapter discusses language attrition among German students in the Netherlands. The experimental group, fifty-two Germans living in the Netherlands, were asked to judge the grammaticality of German infinitive constructions. Among the constructions were both correct ones and some that would not be considered correct in Standard German but were similar to structures in Dutch. Their answers were found to differ significantly from a German control group with no contact with Dutch. The chapter explains this difference between the two groups with reference to the transfer from the second language (Dutch) to the first language (German) within the experimental group. It discusses the interpretation of these results and their importance for general conclusions about language attrition, as well as the impact of a number of extralinguistic factors, such as contact with the first and second language and attitude on the degree of attrition.

Introduction

UNDER CERTAIN CIRCUMSTANCES, an individual can lose proficiency in his or her mother tongue. This phenomenon is referred to as language attrition, and can be defined as "the non-pathological decrease in proficiency in a language that had previously been acquired by an individual."[1] Language attrition is often the outcome of living in a new place where a different language is spoken. This chapter explores first-language attrition among German students living in the Netherlands. This group is special in a number of respects. In contrast to the populations that have traditionally been studied, e.g., Germans who moved to New Zeeland or the United States,[2] this group can easily travel back and forth between Germany and the Netherlands. Furthermore, they have access to a variety of German-language media, including several television programs and newspapers. Another difference between the Germans in this study and immigrants who went overseas is that the latter commonly intended to stay in their new environment to start a new life. In contrast, the German students in this study went to the Netherlands in order to pursue their studies with the plan to return to Germany after receiving their degree. This group is particularly interesting because the focus of this study is to investigate the influence of their second language—Dutch—on German as their first language.

The influence of a second or foreign language on the mother tongue has only recently been included as part of the research on transfer.[3] Transfer is used in reference to the psychological process in which prior learning is carried over into a new learning situation.[4] Often, transfer effects have been studied within the area of second-language acquisition, where the main interest has been on how learning a second language is shaped by the processes and rules of the first language. This chapter explores the inverse effect, namely the influence of the second language on the first, guided by the interlanguage perspective in the research on attrition,[5] which holds that changes in the speaker's first language are due to interference from the second. This perspective on language attrition is inspired by Mike Sharwood Smith,[6] who argues that transfer is one of the most important sources for language attrition. Herbert Seliger[7] suggests that less complex and more widely used rules in the second language may replace those rules in the first that are more complex and less often applied.

Transfer effects of Dutch as a second language on German as a first language have been studied before by Ruth Brons-Albert.[8] She detected the heavy transfer of Dutch rules onto the German by her participants who had stayed in the Netherlands for a period of time varying between half a year and twenty-five years. One of the most frequent deviations from Standard German she found was the overgeneralization[9] of the German infinitival complementizer *um* (*Ich habe keine Lust* *um *ins Kino zu gehen*).[10]

While Brons-Albert's observations are based on spontaneous speech data, the present study was conducted with experimental data in order to get a more detailed picture of the transfer of infinitival clauses. The aim was to find out whether the overgeneralization of the complementizer can also be detected in the task of grammaticality judgments of Germans living in the Netherlands.[11] The study subjects were given some German sentences that followed a German rule for the use of the complementizer and some that followed the Dutch rule, thus deviating from Standard German.

The following section provides an overview of linguistic rules for Dutch and German infinitival constructions and then discusses the grammaticality judgment task conducted and its results.[12] This is followed by examining which extralinguistic factors may influence language attrition and a report on a questionnaire study conducted with the same group to be able to account for some of these factors.

Infinitival Constructions in Dutch and German

There are both variation and overlap between the use of the German and the Dutch infinitival constructions. The German complementizer *um* is used in a subset of cases where its Dutch cognate *om* is used. In both languages, the complementizer must obligatorily be used when the infinitival construction that is introduced by the complementizer expresses the purpose or goal of the proposition in the main clause (*Markus treibt Sport,* um *fit zu bleiben /Hij werkt* om *geld te hebben* [He works in order to have money]).

Furthermore, the complementizer can occasionally be used in so-called prospective constructions in both Dutch and German. In those cases, the infinitive clause describes a state of affairs that has not been realized at the moment of speaking and does not indicate a reason or purpose. Even though this construction is not further considered in this chapter, because it is not accepted by all native speakers of the respective languages, it is included here to give a complete overview of the use of the complementizer (*Karl ging in die Stadt,* um *dort von einem Auto überfahren zu werden*[13] */ Karel ging de stad in* om *daar door een auto overreden te worden* [Karl went to the city where he got run over by a car]).

Furthermore, German *um* and Dutch *om* are obligatorily used in a number of phrases such as German *um die Wahrheit zu sagen*, respectively Dutch *om de waarheid te zeggen* [to tell the truth]. These uses, which coincide in the two languages, are also not further considered here.

According to Abraham ten Cate, Hans G. Lodder, and André Kootte,[14] the use of the German complementizer is ungrammatical in all other cases. It should be noted, though, that Germans sometimes use *um* in colloquial speech when there is no strict purpose-consequence relationship between the subordinate and the main clause (*Ich habe keine Zeit,* [um] *in die Stadt zu gehen*).

There is only one additional case in which *um* can be used optionally in German. This case is the consecutive construction, i.e., when the infinitive clause describes the consequence of what is mentioned in the main clause (*Michael war klug genug* [*um*] *seinen Fehler zuzugeben*).[15] Typically, the complementizer is omitted in written German.

The Dutch complementizer *om* is used more widely than its German counterpart. There is a high number of contexts in which the Dutch complementizer is optional, e.g. *Ik ben blij (om) te horen dat je beter bent* [I am delighted to hear you're better].[16] The use of optional *om* in Dutch is not arbitrary, though. Maurice Vliegen[17] shows that speaker subjectivity is the main factor driving its use. Referring to *om* after verbs such as *aanbevelen* (recommend) and *adviseren* (advise), Vliegen[18] points out that the use of the complementizer indicates strong speaker expectations. The speaker expects the proposition expressed by the infinitival clause to be realized. Suffice it to say, for the purposes of this chapter, that the use of the Dutch complementizer depends not only on syntactic rules, but also on pragmatic factors such as speaker subjectivity.

In summary, it should be noted that the use of the Dutch complementizer *om* forms a superset of the use of German *um*. Dutch furthermore has a high number of contexts where *om* can be used optionally.

Grammaticality Judgment Task

The present study started with the following research questions:

- Can the overgeneralization of German *um* by German speakers in the Netherlands as observed in spontaneous speech also be detected in grammaticality judgments?
- What role do extralinguistic factors play in the attrition of the complementizer?

The experimental group consisted of fifty-two Germans who had been living in the Netherlands for between 0.7 and 11.5 years. The mean length of stay was 4.2 years (standard deviation 2.3 years). All of the participants were (former) university students of various subjects. Most of them came to the Netherlands to study because they could not study the topic of their choice in Germany. Despite coming from different parts of Germany, the participants were all speakers of Standard German. All participants came to the Netherlands after puberty; the age at arrival varied between nineteen years and thirty-two years (mean twenty-two years, standard deviation three years).

All participants in this experimental group had at least a good knowledge of Dutch. Most of them had passed the Staatsexamen Nederlands als Tweede Taal (NT2)—Programma II, the highest exam for Dutch as a second language and a prerequisite for most university programs in the Netherlands. For students of music or applied arts, no formal language test is required: eleven participants (8.5 percent) had not taken this exami-

TABLE 1 Number of mistakes per group

Group	Participants	Mean	Standard Deviation	Standard Error Mean
Experimental	52	6.1	4.8	.66
Control	38	1.6	1.8	.28

nation. Eight other students (6.2 percent) did not indicate which programs they were enrolled in. As these participants did not behave significantly different on the grammaticality judgement test, they were treated as though they belong to the same group as the others. This experimental group was compared to a German control group, consisting of thirty-eight participants. The control group was composed of students from the University of Cologne who came from various regions in Germany.

A specific type of a grammaticality judgment task, a "grammaticality preference task," was used to test the students' knowledge of German. The participants were exposed to thirty-five pairs of sentences, one with *um*, and the other without (*Michael hat probiert um Daniela anzurufen / Michael hat probiert Daniela anzurufen*) The students were asked to indicate whether both sentences, only one of them, or neither was correct.[19] They were told that the sentences had identical meaning.

A grammaticality judgment task was chosen in order to tap into the participants' linguistic competence. This choice assumed that the participants, if explicitly asked to give judgments, might judge those uses as incorrect, even though they may use them in their speech.

The participants' answers were categorized into correct and incorrect answers according to the predictions made by standard grammar.[20] The experimental group was compared to the German control group by means of an independent-samples t-test.[21] Table 1 displays the group statistics. Missing values were replaced by the mean group score per item.

Table 1 shows that the group of Germans living in the Netherlands (the experimental group) made more mistakes than the control group of Germans without contact with the Dutch language. By means of Levene's Test for Equality of Variances it was tested whether the sample variances differed significantly. The difference between the groups after a two-tailed test was indeed significant: $t(68.2) = 6.3$, $p < .000$.

Extralinguistic Factors

The behaviour exhibited by the experimental group was quite heterogeneous. Their standard deviation was three times as high as that of the control group. A further research question, therefore, was whether the variance in the performance of the experimental group could be accounted for by extralinguistic factors.

Barbara Köpke and Monika Schmid[22] summarize the most important extralinguistic factors that can influence language attrition. Two of them are age of onset of second-language acquisition and age of onset of attrition. The point in time when the individual moves into the new second-language environment marks the potential onset of language attrition. Evidence indicates that there is considerably more attrition in individuals who emigrated before puberty.[23]

Furthermore, there are indications that level of education can influence attrition, although it is not yet clear in which way this might occur,[24] as prior research has produced conflicting results. Koen Jaspaert and Sjaak Kroon[25] found an effect of education level on attrition, whereas Kutlay Yağmur[26] found the same effect of the variable in both the attriters and the non-attriter control group.

Another variable to take into account is the time since the onset of attrition. It is not clear yet whether this factor has an impact on language attrition. Kees de Bot, Paul Gommans, and Carola Rossing[27] and Aviva Soesman[28] suggest that the factor of time since migration might only have an effect if this implies little or no contact with the first language. Several studies[29] show evidence for the hypothesis that attrition is caused by lack of contact with the first language. Furthermore, it is often argued that language retention is caused by continuous use of the first language. Monika Schmid[30] calls attention to the methodological problems that are connected to this factor, since research has to rely on self-reported data, which are by nature subjective. Contact with the first language might even increase the degree of attrition if the nature of contact is mostly with other immigrants who show comparable signs of attrition.[31]

Finally, attitudes toward both the first and second languages need to be considered. These are strongly interwoven with language use, because positive attitudes toward the first language lead to increased use, whereas negative attitudes lead to avoidance.[32]

Four factors in relationship to attrition affect the study discussed in this chapter: time spent in the second-language environment, contact with the first language (German), contact with the second language (Dutch), and attitudes toward maintenance of the first language. The other factors mentioned above (level of education of the participants, age of second-language acquisition, and age of beginning first-language attrition) did not play a role because they were relatively constant, considering that all participants had moved to the Netherlands after puberty, which coincides with the age of second-language acquisition and potential first-language attrition. Furthermore, as all participants were university or college students, their level of education was relatively high.

The factors were tested in a questionnaire that the participants were asked to fill in after they had done the grammaticality judgment test. The factor of time spent in the second-language environment could simply be investigated by asking the participants to fill in the months of residence in the Netherlands in the questionnaire. Information about their contact with both languages was elicited through questions, for example, about exposure to German/Dutch media and contact with German/Dutch speakers among their friends and family. The last set of questions gathered information on their attitude toward first-language maintenance.

Based on the answers from the questionnaire, the effect of the four extralinguistic variables on the performance of the experimental group was measured by means of a multiple regression analysis. The only variable that turned out to be significant was "contact with Dutch," which could account for 17 percent of the variance in the performance of the experimental group.

Discussion

This study has examined language attrition among Germans living in the Netherlands by investigating transfer from Dutch infinitival constructions into German. Furthermore, the influence of a number of extralinguistic factors on first-language attrition was explored.

The first language of native speakers of German can undergo significant changes in a relatively short time even if immigration has taken place after puberty. Changes were visible even among language users who had lived in the Netherlands for as little as eight months. The variable length of stay in the Netherlands was not a predictor for language attrition. Furthermore, it can be concluded for the participants of the study that attrition has passed the level of performance, since their knowledge about their native language, measured in the grammaticality judgment task, had also changed.

As a note of caution it needs to be pointed out that previous research has not yet been able to convey what exactly is measured in a grammaticality judgment task, nor could the relationship be established between knowledge measured by grammaticality judgment tasks and other domains of knowledge, such as the active use of rules in a language. It would be interesting to investigate, therefore, whether the participants' production of infinitive clauses correlates with their judgments as investigated in this study.

A further question raised by the results of this study is whether the judgments on infinitive clauses are representative in terms of estimating the participants' overall degree of attrition. No straightforward answer to this question can be given on the basis of this study. It is known from contact linguistics that there seems to be a hierarchy of elements that are transferred from one language to the other—the borrowing scale.[33] According to this scale, structural borrowing of, for example, word order presupposes lexical borrowing. It was argued in this chapter that the mistakes of the experimental group resulted from transfer of the Dutch rule for infinitive clauses to German. Structural transfer as encountered in this study thus presupposes influence in areas of the language system that encode lexical knowledge. Future research must verify whether this implicational relationship indeed holds true for language attriters.

In summary, this study has shown that first-language attrition can also occur if people moving to a new place have regular contact with the first language and its culture. Furthermore, the extent of contact with German did not turn out to be a predictor for language attrition. The extralinguistic factors measured in this study hardly had an effect on the amount of language attrition. The only variable that did have a significant impact on attrition was the extent and quality of contact with Dutch. This factor accounted for 17 percent of the variation in the experimental group. The rest of the variation remains unexplained. Since the variance in the performance of the experimental group could not be accounted for by the extralinguistic variables measured in this study, the question of what causes the individual differences between participants in the experimental group remains.

Notes

1 Köpke and Schmid, "First Language Attrition," 5.
2 See Hulsen, *Language Loss*; Smits, *Disintegration of Inflection*.
3 See Cook, *Effects of the Second Language*.
4 Gass and Selinker, *Second Language Acquisition*, 66.
5 Researchers have approached first language attrition with different focuses, including regression, simplification, interlanguage, and universal grammar. For an overview, see Köpke and Schmid, "First Language Attrition," 2004.
6 Sharwood Smith, "First Language Loss."
7 Seliger, "Language Attrition," 237.
8 Brons-Albert, "Verlust der Muttersprache," "Interferenzfehler."
9 Overgeneralization refers to a process by which a linguistic rule extends to language material that is normally not affected by this rule.
10 The asterisk is used to indicate that the structure deviates from the standard language.
11 For a critical review of grammaticality judgment tasks as a means of studying attrition see Altenberg and Vago, "Role of Grammaticality Judgments."
12 This section is based, in part, on Ribbert and Kuiken, "L2-Induced Changes."
13 Eisenberg, *Duden*, 637.
14 Ten Cate et al., *Deutsche Grammatik*, 130.
15 Ten Cate et al., *Deutsche Grammatik*, 130.
16 Klooster, *Grammatica*, 256.

17 Vliegen, "Het facultatieve *om* na illocutionaire werkwoorden"; Vliegen, "Die *om te-*Konstruktion."
18 Vliegen, "Het facultatieve om na illocutionaire werkwoorden," 36–37.
19 There was also a "don't know" option available for some sentences. These sentences were excluded from the results.
20 Eisenberg, *Duden*.
21 This is a frequently used statistical test to establish whether two groups differ significantly in one variable (all other variables being controlled).
22 Köpke and Schmid, "First Language Attrition," 8–15.
23 See, for example, Nicoladis and Grabois. "Learning English and Losing Chinese."
24 See Köpke and Schmid, "First Language Attrition," 10–11.
25 Jaspaert and Kroon, "Social Determinants."
26 Yağmur, *First Language Attrition*, 91.
27 de Bot, Gommans, and Rossing. "L1 Loss in an L2 Environment," 94.
28 Soesman, "Experimental Study," 190.
29 For example, de Bot, Gommans, and Rossing. "L1 Loss in an L2 Environment"; Köpke, *L'attrition de la première langue*.
30 Schmid, *First Language Attrition*, 23.
31 For a discussion on the impact of code-switching on language change, see Backus, "Codeswitching and Language Change."
32 See, for example, Schmid, *First Language Attrition* on the case of German Jews; and see also chapter 39.
33 Thomason, *Language Contact*, 70.

Works Cited

Altenberg, Evelien P., and Robert M. Vago. "The Role of Grammaticality Judgments in Investigating First Language Attrition." In *First Language Attrition: Interdisciplinary Perspectives on Methodological Issues*, edited by Monika S. Schmid, Barbara Köpke, Merel Keijzer, and Lina Weilemar, 105–29. Amsterdam: John Benjamins, 2004.

Backus, Ad. "Codeswitching and Language Change: One Thing Leads to Another?" *International Journal of Bilingualism* 9, no. 3/4 (2005): 307–40.

Brons-Albert, Ruth. "Interferenzfehler in der Muttersprache von in den Niederlanden lebenden Deutschen." In *Nachbarsprachen in Europa*, edited by Bernd Spillner, 96–104. Frankfurt: Peter Lang, 1994.

Cook, Vivian. *Effects of the Second Language on the First*. Clevedon: Multilingual Matters, 2003.

de Bot, Kees, Paul Gommans, and Carola Rossing. "L1 Loss in an L2 Environment: Dutch Immigrants in France." In *First Language Attrition*, edited by Herbert W. Seliger and Robert M. Vago, 87–98. Cambridge: Cambridge University Press, 1991.

Eisenberg, Peter. *Duden. Grammatik der deutschen Gegenwartssprache*, Band 9. Mannheim: Dudenverlag, 1998.

Gass, Susan, and Larry Selinker. *Second Language Acquisition: An Introductory Course*. Mahwah, NJ: Lawrence Erlbaum Associates, Publishers, 2001.

Hulsen, Manon. *Language Loss and Language Processing: Three Generations of Dutch Migrants in New Zealand*. PhD diss., Radboud Universiteit Nijmegen, 2000.

Jaspaert, Koen, and Sjaak Kroon. "Social Determinants of Language Loss." *ITL: Review of Applied Linguistics* 83/84 (1992): 75–98.

Klooster, Wim. *Grammatica van het hedendaags Nederlands. Een volledig overzicht.* Den Haag: Sdu Uitgevers, 2001.

Köpke, Barbara. *L'attrition de la première langue chez le bilingue tardif: Implications pour l'étude psycholinguistique de bilingualisme.* PhD diss., Université de Toulouse-Le Mirail, 1999.

Köpke, Barbara, and Monika S. Schmid. "First Language Attrition: The Next Phase." In *First Language Attrition: Interdisciplinary Perspectives on Methodological Issues,* edited by Monika S. Schmid, Barbara Köpke, Merel Keijzer, and Lina Weilemar, 1–45. Amsterdam: John Benjamins, 2004.

Nicoladis, Elena, and Howard Grabois. "Learning English and Losing Chinese: A Case Study of a Child Adopted from China." *International Journal of Bilingualism* 6, no. 4 (2002): 441–54.

Ribbert, Anne, and Folkert Kuiken. "L2-Induced Changes in the L1 of Germans Living in the Netherlands." Unpublished manuscript, Radboud University Nijmegen, 2007.

Schmid, Monika S. *First Language Attrition, Use, and Maintenance: The Case of German Jews in Anglophone Countries.* Amsterdam: John Benjamins, 2002.

Seliger, Herbert W. "Language Attrition, Reduced Redundancy and Creativity." In *First Language Attrition,* edited by Herbert W. Seliger and Robert M. Vago, 227–40. Cambridge: Cambridge University Press, 1991.

Sharwood Smith, Mike A. "On First Language Loss in the Second Language Acquirer: Problems of Transfer." In *Language Transfer in Language Learning,* edited by Susan Gass and Larry Selinker, 222–31. Rowley, MA: Newbury House, 1983.

Smits, Caroline. *Disintegration of Inflection: The Case of Iowa Dutch.* PhD diss., Amsterdam Vrije Universiteit, 1996.

Soesman, Aviva. "An Experimental Study on Native Language Attrition in Dutch Adult Immigrants in Israel." In *Dutch Overseas: Studies in Maintenance and Loss of Dutch as an Immigrant Language,* edited by Jetske Klatter-Folmer and Sjaak Kroon, 181–94. Tilburg: Tilburg University Press, 1997.

ten Cate, Abraham P., Hans G. Lodder, and André Kootte. *Deutsche Grammatik. Eine kontrastiv deutsch-niederländische Beschreibung für den Zweitspracherwerb.* Bussum: Coutinho, 1998.

Thomason, Sarah Grey. *Language Contact: An Introduction.* Edinburgh: Edinburgh University Press, 2001.

Vliegen, Maurice. "Die *om te*-Konstruktion im Niederländischen und die *um zu*-Konstruktion im Deutschen. Ein Vorschlag zur Bedeutungsbeschreibung." *Leuvense Bijdragen* 93 (2004): 179–220.

———. "Het facultatieve *om* na illocutionaire werkwoorden." *Nederlandse Taalkunde* 6, no. 2 (2001): 112–32.

———. "Verlust der Muttersprache in fremdsprachiger Umgebung." *InfoDaF* 19, no. 3 (1992): 315–25.

Yağmur, Kutlay. *First Language Attrition among Turkish Speakers in Sydney.* Tilburg: Tilburg University Press, 1997.

TWENTY-THREE

Der Onkel aus Amerika:
The German Emigrant as a Figure of
Speech and Fictional Character

Carsten Würmann

The "uncle from America" has been a figure in German culture for more than two hundred years. The following analysis examines the function of this figure in literature and film, showing how the representation of the uncle influences the social construction of migration, the hopes and dreams of the ones who wanted to leave or the self image, and the expectations of the emigrants. The origins of this character are briefly discussed before demonstrating how, in an eighteenth-century drama, the character of the rich uncle illustrates utopian thoughts about society. Since the beginning of the nineteenth century, the figure has been quite present in German popular culture, appearing mainly in comedies and comic operas, as well as in novels. The literary examples of the early twentieth century show how the uncle emerged as a central figure of contemporary views about America. A closer look at some films from the Weimar, Third Reich, and West German eras will reveal how the relationship to the United States and to a modernity that was regarded as typically American was reflected through this character.

The Proverbial Rich Uncle

IN GERMAN AN UNCLE FROM AMERICA is *ipso facto* a rich man. Wolf Friedrich's *Moderne deutsche Idiomatik* defines the "*Onkel aus Amerika*" as a "*steinreicher Mann.*" Hans Schemann's *Deutsche Idiomatik* of 1993 offers German phrases in context and puts the uncle in the following: "*Der Alfons hofft wohl auf einen reichen Onkel aus Amerika, der ihm ein paar*

Millionen vermacht, was? Oder wie will er sonst aus seinen Schulden jemals wieder herauskommen?"[1] The uncle from America became a metaphor for a rich relative, the image of the successful emigrant, who made his fortune overseas.[2] This idiomatic expression not only integrates reminiscences of old legends and fairy tales, but also refers to the historic cultural experience of the German mass emigration to North America. Metonymically, the uncle represents all the emigrated relatives, be they uncles or aunts, desperate siblings, or even lost sons and fallen daughters, while America principally stands for all the countries beyond the ocean, although it mainly refers to the United States of America, the destination of 90 percent of German emigrants in the nineteenth and early twentieth centuries.

This uncle is not only the legendary hero of many family stories. The rich uncle belongs to a collection of images that are part of a cultural concept of America—like the Native American as the "noble savage," like the lonesome heroes, trappers, outlaws, cowboys, and sheriffs of the wilderness and Wild West, like the successful or failed homesteader and the American millionaire. In all European literature, the narratives based on this conception are told in a quite similar manner: usually, America is the other as related to the different self-images and constructions of identity of Europeans.[3]

Origins of a Reputation

How did the uncle gain his reputation? In his dictionary of proverbial idiomatic phrases, Lutz Röhrich explains the impact that emigration had on the mentality of contemporaries left behind in the old country, who had a quaint idea of the life of their relatives in America and were convinced that they had all become incredibly rich, because "*zunächst jeder, der wollte, im Land der unbegrenzten Möglichkeiten sein Glück machen und reich werden konnte.*"[4] It seems to be an open question whether this golden age of immigration ever existed. But if one supposes that the ubiquitous appearance of a historical phenomenon is the prerequisite for common linguistic use, the possible genesis of the character could be dated to the second half of the nineteenth century when nearly five million Germans emigrated to America, making it likely that almost every German had at least one American relative. Without underestimating the influence of the historical situation on the development and circulation of idiomatic phrases, in this case the explanation does not seem to be sufficient. The American uncle makes his first appearances in German-language literature a few decades before the phenomenon of mass emigration.

American Virtue versus European Vice

Karl Gotthelf Lessing is one of the first German-language authors to use the uncle from America as a literary character. The protagonist of his 1780 comedy *Die Mätresse* is Otto von Kronfeld, an emigrant to America who returns as a wealthy man. He is the one who brings this drama about class distinction, prejudices, and seduction to a happy conclusion. Otto's nephew, Graf von Mannhof, had started an affair with the farmer's daughter Juliane with a false promise to marry her. Otto, after having assured himself of Juliane's respectability, rejects his nephew and makes sure that truly honourable behaviour and not the conventional sense of honour is rewarded. As a man who is friendly, kind, and free from any social prejudices, Otto represents a concept of an enlightened spirit linked to Rousseau's ideas of a simple and virtuous life. The wealth that gives him the opportunity to follow his own ideas as well as intellectual impartiality is a result of his American experience. America is imagined as a utopia, and European culture is characterized by arrogance and moral double standards.

From Vaudeville to Germany

In the 1810s and '20s, the uncle character became popular mainly due to his appearance in French comedies, the Vaudevilles, which would become known all over Europe. *Le Trésor de la langue française*,[5] a dictionary for the French language of the nineteenth and twentieth centuries, notes that the French equivalent, *l'oncle d'Amérique*, is a character in a drama or a novel. This uncle, who emigrated to America and became rich, unexpectedly returns and brings luck to his people. In a broader sense, he is a character who appears just at the right moment to solve family or financial problems.

The American uncle keeps his place in European popular culture throughout the nineteenth century. First on stage and then in novels and short stories, he assumes certain roles and functions. His return visits from America are events. His accumulated wealth from which the relatives hope to benefit arouses desires and causes conflicts. This stereotypical character allows and encourages a lucky turn of events and facilitates the denouement of the plot. In so doing, the role and appearance of the character have ironic traits and play on clichés. The prospect of assumed wealth reveals manners and behaviour that are ridiculed and caricatured. In Viktor Blüthgen's novel *Der Onkel aus Amerika* of 1897, David Jonathan Künzel announces in a letter to his old hometown somewhere in northern Germany that, after having lived fifty-two years in America, he wants to spend the rest of his life with his relatives in his old homeland. He does not pretend to be rich; he just suggests it with some remarks and hints. His relatives, who are not poor themselves, do not ask further questions. They take his wealth for granted and try everything to please him and make sure they receive his inheritance. When, after eight years, he finally dies, his treasure turns out to be worthless: false jewellery and self-made stock market certificates. A letter discovered after his death narrates how his life was full of hardship, that is to say closer to the experiences that the majority of the emigrants had to endure.

Between Winnetou and Nick Carter

In the above literary examples a real America or authentic emigrant experiences are rarely presented. The stories of the rich uncle, even when they are told tongue in cheek, reinforce the proverbial dream of material fortune, which since the early nineteenth century was revived and propagated in books and pamphlets for potential emigrants mainly from the lower classes. In the image of the uncle, the American dream remained believable despite the fact that at the beginning of the twentieth century several million Germans had tried to live this dream with sometimes nightmarish consequences.

Over the course of the nineteenth century, multiple images and ideas of America began to circulate. This was fed by stories in adventure books such as James Fennimore Cooper's Leatherstocking tales, Karl May's *Winnetou*, and *Groschenromane*, by articles and reports in newspapers and magazines, and by the famous Wild West Shows. The effect of these popular images is seen in Max Brod's movie draft from 1914: *Ein Tag aus dem Leben Kühnebecks, des jungen Idealisten*. This movie illustrates the imagination of a young man inflamed by incidents of daily life. A letter announces the arrival of an uncle from America:

> *In seiner einsamen Nachmittagsstube, über Schulhefte hin träumt nun Küh-nebeck das Eintreffen des Dollar-Wundermannes ... Bahnhofshalle. Aussteigen. Kühnebeck eilt dem Onkel entgegen, der ihn allerherzlichst an sein Herz drückt. Nun hat alle Sklaverei ein Ende. Denn der Amerikaner trägt nichts weniger als einen Papierkegel-Hut mit sämtlichen Sternen der Union auf dem Kopf, das Geld fließt wie unter automatischem Druck aus seinen beiden aufgeblähten Hosentaschen und zwei lange Linien von Goldmünzen bezeichnen auf der Straße sein Kielwasser, in dem sich die lustigen Delphine des Großstadtpub-likums balgen.*[6]

In the reality, the uncle turns out to be less spectacular than the carnival figure of which the boy was dreaming. Nonetheless, when the boy—still fascinated by the Wild West and the detective stories of Nick Carter and Karl May—causes the arrest of an old adversary of the uncle, an

"Apache," at that time a common slang word for a criminal, the uncle shows his gratitude by showering his nephew with gold and money.

In *Der Verschollene* Franz Kafka systematically deconstructs stereotypes of the contemporary discourse on America.[7] The uncle appears at a crucial moment. He welcomes the seventeen-year-old Karl Roßmann, "*der von seinen armen Eltern nach Amerika geschickt worden war, weil ihn ein Dienstmädchen verführt und ein Kind von ihm bekommen hatte*"[8] on the boat. At first the uncle combines all the attributes one would link to the cliché of an emigrant who has made it: his business is doing very well, he is a senator, and, in the course of his assimilation, he replaces the German-sounding name Bendelmayer with his middle name Jakob. In his behaviour he corresponds to the image of an America that is free from old social and moral conceptions. Therefore, he can act differently than Roßmann's parents, who had disowned their son. The modern, liberal, and open-minded America is contrasted with blimpish and backward Europe. During the first weeks the uncle is very kind to Karl. But after the nephew acts against the wishes of his uncle by accepting the invitation of his uncle's business partner, he is rejected. This rejection is reported to Karl by a letter from his uncle. Unlike the usual tradition of the uncle from America, the letter does not mark the end of all sorrows and worries but the beginning of the decline. In *Der Verschollene* the classic story of the emigrant and the traditional character of the uncle are reversed.

Before World War I the figure of the rich uncle had entered into public debate via the change of Uncle Sam to Onkel Sam, exemplified by the title of a 1904 travel book on America written by Karl Zimmermann: *Onkel Sam. Amerikanische Reise- und Kulturbilder.* This transformation of the character was meant partly to be facetious, but it was to an astonishing degree also serious and politically naive. Facing devastating defeat in the autumn of 1918, the German public focused their hopes on President Woodrow Wilson's Fourteen Point peace plan.[9] The oft-told popular story of the timely appearance of the rich uncle from America offers at least one possible reason for the amount of blind confidence and belief in authority that was offered to President Wilson and his plan.

In the 1920s America remained the preferred destination for German emigrants despite its more rigid immigration policies, but for people during the years of the Weimar Republic, America stood for much more than a way out of the crisis. After the nightmare of World War 1 the German masses, as well as the European, sought, as Wolfgang Schivelbusch puts it, "*ihr Heil in der amerikanischen Traummaschine.*"[10] In the Weimar Republic, Americanism was a widely discussed phenomenon, a metaphor and an example for the process of modernization in all levels of the society.[11]

The Uncle as Simulation

In 1932, in a Germany at the end of an overheated love affair with America, at the apex of an economic crisis and on the verge of a civil war, Carl Boese made the comedy *Man braucht kein Geld*. The appearance of the American uncle in this film creates a cheerful play on stereotypes that reverses the relationship between modern America and old Europe and that at the same time proves the historical function of the uncle character. In retrospect the opening scenes appear as a bitter, albeit valid, satire of contemporary life in Germany. At first, we see the splendid portal of a bank and while the opening credits appear we can hear the melody of "Üb immer Treu und Redlichkeit." The title of this Protestant church hymn—played every half hour by the chimes of the Garnisonkirche in Potsdam between 1797 and 1944—is an imperative for a Christian life and in Prussian Germany had become a motto for a respectable life in general. Here, it is just an ironic allusion to a long-gone past when integrity and honesty were guiding principles for a business conduct rewarded with success and wealth. In this movie, the bank of the fictitious town of Groditzkirchen is closed. The cash boxes are empty—in the safe is just the breakfast of the director. There is only one hope left: the uncle from America. The Brandts, a business family who is jointly responsible for the financial collapse, have invited their old uncle Thomas Hoffmann from Chicago. Convinced that he is a millionaire, the family and the bank await anxiously a cable announcing the arrival of the uncle. Only the clerk Schmidt, played by Heinz Rühmann, remains skeptical:

EXCERPT 1

BANKDIREKTOR: *Sie glauben nicht an das Kabel.*

SCHMIDT: *An das Kabel schon, nicht aber an den reichen Onkel.*

BANKDIREKTOR: *Solange Sie mein Angestellter sind, haben Sie an den Onkel zu glauben. Der reiche Onkel ist unsere letzte Rettung.*

SCHMIDT: *Also bitte, ich glaub's, aber nur rein dienstlich, als Privatmann nicht.*

BANKDIREKTOR: *Wieso?*

SCHMIDT: *Wieso? Reiche Onkels kommen doch überhaupt nur in Lustspielen vor, aber unsere Pleite hier ist doch eine Tragödie.*

Indeed it looks like tragedy because the rich uncle turns out to be a poor man. But now Schmidt arranges the scene. He tells the Brandts to keep silent so that the sad truth does not come out. With seven huge suitcases, the uncle moves into the best hotel in town. A gold ten-dollar tip for the boy suffices to convince the whole community that the uncle is credit-worthy. Now his signature is good enough to establish a new oil company. Schmidt arranges the clichés to create a perfect illusion. The plan succeeds: everyone is investing again and the economy is booming. The small town develops with "American" speed into a flourishing big city.

The uncle, played by the Austrian comedian Hans Moser, could hardly be further from the image of the dynamic American. He is in all regards the reverse of the dominant popular image: he returns as a poor man and he sticks to his old-fashioned moral standards. He deeply mistrusts the swindle that created the wealth and he places much emphasis on always being an honourable human being. He does not like the booming Groditzkirchen at all; it is too loud and busy for him. He wants to go back to Chicago, which he remembers as a peaceful and quiet place. Thus it is not the industrial and business city of Chicago that shelters the idea of Americanism or modernity in its purest form, but rather Germany or, at least, Groditzkirchen. Here the people have understood the signs of the time and act accordingly. Schmidt realizes that the common perception of America is simply made up of clichés and stereotypes—and he uses this to manipulate the situation. But as long as the uncle delivers and lives up to expectations, this way of solving a crisis works, at least in this comedy.

From *Onkel* Sam to *Onkel* Shylock

The National Socialists competed with the U.S. and tried to create a specifically German modernity—a process that, to continue the metaphor, can be regarded as the emancipation from the uncle. Americanism in the Third Reich had negative connotations and characterized for Nazis the excesses of modernity, which in their own minds they had overcome.[12] Americanism, and thus modernity, could only be justified as a means to an end: they had to be compatible to the "higher" aims of the Nazi *Volksgemeinschaft*.

While German Jews and other refugees tried desperately to emigrate to the United States, the National Socialist regime endeavoured to destroy the old myth of successful emigration by trying to reverse that myth. The novel *Der verlorene Sohn* by Luis Trenker fits in this context. It was serialized in the best-selling German weekly *Berliner Illustrirte Zeitung* in 1934 and reflected the efforts of the NS-Auslandsorganisation to entice the return of Germans from America.[13]

The movie *Fünf Millionen suchen einen Erben* from 1938, another comedy by Boese and starring Heinz Rühmann, illustrated this overcoming of the uncle and America. An American uncle hands five million dollars to his nephew Peter Pett on condition that he is happily married. That is the extent that the uncle character plays in this movie—he is dead before the movie starts. The central scene of the movie is the encounter that the nephew has with a most attractive America. The camera indulges in images of a modern and glamorous city landscape: roof gardens, seas of lights, sky-scrapers, grand hotels. The camera moves across the New York skyline and the Statue of Liberty. But all this cannot dissuade Peter Pett from wishing for his immediate return to Germany. He defies all attempts to defraud him: he resists the temptations of the new world and brings back the money safely. In this movie, and from the viewpoint of the Nazis, America, with its pathological appearances of the modern, is situated far beyond the ocean; it has no effect on a good German and does not have anything to do with Germany anymore.[14]

For tactical reasons the Nazi regime was very reserved with anti-American propaganda at the beginning of the Third Reich. Henry Ford, for instance, represented for the Nazis the good American—a kind of good uncle—and was treated positively in the German press until 1939.[15] This changed after the U.S. joined the war against Germany, and in the propaganda fight against the American myth, the Nazis concentrated mainly on President F.D. Roosevelt. The agitation against this president, who was said to have started the war together with the Jews, stood in the centre of an anti-Americanism in which traditional elements were combined with anti-Semitic stereotypes, and Uncle Sam was turned into Uncle Shylock.[16]

The Good Uncle

Shortly after World War II, the character of the rich uncle from America returned to his former glory as a positive representation. Not only did many Americans support their relatives (and not only them) with care packages and money, but the U.S. as occupying power also began to play a role that could quite easily be paralleled with the image of the uncle as benefactor. America was a kind of uncle who, out of affection or for old time's sake, helped his nieces and nephews (at least in the West) to reconstruct their country in peace and offered them a peaceful and wealthy life. In the late 1940s and early '50s America became once again an attractive country for emigration, especially for German-speaking refugees from eastern Europe. This changed, however, as the economic situation in West Germany improved rapidly in the 1950s. Thus, while the real American relatives became fewer or more remote, the uncle continued to play a role in popular culture as well as becoming a metaphor in political discourse.

The relationship between West Germany and the United States remains to this day a very close one militarily, politically, economically, and culturally. At least from the German perspective, this relationship still has a special, singular character. To criticize or praise American politics and lifestyle has been a central point of the ideological objectives of many political parties and movements since the 1950s. Their discussions and arguments offer the whole range of positive and negative connotations, and these discourses of criticism or affirmation bear traces of family disputes. However, the uncle seldom appears in this context. The character and figure of the uncle might seem a little bit old-fashioned, but it can still be employed to great effect. Hans Scheibner, a German cabaret artist, started a satirical comment on the visit of George W. Bush in 2005 with the sentence: *"Ach, war das eine Aufregung. Wir hatten Besuch aus Amerika. Unser reicher Erbonkel hatte sich angesagt."*[17]

The Return of the Uncle in the Heimat

How much this American uncle has been part of the German history of the twentieth century is illustrated by the television series *Heimat—eine deutsche Chronik* by Edgar Reitz. Shown for the first time in 1984, it marks a climax of the popular interest of German society in their personal family histories and the history of the daily life of their parents and grandparents. The series tells the story of the family Simon in the fictitious village Schabbach in the Hunsrück region from 1919 to the 1980s. The series aspired to more than just entertainment as emphasized by the second part of the title *Eine deutsche Chronik*.

Through the character of Paul Simon the stereotypes of the "uncle from America" tradition are integrated into the family saga and at the same time intertwined with certain aspects of the German economic and political history. Since returning from World War I, Simon is dissatisfied with village life—he longs for distant lands. At the end of the first episode, Simon leaves his wife and children and heads for America. His family learns this only ten years later when his first letter arrives. The letterhead shows the sketch of a factory, and beneath it the title "Simon Electric Company, Detroit, USA." Simon has found his fortune in America. His first attempt to visit in 1939 fails, but in 1945—episode five—the Americans are occupying the Hunsrück. Two years later, Simon returns and displays the trappings of a successful emigrant. Arriving in a huge and expensive car with an African American chauffeur, Simon is now a grand man in the prime of life wearing a hat that reminds one of the Wild West. The whole village marvels at the car, and the nephew Horst runs to the local American headquarters and breathlessly tells an American soldier, that "my *Onkel*, you know, is the *Millionär* in America, Detroiett, Simon Electric" and now he is in Schabbach. Everyone gazes with admiration at the "American" who invites the whole village to a feast where everyone gets enough to eat.

This is not just the staging of a family memory. In the movie, even Simon refers to a bigger context when he is hiring an American military band to play for the village. On the table in the middle of the hall, Simon arranges his presents (*"Die Groceries dort ham mich ein paar Dollars gekost."*) and the camera devoutly absorbs these groceries—American white bread, milk powder, oatmeal, cartons of Lucky Strike cigarettes—all symbols of American wealth in 1940s Germany. The people of Schabbach grab at these delicacies while Simon makes his speech in a strange mixture of dialectal German sprinkled with American words. He tells the story of how he made it all by himself in this foreign country and became wealthy. By this he justifies his decision to leave as the better one, once again providing approval for the old myths of emigration.

Conclusion

The "uncle from America" is a figure with a very long tradition in German popular culture. This character represents a complex story of migration, but the implicit connections to the "promised land" aside, his story remains too undetermined to be of real use for an analysis of the history of migration. On the other hand, this vagueness could be regarded as the main reason for the success of the character. The rich uncle from America is an ideal canvas for the hope to achieve wealth and a better life, a central motive for emigration. In the stories and films examined in this chapter, these material expectations are linked to the character of the uncle. While this character was sometimes comical, it could also be employed in satirical or at least slightly ironic situations.

The film examples show that the American uncle could also serve as a figure to reflect the economic, political, and cultural relationship to the United States in the twentieth century, reflecting the special transatlantic relationship between Germany and the United States that is characterized by a strange mixture of proximity and distance, fascination and disgust, and charged with huge expectations of material support.

The author thanks Heide Wurmann for proofreading and correcting his German English. Widmen möchte ich diesen Aufsatz meinem Onkel Erich Wurmann.

Notes

1   Schemann, Deutsche Idiomatik, 599.
2   Röhrich, *Lexikon,* 79.
3   Schmitz, "Nordamerikanisch-deutsche Literaturbeziehungen," 162–63.
4   Röhrich, *Lexikon,* 79.
5   Centre National de Recherche Scientifique, *Trésor.*
6   Brod, "Tag aus dem Leben Kühnebecks," 67–68.
7   Heimböckel, "'Amerika im Kopf.'"
8   Kafka, *Der Verschollene,* 7.
9   Schivelbusch, *Kultur der Niederlage,* 237.

10 Schivelbusch, *Kultur der Niederlage*, 303.
11 Otto, *Deutsche Amerika-Bilder*, 5.
12 Gassert, *Amerika im Dritten Reich*, 27.
13 Gassert, *Amerika im Dritten Reich*, 237.
14 Gassert, *Amerika im Dritten Reich*, 233–34.
15 Gassert, *Amerika im Dritten Reich*, 148.
16 Diner, *Verkehrte Welten*, 89.
17 Scheibner, "Onkel aus Amerika."

Works Cited

Blüthgen, Victor. *Zigeunerweisen. Der Onkel aus Amerika. Zwei Erzählungen.* Berlin: Weichert's, 1897.

Brod, Max. "Ein Tag aus dem Leben Kühnebecks, des jungen Idealisten." In *Das Kinobuch. Kinodramen von Bermann* u.a., 65–69. Leipzig: Kurt Wolff Verlag, 1914.

Centre National de la Recherche Scientifique. *Trésor de la Langue Française: Dictionnaire de la langue du XIXe et du XXe siècle (1789–1960).* Volume 12, Natation-Pénétrer. Paris: Gallimard, 1986.

Cooper, James Fenimore. *Cooper's sämmtliche Werke. Uebersetzt von Mehreren und herausgegeben von Christian August Fischer.* Frankfurt am Main: Sauerländer, 1826–50.

Diner, Dan. *Verkehrte Welten. Antiamerikanismus in Deutschland. Ein historischer Essay.* Frankfurt: Eichborn, 1993.

Friederich, Wolf. *Moderne deutsche Idiomatik. Systematisches Wörterbuch mit Definitionen und Beispielen.* Munich: Max Hueber, 1966.

Fünf Millionen suchen einen Erben. Directed by Carl Boese. Berlin: Majestic-Film GmbH, 1938.

Gassert, Philipp. *Amerika im Dritten Reich. Ideologie, Propaganda und Volksmeinung 1933–1945.* Stuttgart: Franz Steinert, 1997.

Heimböckel, Dieter. "'Amerika im Kopf.' Franz Kafkas Roman Der Verschollene und der Amerika-Diskurs seiner Zeit." *Deutsche Vierteljahrsschrift für Literaturwissenschaft und Geistesgeschichte* 77, no. 1 (2003): 130–47.

Kafka, Franz. *Der Verschollene.* Edited by Jost Schillemeit. Frankfurt: Fischer, 1983.

Lessing, Karl Gotthelf. *Die Mätresse.* Lustspiel. 1887. Nendeln: Kraus, 1968.

Man braucht kein Geld. Directed by Carl Boese. Berlin: Allianz-Tonfilm, 1931.

May, Karl. *Winnetou der Rote Gentleman. Band 1 und 2.* Freiburg im Breisgau: Friedrich Ernst Fehsenfeld, 1893.

Otto, Viktor. *Deutsche Amerika-Bilder. Zu den Intellektuellen-Diskursen um die Moderne 1900–1950.* Munich: Fink, 2006.

Reitz, Edgar. *Heimat.* 1981–84. Leipzig: Arthaus, 2004.

Röhrich, Lutz. *Das große Lexikon der sprichwörtlichen Redensarten.* Volume 1. Freiburg: Herder, 1991.

Schemann, Hans. *Deutsche Idiomatik. Die deutschen Redewendungen im Kontext.* Stuttgart: Klett, 1993.

Schivelbusch, Wolfgang. *Kultur der Niederlage. Der amerikanische Süden 1865. Frankreich 1871. Deutschland 1918.* Frankfurt: Fischer, 2003.

Schmitz, Walter. "Nordamerikanisch-deutsche Literaturbeziehungen." In *Literatur-lexikon*, edited by Walter Killy. Volume 14, *Begriffe, Realien, Methoden*, edited by Volker Meid, 162–70. Gütersloh: Bertelsmann, 1993.

Scheibner, Hans. "Der Onkel aus Amerika." Scheibner wochenweise. <www3.ndr .de/ndrtv_pages_std/0,3147,OID1098978_REF2398,00.html> (March 2008).

Trenker, Luis. *Der verlorene Sohn*. Berlin: Ullstein, 1934.

Zimmermann, Karl. *Onkel Sam. Amerikanische Reise- und Kulturbilder*. Stuttgart: Strecker und Schröder, 1904.

TWENTY-FOUR

"Ich will nach Amerika, mir eine neue Heimat suchen"*
The Emigration of Expellees in Post-1945 West German Film

Hanno Sowade

In the first years of the Federal Republic of Germany (FRG), 230,000 refugees and expellees emigrated. Compared to the eight million refugees and expellees in the country at the time, this is a relatively small number. Nevertheless, the topic of emigration is generally underrepresented in West German film of this period. The contemporary reception of films such as the very popular *Grün ist die Heide* (1951) and *Ännchen von Tharau* (1954), but also the realistic comedy *Mamitschka* (1955), allows us to draw conclusions about the impact of the emigration experience. It is remarkable that some films found favour with local audiences and expellees alike, whereas others were appreciated by neither group. Whether or not emigration was shown in a positive light did not seem to matter for audiences of the 1950s; it was more important that emigration was depicted in accordance with contemporary social norms that were also in line with the general behaviour encouraged by the government. Thus, the picture painted of emigration in these films reflects the economic circumstances of the country and societal views held by the wider viewing public.

MILLIONS OF GERMANS WERE ON THE MOVE at the end of World War II and shortly afterward. A census in the FRG on 13 September 1950 counted 7,977,000 people from the former German territories in the east, Czechoslovakia, and other countries from which they were expelled,

---

* *Grün ist die Heide.*

constituting 16.1 percent of the population. In the course of the following two decades this number rose to almost 9.6 million—excluding the refugees from the German Democratic Republic (GDR)—because of births and late migration.

At first the British and American Allied authorities assumed responsibility for the refugees and expellees (from hereon referred to simply as expellees) in West Germany because repatriation was not an option. The camps and temporary accommodations that housed millions of people had the potential for social unrest. The American Military Government Regulations of 1946 stated how the problem must be addressed: "These persons [refugees and expellees] will be absorbed integrally into the German communities."[1] Thus the creation of new minorities had to be avoided. The emigration of expellees, at least to abate the situation, was prevented by the American and British authorities. Only certain groups, mainly displaced persons (DPs) and applicants who had relatives abroad, received permission to emigrate. German clerical and political organizations welcomed a "planned" emigration in principle, but raised concerns about the exit of young, qualified personnel because it would threaten the rebuilding of Germany. They argued for the emigration of whole family units so that people unfit for work would not be left behind and become a burden for the social networks in Germany. The church in particular viewed the emigration of single women as especially dangerous. However, there appears to have been "*ein sehr großer Drang*" among expellees to emigrate.[2]

The commitment in the Military Government Regulations to integrate expellees in German postwar society was also implemented as a requirement for the early movie production under the direction of the American and British authorities. The Anglo-American newsreel *Welt im Film* depicted expulsion and flight only in passing in order to avoid giving expellees a special status in society. In the annual reviews of the year's events (1946–48), the topic was only touched upon in two reports of one minute's duration. The large migration of expellees was consequently not mentioned; instead they foregrounded the successful rebuilding of Germany and the achievements of the Allied powers. The topic of expulsion was also not part of the concept of documentary films, of which about one hundred and twenty were planned in 1946–47.

Only two documentaries by the Allied powers focused on flight and expulsion and their consequences: *Asylrecht* (1949/50) and *Eine Kleinstadt hilft sich selbst* (1950). Emigration as a path to finding a new livelihood did not play a role in either of them. As the title *Eine Kleinstadt hilft sich selbst* suggests, this film demonstrated how a small town in southern Germany successfully overcame post-war problems. Here the situation of expellees was a sub-topic of the film: they were significantly worse off than the local community. Very much like the ideal expellees of the Anglo-American plans, they did not contemplate a new existence abroad, they suffered their fate without complaint and with modesty, and made tireless efforts to integrate and advance in their new West German homeland. Both documentaries got a lukewarm reception by the audience. The internationally very successful film *Asylrecht* did have a difficult run in German cinemas. *"Der Dokumentarfilm 'Asylrecht' zeigt in erschütternden Szenen das Gesicht dieser 'verlorenen Generation.' Kein Kino will ihn spielen, kein Publikum sehen,"* the *Evangelische Filmbeobachter* claimed in 1950.[3] The film quickly fell from view as audiences in the FRG wanted to see different movies.

No West German movie on expellees was produced in 1949. As required by the Allied powers, the coming to terms with expulsion and flight did not exist as a subject of German film, and certainly not as a separate genre. Expellees were depicted in supporting roles in numerous productions, however, for example *Film ohne Titel* (1947) by Rudolf Jugert, *In jenen Tagen* (1947) by Helmut Käutner, and *Liebe 47* (1949) by Wolfgang Liebeneiner. Statements such as *"Schlimmer wie die Zigeuner"* or *"Seien Sie froh, Flüchtlinge sind Menschen zweiter Klasse"* from the movie *Film ohne Titel* allude to the everyday reality of refugees.

After the establishment of the FRG, the Allies gradually removed restrictions from movie production and the film industry was in a better position to react to the demands of its audience. Generally, one criterion for the success of a movie is the ability to reflect effectively the prevalent collective attitudes toward life and the Zeitgeist. One quarter of German film production from 1949 to the mid-60s consisted of *Heimatfilms*—sentimental films with a regional setting. One such film, *Grün ist die Heide*, became the most successful German film of the 1950s and by 1959 had attracted nineteen million viewers.

The spectrum of the depiction of expellees in West German movies after World War II is extraordinarily wide. An analysis of films such as *Grün ist die Heide, Ännchen von Tharau*, and *Mamitschka* demonstrates similarities: each film deals with the topic of emigration in the context of the fate of expellees and their efforts at integration. Each film will be analysed in turn.

Grün ist die Heide is a remake of a film from 1932 (see Box 1). However, the themes of integration and emigration appear only in the new postwar version written by Bobby Lüthge. The topic of the expulsion and integration of refugees was depicted in the story of the forester and his love (played by the dream couple of the German postwar cinema, Sonja Ziemann and Rudolf Prack), as well as through the experiences of the expelled land owner Lüder Lüdersen. The love story of the refugee Nora

BOX 1

GRÜN IST DIE HEIDE (1951)

DIRECTOR: Hans Deppe

SCRIPT: Bobby E. Lüthge

The former Silesian land owner Lüder Lüdersen (Hans Stüwe) finds refuge with his cousin at a moated castle in the Lüneburger Heide after his flight from the east. Lüdersen cannot bear the loss of his forest and becomes a poacher. The young forester Rainer (Rudolf Prack) falls in love with Lüdersen's daughter Helga (Sonja Ziemann). Rainer makes it his task to track down the poacher. Helga, on the other hand, wants to protect her father and persuades him—despite her own reservations—to move to town. When a country constable is found murdered, the situation gets worse. At the same time, a circus is in town, in which Helga's former friend, Nora von Burkwitz (Maria Holst), performs dressage in order to earn money for her emigration to America. Lüdersen gives a thank-you and farewell speech at a fair, and a Silesian costume group sings a song about the *Riesengebirge*. Prior to his departure he goes for a walk in his beloved forest. There he meets another poacher from the travelling circus. Before the poacher is arrested as the real perpetrator, he shoots Lüdersen. Lüdersen is injured, but at least he is now exonerated. Helga and forester Rainer now await a happy future. Nora also has the prospect of a happy future shared with the district judge (Willy Fritsch) in his Heimat.[4]

von Burkwitz and the local district judge is the second plot strand that foregrounds the theme of emigration. Interestingly, the total length of screen time for Nora and the district judge equals that of Helga and Rainer. A number of scenes show why Nora wants to emigrate, how the district judge courts her, and how she starts building her future in Germany at the (happy) end.

The dramaturgy in *Grün ist die Heide* relies on a number of typical images and clichés, which the contemporary audience understood immediately, such as a young woman as expellee and a financially and socially well-established man as the representative of the admitting West German society. The planned emigration seems more like the desperate idea of a tomboyish, young, single woman than a well thought-out plan for building a life. Her work in a circus, which is by definition at the fringes of society, emphasizes this. Nora's admission *"Ich finde es nicht nett hier in der sogenannten Heimat, gar nicht!"* comes across as defiant protest. However, her reservations are remedied in the course of the film and it comes to a double happy ending: she finds her happiness in a new relationship and she is spared emigration. Thus, the film subtly connects her love to a local with her revived love for the *Heimat*, which had been submerged by the experience of her flight. Emigration to America is no longer necessary.

The Heimatfilm *Ännchen von Tharau* depicts emigration plans of a different group, the older, destitute expellees for whom building a new life was fraught with particular material and non-material problems. The portrayal of expellees in this film is multilayered. In the plot line that focuses on Gru Gutjahn, two scenes are key. One shows the local innkeeper organizing a film evening and showing a movie about the lost territories of East Prussia. The emotional portrayal of wistful memories makes it clear that this loss is still very much felt by the older generation from East Prussia such as Gru and the people around her and that they have not found a new *Heimat* in the West. In the second scene, Gru informs Ännchen about a letter from her son, who lives in America with his family. The letter also contains travel documents for Gru to emigrate to Texas. Gru sees her future with her children and grandchildren there. In her opinion, her departure is also positive for Ännchen, who cares for the elderly lady: "*Seien Sie froh, dass Sie mich los werden, wo Sie so viel Mühe mit mir gehabt haben.*"

The extraordinary popular success of the films *Grün ist die Heide* and *Ännchen von Tharau* enables us to draw conclusions about how the German public dealt with the topics of emigration and integration of displaced persons in the mid 1950s. It seems that locals and expellees shared some common ground in their interpretation. *Grün ist die Heide* shows love stories in an idealized natural world. *Ännchen von Tharau* does the same in the environment of an intact small town that is close to nature. The

BOX 2

ÄNNCHEN VON THARAU (1954)

DIRECTOR: Wolfgang Schleif

SCRIPT: Heinz Otto Jahn, Wolfgang Schleif

A number of expellees live in a small town in the wine-growing district around Würzburg and try to secure their existence. The inherent problems of integration, the wistful memories of the former *Heimat*, and the many different ways of solving these problems—for example, the plans of Gru Gutjahn, played by Margarete Haage, to emigrate—mould every-day life. The expellee Anna Wittkuhn/Ännchen (Ilse Werner) works as a waitress in the local tavern to make a living for herself and her son, Utz (Klaus-Ulrich Krause). She is so popular that she is celebrated in the song "Ännchen von Tharau." The young, affluent vineyard owner Adrian Rotenbach (Helmuth Schneider) asks for her hand. Ännchen is reluctant to accept because she is not the biological mother of Utz. During her flight, she was given the child by his dying mother together with a picture of the father, Ullrich Lessau (Heinz Engelmann). When the missing Lessau arrives in the town, a very complex love story ensues. The film ends with Ullrich, Ännchen, and Utz forming a happy family.

destroyed cities of the early 1950s did not feature much in these productions; instead nature is a metaphor for an ideal world and the *Heimat*.
Problems in living together and with integration were only cautiously
hinted at. Individual story lines underscored successful integration.
Expellees who needed help and support were stereotypically cast as women.
It is interesting to note that these films depicted emigration both as an ideal
opportunity for the refugees to build a new life and as an error of judgement. They achieved this by linking this portrayal with generally accepted
behaviour patters. The plot in *Grün ist die Heide* reflects the social and
moral conventions of the time. A single woman could only find fulfillment in marriage, not by emigrating on her own. With its positive depiction of the abandonment of emigration plans, the plot also corresponded
to the political and economic priorities of preventing young, employable
people from emigrating in order to protect the German labour market and
economy. On the other hand, *Ännchen von Tharau* shows the emigration
of Gru Gutjahn, for which she is ready with the receipt of the travel documents, in a positive light. The wish of an elderly lady to be reunited with
her family abroad found wide acceptance among the German population
of the 1950s. The departure of an elderly expellee who could no longer
contribute to the economy and therefore would depend on benefits is
portrayed as a relief for society. Interestingly, Ännchen, a hard-working
expellee who is trying to build her own life and is not yet a member of the
local community, is the one who is relieved of the burden to care for Gru.
This way the film avoids potential conflict between the needy refugees
and the ostensibly antisocial host society.

Locals and expellees read both films each in their own way and understood the films' messages in different ways: from "we have integrated
them" to "we have made it." The *Heimatfilm* gave fledgling West German
society a sense of orientation with respect to traditional values. The refugees
in the successful German postwar movies were a stabilizing factor for society. They accepted their fate without complaint, had the will to build a
new life, and made every effort to integrate successfully or to find a new
home for themselves—in Germany or abroad.

The fate of expellees, however, was underrepresented as a subject in
film; even in the *Heimatfilm* it was only touched upon.[5] During the Allied
occupation from 1945 to 1949, audiences were hardly interested in the
depiction of contemporary problems because locals and refugees alike
did not want to be confronted with reality in the movie theatre. The lack
of success of *Mamitschka* (1955), a feature film by the Bohemian Rolf
Thiele, is an indication of that. Thiele staged the trials and tribulations
of an ethnic German family from Bohemia using comedic and tragic
elements.

BOX 3

MAMITSCHKA (1955)

DIRECTOR: Rolf Thiele

SCRIPT: Rolf Thiele

In the refugee camp, the Navratils, a family of eight from Bohemia, learn that they have been allocated an apartment in another town, where the father, Tatinek (Rudolf Platte), also finds work. Under Mamitschka's (Mila Kopp) leadership they move there. When they arrive in the small and run-down apartment, they are greeted with astonishment and rejection. Only to avoid having to share the kitchen does the landlord give them another room for cooking. It takes a lot of effort for Mamitschka to muddle through. However, they are also responsible for a number of ensuing problems themselves. After an initial confrontation, the family finds a real friend in the shy, German-American soldier Paul Wilborn (Klaus Behrendt), who is in love with daughter Rosa (Jester Naefe). When Tatinek is fired from his factory job because of a petty crime, all begins to break down. But then a lottery win changes everything. But even though Mamitschka tries to use the money wisely, she does not manage. The steady decline culminates in a deadly motorcycle accident involving two of the children. After overcoming the initial shock, the family decides to start afresh and emigrate with the help of their friend Wilborn.[6]

Austrian and Swiss film critics reacted positively to this problem-oriented film. However, the plot with dialogue such as *"In meine Küche kommt mir niemand herein, das sage ich gleich!...Tatinek, bring das Papier, wo steht von Küchenbenutzung"* focused on the opposition of locals and refugees, which did not find grace with German audiences. When it becomes apparent that, after the transition period in the camp, the family's attempts at integration will fail, their decision to emigrate can almost be described as logical consequence. In a key scene, Mamitschka, Tatinek, Rosa, and Wilborn debate the future fate of their family and decide to start afresh in America. Mamitschka says: *"Na gut. Gehen wir nach Amerika ... Amerika ist groß, hat genug Platz für alle, die Heimat verloren haben. Deutschland ist so voll von Flüchtlingen, hat nicht genug Platz für alle."*

When they leave town wearily, but with great hopes for their future in America, it is framed in a shot similar to their optimistic, if somewhat skeptical arrival: they walk through the town gate and the song "Mamitschka" is played. Neither the local nor the expellee audience would have expected a positive perception of emigration as the one in *Grün ist die Heide* or *Ännchen von Tharau*: the hosts saw themselves accused of not having integrated the refugees, whereas the refugees, on the other hand, had not succeeded in building their own life in Germany through calm commitment and hard work.

Officials also viewed the film skeptically. The Bürgschaftsgesellschaft für Filmkredite had its doubts and refused to provide a financial guarantee at first, because the film focuses on "*das Flüchtlingsmilieu ... im Gegensatz zu den Bemühungen der Bundesregierung nicht die Eingliederung, sondern die Isolierung der Flüchtlinge.*"[7]

The efforts by the Bundesministerium für Vertriebene, Flüchtlinge und Kriegsgeschädigte explicit use of the media. The ministry provided slides and films that were used not only by expellee organizations but also by schools and other educational institutions as well as by the army. By 1960 their film archive had expanded to eighty-one films, of which fifty-four can be classified as *Heimatfilm*. Lending was brisk, particularly in the first half of the 1950s. Still, in 1958 the Konferenz der Landesfilmdienste reported 1,600 screenings with more than 80,000 viewers. Most *Heimatfilme* showed people, towns, and rural areas of the expellees' homelands before 1945. A noteworthy number of films depicting the integration of expellees did not exist. Only the film *Guarapuava* shows the settling of about five hundred German refugees from southeast Europe in the Brazilian primeval forest. Since the Swiss financed this emigration, it can be assumed that this sixteen-minute documentary was also produced on their initiative.[8]

In 1955, the ministry started a large-scale attempt "*zur Schaffung eines Filmstreifens, der das Vertriebenen-Problem behandelt, mit Hilfe von Autorenanschreiben geeignete Entwürfe zu erhalten.*"[9] The choice of genre—short film, documentary, or feature film—was up to the authors. However, the parameters for content were more restrictive: the significance of expellees and refugees for the *Wirtschaftswunder*, their endurance of the hardships of the initial years, and the great sense of responsibility and tolerance on the part of both local residents and refugees. Emigration was clearly not a topic mentioned by the ministry. The project was largely accepted by potential authors. Of the forty invited to submit scripts, the overwhelming majority did so. A further twenty unsolicited scripts brought the total number to sixty. However, a thorough assessment by four panels of consultants showed that none of the projects had sufficient artistic merit to be produced. Instead the ministry had to continue to rely on its film archive to show "*den Vertriebenen und Flüchtlingen die alte Heimat ... Zugleich aber dienen diese Filme auch dazu, die Einheimischen mit den Kulturdenkmälern und der Landschaft in Ost- und Mitteldeutschland vertraut zu machen.*"[10]

For a long time, it was a widely held view that the refugees and expellees would be integrated quickly into the life of the FRG after World War II. However, this was an ambivalent and complex process. The economic, social, and political integration of the expellees—the construction of a new *Heimat*—was a different process for each individual depending on origin, age, and educational background. Approximately 230,000 refugees and expellees were trying to find this new *Heimat* abroad, the main destination being Canada followed by the United States and Australia. Emigrants born in West Germany, on the other hand, preferred the United States. In view of the total number of refugees and expellees of eight million in West Germany in 1950, the proportion of expellees who eased Germany's refugee problem through emigration is small. Emigration was restricted during the time of Allied occupation, thereby preventing large groups from leaving. Only after the founding of the Federal Republic of Germany were the quotas for emigrants increased, but at this time Germany had become the country of the *Wirtschaftswunder* and human resources were urgently needed.

It was during this phase that the feature films that depicted the topic of emigration were produced. It is remarkable that these films were received similarly by expellees and locals alike. Either the films met with approval by both audiences or they flopped. Emigration could be shown in commercially successful films in a positive or negative light. It was more important whether the concept of emigration in the film related to widely accepted, binding social norms and motives, which often corresponded to officially encouraged behavioural patterns. Young, employable people had to be retained for the German economy, whereas people who were no longer productive could leave. A film such as *Mamitschka*, which attempted to depict the fate of expellees using fewer clichés and more realistic portrayals, was not appreciated by the wider audience, which preferred "*leichte und bunte Unterhaltungsfilme.*"[11] The reasons for emigration by a whole family are understandable in the light of eight million expellees in the country, but they were in direct opposition to the economic interests of Germany. Thus the view of emigration accepted by the audience was in accordance with the economic interests of the country on the one hand, and the relatively small number of émigrés on the other. The projects and measures undertaken by the Bundesministerium für Vertriebene, Flüchtlinge und Kriegsgeschädigte were, of course, in line with the interests of the whole state. The films hardly ever referred to emigration, certainly not as a possible solution to existing problems. How many expellees would have left Germany had there been a less restrictive American or Canadian emigration policy between 1945 until the start of the economic upswing in the early 1950s is a matter for speculation, as is the possible representation of this emigration in German feature films.

This chapter has been translated from German by Mathias Schulze and James M. Skidmore.

Notes

1 Military Government Regulations, Title 20, quoted in Schraut, "Flüchtlingsbild," 353.
2 "Deutsche Auswanderung in der Nachkriegszeit," Maas, 18 January 1954, Staatsarchiv Bremen (STAB) 4.35/4 Handakten Dr. Maas. See also "Gemeinsamer Schritt der Ministerpräsidenten zur Auswanderungsfrage" mit drei Anlagen, 14 March 1949, STAB 3-A.4. Nr. 671; "Die Eingliederung der Flüchtlinge in die deutsche Gemeinschaft," Sonne-Kommission, 21 April 1951, STAB 3-R.1. m. Nr. 211 [19].
3 Stettner, "Deutsche," 160.
4 Stettner, "Deutsche," 161.
5 See also Der Bundesminister für Vertriebene, Flüchtlinge und Kriegsgeschädigte an Herrn Hasselbach, 28 February 1955, Bundesarchiv Koblenz (BAK) B 150/ 6989 Heft 2.
6 Stettner, "Deutsche," 163–64.
7 Stettner, "Deutsche," 167.
8 See "Filmliste des Bundesministeriums für Vertriebene, Flüchtlinge und Kriegsgeschädigte," Bonn, Stand: April 1967, BAK, B 106/27697; Konferenz der Landesfilmdienste für Jugend und Volksbildung, Zusammenfassung der Einsatzberichte der Landesfilmdienste, 1 July 1958, BAK, B 150/3377 Heft 2.
9 Bundesministerium für Vertriebene, Flüchtlinge und Kriegsgeschädigte an das Kulturwerk der vertriebenen Deutschen e.V., betr. Begutachtung von Filmmanuskript-Entwürfen, 21 September 1955, BAK, B 150/3365 Heft 3.
10 Der Bundesminister für Vertriebene, Flüchtlinge und Kriegsgeschädigte, Filmprojekt, betr. Filme aus den ostdeutschen Siedlungsgebieten, BAK, B 150/3377 Heft 2.
11 Anschreiben mit Einnahmen-Abrechnung Mamitschka, Saarfilm-Union Saarbrücken, 12 December 1956, Dokumentations- und Forschungsstelle Medien, FH Hannover, Fachbereich IK Kulturarchiv (116).

Archival Material

Bundesarchiv Koblenz (BAK), B 106/27697; B 150/3377 Heft 2. B 150/3365 Heft 3.
Dokumentations- und Forschungsstelle Medien, FH Hannover, Fachbereich IK Kulturarchiv (116).
Konferenz der Landesfilmdienste für Jugend und Volksbildung, Zusammenfassung der Einsatzberichte der Landesfilmdienste, 1 July 1958, Bundesarchiv Koblenz.
Staatsarchiv Bremen (STAB) 4.35/4 Handakten Dr. Maas.

Works Cited

Ännchen von Tharau. Directed by Wolfgang Schleif. Berlin: Filmstudios Berlin Tempelhof GmbH, 1954.
Asylrecht. Directed by Rudolf Werner Kipp. Berlin: Deutsche Dokumentarfilmgesellschaft mbH, 1949.
Film ohne Titel. Directed by Rudolf Jugert. Grünwald, Germany: Bavaria Filmstudios, 1947–48.
Grün ist die Heide. Directed by Hans Deppe. Berlin: Berolina, 1951.

Mamitschka. Directed by Rolf Thiele, Göttingen: Filmatelier Göttingen, 1955.

Schraut, Sylvia. "Das Flüchtlingsbild im westdeutschen Nachkriegsfilm der Besatzungszeit." In *Die Flüchtlingsfrage in der deutschen Nachkriegsgesellschaft,* edited by Sylvia Schraut and Thomas Grosser, 193–214. Mannheim: Palatium, 1996.

Stettner, Peter. "'Sind Sie denn überhaupt Deutsche?' Stereotype, Sehnsüchte und Ängste im Flüchtlingsbild des deutschen Nachkriegsfilms." In *Zwischen Heimat und Zuhause. Deutsche Flüchtlinge und Vertriebene in (West-) Deutschland 1945–2000,* edited by Rainer Schulze, 156–70. Osnabrück: Secolo, 2001.

TWENTY-FIVE

German Diaspora Experiences in British Columbia after 1945

Christian Lieb

German immigrants to British Columbia in the 1950s had a different experience than their contemporaries elsewhere in Canada. Within this ethnic group, diverse patterns of immigration and integration into the host society are discernible. Although the Canadian mainstream would characterize all of them as Germans, information gleaned from interviews with these immigrants strongly questions the existence of a single German Canadian or German diaspora identity. Ethnic Germans, many of whom were sponsored by relatives and friends who came to Canada before or just after World War II, often joined or were joined by entire extended families, unlike German nationals who had no previous connections to Canada and came either on their own or in small family units. Ethnic Germans also tended to preserve their traditions and language, and to participate actively in German clubs and churches, whereas individuals born in Germany were more likely to switch to English as the home language and to socialize with Canadians. Regardless of the initial differences in the patterns of integration between ethnic Germans and German nationals, however, their children have become Canadians.

Immigration

IN A SEPTEMBER 1951 MEMORANDUM, Dr. Werner Dankwort, the German ambassador in Ottawa, described his impressions of a trip to the four western provinces where he met with representatives of the German community. He found a noticeable difference between prewar

305

immigrants who stressed their Canadian identity and avoided associating with German organizations because of the pressures they experienced during the war, and "recent immigrants," who were mainly part of "German minorities from Russia, the smaller states along its margins and the successor states of the Austrian Empire."[1] Because they usually knew little English and hardly anything about the Canadian way of life, they sought to associate with other Germans. Concentrated in southern Ontario, the Prairie provinces, and British Columbia, they took the lead in cultivating "German traditions" and in running German associations.[2] The ambassador believed their concern for preserving their German heritage resulted from a long experience in fighting for their identity while living in an alien environment for generations.

Given Canadian immigration policy, the vast majority of Germans who were allowed into the country between 1945 and September 1950 were eastern European refugees.[3] Only after Canada completely lifted its ban on the immigration of former enemy aliens in September 1950 did German nationals begin to arrive in significant numbers, reaching a peak of 23,000 annually in the years between 1950 and 1957.[4] Thus when Dankwort travelled to western Canada, most German nationals were recent immigrants who were not well enough established to finance and support their own ethnic clubs and churches, and the ambassador's observations were at least partly based on the fact that early postwar German immigration to Canada was, like the migrations before and between the wars, dominated by ethnic Germans (German-speaking populations born outside of the 1937 borders of Germany).[5] This link is also reflected in Alexander Freund's assessment that this postwar migration was "economically, politically, socially, and culturally connected to earlier, simultaneous, and later migration streams."[6] Especially in the early postwar years, Ottawa's policies were clearly biased toward healthy young refugees with existing family connections in Canada who could sponsor them by loaning money to pay for their passage from Europe.[7] Even after September 1950, three quarters of the immigrants were sponsored by relatives, the Canadian government, religious organizations, and farmers, while only one quarter were able to pay their own passage. Most of the latter, however, arrived toward the end of the decade. Given the nature of migration in the interwar period, almost all immigrants sponsored by family members in Canada were ethnic Germans, while people born in West Germany were overrepresented in the group who paid their own passage or were supported by their family in Germany.

Family connections, not displacement *per se* or the chilly reception these displaced persons received in West Germany, contributed to making Germans one of the largest immigrant groups between 1950 and 1990, not only in Canada as a whole, but also in British Columbia, where close to a quarter of all German postwar immigrants now reside.[8] While the number of German immigrants declined significantly after the 1950s, British Columbia increasingly became their preferred destination.[9] Based on fifty personal interviews,[10] published biographies, and government records, this chapter addresses the immigration and integration of the German diaspora in British Columbia, especially Vancouver Island, the Lower Mainland, and the Okanagan Valley. It focuses on the challenges and coping strategies of these German immigrants, as well as the significant differences between the experiences of ethnic Germans and German nationals in terms of settlement and assimilation.

Integration

Dankwort's assessment that German organizations were often in the hands of ethnic Germans because they had a tradition of preserving their German identity in eastern Europe was certainly correct for British Columbia. He could have added two other possible explanations. First, since many of the ethnic Germans came to Canada with their extended families, they continued to speak German and celebrate traditional holidays. Second, German nationals had a more immediate connection with the Hitler dictatorship and likely felt some guilt or shame. As a result, they were generally less inclined to lead these organizations, if they joined them at all. Ethnic Germans, in contrast, could point to the loss of their homes and the horrors of the trek westward to justify their role as victims of the war, not perpetrators, a prominent theme in their life stories. Therefore, they had little reason to feel ashamed or guilty of their German identity and did not readily give up their language and customs.

Like most other ethnic Germans, Reinhold P., born in Romania, and Richard P., born in Poland, reflect this sentiment by expressing pride in being both German and Canadian,[11] whereas Lucia F., born in Hesse, displayed the opposite: "Usually, I would tell people that I was one of those 'bloody Germans.' I was always afraid of people's reactions when they found out, though my family never had anything to do with the Nazis."[12] There is a discernible tendency for German nationals to keep their distance from German organizations in an attempt to integrate into the Canadian mainstream. As a result, not all German-speaking immigrants made similar use of the developing ethnic support networks in British Columbia. German nationals who could maintain ties to family still in Germany did not have the emotional need to bring their old traditions with them. Moreover, people born in West Germany usually had the option to return home if they did not succeed in Canada. Rolf and Brigitte U., for example, even had a return ticket as insurance against failure.[13] Others had a place to return to, although not necessarily the financial means. Since ethnic Germans had lost everything in Europe, they were more likely to attempt to recreate their lost home in North America through churches and clubs. Most of the ethnic German immigrants were sponsored by relatives and sometimes by friends who had immigrated in the 1920s and in turn would sponsor their own extended families. Thus they established a pattern of chain migration to the farming areas in Alberta and, to a lesser degree, to Manitoba and Saskatchewan. Of a total of forty-eight respondents in this study, sixteen went immediately to British Columbia, while twenty-nine went first to the Prairie provinces. However, British Columbia soon attracted many of them. Within the first five years of their arrival, thirty of these immigrants resided in British Columbia; most of the remaining eighteen came later to the Okanagan, Lower Mainland, or Vancouver Island for their retirement.

A common reason for moving to British Columbia was to escape the long, cold Prairie winters. Apart from the more familiar climate, the landscapes of the Okanagan Valley evoked memories of home for several. Irene S. and Erwin K. found the area strikingly similar to their former homes in western Hungary, and Mina S. and her husband moved to Kelowna because the countryside "with all the fruit trees" was reminiscent of the scenery along the Rhine.[14] For others, it was the fulfillment of a dream to live in view of the Coast Mountains in Vancouver, or on an island as in the case of Caroline L.'s husband, who gave up a position as a manager of a feed mill in Alberta to work in the engine room of a ferry simply because it allowed him to live on Saltspring Island.[15]

In the early 1950s, there were also good job opportunities on the West Coast for men who wanted to establish themselves in agriculture, or were willing to work in construction, logging, and sawmills. For women, jobs as domestics, waitresses, house cleaners, and kitchen helpers were available. In addition, Vancouver Island was a paradise for gardeners.[16] Few of these jobs required English skills and for many immigrants the first two years in a low-paying position seemed unavoidable in order to learn the language and the customs, which were valuable assets for later careers. In contrast to Freund's findings, most of the immigrants in this sample did not deny that they were exploited and fought for higher wages or sought better employment opportunities once they improved their command of the language and familiarized themselves with practices in Canada.[17]

West Germans were more likely to have some knowledge of English when they arrived in Canada. This often allowed them to develop their language skills quickly and thereby improve their employment prospects and integration. For example, Christian S., who had learned English in high school in Germany and attended university in Hannover for three semesters, readily secured a job as a draftsman in Winnipeg. With this income he financed university studies, graduated as an engineer, and soon found employment with the Canadian government.[18] Others, like Günther B., used their English skills to start their own successful businesses.[19] Most of the immigrants interviewed in British Columbia, however, did not return to their old professions, partly because many of those with an agricultural background either did not want to start their own farms or could not afford to do so until they were already well established in another profession.[20] Those who had learned a trade often found that their certificates and credentials were not recognized in Canada.

For many immigrants the first one or two years were difficult unless they came to a well-established family in Canada. The living conditions were very basic and first jobs often strenuous, underpaid, and exploitative, but many German immigrants, in particular the refugees, claimed that they felt at home in Canada within a year, partly because they had more spacious accommodation than in Germany and finally had enough to eat. Since most of the ethnic Germans had family and friends in Canada and no roots in Germany, none of them regretted the decision to immigrate. German nationals, however, usually had most of their family and friends in Germany, so the decision-making process was more complex, especially when the beginning proved more difficult than expected. In particular when they left behind secure jobs it took significantly longer to overcome homesickness and self-doubt about whether emigration was the right decision. There was some re-migration, but those who stayed generally made a strong commitment to become Canadians. Later, their circle of friends usually included many Canadians; they were more likely to switch to English as their home language; and, in a few cases, they would even convert from Lutheranism or Catholicism to Anglicanism. For example, Christian S. states that he and his wife never attended "any German Lutheran church. Very early on, we got involved with the Anglican Church of Canada, which has become a home to us. We were quite determined to integrate and did not want to be a separate entity in a foreign environment."[21]

Once immigrants had adjusted to Canadian conditions and started learning the language, establishing a home, and making friends, they began to put down roots in their new home country. Their children, however, often confronted situations in schools where their classmates equated their German background with Nazism. Olga S. remembers that "back in the 1950s in Canada, being German was not something you would make public. In the school system there was no distinction. If you were German you were a Nazi and as a child I knew that that was not something I wanted to be."[22] As some of the interviews show, this stigmatizing led to children either getting into fights in the schoolyards or trying to reject their

German background in order to fit in. Leo K. recalled being "called Nazi. It did two things for me, really. It made me want to learn how to speak English very quickly to avoid being identified as German and it gave me the ability to run very fast. I was beaten up because I was a Kraut."[23]

Given the children's experiences, it seems surprising to note that few of the adults remember experiencing discrimination. This might be partially explained by their initial lack of English skills, but may also have resulted from the fact that in their initial low-paying labouring positions, they did not compete with established Canadian workers. When they applied for managerial positions, however, a few adults encountered jealous Canadians who feared competition. Klay S. experienced physical and mental abuse for being German, especially at a job interview with a television station in Vancouver. At a different company the boss simply told him that he would not hire Germans at a managerial level.[24]

The Development of German Ethnic Organizations in British Columbia

In the Prairies, a network of German clubs existed in the early 1950s, but in British Columbia there were basically only two, the Vancouver Alpen Club and the German club in Osoyoos. In most other locations, including the Okanagan and Vancouver Island, no German clubs and churches existed at the time. Therefore, many of the early social networks were limited to family connections and friendships. Lilli G., who had been sponsored by her aunt and uncle with whom she stayed after her arrival in the Okanagan, remembers how the younger German people met every Sunday at the Muller farm in Rutland just outside of Kelowna and then drove to the park to play games. Lilli and her sister, Lydia P., also met their future husbands, both ethnic Germans, at a privately organized German New Year's dance in Vernon.[25]

By the early 1960s, however, German immigrants were sufficiently well established to start their own ethnic organizations. Rolando Ernesto Sartorius, a German from Mexico who owned a delicatessen in Victoria, organized German movie nights in a local theatre for the recent immigrants.[26] His delicatessen and others in downtown Victoria also served as informal information exchanges that helped, for example, to spread the idea of establishing the Harmonie Choir in 1961 and the Edelweiss Club in 1970. The initiative for both the choir and the club came largely from German immigrants who had participated in German ethnic clubs in Ontario or the Prairies and wanted to establish similar organizations in their new hometowns. As Liesel Schumacher notes: "People from the prairies came in, and in those areas there were many flourishing German clubs. The new arrivals wanted the same here. The best supporters were and still are

Germans from the eastern part of Europe with a long tradition of religious as well as social organizations."[27] According to Schumacher, the drive to establish a German club in Victoria, therefore, came from within the community and had little to do with Canada's adoption of multiculturalism at the end of the 1960s. Horst Kopplin, who later became president of the Edelweiss Club, states that the club's founding resulted from an "influx of Germans from all over Canada ... [who] had been members of clubs with a wider range of interests on the mainland."[28]

Once the Victoria Edelweiss Club was formed, it also assisted new immigrants to adjust to life in Canada. Schumacher, the president of its Ladies Group, recalled that not only did an ethnic club preserve language and traditions, but it also made it easier to adjust to life in Canada. She explained that "it has always been a great help. As a group we have been facing similar problems and therefore have always been able to help each other in finding solutions. It also has helped our children to better understand their German heritage. We truly feel that we are German-Canadians!"[29] This assessment coincides with Rolf U.'s explanation that the clubs created a second home for recent immigrants and, therefore, made it easier for them to get accustomed to their new lives in Canada.[30]

The various Christian churches were also not idle in dealing with the influx of German immigrants and in establishing new congregations in British Columbia. Catholics, Baptists, and Lutherans founded German-language congregations while the initiative in some cases came from the immigrants themselves. For example, in the 1950s, Alcan's new company town of Kitimat attracted many immigrant families from western and northern Europe including a significant number of Lutherans. Since there were no church services, Alcan employee Wilfried Langen contacted the Western Canada Synod in Winnipeg and provided a list of fifty people who would support the establishment of a Lutheran congregation. He estimated that there were about two hundred Lutheran workers in Kitimat and an unknown number of family members. The vast majority of those listed were German immigrants, but also included were five Norwegians and one Danish couple. Partly in response to the request, the Lutheran Church provided eighty thousand dollars to develop a bilingual or multilingual church in Kitimat in 1955.[31]

Around the same time, in 1954–55, the Western Canada Synod investigated the possibility of establishing a German mission in Victoria. After retiring from the presidency of the synod, Reverend Julius Bergbusch accepted the task of building this new bilingual German English church in 1955. As a mission, it initially received financial support directly from the synod since the recent immigrants did not have the means to pay for their own church. Moreover, because the German government had deducted church taxes directly from personal income, German nationals were not accustomed to donating directly to churches. By 1960, however, the congregation was able to purchase its own building, the Good Shepherd Lutheran Church, which provided a morning service in English and the main service in German.[32]

Bergbusch not only took care of the spiritual needs of his congregation, but he also helped them adjust to life in Canada by giving new immigrants English and driving lessons or by accompanying some—not necessarily all Lutherans—as translator to job interviews or on house-hunting expeditions. In at least a couple of cases, he also supported the immigration of fiancées of members of his congregation through the Lutheran World Relief Organization and assured worried parents that their daughters would stay well protected in his parsonage until the wedding day.[33] Bergbusch's wife, Mary Magdalene, remembered in a 1981 interview that when German immigrants arrived in Victoria, the immigration department would inform Bergbusch so that he could meet them and arrange temporary shelter. One young immigrant family, for example, came to the Bergbuschs with only five dollars in cash and a tent they had planned to pitch within walking distance of the harbour. Instead they stayed at the parsonage until they found work and could pay for their own accommodations while neighbours provided them and other immigrants in need with blankets, furniture, and various household items.[34] Not everyone who took advantage of the social network provided by the Bergbuschs was interested in the church. Mary Bergbusch seemed resentful of the fact that "many showed little or no interest or even enmity for the church," although "they were very pleased when my husband let them use his car for driving lessons and taught them to speak English so they could find jobs."[35] The Bergbuschs continued to work with the Good Shepherd congregation until 1967 when Reverend Bergbusch retired at the age of seventy.

Although most German immigrants to Canada learned enough English within a few years to communicate effectively at work and in their daily lives, there appears to be a noticeable difference between ethnic Germans and German nationals in the emphasis on the use of German at home. In many ethnic German families, the parents insisted on German as the home language, and when that became impossible—usually when two children were in school and started to speak English with each other—they often demanded that only German be spoken around the dinner table. Ethnic German parents were also more likely to send their children to German Saturday school as a means of preserving their heritage.[36] Although this was also important for families from Germany, they usually accepted the unwillingness of their children to learn German and were more likely to switch to English as their home language, as in the case of

Christian S. who encouraged his children to learn German but did not insist on it.[37]

Today, the German clubs and choirs are in decline due to an aging membership. German immigration to Canada has dropped significantly to an average of only about fifteen hundred per year in the 1970s to '90s. Its nature has also shifted noticeably in terms of occupational background and destination within the country.[38] While many of the immigrants in the 1950s either had an agricultural or trade background and arrived with one or two suitcases, later immigrants were generally better educated, usually already spoke English, and came with a substantial portion of their household effects. The older immigrants, with a mix of pride in their own achievements after initial hardship and some jealousy for the easy beginnings of the newcomers, often refer to these later arrivals as "*Container-deutsche.*"[39] Many of these new immigrants did not join the clubs and churches established by their predecessors, and ethnic organizations no longer profited even from this small infusion of younger people from Germany.

As a result, the German diaspora in British Columbia, defined as the organized network of people identifying as Germans, is disappearing. With the significantly reduced volume and changing nature of immigration, postwar ethnic churches and clubs have gradually found themselves catering to aging and often very traditional groups that hold little appeal for the second and third generations. Although some believed that the only way to preserve the German clubs was to "try to instil our traditions and values into the second generation,"[40] it seems that German language and tradition hold only a limited attraction for the children of the postwar immigrants in Canada. It is, therefore, likely that most German organizations, at least in British Columbia, will disappear within the next decade or two. Even though they provided an important network for immigrants in the past, they are no longer useful to the small number of new arrivals or the second generation.

Notes

1 Dr. Werner Dankwort memorandum, Ottawa, 26 September 1951, Library and Archives Canada (LAC) MG31–H39, Kurt von Cardinal fonds, vol. 1, Correspondence Immigration II, translation from German original.

2 Ibid.

3 For a detailed description of Canada's immigration policy, see Steinert, *Migration und Politik,* 79–81 and 105–09; Schmalz, "Statistical Overview," 8–9.

4 For changes in Canadian immigration policy, see Sauer, "A Matter of Domestic Policy?"; Avery, "Canadian Immigration Policy," 51–53.

5 For Canada's immigration policy toward German nationals in the interwar period, see Wagner, *A History of Migration,* 164–68; Lehmann, *The German Canadians,* 157–60.

6 Freund, *Aufbrüche*, 509–10.

7 For changes in Canadian immigration policy with respect to Germans, see Schmalz, "Statistical Overview," 14–15.

8 *Immigration Research Series*, 1–4.

8 *Citizenship and Immigration Statistics*, 58, Table IM13.

10 These personal interviews were conducted between the summer of 2005 and the summer of 2006, mostly in the private homes of the interviewees, but in some cases also at the Lutheran Church in Kelowna and at the University of Victoria. All participants volunteered for the interviews, either by responding to newspaper ads or after hearing about the project through churches, clubs, friends, and neighbours. Interviews were approximately one to three hours long and were conducted either in German, English, or a mix of both, depending on the preferences of the participants.

11 Reinhold P. and Richard P., interviews.

12 Lucia F., interview.

13 Rolf and Brigitte U., interview.

14 Mina S., Erwin K., and Irene S., interviews.

15 Caroline L., interview.

16 Bernhard D. Interview. For the experiences of domestics in Vancouver, see Freund, "Identity in Immigration"; Oberle, *Finding Home*; Rudolph, *Landscape of My Life*.

17 Freund and Quilici, "Exploring Myths," 167.

18 Christian S., interview.

19 Günther B., interview.

20 Mina S., interview. Also Freund, *Aufbrüche*, 489.

21 Christian S., interview.

22 Olga S., interview.

23 Leo K., interview.

24 Klay S., interview.

25 Lydia P. and Lilli G., interviews.

26 Erwin and Leona Koslowski, interview with Elizabeth M. Mayer, *The Story of the Victoria Edelweiss Club*. BC Archives, 1983, transcript, 1.

27 Liesel Schumacher, interview with Elizabeth M. Mayer, *The Story of the Victoria Edelweiss Club*. BC Archives, 1983, transcript, 11.

28 Horst Kopplin, interview with Elizabeth M. Mayer. *The Story of the Victoria Edelweiss Club*. BC Archives, 1983, transcript, 19.

29 Liesel Schumacher, interview, transcript, 16.

30 Rolf U., interview.

31 Correspondence between Wilfried Langen, Pastor Julius Ernst Bergbusch, and Pastor W.A. Mehlenbacher, 15 October 1954 to 15 April 1955, LAC MG30–D 213, Julius Ernst Bergbusch fonds, vol. 2.

32 *Der Synodalbote*, January 1961, 4–5, NAC MG 30–D 213, Julius Ernst Bergbusch fonds, vol. 4.

33 Correspondence between Julius Ernst Bergbusch and Ellen Meyer, 2 February 1958, Karin Nessl, 26 February 1958, and Erwin Nessl, 1 April 1958, NAC MG 30–D 213, Julius Ernst Bergbusch fonds, vol. 2.

34 Mary Magdalene Bergbusch, interview with Elizabeth M. Mayer, *Germans in British Columbia Collection* (tape 3880:1), BC Archives, 7 August 1981, transcript, 11.

35 Mary Bergbusch, interview, transcript, 12.

36 For a discussion of language retention in Vancouver, see Gumpp, "Language Loss and Language Retention." However, her finding that Germans quickly switched

to English as their home language does not coincide with the data from the interviews conducted for this chapter. A majority of the interviewees outside of mixed marriages still use German or at least a mix of German and English as their home language and many of the second generation still have a working knowledge of German.

37 Christian S., interview.
38 *Immigration Research Series*, 1, 4; *Citizenship and Immigration Statistics*, 58, Table IM 13.
39 Brigitte U., interview. "*Containerdeutsche*" refers to the fact that these later German immigrants shipped their possessions in containers.
40 Horst Kopplin, interview, transcript, 22.

Interview Sources

The sixteen interviews, unless otherwise indicated, were conducted by Christian Lieb and are in his possession.

Arnold H., Courtenay, BC, 22 April 2006.
Bernhard and Gertrud D., Duncan, BC, 23 October 2005.
Caroline L. (pseudonym), Sidney, BC, 25 August 2005.
Christian S., University of Victoria, Victoria, BC, 5 August 2005.
Erwin K. (pseudonym), Vernon, BC, 11 October 2005.
Günther B., Summerland, BC, 9 October 2005.
Irene S., Kelowna, BC, 14 October 2005.
Klay S., Steveston, BC, 1 September 2005.
Leo K., interviewed by Jenny Clayton, Kelowna, BC, 15 October 2005.
Lilli G., Kelowna, BC, 15 October 2005.
Lucia F., Sidney, BC, 9 August 2005.
Lydia and Reinhold P., Kelowna, BC, 16 October 2005.
Mina S., Kelowna, BC, 15 October 2005.
Olga S., interviewed by Jenny Clayton, Christ Evangelical Lutheran Church, Kelowna, BC, 16 October 2005.
Richard P., Kelowna, BC, 16 October 2005.
Rolf and Brigitte U., Victoria, BC, 15 October 2005.
Willi G., Vancouver, BC, 27 May 2006.

Archival Sources

Bergbusch, Mary Magdalene. Interview with Elizabeth M. Mayer. *Germans in British Columbia Collection*, British Columbia Archives (tape 3880:1), 7 August 1981, transcript.
Julius Ernst Bergbusch fonds (Library and Archives Canada MG 30/D 213), vols. 2 and 4.
Kopplin, Horst. Interview with Elizabeth M. Mayer. *The Story of the Victoria Edelweiss Club*, British Columbia Archives, 1983, transcript.
Koslowski, Erwin and Leona. Interview with Elizabeth M. Mayer. *The Story of the Victoria Edelweiss Club*, British Columbia Archives, 1983, transcript.
Library and Archives Canada (LAC). Kurt von Cardinal fonds (MG 31/H 39), vol. 1, Correspondence Immigration II.

Schumacher, Liesel. Interview with Elizabeth M. Mayer. *The Story of the Victoria Edelweiss Club*, British Columbia Archives, 1983, transcript.

Works Cited

Avery, Donald. "Canadian Immigration Policy towards Europe 1945–1952. Altruism and Economic Self-Interest." *Zeitschrift der Gesellschaft für Kanada-Studien*, 1 (1986): 37–56.

Citizenship and Immigration Statistics 1996. Ottawa: Government Publication, 1999.

Freund, Alexander. *Aufbrüche nach dem Zusammenbruch. Die deutsche Nordamerika-Auswanderung nach dem Zweiten Weltkrieg*. Osnabrück: V&R unipress, 2004.

———. "Identity in Immigration: Self-Conceptualization and Myth in the Narratives of German Immigrant Women in Vancouver, BC, 1950–1960." MA thesis, Simon Fraser University, 1994.

Freund, Alexander, and Laura Quilici. "Exploring Myths in Women's Narratives." *BC Studies*, 105–106 (1995): 159–82.

Gumpp, Ruth. "Language Loss and Language Retention among German Postwar Immigrants in Vancouver, 1945–1971." *Deutschkanadisches Jahrbuch / German-Canadian Yearbook*, 14 (1995): 75–88.

Immigration Research Series, Profiles Germany: German Immigrants in Canada. Ottawa, Government Publication, 1996.

Lehmann, Heinz. *The German Canadians, 1750–1937. Immigration, Settlement, and Culture*, translated, edited, and introduced by Gerhard P. Bassler. St. John's, NF: Jesperson Press, 1986.

Oberle, Frank. *Finding Home: A War Child's Journey to Peace*. Surrey, BC: Heritage House, 2004.

Rudolph, Erna. *The Landscape of My Life*. Garibaldi Highlands, BC: Harmony House, 2004.

Sauer, Angelika E. "A Matter of Domestic Policy? Canadian Immigration Policy and the Admission of Germans, 1945–50." *Canadian Historical Review* 74, no. 2 (1993): 226–63.

Schmalz, Ron. "A Statistical Overview of the German Immigration Boom to Canada, 1951–1957." *Deutschkanadisches Jahrbuch/German-Canadian Yearbook*, 16 (2000): 1–38.

Steinert, Johannes-Dieter. *Migration und Politik. Westdeutschland—Europa—Übersee 1945–1961*. Osnabrück: Secolo Verlag, 1995.

Wagner, Jonathan. *A History of Migration from Germany to Canada, 1850–1939*. Vancouver: University of British Columbia Press, 2006.

TWENTY-SIX

The German Language in the South Seas

Language Contact and the Influence of
Language Politics and Language Attitudes

Stefan Engelberg

Between 1884 and 1900, Germany established protectorates in large areas of the South Pacific. The authorities assumed that the linguistically extremely diverse areas would pose communication problems. Thus the question arose whether German should become the lingua franca in the South Pacific. After a controversial discussion, the German government implemented language policies to promote the German language in the colonies. This chapter shows why, on the one hand, German language policies were doomed to failure and why, on the other, they unintentionally supported other linguistic developments such as the introduction of borrowing from German into indigenous languages, the development of German settler varieties, and the spread of pidgin languages.

Historical Background of German Language Contact in Oceania

GERMAN SPEAKERS STARTED TO VISIT the South Pacific in the late eighteenth century. Explorers such as Georg Forster on James Cook's ship *Resolution*, Adelbert von Chamisso on Otto von Kotzebue's *Rurik*, or Ferdinand Hochstetter on the Austrian ship *Novara* raised awareness about the Pacific in Europe. They were followed by companies that were primarily trading in copra, but also in bêche-de-mer, sandalwood, coffee, and other plantation products. Companies such as Hernsheim, Hennings, and, above all, Godeffroy & Son and its successor, the Deutsche Handels- und Plantagengesellschaft, dominated trade in the South Pacific in the

1860s and '70s and prepared the way for the annexation of large parts of the South Pacific by the German Empire. In 1884, the northeastern part of New Guinea, the Bismarck Archipelago, and the North Solomon Islands became a German protectorate, followed by the Marshall Islands in 1885, Nauru in 1888, the Carolines and the northern Marianas in 1889, and Western Samoa in 1900. All the islands mentioned above—except for Samoa, which became the province German Samoa—formed the province German New Guinea. The establishment of a German administration was accompanied by increasing efforts by German missions, which supplemented or replaced older missions from Spain, the United States, Australia, Great Britain, and France.

In the early twentieth century, the province of German New Guinea had an indigenous population of about 600,000. In German Samoa, 35,000 indigenous inhabitants were counted. The German population, however, was small. Toward the end of German rule in the South Pacific, about one thousand Germans lived in German New Guinea and three hundred and fifty in German Samoa.[1]

The South Pacific, with its three major geographical areas of Micronesia, Polynesia, and Melanesia, is known for its linguistic diversity. There are more than one thousand languages of two language families—the Austronesian (spoken in most parts of the South Pacific) and Papuan languages (New Guinea and circumjacent islands). In the German provinces of the Pacific, between four hundred and five hundred different languages were spoken. English-based pidgins (i.e., structurally simplified languages, which develop in contact situations among people who do not share a language for communication) started to spread in the South Seas in the nineteenth century. They spread unevenly in the German provinces with a stronghold in parts of Melanesia.

This linguistic situation in which German traders, settlers, missionaries, and civil servants lived was the starting point for discussions among German colonialists about the role of the German language in the South Sea provinces. Should it become the lingua franca?

German Colonialist Language Policies

Beginning in the mid 1880s, colonial circles in Germany discussed which language might best meet the administrative, economical, and social needs of the German colonies. Among the options for a lingua franca were German, English, Pidgin English, and several indigenous languages.

Varieties of Pidgin English—despite their popularity among the indigenous and the European populations—did not have many supporters in politically influential circles. The bad reputation of pidgin is reflected in numerous comments such as the following: "a rotten English, mixed with scraps from other languages"[2] and "the locals twist and muddle the words in flowery compositions into the few concepts their dim-witted mind uses."[3] It was considered "gibberish" with a "cannibalistic primitivity of expression"[4] that the Germans "learn in a ghastly shape from their own coloured workers."[5] Thus, it was concluded that Pidgin English "should be suppressed the sooner the better" since "it could neither serve as a regular lingua franca nor as a carrier of culture."[6]

Indigenous languages as lingua francas were favoured by missionaries. According to mission policies, the native language of the students was supposed to be used in elementary school and, above all, in religious instruction. Since in some regions the density of languages was so high that students of different mother tongues shared a classroom, the missions either used a pidgin or started to develop certain indigenous languages into lingua francas, e.g., Kâte and Yabem on New Guinea and Tolai in the Bismarck Archipelago.[7] The use of these languages as lingua francas was restricted to the context of schooling and missionary work. Plans to expand them into other domains of colonial life were opposed by the German settlers who were not willing to learn indigenous languages: "You cannot ask of a farmer and his workers, who earn their bread in the sweat of their brows, to go to school after a day's labour."[8] Moreover, most of the indigenous languages were considered difficult to learn. Consequently, what was reported from the Marshall Islands held true for most German settlers: "There is hardly a white man on the Marshall Islands who—even though a resident for years—has mastered the language."[9]

This reluctance to learn indigenous languages was often combined with a negative attitude toward them. Since the "simple languages of these peoples" were thought to have only a certain value for science, "we, as the higher developed people, are obliged to document them, before we destroy them."[10] In the vein of social Darwinism, indigenous languages were considered doomed to extinction. Those languages that "are too weak in the struggle for life may disappear; there are no immortal literary works that would die with them."[11]

Thus colonialists remained trapped in the contradiction that indigenous languages were considered too complicated to learn and too simple to transport the cultural values of the colonizing nation. It was not only for linguistic reasons that the use of indigenous languages was not promoted by the German government. It was also feared that the spread of indigenous languages might contribute to the development of national, anti-colonial sentiments among the indigenous population.

Since the German Empire was committed to the unity of state, nation, and language, one might assume that colonialists in Germany may have unanimously opted for German as a lingua franca. However, the language policies developed and adopted in Germany were not transferred automatically to the colonies. In the colonies, the teaching of German was not always welcomed by settlers, who were afraid that they would not have the language to themselves and that the natives might eavesdrop and spread about what they had heard.[12] Moreover, some politicians were afraid that the knowledge of spoken and written German might help indigenous people to interfere in German politics and to promote national aspirations. The German language was also viewed as a symbol of social distance between the German and indigenous populations. Thus it was recommended that the Germans learn the indigenous languages so "that by keeping the natives away from our language community we draw the line between us and them."[13] Expressing feelings of western supremacy, the Germans also pondered "whether our beautiful German mother tongue would improve by forcing it onto other people who will never learn to understand it in its entire beauty and will at best distort it."[14]

However, politicians in Germany favoured the use of German as a lingua franca. Nationalistic sentiments led to demands such as the following: "In German colonies—the German language!" "English advances into British protectorates, French expands into the French ones—partially without human intervention, partially assisted by the governments. We cannot be left behind."[15] Apart from political arguments, there was also economic reasoning. Making German the leading language in the South Pacific could be advantageous for international trade. Again, ideas of western supremacy slipped into the discussion: "It is only by learning a world language that the native will become a '*Kulturmensch.*'"[16]

Political Measures Taken

In the end, the discussions in Berlin were dominated by arguments that placed the language question within the context of imperialistic rivalry. This also meant that activities by influential circles such as the German Colonial Society were directed against English and Pidgin English but not against the indigenous languages. These were granted their own status to serve a local purpose and their scientific study was supported financially. In general, politicians in Berlin were not really aware of the linguistic situation in the South Pacific colonies, and language policies were based less on the wish to comply with the communicative needs of the inhabitants of the colonies than on a fundamental expansionist, imperialistic attitude.

The political measures had the goal of establishing German as a lingua franca. However, these were compartmentalized activities without an overarching concept. The Colonial Department of the German Foreign

Office issued a decree that intervened in the school curricula in the colonies. It demanded that if a language other than the indigenous languages was taught, German had to be included into the curriculum.[17] As a consequence, even the non-German missions were not allowed to teach English as the first foreign language. In Samoa, the governor amended the decree by prohibiting English as the language of instruction in favour of Samoan.[18] One method to promote the German language was the establishment of government schools in which German gained a prominent role as a subject and as a language of instruction. However, only four government schools were founded in the two provinces, while 756 schools were run by the missions. In the two German provinces, 98 percent of the students were educated in mission schools,[19] which were subsidized only to a small extent for teaching German. Furthermore, the budgets of the provinces of German Samoa and German New Guinea contained a fund of 5,000 and 12,000 German marks, respectively, for promoting the German language—the Fonds zur Verbreitung der deutschen Sprache. Financial rewards went to indigenous students for excellent knowledge of German, to indigenous civil servants for improvement of their German, and to German clubs in the colonies for efforts in language cultivation.

The Language Use of Traders and Settlers

Despite all these efforts, the reality was that the language of the multinational society of traders and settlers in the South Pacific was English. Pidgin English was widely spoken as well, in particular between European and indigenous inhabitants. The attempt to establish German in these domains failed because there was no communicative deficit that pro-German language policies could have addressed. Contemporary reports document how deeply English and Pidgin English were rooted in the South Pacific communities. A missionary reports from the Marshall Islands: "Though the Germans used their own language in conversing among themselves, the natives were all addressed in English. One of the members of the firm [the Deutsche Handels- und Plantagengesellschaft], in discussing the desirability of the natives learning German, said to me, 'There is no need of teaching them German, they all know English.'"[20] A letter referring to the Caroline Islands attests that the "missionaries are doing their best to satisfy the government according to our instructions. German is already taught in some of the schools; the missionaries are studying German so that they can do this better. (The Germans on Ponape use English as a means of intercourse and do not seem to care for German.)"[21]

German and the Administration

Within the administrative domain, there was an attempt to strengthen the role of German by using it for special purposes.[22] Decrees were usually published in German and partly in local languages; the courts used German in their proceedings, using interpreters if necessary; indigenous civil servants were expected to learn German, and special language classes were established for the police force. Nevertheless, the police force—usually composed of men from different linguistic backgrounds—preferred pidgin when talking among themselves. German became only the language of commands. It is frequently reported that German civil servants even used pidgin when talking to the locals. A missionary from Nauru remarked on the efforts of the German government to eradicate Pidgin English by pointing out that this "is of course not an easy matter as not only English-speaking whites use it in their daily dealings with the natives, but the writer has more than once heard German Government Officials converse with their protégées in this peculiar dialect."[23] As a consequence, the use of German in the centres of German administration (Apia on Samoa, Ponape in the Carolines, Rabaul in the Bismarck Archipelago) was mostly restricted to the immediate surroundings of the German officials, that is, to their employees and domestic servants.

German in School and Missions

Due to the language decree of 1898, most mission schools taught German. However, only about 35 percent of the schools in the two provinces were run by German missions. Even in those, 60 percent of the classes were taught by indigenous teachers. Thus only about 15 percent of school lessons were given by native speakers of German. For the non-German missionaries, the obligation to teach German posed serious problems. A missionary from the Boston mission points out in a letter to the mission secretary that the appointment of a German is necessary, because "I cannot teach it at all well, however, as I pronounce very badly and cannot read even the easiest little story without my German English dictionary. I am giving the girls easy stories to translate. Mr. Gray and I are trying to do a little studying together at least twice a week but it is hard to find time for it."[24] Thus it is no wonder that the results of these German lessons did not go beyond learning a few German songs, as a missionary from Kosrae claims not without irony:

> We have made use of our English readers and Bible stories. After reading the English, the scholars have been required to translate what they have read into their own language. An effort has been made to use the German Readers in the same way but, as you realize, to become a teacher of German means that one must be familiar with the German language.

> During the past few years, the girls have been taught to sing equally as many German hymns and songs as they have English.[25]

This impression is corroborated by a visitor on Kosrae who was impressed by some beautifully performed German songs, "the contents of which probably remain unintelligible to the singers."[26]

The situation was different in the government schools and some of the German mission schools. In particular, in cases where German was not only subject but also language of instruction, the German language gained a certain functional value in the vicinity of the schools. The German Capuchins report from the Palau Islands that the students "have advanced so far in German that they can serve as interpreters for government officials, travellers, etc."[27] The success of German in educational contexts depended also on the language attitudes displayed by the students. From Kosraean schools, run by the Boston mission, it is reported that "English is very much desired by the scholars ... German is tolerated by the scholars, for the sake of the English, but there is no enthusiasm over it."[28] In Palau, the German Capuchins claimed that students showed a positive attitude toward German: "The students show the most interest in German and geography. Every German word gets written into an exercise book right away."[29]

In summary, domains in which German functioned as a second language were limited to the households of the German settlers, traders, and planters, to the lower levels of administration, and to the vicinity of the missions. Beyond that, German never became a lingua franca in the South Seas. This was due to the qualitatively inadequate language instruction, the low number of native speakers of German, and, therefore, the rare opportunity to practise German, the widespread use of pidgins, and the language choice of many Germans who preferred English or pidgins.

German Loanwords

Considering the low functionality of German in Oceania, the influence of German on the indigenous languages could only be minimal. Yet the influence is still noticeable today. Many languages contain at least a handful of German loanwords. An investigation of sixteen of the twenty-five languages spoken in Micronesia[30] resulted in the detection of German loanwords in all but two of them (Kosraean and Chamorro). Table 1 contains some examples.

There are remarkable differences concerning the number of loanwords. While Kosraean in eastern Micronesia does not have any German loanwords, at least thirty-five were found in Palauan on the western fringe of Micronesia. The differences are due to the following conditions, which were prevalent, for example, in Palau but not in Kosrae: a comparatively

TABLE 1   Examples of German loanwords in indigenous
languages in Oceana

Language	Lexical Item	Source	Translation
Carolinian	*fayérabwaw*	*Feuerbaum*	flame tree, poinciana
Chuukese	*kkumi*	*Gummi*	rubber
Kapingamarangi	*situnte*	*Stunde*	hour
Marshallese	*kapel*	*Gabel*	fork
Mokilese	*Dois*	*deutsch*	Germany
Nauruan	*esel*	*Esel*	donkey
Nukuoro	*situnte*	*Stunde*	hour
Palauan	*chausbéngdik*	*auswendig*	know thoroughly, memorize
Ponapean	*sirangk*	*Schrank*	cabinet, particularly one in which food is stored
Puluwatese	*siike*	*Ziege*	goat
Sonsorol	*dioka*	*Tapioka*	tapioca
Tobi	*dioka*	*Tapioka*	tapioca
Ulithian	*rat*	*Rad*	bicycle
Woleaian	*kaantiin*	*Kantine*	store, shop, booth
Yapese	*sitiraf*	*Strafe*	punishment

high functionality of German as a second language, little competition
with English, and a positive attitude toward German. Thus while German
language policies did not establish German as a lingua franca in the South
Seas, they had consequences for the lexicon of the indigenous languages,
which survived the times of German colonialism.[31]

Settler Varieties of German

Reports from different parts of the German South Seas indicate that English and Pidgin English must have had a considerable influence on the German spoken by the settlers. Contemporary accounts, in
particular from Samoa, complain that "our German here is strongly mixed
with pieces from English."[32] In Samoa, a particular variety of German
seemed to have developed that I will call Samoan Settler German. Because
it was mainly a spoken variety, evidence is hard to come by and the traits
of Settler German must be reconstructed from written sources: a strong
lexical influence from English, a grammatical influence from English,
and a certain lexical influence from Samoan. The lexical influence from

English is evident in loanwords such as *Schweinefenz* (hog fence), *Wharf* (wharf), *Bicycle, Halfcast.* The grammatical influence is evident, first, in adopting the structure of certain English prepositional constructions (e.g., *in meiner Meinung* for "in my opinion," instead of standard German *meiner Meinung nach*); second, in using English word order (e.g., by allowing more than one phrase in front of the finite verb); third, in simplifying the German gender system; and fourth, in loan translations of English idioms (e.g., *sage* derived from "let's say"). The lexical influence from Samoan is mainly restricted to words expressing culture-specific concepts such as *matai* (head of the family), *tofiga* (official duty or function), *pulenuu* (mayor), *faamasino* (village judge or judge), and *pule* (authority or power). Samoan Settler German is a result of certain language attitudes and language policies. In trying to elevate a minority language (the language of the colonial power) to a lingua franca, colonial language policies concentrated their efforts almost exclusively on the indigenous population and overlooked the fact that many of the few native speakers of this minority language had already made other language choices (English, Pidgin English, Settler German).

The Development of Pidgin and Creole Languages

Toward the end of the nineteenth century, German-based pidgin and creole languages began to develop in some areas of the German South Seas.[33] Among them were Ali Pidgin German, spoken on Ali, an island off the shore of New Guinea,[34] and Unserdeutsch (literally "our German") in northern New Britain. Unserdeutsch is a creole language that was spoken in the vicinity of the mission school of Vunapope, which also served as an orphan home.[35] In Vunapope, as in Palau, German was taught intensively and was used as the language of instruction. Yet, while the linguistic background in Palau was uniform—Palauan was the only language spoken—the students in Vunapope came from families with many different native languages. In this regard, German could assume a function that went beyond classroom instruction. However, while standard German was taught in school, a German-based creole developed as a vernacular in the vicinity of the school. This creole was passed on through several generations. Obviously, communicative needs and decisions made by the speakers thwarted the official attempts to promote standard German as a lingua franca.

Even more remarkable is the connection between German colonial politics and the history of Tok Pisin, the English-based pidgin spoken in New Guinea.[36] From the 1860s on, there was a great demand for workers on the German plantations in Samoa, so that workers were recruited from the Bismarck Archipelago (after 1879 and again after 1900), the Gilbert and

Ellice Islands (1867–1880), the North Solomon Islands (after 1880), and the New Hebrides (1878–1885). Under these conditions, a stable English-based pidgin originated—Samoan Plantation Pidgin. It was used among the Melanesian and Polynesian workers, and between the workers and the German and German Samoan employees of the Deutsche Handels-und Plantagen-Gesellschaft. Between 1879 and 1913, about 6,000 workers returned to the islands of the province of German New Guinea after their contracts had expired. Due to labour migration between the Bismarck Archipelago and New Guinea, the pidgin spread and became what was later known as Tok Pisin. During the times of German administration, this pidgin underwent lexical extension and relexification of English words on the basis of German. About one hundred and fifty lexemes of German origin can be traced, among them *ananas* (pineapple), *balaistip* (pencil), *beten* (pray), *bigelaisen* (iron [for ironing]), *donabeta* (cry of admiration or anger), *esik* (vinegar), *gever* (rifle), *gumi* (rubber), *lupsip* (airship), *malen* (paint), *palmen* (palm trees), *saiskanake* (derogative, literally "shit kanaka"), *saitung* (newspaper), *sange* (pliers), *sikmel* (sawdust), *soken* (socks), *svesta* (sister), and *turm* (tower). While German colonial politics aimed at suppressing the use of pidgin, their economic policies, which were tied to a high degree of work migration, had quite the opposite effect and helped to spread and develop pidgin languages.

Conclusion

In spite of a controversial discussion in the colonies about the role that the German language should assume in the South Pacific, politicians in Berlin opted for the spread of German in the colonies. Ultimately, the official German language policies were not successful. German did not become the lingua franca of the South Pacific. However, the efforts to spread German throughout the South Pacific were not without consequences, even though they were not the ones initially intended: indigenous languages were enriched by German loanwords; settler varieties emerged under the influence of English and local languages, and pidgin languages developed and spread through the German provinces. The failure of German language politics was due to several factors. There was no promising concept for the promotion of German. The necessary financial efforts were not made with the consequence that language education was insufficient. Too few native speakers of German populated the colonies in order to provide opportunities to speak German. Finally, the European and indigenous inhabitants of the colonies had already made other language choices that fulfilled their communicative needs.

Notes

1 Schnee, *Deutsches Kolonial-Lexikon.*
2 Baessler, *Südseebilder,* 23. All translations from German sources into English are by the author.
3 Spiegel von und zu Peckelsheim, *Kriegsbilder aus Ponape,* 47.
4 Jacques, *Südsee,* 96.
5 "Der Kampf um die deutsche Sprache," 456.
6 Deutscher Reichstag, 10. Legislaturperiode 1900–1903, 2. Sitzung, 8. Anlagenbuch, Aktenstück 814.
7 Wurm, *New Guinea Area Languages,* 833ff.
8 Friederici, "Pidgin-Englisch," 95.
9 Erdland, "Der gegenwärtige Stand der katholischen Mission," 488.
10 Weck, *Die Sprache im Deutschen Recht,* 119.
11 Sembritzki, "Deutsche Sprache," 128.
12 Friederici, "Pidgin-Englisch," 97.
13 Kindt, "Sollen die Eingeborenen," 283.
14 Schlunk, *Das Schulwesen,* 93.
15 Sembritzki, "Deutsche Sprache," 128.
16 Sembritzki, "Deutsche Sprache," 128.
17 Deutsche Kolonialgesetzgebung IV 1898/99, Nr. 75.
18 Samoanisches Gouvernementsblatt, Bd. III, Nr. 9, 15 June 1901.
19 Schlunk, *Die Schulen.*
20 Jenny Olin, "Letter to Dr. Judson Smith, Kusaie, Caroline Islands, August 9, 1902." Papers of the American Board of Commissioners for Foreign Missions (ABC), 19.4, vol. 16, Letters J–P.
21 "Proposed Transfer of Micronesia, December 1902." ABC 19.4, vol. 11 (Micronesia Mission 1890–1899), Letters A–K.
22 For information provided in this section see Engelberg, "Influence of German."
23 Rev. Ph. A. Delaporte, Mrs. Salome Delaporte, Miss Maria Linke, *Tenth Annual Report of the Nauru Mission.* Nauru, Marshall Islands: Nauru Mission-Press (1911). ABC 19.4, vol. 18, part 1, Documents Reports Letters.
24 "Letter to R. Jackson Smith, Oua, Ponape, June 12, 1903." ABC 19.4, vol. 11, Letters A–K.
25 Louise E. Wilson, "Letter to Judson Smith, D.D., Kusaie, Caroline Islands, August 2nd, 1902." ABC 19.4, vol. 17, Letters R–W.
26 Sarfert, *Kusae,* 421.
27 Placidus, "Die Schule in Korror," 56.
28 Jenny Olin, "Letter to Dr. Judson Smith."
29 Placidus, "Die Schule in Korror," 56.
30 See Gordon, *Ethnologue: Languages of the World.*
31 For more information, see Engelberg, "Influence of German," "Kaisa, Kumi, Karmoból."
32 Zieschank, *Ein Jahrzehnt in Samoa,* 57.
33 The term "creole languages," in contrast to pidgins, is usually reserved for first languages used by native speakers, i.e., they are often distinguished from pidgins by their status as the native language of their speakers.
34 See Mühlhäusler, "Bemerkungen."
35 See Volker, "Birth and Decline."
36 See Mühlhäusler, "Bemerkungen."

Archival Material

Deutsche Kolonialgesetzgebung ɪᴠ 1898/99, Nr. 75.
Deutscher Reichstag, 10. Legislaturperiode 1900–1903, 2. Sitzung, 8. Anlagenbuch, Aktenstück 814.
Papers of the American Board of Commissioners for Foreign Missions (ABC),
19.4. vols. 11 (Micronesia Mission 1890–1899), 16 (Micronesia Mission 1900–
1909), 17 (Micronesia Mission 1900–1909), 18 (Micronesia Mission 1910–
1919).
Samoanisches Gouvernementsblatt, Bd. ɪɪɪ, Nr. 9, 15 June 1901.

Works Cited

Baessler, Arthur. *Südsee-Bilder.* Berlin: Asher & Co., 1895.
"Der Kampf um die deutsche Sprache und das Deutschtum in den Deutschen
Kolonien." *Deutsche Kolonialzeitung* 20 (1903): 455–57.
Engelberg, Stefan. "The Influence of German on the Lexicon of Palauan and
Kosraean." In *Selected Papers from the 2005 Conference of the Australian Lin-
guistic Society,* edited by Keith Allen. Melbourne, 2006. <au.geocities.com/
austlingsoc/proceedings/als2005/engelberg-german.pdf> (March 2008).
———. "Kaisa, Kumi, Karmoból. Deutsche Lehnwörter in den Sprachen des Süd-
pazifiks." *Sprachreport* (4/2006): 2–9.
Erdland, August. "Der gegenwärtige Stand der katholischen Mission auf den Mar-
shall-Inseln." *Monatshefte zu Ehren unserer lieben Frau vom hlst. Herzen Jesu* 20
(1903): 487–89.
Friederici, Georg. "Pidgin-Englisch in Deutsch-Neuguinea." *Koloniale Rundschau*
2 (1911): 92–106.
Gordon, Raymond G., Jr., ed. *Ethnologue: Languages of the World.* 15th edition. Dal-
las: SIL International, 2005. <www.ethnologue.com> (March 2008).
Jacques, Norbert. *Südsee. Ein Reisebuch.* Munich: Drei Masken Verlag, 1922.
Kindt, Ludwig. "Sollen die Eingeborenen und die fremden Arbeiter in unseren
Kolonien die deutsche Sprache erlernen?" *Zeitschrift für Kolonialpolitik, Kolo-
nialrecht und Kolonialwirtschaft,* 6 (1906): 281–84.
Mühlhäusler, Peter. "Bemerkungen zum 'Pidgin Deutsch' von Neuguinea." In
*Deutsch im Kontakt mit anderen Sprachen, German in Contact with Other Lan-
guages,* edited by Carol Molony, Helmut Zobl, and Wilfried Stölting, 58–70.
Kronberg: Scriptor, 1977.
Placidus. "Die Schule in Korror." In *Aus den Missionen der rhein.-westf. Kapuziner-
Ordensprovinz auf den Karolinen-, Marianen- und Palau-Inseln in der deutschen
Südsee. Jahresbericht 1911,* edited by Kilian Müller, 55–57. Oberginingen:
1911.
Sarfert, Ernst. *Kusae, Ergebnisse Der Südsee-Expedition 1908–1910. II. Ethnographie:
B. Mikronesien, Bd. 4.* Hamburg: Friederichsen, 1920.
Schlunk, Martin. *Das Schulwesen in den deutschen Schutzgebieten.* Hamburg: L. Frie-
derichsen & Co., 1914.
———. *Die Schulen für Eingeborene in den deutschen Schutzgebieten am 1. Juni 1911.
Auf Grund einer statistischen Erhebung der Zentralstelle des Hamburgischen Kolo-
nialinstituts.* Hamburg: L. Friederichsen & Co., 1914.

Schnee, Heinrich, ed. *Deutsches Kolonial-Lexikon.* 3 Volumes. Leipzig: Quelle & Meyer, 1920.

Sembritzki, Emil. "Deutsche Sprache in deutschen Kolonien." *Deutsche Kolonial-Post (Beilage)*, 8 (1913): 128–29.

Spiegel von und zu Peckelsheim, Edgar Freiherr. *Kriegsbilder aus Ponape. Erlebnisse eines Seeoffiziers im Aufstande auf den Karolinen.* Stuttgart: Union Deutsche Verlagsgesellschaft, 1912.

Volker, Craig. "The Birth and Decline of Rabaul Creole German." *Language and Linguistics in Melanesia*, 22 (1991): 143–56.

Weck, Hermann. *Die Sprache im deutschen Recht.* Berlin: Heymanns, 1913.

Wurm, S.A., ed. *New Guinea Area Languages and Language Study.* Canberra: Australian National University, Research School of Pacific Studies, 1977.

Zieschank, Frieda. *Ein Jahrzehnt in Samoa (1906–1916).* Leipzig: Haberland, 1918.

TWENTY-SEVEN

Migration, Gender, and Storytelling

*How Gender Shapes the Experiences
and the Narrative Patterns in
Biographical Interviews*

Brigitte Bönisch-Brednich

This chapter offers a short overview of the issues raised by German women and men in interviews and of the different ways they referred to their immigration experience. This analysis is based on a comprehensive research project on the oral history of German immigration to New Zealand. The primary sources are interviews with 102 immigrants (forty-two men and sixty women) who came to New Zealand between 1936 and 1996. The project found that both genders construct their life story in terms of accomplishment and success, but describe this overall achievement quite differently. Generally speaking, men construct their stories in terms of their work and professional development, and women describe their emotional experiences in more detail. The project also found that the act of telling emigration stories contributes significantly to people's ability to feel confident in their choice to leave Germany for a new life in New Zealand.

Introduction

RESEARCH ON MIGRATION, CERTAINLY PROJECTS done during the past fifteen years, utilize gender as both a methodological framework and an analytical one. Women and men are usually both included in interview and questionnaire samples, as well as in the historical sources, although sometimes a single sex is exclusively chosen for a detailed analysis. In recent studies that are methodologically based in oral history, men and women are as a rule interviewed in equal proportions. It is, therefore, surprising that there are few specific attempts to compare the migration experiences of the female and male migration experiences to explore the different ways men and women might reflect on and narrate about these central biographical experiences.[1] This chapter discusses the following main questions: What differential importance does the decision-making process to emigrate have in the memory of men and women, and how are these decisions explained and justified? How are the stories of integration told, and what memories are considered important—particularly those that constitute the turning point? What are the key stories in male and female narratives?[2] And how do women and men reflect on the impact of migration on their own personality, their personal growth, and so on?

These questions form the basis for this comprehensive research project on the oral history of German immigration to New Zealand, which was part of a long-term ethnographic study, involving participant observation, a field diary, and interviews with focus groups, as well as interviews with couples, families, and single individuals. For this particular research project, interviews were conducted with 102 immigrants between 1996 and 1998, with the average duration of ninety minutes. Of those interviews, 90 percent were conducted in German, so most of the quotations given in this chapter have been translated by the author, who conducted them all herself in an informal, open style. A guideline of questions was used, if necessary, starting always with the question "Why New Zealand?"

Who Decides?

A very important aspect of the way individuals assess their own emigration experience is the decision-making phase, when the new place of residence and the entire future of the person and perhaps his or her family are being determined. Where emigration took place in a family situation, a collectively used "we" in the interviews made it difficult to work out how the decision process took place. Frequently, in fact, the crucial discussion inside the family group or the couple was usually covered up in a joint "we decided," "we went," "we expected." Although it is not possible to make a thorough analysis of such a decision on the basis of the interview technique chosen for this project, it is possible to express doubts about the reality of a meaningful collective "we" in decision making. In most cases, certain phrases point toward the man as the main motivator in the wish to emigrate. Women would sometimes provide a clue, saying something like "and then Werner came home and said ..." Men, too, often went on exploratory forays to New Zealand, leaving the women staying at home to manage the family. Men would talk about their initiatives in finding a job in New Zealand, including preliminary inquiries, and of having presented job offers as surprises to the families.

The usual family "contract" often made before leaving was that after a period of two years or so the decision would be reconsidered by every single family member. But this contract often no longer applied after a short time in New Zealand. Meanwhile, it was usually the women who had the greatest adjustment problems, with men and children adapting faster and easier to the new living conditions, especially as a result of their work and school experiences.

Thus from a feminist perspective emigration often became counter-productive, leading women into isolation and financial dependency during the first years after arrival. Most women who came with their families did not start jobs until three to five years after arriving. This was frequently described as the turning point in their immigrant biography. A job would open up new social networks, and improve their English skills, and thereby make them more confident and content. In retrospect, however, about half of the interviewed women would say that they were glad to have had the "home alone" experience, believing that having survived such hard and lonely times had improved their lives by giving them the opportunity to discover hidden strength in their characters. In short, they reinterpreted it as a positive experience. The other half said that although they were now happy and could laugh about their early years and tears, they would not be prepared to go through the process again, as it had been such a hard experience at the time.

Since the 1980s, increasing numbers of young women have travelled on their own, and a sizable number have decided to emigrate and live in New Zealand. The way in which they remember their migration, and how they dealt with the period of arriving and settling in, is completely different from that of women with families. They gave some very firm statements in the interviews about the reason for going to New Zealand in the first place, and in some cases their determination to follow through on emigration to New Zealand:

EXAMPLE 1

I travelled for three years and the conclusion of those three years, when I was on a journey around the world, was New Zealand. I was travelling by myself. And the country simply fascinated me ... And then I went back, actually with the idea that I would save some money and then come back here as quickly as possible. And then I met Rolf and made it clear to him from the beginning that I was going to go to New Zealand and if there had been no interest of any kind in that I would not have gone into a relationship. Oh well, New Zealand was more important than a relationship with a man who was not interested in New Zealand. [Ingrid]

Explaining Decisions

Although on the surface many women had been making confident decisions about emigration, there seems to be more need for them than for men to have thought long and hard since their arrival about why they decided to emigrate and stay in New Zealand. Certainly, an overall set of reasons for emigrating in the 1980s and '90s was used equally by men and women—the nuclear danger in Europe, for example, and environmental pollution, overpopulation, and everyday racism. But while this set of explanations was widely used, together with comments on the qualities of New Zealand compared to Germany, women quite often also had decision-making stories of another kind. These placed their reasons for emigration somewhat apart from the general reasons used by both genders, fixing them on a plane reflecting the workings of fate or supernatural powers having taken a lead in their lives.

EXAMPLE 2

I wanted, from childhood on, to see the other side of the world. I just had this idea. My father was always talking about the Antipodes and that sort of thing. And as a child I always thought: so what is an antipodean? And I thought about the way their feet pointed up towards ours and I had all sorts of fantasies. And it never left me, this urge to find out what's going on at the other side of the world. [Inge]

For other women this phase of discovering the world, and the dreams that went along with it, came during puberty. Fantasies about world travel and about another, exotic life are remembered again and again in migration narratives and with hindsight obtain meaning:

EXAMPLE 3

When I was—how old was I then?—when I was about fifteen or sixteen we did something about New Zealand at school. And also I had a friend back then, a girl called Martina … and then I said to her back then: "One day I'm going to marry someone who comes from America or New Zealand." And I was fifteen then. And of course she thought that was silly and said, "Oh, rubbish," and I said "Ah, you'll see." [Rachel]

These reminiscences from childhood and girlhood are a pattern of explanation used frequently to add to the reasons for emigrating that both genders provided. Other memories, which are narrated either in this connection or independently, also constitute spiritually significant scenarios of migration. The moment of arrival in New Zealand, feelings of inner confirmation at that time, are of great significance to many women. Arrival is not just interpreted as a normal part of migrating, but is also given the meaning of spiritual arrival. Some simply describe this as an intense feeling of having come home. Men, on the other hand, do little more than carefully present their decision to emigrate in rational terms, using generally the set of explanations mentioned above. If they have additional reasons, these are things such as the overall wish for a new challenge, often having had the feeling that their life in Germany seemed to have reached a point where they had achieved everything they wanted and that this stalemate had been reached too early in life. As already noted, in family situations it is men who motivate the decision to emigrate. Women's spiritual reasons may be empowering reactions to this.

Narratives of Integration

In general, well-known gender-specific patterns of narration[3] can be detected in stories about the familiarization phase. Women tell stories very subjectively, narrating their feelings and personal experiences (including those of the family); men tend rather to emphasize their specific reasons for emigrating and narrate along the lines of their professional careers, as well as reflecting on political, historical, and general topics (for example, the logistics involved in emigration). Such different patterns create distinctive topic and narrative worlds. For women the most important topics are homesickness, problems with integration, the health of aging parents at home, the progress of their children, and assessments of their own development since emigrating. Weaknesses and mistakes (misinterpreting "ladies a plate" or "bring a plate" as a request to bring an empty plate to a function rather than a request to bring a dish that guests can share)[4] are detailed and discussed. Exemplary stories often reflect a symbolic meaning for a person's life.

Men, on the other hand, construct their immigration narratives more as success stories. Homesickness is not one of their topics, and bonds with Germany are often made objective rather than personal by such matters as emphasizing responsibility for aging parents. Any expression of an inner desire to go back is immediately blocked off by reference to the fact that it is financially impossible to do so. They focus on ongoing integration, especially in the form of the various steps in their career or of their own social progress. Initial difficulties in the workplace are usually described as closely associated with language problems, and a lack of professional discipline among their New Zealand colleagues. Quite a few men talked about suffering the "tall poppy syndrome"—a pejorative term for attracting criticism because of social success, related to attitudes of social levelling—and about having problems to make friends at work and so on. But they talked about this more in passing rather than emphasizing it. At the same time, their reporting is often peppered with humorous remarks, suggesting that today it is possible to smile about it all and that therefore these problems are things of the past.

In general men speak more about their career and their success, while women who have immigrated with a family speak of both homesickness (often referring to absent things) and overcoming it. Women who immigrated alone talk about gaining strength and the development of their personality. These three variants are now presented in more detail.

Masculine Success Stories

In contrast to many women, men give only limited space to describing problems, doubts and homesickness. It cannot be assumed, however, that homesickness is an exclusively female topic. Men do talk about problems and express self-doubts, albeit indirectly. But in their descriptions of the arrival and familiarization phases, they use fundamentally different narrative techniques from those of women. One receives, on the surface, the impression that they had basically fewer problems and more or less quickly "had the matter in hand." Their first years in New Zealand are narrated less as periods of emotional difficulty and more in relation to their first jobs, their wages, and the subsequent steps in their careers; in some cases this employment-related range of subjects is extended to other spheres, such as political or club activities. Initial difficulties with such matters as language, lower wages, and the casual attitude to work of their new colleagues serve especially to emphasize their subsequent improvement in English-language skills, increased wages, and adaptation to the new world in the context of the networks that were built up.

EXAMPLE 4

The language was the biggest problem. My first job was for a consultancy company and I had been working there for two weeks when they put me into a firm and I was sitting there at a big board meeting where they were all telling me what they wanted to do and I didn't understand anything at all about what they wanted me to do. But they were paying one hundred dollars an hour for me. And I sat there and the third time I asked a question I thought, I just can't go on; I can't ask four times, no. It was an absolute nightmare. That was not good. [Wulf]

When stories about first jobs are being told by men, an effort to record the subjective side of the experience is carried out using objectively measurable statements. Since one hundred dollars an hour were being paid for Wulf, it is perfectly credible that he was suffering from some kind of pressure. From a masculine narrative point of view there is often the suggestion that feelings are only credible in terms of precise basic facts relating to earnings, time, and time management.

In the interviews with men, often a lot of time is spent describing such matters as the founding of a firm or taking the various stages of a career as the basic structure of a life, with only a few small remarks being injected about states of mind or personal development. For example, one interviewee, between descriptions of two different contracts with companies, mentioned in passing that his marriage with the woman who had emigrated with him had ended around the same time as the two jobs. Indeed, questions about personal development are very often answered with stories about work. This does not necessarily mean that interviewees want to evade such questions, but rather that working for a living plays a fundamental role in personal states of mind, and that self-assessment depends a great deal on the working part of daily life.

Even if some men deliberately pushed the topic of work to the margins, their narrative techniques remain similar. In the case of so-called dropouts into alternative lifestyles, their narrated biographies tell of successfully leaving conventional society and of successful personal development. Even here, feelings such as unhappiness or detailed descriptions of crises do not take up much space, and short remarks must suffice in the course of detailed descriptions.

> **EXAMPLE 5**
>
> And that's a matter of fate, where you happen to be. Things can't go on in Germany the way they are now, because the country changes you. The main thing is that it changes you into having more freedom. You suddenly discover, we could do that too and you don't need that at all. There are all the things you no longer have to do, that you have to do when you're in Germany. You don't need any insurance policies, for example. I haven't got a single insurance policy! You don't have to. I just live. I have very few extra costs. [Arne]

Often, in fact, it is only by reading between the lines that one can detect specific problems that arise in the life of a dropout. For example, Arne comments that it is indeed the fulfilment of a dream to own a house on the hill with a view of the ocean, but he adds that in the lonely region where he now lives there is a lack of intellectual stimulation, or, as he describes it in his own words:

> **EXAMPLE 6**
>
> The landscape is such an incredibly powerful presence here, and such a source of strength, and every day, every day I am on my "rebounder" out there. I always make a hop and look out

> [laughs], do my exercises, because at my age I have to do them slowly, and then I always tell myself how happy I am that I can afford to do that, to live here. Really, you just have to do that, it can get dead boring if you don't create that in your consciousness every day afresh. What else can one do here? [Arne]

When one compares the narrative techniques of men and women, it becomes clear that there are gender-specific differences in their forms of statement. This does not mean that it is impossible to tell whether a man is happy, unhappy, or both about his emigration. It is just that the messages are packed in masculine narrative codes. To decode them, at least for me as a female listener, it is necessary to go through the entire conversation again and again, listening very carefully. Women, on the other hand, generally make very clear and meaningful statements about their personal feelings and their emotional development. This makes it difficult to reconstruct what would generally be considered a conventional curriculum vitae from their interviews. For example, one can only indirectly find out anything about an individual's financial situation or specific dates demarcating the end or beginning of certain biographical shifts. On the other hand, there seems to emerge the structure of a female version of narrated biographies where very personal memories and emotions create the frame of a life's narrative. Such memories and recollections form the base of central fundamental experiences such as emigration—and these emotional points of reference are more easily observed in women's interviews than in men's.

Female Homesickness Stories

To recapitulate, the fact that women speak quite openly about their feelings during the immigration process constitutes a profound difference from the masculine style of narration. Articulating both negative and positive feelings points to a strong inner preoccupation with one's own history; it also reflects the presence of narrative items that have already been used in endless conversations with woman friends, relatives, and other people. The term generally best used to name the problematic aspect of emigration is homesickness. There were narrations of homesickness not only in the interviews but also in many informal conversational situations, and homesickness is referred to in most female group conversations.

Suffering from homesickness is closely related to the intensity of bonds with Germany, and the real extent to which the decision to emigrate was shared by the women in partnerships. When families emigrate the traditional gender roles that are already in place are very frequently reconstituted or reinforced in the new country. In the case of families that emigrated during the 1980s and '90s, especially, the children were often still infants or were just reaching primary school age. In such cases the women had already given up their professional careers in Germany, or they no longer practised their professions when they reached New Zealand. As a rule, then, organizing emigration meant concentrating on looking for a position for the man or helping him settle happily into prearranged work. The woman, meanwhile, took over the tasks of finding a suitable flat or house, unpacking the container, and looking after the children. This led to rapid and profound isolation in surroundings where the woman neither understood the language nor felt familiar with cultural codes. In addition, for mothers it was often a shock that the all-day schools[5] made it unnecessary to look after the children with the same intensity.

EXAMPLE 7

And here in New Zealand, from the very beginning the children were away from nine or half-past eight until half-past three, if you include their way to and from school, and I was by myself all day! And then, when the container arrived I first had a bit of time to unpack and decorate the rooms and so on, and when I had done that, I thought, what now? Nothing ... Get a bit angry, cry a bit, and things like that. That was just unavoidable, really ... I was feeling very homesick. [Bea]

While women often spoke at length of their feelings of despair and homesickness, they also told of their attempts to hide this from their children, and sometimes from their partners as well. Moreover, these descriptions were often followed by descriptions of the moment when their destiny took a turn for the better. The disappearance of homesickness is usually coupled with taking up work. While this was often just an ordinary job, sometimes it was training for a new career. Some kind of unpaid activity also constituted a departure from homesickness; finding any kind of meaningful task strengthened the woman's self-esteem, led to a rapid improvement in English-language skills and to new acquaintances, and, ultimately, meant faster integration into the new way of life. Even so, work activities constituted only one strand in their emigration narratives; others included their circle of friends, the lives and development of their children, and (again and again) their own state of mind—culminating in contentment and even happiness.

Finally, talking about homesickness, and about the earliest years and their associated trials, serves to emphasize the success of one's emigration biography. Describing homesickness by narrating, remembering, and recapitulating pain is extremely important: it is not only part of one's own life story, it is above all a part that has been mastered, and so while it constitutes a stark contrast with one's life today, it is also the foundation for current happiness. Almost all women interviewees state that in the end they have profited from emigrating, even if the path they followed was considerably harder to get through than that of their husbands and children, and even if half of them would not want to experience such difficulties again.

Stories of Personal Growth and Cathartic Experience

One of the final prepared questions in the interviews inquired whether the emigrants would do it again. Very often this topic had already been raised by the interviewees themselves as part of their self-analysis, for it seemed to be necessary for them to reflect on the impact migration has on one's personality and personal growth. Indeed most interviewees of the 1980s and '90s would put it in exactly such terms. This topic is often closely combined with a reflection on the (sometimes former) partner with whom emigration was planned and carried out. Many women feel that their emigration story—whether happy or otherwise—is very relevant or even central to their personal development and their general biography. In particular, if they emigrated by themselves, homesickness usually has no great role to play in their narrations. Rather, the emphasis is on opportunities for personal development and getting to know one's own strengths. These are described not so much in terms of a professional career as in those of cognitive processes, extending horizons, and the conviction that life in New Zealand has been better than it would have been in Germany.

EXAMPLE 8

For me it was like this: because I was so much alone here and so dependent on myself, you just have to do it somehow, you are driven to your own limits. And then I noticed, "hey, action— I can really do that," you know? And that gives you so much strength, you know. I'm a completely different person here from the one I was in Germany. You know, much, much stronger. [Sina]

In spite of their more restrained narrative style, a number of men also suggest that they have been through development processes of this kind. As might be expected, these are not told directly and with the same enthusiasm as that of women, but expressed in a more impersonal way. One such statement might be, for example, that "emigration can be recommended to others because of the quality of experience it brings with it." In using this style there is an underlying suggestion that these experiences can be generalized across all emigrants. With such a rhetorical trick, the individual's personal experiences are neutralized to a sufficient degree to let them be expressed in a covert way. It seems to say: this could happen to everybody and, therefore, I can talk about it, too.

EXAMPLE 9

You fall on your face now and then, it's true. But it's a really great space for personal growth. I can only recommend it [laughs]: New Zealand! [Werner]

Conclusion

One overall conclusion from analysing a number of autobiographical stories on migration is that both genders construct their life story as one of achievement and success. Men and women mostly describe their migration enterprise as an enriching experience of great value for their lives. But the way in which men and woman describe this overall achievement is very different.

Men construct their stories along the lines of their work experiences and professional successes, mentioning their emotional experiences more in passing; they tend to present their story as a more or less linear narrative, emphasizing "good" or funny success stories. Women who emigrated with their families often describe the time of arrival and integration as a period of (passive) endurance, dealing with sadness, the feelings of loss and of feeling lost. But all of them contrast this period with their current happiness and confidence and the emergence of new, strong sides to their personalities. Women who emigrated as single persons also describe initial feelings of loneliness and hardship, although this period passed relatively quickly and was soon interpreted as a positive and enriching experience of gathering new qualities and gaining new facets to their personalities.

Telling stories of one's own emigration experiences is a crucial part of the everyday life of German immigrants to New Zealand. It is vital for their contentment and their confidence that their decision to emigrate is reflected upon as a positive one. All interviews used for this article were conducted with immigrants of the last twenty years, and this periodization has added an extra factor to immigrant interpretation of migration as a positive move in life. Migration is considered to be a vital and desirable part of modern concepts of lifestyle, part of a globalized, easy-moving, interconnected world. Nonetheless, interviewing such migrants reveals that the process of moving, of changing locations and continents, is clearly connected with difficulties and anxiety, and requires a lot of emotional energy and hard work.

Narrating biographies, and the constant recreating of biographies on an everyday basis, enables people to feel more secure and assured about their processes of moving and settling. They can even feel more secure about darker periods and challenging phases in their life stories. Telling stories about one's migrant life, then, is vital for gaining emotional security and happiness, but women handle that task quite differently from men. Although both genders come—in the final analysis—to the same (positive) conclusion, migration is and will probably remain a different story for men and women.

Notes

1 For recent (international) attempts to address the problem, see Anthias, "Metaphors of Home"; Leckie, "Silent Immigrants?"
2 The analytical approach taken for this study is much inspired by Albrecht Lehmann, who established the field of biographical narratives as "Bewusstseinsanalyse" and following the author's discussion on the principles of analytical frameworks in ethnographic writing. See Lehmann, "Bewusstseinsanalyse," *Erzählstruktur, Reden*; Bönisch-Brednich, "Being German," "Quelle und Feld," "Überlegungen," "Poetik."
3 For a discussion of gender specific patterns of narration and story telling refer to Stahl, *Literary Folkloristics*, 1987; Zaborowska, *How We Found America*, 1995; Tannen, *You Just Don't Understand*, 1990.
4 For specifically female issues on the every-day culture of New Zealand life, refer to Park, *Ladies a Plate*, 1991.
5 In Germany, schools are run half day, and with limited arrangements for childcare it is very often necessary for one parent to stay home or work half time.

Interview Sources

Interviews with 102 immigrants, all conducted by Brigitte Bönish-Brednich and in her possession, including specifically the following (some pseudonyms have been used at the subjects' request):

Arne, 6 December 1996.
Bea and Wulf, 18 October 1996.
Inge, Ingrid, and Sina, 31 May 1996.
Rachel, 7 May 1996.
Werner, 12 October 1996.

Works Cited

Anthias, Floya. "Metaphors of Home: Gendering New Migrations to Southern Europe." In *Gender and Migration in Southern Europe. Women on the Move*, edited by Floya Anthias and Gabriella Lazardis, 15–47. Oxford: Berg, 2000.

Bönisch-Brednich, Brigitte. "Being German in Wellington: Female Perspectives." In *Oral History New Zealand*, edited by Megan Hutching, Linda Evans, and Judith Byrne, 11: 23–29. Wellington: National Oral History Association of New Zealand, 1999.

———. "'Die Quelle und das Feld?' Zum Gebrauch von Metaphern in der heutigen Volkskunde." In *Symbole. Zur Bedeutung der Zeichen in der Kultur*, edited by Rolf Wilhelm Brednich, and Heinz Schmitt, 373–86. Münster: Waxmann, 1997.

————. "Überlegungen zur Kunstform des ethnographischen Erzählens. Die Faszination des Dorfes Átány." In *Zeitschrift für Volkskunde* 102 Jahrgang (2006), 1–15.

————. "Zur Poetik des Fachs. Wie man sich in die Nähe schreibt." In *Dazwischen. Zur Spezifik volkskundlicher Empirien*, edited by Klara Löffler, 65–74. Vienna: Institut für Europäische Ethnologie, 2001.

Leckie, Jaqueline. "Silent Immigrants? Immigration and Ethnicity in New Zealand." In *Immigration and National Identity in New Zealand: One People—Two—Peoples—Many Peoples?*, edited by Stuart Greif, 50–76. Palmerston North: Dunmore Press, 1995.

Lehmann, Albrecht. "Bewusstseinsanalyse." In *Methoden der Volkskunde. Positionen, Quellen, Arbeitsweisen der Europäischen Ethnologie*, edited by Silke Göttsch and Albrecht Lehmann, 233–49. Berlin: Reimer Verlag, 2001.

————. *Erzählstruktur und Lebenslauf. Autobiographische Untersuchungen*. Frankfurt: Campus, 1983.

————. *Reden über Erfahrung. Kulturwissenschaftliche Bewusstseinsanalyse des Erzählens*. Berlin: Reimer Verlag 2007.

Park, Julie. *Ladies a Plate: Changes and Continuity of New Zealand Women*. Auckland: Auckland University Press, 1991.

Stahl, Sandra K.D. *Literary Folkloristics and the Personal Narrative*. Bloomington, IN: Indiana University Press, 1987.

Tannen, Deborah. *You Just Don't Understand: Women and Men in Conversation*. New York: Morrow, 1990.

Zaborowska, Magdalena J. *How We Found America: Reading Gender through East-European Immigrant Narratives*. Chapel Hill: University of North Carolina Press, 1995.

TWENTY-EIGHT

The Domestication of Radical Ideas and Colonial Spaces

The Case of Elisabeth Förster-Nietzsche

Karin Bauer

This chapter explores Bernhard Förster's and Elisabeth Förster-Nietzsche's pursuit of the colonial dream in Paraguay. It outlines and contextualizes Förster's political and colonialist ideas and asks what motivated Förster-Nietzsche to participate in his enterprise. With an eye on the role of women in the male colonial project, it examines Förster-Nietzsche's contribution to this venture and her evolving role within the colony. The analysis demonstrates how female strategies of domestication simultaneously further and undermine the notion of female complicity with the colonial enterprises of men. Förster-Nietzsche's case offers not only broader insight into the multiple functions of what Ann McClintock termed the "traitorous cult of domesticity," but also into the peculiar relationship between domestication, domesticity, and the feminine exercise of power.

IN 1885, AT THE AGE OF THIRTY-NINE, Elisabeth Nietzsche, the infamous sister of the famous philosopher, married Bernhard Förster. In the spring of the following year, when the couple left Germany to found the settlement colony Nueva Germania in Paraguay, Förster-Nietzsche was optimistic about her future and keen to break away from the narrow confines of provincial life in Germany. She later inflated her claim to fame by maintaining to have been "the only woman in Germany who herself colonized."[1]

Based on published and unpublished materials housed at the Goethe-Schiller Archive in Weimar, this exploration of Förster's and Förster-

345

Nietzsche's pursuit of the colonial dream will proceed in three stages: First, I will outline and contextualize Förster's political and colonialist ideas; second, I will ask what motivated Förster-Nietzsche to participate in Förster's enterprise; and third, I will analyse Förster-Nietzsche's contribution to this venture and her evolving role within the colony. With a focus on the role of women in the male colonial project, this chapter will examine Förster-Nietzsche's various activities in an effort to tease out the feminine adaptations of what is usually coded as one of the ultimate male projects. In particular, it examines the ambiguous role that domesticity plays in the colonial venture and demonstrates how female strategies of domestication simultaneously further and undermine the notion of female complicity with the colonial enterprises of men. In the final analysis, Förster-Nietzsche's case offers broader insight not only into the multiple functions of the "traitorous cult of domesticity,"[2] but also into the peculiar relationship between domestication, domesticity, and the exercise of power.

Clearly, Förster's grandiose plans to colonize Paraguay were in need of domesticating influences in order to be perceived as a viable project by a wider public. Förster was a crude thinker and agitator who had had numerous charges of insult and assault laid against him. His virulent anti-Semitism and notoriety in creating disturbances and inciting violence against Jews constituted his claim to fame. After several disciplinary warnings from the Prussian Ministry of Education his anti-Semitic provocations finally led to his dismissal from teaching. Too outspoken for the German Reich, Förster had become a political liability. His world view consisted of a mixture of racial theories, vegetarianism, hygienism, vitalism, anti-Semitism, anti-capitalism, anti-modernism, anti-socialism, and anti-liberalism. These views were based on a regressive view of history, apocalyptic visions of the decline of German civilization, and the vague notion of a needed return to a mythic German origin. A devoted disciple of Wagner, Förster's writings were unoriginal appropriations of Wagnerian ideals, foremost among them the 1881 pamphlet *Das Verhältnis des modernen Judenthums zur deutschen Kunst,* which is based on Wagner's 1849 tract *Judaism in Music.*

Inspired by Wagner's ideas of a German cultural renewal, without a job, and profoundly alienated by the modernization of German society, Förster saw, paradoxically, the only possibility for the survival of Germanness in leaving Germany. Förster opposed immigration to the United States because of its tendency to assimilate immigrants, and in 1883 he set out on his first Paraguay expedition to explore the possibility of establishing his German community there. Förster yearned for a simpler life in opposition to the pollution he experienced in Germany: "noise, bad air, and the vice of the big cities … newspaper humbug … trivial novels … the beer hall ... Through physical labour, fresh air, the avoidance of fashionable poisons and through a more natural way of life, health, and beauty must be won back."[3]

At the time, clubs and associations in support of colonization were springing up all over Germany, and Förster's colonial aspirations spoke to the frustrated desires of certain segments of society disappointed that Germany had not aggressively pursued the acquisition of colonies. For Förster, it was a question of Aryan virility to spread the Germanic seed, and the lack of interest on the part of the German government served as further proof of the decadent decline of German values and strengths.

Germany had a long tradition of overseas settlements, missionary work, and commercial activity, but state-sponsored colonialism began only in 1884 when Bismarck—more or less reluctantly—proclaimed areas of Southwest Africa, Togo, and Cameroon to stand under German protection. This move gave an enormous boost to the activities of the Deutschen Kolonialgesellschaft, which had promoted emigration and settlement colonialism since the 1860s. The Försters hoped that with the aid of the Kolonialgesellschaft their lobbying efforts would eventually succeed in securing sponsorship of their enterprise by the German government.

Bismarck's stamp of approval set in motion an eruption of colonial fantasies that had been latently in the making since the eighteenth century. Susanne Zantop argues that the lack of real colonies and colonial power did not hinder the development of colonial fantasies, but allowed them to develop unhampered by experiences that may have offered a reality check. German colonial discourse "established itself not so much as 'intellectual authority' ... over distant terrains than as mythological authority over the collective imagination."[4] Thus Germany could also nurture the fantasy that in comparison to France, England, and Spain, it was a nation of kinder and gentler colonizers.

The Försters situated their enterprise between an aggressive anti-modernist stance, on the one hand, and, on the other, the evocation of pastoral bliss and the peaceful colonial farm that served as one of colonialism's master fantasies covering up latent imperialist expansionism.[5] Seemingly harmless and with nothing but good intentions, Förster hoped to find in South America the soil upon which to sow the seed of German culture: "Colonization we understand as: Transplanting our own culture onto a new, fertile ground ... under preclusion of everything accidental, artificial, and inauthentic and with the determined and conscious emphasis upon the authentic, eternal, and valuable of our folk."[6] Yet while this colonial enterprise seemed to be motivated by the wish to establish an Aryan brotherhood of farmers who would live a simple life in a kind of splendid isolation, the ambitions of both Försters clearly went beyond a life in rural bliss toward establishing a counter-empire with themselves installed as benevolent rulers.

Förster-Nietzsche intuitively—if not intellectually—understood the various ambivalences inherent in the colonial enterprise and took it on as her task to cover them up and mask contradictions, conflicts, and disagreements. To this end, she involved herself in Förster's plan from its inception by collecting signatures for various petitions, mailing flyers and requests, and lobbying for the cause through the local Wagner Association. Facing the life of an old maid in Naumburg, her work seemed to be aimed at wooing Förster. During his first exploration of Paraguay, Förster-Nietzsche sent him many admiring letters that effected, finally, their engagement via correspondence.

Immediately, Förster-Nietzsche took on the responsibility for her fiancé's domestic well-being: she insisted on sending him money so that he could hire a servant to take care of his personal needs. However, Förster-Nietzsche's civilizing mission does not end with the domestication of the male body and its needs, but extends to the domestication of ideas. Förster's radical nationalist and anti-Semitist ideas needed to be toned down in order to sell his colonialist project to a broader public. Förster-Nietzsche began to edit Förster's writings and attempted—at the risk of arguments and marital strife—to turn his racist rhetoric into romanticizing kitsch.

In Förster-Nietzsche's estimation, Förster's colonial fantasy was in need of the practical and domesticating influence of a woman. The translation of Förster's ideas into reality would have to rely heavily on female labour and the success of the colony would depend on the ability of German women to bear children, to run households adhering to German standards, and to establish a culture of respectability.[7] Although her rhetoric indicates that she was ready to take on the task of domestication, she was not content with a supporting role. Soon, she found her own strategies of exercising power—strategies that on the surface adhered to the limited role accorded to women, but which, in reality, aimed to undermine and circumvent those limits. She accepted the domestic realm as her sphere of influence, but saw colonization as a way to expand the boundaries of the domestic realm—and thus her sphere of influence—into the jungle.

Claiming to favour Förster's *National Education* (*Über nationale Erziehung: Ein Versuch*) over Nietzsche's *Zarathustra*, she flattered him and expressed allegiance to him rather than to her brother whose "entire world view goes against my grain."[8] She made it clear that she not merely preferred Förster's ideas, but also identified with them. If she were a man and not bound by the constraint society places upon women, she would take on Förster's task. Förster-Nietzsche could not have known that one day soon she would indeed do that. For now, she served encouragement to Förster and projected herself as his soul mate and female Doppelgänger.

Eager to define her own role in the colonial project, Förster-Nietzsche sought an emancipatory space for herself and an outlet for her ambitions: "Is it not better to go under while being useful to others, strong and striving, and to give value to one's existence rather than to wither away in Naumburg?"[9] "Finally and for once I, too, want to be free and independent. Over there I can do what I want; there, we will make our own laws."[10] While identifying with Förster's colonial fantasy, the emphasis of Förster-Nietzsche's assertions lay on herself and her own interests. First and foremost she sought an appropriate outlet for her own ambitions to transcend ordinary existence. Like other women involved in colonial enterprises, Förster-Nietzsche hoped that her husband's colony would be an outlet for her aspirations—aspirations that find satisfaction not in the domestic realm but in the exercise of power. "Maybe our attempt at colonization is just this: to stamp our seal onto a community, to be surrounded by a large number of people whom we want to make happy in our own way; and to make people happy means to rule over them."[11]

Although she would have never admitted it in public, the daily reality of living in Paraguay and later in the colony quickly dampened Förster-Nietzsche's idealism, and she soon found out that her command did not make people happy. Colonial fantasy confronted reality, and this reality turned out differently from what she had imagined. From the beginning, the conditions under which the colonial adventure was undertaken were harsh: their trip by ship was gruelling and Förster-Nietzsche appeared to have suffered a miscarriage.[12] When the Försters finally arrived in Asuncion, they rented a house in a place named Tuyu-cua, which means "dirt hole." Nevertheless, Förster-Nietzsche claimed that the area was charming and that she could stay there for the rest of her life.

The Förster's moved to the site of Nueva Germania only in March 1888, nearly two years after their departure from Germany. Förster-Nietzsche was elated by her arrival in her "dukedom," as she liked to call Nueva Germania. The welcoming festivities in honour of the their arrival included speeches, songs, poems, and the formal taking possession of their new home, Försterhof. "On the 5th of March we arrived in our marvellous new home. We entered like kings. Mr. Enzweiler, a very industrious and capable colonist, gave a nice speech and a toast to the mother of the colony [*Koloniemutter*] that warmed my heart."[13] While she gladly accepted the role as mother of the colony, her ambitions clearly surpassed her maternal urges. Förster-Nietzsche had grander visions for herself. It is interesting to note her description of herself as "king"; she did not describe herself as the *Koloniemutter*, nor did she describe their arrival as that of a king and a queen. In another instance of male identification, she again became Förster's double and projected herself as Förster's equal and into the role of king. To accent her aristocratic role, she adopted unofficially the name Eli de Förster, which was printed on her letterhead and calling card.

Förster-Nietzsche's glorifying narration of her seemingly triumphal entrance into Nueva Germania is also noteworthy for what is absent: namely, with the exception of two peons crying for joy, the colonized people have no place in her description. Instead, there are beautifully decorated houses, horses, handsome colonists, and pretty German girls carrying flowers. In line with the mythologies of colonization at the time, Förster-Nietzsche portrayed the colony as a depopulated "blank space for a new beginning" ready "for the creation of an imaginary national self."[14] Not shying away from clichés, in an article published in the *Bayreuther Blätter* in 1888, Förster-Nietzsche describes how Germanness takes possession of the geographic, acoustic, and emotional territory:

> The song of German men swells up in a nearby garden. Amazed by these strange new sounds, the tops of the jungle trees tremble! For twenty years, deep silence reigned here, and now this strange new life ... now— one can hear it quite well—everybody sings along, and wholesomely and strongly, with love, pride and longing, the sound caries far, all the way up into the starlit southern sky, into the mysterious dark of the towering jungle: "Germany, Germany above everything, above everything in the world."[15]

After an enduring silence, the patriotic German song of men awoke the Paraguayan jungle and found it ready to be cultivated under the guardianship of German civilization. The colonized land was a blank space on the map that demanded inscription by its new occupant and master. Colonizing the sonic space of the jungle, German song carried German virtues into the mysterious darkness of nature. Male labour and song would thus prepare the way for the civilizing mission of extending the boundaries of domestic bliss deeper into the jungle.

However, the reality behind the descriptions of the "glorious timber forest" and the "charming huts" of the colonists soon caught up with Förster-Nietzsche. By promising to settle 140 families within two years in his colony, Förster had secured the land from the government of Paraguay. Essentially, he sold land to colonists that he did not own. According to varying estimates, he was never able to settle more than about forty families. Förster vastly underestimated the kinds of resources it would have taken to establish an economically functional colony, and little more than wishful thinking seemed to have sustained the colonial dream. The land was a two- to three-day trip downstream from Asuncion, but Förster did not grasp the economic implications of this isolation. He underestimated the money needed to prepare the land for agricultural use and to build the infrastructure necessary to connect the community to the markets in Asuncion. Soon other problems arose: the deforested ground of the area proved to be unsuitable for most crops; cattle died of disease; colonists, too, became ill and some died; the climate was inhospitable and the colony was cut off from the outside during the raining season. The rest of the time, the water level in the river was not high enough to permit ship traffic. One of the major obstacles was that few of the settlers had actual experience in agriculture and even fewer had experience in the hot and humid climate. Förster's land distribution scheme left most settler families isolated and hours away from the centre of the colony, which was, of course, Förster-hof, the domicile of the Försters.[16]

Försterhof was larger and better built than the other houses of the colony and indicative of the status the Försters accorded to themselves. "We had a big, airy villa, Uncle Bernhard and I," Förster-Nietzsche would tell her niece thirty years later, "on the edge of the jungle with a grand view of the land, and we would have built such beautiful houses for the natives, too, if we had not been overcome by misfortune."[17] Förster-Nietzsche's recollection points to the importance of establishing a proper domestic space within the vast colonial landscape; however, the "big, airy villa" remained the privileged site of the colonizers.

Förster-Nietzsche was proud of her respectable household, and her domestic agenda provided the impetus for her colonial efforts. To her mother, she wrote: "It's so nice to rule a bit, to set things up, to give orders."[18] She reported in detail on her domestication efforts on two fronts: the colonists and the native population. In general, indigenous people were mentioned in her writings only in terms of their utility as workers. Förster-Nietzsche shared Förster's view, which described the native population in patronizing terms as naive and friendly, but with a tendency to be disloyal and lazy. He suggested that the tendency toward laziness was not entirely the people's fault: "To live without hard labour, a condition that indicates paradise for the lazy Jew, is normal in the tropics … although this kind of existence is deprived and would be intolerable to the Aryan."[19] In Förster-Nietzsche's propagandistic writings, native women were portrayed mostly as well-meaning and marginally attractive labourers. "From early morning on the picturesque figures of the Paraguayan women dressed in white carry their heavy loads … beautiful they aren't, but graceful they are."[20] In her letters to her mother, Förster-Nietzsche criticizes native women for smoking and for lacking self-discipline and control. She also perceives their sexuality—and its culturally different expression—as a threat to the racial and moral fabric of the colony.

Perpetuating the myth of the superiority of the German *Hausfrau*, Förster-Nietzsche complained about the indigenous women's supposed lack of housekeeping skills and attempted to recruit female servants and unmarried German women or families with daughters. Her efforts fit into the emerging fascination with the image of the colonialist *Farmersfrau* and mirror the efforts of various colonialist women's organizations that began to form in the late nineteenth century.[21] As historian Nancy Reagin points out, the myth of German housekeeping played a significant role in the definition of German identity in the colonies. Germanized households served to demarcate the colonists from the colonized, thus creating a community of Germans that resembled the idealized, orderly small towns of the homeland.[22] Thus Naumburg in Paraguay could serve as a slogan to characterize Förster-Nietzsche's domestic zeal.

In her study of gender, race, and sexuality in the colonial contest, Ann McClintock, too, exposes aspects of the cult of domesticity that is an integral part of the colonial enterprise. She identifies domestic colonialism as a site of domination where the myths of racial and national superiority assert and manifest themselves.[23] Like many women in the colonies, Förster-Nietzsche fulfilled her domestic agenda by reverting to the "self-sacrificing graces of white motherhood."[24] While Förster-Nietzsche had no child of her own, she undertook what she called a "*Kulturversuch*," a cultural experiment that may on a personal level have provided her temporarily with a substitute for the child she did not bear. She took in a six-year-old native girl named Carmen and attempted to raise her as a German, initially with little success. But under Förster-Nietzsche's care, Carmen soon improved: "The little one speaks and feels entirely German and shed bitter tears when one of the peons tried to explain to her that she is nothing but a Chamacoco [a native tribe].... 'Mama, I am German, aren't I?' She asked with tears streaming down her face. 'Of course,' I answered, 'yes,' and the brown round face lit up with joy."[25] After her baptism, Carmen is not mentioned again in Förster-Nietzsche's correspondence, and it is thus impossible to ascertain what happened to this cultural experiment and how, in Förster-Nietzsche's estimation, it turned out.

Carmen represented the colonized ideal: an illiterate blank screen, young, innocent, naive, and eager to adopt a German identity. Germanness brings joy to the colonized, and under proper guidance, Carmen learned how to feel and act German. With this cultural experiment and her claim that Germanness can be acquired, Förster-Nietzsche turned Förster's notion of national education into a domestic and domesticating project. By claiming to have educated the girl to become German, Förster-Nietzsche implied that Germanness is not—as her husband asserted—a matter of race or an hereditary trait, but a learned behaviour and thus a constructed identity. Obviously, this constructed identity contradicts the essentialist view of race with which the Försters operate in other contexts. Förster-Nietzsche's cultural experiment emphasized the importance of domestication to the colonial cause and thus presents another variation of the familial narrative that Zantop[26] identified as central to the portrayal and legitimation of the colonizing effort.

However, as conditions deteriorated in the colony, Förster-Nietzsche began to realize that her maternal and mediating role and her pursuit of respectability were being used for the affirmation of the paternalistic master narrative of colonization. "I know quite well that without me this entire founding of the colony would have been a dark and uncertain undertaking."[27] As Förster was mostly absent on his so-called business trips, the colony was increasingly in Förster-Nietzsche's hands. In Förster's absence, she allotted land, seeds, and livestock to the settlers; she made decisions regarding the building of pathways, roads, and community building, planned new industries, and assisted settlers with their bureaucratic tasks. She had to settle disputes among the colonists, and when Förster came home, she had to put up with his bad mood and temper: "One thing is certain: the few years I have been married will cost me ten years of my life."[28]

Financially destitute, the colony did not develop into a communal haven of German virtues. There was little to foster solidarity amongst the colonists, left without a basic infrastructure and in competition for scarce resources. There was too much alcohol and there were not enough German women to maintain domestic order. It was not enough to cultivate the soil and domesticate the natives; the male colonizers, too, were in need of civilizing influences. The Paraguayan reality had put a large question mark behind the imagined community of Aryan brotherhood.

Complaints about the colony soon turned into nasty fights and open revolts. Newspapers in Germany and the *Deutsche Kolonialzeitung* published in Paraguay became the venue for accusations and counter-accusations. Förster-Nietzsche was on the defensive and her writings exhibited a strategy of appeasement. While acknowledging some problems, she absolved herself of the responsibility of wooing people to Nueva Germania under false pretences by stating that colonization is hard work that only a special few are able to accomplish; this said, she continued writing about the colony in romanticizing terms. Adopting the German colonial ur-narrative of sacrifice and heroism,[29] Förster-Nietzsche's rhetorical gestures oscillate between the evocation of martyrdom, domestic bliss, and patriotism. She reached the point of frustration.[30]

Countering every complaint as denunciation, Förster-Nietzsche attributed the failure of the colony to causes outside of her control, either to adventurers or to the German government. Only after the conditions in the colony had deteriorated to the point where its dysfunctionality could no longer be disputed did Förster-Nietzsche occasionally voice to her mother in confidence her dissatisfaction with "Bernchen": "This man fails to understand anything and instead of helping, he promenades around on his horse. The more a woman accomplishes, the more is asked of her."[31]

When the financial situation of the colony with the related issue of the lack of title to the land became untenable, Förster died. Upon his death in June 1889, he immediately turned from being a "horrible egotist" into "my dearest darling" who was killed by the disappointments, treachery, and acts of sabotage he had endured by, among others, inept German politicians, colonists, creditors, the German Colonial Society, and even the anti-Semitic party. Believing herself to have become the executor of Förster's ideas, she settled his debts as best she could and managed to sell Försterhof. Like the colonial venture, marriage now became suspect: "Marriage, after all, was too dangerous and uncertain a sea for me—I will not set sail a second time."[32]

Förster-Nietzsche returned to Germany in 1893 to take care of her brother, who had descended into madness and could no longer object to her attention. Now began her second transformation: Eli de Förster became Frau Dr. h.c. Elisabeth Förster-Nietzsche, her brother's keeper and matriarch of the Nietzsche Archive. She began the work of colonizing, monumentalizing, and domesticating Nietzsche and his ideas and of creating the Nietzsche Archive, a public-domestic space for the desexualized man-child under her control. As she had done with the Paraguayan jungle, Förster-Nietzsche filled this space with German patriotic, male song, and, as the self-proclaimed executor of her brother's legacy, she utilized skills practised in Paraguay. As she herself stated: "Without Paraguay, there would be no Nietzsche archive."[33]

In domesticating Förster's ideas in Paraguay and later Nietzsche's philosophy at the Nietzsche Archive in Weimar, Förster-Nietzsche set in motion a process of dispossession that attempted to counteract her own subordination under the enterprises of men. She domesticated not only the physical space of the colony, but also the intellectual space occupied by men. The ideas of men were too theoretical, abstract, and radical for Förster-Nietzsche and had to be transformed by the practical expertise and domesticating labour of women. To maintain the bourgeois social order, the male body and mind had to be constrained and civilized. Thus, the products of male intellectual labour served as the impetus and foil for realizing the feminine agenda. Exercising a familial tyranny, Förster-Nietzsche facilitated the tenuous triumph of domestication. Förster-Nietzsche's case thus testifies to the unfortunate results of the displacement of a repressed female desire for autonomy and recognition.

The author thanks the Social Science and Humanities Research Council of Canada for the financial support of her work at the Goethe-Schiller Archive. For their generous support of the project, she is indebted to Dr. Roswitha Wollkopf, the staff at the archive, Andrea Dietrich, Ralf Rosmiarek, Dr. Daniela Kraus, Professor Imke Meyer, Hilke Meyer, and Monika Schott-Rajabi.

Notes

1 Goethe-Schiller Archive (GSA) 72/719a. All translations from published sources are by the author.
2 McClintock, *Imperial Leather*, 272.
3 Förster, *Über nationale Erziehung*, 22.
4 Zantop, *Colonial Fantasies*, 7. For a discussion of the concept of "intellectual authority," see Saïd, *Culture and Imperialism*.
5 For explorations of the romanticizing of the farm and the so-called simple life in the colonies, see, for example, Zantop, *Colonial Fantasies*; Wildenthal, *German Women*; and Klotz, *White Women*.
6 Förster, *Deutsche Colonien*, 194.
7 Smith, "Colonialism."
8 Letter to Förster, 24 September 1883, GS 72/1158a.
9 Nietzsche, *Sämtliche Briefe*, III/4, 102.
10 Nietzsche, *Sämtliche Briefe*, III/4, 25.
11 Nietzsche, *Sämtliche Briefe*, III/4, 238.
12 Nietzsche, *Sämtliche Briefe*, III/4, 159.
13 Letter to Franziska Nietzsche, 30 April 1888, GSA 100/533, 1.
14 Zantop, *Colonial Fantasies*, 7.
15 Podach, *Gestalten um Nietzsche*, 154.
16 This account of the conditions in Nueva Germania is based on Daniela Kraus's expertly researched dissertation.
17 Sigismund, *Zarathustras Sippschaft*, 116.
18 Letter to Franziska Nietzsche, 28 March 1888, GSA 100/533, 1.
19 Förster, *Deutsche Colonien*, 74.
20 Förster-Nietzsche, *Dr. Bernhard Försters Kolonie*, 15.
21 Wildenthal, *German Women*, 131.
22 Reagin, "Imagined Hausfrau," 84.
23 McClintock, *Imperial Leather*, 272.
24 McClintock, *Imperial Leather*, 272–73.
25 Förster-Nietzsche, *Dr. Bernhard Försters Kolonie*, 37–38.
26 Zantop, *Colonial Fantasies*.
27 Letter to Franziska Nietzsche, 4 September 1889, GSA 100/533, 2.
28 Letter to Franziska Nietzsche, 9 November 1887, GSA 100/533, 1.
29 Zantop, *Colonial Fantasies*, 21.
30 Podach, *Gestalten um Nietzsche*, 154.
31 Letter to Franziska Nietzsche, 18 March 1888, GSA 100/533, 1.
32 Letter to Franziska Nietzsche, 30 June 1892, GSA 100/533, 2.
33 GSA 72/1064.

Archival Material

Goethe-Schiller Archive (GSA), Weimar.

Works Cited

Förster, Bernhard. *Deutsche Colonien im oberen Laplata Gebiete mit besonderer Berück-sichtigung von Paraguay.* 2nd edition. Leipzig: Fock, 1886.

———. *Über nationale Erziehung: Ein Versuch.* 2nd edition. Leipzig: Fock, 1886.

———. *Das Verhältnis des modernen Judenthums zur deutschen Kunst.* Berlin, 1881.

Förster-Nietzsche, Elisabeth. *Dr. Bernhard Försters Kolonie Neu-Germania in Paraguay.* Berlin: Commissions-Verlag der Aktien-Gesellschaft Pionier, 1891.

Kraus, Daniela. "Bernhard und Elisabeth Försters Neu-Germania in Paraguay: eine antisemitische Utopie." PhD diss., Universität Wien, 1999.

Klotz, Marcia. *White Women and the Dark Continent: Gender and Sexuality in German Colonial Discourse from the Sentimental Novel to the Fascist Film.* Ann Arbor: UMI, 1994.

McClintock, Ann. *Imperial Leather: Race, Gender and Sexuality in the Colonial Contest.* New York: Routledge, 1995.

Nietzsche, Friedrich. *Sämtliche Briefe. Kritische Studienausgabe.* Edited by Giorgio Colli and Mazzino Montinari. Berlin: dtv/de Gruyter, 1986.

Podach, Erich F. *Gestalten um Nietzsche.* Weimar: Erich Lichtenstein Verlag, 1954.

Reagin, Nancy. "The Imagined Hausfrau: National Identity, Domesticity, and Colonialism in Imperial Germany." *Journal of Modern History,* 73, no. 1 (2001): 54–86.

Said, Edward. *Culture and Imperialism.* New York: Vintage, 1993.

Sigismund, Ursula. *Zarathustras Sippschaft.* Darmstadt: Kranichsteiner Literaturverlag, 1992.

Smith, Woodruff D. "Colonialism and the Culture of Respectability." In *Germany's Colonial Past,* edited by Eric Ames, Marcia Klotz, and Lora Wildenthal, 3–20. Lincoln, NE: University of Nebraska Press.

Wagner, Richard. "Judaism in Music." In *Judaism in Music and other Essays.* Translated by W. Ashton Ellis, 51–59. Lincoln, NE: University of Nebraska Press, 1995.

Wildenthal, Lora. *German Women for Empire, 1884–1945.* Durham, NC: Duke University Press, 2001.

Zantop, Susanne. *Colonial Fantasies: Conquest, Family, and Nation in Precolonial Germany, 1770–1870.* Durham, NC: Duke University Press, 1997.

PART THREE

LOSS

TWENTY-NINE

Reasons and Conditions of Population Transfer

The Expulsion of Germans from East and Central Europe and Their Integration in Germany and Abroad after World War II

Hans Lemberg

It is a truism that most of the Germans who immigrated to Canada did not come from Germany proper. Many of them were former citizens of Russia, the United States, of Yugoslavia, Poland, Czechoslovakia, the Baltic states, etc. The notion of "Canadian German" is mostly related to ethnicity. Considering the self-declaration of citizens in censuses, statistics cannot sufficiently categorize the group known as Canadian Germans[1] in both meanings (former citizenship and/or ethnicity), and above all cannot define where they came from and at which date: too complicated are the immigrants' courses of life. But migration historians and the living tradition itself among Canadian Germans assert that there is a large number of immigrants of German origin in Canada, who were affected by acts of forced population transfers somewhere in central or eastern Europe, before they came, or whose parents were affected.

Immigration to Canada and the Germans

FROM THE 1920S UNTIL THE END OF WORLD WAR II Canadian policy was reluctant to admit immigrants from Europe, even persons who were persecuted by totalitarian regimes were normally not admitted or even sent back to Europe.[2] Yet at the end of World War II, the tide turned. Soon a new postwar prosperity and the need of labour, and also the rethinking of racial policy resulted in changing immigration policy. But even then newcomers to Canada were separated out by immigration officers who were more or less guided by changing, sometimes secret, directives that considered racial and ethnic affiliation, nationality, health, occupational qualification, even "character."[3]

As a result, persons identifying themselves as Germans might, in the immigration officers' eyes, be also Russians, Americans, Poles, Yugoslavs, or just displaced persons[4] who were let into the country in times when "proper" Germans were still refused entry as enemy aliens until 1950, when Germans were admitted and immigration from Germany soared. It is thus understandable that often enough, beginning with World War I, Canadians of German origin preferred to hide or to jettison their German part of identity—or that they simply "Canadianized" it in the course of relatively short time.[5]

Even without the masses of people fleeing before the approaching battle fronts and deported to forced labour, there are still millions left who were transferred or expelled because they belonged to a national minority, among them a large number of ethnic Germans, so-called *Volksdeutsche*. A relatively small part of them, but still some hundred thousands, found their way to Canada. A relevant number of today's Canadians are descendants of these resettlers. It might therefore be useful to look at the driving power of—as it has been called—the migration of peoples of our times in central and eastern Europe from the late 1930s and into the '40s.

The Idée Fixe of Ethnically Homogeneous National States

One of the main reasons for the great movements of population during this time was an idée fixe, a thought, that it would be possible to solve problems of minorities in national states with mixed ethnic population just by unmixing them, that is by transferring or exchanging national minorities to their assumed countries of origin, unilaterally or in exchange with other states. This would be managed by treaties, in voluntary or compulsory transfers, with the migrants possibly taking movable property with them, and with or without indemnities for the abandoned and mostly immovable property.[6]

This idea rests on the fundamental transformation of society in the nineteenth and early twentieth centuries, when society in central and eastern Europe underwent a radical change toward equality and democratization. In premodern society only privileged persons were important and nonprivileged people did not count at all in politics; at that time the language used in the society and by the masses of population was irrelevant. Only with the conception of gender equality and with the rise of national movements did language become a more and more distinctive feature. This was the predisposition for the emergence of modern national states, first in the late nineteenth century in the Balkans, so that when the same happened after World War 1 in east-central Europe, it was scoffed as balkaniza-tion. It was only then, in the new democratic era, that inhabitants were not considered but merely counted, and a distinction was made between majority nationalities and the so-called national minorities, that is people of non-dominant ethnic groups. National minorities were now a new phe-nomenon, and there was no previous experience of how to handle them.[7]

Theoretically, it would have been possible to give autonomy rights to the new minorities, but this was not very popular with the founders of the new states who felt victorious. Radical solutions, such as those suggested as early as 1915 by Swiss ethnographer George Montandon were also pos-sible. In his brochure on *Frontières nationales: Détermination objective de la condition primordiale nécessaire à l'obtention d'une paix durable* he saw the only guaranty for future peace in Europe in the creation of ethnically homogeneous national states.[8] There had to be defendable boundaries—and minorities had to be compulsorily exchanged with corresponding minorities from the neighbouring states—or simply expelled to their so-called motherlands. Montandon may not have been widely read, but his idea was in the air.

The Conference of Lausanne and Possible Solutions of Minority Problems

The first massive materialization of this idea was the treaty of Lausanne between Greece and Turkey of January 1923. For the first time in European history a compulsory exchange of populations between two countries was established. This treaty was the prototype for all similar ones in the future. It was also so significant because such high diplomats as the British foreign minister Lord Curzon and Fridtjof Nansen, then League of Nations refugee commissioner, were involved.[9]

Immediately after the initial peace treaty of Sèvres in 1920, a Greek-Turkish war had broken out during which a forceful and chaotic expul-sion of approximately a million Greeks from Asia minor began. The peace negotiations in the winter of 1922/23 were conducted under extraordi-nary time constraints and refugee pressures. It was not easy for Lord Cur-zon to bring Greek and Turkish adversaries together at the conference table. An exposé written by Nansen and read by Curzon asserted that "the quickest and most efficacious way of dealing with the grave economic results which must result from the great movement of populations" must employ the strategy "to unmix the populations of the Near East," a phrase that has become a cliché. They claimed further that this "will tend to secure the true pacification of the Near East."[10]

During the negotiations, many of the refugees found out that they would no longer be allowed to return to their homes, and there were furious demonstrations all over Greece. The participants of the Lausanne conference tried to shift responsibility to others—including Nansen himself. Lord Curzon coined his regret with the famous words: a compulsory exchange of populations is "a thoroughly bad and vicious solution, for which the world would pay a heavy penalty for a hundred years to come."[11]

In the end, the Treaty of Lausanne brought both Greece and Turkey nearer to the ethnic homogeneity of their national states. But it took years to integrate the refugees into their new mother countries and the action was a tremendous financial failure. The relations between Greece and Turkey were not improved in the long run. Yet, in spite of these disadvantages, this compulsory population exchange has been regarded by European public opinion as very successful. It appeared, in a way, to be a possible pattern for future solutions of minority problems elsewhere.

Apparently, during the 1920s there were no more frontier corrections that had to be made, no more populations to be exchanged. Of course there were major minority problems here and there, but to contain them the League of Nations had invented a sophisticated system of minority protection, which somehow worked. Minority discontent was kept within limits, and there was relatively little violence in this field.

In 1929 in England, Professor John S. Stephens held a significant lecture on "Danger Zones of Europe. A Study of National Minorities," in which Stephens pointed out three possibilities for handling minority problems.[12]

The best possibility of all seemed to him to be protection of minorities. However, Stephens was struck by the intense disputes at the time on the complex implications of minority rights and demands for autonomy. The second possibility in Stephens's eyes was the assimilation of national minorities. In December 1925, shortly after the Treaty of Locarno, the League of Nations referee on minority questions, Afranio de Mello Franco, made the startling remark that the purpose of minority protection was *"de préparer, peu à peu, les conditions nécessaires à l'établissement de la complète unité nationale"* (to prepare, little by little, the conditions necessary to establish complete national unity).[13] This was misunderstood as ethnic assimilation in central and eastern Europe because of the ambiguity of the word "nation" in other than western languages. What Mello Franco really meant was that members of minorities had to become loyal citizens of the state. However, often politicians were obsessed with the idea of the assimilation of minorities. As the British foreign secretary Austen Chamberlain put it: "The object of the Minority Treaties … was … to secure for the minorities that measure of protection and justice which would gradually prepare them to be merged in the national community to which they belonged."[14] In Stephens's view there was a third alternative: "To avoid such a result [i.e., assimilation], a high League official has recently said that, failing a workable system for the protection of minorities, it would be necessary to exchange populations—a remedy so drastic when attempted in the Near East that one shudders at the thought of its application to European peoples so much more firmly rooted."[15] No one can know what the various officials thought of this alternative, but evidently it remained in politicians' minds.

There was still a fourth alternative, which John Stephens did not mention and which perhaps did not seem realistic in the late 1920s: the shifting of frontiers. Ten years later this option was the order of the day in central European politics. After seizing power, Hitler had begun to destroy the Versailles system and set about to alter the frontiers of Europe.

Concepts of Population Exchange in the 1930s

The first of these changes was the Anschluss of Austria in March 1938. In consequence, Germany now had common borderlines with Hungary, Yugoslavia, and Italy. So the Axis partnership was burdened more than before with the problem of the South Tyrol. There Fascist Italy had put the German minority under hard assimilatory pressure. If this obstacle for Axis friendship was to be removed now, it was not possible to apply the slogan "Ein Volk, ein Reich, ein Führer" in the way it had been applied at the Munich conference, where the Sudeten minority problem was "solved" by cutting off a territory populated by a minority from Czechoslovakia and by annexing it to Germany.[16]

Accordingly, in South Tyrol for the first time after Lausanne the model of a population transfer by international agreement was applied. In mid 1939 the partners, with Himmler on the German side, began to negotiate. The transfer treaty was signed in October 1939. There were more than twenty additional treaties on transfer issues for South Tyrol between 1939 and 1942. The decision to go or to stay was charged with psychological pressure applied by various agents: the church, the domestic Nazis, fascist government organs in Italy, the SS, and others. As a result, the transfer was watered down, above all when disappointing news came from the destinations of the resettled Tyrolians.[17]

The case of the South Tyrol population transfer had no lasting effects—after the war most of the transferees returned home. But it became a further prototype for population transfer in central Europe.

Shortly thereafter, the immediate threat of war between Germany and Poland illustrates how widespread this idea was. In the last weeks of August 1939, British diplomatic officials made strong efforts with German and Polish governments to effect a population exchange in Upper Silesia and Danzig to relax the tensions between the two countries. British ambassador to Germany Sir Neville Henderson saw "as the sole method of terminating minority disputes an exchange of populations on the same but much easier lines as in South Tyrol"[18]—even if the British consul from Kattowitz was skeptical. He "did not think it was practicable. The population was inextricably mixed. There were many Germans with Polish names and many Poles with German names. The people regarded themselves as Silesians rather than as either Poles or Germans."[19]

Just a week before the outbreak of the war, Ambassador Henderson met with Hitler. The British diplomatic papers contain the remark, "When Herr Hitler talked about Macedonian conditions on his frontier, Sir H. Henderson agreed that the nationality idea being so strong today, the exchange of populations was a very useful solution."[20]

The ideology that state borders had to be identical with ethnographic ones was not only rooted in British thinking, but had also become endemic elsewhere in Europe. Approximately a month later, on 6 October, after the German aggression and the new partition of Poland by Hitler and Stalin, Hitler delivered a speech in the Reichstag that reflected this manner of thinking. The new Reich order was to "correspond with historical, ethnographic, and economic realities." He added that "the most important task is to create a new order of ethnographic conditions, that is a resettlement of nationalities in a way, that at the end of the development there will be better lines of division than nowadays." Somewhat later he added that "the east and southeast of Europe are to some extent filled with non-durable fragments of German population. Exactly here lies the reason for continuous international disturbances ... Therefore it belongs to the task of the far-reaching establishment of order in European life to arrange transfers of populations to remove at least in part the European points of conflict."[21]

Hitler's Resettlement Policy and the SS

This speech of Hitler, which resounded with anti-Semitic and imperialist notes, was the propagandistic prelude for a new wave of resettlements of German population groups from east-central European neighbour states under the slogan "Heim ins Reich." During the months after he made the speech, fifteen international treaties were concluded, the only purpose of which was the so-called *Heimführung* of German ethnic groups.[22]

Before World War II, in the first phase of the South Tyrolean transfer planning, the SS had in mind a two-staged pattern. Transferees had to be brought temporarily into the Reich, and after the conquest of east European territories the resettlers had to be transferred there for purposes of Germanization.

Let us consider two examples. First, the Baltic Germans had lived in their provinces for hundreds of years as a privileged group. With the founding of the national states of Estonia and Latvia after the Russian Revolution they felt degraded as a national minority. When they left their homes in 1940 on the basis of treaties concluded between Germany and the Baltic states, they thought they would be shipped to inner Germany, but on their way they found out that they were directed to the so-called new Eastern Provinces of the Reich, the "Wartheland," that was the hitherto western parts of Poland. A new version of the population exchange model was now being realized. To gain resettling space and buildings for the Baltic transferees, masses of Poles and Jews were deported in hasty and extremely inhuman fashion to the *Generalgouvernement* or directly into ghettos and concentration camps.

In another example, the same destiny was experienced by the Galician Germans. They had come to their regions of settlement in Galicia after the partitions of Poland at the end of the eighteenth century, called by the Austrian emperors to cultivate the region as farmers. After 1918 they were, as a German national minority, citizens of restored Poland. Both of these groups, Balts and Galician Germans, and some others, were uprooted by Hitler's resettlement policy in 1939–40 and made to relocate.[23]

The new wave of wartime population transfer was exacerbated by the creation of new special agencies and their subordination under the SS. The chaos of the plurality of Nazi organizations was intensified. Himmler, the chief of the SS, was appointed Reichskommissar für die Festigung des deutschen Volkstums[24] and, among a jumble of offices and administrative units, it was the SS that managed the population transfers with its characteristic brutality and cynicism. Incidentally, during the SS regime the thought of ethnic homogenization was more and more neglected and substituted by racist and imperialist experiments and crimes.

The national socialist transfer actions can be divided into three periods: 1939 to 1941, the stage of experiments and resettlements without planning; 1941 to 1943, the stage of actions corresponding to planning; 1943 to 1945, the stage of retreat, when nevertheless—until the end of the war—new transfers were constantly initiated, such as the transfer of the Black Sea Germans, who on their way to the northwest were overrun by the Red Army.

During this relatively short time, the German authorities initiated a great variety of settlement measures in various places. There were well-organized repatriations; there even were exchange settlements farm by farm between Poles and Germans and compensation of value differences was envisaged. But far more often there were actions that went out of control or expulsions that were brutal from their beginnings, seen primarily in the systematic degrading of populations in occupied countries (above all of the Poles), the system of forced labour, the extermination of the Jewish people, and the mass murder in concentration camps.

Transfers with the purpose to ethnographically cleanse the enlarged Reich were started not only in the east, but also in other regions, for example in Alsace-Lorraine,[25] and in the south in the annexed regions of Yugoslavia from which Slovenes were transferred.[26]

In the planning stage, grandiose projects were developed, such as the Generalplan Ost, which envisaged the new order of eastern Europe for the postwar era;[27] the substance of these plans was summarized by Karl Hermann Frank in 1941 in his Nazi jargon: "Umvolkung der rassisch Geeigneten, Aussiedlung von rassisch Unverdaulichen, Sonderbehandlung destruktiver Elemente, Neubesiedlung dadurch freigewordenen Raumes mit frischem deutschem Blut."[28]

The traditional idea of creating homogeneous national states by unmixing peoples and bringing state and ethnic frontiers into congruence was furthered among the German allies as well as in the annexed parts of Germany. This included population exchanges between Bulgaria and Romania, between Serbia and Croatia and others. But it is not too much to say that in the short era of Nazi rule this idea of unmixing peoples experienced an enormous leap that was characterized by an hereto unprecedented mixture of cynicism, inhuman pseudo-scientific experimentation with population relocation, and by lawless brutality that time and again ended in genocide. There was even a causal connection between resettlement policy and the Holocaust. Through Hitler's policies the threshold for brutality within the framework of population transfers had been lowered significantly.

Population Transfer Plans with the Allies

On the Allied side, the British designs with regard to the idea of ethnic homogenization of states were much more traditional. But, as remarked earlier, here, too, the idea prevailed that conflicts between states could be eliminated by the exchange or transfer of minority populations. British projects related to disentangling populations developed early and were prepared by memoranda by a think tank of Oxford experts between 1940 and 1942. When additional news of the Nazi crimes in the concentration camps and elsewhere began to leak out, the additional impulse to punish the Germans after the war arose.

The idea of unmixing of populations was so deeply rooted that with the various drafts for new frontier lines between Poland and Germany and with the restoration of Czechoslovakia and Yugoslavia, the number of Germans who had to be expelled in consequence was automatically calculated for each version. These designs were accomplished by the Inter-departmental Committee on the Transfer of German Populations, which was given the task of coordinating planning in the British government. The plans had to be harmonized with the small East European exile govern-ments, with the United States, the European Advisory Commission, the Soviet Union, and other involved parties.[29] In May 1944 British foreign sec-retary Anthony Eden coined the classical formula for the fundamental idea of homogenization of national states: "My own policy w[oul]d be such: ... there sh[oul]d be no national minorities in Europe."[30]

The nearer the day of victory over Germany came and the more the real amount of destruction in Germany was known, the more obvious became the problem of how to house and feed the masses of refugees and transferees who began to pour in from the moment of occupation or liberation. There was no clear idea how to integrate these people at any of the points of destination.

The great population transfers of the 1940s were accompanied by an intensive controversy in the publication field. There were determined advocates such as the well-informed Bernard Newman, who had travelled central and eastern Europe before the war and who in 1943, based on his earlier book *Danger Spots of Europe*, pointed out the necessity of popula-tion exchanges and transfers, writing that "the inconvenience of the few cannot be allowed to prejudice the safety of the many."[31]

Among the many voices advocating the separation of populations were former U.S. president Herbert Hoover and the former U.S. under secre-tary of state Sumner Welles, who looked upon minorities as an "eternal menace to friendly relations between peoples." "Isn't it better," he contin-ues, "considering the appalling tragedy in Europe which we now con-front, to get through with all the heartaches in this generation, when they may be an immediate consequence of planning for a peaceful and hap-pier world, and thus prevent new heartaches in the generations to come?"[32]

But there were also voices vehemently criticizing the concept of unmix-ing during the 1940s, among people affected by exchanges of popula-tions as well as among those in secure western countries. For example, Eugene Kulischer, an immigrant to America who was an expert on migra-tion history and himself affected by forced migration, wrote: "No politi-cal rationalization can obscure the sad reality of a wasteful mass depor-tation of innocent people."[33] In 1946, Kulischer called it a prejudice to assume that a nation should profess the same religion or must consist of people of the same language. "The whole idea of a 'national state' is anti-quated," he wrote, and the exchange of population had by no means the pacificatory effect that had been assumed. Above all, wrote Kulischer, "No artificial ethnic segregation can be durable." The discussion pro and contra population transfer was not only put forward in publications, but also directly, as in a memorable debate in the British House of Lords in March 1944.[34]

Realization of Population Transfer 1945 and After

At the end of the war, with the complete liberation of European states and the division of Germany into occupation zones, it was evident that the plans for ethnic homogenization of central and east European states, envisaged to be accomplished during a period of five to ten years, went far beyond the script written in London or Yalta or Potsdam.[35] Acts of revenge and spontaneous violence, together with the intention of the governments of the liberated states to get rid of as many Germans as soon as possible, resulted in the mixing of methods in which this ethnic cleansing before the term existed was realized.

The larger than expected proportions and the real forms of this transfer can be divided into two stages. The first was the so-called wild expulsions. As in the case of the Anatolic Greeks before the conference of Lausanne, now in Czechoslovakia, in the old and in freshly annexed territories of Poland, and in southeastern Europe, Germans were brutally driven out of their homes in short time, with minimal possessions or no luggage at all. There was chaos: they were expelled by civilians, members of self-appointed militias, but also regular soldiers. The wild expulsions seemed to be spontaneous, but often enough they were officially steered to create a *fait accompli* before international regulations took effect. There were even special authorities to handle the *repatriacija*, the transfer and resettlement of inhabitants. These unregulated expulsions peaked in June and July 1945, when many of the expellees were no longer permitted to cross the borders into neighbouring states or into the occupation zones of Germany, but neither could they return home and were literally in stateless limbo. Many starved to death and there were numerous suicides. In these weeks some of the notorious massacres occurred.

The second of these stages began with the conclusion of the Potsdam conference in August 1945. In Potsdam the victorious Great Three—the United Kingdom, the United States, and Russia—agreed to expel Germans in an "orderly and humane" manner from Czechoslovakia, Poland, and even Hungary, which had jumped into the boat at the last moment. Accordingly, in 1946, after an official moratorium of some months, which was bypassed in many cases, the organized transport of thousands of trains of livestock wagons full of expellees with their minimal belongings began to the borders of the American, British, and Soviet occupation zones of Germany. These transports were indeed orderly, but not always humane. There were many casualties caused by the cold, by epidemic diseases, and by hunger. These transports were increasingly criticized in British public opinion, and official protests were addressed to the Polish authorities. Questions were raised in the British Parliament and the government tried to stop the transports for a while, but were not very successful.

There were various other forms of displacement of people from their homes and uprooting from their social environment. Some of these forms merged into another, as when, for example, a retreat or flight in fear of the approaching front was intended as "voluntary" and transitional. Most refugees in this category hoped to return home when the immediate fighting was over. Many of them tried—often in vain, when Polish soldiers refused them permission to cross the river Oder eastwards. Hence, such refugees became expellees.

Among those hit by flight and expulsion were people who had lived in their home regions for centuries, and also groups that only some years or months earlier had arrived by the resettlements under the Heim ins Reich program. These latter groups now experienced a double or triple displacement in a short period of time, this time in flight before the Red Army or before expulsion by the Poles.

The general situation of Germans—but also of other ethnic groups in the regions damaged by war—was most deplorable. However, it was not only discriminated minorities who starved, there was general misery in all ethnic groups. Epidemic diseases raged; people were exhausted; they suffered from pillage, from the arbitrariness of the provisional and badly staffed authorities, from general lawlessness, and from a lack of legal rights. The legal system, which had been destroyed during the German occupation and the Third Reich, was re-established, first by decrees, and later also through orderly legislation. But this took months, during which there was chaos and interfering forces of local authorities, namely the regular and irregular Polish, Czechoslovak, or Soviet troops, or police forces with contradictory interests. In the hitherto German eastern provinces recently adjudged to Poland, a new Polish administration was gradually installed. As a consequence, a general feeling arose called "Heimatverlust in der Heimat"; many of the Germans were even eager to leave their homes to escape their unbearable situation.[36]

Camps of all sorts belong to the standard equipment of totalitarian and authoritarian systems, the most terrible of which were the Nazi extermination camps. But camps belonged also to the process of population transfers, in the form of either detention camps or camps for compulsory work, where inmates were forced to labour or were rented as slaves. Some of these camps were also called concentration camps, albeit without the character of intended mass killing that distinguished the Nazi ones. Many camps were collecting points for people already expelled from their homes

and expecting transport across state boundaries, with minimal belongings, often in terrible hygienic circumstances. Many detainees in these
camps spent months there, if not years, and often after arrival in the occupation zones of Germany had again to spend the first months, even years,
in camps, although this time camps for refugees.

Integration in the Occupation Zones of Germany and in the Two Germanies

After all this suffering, the refugees and expellees did not find
their paradise in Germany either. Most of the cities and many towns were
heavily damaged by air raids and by the campaigns of the last weeks of the
war; the economy and the population were on their knees, and now the
millions of pauperized refugees and expellees poured in. In some regions,
the population more than doubled.

Local administrations and individuals in the British and American
zones—the French having at first refused to admit refugees in their zone
at all—were often unwilling to welcome newcomers. They were let in only
after hard pressure from the Allied occupation authorities. Indeed, these
authorities and the churches, which began to help first, were anxious to
settle the refugee problem, which was soon felt to be one of the most dangerous social problems. The German authorities, which were slowly reor-
ganising, were also eager to resolve the situation. In the first years of the
Federal Republic of Germany (FRG) some legal measures were enacted,
sometimes taking the Finnish integration of Karelian refugees as a pattern.
These legal measures included the so-called *Lastenausgleich* of 1952, by
which an "equalization of burdens" was at least symbolically initiated; it
also included the *Vertriebenengesetz* of 1953, which concurrently brought
full equality of the expellees and refugees within the West German population, but nevertheless secured their special character and supported their
cultural traditions. In the 1950s, during the economic boom of the *Wirtschaftswunder,* most of the shortcomings in this area were eliminated, and
any remaining refugee camps were dissolved, refugees having been integrated as much as possible—even if often not necessarily employed in
their original professions.[37]

Part of the self-identification of the FRG was actually the great achievement of integrating the refugees and expellees. Indeed—as recent research
has pointed out—there was no *Eingliederungswunder* in terms of a miracle:
the integration, which came about gradually, was brought about only with
much friction and many conflicts, and it took a relatively long time. The
intensity of the problems was nearly comparable to the integration problems of today's millions of foreign migrants living in Germany, one of the
major challenges of our time, the so-called clash of cultures, the self-created
ghettos made up of people of foreign origin in German cities and towns.

One of the predispositions that supported integration into the occupation zones of Germany lay within the expellees themselves. This was the gradual abandonment of any hope of returning "home" after the first decade following the great exodus. People increasingly intended to put down roots in their new homes—notwithstanding the constant insistence on the Recht auf Heimat by the refugee associations even until today.[38]

In the Soviet Zone, the refugee problem was in the beginning extremely critical. The initial wild expulsions crossed mainly the long common frontier with Poland and Czechoslovakia. But with the foundation of the German Democratic Republic (GDR)—marked by the "socialist friendship of peoples"—the problem was declared to be settled once and for all and in a just way.[39] Thus, hopes for returning home were cut off earlier than in the FRG, where they were nourished time and again in official speeches. The large group of refugees and expellees in the GDR were termed *Umsiedler* and had no independent role to play. However, the land reform, which divided large estates into lots that were given to the *Umsiedler*, was a real help for many of them. So this group was integrated instantly de facto. Any remaining problems were suppressed,[40] although they survived longer under the surface than in the West, where it was possible to confess to the special identity of refugees, to cultivate their memories, and to form pressure groups and associations of regional origins (*Landsmannschaften*) with their press organs, museums, and yearly mass meetings. Since 1990, the conditions in the former GDR have been adjusted in this respect to those of the old FRG.

The Integration of German Refugees in Other Countries

After the war many refugees also found shelter in Austria. But Austrian administrations under the Allied occupation regime often passed expellees—in a second wave of expulsion—on to the western zones of Germany. Later, after regaining sovereignty, Austria also enacted a *Lastenausgleich*, and some hundred thousands of remaining expellees lived on in a comparable situation to those in Germany.[41]

Again, the countries in east and central Europe had their corresponding integration problems too: the "ethnic processes," as they were called in communist times, were sometimes much more complicated than those of the two German states—where at least German-speaking people came to other Germans, even if partly from other cultural traditions. In Poland, Czechoslovakia, and elsewhere the evacuated spaces were filled by very different "repatriates" from other countries, often with different languages and different cultural and religious characters.

So, in a way, the population transfers were and are *ein europäisches Thema*, as has repeatedly been pointed out.[42] But of course the theme has never been only a European one. As soon as it was possible, some of the younger refugees tried to find a new life abroad, in western Europe and overseas.

The Canadian example is familiar. After the alleviation of the most restrictive measures against former enemy aliens already in 1946, the Waterloo-based Canadian Society for German Relief began its work. Organizations such as the Trans-Canadian Alliance, and later the German Canadian Congress, were founded. Ethnic German refugees came in as displaced persons; Canadian soldiers brought family members from Europe with them; immigrants came in small religious groups. From the beginning of the 1950s, in growing numbers, individuals immigrated in search of employment and new opportunities. In the 1950s the situation became paradoxical: Canada, like Germany, was experiencing a labour shortage. Hence Canada strengthened the "pull factor," whereas, curiously enough, the German federal government at this time was eager to pass expellees onto other states, while at the same time seeking people with qualifications in Germany itself, so their emigration was by no means encouraged.[43]

To review the ups and downs of Canadian immigration and integration policy after 1945 would be like carrying coal to Newcastle. It is also unnecessary here to compare the integration of German refugees in Germany to, say, Canada. It is evident that there are too many fundamental differences and particularities. Some of those comparisons are the following:

- Germans came into the German zones in huge numbers, well over ten million. To Canada they came—besides some small religious groups— as individuals or families, and their number could be counted in tens of thousands—which is itself a large group for overseas immigration.
- Even if some of the German immigrants in Canada settled in regions where traditionally immigrants of ethnic German origin lived, the official languages of the new country were English and French. That made the effort of acculturation much more difficult. However, with the stigma associated with Germany, the German group in Canada assimilated more quickly and thoroughly, compared with other ethnic groups.
- So-called *Reichsdeutsche*, when coming as refugees from the former eastern provinces to the German occupation zones, had the advantage of remaining in their motherland and simply migrating from one part to another, whereas the *Volksdeutsche* had greater difficulties in acculturating in Germany. Conversely, in Canada the *Volksdeutsche* had the advantage in that they were already admitted to this country in the late 1940s, when German citizens were still rejected as enemy aliens.

It is remarkable that the term *Volksdeutsche* covers a broad range of origins, from the Baltic to the Black Sea Germans, from the Sudeten Germans and the Danube Swabians or the Transylvanian Saxons to the Volynian and Volga Germans, and many others. Many of them had the experience of being relocated two, three, or four times before finally migrating voluntarily to Canada. The gates for German citizens were opened only after 1950, but meanwhile the *Volksdeutsche* could acquire citizenship in the FRG, so that a considerable percentage of German immigrants to Canada—again—were of *Volksdeutsche* origin.

Consequently, it might be possible to presume that it was generally easier to find a new home in the occupation zones of Germany than in an overseas country of emigration with a foreign language of communication, with an unknown system of laws, and a society with different structures. But in some respects the integration of expellees in Germany and of immigrants in Canada also has some comparable traits. Newcomers to central and west Germany from the east who were children or teenagers shortly after the war quickly adapted to their new environment. They suppressed their native dialect or German pronunciation and achieved the diction of their new homes, often past recognition.[44] Is not this attitude comparable to the Canadian Germans, who in 1964 were characterized as "almost painfully unassertive"[45] in regard to their Germanness?

This book is on diasporic experiences. Clearly enough, refugees and expellees in Germany did not—in the ethnical sense of the word—experience a diaspora situation; more likely they did so in a denominational or cultural sense. The "diaspora" situation even in Canada is not indisputable and not always the same. Regularly, year by year and from generation to generation, it fades from sight. What remains is a feeling—more or less distinct—of the family's origins.

For all those whose ancestors experienced forced migration, some of them two or three times in their life, their circumstance can be understood through the events of the twentieth century, during which time their parents or ancestors were moved from their homes in east, central, and southeastern Europe because of an idée fixe, namely the damnable doctrine that minorities are in themselves reasons for conflict, and that peace allegedly can be ensured by ethnic homogenization of national states, or, as it is worded today, by ethnic cleansing.

The author is extremely grateful to Professor David D. John, University of Waterloo, for critically reading an earlier draft of this chapter.

Notes

1 For definitions of Canadian Germans, German Canadians, etc., see Bassler, "German-Canadian Identity"; Zimmer, "Deconstructing"; Isajiw, "Identity"; Frisse, *Berlin, Ontario*, 1–8.

2 For the high degree of suspicions against "aliens" of all kind, for example in Newfoundland, see Bassler, *Sanctuary Denied*.

3 Harzig, *Einwanderung*.

4 Jacobmeyer, *Vom Zwangsarbeiter*.

5 Bassler, "German-Canadian Identity," 93.

6 Lemberg, "Ethnische Säuberung."

7 Lemberg, "Grenzen und Minderheiten."

8 Montandon, *Frontières*.

9 Ladas, *Exchange*.

10 Report by Nansen, 5 February 1923, Public Record Office, London: Political Correspondence of the Foreign Office (FO 371), Box 9092, File E 1131/4/44.

11 Ladas, *Exchange*, 341.

12 Stephens, *Danger Zones*.

13 Schot, *Nation oder Staat*, 16–17.

14 Schot, *Nation oder Staat*, 169.

15 Stephens, *Danger Zones*.

16 In the Munich Agreement there were also previsions for an "Austausch der Bevölkerungen." See Facsimile of p. 4 of the Agreement text in Datner, "Fall Otto," after p. 56.

17 Steurer, *Südtirol*.

18 Henderson to Foreign Office, 25 August 1939, FO 371/2302–C12058/54/18.

19 Minutes by Mr. Makins, 18 August 1939, FO 371/23026–C11649/54/18.

20 Henderson to Foreign Office, 25 August 1939, FO 371/23027–C12058/54/18. For Hitler's remark, but not Henderson's answer, see also *Akten zur Deutschen Auswärtigen Politik*,

21 Hitler, *Der großdeutsche Freiheitskampf*, 82–83.

22 Hecker, *Umsiedlungsverträge*.

23 See Kotzian, *Umsiedler*, 72–126.

24 Koehl, R.L.: RKFDV.

25 Wahl, "Les Expulsions."

26 Ferenc, "Die Massenvertreibung."

27 Madajczyk, *Vom Generalplan Ost*.

28 Drechsler, Hass, and Schumann, "Zwangsaussiedlung," 41.

29 Brandes, *Der Weg*.

30 Lemberg, "Grenzen und Minderheiten," 176; see there the reference to Brandes.

31 Newman, *The New Europe*.

32 Schechtman, *Postwar Population Transfers*, 390.

33 Kulischer, "Population Transfer."

34 See Schechtman, *Postwar Population Transfers*, 394–95.

35 For literature on postwar population transfers see Krallert, *Bibliographie*, and the continuation in Schlau, *Die Ostdeutschen*, 183–279.

36 For the situation of the Germans in Poland from 1945 to 1950, see Borodziej and Lemberg, *Die Deutschen östlich*.

37 Lemberg and Edding, *Die Vertriebenen*.

38 Lemberg, "Geschichten und Geschichte."

39 Hoffmann and Schwartz, *Geglückte Integration?*

40 Lehmann, *Im Fremden.*
41 For literature on refugees and expellees in Austria see Krallert, *Bibliographie,* 753–822.
42 Faulenbach, "Vertreibungen."
43 Koch-Kraft, *Deutsche in Kanada,* 38–49.
44 Mackensen, "Die deutsche Sprache."
45 Quoted by Bassler, "German-Canadian Identity," 93.

Archival Material

Public Record Office, London: Political Correspondence of the Foreign Office (FO):
   Minutes by Mr. Makins, 18 August 1939, FO 371/23026–C11649/54/18;
   Henderson, 25 August 1939 to Foreign Office, FO 371/23027–C12058/54/
   18; Report by Nansen, 5 February 1923, FO 371, Box 9092, File E 1131/4/44.

Works Cited

Akten zur Deutschen Auswärtigen Politik. Serie D, vol. 7. Baden-Baden: 1956.
Bassler, Gerhard P. "German-Canadian Identity in Historical Perspective." In *A Chorus of Different Voices. German-Canadian Identities,* edited by Angelika E. Sauer and Matthias Zimmer, 85–98. New York: Peter Lang, 1998.
——. *Sanctuary Denied: Refugees from the Third Reich and Newfoundland Immigration Policy 1906–1949.* St. John's, NF: ISER, 1992.
Borodziej, Włodzimierz, and Hans Lemberg, eds. *"Unsere Heimat ist uns ein fremdes Land geworden ..." Die Deutschen östlich von Oder und Neiße 1945–1950. Dokumente aus polnischen Archiven.* 4 vols. Marburg: Herder-Institut, 2000–04.
Brandes, Detlef. *Der Weg zur Vertreibung 1938–1945. Pläne und Entscheidungen zum "Transfer" der Deutschen aus der Tschechoslowakei und aus Polen.* 2nd revised and expanded edition. Munich: Oldenbourg, 2005.
Datner, Szymon. "Fall Otto"—"Fall Grün." *Biuletyn Głównej komisji badania zbrodni hitlerowskich w Polsce,* 11 (1960): 5–73.
Drechsler, Karl, Gerhard Hass, and Wolfgang Schumann. "Zwangsaussiedlung und Germanisierung in den Kriegszielplanungen der faschistischen deutschen Monopolbourgeoisie." *Studia Historiae Oeconomicae* 8 (1973): 35–49.
Faulenbach, Bernd. "Vertreibungen—ein europäisches Thema." In *Flucht—Vertreibung—Integration. Begleitbuch zur Ausstellung im Haus der Geschichte,* 189–95. Bonn: Haus der Geschichte, 2006.
Ferenc, Tone. "Die Massenvertreibung der Bevölkerung Jugoslawiens während des Zweiten Weltkrieges und der mißglückte Plan einer Ansiedlung von Slowenen in Polen." *Studia Historiae Oeconomicae,* 8 (1973): 51–76.
Frisse, Ulrich. *Berlin, Ontario (1800–1916). Historische Identitäten von 'Kanadas deutscher Hauptstadt.' Ein Beitrag zur deutsch-kanadischen Migrations-, Akkulturations- und Perzeptionsgeschichte des 19. und frühen 20. Jahrhunderts.* New Dundee, ON: Trans-Atlantic Publishing, 2003.
Harzig, Christiane. *Einwanderung und Politik. historische Erinnerung und politische Kultur als Gestaltungsressourcen in den Niederlanden, Schweden und Kanada.* Göttingen: V&R unipress, 2004.

Hecker, Hellmuth. *Die Umsiedlungsverträge des Deutschen Reiches während des Zweiten Weltkrieges.* Hamburg: Metzner, 1971.

Hitler, Adolf. *Der großdeutsche Freiheitskampf. Reden Adolf Hitlers vom 1. Sept. 1939 bis 10. März 1940.* Munich: Eher, 1942.

Hoffmann, Dierk, and Michael Schwartz, eds. *Geglückte Integration? Spezifika und Vergleichbarkeiten der Vertriebenen-Eingliederung in der SBZ/DDR.* Munich: Oldenbourg, 1999.

Isajiw, Wsevolod W. "Identity and Identity-Retention among German Canadians: Individual and Institutional." In *A Chorus of Different Voices. German-Canadian Identities,* edited by Angelika E. Sauer and Matthias Zimmer, 67–83. New York: Peter Lang, 1998.

Jacobmeyer, Wolfgang. *Vom Zwangsarbeiter zum heimatlosen Ausländer. Die Displaced Persons in Westdeutschland 1945–1951.* Göttingen: Vandenhoeck & Ruprecht, 1985.

Koch-Kraft, Andrea. *Deutsche in Kanada—Einwanderung und Adaption. Mit einer Untersuchung zur Situation der Nachkriegsimmigration in Edmonton Alberta.* Bochum: Brockmeyer, 1990.

Koehl, R.L. *RKFDV. German Resettlement and Population Policy 1939–1945: A History of the Reich Commission for the Strengthening of Germandom.* Cambridge, MA: Harvard University Press, 1957.

Kotzian, Ortfried. *Die Umsiedler. Die Deutschen aus West-Wolhynien Galizien, der Bukowina, Bessarabien, der Dobrudscha und in der Karpatenukraine.* Munich: Langen Müller, 2005.

Krallert, Gertrud. *Kommentierte Bibliographie zum Flüchtlings- und Vertriebenenproblem in der Bundesrepublik Deutschland, in Österreich und in der Schweiz.* Vienna: Braumüller, 1989.

Kulischer, Eugene Michel. "Population Transfer." *South Atlantic Quarterly* 45, no. 4 (1946): 403–14.

Ladas, Stephen P. *The Exchange of Minorities: Bulgaria, Greece and Turkey.* New York: Macmillan, 1932.

Lehmann, Albrecht. *Im Fremden ungewollt zuhaus. Flüchtlinge und Vertriebene in Westdeutschland; 1945–1990.* 2nd edition. Munich: Beck 1993.

Lemberg, Eugen, and Friedrich Edding, eds. *Die Vertriebenen in Westdeutschland. Ihre Eingliederung und ihr Einfluss auf Gesellschaft, Wirtschaft, Politik und Geistesleben.* 3 volumes. Kiel: Hirt, 1959.

Lemberg, Hans. "Ethnische Säuberung": Ein Mittel zur Lösung von Nationalitätenproblemen?" *Aus Politik und Zeitgeschichte. Beilage zur Wochenzeitung Das Parlament.* 6 November 1992: 27–38.

———. "Geschichten und Geschichte. Das Gedächtnis der Vertriebenen in Deutschland nach 1945." *Archiv für Sozialgeschichte* 44 (2004): 509–23.

———. "Grenzen und Minderheiten im östlichen Mitteleuropa—Genese und Wechselwirkungen." In *Grenzen in Ostmitteleuropa im 19. und 20. Jahrhundert. Aktuelle Forschungsprobleme,* edited by Hans Lemberg, 159–81. Marburg: Herder-Institut, 2000.

Mackensen, Lutz. "Die deutsche Sprache in und nach der Vertreibung." In *Die Vertriebenen in Westdeutschland. Ihre Eingliederung und ihr Einfluss auf Gesellschaft*

Wirtschaft Politik und Geistesleben, edited by Eugen Lemberg and Friedrich Edding, 3: 224–71. Kiel: Hirt, 1959.

Madajczyk, Czesław, ed. *Vom Generalplan Ost zum Generalsiedlungsplan*. Munich: Saur, 1994.

Montandon, George. *Frontières nationales. Détermination objective de la condition primordiale nécessaire à l'obtention d'une paix durable*. Lausanne: Imprimeurs réunis SA, 1915.

Newman, Bernard. *Danger Spots of Europe*, London: Hale, 1938.

———. *The New Europe*, London: Hale, 1943.

Schechtman, Joseph B. *Postwar Population Transfers in Europe 1945–1955*. Philadelphia: University of Pennsylvania Press, 1962.

Schlau, Wilfried. *Die Ostdeutschen. Eine dokumentarische Bilanz, 1945–1995*. Munich: Langen Müller, 1996.

Schot, Bastiaan. *Nation oder Staat? Deutschland und der Minderheitenschutz. Zur Völkerbundspolitik der Stresemann-Ära*. Marburg: Herder-Institut, 1988.

Stephens, John S. *Danger Zones of Europe: A Study of National Minorities*. London: L. and Virginia Woolf, 1929.

Steurer, Leopold. *Südtirol zwischen Rom und Berlin 1919–1939*. Vienna: Europaverlag, 1980.

Wahl, Alfred: "Les Expulsions en Alsace et en Lorraine (1940–1944)." *Studia Historiae Oeconomicae* 8 (1973): 107–16.

Zimmer, Matthias. "Deconstructing German-Canadian Identity." In *A Chorus of Different Voices. German-Canadian Identities*, edited by Angelika E. Sauer and Matthias Zimmer, 21–39. New York: Peter Lang, 1998.

THIRTY

Emigration and *Wiedergutmachung*
The Social History of Jewish Entrepreneurs from Frankfurt, 1933–1963

Benno Nietzel

This chapter deals with the social history of the emigration of Jewish entrepreneurs from Frankfurt during the Nazi era and analyses the impact of restitution and indemnification on their lives in exile. First, the diminishing possibilities of property transfer from Germany are described. The loss of large parts of their property was responsible for the precarious economic situation of Jewish emigrants in their countries of exile and made a new entrepreneurial beginning difficult. Only few Jewish emigrants succeeded to re-establish themselves as independent entrepreneurs, while many failed completely to earn their livings on their own again. This group depended heavily on payments from the German *Wiedergutmachung* after 1945. Restitution and indemnification proceedings allow a deeper insight into the material circumstances of Jewish emigrants during the 1940s and '50s, which were grimmer than has previously been described by emigration research. Restitution payments were usually low, but contributions granted through the indemnification program could serve as a pension for many Nazi victims who were no longer able to work.

THE EXPULSION OF JEWISH CITIZENS from Germany during the Nazi era as a phenomenon of forced emigration has always been an important area of historical research. The different waves of emigration, corresponding to the changing policy of the Third Reich toward Jews, have been precisely described. But Jewish emigration was more than a mere reaction to government policy.[1] Despite the growing pressure on German Jews, the increasingly discriminating tax and currency laws of the Nazi government made emigration extremely unattractive and the progressive economic weakening of German Jews restricted their possibilities to find foreign countries that accepted them as immigrants.[2] Most countries showed themselves indifferent to the persecution of Jews in Germany during the 1930s and restricted rather than opened up their immigration policy.[3] With the outbreak of World War II, the possibilities of emigration were reduced to a minimum. When the persecution in Germany reached its first peak in 1938 with mass arrests during the summer, the notorious November pogroms, and the final termination of Jewish economic activity, the majority of Jewish citizens were still in the country, and many of them failed to find a way to emigrate.[4]

While much has been written about the circumstances of flight and expulsion from Germany, historical research has only recently turned toward the life of Jewish refugees in exile. Traditional emigration research has concentrated mainly on the fate of prominent personalities from politics, arts, and sciences and for a long time neglected the masses of "ordinary" refugees.[5] The latest findings indicate that from the perspective of that majority, the end of World War II did not mean a caesura. For many emigrants, life in the free parts of the world meant economical suffering and social decline.[6] Even well-to-do Jews usually failed to transfer significant parts of their property abroad. Jews who did not manage to escape from Germany until 1938 or later were often left completely impoverished. It took many of them years of hard work to reach an adequate standard of living again.

After 1945, Jewish Holocaust survivors lived all over the world. In Germany itself, there were some 20,000 survivors of German origin, apart from masses of displaced persons.[7] This group of Jewish survivors of German origin formed a nearly negligible minority in German postwar society, and their fate and needs were mostly ignored. However, the emigrants from Germany of the 1930s were not only ignored, but were almost completely forgotten, their stories suppressed and distorted. Many Germans believed in a grotesque stereotype of the Jewish emigrant, living a comfortable life abroad, while they themselves suffered during the war and afterward, and, therefore, felt as though they were the real victims of the Nazi dictatorship and World War II.[8] The forgotten lives of these emigrants, the material circumstances of their new existence in exile, and their difficult relationship to Germany are the subject of this chapter.

The Jewish entrepreneurs of Frankfurt were forced to sell or liquidate their firms by the beginning of 1939. Those who managed to emigrate were scattered all over the world. This chapter examines the relationship of these Jewish emigrants toward Germany as their country of origin and, therefore does not follow the traditional questions of emigration research concerning acculturation and integration in the countries of destination or their impact on national culture and arts. Moreover, in the context of this chapter, this group is referred to not so much as Jews than as entrepreneurs, a group about whom not much is known so far. Jewish emigrants still had strong links to their German homeland, if their former enterprises had survived the war economically. They got in contact with Germany during the process of the so-called *Wiedergutmachung*. The economic situation and activities of Jewish entrepreneurs-in-exile set up the social background of the conflicts about restitution of property during the first years after the war. Additionally, payments granted during *Wiedergutmachung* had a significant impact on their lives. These assumptions led to the following questions: What were the possibilities of property transfer for Jewish entrepreneurs during their emigration process? What was the economic situation in exile and was a new entrepreneurial beginning possible? What was the impact of restitution and indemnification as elements of *Wiedergutmachung* on the lives of Jewish emigrants, both economically as well as in a symbolic way?

Property Transfer and the Situation in Exile

It is well known that during the Nazi era the possibilities of property transfer were extremely restricted by discriminatory taxes and currency regulations.[9] People who considered emigration from Germany faced the loss of large parts of their property. The *Reichsfluchtsteuer* as an emigration tax had been established in the last years of the Weimar republic and amounted to one quarter of a person's property.[10] The fee for currency exchange increased rapidly and amounted to as much as 96 percent of the exchanged amount in 1939. Furthermore, the transfer of personal items was strictly restricted. Government officials rigorously searched and listed personal property of Jewish emigrants.[11] This administrative practice was accompanied by massive corruption, blackmail, and personal theft by state and party officials.[12]

Strategies of property preservation and transfer were often combined with strategies of structural adaptation of Jewish enterprises in order to avoid Nazi persecution.[13] For example, Jewish owners tried to withdraw from visible fields of business and cooperated with non-Jewish owners who represented the company in public. If it was possible to plan emigration in the long term, Jewish owners sometimes arranged for a gradual transition, working for their company as representatives or branch managers abroad for some time before they finally retired. Such an arrangement offered various possibilities of property transfer. But it is also clear that only those emigrants with international business contacts could adopt such a strategy. Those who prepared for emigration early had much better chances than those who fled from Germany after the November 1938 pogroms. In the sample analysed, more than half of the people did not leave the country until the second half of 1938. While certain professional groups such as civil servants, doctors, and lawyers were already driven out of their positions during the first years of the Nazi regime, a legal prohibition of Jewish commercial activity was not enacted before November 1938.[14] Jewish firms vanished comparatively early in small and medium-sized cities. But Frankfurt, with the second largest Jewish community in Germany, provided much more room for the activities of Jewish entrepreneurs, of whom the majority could survive until the second half of 1938. But after that, the manifest danger of Nazi persecution pushed Jewish business owners to emigrate. The loss of property sometimes seemed to be a secondary consideration.

It can, therefore, be assumed that the overwhelming majority of Jewish emigrants arrived in their countries of destination completely impoverished. At this stage of research, it is hardly possible to differentiate the possibilities of economic activity for each country of destination. More than half of the Jewish entrepreneurs went to the United States, nearly half of them settling in New York City.[15] This enormous concentration is not surprising. Immigrants could rely on relatives and friends and receive help from the various relief organizations located there. The social situation and the economic difficulties of the emigrants have already been described, but entrepreneurs as a specific group among the emigrants also faced specific difficulties. Used to the traditional economic independence that German Jews had always sought, it was hard for them to earn their living as workers or clerks. A new entrepreneurial beginning was impeded both by lack of capital and by lack of knowledge about local business practices and customs in the countries of exile. The German commercial training offered an insufficient preparation for the new challenges. Martin M., for example, a machine tools merchant who sold his firm to one of his employees and emigrated via Great Britain to New York in 1938, turned to his former occupation at first, but had to give up soon "*weil das Geschäft hier ganz anders lag als drüben.*"[16] It took him several attempts in different branches of business until he finally made a living as a small shopkeeper. But even if emigrants managed to establish themselves in a business they were familiar with, their new enterprises often remained small.[17] However, it is true that there were some examples of spectacular success of emigrants starting a new business, as in the case of Thomas Bicks, who worked his way up from a farm boy to Canada's largest producer of canned food.[18] But this career is exceptional, as integration in the country of exile usually meant decline to economic dependency in fast-changing, unstable employments in unfamiliar fields of work. Moreover, the analysed sample shows that a large part of about 40 percent of the emigrants failed completely to earn their livelihood on their own. They depended on social security, on help from relatives, and on payments from the German *Wiedergutmachung*, which was gradually established after 1945.

Restitution of Enterprises, 1945–55

After the occupation of Germany by Allied forces and the establishment of military government, for the first time it became possible to legally proceed against Nazi injustice and to claim compensation. Not surprisingly, to start with, Jewish entrepreneurs focused mainly on their looted firms in Germany. In postwar Frankfurt, there were several hundred of more than two thousand formerly Jewish firms that were still run by the non-Jewish purchasers. The American military government was particularly active in the field of investigation and seizure of Jewish property, and consequently promoted a fast and complete restitution of these properties. Military Government Regulation Number 59 of November 1947 set up the legal framework.[19] According to the law, former owners of enterprises in Germany could claim the restitution of their property or indemnification to be granted by the respective purchasers. These proceedings are of particular interest as they brought the Jewish Nazi victims into contact again with the people who had profited from their persecution or had unscrupulously exploited it.[20] It has, therefore, been said that restitution proceedings could be understood as a dialogue between victims and offenders and offered room for reconciliation.[21] But this assumption can be doubted for several reasons. First, restitution legislation did not attempt an understanding between the parties in an interpersonal sense. Jews did not need to confront their adversaries during the proceedings nor did they need to reconstruct the circumstances of property transactions in detail. Second, the social and psychological climate in German postwar society made reconciliation unlikely. The internal restitution program was strongly rejected by large parts of German society and only the conviction of the western Allies prevented a revision of the decree that would have protected German purchasers of Jewish property against claims of the former owners.[22] It can, therefore, be argued that the cultural dimensions of restitution proceedings have been overestimated to some extent, while a social historical approach shows that the courses and results of these proceedings were above all determined by the economic situation of the people involved.

Flexible solutions were possible regarding the amount as well as the form of compensation. This led usually to a speedy resolution, but did not necessarily serve the interests of the Jewish claimants. If they found themselves in economic difficulty and strongly needed liquid assets, they often had to accept unfavourable settlements. If proceedings had to be closed quickly, it was impossible to determine the real value of the property in question at the moment of its transfer. It was also impossible in these cases to reconstruct the circumstances of property transfers in order to shed light upon the force and violence applied during these affairs. Although of minor importance for the decision on restitution, for many Jewish claimants, these aspects were of particular personal importance, and often the focus of persistent and aggressive resistance of the non-Jewish opposing parties, who were thus able to block or delay a settlement. Many claimants were forced to forego moral restitution in favour of financial compensation. A good example for this is the case of the textile store of Leonhard K. The enterprise was one of the most reputable in the textile sector in Frankfurt, employing up to eighty people during the 1930s. In 1938, the owner was forced to sell the firm and fled completely impoverished to the Netherlands after the November pogrom. He died there shortly after the end of the war. His son, who had already emigrated to the Netherlands in 1933, inherited the claim to his father's business. He had founded his own enterprise in exile and was, therefore, heavily indebted. While he quickly needed liquid assets, the opposing party played for time, so that he finally had to accept a payment of 9,500 DM, having started into the proceedings with a claim of over 300,000 DM.[23]

It can be said that the balance between the parties involved in restitution proceedings was to some extent uneven. Until the closing of proceedings the status quo was maintained, so that the present owners of formerly Jewish firms could continue to collect all profits and delay the proceedings or diminish compensation payments.[24] But the picture that historical research has drawn of the Nazi profiteer who thrived by exploiting the persecution of the Jews does not always match reality. Many purchasers of Jewish firms had lost these properties during the war and were in economic difficulties themselves. Even if it was possible, under the conditions described, to determine the worth of the properties adequately, compensation payments had to be assessed according to the economic possibilities of the debtor. This can be illustrated by the example of the cheese wholesaler Henry T., owner of a reputable enterprise in Frankfurt with customers all over Germany. The business was sold in 1938 but was shut down when the non-Jewish purchaser was drafted into the army. The enterprise no longer existed after the war. The claim of the Jewish owner was for more than 60,000 DM, but even after tenacious negotiations he could not get more than 1,500 DM from the now impoverished purchaser.[25]

The attitude of Jewish emigrants toward their former enterprises in Germany and toward Germany in general is difficult to assess. However, 80 percent of restitution proceedings resulted in compensation payments instead of the restitution of the actual properties. Although these enterprises had often been the lifework of the emigrants and their standard of living in exile remained low, almost none wanted to return to their former homeland. In the cases in which property was restituted, mostly shares of stock corporations or capital companies were returned. Only a handful of Jewish individuals who returned to Germany took over their former enterprises. Restitution, therefore, turned into the opposite: instead of revoking the property transfers of the Nazi era, it completed them. The new distribution of property was confirmed with Jewish claimants liquidating the remaining assets in Germany and cutting links to their former homeland.

The Impact of Indemnification, 1955–63

Individual restitution of enterprises was nearly finished by the middle of the 1950s. In 1954, more than 90 percent of the proceedings were already closed. From the perspective of the Jewish entrepreneurs, restitution was followed by the state program of indemnification that was implemented during the late 1950s. Indemnification for Nazi victims was based on several federal laws of 1949 and later standardized in the German indemnification law of 1956. The indemnification system replaced the welfare program for Nazi victims of the early postwar period, admitting legal claims for compensation payments. Claims were divided into different categories, referring to different kinds of sufferings, namely the loss of liberty, health defects, the loss of life, the loss of property, and damages inflicted upon economic and professional growth.[26] The following discussion focuses on the latter category, because it included all damages that resulted from the restriction and termination of Jewish commercial activity. Compensation payments in this category were usually among the first payments to be granted to the claimant, but because it took time to process the applications, the first payments were not granted before the mid 1950s. Although the process of indemnification for economic damages was mostly finished in 1963, it was not uncommon for the whole procedure to take up to fifteen years, in some cases even considerably longer.

As has been seen, the settlement payments that could be reached by Jewish emigrants usually did not correspond to the real value of the properties in question. The payments could not provide permanent financial security for people in economic difficulties. This assumption is confirmed by the high number of applications for advance payments or for expedient treatment of cases to the indemnification administration. Later critics of the German indemnification program considered mainly the practice of the medical examination, which was often humiliating for Nazi victims, and the explicit exclusion of certain groups of persecuted persons.[27] But for many of the applicants, it was the length of the bureaucratic process that caused frustration and anger, especially in cases of economic distress. Proofs and records had to be submitted that no one who had fled from Germany could have kept. Proof of former financial and economic circumstances was also a symbolic fight for recognition and dignity for many applicants. The abovementioned Henry T., who had managed to earn his living as a manual worker in New York, fought for ten years with the German administration and courts for the acceptance of the fact that he once ran a profitable and reputable enterprise in Frankfurt. Without the support of a lawyer, he took the case through all levels of jurisdiction before he was finally awarded the maximum possible amount for economic damages (40,000 DM).[28] The fact that for many Jewish victims the assertion of their claims was of enormous personal importance is confirmed by cases in which applicants intensively applied themselves to the proceedings for years, even if they did not depend on the compensation financially.[29] At the same time, *Wiedergutmachung* was something Nazi victims avoided talking about and, therefore, the topic rarely appears in autobiographies and memoirs.[30]

The analyzed sample of people illustrates that many Jewish entrepreneurs failed to earn a living even twenty years after their emigration from Germany. It becomes clear that the social history of emigration can be studied insufficiently by using interview methods, which is a dominant approach in current emigration research. Interviews can only focus on people who emigrated as children or young people and, therefore, were in many respects much more predestined for social and economic rehabilitation. Moreover, it can be assumed that people who look back on a successful integration in their new homelands agree to a higher degree to be interviewed about their immigration experiences than others.

The emigrants studied for this chapter were born between 1870 and 1900, were affected by Nazi persecution during the most productive period of their lives, and were of retirement age after the war. Many of them lacked the ability to work for health reasons. They often had to live on the sale of any property they managed to transfer from Germany. It seems that the circumstances of this generation of emigrants have been underexposed. This study relied on case files of restitution and indemnification proceedings, which allowed a deep insight into the material circumstances of emigrants and which should, therefore, be consulted more often by emigration researchers.[31]

Contributions granted during restitution and indemnification were vitally important for the group of emigrants under consideration here. It was, therefore, disastrous that *Wiedergutmachung* developed against the needs of Nazi victims. In the first years after the war, when economic difficulties were most urgent, only moderate payments could be obtained. Contributions granted during the indemnification program did increase later. For most applicants, they served as a pension rather than a support for economic rehabilitation. Applicants could select a life-long pension instead of one single payment, and many chose this option.

Because *Wiedergutmachung* contributions were paid ten years after the end of Nazi rule, in many cases they did not reach the Jewish survivors. Moreover, it is self-evident that not all damages and injustices suffered could be healed by financial compensation. The length and the bureaucratic proceedings of *Wiedergutmachung* led to indignation and annoyance among the survivors. The indemnification program has, therefore, even been called a "war against the victims" by later critics.[32] But there are also indications of a changing image of Germany among Jewish emigrants, caused by the increase of payments and the rising reliability of the indemnification system during the 1960s.[33] This has certainly been one reason among others why some Jewish emigrants were willing to visit their former homeland in the 1970s and '80s for the first time after 1945. Most of the emigrated entrepreneurs from Frankfurt, of course, had by then already died.

Notes

1 Contrary to that: see, Strauss, "Jewish Emigration from Germany," 316.
2 Diner, "Die Katastrophe vor der Katastrophe."
3 Kieffer, *Judenverfolgung in Deutschland.*
4 Wetzel, "Auswanderung aus Deutschland."
5 Benz, "Das Exil der kleinen Leute."
6 Quack, *Zuflucht Amerika,* 115–48.
7 Jacobmeyer, "Jüdische Überlebende"; Geis, *Übrig sein.*
8 Nietzel, "Die jüdische Presse"; Moeller, *War Stories.*
9 Bajohr, *Arisierung,* 189–95, 208–16; Meinl, "*Schalom.*"
10 Mußgnug, *Reichsfluchtsteuer.*
11 Friedenberger, "Rolle der Finanzverwaltung"; Meinl and Zwilling, *Legalisierter Raub,* 110–18.
12 Bajohr, *Parvenüs und Profiteure,* 101–36.
13 Herbst, "Banker in einem prekären Geschäft."
14 *Erste Verordnung.*
15 Lowenstein, *Frankfurt on the Hudson.*
16 Affidavit Martin M., 29 November 1955, Hessian State Archive (HSA), Wiesbaden, 518, P 1361, 5: 56.
17 For example, Susemihl, *and it became my home,* 114–23.
18 Susemihl, *and it became my home,* 202–06.
19 Schwarz, *Rückerstattung;* Goschler, *Wiedergutmachung,* 91–148.
20 Goschler, "Auseinandersetzung," 340.
21 Winstel, "Über die Bedeutung," 200–03, 208.
22 Lillteicher, *Raub, Recht und Restitution,* 135–78.

23 Institute for City History (ICH), Frankfurt, Magistratsakten, 9797; HSA, 519/1, Wi-
    Ffm-A 6598.
24 Lillteicher, "Rechtsstaatlichkeit und Verfolgungserfahrung," 144–46.
25 HSA, 519/1, Wi-Ffm-A 4549.
26 Brunn, Giessler, and Klee, *Bundesentschädigungsgesetz;* Giessler, Gnirs, and Heben-
    streit, *Bundesentschädigungsgesetz.*
27 Pross, *Wiedergutmachung,* 297–321.
28 HSA, 518, P 1891, 14.
29 See, for example, Roseman, *Past in Hiding,* 401–06.
30 Winstel, *Verhandelte Gerechtigkeit,* 289.
31 Eichler, "Entschädigungsakten"; Grau, "Entschädigungs- und Rückerstattungsak-
    ten"; Pusch, "es tut mir leid."
32 See, for example, the title of Pross, *Wiedergutmachung.*
33 Winstel, "Über die Bedeutung," 208.

Archival Material

Institute for City History (ICH), Frankfurt on Main. Magistratsakten.
Hessian State Archive (HSA), Wiesbaden. Entschädigungsbehörde (Abt. 518); Lan-
    desamt für Vermögenskontrolle und Wiedergutmachung (Abt. 519).

Works Cited

Bajohr, Frank. *"Arisierung" in Hamburg. Die Verdrängung der jüdischen Unternehmer
    1933–1945.* Hamburg: Christians, 1998.
————. *Parvenüs und Profiteure. Korruption in der NS-Zeit.* Frankfurt: Fischer, 2001.
Benz, Wolfgang. "Das Exil der kleinen Leute." In *Das Exil der kleinen Leute. Alltagser-
    fahrungen deutscher Juden in der Emigration,* edited by Wolfgang Benz, 7–37.
    Munich: Beck, 1991.
Brunn, Walter, Hans Giessler, and Heinz Klee. *Das Bundesentschädigungsgesetz,*
    vol. 1. Munich: Beck, 1981.
Diner, Dan. "Die Katastrophe vor der Katastrophe. Auswanderung ohne Einwan-
    derung." In *Zerbrochene Geschichte. Leben und Selbstverständnis der Juden in
    Deutschland,* edited by Dirk Blasius and Dan Diner, 138–60. Frankfurt: Fis-
    cher, 1991.
Eichler, Volker. "Entschädigungsakten—Zeitgeschichtliche Bedeutung und
    Möglichkeiten der Erschließung." In *Vom Findbuch zum Internet. Erschließung
    von Archivgut vor neuen Herausforderungen. Referate des 68. Deutschen Archiv-
    tags,* 221–29. Siegburg: Schmitt, 1998.
*Erste Verordnung zur Ausschaltung der Juden aus dem deutschen Wirtschaftsleben vom
    12.11.1938,* Reichsgesetzblatt I 1938, 1580.
Friedenberger, Martin. "Die Rolle der Finanzverwaltung bei der Vertreibung, Ver-
    folgung und Vernichtung der deutschen Juden." In *Die Reichsfinanzverwal-
    tung im Nationalsozialismus. Darstellung und Dokumente,* edited by Martin
    Friedenberger, Klaus-Dieter Gössel, and Eberhard Schönknecht, 10–94.
    Bremen: Temmen, 2002.
Geis, Jael. *Übrig sein—Leben "danach." Juden deutscher Herkunft in der britischen und
    amerikanischen Zone Deutschlands 1945–1949.* Berlin/Vienna: Philo, 2000.

Giessler, Hans, Otto Gnirs, and Richard Hebenstreit. *Das Bundesentschädigungsgesetz*, volume 2. Munich: Beck, 1983.

Goschler, Constantin. "Die Auseinandersetzung um die Rückerstattung 'arisierten' jüdischen Eigentums nach 1945." In *Die Deutschen und die Judenverfolgung im Dritten Reich*, edited by Ursula Büttner, 339–56. Hamburg: Christians, 1992.

———. *Wiedergutmachung. Westdeutschland und die Verfolgten des Nationalsozialismus (1945–1954)*. Munich: Oldenbourg, 1992.

Grau, Bernhard. "Entschädigungs- und Rückerstattungsakten als neue Quelle der Zeitgeschichtsforschung am Beispiel Bayerns." *Zeitenblicke* 3, no. 2 (2004). <www.zeitenblicke.historicum.net/2004/02/grau> (March 2008).

Herbst, Ludolf. "Banker in einem prekären Geschäft. Die Beteiligung der Commerzbank an der Vernichtung der jüdischen Gewerbetätigkeit im Altreich (1933–1940)." In *Die Commerzbank und die Juden 1933–1945*, edited by Ludolf Herbst and Thomas Weihe, 74–137. Munich: Beck, 2004.

Jacobmeyer, Wolfgang. "Jüdische Überlebende als 'Displaced Persons.'" *Geschichte und Gesellschaft* 9 (1983): 421–52.

Kieffer, Fritz. *Judenverfolgung in Deutschland—eine innere Angelegenheit? Internationale Reaktionen auf die Flüchtlingsproblematik 1933–1939*. Wiesbaden: Steiner, 2002.

Lillteicher, Jürgen. "Rechtsstaatlichkeit und Verfolgungserfahrung. "Arisierung" und fiskalische Ausplünderung vor Gericht." In *"Arisierung" und Restitution. Die Rückerstattung jüdischen Eigentums in Deutschland und Österreich nach 1945 und 1989*, edited by Constantin Goschler and Jürgen Lillteicher, 127–59. Göttingen: Wallstein, 2002.

———. *Raub, Recht und Restitution. Die Rückerstattung jüdischen Eigentums in der frühen Bundesrepublik*. Göttingen: Wallstein, 2007.

Lowenstein, Steven M. *Frankfurt on the Hudson: The German-Jewish Community of Washington Heights 1933–1983, Its Structure and Culture*. Detroit: Wayne State University Press, 1989.

Meinl, Susanne. "'*Schalom*—meine Heimat.' Stationen der Flucht aus Deutschland." *Exilforschung* 19 (2001): 41–64.

Meinl, Susanne, and Jutta Zwilling. *Legalisierter Raub. Die Ausplünderung der Juden im Nationalsozialismus durch die Reichsfinanzverwaltung in Hessen*. Frankfurt/New York: Campus, 2004.

Moeller, Robert G. *War Stories: The Search for a Usable Past in the Federal Republic of Germany*. Berkeley/Los Angeles: University of California Press, 2001.

Mußgnug, Dorothee. *Die Reichsfluchtsteuer 1931–1953*. Berlin: Duncker & Humblot, 1993.

Nietzel, Benno. "Die jüdische Presse und die Debatte um die Rückerstattung entzogenen Eigentums 1945–1952." In *Zwischen Erinnerung und Neubeginn. Zur deutsch-jüdischen Geschichte nach 1945*, edited by Susanne Schönborn, 135–59. Munich: Meidenbauer 2006.

Pross, Christian. *Wiedergutmachung. Der Kleinkrieg gegen die Opfer*. Frankfurt: Athenäum, 1988.

Pusch, Thomas. "'… es tut mir leid um Deutschland!' Die Entschädigungsakte als Quelle für die Exilforschung." *Informationen zur Schleswig-Holsteinischen Zeitgeschichte* 33/34 (1998): 189–212.

Quack, Sibylle. *Zuflucht Amerika. Zur Sozialgeschichte der Emigration deutsch-jüdischer Frauen in die USA 1933–1945.* Bonn: Dietz, 1995.

Roseman, Mark. *A Past in Hiding: Memory and Survival in Nazi Germany.* London: Allen Lane, 2000.

Schwarz, Walter. *Rückerstattung nach den Gesetzen der Alliierten Mächte.* Munich: Beck, 1974.

Strauss, Herbert A. "Jewish Emigration from Germany: Nazi Policies and Jewish Responses (I)." *Year Book Leo Baeck Institute* 25 (1980): 313–61.

Susemihl, Geneviève. "*… and it became my home.*" *Die Assimilation und Integration der deutsch-jüdischen Hitlerflüchtlinge in New York und Toronto.* Münster: Lit, 2004.

Wetzel, Juliane. "Auswanderung aus Deutschland." In *Die Juden in Deutschland 1933–1945. Leben unter nationalsozialistischer Herrschaft,* edited by Wolfgang Benz, 4th edition, 413–98. Munich: Beck, 1996.

Winstel, Tobias. "Über die Bedeutung der Wiedergutmachung im Leben der jüdischen NS-Verfolgten. Erfahrungsgeschichtliche Annäherungen." In *Nach der Verfolgung. Wiedergutmachung nationalsozialistischen Unrechts in Deutschland?* edited by Hans Günter Hockerts, and Christiane Kuller, 199–227. Göttingen: Wallstein, 2003.

———. *Verhandelte Gerechtigkeit. Rückerstattung und Entschädigung für jüdische NS-Opfer in Bayern und Westdeutschland.* Munich: Oldenbourg, 2006.

THIRTY-ONE

Dissolving the German Diaspora in Poland

A Different Approach

Dieter K. Buse

The Nazi regime took the decisive steps, starting September 1939, to dissolve the German diasporas that had existed for more than a hundred years in Poland and eastern Europe. The preoccupation of historians and the German public with the forced migrations of 1944–45 has twisted the understanding of the larger ethnic cleansing process that was practised during World War II. By examining the fate of one set of villages in the area of Paprotsch, whose existence had been tested during the nineteenth and early twentieth centuries, this chapter employs a different approach. It illustrates that the decisive events in destroying the diaspora occurred well before the flight of the population and deportations at war's end. The Nazi state and its practice of racial ideology refused to tolerate the ethnic German enclaves in their old form; the postwar forced migrations of 1944–45 are merely an epilogue to a longer story.

ON 21 FEBRUARY 1939, IN GROSS PAPROTSCH, Poland, twenty-five-year-old Robert Schütz married the twenty-one-year-old Emilie Buse. A son was born within three months. The birth so soon after marriage would not have been scandalous in a rural society where such events were fairly common.[1] Much more momentous would have been the beginning of World War II, when Robert and an older brother, Emil, were incarcerated by the Polish authorities at Bereza Kartuska, a concentration camp in northeast Poland. They were able to leave in mid-September 1939, when the German military approached and the Polish guards ran away. On their return to Paprotsch the brothers found their village vacated, the ethnic Germans having been evacuated by the German military to the area of Ortelsburg in East Prussia.[2] The Nazi regime and the Wehrmacht thus took the decisive step—there were previous lesser ones—toward dissolving a German diaspora that had lasted for nearly one hundred and forty years, one of the few instances where ethnic Germans were not so readily assimilated. Paprotsch's path to dissolution offers an opportunity to rethink German diasporas.

Making a German Diaspora

After the division of Poland between Austria, Prussia, and Russia in 1795, the Prussian military surveyed its newly acquired territory, and soon publicists were extolling the area's potential and pointing to the Polish serf economy as a problem, but one that could be overcome.[3] Within a few years new villages were being planned for those areas unoccupied by Poles, and a process of colonization was under way.[4] Although hundreds of such colonies were planned and tens established, of special interest is one group placed in low-lying bushy lands approximately one hundred kilometres northeast of Warsaw. By 1805 four small agricultural settlements were being developed for about one hundred families.[5] The colonists, mostly from northern Brandenburg, Mecklenburg and the Pfalz, received lands, travel and living subsidies plus lumber for buildings in a system calculated to produce stable, fairly self-sufficient units. The four colonies of Louisenau, Mecklenburg, Wilhelmsdorf and Königshuld, plus nearby Silberwald (created slightly later), would in the nineteenth century have Polish designations. For convenience they will be termed the Paprotsch (Paproć is Polish for fern) area settlements after the largest village. The German colonists eventually spoke of Gross Paprotsch (Polish: Paproć Duża) with its sub-village of Klein Paprotsch (Paproć Mława). The Prussian state's detailed colonial lists of 1806 provide evaluations of the original colonists, including their good agricultural abilities and upright moral character. They enumerate the family members, their possessions and the allotted land according to assumptions about large farms' necessities, cottagers' needs, and villages' desired attributes. The latter appeared in provisions for a church with parson, school with teacher, and special trades such as miller and blacksmith. The Prussian bureaucrats listed in summary reports what had been achieved by 1806 in terms of buildings, cultivation and husbandry.[6] Within a decade, colonies of Germans had been solidly established among many Poles and few Jews.

The wars of the Napoleonic era altered the situation. As a result of Napoleon's defeat of Prussia in 1807, the colonized Prussian territory was placed under the administration of the Saxon king as part of the Duchy of Warsaw, who continued the colonization efforts. Perhaps due to the insecurities of warfare, some of the original colonists returned to their homelands; others went further east into Russia, forming new ethnic diasporas.[7] After Napoleon's defeat in 1813 the colonized Polish areas fell to Russia as part of the Kingdom of Poland. Again some colonists left but most stayed, creating a diaspora of ethnic Germans within Russian Poland.[8] State borders cut them off from their "homeland," religious differences as Lutherans set most of them off from their Polish Catholic neighbours, and language set them off from Poles and Russian bureaucrats, and perhaps also from Jewish traders. The colonies faced possible extinction, assimilation, or isolated preservation.

Maintaining a Diaspora

The enclaves of Germans in Russian Poland kept their homeland identity for well over a hundred years. A teacher who arrived from Germany before World War I to take up a post in the Paprotsch villages was surprised about the extent to which the Mecklenburg Low German language and customs were in evidence.[9] In 1937, by which time Poland administered the area with less tolerant linguistic laws, a distant relative of some of the colonists travelled in the region to research the migratory spread of Mecklenburgers in eastern Europe.[10] She sketched the crossed horses heads on the wooden buildings similar to Lower Saxony and Mecklenburg and noted that the diasporas had managed to survive a surprisingly long time even though some had "gone under" in Polish urban milieus.[11]

Some tentative suggestions might help explain this diaspora's lengthy survival. Language, religion, Russian policies, and economic self-sufficiency sustained the enclaves. The Russian state employed Russian as a bureaucratic language, while the local Catholic church used Polish for church registers (including for the Lutherans), but both institutions tolerated German usage at home, in school, at church, or for social activities. Few restrictions seem to have been placed on the colonies in terms of language until the 1870s when Russian schooling slowly became the norm (although Low German remained a common language in the community). Agrarian self-sufficiency in terms of home-grown and preserved foodstuffs, clothing from flax and animal skins, and limited external commercial contacts reinforced isolation. Some genealogical charts indicate high rates of cousin marriages and linked families.[12] In 1835 the Paprotsch colonies had 318 families with 1,481 persons, but by World War I they had increased to nearly 3,000.[13] Perhaps population increase and agricultural productivity were the beginnings of their undoing, since the former eventually encouraged emigration while the latter necessitated wider trading networks. Until World War I the colonies survived and partially thrived as self-contained and fairly homogeneous enclaves.

Dissolving a Diaspora

Influenced by the Polish revolt in 1863, Russia began instituting policies aimed at nationalizing ethnic minorities. During the 1870s military service became compulsory and Russian became the main language taught in schools. More important in the context of population growth were decrees against the purchase of land by Germans in Poland.[14] Young people began considering emigration, and before World War I a substantial number took this step.[15] While it is not clear who initiated it or when, a chain of migration was underway. This chain would become much larger in the interwar period, perhaps due to the nationalizing policies of the new Polish state. In numerous ways that state's educational and religious policies were discriminatory; in general they aimed at assimilating six million Ukrainians, three million Jews, and approximately a million Germans. Although minority rights were protected in theory, in practice the Polish state undermined schooling in anything but Polish.[16] Pressures were also exerted on the Lutheran church to be run by Polish leaders, not German ones.

The precise nature of ethnic relations at the community level is difficult to recover. In the first part of the twentieth century most Paprotschers were bilingual and in later oral accounts they spoke of mostly cordial relations with Polish neighbours and Jewish traders. Marriage within the religious and ethnic group suggests that this community kept to itself as it adapted to various regimes. Among the reasons for strength of local identity and seeing Paprotsch as *Heimat* would have been the mass deportation of the Germans of Russian Poland—some 400,000 persons—to the Russian interior during World War I.[17] Males of military age were deported starting in September 1914, followed by families in February 1915. A contemporary account claimed that "Gross Paprotsch is completely gone: of the 5600 souls no one is left ... the school in Paprotsch burned down."[18] By 1918 they were allowed to return, although some only came back in 1920–21 due to the Soviet-Polish border dispute. Some of that fighting occurred directly in Paprotsch. Only a few houses remained standing and the returning villagers had to reclaim their land and rebuild farm buildings and housing. A substantial number had died during the deportation and exile.[19] Having to recreate their existence probably reinforced their attachment to the area.

The pre–World War II diaspora was a traditional agricultural society. Visitors in 1937 found many low-beam buildings. Low German was spoken and schooling in German and Polish to about age twelve was normal.[20] A summary on the church community published in 1939 found services well attended and communal endeavours reinforced by choirs, a brass band, and bible study classes.[21] Weddings, harvest celebrations, Christmas, and Easter reinforced religious unity and ethnic identity, although more as Mecklenburgers than Germans. By 1937 the population had only regained mid-nineteenth-century levels with some 1,355 church members in 296 households.[22] If only property is considered, Paprotsch proved to be a Germanic holdout as Poles had increased their land holdings in the surrounding area. In the long run this German diaspora within Poland would have disappeared for two reasons: Poles were buying up German property, which would have resulted in emigration or assimilation, and a transition to a modern, engine-powered, and market-oriented agriculture requiring few labourers would have increased assimilation and migration to the cities. Warfare interrupted those trends and drastically altered the dissolution process.

September 1939: Traumas and Treks

When Germany invaded Poland in the fall of 1939 the situation of Germans in Poland became precarious. One might think the opposite, since the German military quickly won the war, but some Germans had reason for anxiety, partly because of the manner in which ethnic minorities in Poland had been treated as second-class citizens in the interwar era. Ethnic relations became especially tense in the weeks before the war as some German families were deported, and the Polish state as well as some Polish individuals planned to apprehend anyone who might be disloyal to Poland or somehow support the German military, actions that were implemented once the war began.[23] Mostly without evidence, the Polish state and some individuals struck out against the "strangers in their midst," who had been there over a hundred years. Oral accounts by contemporaries indicate that some Germans were taken, beaten, and placed in holding camps such as Bereza Kartuska.[24] At least five Paprotschers (Emil and Robert Schütz and Adolf, Franz, and Wanda Schultz) were among those forcibly moved, a small first step in the physical dissolution of German diasporas.

By 12–13 September the front had reached the Paprotsch area and the villages came under the rule of the German military. The inhabitants were given limited choices: move to East Prussia under German protection or await their fate with the advancing Soviets who had been allotted half the district (3,507 of 7,014 inhabitants) in the proposed division of Poland.[25] Nearly all villagers decided to move, and had a week to pack their possessions and to prepare for the trek to southern East Prussia, territory taken from northern Poland. The Paprotschers were distributed in the area around Ortelsburg, near Johannisberg, Sensburg, and further west near Thorn. Some remember helping with the potato harvest before they were allotted farmland, mostly taken from Poles.[26] Many received holdings in the Soldau (Działdowo) area of East Prussia. This small town sat in the border region lost to Germany in 1920, but was reattached to East Prussia in September 1939. The Paprotschers, used to living in a set of villages within fifteen kilometres of one other, were now dispersed over an area of over fifty kilometres.

The quality of land and farms received was of great interest to the resettlers. In one case the land was rocky, good only for running a few goats; the craftsman who had received it insisted on a better location. In another case, due to the death of the family head—Robert Schütz, who died in July 1942 on the eastern front—information about the quality of the land was recorded in his widow's request in 1944 to give up the farm yet keep inheritance rights for a future allotment for her sons. The bureaucrat reviewing the case wrote that this family had held three hectares in Paprotsch and had been allotted twelve near Soldau. He admitted that the land was located three kilometres from the farmyard in Soldau, and that the soil was perhaps only good for reforestation and, therefore, not profitable. Furthermore, the wife was incapable of running it.[27] Instead of farming or following their trades, the Paprotschers had to rebuild their lives dependent upon bureaucratic decisions.

Bureaucratic Evaluations

Ethnic sorting undertaken by the Nazi regime affected the lives of the Paprotschers. In June 1940, they were evaluated for purposes of becoming German citizens. The Nazi resettlement offices employed four categories to assess racial purity. Category 1 applied to those Germans who had been Reich citizens before 1919 and thus almost automatically deemed racially acceptable. Category 2 designated *Volksdeutsche*, or ethnic Germans, who had lived outside the Reich but were found to be racially untainted. Category 3 identified those of German background but who had some "shortcomings" such as intermarriage with other ethnic groups or were unfamiliar with German cultural norms, including linguistic and homemaking skills. Category 4 identified those who had been racially "defiled" or were regarded as renegades because of sympathizing with other ethnic groups. Only those in the first two categories received citizenship, although the review practice became less stringent as labour needs increased during 1943 and 1944. Most Paprotschers were placed in the second and third categories, thus some were considered not to be full-blooded Germans.

Documents used to assess the Paprotschers illustrate the arbitrary bureaucratic evaluations. In one case, Gustav Buse, born during September 1901 in Gross Paprotsch and brother of Emilie (married to Robert Schütz), had a cousin with the same name, born 1907 in Malkinia, but whose parents were from Paprotsch and Silberwald. Both Gustavs were carpenters. During the resettlement the former was assigned to a farm in Seeben in the district of Neidenburg close to where his parents were assigned.[28] For both, the bureaucrats evaluated their German as "good" or "very good" and noted that it was the common language in the families. In the initial evaluation during June 1940 of the first Gustav, the bureaucrat had "reservations about inherited biological traits." Later another bureaucrat reviewed the case and noted that reference should be made to the "medical reports of the other members of the Buse family." Later the first Gustav would be granted citizenship without reservations. On the application the bureaucrat entered "applicant German; speaks German; attended Russian school." On the application of the second Gustav, the bureaucrat commented that Gustav had been a member of the ethnic lobbying group, the Deutscher Volksverband in Poland, since 1935. He attained his citizenship immediately in June 1940; he had been assigned half a house in Soldau from which he practised carpentry.[29] Of interest is the family background because his mother, Ottilie Medbeck, also happened to be Emilie Schütz's mother (hence simultaneously cousins and in-laws), and who had died on the return from Russia in 1920.

If the case of Ludwig Buse born in 1877 in Gross Paprotsch is considered, this farmer's parents, too, came from the Paprotsch colonies and both died in Russia.[30] His wife's parents included a Buse, but the file had question marks about her origins. Both her parents had died during the return from Russian deportation. Although the family spoke German well, Ludwig's application was held over and only in September 1940 did he receive citizenship. In this case the bureaucrat noted "*Volksdeutscher*; speaks good German; attended German school; parents German, wife German; child speaks good German." As in the case of the first Gustav Buse, the first evaluating bureaucrat had "reservations about inherited biological traits." Another Ludwig Buse born in Gross Paprotsch in 1903 and who now was in the Neidenburg district offers another case of delayed citizenship.[31] Undoubtedly his citizenship was delayed despite his claimed activity on behalf of *Deutschtum* because two children of his father's brother were dwarfs.

Although the Paprotschers had lost their own agricultural or artisan holdings, they would have shared the experience of taking property from the Poles. The attitudes of the resettlers are not well known, although some felt guilty about receiving the property of others.[32] However, they justified it by saying that their own lands and farms and houses had been turned over to others. Another common experience was the influx of teachers, nurses, and others sent to bring German culture to the ethnic Germans. Starting in late 1940 the first batch of fifty women settler-aides (*Ansiedlerbetreuer*) arrived in East Prussia,[33] and eventually some thousand officials from various Nazi organizations operated kindergartens, cleaned Polish homes taken for German resettlers, and taught home economics. Some of the ethnic Germans resented the arrogance and assumptions of that program.[34]

Why did the Paprotschers not return to their *Heimat* behind the advancing German troops after June 1941? They were not given that choice. The answer underscores that the resettlers had little control over their fate. The first major step in dissolving the diaspora of Polish Germans had been taken by forcing them to move, and the second by reviewing the Polish Germans for racial traits of Germanness as well as political activities on behalf of it. Sometimes having craft skills resulted in further assigned moves. The third step was the Heim ins Reich program through which hundreds of thousand of Germans from various diasporas were moved and resettled. The Polish Germans could have known little of the Nazi planners' concepts of model racial settlements. Those plans included the assumption that their original areas of settlement were to be completely revamped so that no return to the Paprotsch style of existence would have been possible had the Third Reich lasted longer. Studies are just beginning to recover the racial *Dorfgemeinschaften* [village communities] drafted by Nazi architects and town planners. This reordering of the east viewed the populace, including ethnic Germans, as pawns to be moved, directed, and homogenized at will. The architectural planning and some of the movement of people into new establishments was being realized by 1943–44.[35] Villages such as Paprotsch were to be replaced by model ones designed according to vague "Germanic" principles of order and aesthetics.

In late 1944 some Paprotschers saw that the war's end was near and made arrangements to flee. In early 1945 many did leave and ended up all over western and central Germany, amounting to another dispersal of the Paprotsch community. As refugees, small family groups tried to maintain ties and established themselves in clusters of Paprotscher in Schleswig-Holstein, near Heidelberg and in the Ruhr valley; some also migrated overseas. These communities would disappear within a generation as intermarriage with other ethnic groups closed the coffin on Paprotsch. However, neither the flight nor the expulsions at war's end provided the main acid to dissolve the Polish diasporas. The Nazis' racial war provided the main impetus and their ultimate plans—if implemented—would have prevented any return to ethnic enclaves.

Epilogue and Different Approach

Although some Paprotscher descendants still hold clan meetings, those who experienced the Polish diaspora are dying off. In their collective memory they have focused on their own victimization. Many ethnic Germans were victimized, but they have been reluctant to put their experiences in the context of the victimization of Poles and Jews and only recently have they begun to acknowledge that their victimization had German sources. They would probably not agree with a historian's outlook that it was not the fleeing and deportations at war's end, but long-term demographics, Russian and Polish state policies, and emigration that set the parameters for dissolution. Their descendants might agree that Reich Germans, through Nazi warfare and practices of ethnic cleansing, destroyed their diaspora. Polish state policies may have increased inter-ethnic tensions just as earlier Russian wartime deportations underscored ethnic differences and fostered national attachments. But only the moves forced by the Nazi state meant assimilation with Germans in and from the Reich. The Nazi practices and plans for the east included a horrendous ethnic cleansing of non-Germans that ultimately led to a reverse ethnic cleansing and terminated the *Volksdeutsche* diasporas.

Most accounts place this subject in the context of twentieth-century population transfers or begin the story with the expulsions at the end of the war. This chapter's approach is different: it underlines that the dissolution began with the outbreak of World War II and it places responsibility on the German state in its Nazi form for implementing the destruction of the German diasporas in eastern Europe. That state and its practice of racial ideology refused to tolerate the Paprotsch enclaves in their old form any more than the Poles did later. The postwar forced migrations of 1945–46 are mainly an epilogue to a longer story, and the historians' focus on victimization requires that the various forms of victimization undergo greater clarification. That will occur only when the period before 1945 and the displacement of Poles are given as much attention as the treks, rapes and looting of 1945.[36]

The author is grateful to Adolf Buse, Judith M. Buse, Lisa J. Buse, and Karl Krueger for research and editorial assistance.

Notes

1   This case is taken from the personnel file and application to obtain German citizenship during June 1940 of one family (Robert Schütz and Emile née Buse) in the Einwanderungs-Zentralstelle (EWZ) collection. Copies of these documents at the Berlin Documentation Centre in the Bundesarchiv Berlin are available through the Family History Centers of the Church of Latter Day Saints; film numbers

1796768–70 cover the Paprotsch area villages. Some of the individuals mentioned are immediate and distant relatives of the author.

2   Interview by Adolf Buse with Emil Schütz and citizenship file 175752 of EWZ collection.

3   Detailed topographical maps, noting number of dwellings in each village and unoccupied lands at Paprotsch site, are in the map collection of the Staatsbibliothek Berlin.

4   For Prussian administrative policies and practices see the works of Ingeburg Bussenius, especially Hubatsch and Bussenius, *Urkunden und Akten*, 501–17, on types of colonists sought.

5   The detailed colonial lists are in the Geheimes Preussisches Staatsarchiv (GPS), Berlin, II, VI, 1104 "Nachweissung der Kolonisten auf dem platten Lande 1806"; folio pp. 4–6 provide an overview; pp. 82–129 tabulate individual colonists, their families, possessions, skills, and moral character as well as the state of development in terms of land worked and buildings erected.

6   See GPS II, VI, 1104 "Nachweissung der Kolonisten auf dem platten Lande 1806," 82ff.

7   See Müller, *Preussische Kolonisation*, 25ff.

8   Colonists who returned to Prussia listed in Pokrandt, "Deutsche Rückwanderung aus Mittelpolen," 105ff, especially 140–42.

9   Schmit, "Siedlungsgeschichte von Gross-Paproc," a serialized memoir rich in details of daily life.

10   Müller, *Mecklenburger*, 310ff, emphasizes the Paprotsch villages.

11   See Müller, "Mecklenburger wandern nach Polen," 88. She claims that in "1936 the descendants of the colonists were spread over 23 villages in the region" (106); she used some church registers to determine origins. Her writings included accolades to the Führer and racist assumptions about health and blood lines.

12   Volker F. Hahn, a genealogist specializing on Paprotsch, has constructed such charts, but the EWZ files provide the most evidence of cousin intermarriage.

13   See Kersten [Paprotsch pastor], "100 Jahre," 50.

14   Pytlak, *Kolonisationsbestrebungen*, 23ff, notes decree of 1887, renewed in 1892.

15   Search Paproć in <www.ellisislandrecords.org> or <www.angelfire.com/ks/gerrus/ShipsBaltNov1910.htm>.

16   The literature on Polish German relations is vast but focused mostly on state relations. For treatment of German minorities see Blanke, *Orphans of Versailles*, and Bergen, "'Volksdeutschen' of Eastern Europe," 70ff. See also contemporary accounts by Kneifel, *Die evangelisch-augsburgischen Gemeinden in Polen 1555–1939*, which is less anti-Polish than Kneifel, *Die evangelisch-augsburgischen Gemeinden der Kalischer Diözese*.

17   Hardly known, the deportation is detailed by Lohr, *Nationalizing the Russian Empire*, ch. 5, "Forced Migrations."

18   Holtz, *Krieg und die Evangelisch-Lutherische Kirche*, 9–11.

19   See Rendtorff, *Polen: Unpolitische Kriegsbilder*, 10ff.

20   Müller, *Mecklenburger*, 17ff.

21   See Kersten, "100 Jahre," 49ff.

22   See Kersten, "100 Jahre," 51, and Wichert, *Gross Paprotsch und Umgebung*, passim.

23   See Menn, *Auf den Straßen des Todes*, particularly the chapter on "Schandfleck Polens: Bereza Kartuska," although it is biased.

24   Sleszynski, *Obóz odosobnienia w Berezie Kartuskiej*, 109–11, claims around 3,100 persons were incarcerated in August 1939; it closed on September 18.

25 See *Statistisches Gemeindeverzeichnis des bisherigen polnischen Staates* (Berlin, October 1939), 75, 100.

26 Based on interviews with Emilie Schütz, but well substantiated by the EWZ documents that reveal places of residence in mid June 1940 when most were processed for citizenship.

27 Based on EWZ file 175851.

28 Based on EWZ file 175661.

29 Based on EWZ file 175681.

30 Based on EWZ file 175630.

31 Based on EWZ file 175670.

32 Based on interviews with Emilie Schütz and Helene Weirauch.

33 Harvey, *Women and the Nazi East*, has written extensively on this subject, from the perspective of the questionable publicity materials of the Nazis. She seeks to demonstrate women's agency for those imposing the Germanization, but seems to see no female initiatives or choices for the subjects receiving the ideology. Yet she acknowledges what evacuation policies meant: "As ever, the ethnic Germans were pawns in the schemes of the SS planners" (284). Compare O'Donnell, Bridenthal, and Reagin, *Heimat Abroad*, especially chapters 2 and 6 on identity and ethnic cleansing.

34 The memoir of a teacher who worked in East Prussia and visited the Paprotsch area is instructive since she observed a ghetto and commented on relations to Poles. See Peyringhaus, *Stille Jahre in Gertlauken*.

35 Hartenstein, *Neue Dorflandschaften*, 17, notes that the people were hardly considered in the revamping to be undertaken.

36 Standard historical accounts of Germans in Poland do not consider this particular group of Germans. Exemplar is Brandes, *Der Weg zur Vertreibung*, which is superb but limited to population transfer planning. Nearly all others begin in late 1944 or early 1945, for example, Nitschke, *Vertreibung und Aussiedlung*. Typical consequences of the narrow approach appear in Schulze, "Politics of Memory."

Interview Sources

Four interviews conducted by the author and in his possession:

Dams, Olga. Barrhead, May 1985.

Schütz, Emil. Winnipeg, May 2000.

Schütz, Emilie. Rendsburg, April, August 2004.

Weirauch, Helene. Stelle, June 1986.

Archival Material

Einwanderungs-Zentralstelle (EWZ) collection. Family History Center of the Church of Latter Day Saints; film numbers 1796768–70; originals in Berlin Documentation Center.

Geheimes Preussisches Staatsarchiv (GPS), Berlin, II, VI, 1104. "Nachweissung der Kolonisten auf dem platten Lande 1806."

Works Cited

Bergen, Doris L. "The 'Volksdeutschen' of Eastern Europe." *Yearbook of European Studies* XIII (1999): 70–92.

Blanke, Richard. *Orphans of Versailles: Germans in Western Poland, 1918–1939.* Lexington, KY: University of Kentucky Press, 1993.

Brandes, Detlef. *Der Weg zur Vertreibung 1938–1945. Pläne und Entscheidungen zum Transfer der Deutschen aus der Tschechoslowakei und aus Polen.* Munich: Collegium Carolinum, 2001.

Hartenstein, Michael A. *Neue Dorflandschaften. Nationalsozialistische Siedlungsplanung in den "eingegliederten Ostgebieten" 1939 bis 1944.* Berlin: Köster, 1998.

Harvey, Elizabeth. *Women and the Nazi East: Agents and Witnesses of Germanization.* New Haven, CT: Yale University Press, 2003.

Holtz, Edmund. *Der Krieg und die Evangelisch-Lutherische Kirche in Polen.* Lodz: Deutsche Staatsdruckerei, 1916.

Hubatsch, Walther, and Ingeburg Bussenius, eds. *Urkunden und Akten zur Geschichte der Preussischen Verwaltung in Südpreussen und Neuostpreussen 1793–1806.* Frankfurt: Athenäum, 1961.

Kersten, R. "100 Jahre der Gemeinde Gross-Paprotsch?" *Hausfreund. Evangelischer Volks-Kalender für das Jahr 1939*: 50.

Kneifel, Eduard. *Die evangelisch-augsburgischen Gemeinden der Kalischer Diözese.* Plauen: Günther Wolff, 1937.

———. *Die evangelisch-augsburgischen Gemeinden in Polen 1555–1939.* Vierkirchen: Selbstverlag, 1971.

Lohr, Eric. *Nationalizing the Russian Empire: The Campaign Against Enemy Aliens during World War I.* Cambridge, MA: Harvard University Press, 2003.

Menn, Fritz, ed. *Auf den Straßen des Todes. Der Leidensweg der Volksdeutschen in Polen.* Leipzig: Hase & Koehler Verlag, 1940. <www.wintersonnenwende.com/scriptorium/deutsch/archiv/strassendestodes/adsdtoo.html> (March 2008).

Müller, August. *Die Preussische Kolonisation in Nordpolen und Litauen 1795–1807.* Berlin: 1928.

Müller, Martha. *Mecklenburger in Osteuropa; ein Beitrag zu ihrer Auswanderung im 16. bis 19. Jahrhundert.* Göttingen: Gottfried Herder Institut, 1972.

———. "Mecklenburger wandern nach Polen (1795) und kehren heim (1940)." *Jahrbuch des Deutschen Ausland-Instituts zur Wandersforschung und Sippenkunde* V (1940/41): 88–109.

Nitschke, Bernadetta. *Vertreibung und Aussiedlung der deutschen Bevölkerung aus Polen, 1945–1950.* Munich: Oldenbourg, 2004.

O'Donnell, Krista, Renate Bridenthal, and Nancy Reagin, eds. *The Heimat Abroad: The Boundaries of Germanness.* Ann Arbor: University of Michigan Press, 2005.

Peyringhaus, Mariane. *Stille Jahre in Gertlauken.* Berlin: Siedler, 1985.

Pokrandt, Alfred. "Deutsche Rückwanderung aus Mittelpolen nach 1815." *Deutsche Monatshefte in Polen* III (1936), 105–46.

Rendtorff, Franz. *Polen: Unpolitische Kriegsbilder.* Leipzig: 1916.

Schmit, Michael. "Siedlungsgeschichte von Gross-Paproc und den Tochtergemeinden." *Weg und Ziel* (1959–60) (serialized in no. 10 [1959], 6–7; no. 1

[1960], 4–5; no. 2 [1960], 4–5; no. 3 [1960], 4–5; no. 4 [1960], 8–9; no. 5 [1960], 7; no. 6 [1960], 6; no. 7 [1960], 8–9; no. 8 [1960], 4–5).

Schulze, Rainer. "The Politics of Memory: Flight and Expulsion of German Populations after the Second World War and German Collective Memory." *National Identities* VIII (2006): 367–82.

Sleszynski, W. *Obóz odosobnienia w Berezie Kartuskiej 1930–1939.* Bialystok: 2003.

Statistisches Gemeindeverzeichnis des bisherigen polnischen Staates (Berlin, October 1939), 75, 100.

Wichert, L. *Gross Paprotsch und Umgebung.* Himbergen: Selbstverlag, 1998.

THIRTY-TWO

Suffering in a Province of Asia

The Russian German Diaspora in Kazakhstan

J. Otto Pohl

By 1989, nearly a million Russian Germans lived in Kazakhstan. They constituted the third largest nationality in the territory after Russians and Kazakhs. At almost six percent of the population, the Russian Germans played an important role in the economic development of the republic. The vast majority of Russian Germans from Kazakhstan are the descendants of deportees during World War II. During the fall of 1941, the Stalin regime deported more than 850,000 Russian Germans eastward. Close to 400,000 of these deportees ended up in Kazakhstan. Here the Soviet government subjected them to inhumane living conditions of severe material poverty and denial of basic human rights. Only in the mid-1950s, after Stalin's death, did their status improve significantly. Despite these improvements, the Russian Germans continued to suffer from official discrimination. They could not return to their former places of residence; they only had access to a few token German-language publications; and they remained largely excluded from receiving higher education and white collar jobs. This discrimination made it impossible for the Russian Germans to adopt Kazakhstan as a new homeland. It continued to be a land of involuntary exile and suffering.

We do not want you to be uninformed, brothers, about the hardships we suffered in the province of Asia. We were under great pressure, far beyond our ability to endure, so that we despaired even of life. Indeed, in our hearts we felt the sentence of death.[1]

Russian Germans have lived in Kazakhstan for more than 120 years. In 1882 colonists from other regions of the Russian Empire established the first Russian German settlements there. By 1900 they had established 110 separate colonies in Kazakhstan.[2] During the first decades of the twentieth century, Russian Germans from the western regions of the Russian Empire continued to migrate east to Kazakhstan in search of farmland. By 1926, their population numbered 51,102.[3] The voluntary nature of this settlement contrasts sharply with the involuntary settlement of more than 400,000 Russian Germans in Kazakhstan during the 1940s.

Racism in the USSR

Soviet nationality policy during the 1920s and '30s aimed at integrating the various peoples of the USSR by granting each ethnic group its own territorial unit to promote a socialist version of its culture.[4] These administrative territories served as pseudo nation-state formations for their titular nationalities. The larger units had their own flags, anthems, constitutions, and other symbolic trappings. Even the smaller territories, however, promoted their titular nationalities through affirmative action and supporting education and the media in their native language. These cultural infrastructures aimed to construct socialist versions of the histories of the various ethnic groups in the USSR linked to the specific territories they inhabited. Almost every ethnicity in the Soviet Union thus received a specific territory with an administration geared toward promoting its national culture and historical ties to that land. This was true even of nationalities descended from immigrants such as the Russian Finns, Russian Koreans, and Russian Greeks, all of which received national *raions* [districts]. The Soviet government granted the Russian Germans a number of *raions* as well as the Volga German Autonomous Soviet Socialist Republic.

During the 1930s, ethnic categories became racialized in the USSR as the regime increasingly came to view culture as primordial rather than an environmentally acquired set of beliefs and practices. The Stalin regime came to associate extraterritorial nationalities within the Soviet Union with the states from which their ancestors emigrated. This association posited that the ethnic origins of these Soviet citizens made them and their descendants inherently "politically unreliable." No amount of Sovietization could in practice erase this primordial cultural association.[5] Francine Hirsch has observed: "Soviet leaders were concerned that these nationalities could not be 'reinvented' as Soviet nations—national in form, but socialist in content—because other states or class enemies had 'control' over the histories and traditions that shaped their national consciousness."[6] The Russian Germans constituted the largest extraterritorial nationality in the USSR. They also had an ethnic association with the Soviet Union's most formidable ideological and military opponent in Europe. As the 1930s progressed they came under increasing repression due to their ancestral origins in central Europe.

The Soviet concept of nationality developed along a peculiar path and resulted in the creation of racial categorizations considerably different from those in other countries. Race is a social category that distinguishes people based upon their biological descent from groups of people defined by shared signifiers. These groups do not have to be marked by skin colour or other phenotypes. Other signifiers such as religion, language, or geographical origin can also mark these groups. Several important factors define a categorization as racial as opposed to ethnic or national, in particular that race is inherited automatically at birth, is unchangeable, and is passed on to one's children by mere virtue of descent.[7] The Soviet Union developed a system of racial categorization that relied upon distinguishing between people on the basis of their biological descent using signifiers other than physical phenotypes.

The Soviet category of nationality originally corresponded to ethnic heritage. A classification they generally distinguished by language. Nationality did not refer to citizenship as the term does in the English-speaking world. Every Soviet citizen had a recognized legal nationality such as Russian, Ukrainian, Uzbek, German, Jewish, etc. Throughout the Soviet period, individuals had to fill out their nationality on all applications and forms. This practice has persisted in many of the USSR's successor states. In 1932, the Soviet government introduced internal passports that listed the carrier's nationality on the fifth line. Initially, individuals could specify which nationality they wished to have entered into this document. On 28 April 1938, the NKVD (Soviet secret police) changed nationality from a chosen ethnic identification to an imposed racial identification.[8] Nationality from this point on became inherited. The Soviet government began to register the children of people listed as Germans in their identification documents automatically as Germans. The nationality entry no longer specified an individual's primary language or cultural background. Rather it specified biological descent from an ethnolinguistic group.

Early Russian German Deportations and the Great Terror

The summer of 1936 witnessed the first deportations of Russian Germans to Kazakhstan based solely upon their nationality. At this time the Soviet regime decided that extraterritorial nationalities in the border regions of the USSR posed a threat to the security of the state. In particular, the regime distrusted the Russian Germans and ethnic Poles living in western

Ukraine near the borders of Poland. It considered them to be potential spies and saboteurs with dubious loyalty toward the Soviet Union. Between 20 February and 10 March 1935, the NKVD forcibly removed 1,903 Russian German families from this region to the eastern regions of Ukraine.[9] The regime followed this partial resettlement with the deportation of 26,778 Russian German and Polish people from the same region to special settlements in northern Kazakhstan in June 1936[10] and another 12,975 people in September. These operations—the first purely ethnically motivated deportations in the USSR—cleared the Ukrainian border region of its Russian German and ethnic Polish minorities.

Between 1937 and 1938, the Stalin regime engaged in a murderous campaign of mass executions. Known as the Great Terror, this colossal bloodletting disproportionately targeted and killed extraterritorial nationalities such as the Russian Germans on the basis of their foreign ethnic heritage. In these two years the Stalin regime sentenced 681,692 people to death by firing squad.[11] National operations aimed at eliminating foreign spies from specific nationalities constituted more than a third of these death sentences. The "German Operation," launched on 25 July 1937, specifically targeted Russian Germans as being agents of Nazi Germany and lasted until 15 December 1938.[12] In total it resulted in 55,005 convictions of which 41,898 received death sentences. Russian Germans constituted around 38,000 of these convictions with 29,000 (2.5 percent of the total Russian German population) leading to execution. In 1937–38, the Stalin regime convicted a total of around 70,000 Russian Germans in various operations, more than 5 percent of their total population. The NKVD shot over 53,000 of these men and women, close to 3.5 percent of all Russian Germans in the USSR.[13]

The Nazi invasion of the Soviet Union sealed the fate of the Russian Germans. The Stalin regime already wrongly associated the Russian Germans with the German state. Nazi Germany's attack on the USSR provided the provocation for the Soviet regime to enact a brutal revenge against its own citizens of German descent. The Stalin regime falsely accused the entire Russian German population of being traitors awaiting orders from Nazi Germany.[14] It then proceeded to ethnically cleanse the western Soviet Union of Russian Germans. During the fall of 1941, the NKVD rounded up the entire Russian German population in the European USSR that remained under its control, forcibly loaded them into cattle cars, and transported them east to Kazakhstan and Siberia. The deportations started in Crimea on 15 August 1941.[15] The Stalin regime then systematically removed the Russia Germans from their homes in the Volga, Leningrad, Moscow, Rostov, the Kuban, the Caucasus, Ukraine, and other western regions of the USSR. By 25 December 1941, the NKVD had deported 856,168 Russian

Germans in a massive act of ethnic cleansing.[16] The Russian Germans could only take a limited amount of food, clothing, utensils, and rugs with them into exile.[17] The Soviet government appropriated all immovable property, including harvested grain, and issued the deportees vouchers in exchange. The deportees permanently lost their homelands, farms, houses, furniture, churches, cemeteries, libraries, livestock, and much of their personal property.

The Special Settlement Regime

The journey into exile took place under extremely unhealthy conditions. The train wagons carried an average of more than 40 deportees each[18] and took several weeks to reach their destinations. Overcrowded and unsanitary conditions led to many deaths especially of children from gastrointestinal diseases, mange, and measles.[19] Many deportees suffered from malnutrition and dehydration.[20] The surviving Russian Germans arrived in exile traumatized and weakened by hunger and sickness. The Stalin regime immediately placed the deported Russian Germans in Kazakhstan and Siberia under special settlement restrictions. They came under the surveillance and administration of NKVD special commandants in August 1941. The Russian German deportees could not leave their assigned places of settlement without written permission from these commandants[21] and had to register with these commandants at least once a month starting in February 1944.[22] The NKVD commandants enforced a separate legal system upon the special settlers and administered their housing and job assignments. These commandants wielded enormous arbitrary power over the lives of the special settlers. After World War II, the Stalin regime extended the special settlement restrictions to 146,590 of the 250,354 Russian Germans who were already living east of the Urals before 1941.[23] These new special settlers included almost the entire prewar Russian German population of Kazakhstan and Central Asia, but only a few thousand in Siberia.[24] The vast majority of the Russian German population of the Soviet Union thus came to suffer under this system of legal discrimination.

A mass increase in the Russian German population of Kazakhstan occurred during World War II as a direct result of Stalin's forced dispersal of their population across Eurasia. In 1941, prior to the Nazi invasion of the USSR, around 92,000 Russian Germans lived in Kazakhstan.[25] Between September 1941 and January 1942, the Stalin regime deported 385,785 Russian Germans from the Volga, Ukraine, Crimea, the Caucasus, the Kuban, Moscow, Rostov, and Tula to Kazakhstan.[26] This number represents nearly half the number of Russian Germans surviving the train journey into exile. The other half of this remaining population ended up in Siberia. The Soviet government settled most of the Russian German deportees sent to Kazakhstan in its cold northern oblasts. The oblasts receiving the most Russian German deportees with more than 30,000 each before December 1941 were Akmola, North Kazakhstan, Pavlodar, Semipalatinsk, and Kustannai.[27] These harsh steppe regions closely resembled the Siberian lands to Kazakhstan's immediate northeast in their physical geography and climate.

Already by October 1941 a severe housing crisis had developed in Kazakhstan as a result of the arrival of the deported Russian Germans. The Soviet government initially settled almost all the Russian Germans exiled to Kazakhstan on already existing kolkhozes (collective farms). In Jambul Oblast for instance a full 30 percent of the housing available for the 33,000 newly arrived Russian Germans had no glass in their window frames or working doors.[28] In Kustannai Oblast the majority of structures used to house Russian German deportees needed significant repair, but a severe shortage of construction materials prevented such work.[29] As early as 12 September 1941, Russian German deportees had used up all empty housing and extra space in occupied houses in South Kazakhstan Oblast.[30] A large number of Russian Germans in the oblast thus had no proper shelter and had to live in earth huts and dugouts. This pattern held throughout Kazakhstan. The Soviet authorities quartered the majority of Russian Germans exiled to Kazakhstan in already occupied Kazakh houses in extremely overcrowded conditions.[31] By November 1941, 65.26 percent of Russian German deportees in Pavlodar Oblast and 63.59 percent in Semipalatinsk Oblast lived under such conditions.[32] This situation also put a burden upon the native Kazakh population. They found themselves forced to share their homes with strangers. In most cases, the Kazakh collective farmers and Russian German deportees lacked any common language and could not communicate with each other despite living in the same buildings.

For the Russian German deportees, lack of food proved to be an even greater problem than finding proper shelter. Only after being integrated into kolkhozes could they receive food in exchange for labour. In many cases this took weeks or even months. In the meantime their only sources of food consisted of the vouchers issued by the Soviet government in exchange for grain confiscated during the deportations, bartering their few possessions with the local population, begging, and theft. Initially the Kazakh authorities refused to issue grain in exchange for the vouchers.[33] Only after an 11 November 1941 decree by the Peoples Commissariat of Procurement did the authorities start to honour the vouchers and issue each Russian German deportee who was capable of physical labour a minimal amount of grain.[34] The vouchers could not be used to acquire any other food items than grain. An even more acute food problem accrued to the sizable portion of Russian German special settlers in Kazakhstan without any grain vouchers. Deportees who had worked outside of kolkhozes in waged or salaried positions, for example urban Russian Germans, received no vouchers. Also a large number of kolkhoz workers, e.g., the 50,000 Crimean Germans deported to Kazakhstan,[35] failed to receive any vouchers during their deportation. In Semipalatinsk Oblast, some 46 percent of the Russian Germans had no grain vouchers.[36] A majority of the 23,832 Russian German exiles in South Kazakhstan Oblast also did not have food vouchers.[37] Starvation quickly ensued among those Russian Germans without vouchers. In the village of Frunze, South Kazakhstan Oblast, eighty-four Russian German children perished from malnourishment by mid-November 1941.[38] A large, but unknown, number of Russian Germans died from hunger and disease during their first months of exile in Kazakhstan.

Even after being integrated into the kolkhoz structure of Kazakhstan, the Russian Germans faced severe food shortages and constant hunger. In October 1941, kolkhozes in East Kazakhstan Oblast only issued 200–400 grams of bread a day to Russian German workers.[39] These minimal rations frequently had to be divided among a large number of children and other non-working dependants. Russian German special settlers in Kazakhstan thus resorted to bartering away the few possessions they brought with them into exile for food.[40] After exhausting their meagre possessions, many of them resorted to begging and stealing to acquire food.[41] As late as February 1946, the Soviet government had to provide significant food aid to Russian German deportees in Tsyurupinsk District, Pavlodar Oblast to prevent their death from starvation.[42] These food shortages persisted among the Russian Germans despite an increase in overall food production in Kazakhstan in 1941–46.[43] Only several years after the end of World War II did the Russian Germans in Kazakhstan manage to obtain an adequate supply of nourishment.

After the Special Settlement Regime

After the death of Stalin in 1953, the Soviet government began dismantling the special settlement regime. On 13 December 1955, the Soviet government freed the last remaining Russian Germans from the jurisdiction of the special settlement regime and surveillance of the Ministry of Internal Affairs—the successor to the NKVD and predecessor of the KGB.[44] The same decree that ended the special settlement restrictions for the Russian Germans, however, also prohibited them from returning to their former homes or seeking restitution for property confiscated during the deportations. It also did not annul the false charges of treason against the Russian Germans.

The Russian Germans in Kazakhstan progressively lost much of their German language and culture from the 1950s onward while still suffering discrimination on the basis of their German descent. German-language publications and education had been completely banned during the special settlement era. In the 1950s and '60s the Soviet government made a few token concessions in these areas. But these half-hearted measures proved insufficient to halt the replacement of German with Russian as the primary language of the Russian Germans. By 1991, only around 15 percent of all Russian Germans in the USSR had a good command of spoken German.[45] This small percentage consisted largely of those born before the deportations. More recent generations had little opportunity to learn the language.

Despite adopting the language and many other attributes of the dominant Soviet Russian culture, Russian Germans continued to experience discrimination on the basis of their German origins in Kazakhstan. For example, they suffered from anti-German discrimination in university admissions. Only 4.3 percent of Russian Germans in Kazakhstan had university degrees in 1979 versus 11.7 percent of the population of the republic as a whole.[46] By 1989, the proportion of Russian Germans in Kazakhstan over the age of fifteen with postsecondary education was still only 5.7 percent.[47] Only 22.4 percent had completed secondary school and 8.4 percent had not finished grammar school. The Soviet government sought to prevent the development of a large Russian German educated class in order to deprive the group of national leadership and keep its population tied to the agricultural economy.

This strategy had considerable success. Russian German political activism remained limited during the Soviet era. Not until after a 1964 Soviet decree annulled the charges of treason against the Russian Germans, but did not allow them to return to their former homes, did an organized movement for full rehabilitation arise among the Russian Germans.[48] In the fall of 1964, a movement to petition the Soviet government for the restoration of the Volga German ASSR and equal rights for Russian Germans formed at a meeting in Frunze (now Bishkek), Kyrgyzstan.[49] This movement sent three delegations to Moscow to plead their case with the Soviet leadership before it completely disintegrated in 1968.[50] The autonomy movement lacked the ability to successfully mount a sustained challenge to Soviet policies of racialized discrimination against Russian Germans.

The Emigration Movement

In 1972, a new political movement arose among the Russian Germans. It developed after new legislation granted partial rehabilitation to the Russian Germans. On 3 November 1972, the Soviet regime finally removed the official residency restriction that still confined the entire Russian German population to those areas of the USSR east of the Urals.[51] This legislation, however, offered little in the way of concrete rights. By this time the former homes of the Russian Germans had long been taken over by Russians hostile to any German return. The new Russian German movement had abandoned the idea that they could ever achieve equal rights with other nationalities in the USSR. Instead they fought for the right to emigrate from the Soviet Union and settle in West Germany.[52] Kazakhstan became a major centre for this movement. Although the Soviet government allowed 63,204 Russian Germans (3.4 percent of the 1970 population) to leave the USSR between 1971 and 1980 partially in response to this movement, it also ruthlessly repressed its leadership.[53] From 1974 to 1977, the Soviet legal system sentenced more than forty Russian German emigration activists to terms of incarceration ranging from six months to three years.[54] Half of these trials occurred in Kazakhstan. In 1977, the Soviet state tried twelve Russian Germans in Alma-Ata (now Almaty) on charges of "slandering the USSR." This repression largely succeeded in decapitating and ending the movement.

In 1987, the Soviet government removed all restrictions on emigration. The Russian Germans could now freely leave the Soviet Union and settle in West Germany. Between 1986 and 1990, a total of 308,537 Russian Germans arrived in West Germany from the USSR.[55] A large number of these emigrants came from Kazakhstan. From 1989 to 1990 alone the Russian German population of Kazakhstan dropped by more than 40,000.[56] A mass exodus of Russian Germans from Kazakhstan had begun.

Independent Kazakhstan

In 1991, the Soviet Union broke up into its component republics. Kazakhstan became an independent state for the first time in its history. The newly independent Kazakh state, however, maintained and even intensified the Soviet-era discrimination regarding jobs, education, and cultural outlets.[57] The Nazarbayev regime instituted a policy of Kazakhization aimed at solidifying Kazakhstan as a Kazakh national state by granting preference to the Kazakh language and ethnic Kazakhs in all spheres of public life.[58] The regime has kept the old Soviet system of nationality classifications and replaced Russians with Kazakhs as the "leading nationality." Kazakhstani passports and identification cards still have entries for nationality based on the old racialized Soviet criteria.[59] Officials continue to routinely demand proof of nationality in filling out paperwork even though Kazakhstani law no longer requires this information be provided. This discrimination has reinforced the desire of

Russian Germans in Kazakhstan to settle in Germany. Russian Germans continued to leave Kazakhstan in large numbers during the 1990s. Between 1992 and 1996, a total of 558,460 Russian Germans from Kazakhstan—56 percent of all Russian Germans arriving in Germany from the former USSR—settled in Germany.[60] The last Soviet census in 1989 counted 957,518 Russian Germans in Kazakhstan.[61] They represented the third largest nationality in Kazakhstan at 5.8 percent of the population. Ten years later the first census of independent Kazakhstan counted only 353,441 Russian Germans remaining in Kazakhstan. Although they were still the fifth largest nationality in the country they now only constituted 2.4 percent of the population. In the seven years since the census, substantial numbers of Russian Germans have continued to leave Kazakhstan.

It is clear that the overwhelming majority of the Russian Germans have decided that being German citizens in Germany is preferable to being second-class Kazakhstani citizens. Historically Kazakhstan has been a land of bondage and suffering for the Russian Germans. Few of them regard it as a national homeland.

Notes

1   Second Corinthians 1:8–10, NIV.
2   Wolf and Frank, "No Future," 154.
3   Buchsweiler, *Collection of Soviet Documents*, 24, table 1.
4   Martin, "Affirmative Action Empire."
5   Weitz, *Century of Genocide*, 97–98.
6   Hirsch, "Race," 38.
7   Weitz, *Century of Genocide*, 97–98.
8   Martin, *Affirmative Action Empire*, 450.
9   Martin, *Affirmative Action Empire*, 330.
10 Document reproduced in Polian, *Ne po svoei vole*, 89.
11 Martin, *Affirmative Action Empire*, 338.
12 Okhotin and Roginskii, "Iz istorii 'nemetskoi operatsii,'" 70–71.
13 In contrast, the political conviction rate for the USSR as a whole during these years was 0.84 percent and the execution rate was 0.43 percent. Percentages based upon 1,344,926 convictions and 681,692 executions on cases of the NKVD in the USSR during 1937 and 1938 out of a 1937 population of 162 million. Popov, "Gosudarvennyi," 28, table 3.
14 Bugai, *Iosif Stalin-Lavrentiiu Berii*, 37–38, doc. 3.
15 Bugai, *Deportatsiia narodov kryma*, 79, doc. 48.
16 Milova, *Deportatsii narodov*, doc. 63–69, 9.
17 Bugai, *Iosif Stalin-Lavrentiiu Berii*, 43–47, doc. 10.
18 Milova, *Deportatsii narodov*, vol. II, 153–58, doc. 49.
19 Vol'ter, *Zona polnogo pokia*, 64.
20 Milova, *Deportatsii narodov*, vol. II, 218–19, doc. 57.
21 Bruhl, *Nemtsy v zapadnoi sibiri*, vol. II, 107.
22 Bakaev, *Ssylka kalmykov*, 144–45, doc. 145.
23 Berdinskikh, *Spetsposelentsy*, 339–42, docs. 8 and 9.
24 Berdinskikh, *Spetsposelentsy*, 338–39, doc. 7.

25 Eisfeld and Herdt, *Deportation*, 45–46, doc. 24.
26 Bugai, *Iosif Stalin-Lavrentiiu Berii*, 74–75, doc. 43 and 44; Milova, *Deportatsii narodov*, vol. II, 47–51, doc. 8.
27 Milova, *Deportatsii narodov*, vol. II, 147–48, doc. 47.
28 Milova, *Deportatsii narodov*, vol. II, 216, doc. 57.
29 Shtraus and Pankrats, *Svidetel'stva prestuplenii*, 151.
30 Karpykova, *Iz istorii nemtsev Kazakhstana*, 97–98, doc. 45.
31 Milova, *Deportatsii narodov*, vol. II, 216–23, doc. 57.
32 Bugai, *Iosif Stalin-Lavrentiiu Berii*, 66–67, doc. 34; 70, doc. 39.
33 Shtraus and Pankrats, *Svidetel'stva prestuplenii*, 151–52.
34 Milova, *Deportatsii narodov*, vol. II, 227–30, doc. 61.
35 Milova, *Deportatsii narodov*, vol. II, 231–36, doc. 62.
36 Shtraus and Pankrats, *Svidetel'stva prestuplenii*, 151–52.
37 Karpykova, *Iz istorii nemtsev Kazakhstana*, doc. 53, 108–10; Milova, *Deportatsii narodov*, vol. II, 147–48, doc. 47.
38 Karpykova, *Iz istorii nemtsev Kazakhstana*, 108–10, doc. 53.
39 Shtraus and Pankrats, *Svidetel'stva prestuplenii*, 148–49.
40 Toews, *Journeys*, 77–78; Bachmann, *Memories*, 34–35; 45.
41 Bachmann, *Memories*, 43–45; 59.
42 Shtraus and Pankrats, *Svidetel'stva prestuplenii*, 212–14.
43 Mately, "Agricultural Development," 302–04.
44 Document reproduced in Auman and Chebotareva, *Istoriia rossiiskikh nemtsev*, 177.
45 Dietz and Hilkes, *Russlanddeutsche*, 52–58.
46 Shtraus and Pankrats, *Svidetel'stva prestuplenii*, 238–39.
47 Krieger, "Intellektuelle Rückentwicklung," 14, table 3.
48 Auman and Chebotareva, *Istoriia rossiiskikh nemtsev*, 178–79.
49 Fuchs, *Rokovye dorogi*, 165.
50 Schmaltz, *Reform*, 113–86.
51 Auman and Chebotareva, *Istoriia rossiiskikh nemtsev*, 180.
52 Pinkus and Fleischhauer, *Die Deutschen in der Sowjetunion*, 507–14.
53 Polian, *Ne po svoei vole*, 169, table 12.
54 Pinkus and Fleischhauer, *Die Deutschen in der Sowjetunion*, 517–18.
55 Polian, *Ne po svoei vole*, 169, table 12.
56 Oka, "Korean Diaspora," 95, table 1.
57 Wolf and Frank, "No Future," 157–60.
58 Oka, "Korean Diaspora," 92–93; United States Department of State, "Kazakhstan."
59 Dave, *Minorities*, 15.
60 Polian, *Ne po svoei vole*, 170, table 13.
61 Oka, "Korean Diaspora," 94, table 1.

Works Cited

Auman, V.A., and Chebotareva, V.G., eds. *Istoriia rossiiskikh nemtsev v dokumentakh (1763–1992 gg.)*. Moscow: MIGP, 1993.

Bachmann, Berta. *Memories of Kazakhstan: A Report on the Life Experience of a German Woman in Russia*. Translated by Edgar Duin. Lincoln, NE: American Historical Society of Germans from Russia, 1983.

Bakaev, P.D., ed. *Ssylka kalmykov: Kak eto bylo: Sbornik dokumentov i materialov*. Elitsa: Kalmytskoe knizhnoe izd-vo, 1993.

Berdinskikh, V.A. *Spetsposelentsy: Politcheskaia ssylka narodov Sovetskoi Rossii*. Moscow: Novoe literaturnoe obozrenie, 2005. .

Bruhl, V.I. *Nemtsy v zapadnoi sibiri*. Topchikha: Topchikhinskaia tip., 1995.

Buchsweiler, Meir, ed. *A Collection of Soviet Documents Concerning Germans in the USSR*. Jerusalem: Hebrew University, Majorie Mayrock Center for Soviet and East European Research, 1991.

Bugai, N.F., ed. *Deportatsiia narodov kryma: Dokumenty, fakty, kommentarii*. Moscow: Insan, 2002.

———, ed. *Iosif Stalin-Lavrentiiu Berii: "Ikh nado deportirovat'" Dokumenty, fakty, kommentarii*. Moscow: Druzhba narodov, 1992.

Dave, Bhana. *Minorities and Participation in Public Life: Kazakhstan*. Bishkek, Kyrgyzstan: United Nations Office of the High Commissioner for Human Rights, 2004.

Dietz, Barbara, and Peter Hilkes. *Russlanddeutsche: Unbekannte im Osten: Geschichte, Situation, Zukunftsperspektiven*. Munich: Olzog Verlag, 1992.

Eisfeld, Alfred, and Viktor Herdt, eds. *Deportation, Sondersiedlung, Arbeitsarmee: Deutsche in der Sowjetunion 1941 bis 1956*. Cologne: Verlag Wissenschaft und Politik, 1996.

Fuchs, V. *Rokovye dorogi povolzhskikh nemtsev 1763-1993 gg*. Krasnoiarsk Krai: Vozrozhdenie, 1993.

Hirsch, Francine. "Race without the Practice of Racial Politics." *Slavic Review*, 61, no. 1 (2002): 30–43.

Karpykova, G.A., ed. *Iz istorii nemtsev Kazakhstana (1921–1975), Sbornik dokumentov iz arkhiva presidenta respubliki Kazakhstan*. Almaty-Moscow: Gotika, 1997.

Krieger, Viktor. "Intellektuelle Rückentwicklung der Russlanddeutschen in der Sowjetunion." *Volk auf dem Weg*, no. 3/2006 (2006): 12–14.

Martin, Terry. "An Affirmative Action Empire: The Soviet Union as the Highest Form of Imperialism." In *A State of Nations: Empire and Nation-Making in the Age of Lenin and Stalin*, edited by Ronald Grigor Suny and Tarry Martin, 67–90. Oxford: Oxford University Press, 2001.

———. *An Affirmative Action Empire: Nations and Nationalism in the Soviet Union, 1923-1939*. London: Cornell University Press, 2001.

Mately, Ian. "Agricultural Development (1865–1963)." In *Central Asia: 130 Years of Russian Dominance*, edited by Edward Allworth, 266–308. Durham, NC: Duke University Press, 1994.

Milova, O.L., ed. *Deportatsii narodov SSSR (1930-1950-e gody), Chast' 2. Deportatsiia nemtsev (Sentiabr' 1941-Fevral' 1942 gg.)*. Moscow: RAN, 1995.

Oka, Natsuko. "The Korean Diaspora in Nationalizing Kazakhstan: Strategies for Survival as an Ethnic Minority." *Korean and Korean American Studies Bulletin*, 12, nos. 2–3 (2001): 89–113.

Okhotin, Nikita, and Roginskii, Arsenii. "Iz istorii 'nemetskoi operatsii' NKVD 1937-1938 gg." In *Nakazannyi narod: Repressi protiv rossiiskikh nemtsev*, edited by I.L. Shcherbakova, 35–74. Moscow: Zve'ia, 1999.

Pinkus, Benjamin, and Fleischhauer, Ingeborg. *Die Deutschen in der Sowjetunion: Geschichte einer nationalen Minderheit im 20 Jahrhundert*. Baden-Baden: Nomos Verlagsgesellschaft, 1987.

Polian, Pavel. *Ne po svoei vole: Istoriia i geografiia prinuditel'nykh migratsii v SSSR.* Moscow: OGI-Memorial, 2001.

Popov, V.P. "Gosudarvennyi terror v sovetskoi rossi 1923–1953 gg. (Istochniki I ikh interpretatsiia)," *Otechestvennye Arkhivy,* no. 2 (1992): 20–31.

Schmaltz, Eric. *Reform, "Rebirth," and Regret: The Early Autonomy Movement of Ethnic Germans in the USSR, 1955–1989.* PhD diss., University of Nebraska, 2002.

Shtraus, A., and Pankrats, S., eds. *Svidetel'stva prestuplenii.* Bishkek: Ilim, 1997.

Toews, John B. *Journeys: Mennonite Stories of Faith and Survival in Stalin's Russia.* Winnipeg: Kindred Productions, 1998.

United States Department of State. "Kazakhstan: Country Reports on Human Rights Practices, 2004." Bureau of Democracy, Human Rights, and Labor. <www.state.gov/g/drl/rls/hrrpt/2004/41689.htm> (February 2008).

Vol'ter, G.A. *Zona polnogo pokia: Rossiiskie nemtsy v gody voiny i posle nee: Svidetel'stva ocheviedetsev.* Moscow: LA Varig, 1998.

Weitz, Eric. *A Century of Genocide: Utopias of Race and Nation.* Princeton: Princeton University Press, 2003.

Wolf, Markus, and Frank, Alexander. "No Future for the Ethnic Germans in Kazakhstan?" *Aussenpolitik,* 44, no. 2 (1993): 153–62 <people.freenet.de/Wolf/1993aengl.html> (February 2008).

THIRTY-THREE

The Nationalization Campaign and the Rewriting of History

The Case of Blumenau

Méri Frotscher Kramer

During the Estado Novo ("New State," 1937–45), the Brazilian government practised an authoritarian nationalization policy to forge a greater sense of national unity. The government undertook many measures against different populations in order to homogenize them. This was intensified with Brazil's entry into World War II in 1942. Blumenau, located in the state of Santa Catarina, known in Brazil and Germany as the most successful of the German colonies in Brazil, was a focal point of the nationalization campaign and of the repression of Germans and their descendants. These facts influenced not only Blumenau's political, economical, and cultural life, but also the regional historiography. The change of the historical discourse is the subject of this chapter.

Blumenau's Past

The colony of Blumenau, founded in 1850 by Dr. Hermann Blumenau and mainly populated by German-speaking immigrants from middle and eastern Europe, soon became known as the most successful colony in Brazil. When, in 1917, Brazil declared war on Germany, the state intervened for the first time directly in German settlements: the press was nationalized and censored, and German schools were closed.[1] Although the situation normalized after World War I, fears of intervention persisted. From 1937, under Getúlio Vargas's Estado Novo, the state intervened throughout Brazil in order to integrate the regions, intervention becoming severe oppression in the case of Blumenau when Brazil declared war again on Germany in 1942.

Even before Vargas's dictatorship, the government had used nationalization to fight regionalism. With the revolution of 1930, Blumenau suffered greatly as the Republican Party, whose members were from the Itajaí valley and mostly German Brazilians, lost to the Liberal Party, whose core came from the highlands. In 1934, the Liberals increased their presence in Santa Catarina's state government, reducing the territory of Blumenau to 1,650 square kilometres (just 16 percent of its former size and now consisting only of its old districts of Blumenau-sede and Massaranduba). The prefect of Santa Catarina, Aristiliano Ramos, justified this as rationalization of the administration and as part of the nationalization process. Obviously, these measures were meant to weaken further the old elites who stood for carrying on the legacy of Dr. Blumenau. The municipal elections in 1936 were another sign of political change. The Integralist Party (Aliança Integralista Brasileira—founded in October 1932 and a right-wing movement inspired by European fascism) won in Blumenau and in other municipalities, indicating the rise to power of a new middle class.

Vargas's putsch in 1937 resulted in the strengthening of the executive, centralization of administration, economic intervention, and the founding of an umbrella labour organization controlled by the state. This nationalization policy affected all of Brazil as it also involved propaganda, censorship, and the control of the press. The pressures to nationalize became stronger for Blumenau's people, who were attracted to Nazi Germany and its ideology; increasingly, German and Nazism became synonymous in Brazil.

When Blumenau's NSDAP group was affected by the ban of foreign parties and conflict arose because of this, the demand for *Gleichschaltung* of the various German associations as a response did not take place because the old and new elites were not interested in power sharing.[2] The Vargas government had many commercial relations with Germany, and indeed was quite sympathetic to Hitler's Germany and to the German Brazilians, and some Brazilian military and civil elites had a strong affinity for Nazism. But the idea that Germans in Brazil could become a parallel power within Brazil was one of their greatest fears.[3] Until 1941, the Brazilian government fought Nazism internally, but Vargas preferred a policy that alternated between favouring the United States and Germany. In the end, however, against the background of strong economic interests, Vargas sided increasingly with the United States.

Visiting Blumenau in 1940,[4] Vargas spoke about Blumenau's economic importance and the necessity of discipline and diligence to modernize Brazil, indirectly praising the German Brazilian colonists.[5] On another occasion he emphasized that his sympathies did not mean that the state would tolerate foreign influences and that his goal was "to create only one Brazilian race with one language and culture."[6]

Nationalization was one of the main characteristics of the Estado Novo's model of industrial development as it was to prevent the supremacy of foreign interests in Brazil's key industries.[7] To reinforce the government's attitude toward Blumenau's inhabitants, also in 1940, the prefect of Santa Catarina, Nereu Ramos, dedicated a statue to its founder, with the appropriate inscription: "To Dr. Blumenau, a foreigner who could love Brazil."[8] This sounded like a warning to the German Brazilians, who in the view of the government did not love Brazil enough.

This attitude was also expressed by army and police officers writing about the nationalization campaign. They even used the expressions "foreign cysts" for German settlements and "internal enemy"[9] for Germans and their descendants, who were accused of being Nazis. This fight for nationalization was carried out on a number of fronts. A special army unit was set up in Rio de Janeiro in 1939, consisting of soldiers from Brazil's northeast and southeast. Their mission was to fight Nazism and to "convert" the foreigners and their descendants to the national spirit. In the same year, they were sent to the Blumenau area, where they behaved like occupiers: symbolically billeting in Blumenau's best shooting club, marching through the town, placing themselves in German schools, and calling up sons of colonists to serve in other regions of Brazil so as to integrate them into the nation. The army's presence in areas of German settlement was also a way to make the colonists' children feel Brazilian and to impose on them the Portuguese language.

When Brazil sided with the U.S. and declared war on Germany in 1942, the Germans were increasingly repressed. Clubs were closed; it was forbidden to speak German; many people were arrested; and some were tried at the Tribunal of National Security and even held in so-called concentration camps, mainly because of political intrigue, but also just for speaking German. Some tradesmen and businesspersons in Blumenau—Germans or their descendants—were placed on blacklists, furnished by the U.S. government. These lists included persons or firms that were charged with having commercial contacts with the Axis powers. Some of these firms were managed by "inspectors" placed there by the government. This, for example, happened in Hering's Company, the biggest textile enterprise in Blumenau,[10] a family business managed by Curt Hering, mayor between 1923 and 1930 and very influential in Blumenau's cultural life.

Nazism and the cultivation of the German language and tradition were considered a threat to national unification. The Brazilian government invested in education, patriotism, and political propaganda to build a

Brazilian identity. To this end, the majority of private and county-admin-istered schools were nationalized. In 1936, Blumenau and its rural area had had thirty-five private and thirty-six public schools,[11] but by 1943 there were only three private schools but seventy-six public schools.[12] Visiting Blu-menau in 1939, Nereu Ramos affirmed that school and army were the "foundation" on which the Brazilian nation would be built.[13] To foster the national spirit, militarism and uniforms were given prominence, and fly-ing the Brazilian flag and marching in parades through the town would soon be part of everyday life. Most important for establishing the nation was the Portuguese language.[14]

In addition to the schools, the many cultural and sports clubs became the targets for nationalization. They were not only meeting points for leisure and social activities, but also establishments of local powers and, as such, of Germanness. In order to survive, many clubs used the strategy of giving themselves new statutes, accentuating sports and recreation to the detriment of cultural activities. The churches also had to hold services in Portuguese. Postal services were censored, publishing in German was forbidden, and all printing and circulation of books was controlled.[15] The government prohibited discourses that honoured *Deutschtum*; instead, materials with a Brazilian nationalist content were published, and a cult of national heroes was introduced.

The Reinterpretation of the Past

Before World War II, various authors dedicated themselves to historical writing about Blumenau. Their main themes were the cultiva-tion of the jungle, the development of the colony, and biographies of Blu-menau's famous inhabitants, like its founder and the naturalist Dr. Fritz Müller, publications that were almost always appreciative of the German element. Until the 1930s it was possible to publish texts that explained Blu-menau's economical development on the basis of its "racial purity." For instance, in 1929, on the centenary of German immigration to Santa Cata-rina, G. Arthur Koehler, the owner of *Der Urwaldsbote*, praised the aware-ness of the inhabitants of Blumenau and of other municipalities of their identity, which they preserved through schools, cultural clubs, language, and customs. Blumenau, he wrote, prospered because of "the ability of Hermann Blumenau to lead the colony," and he accentuated that "it was not assimilation that made model colonies at the banks of the Itajaí River, but the possibility of maintaining their individuality made the new colonists into brave pioneers."[16]

The local publications of the time were preoccupied with maintaining *Deutschtum* and *Deutschbrasilianertum*. A *Deutschbrasilianer* was someone who held Brazilian citizenship, but had a German national consciousness.[17] Despite its cultural diversity, Blumenau was sometimes represented as an exclusively German ethnic community: The *Urwaldsbote*, the *Blumenauer Volkskalender* (published 1934–38), and the *Deutschbrasilianische Jugendzeitung* (published between August 1935 and July 1936) even postulated the idea that they were still a part of the *"deutsche Volksgemeinschaft."* Most Brazilian politicians and intellectuals at the time did not accept this at all.

During the Estado Novo, manifestations of German or German Brazilian identity were not tolerated; Germans and their descendants were, in the eyes of the government, resisting cultural assimilation. The writers of that time defended the necessity of cultural assimilation and rehabilitated the Mestizo—children from the union of one Amerindian and one European parent or of Mestizo parents—in Brazil's history. Chiefly through the work of the sociologist Gilberto Freyre, the Mestizo became the prototype of Brazil's national identity.[18] These ideas influenced the local historiography,.especially through those writers who took part in the nationalization program. One of them, the ex-army officer and civil servant Theobaldo Jamundá, wrote about Blumenau, honouring the Mestizo as helper and adviser to the first colonists: "This Mestizo always preceded the Europeans, even guided them and taught them how to succeed in the rough nature without the artifices of civilization."[19] Jamundá accentuated the role of the Mestizo, having Portuguese and African roots, in order to connect the history of the Itajaí valley with the Brazilian nation, discrediting the German immigrants as "thankless guests,"[20] with "rough racism"[21] and resisting assimilation.

The end of Estado Novo and the return to democracy in October 1945 did not mean that all changes were reversed or without effect. Speaking German was no longer forbidden, but official organs and others still maintained that the German Brazilians should "brazilianize" themselves (*abrasileirar-se*). In Blumenau, traumas and resentment due to violence, persecution, abuse, and conflict during World War II still existed, but were not openly discussed, as they evoked feelings of discomfort; the repression and the themes of Nazism and nationalization remained taboo subjects.

The most important change, however, was the impossibility of defending the maintaining of a German identity. That German was spoken in public again renewed discourses about the necessity of brazilianization. In 1946, the local magazine *O Vale do Itajaí* published a diatribe by Osias Guimarães, demanding a decision from the Germans and their descendants to either "speak German and be dominated by people from outside, with the risk of prison, extortion, and other absurdities," or "to speak Portuguese well, to try to know better the homeland, to have honest and sincere friends, and then occupy posts of their legitimacy."[22] During World War II, some German-speaking civil servants had been replaced by 'Brazilians,' and many civil servants, employees, and self-employed of Portuguese descent had moved to Blumenau, hence the phrase "people from outside."

Parts of Blumenau's German Brazilian elites soon realized the advantage of affirming their Brazilian identity as a political and economical strategy. So, in the 1947 democratic elections, they regained power. The União Democrática Nacional (UDN) won, and the new mayor was of German descent. This success and the following UDN electoral victories in Blumenau were politically and culturally very significant because they showed that the majority rejected the Partido Social Democrático—nicknamed "party of the insiders," as it included Nereu Ramos, the former prefect and architect of the Estado Novo in Santa Catarina.

However, the preoccupation with the assimilation of German descendants persisted in many political and intellectual circles of Santa Catarina. At the First Congress of Catarinense History, in 1948, it became obvious that the time of nationalization was remembered as a time of confrontation between the Luso-Brazilian—the Azorean descendants at Santa Catarina's coast who are pejoratively called *caboclos* (indolent and carefree) by those in the Itajaí valley—and the prevailing German culture.[23] Gilberto Freyre's ideas during World War II concerning the Luso-Brazilian culture had had a great impact. Freyre was obviously influenced by the anti-German ideas of that time.[24] At this congress, the Luso-Brazilians were now described as founders of Luso-Brazilian culture in the state, appreciated because of their inclination to cultural assimilation, and as men who took part in the creation of the Brazilian identity in Santa Catarina.[25] Until Blumenau's centennial festivities in 1950, the Brazilian press vacillated on the subject of Germans in Blumenau. *O Cruzeiro*, the most important Brazilian illustrated review, renewed the polemic about the use of the German language in Blumenau,[26] but the answer from the local press and representatives of the Itajaí valley was fast and fierce: The lawyer and representative Max Tavares D'Amaral—who had married into the Hering family in 1941—accused the writer of the article of being "thoughtless," "prejudiced," and "ignorant" on the subject, and to be afflicted with an "inferiority complex."[27] Antônio Konder Reis—a member of the Konder oligarchy, which had dominated the state prior to the 1930 revolution, and another deputy of the Itajaí valley—even indicated that the "campaign against the German colonization in Santa Catarina" was caused by envy. He defended the German Brazilians and recalled the former repression against them, criticizing "the regrettable confusion that was made between Germans and Nazis, because only 10 percent of the colonists had sympathies for Nazism."[28] He remembered the German contributions to the state's economy and to "society and the arts." This discourse was not new

and was often used to affirm the German Brazilian identity, thus defending the German Brazilians when they were criticized.

After Blumenau's centennial festivities in 1950, a commemorative book
was printed that showed all aspects from Blumenau's point of view. It reaf-
firmed its economical contribution, celebrated it, and referred to all Blumenau inhabitants. The elites, descendants of the old German Brazilian
oligarchies as well as some who came to power during the Estado Novo,
celebrated the town's progress and their own economical power. The patriotism of the German Brazilians in the past was emphasized by reprinting
articles of the Catholic priest Emmendoerfer and of the late Curt Hering,
honouring the participation of the immigrants and their descendants in
wars for Brazil, for example the war against Paraguay (1865–70), the bat-
tles for the consolidation of the Republic (1889), and the participation in
World War II.[29] Through the emphasis on bloodshed for Brazil and the
"value and patriotism" of people from Blumenau, Brazil was shown as a
homeland of immigrants and their descendants.

The question of assimilation was not only a matter of the municipality's past. Max Tavares D'Amaral, who had defended Blumenau in public before, wrote an article discussing the problem of "assimilation and
acculturation"[30] of foreigners and descendants at present. He explained
how this problem had been handled so far and emphasized the importance of the "emotional assimilation" to the "Luso-Brazilian tradition" without using force. He often cited Freyre's book *O mundo que o português
criou* (The World That the Portuguese Founded), written in 1938, considering Freyre a "great authority" on this theme. According to Freyre,
Portuguese culture was capable of assimilating other cultures, and Blumenau was a "new Brazilian" town, because a process of assimilation was
going on. This could be seen in the gestures, in the manner of walking,
in the practice of "traditional Brazilian" behaviour. For him, the German descendants were already "half converted" or "on their way" to
"*brasilidade*."[31]

To build his argument, D'Amaral referred to the book of Freyre that
was published before World War II, not to his anti-German writings during the conflict. In this way, D'Amaral stressed "the feeling of Brazilianness"
of the Itajaí valley inhabitants. Although he used the words *assimilation* and
acculturation, terms often heard during the nationalization campaign, he
did not defend the complete assimilation of German immigrants to the
"Luso-Brazilian tradition." He argued that Luso-Brazilians should incor-
porate positive habits and customs of the foreigners and defended the
cultural plurality as positive and necessary for Brazil's progress.[32] By so
doing he indirectly criticized the authoritarian attempts of cultural homogenization during the nationalization campaign.

D'Amaral's text exemplifies some changes of the discourse about the inter-ethnical relationships and the assimilation of German descendants. While in 1929, on the German colony's centenary, the maintenance of ethnical borders was still affirmed, now the necessity of acculturation was defended. The nationalization's campaign had not been completely in vain.

This was quite noticeable from the contents of the commemoration book where old ideas about Blumenau's past and its identity were affirmed, but also new insights brought forward. The industrialist Ingo Hering— Curt Hering's son and successor—wrote an article about Blumenau's development, emphasizing as its reason the "technical abilities" of the immigrants and their "initiative" to change forest into an industrialized region.[33] He did not say German immigrants, but immigrants in general, thereby not alluding to the subject of implicit German superiority. In 1937, on Colonist Day, for example, Ingo Hering had expressed in public an anti-assimilation position,[34] but in 1950, he did not.

Other authors, formerly connected to the Estado Novo, also participated in the commemoration book. José Ferreira da Silva wrote about Blumenau's history, but in a factual manner, focusing on the historical description of the nineteenth century.[35] Paulo Malta Ferraz, a police officer in the region during the Estado Novo from 1942 to 1946, emphasized in his article the contribution of the Brazilian Empire to Blumenau's development: the governmental loans in 1851 and 1855, and the cession of the colony Blumenau to the government in 1860 were cited as fundamental facts for its success. Ferraz also affirmed the importance of the "national element" in the local history, as during the Estado Novo, and Angelo Dias, the "fearless *caboclo*" who guided Dr. Blumenau, was also mentioned. With the same intention, Ferraz named the "bold Brazilians" who defended the colony against the Indians.[36] Jamundá, known in some German Brazilian circles as *Deutschfresser*, was by this time director of the agricultural school in Blumenau and wrote harmlessly on agricultural themes.

Despite the different themes and positions, the commemoration book emphasized Blumenau's progress and presented an image of what it meant to be "good Brazilians" now and then. In order to stay in power, the local elites had to adapt their discourses in public and to negotiate their identities, which they did successfully. Proclaiming Blumenau's progress and Brazilianness became the most important elements in the representation of the municipality in the 1950s.

Conclusion

The nationalization campaign was not able to completely replace German with Portuguese, but made it impossible to defend *Deutsch-*

tum and *Deutschbrasilianertum* in the public sphere. The repression during the nationalization period and the decline of Nazi Germany made criticism of the assimilation of German descendants no longer tolerable. Traumas, hatred, and resentment still persisted, but were not openly discussed. The change from defending the *Deutschtum* to affirming the Brazilianness was necessary so soon after World War II to be able to return industrialists of German descent to local government. This does not mean that all of them totally accepted the discourse of complete assimilation. For those who were not in power during the Estado Novo, the affirmation of Brazilianness was more a defensive action than an act of conviction.

A considerable change is visible in the discourses about Blumenau's cultural identity on these two centenary commemorations. While in 1929 the pride of being German descendants was celebrated, in 1950 it was the pride of being from Blumenau, namely being hard-working and Brazilian. The superior ability to work, in the past explicitly conferred on German descendants, now was associated with all inhabitants and taken as the main reason for the municipality's progress. Thus, a small progress in the building of a hybrid identity can already be recognized.

Over time, even if German was spoken less or, in many cases, given up, it was no longer the language but other criteria that were used to build a German Brazilian identity: the German ancestry above all and a "German concept of life," including being hard working. Especially since the first Oktoberfest in 1984—today the second biggest festival in Brazil and one of the largest Oktoberfests in the Americas—Blumenau is commonly known as the Brazilian Germany. Ironically, this image, which caused repression and violence in the past, nowadays attracts thousands of Brazilian tourists to Blumenau every year.

Notes

1 Seyferth, "Os imigrantes," 199.
2 Moraes, *Konflikt und Anerkennung;* Müller, *Nationalsozialismus in Lateinamerika.*
3 D'Araújo, *O Estado Novo,* 37.
4 Frotscher, "A visita de Getúlio Vargas," 27–38.
5 "O discurso de Blumenau," 1.
6 Politisches Archiv des Auswärtigen Amtes, Berlin, R 104939, Political report of the German Embassy in Brazil, Rio de Janeiro, 30 March 1938, p. 2.
7 D'Araújo, *O Estado Novo,* 44.
8 Frotscher, "Mãos que esculpem a memória no espaço urbano," 105–30.
9 For example, Jamundá, *O Itajaí-Açu e outras águas,* 52.
10 Frotscher, "A Segunda Guerra Mundial," 1–11.
11 Klug, "A escola teuto-catarinense," 223.
12 See *Relatórios dos negócios administrativos do município de Blumenau apresentados ao interventor federal no Estado, Nereu Ramos.*
13 Ramos, *A obra nacionalizadora do Estado Novo,* 12.
14 Campos, "As intervenções do Estado," 149–66.

15 Frotscher, "Intervenções do Estado," 74–88.
16 Koehler, "Die vor uns waren," 15. Translations from German are by the author.
17 Seyferth, *Nacionalismo e identidade étnica,* 214–19.
18 Ortiz, *Cultura brasileira e identidade nacional,* 41.
19 Jamundá, *Indaial,* 20.
20 Jamundá, *Indaial,* 19.
21 Jamundá, *O Itajaí-Açu e outras águas,* 10.
22 Guimarães, "Aviso aos blumenauenses."
23 Boléo, *O congresso de Florianópolis,* 47, quoted in Flores, *A farra do boi,* 115.
24 Freyre, *Uma cultura ameaçada,* 56 and 61, quoted in Falcão, *Entre ontem e amanhã,* 179.
25 Flores, *A farra do boi,* 133.
26 Queiroz, "Olhos Azuis," used expressions such as "racial canker," "upside down Brazil," "border of the Brazilian nation," "a foreign and unfriendly country" in her article entitled "Blue Eyes."
27 "Notável discurso," 1.
28 Reis, "Em defesa da colonização alemã," 242.
29 Emmendoerfer, "Blumenau no exército nacional"; C. Hering, "O 28 de julho de 1893."
30 D'Amaral, "Assimilação e aculturação," 355.
31 Freyre, *O mundo que o português criou,* 35–36.
32 D'Amaral, "Assimilação e aculturação," 363.
33 I. Hering, "Desenvolvimento da indústria blumenauense," 161.
34 I. Hering, "Dialog über den 'Dia do Colono,'" 38–42.
35 Silva, "Blumenau."
36 Ferraz, "A contribuição do governo," 139.

Archival Material

Politisches Archiv des Auswärtiges Amt, Berlin. R 104939. Political report of the German Embassy in Brazil. Rio de Janeiro, 30 March 1938.
Relatório dos negócios administrativos do município de Blumenau apresentados ao interventor federal no Estado, Nereu Ramos. Blumenau: 1937, 1938, 1939, 1940, 1941, 1942, and 1943.

Works Cited

Boléo, Manuel de Paiva. *O congresso de Florianópolis, comemorativo do bicentenário da colonização açoriana.* Coimbra: Coimbra Ed. Ltda, 1950.
Campos, Cynthia Machado. "As intervenções do Estado nas escolas estrangeiras de Santa Catarina na era Vargas." In *História de Santa Catarina: estudos contemporâneos,* edited by Ana Brancher, 149–66. Florianópolis: Letras Contemporâneas, 1999.
D'Amaral, Max Tavares. "Assimilação e aculturação dos estrangeiros e seus descendentes no Vale do Itajaí" In *Centenário de Blumenau. 1850–1950,* 355–63. Blumenau: Edição da Comissão de Festejos, 1950.
D'Araújo, Maria Celina. *O Estado Novo.* Rio de Janeiro: Jorge Zahar Ed., 2000.
Emmendoerfer, Ernesto. "Blumenau no exército nacional." In *Centenário de Blumenau. 1850–1950,* 437–45, Blumenau: Edição da Comissão de Festejos, 1950.

Falcão, Luiz Felipe. *Entre ontem e amanhã: diferença cultural, tensões sociais e separatismo em Santa Catarina no século XX*. Itajaí: Ed. Univali, 2000.

Ferraz, Paulo Malta. "A contribuição do governo e do elemento nacional na colonização de Blumenau," In *Centenário de Blumenau. 1850–1950*. Blumenau: Edição da Comissão de Festejos, 1950, 139.

Flores, Maria Bernardete Ramos. *A farra do boi: palavras, sentidos, ficções*, 2nd edition. Florianópolis: Ed. UFSC, 1998.

Freyre, Gilberto. *O mundo que o português criou*. Rio de Janeiro: José Olympio Editora, 1940.

———. *Uma cultura ameaçada: a luso-brasileira*. Recife: Gabinete Português de Leitura de Pernambuco, 1940.

Frotscher, Méri. "A Segunda Guerra Mundial e as intervenções do Estado na esfera de produção: o caso da Cia. Hering de Blumenau." In *Anais do Simpósio Muitas faces de uma guerra: 60 anos do término da Segunda Guerra Mundial e o processo de nacionalização no Sul do Brasil*, 2005. <www.cce.udesc.br/cem/simposioudesc/anais/st4/st4meri.doc> (March 2008).

———. "A visita de Getúlio Vargas a Blumenau em 1940 e seus significados." *Blumenau em Cadernos*, no. 11/12 (1998), 27–38.

———. "Intervenções do Estado na imprensa de Blumenau (1937–1945): Nacionalização, controle político e ações das elites locais." *Blumenau em Cadernos*, no. 1/2 (2005): 74–88.

———. "Mãos que esculpem a memória no espaço urbano: investimentos em monumentos em Blumenau na primeira metade do século xx." In *História e poder: a reprodução das elites em Santa Catarina*, edited by Waldir Rampinelli, 105–30. Florianópolis: Insular, 2003.

Guimarães, Osias. "Aviso aos blumenauenses," *Revista O Vale do Itajaí*, no. 17 e 18 (August 1946): n.p.

Hering, Curt. "O 28 de julho de 1893," in *Centenário de Blumenau. 1850–1950*, 440–43. Blumenau: Edição da Comissão de Festejos, 1950.

Hering, Ingo. "Desenvolvimento da indústria blumenauense," in *Centenário de Blumenau, 1850–1950*, 161–72, Blumenau: Edição da Comissão de Festejos, 1950.

———. "Dialog über den ´Dia do Colono.'" in *Unser ist heute der Tag! Festbüchlein zum 25. Juli*, edited by Blumenauer Lokalauschuss, 38˚–42. Blumenau: G.A. Koehler Verlag, 1937.

Jamundá, Theobaldo C. *Indaial, município do Vale do Itajaí-Açu*. N.p, 1943.

———. *O Itajaí-Açu e outras águas: ensaio histórico-descritivo*. Blumenau: Tipografia e Livraria Blumenauense, 1945.

Klug, João. "A escola teuto-catarinense e oprocesso de modernização em Santa Catarina—a ação da igreja luterana através das escolas (1871–1938)." PhD thesis. São Paulo: Universidade de São Paulo, 1997.

Koehler, G.A. "Die vor uns waren." in *Zur Jahrhundertfeier*, edited by G. Artur Koehler, 14–18. Blumenau, Verlag G.A. Koehler, 1929.

Moraes, Luis Edmundo de Souza. *Konflikt und Anerkennung: die Orstsgruppen der NSDAP in Blumenau und in Rio de Janeiro*. Berlin: Metropol Verlag, 2005.

Müller, Jürgen. *Nationalsozialismus in Lateinamerika: die Auslandsorganisation der NSDAP in Argentinien, Brasilien, Chile und Mexiko, 1931–1945*. Stuttgart: Verlag Hans-Dieter Heinz, Akademischer Verlag, 1997.

"Notável discurso do deputado Max Tavares D'Amaral." *Revista O Vale do Itajaí*, no. 50 (1949), 1.

"O discurso de Blumenau." *Jornal Cidade de Blumenau*, no. 44 (1940): 1.

Ortiz, Renato. *Cultura brasileira e identidade nacional*, 5th edition. São Paulo: Brasiliense, 1994.

Queiroz, Rachel de. "Olhos Azuis." *Revista O Cruzeiro*, no. 19 (1949): n.p.

Ramos, Nereu. *A obra nacionalizadora do Estado Novo. Discurso pronunciado em Blumenau, no dia 21 de maio de 1939*. Florianópolis: Imprensa Oficial do Estado, 1939.

Reis, Antônio Carlos Konder. "Em defesa da colonização alemã." In *São Pedro de Alcântara. 1829–1999. Aspectos de sua história*, edited by Toni. V. Jochen, 233–46. São Pedro de Alcântara: Coordenação dos Festejos, 1999.

Seyferth, Giralda. *Nacionalismo e identidade étnica: a ideologia germanista e o grupo étnico teuto-brasileiro numa comunidade do Vale do Itajaí*. Florianópolis: FCC, 1982.

———. "Os imigrantes e a campanha de nacionalização do Estado Novo." in *Repensando o Estado Novo*, edited by Dulce Pandolfi, 199–228. Rio de Janeiro: FGV, 1999.

Silva, José F. da. *Blumenau: notícia estatístico-descritiva*. Florianópolis: Imprensa Oficial do Estado, November 1939.

THIRTY-FOUR

Pennsylvania German in Kansas

Language Change or Loss?

Jörg Meindl

Pennsylvania German (PG), spoken mainly by Amish and Mennonites in the United States and Canada, is an immigrant language in contact with American and Canadian English. PG is of special interest for research on language change because it is maintained by some groups but subject to language loss in other groups; therefore, an understanding of the development of PG can help to solve the problem of predicting the outcome of language change. This chapter uses the specific situation of a PG speech community in Kansas to describe the necessary components for an analysis of language change processes. It shows that the use of linguistic evidence as a predictor of language maintenance, including language change, or language loss can only succeed when the data, on which this evidence is based, are compared to data from other German dialects. In addition to language-internal factors, extralinguistic factors and the sociolinguistic context of the speech community also need to be considered as factors for language maintenance and loss.

Introduction

Language change is a natural process and not necessarily a sign of language loss, defined here as language use shifting toward the dominant language. Research on language loss has identified numerous linguistic processes as evidence of language change but many appear with both decaying languages as well as with languages not threatened by loss.[1] Using the example of PG in an Old Order Amish speech community in

431

Anderson County, Kansas (Kansas PG), this chapter will discuss several linguistic processes and features, which could be seen as an indication of language loss but are not necessarily evidence of loss if they are looked at in isolation. This analysis of these processes and features confirms the results of other studies on PG that have shown that PG is maintained in sectarian Anabaptist groups, which is in the more conservative groups such as Old Order Amish, while it is abandoned in non-sectarian groups[2] (cf. chapter 2). Analysing the potential evidence of language loss can help determine what is needed to predict language loss in immigrant languages.

A considerable amount of research has already been done about PG in different areas of the United States and Canada, but not very much is known about PG speakers in Kansas. This chapter is based on data from the early stages of an ongoing research project. The data are drawn from translation tasks[3] and short interviews with nine speakers and field observations from several visits to the Amish community from May to August 2006. These are preliminary findings due to the limited number of informants and the use of translation tasks and interviews rather than naturally occurring conversation. Nevertheless, the study can give an insight into ongoing developments in PG in Kansas and suggest further research avenues.

Language Change and Language Loss

In ongoing processes of language change, it is difficult to predict whether the change is going to result in maintenance or loss. It can also be difficult to distinguish whether an observed change is caused internally by the language structure itself or externally by contact with another language. The results can be identical. An example is the loss of the dative case in PG, which some researchers attribute to contact with English, while others point out that several German dialects reduce their case inventory in a similar way but without having contact to English.[4] This shows that an external influence (e.g., contact with English) as well as internal structural characteristics of German dialects could be at the heart of the dative loss. With regard to PG, most researchers now assume dative case loss to be caused by the structural evolution of German dialects, accelerated by the contact with English.[5]

Language loss takes place in language contact situations involving bi- or multilingual speakers who give up their first language in favour of the contact language. Language loss can be observed when the linguistic structure of the first language converges with that of the contact language. Consequently, linguistic contact phenomena such as code-switching, lexical borrowing, loan translations, and grammatical interferences in areas such as word order have been described as crucial indicators of possible language loss.[6] Such contact phenomena indicate language loss when they result in "ungrammatical" sentences or reduce the functionality of the language.[7] They are neither the only signs of language loss[8] nor do they always indicate linguistic loss, since they can also be a communicative enrichment.[9] Another indication that language loss is underway can be extreme variability,[10] while a certain degree of variability or variation is a common phenomenon in language change and does not necessarily indicate loss.[11]

Linguistic evidence alone may, therefore, not be sufficient to predict the loss of a language. As Jane Hill concludes, the same linguistic processes may appear in maintained languages as well as in dying languages, and they often only differ in speed.[12] This suggests that we need to examine not only what is changing but also how the changes occur. Language loss is likely in progress when the core structure of the language has been converted to the contact language. Furthermore, the loss of the functionality of the language can be used as a marker of language loss,[13] although sometimes functional losses in one sector are compensated in other sectors.[14] A marker for functional loss is a lack of productivity: when a language shows no innovations, it is not able to adjust to changing communicative needs and thus cannot survive.[15]

Ethnographic Profile of Kansas Pennsylvania Germans

In Kansas, PG speakers live in different Anabaptist groups with different degrees of religious conservatism, with the Old Order Amish as the most conservative group. There are two Old Order Amish church districts in Anderson County in eastern Kansas, which are the focus of this study. There are also six church districts in Reno County around Yoder and Partridge in southeastern Kansas. Four new districts were founded since 2005 in northeastern (Washington County) and southeastern Kansas (Bourbon and Labette Counties). In Anderson County, forty Old Order Amish families live west of the county seat Garnett. While several other Amish settlements in Kansas failed, the Anderson County districts have managed to maintain their settlement since 1903.[16] The two church districts in Anderson County exhibit a lifestyle typical of Old Order Amish groups, with the horse and buggy as major means of transportation, a dress code, church services held at members' homes, no electricity in the house, and restrictions on the choice of profession—the Anderson County Amish are mainly farmers and carpenters. Living in Kansas has required the group to change from the old lifestyle: because conditions in Kansas make farming by horse difficult, machinery has been allowed for farming since the 1930s. Furthermore, the telephone has been allowed on the farm property (but not in the house) to keep the carpentry shops connected to customers.

Linguistic Profile of Kansas Pennsylvania German

The linguistic profile of the Anderson County Amish is typical of Old Order Amish.[17] PG is the dominant language in the domains of church service and family life, and also very important for in-group communication. During church service, the sermons are entirely in PG, with a considerable number of English loan words and expressions. The hymns and the bible text are in Standard German, which is not used otherwise. All domains exhibit some code-switching—the purposeful alternation of two or more languages in a single conversation—with the highest amount occurring in in-group communication. The informants report that children speak PG as their first language, while picking up some English words or phrases from family members, and later use English in public school. The PG in Anderson County contains many English words with or without a German-based equivalent, furthermore some English grammar. Therefore, the PG in Anderson County can be categorized as a "composite language,"[18] integrating elements from two languages in its structure, and linguistically not completely separated from both languages.[19]

Speech communities of the Old Order Amish in Kansas have fluent speakers of PG in all generations and a relatively strict domain structure: PG speakers clearly associate certain domains (church service, family, interaction with customers, etc.) with the dominance of one language. This phenomenon has often been described as diglossia. Language use in PG speech communities in Kansas can thus be categorized as stable bilingualism.[20] Stable bilingualism has been described as ensuring the use of PG but at the same time supporting more linguistic change than in speech communities without clear domain structure. While several scholars regard stable bilingualism as a starting point for language loss,[21] Eric Hamp points out that stable bilingualism enables speakers to use repair strategies that can help to maintain their first language, including what he calls "healthy repair." Such repairs adapt some phonological features of the minority language to the contact language, enabling contact of the languages without converging them completely.[22]

Kansas PG exhibits several possible markers of language loss as described in the research literature. Influences from English (contact phenomena) can be found mainly in the lexicon but also on other language levels. Speakers use many loan words. Certain words exist only as English loans while others have PG equivalents. In contrast to Roger Andersen's hypothesis that mainly uncommon words with a low frequency of usage are replaced by loans,[23] observation and interview data show that PG in Kansas has many English words that are frequently used and can be considered a core part of the vocabulary. This includes the English words for weekdays, months, and numbers, different designations for relatives (such as mother, father, aunt), certain vegetables, some furniture items, and terms for technological innovations. Furthermore, common verbs are borrowed (e.g., to farm, to teach, to be concerned, to realize, to figure).

English loans appear on different degrees of phonological, grammatical, and morphological integration into the PG system. Verbs are inflected according to PG grammar, and the verb morphology follows Standard German rules. This means, for example, that German prefixes are added to English verb stems, e.g., *drowelde* (welding to it) and *druffwelde* (welding on top). Sometimes German verbs are rendered as prefix-verb with English elements, e.g., *readykrigge* (to get something finished). The specific pattern of German past participle formation is also applied to English loans: the prefix *ge-* is added or omitted according to the German rule that only verbs with a stressed first syllable form the past participle with a prefix (*gejudged* or concerned) and inserted between prefix and verb root (e.g., *rausgegushed*). The assignment of the auxiliary verbs "to have" and "to be" usually also follows German rules.

Loan translations (such as *rausdrehe* for English "turning out") exist for individual words as well as longer expressions. A semantic reduction of the German lexicon can be observed with the lack of the distinction between the two different verbs for the English "to know," which are in PG *wissə* (Standard German *wissen*) and *kennə* (Standard German *kennen*). Some speakers use *wissə* relating to a person, where according to Standard German grammar *kennə* should have been used. The main source of contact phenomena in the syntax are loan translations of expressions (calques). Expressions are mostly transferred into PG while partly or completely maintaining English word order:

EXAMPLE 1

Wenn du usch ihn bessə gwissd hedschd, wär schdoff bessə ausgedreht unn du wärschd bessə ab. [INFORMANT 2]
[TRANSLATION OF WENKER SENTENCE 18: If only you had known him! Things would have turned out differently and you would be better off.]

In approximately 80 percent of the possible sentences in the data collected for this study, prepositional phrases and time expressions appear at the post-position behind the infinitive or past participle in analytical constructions, as observed also by Barbara Meister Ferré.[24] The speakers in these data also move reflexive expressions into post-position, as in example 2c below. However, most of the data used for this analysis came from a translation task where post-positioning agrees with English syntax, and thus the interpretation as a sign of convergence to English is problematic. Since translation tasks have several drawbacks for analyses of this kind,[25] more data from different task forms are needed for a thorough analysis.[26] A second problem is that sentences with post-positioning, as the following three examples, are also common in spoken Standard German and in other German dialects without any contact to English.[27]

EXAMPLE 2

a. *In de winder dihn die druggene bledder rumfliege in di luft.* [INFORMANT 1]
   [TRANSLATION OF WENKER SENTENCE 1: In the winter the dry leaves fly around in the air.]

b. *Wu ma hääm kumme sinn ledschd nacht...* [INFORMANT 3]
   [TRANSLATION OF WENKER SENTENCE 24: When we got home last night...]

c. *...awwə sie henns geduh sich selwə* [INFORMANT 1]
   [TRANSLATION OF WENKER SENTENCE 20: ... but they did it themselves]

Simplification processes that have parallels in other German dialects can be observed in the morphosyntax. The simple past tense exists only for the verb "to be" and verb endings are reduced. Kansas PG has not completely established a unified plural ending as in other PG speech communities.[28] Case endings are widely reduced; the accusative and nominative seem to form a common case, except for personal pronouns; the genitive case is not used; the dative case is usually merged with the accusative or common case; however, some dative forms are retained after the prepositions *mit* or *zu*. Furthermore, relative pronouns in Kansas PG do not show case or gender distinction anymore; only unified singular (*des, es, was*) and plural forms exist (*die, wu*).

Because all these phenomena are not exclusive to dialects in contact with English, they are not necessarily caused by contact with English. Some of them, however, result in partial convergence with English. Kansas PG also exhibits processes that establish or maintain a distinct structure different from English. For example, all German tenses (except simple past), passive voice, and subjunctive mood are maintained. Subordinate clauses (e.g., relative clauses) are not eliminated and the word order in these clauses maintains the typical German final position of the finite verb. Additionally, Kansas PG shows a significant use of *duhn* (to do) plus an infinite verb replacing finite verbs. Some scholars have ascribed to *duhn* an emphatic or aspectual function, similar to the English "to do" paraphrase.[29] However, the PG structure is not restricted to an emphatic function or to aspect and, as several phenomena described before, can also be found in dialects in Germany itself.[30] The "duh" paraphrase is restricted to present tense and the majority of the sentences are still constructed with finite verbs. Furthermore, it seems to be used interchangeably with finite verbs by the same speaker in free variation.

EXAMPLE 3

a. *Ich deed sache die helft vun dem dihn baure unn die anner helft duhd dairye unn some wu dairye dihn oda melke dihn dihn ah baure.* [INFORMANT 1, INTERVIEW]
[I would say half of them do farming and the other half does dairying and some who do dairying or milking also do farming]

b. *Die die baure die deede äh weeze unn korn those are the main crops. Si deede wann se dairye henn widder mee korn wachse vielleicht fer silage.* [INFORMANT 1, INTERVIEW]
[Those who farm would do wheat and corn, those are the main crops. They would, if they do dairy, they have again more wheat and corn growing, maybe for silage.]

Distinct from both Standard German and English is also the existence of a progressive with *am* or *an* plus an infinitive verb (*Ich bin am älda were alle daag* [INFORMANT 4] [I'm getting older every day]). The formation of a progressive has sometimes been attributed to the influence of English. Like the *duhn* paraphrase, however, it is a structure that can also be found in German dialects in the linguistic motherland.

Conclusion

The analysis of Kansas PG has shown that several simplifications of the linguistic structure have occurred. However, many of these simplification processes happen in a similar way in other German dialects, sometimes in Standard German and also in other languages.[31] Some of these simplification processes result in partial convergence with American English. Loan words and code-switching infuse English vocabulary into PG and sometimes these loans replace PG equivalents. Loan words are often morphologically and phonologically integrated into the PG system. Loan translations import American English syntax, although restricted to these expressions and rarely spreading into the German system. The highest level of convergence, besides in the lexicon, can be seen in the morphology, where the dative case is seldom used and nominative and dative cases show a tendency to become a common case. The progressive construction and the *duhn* paraphrase differ from Standard German and have analogous structures in English, but they also differ from English in usage and in the way they are formed.

PG in Kansas has basically kept its German linguistic structure, since all moods, voices, and tenses except simple past are maintained. Noun plurals resist the English unified plural ending, and the German phonology is mainly unchanged. Furthermore, the verb-final word order in subordinate clauses remains intact, as does the positioning of infinitives and past participles (with a few post-positioned participles in some cases).

The changes that are taking place in Kansas PG are mainly predictable and do not exhibit a large amount of variability. Ongoing simplification does not always result in convergence with English, but sometimes develops distinct forms separate from either Standard German or English. Most of the changes parallel developments in German dialects that have no contact to English. Therefore, they cannot be attributed exclusively to English influence. These developments are more likely a result of the structure of Germanic or Indo-European languages, perhaps accelerated by the influence of English.[32]

Contact phenomena and simplification often fulfill a function for PG, e.g., by expanding expressive possibilities, enabling innovation or repair to fill gaps in the lexicon. Taken as a whole, contact phenomena in Kansas PG rarely reduce the functionality of the language but rather add communicative options. Miriam Ben-Rafael has already suggested that contact phenomena might not be the crucial factor in language loss.[33] PG in Kansas—spoken fluently by people of all generations—shows that convergence processes can help maintain a language by enabling the usage in a changing communicative environment.[34] The reasons why this language is not lost in this community may be found in the attitude of the speakers toward their language rather than in linguistic markers alone. For PG speakers, the motivation to speak PG is the wish to maintain their distinct Anabaptist identity.[35]

This analysis of PG in Kansas shows that predictions whether a changing language is in the process of language loss require five procedures. First, comparison with the linguistic motherland or other speech islands must be done to be able to interpret the ongoing linguistic phenomena. Second, the factor of productivity should have a prominent position: does a language innovate and integrate influences from the contact language or do the speakers simply switch languages? Third, the linguistic changes must be analysed in the context of extralinguistic factors. These factors include the frequency of use of the language, the structure of bilingualism in the community, attitudes, and the strength of the ethnic and cultural identities. Fourth, loan words and other contact phenomena should not automatically be seen as disturbance in the linguistic system but rather as a part of the specific grammar of the examined language. English loans are a part of the Kansas PG lexicon; as one informant in Garnett expressed it: "We have a lot of English in our German, but that is how it has always been." Fifth, the functionality of the language should be at the centre of the analysis. As long as the language has a function and uses the contact language as a source for innovation, it may be maintained. Since the Old Order Amish in Kansas integrated English influences into their language and Kansas PG fulfills an important function as an identity marker in the speech community, it will survive—not necessarily in spite of linguistic change, but because this change helps the PG speakers to adapt to new communicative needs.

Notes

1   For phonology, see Hamp, "On Signs of Health," 201; for lexicon, see Sasse, "Language Decay," 68; for semantics, see Hutz, "Is There a Natural Process?" 198–99.
2   Louden, "Syntactic Change," 81–85.
3   The translation task consisted of forty sentences designed by the German dialectologist Georg Wenker in the 1870s (so-called Wenker sentences) in an English version and a word list, both as used in the Linguistic Atlas of Kansas German Dialects project at the University of Kansas. The material is accessible at <www2.ku.edu/~germanic/LAKGD/Atlas_Intro.shtml> (March 2008).
4   For an overview of the discussion see Keel, "Reduction and Loss," 94–95, 101.
5   Huffines, "Convergence and Language Death," 17.
6   Sercombe, "Language Maintenance," 3–4.
7   Sasse, "Language Decay," 76..
8   Sasse, "Theory," 16.
9   Köpke and Schmid, "Language Attrition," 32; Ben-Rafael, "Language Contact and Attrition," 183.
10   Sasse, "Language Decay," 76.
11   Sercombe, "Language Maintenance," 2.
12   Hill, "Social Function," 149.
13   Sasse, "Theory," 16.
14   Hill, "Social Function," 155.
15   Sasse, "Language Decay," 69.
16   See Luthy, *Amish in America*.
17   See for example Huffines, "Pennsylvania German"; Meister Ferré, *Stability and Change*.
18   In analogy to Myers-Scotton's concept of "composite matrix language"; see also Fuller "Borrowing Trouble," 193.
19   Gardner-Chloros, "Code-Switching," 69.
20   Fishman, "Measurement and Description"; Louden, "Syntactic Change," 85.
21   Brenzinger and Dimmendaal, "Social Contexts," 3–4.
22   Hamp, "On Signs of Health," 204.
23   Andersen, "Linguistic Attributes," 97.
24   Meister Ferré, *Stability and Change*, 106–07.
25   Yağmur, "Issues," 141–43; Huffines, "The Function of Aspect," 140, 142, 151.
26   Meister Ferré, *Stability and Change*, 110.
27   Meister Ferré, *Stability and Change*, 104.
28   Meister Ferré, *Stability and Change*, 30.
29   For an overview see Huffines, "The Function of Aspect," 14–50.
30   Costello, "Periphrastic Duh Construction," 243.
31   Huffines, "Convergence and Language Death," 17.

32 Huffines, "Convergence and Language Death," 17.
33 Ben-Rafael, "Language Maintenance," 166.
34 See Meister Ferré, *Stability and Change*, 112.
35 Huffines, "Pennsylvania German," 55.

Interview Sources

Nine Old Order Amish Pennsylvania German speakers in Anderson County, Kansas. Interviews by Jörg Meindl, May to August 2006.

Works Cited

Andersen, Roger W. "Determining the Linguistic Attributes of Language Attrition." In *The Loss of Language Skills*, edited by Richard D. Lambert and Barbara F. Freed, 83–118. Rowley, MA: Newbury House, 1982.

Ben-Rafael, Miriam. "Language Contact and Attrition." In *First Language Attrition: Interdisciplinary Perspectives on Methodological Issues*, edited by Monika S. Schmid, Barbara Köpke, Merel Keijzer, and Lina Weilemar, 165–87. Amsterdam: John Benjamins, 2004.

Brenzinger, Matthias, and Gerrit J. Dimmendaal. "Social Contexts of Language Death." In *Language Death*, edited by Matthias Brenzinger, 3–5. Berlin: Mouton de Gruyter, 1992.

Costello, John R. "The Periphrastic Duh Construction in Anabaptist and Nonsectarian Pennsylvania German." In *Diachronic Studies on the Languages of the Anabaptists*, edited by Kate Burridge and Werner Enninger, 242–63. Bochum: Brockmeyer, 1992.

Fishman, Joshua A. "The Measurement and Description of Widespread and Relatively Stable Bilingualism." *The Modern Language Journal* 53, no. 3 (1969): 152–56.

Fuller, Janet M. "Borrowing Trouble: Convergence in Pennsylvania German." In *Studies in Contact Linguistics: Essays in Honor of Glen G. Gilbert*, edited by Linda L. Thornburg and Janet M. Fuller, 189–204. New York: Peter Lang, 2006.

Gardner-Chloros, Penelope. "Code-Switching in Community, Regional and National Repertoires: The Myth of the Discreteness of Linguistic Systems." In *One Speaker, Two Languages*, edited by Lesley Milroy and Pieter Muysken, 68–89. Cambridge: Cambridge University Press, 1995.

Hamp, Eric C. "On Signs of Health and Death." In *Investigating Obsolescence*, edited by Nancy C. Dorian, 197–210. Cambridge: Cambridge University Press, 1989.

Hill, Jane H. "The Social Function of Relativization in Obsolescent and Nonobsolescent Languages." In *Investigating Obsolescence*, edited by Nancy C. Dorian, 149–64. Cambridge: Cambridge University Press, 1989.

Huffines, Marion L. "Pennsylvania German: Maintenance and Shift." *International Journal of the Sociology of Language* 25 (1980): 43–57.

———. "The Function of Aspect in Pennsylvania German and the Impact of English." In *Yearbook of German-American Studies* 21 (1986): 137–54.

————. "Convergence and Language Death: The Case of Pennsylvania German." In *Studies on the Languages and the Verbal Behavior of the Pennsylvania Germans II,* edited by Werner Enninger, Joachim Raith, and Karl-Heinz Wandt, 17–28. Stuttgart: Franz Steiner, 1989.

Hutz, Matthias. "Is There a Natural Process of Decay?" In *First Language Attrition: Interdisciplinary Perspectives on Methodological Issues,* edited by Monika S. Schmid, Barbara Köpke, Merel Keijzer, and Lina Weilemar, 189–206. Amsterdam: John Benjamins, 2004.

Keel, William D. "Reduction and Loss of Case Marking in the Noun Phrase in German-American Speech Islands: Internal Development or External Interference?" In *Sprachinselforschung. Eine Gedenkschrift für Hugo Jedig,* edited by Nina Berend and Klaus J. Mattheier, 93–104. New York: Peter Lang, 1994.

Köpke, Barbara, and Monika S. Schmid. "Language Attrition: The Next Phase." In *First Language Attrition: Interdisciplinary Perspectives on Methodological Issues,* edited by Monika S. Schmid, Barbara Köpke, Merel Keijzer, and Lina Weilemar, 1–43. Amsterdam: John Benjamins, 2004.

Louden, Mark L. "Syntactic Change in Multilingual Speech Islands." In *Sprachinselforschung. Eine Gedenkschrift für Hugo Jedig,* edited by Nina Berend and Klaus J. Mattheier, 73–92. Frankfurt: Peter Lang, 1994.

Luthy, David. *The Amish in America: Settlements that Failed.* Aylmer, ON: Pathway Publishers, 1986.

Meister Ferré, Barbara. *Stability and Change in the Pennsylvania German Dialect of an Old Order Amish Community in Lancaster County.* Stuttgart: F.C.W. Vogel, 1994.

Sasse, Hans-Jürgen. "Language Decay and Contact-Induced Change: Similarities and Differences." In *Language Death,* edited by Matthias Brenzinger, 59–80. Berlin: Mouton de Gruyter, 1992.

————. "Theory of Language Death." In *Language Death,* edited by Matthias Brenzinger, 7–30. Berlin: Mouton de Gruyter, 1992.

Sercombe, Peter. "Language Maintenance and Shift: A Review of Theoretical and Regional Issues with Special Reference to Borneo." In *Methodological and Analytical Issues in Language Maintenance and Language Shift Studies,* edited by Maya Khemlani David, 1–19. New York: Peter Lang, 2002.

Yağmur, Kutlay. "Issues in Finding the Appropriate Methodology in Language Attrition Research." In *First Language Attrition: Interdisciplinary Perspectives on Methodological Issues,* edited by Monika S. Schmid, Barbara Köpke, Merel Keijzer, and Lina Weilemar, 133–64. Amsterdam: John Benjamins, 2004.

THIRTY-FIVE

Wernher von Braun and Arthur Rudolph

Negotiating the Past in Huntsville

Monique Laney

After Germany's capitulation in 1945, hundreds of engineers, scientists, and technicians were brought to the United States from postwar Germany as a form of "intelligence reparations" under Operation Paperclip. Approximately 118 of them had worked with Wernher von Braun in Peenemünde, designing V-2 rockets. After an initial four years in El Paso, Texas, where their families joined them within the first two years, most of them moved to Huntsville, Alabama, where they later worked for the National Aeronautics and Space Administration (NASA) on the Apollo program. The following chapter is based on a larger interdisciplinary dissertation project that primarily uses interviews conducted with German and non-German residents of Huntsville to understand the impact of this national endeavour on the formerly small cotton town in the U.S. South. The essay focuses on two prominent figures in this group, Dr. Wernher von Braun and Dr. Arthur Rudolph, who epitomized the extremes between which sentiments toward this German community in Huntsville vacillate. Where von Braun symbolizes the vision and success of the pioneering years of the space program, Rudolph signifies an unwelcome reminder of the engineers' past in Nazi Germany.

OPERATION PAPERCLIP, A SECRET post–World War II U.S. military operation, brought hundreds of German and Austrian specialists to the United States between 1945 and the late 1950s. Most of these specialists had worked in Peenemünde, Germany, a rocket development and test site established in 1937, where they had been designing V-2 rockets during the war. In the last years of the war slave labourers from the Mittelbau

Dora concentration camp were used to build the V-2s. Soon after the end of the war, the rocket specialists were brought to Fort Bliss, Texas, under the secret military program, Project Overcast, for short-term military exploitation, while many of their dependants were under U.S. military care in Landshut, Germany.[1] The project name was later changed to Paper-clip, and after the first year or two the families were brought to Fort Bliss as well. In 1946 the first group of engineers and technicians were prom-ised long-term employment with the U.S. Army and eventual citizenship for themselves and their families. Most of them followed the army, which moved its program to Huntsville, Alabama, in 1950, and were naturalized as American citizens by 1955.

Initially, the purpose of the military operation was to use the special-ists' expertise to help the war effort against Japan and to deny them to the Soviet Union and other allies. Once Japan had surrendered, the goal shifted primarily to deny their expertise to the Soviet Union. During the first years they worked on guided and ballistic missile technology, which led to the development of intercontinental ballistic missiles (ICBM). In 1960, most joined NASA under the leadership of von Braun to work on the Apollo program. Many were "forcibly retired" in the early 1970s as part of a general workforce reduction measure by NASA headquarters.[2] Shortly afterward, the U.S. Justice Department formed the Office of Special Inves-tigations (OSI) in 1979 to investigate and denaturalize or deport former Nazis who had entered the United States fraudulently. One of the retired German team members and former production manager for Peenemünde, Dr. Arthur Rudolph, was brought in for questioning by this office. In 1984 Rudolph and his wife left the United States after he signed a statement agreeing to give up his U.S. citizenship and move back to Germany. Many attempts have been made to clear his name, but so far they have been unsuccessful. Rudolph died in 1996.

This chapter is based on a dissertation project that leans heavily on inter-views with both German and non-German members of the Huntsville community, while emphasizing an interdisciplinary approach to answer broader questions.[3] Sources include archival material, newspaper and magazine articles, personal correspondence, documentary films, as well as public presentations and social gatherings organized by or for the German group in Huntsville. Different disciplinary tools are applied, including methods and theories developed in anthropology, sociology, history, and cultural studies. The overarching question is always the same: How do these sources construct the past, and how do they negotiate the presum-ably divergent roles of the German rocket specialists? The preliminary research results concerning the particular roles of Dr. Wernher von Braun and Dr. Arthur Rudolph are used here in the construction of a "usable past."

"German Scientists Bring Knowledge and
Pumpernickel to Huntsville"

In Huntsville and at NASA, the German specialists are considered the "visionaries" and "pioneers" that made the space program a reality. The town changed dramatically after the arrival of the German families and the many engineers, scientists, and technicians who followed them to support the Army's program and later NASA, as is indicated by a newspaper headline of 1954: "German Scientists Bring Knowledge and Pumpernickel to Huntsville."[4] Huntsville's population more than doubled over the following two decades. A small town, once known as the watercress capital of the world and heavily reliant on the cotton industry, Huntsville soon became known as Rocket City for its new technical industry related to the space program. The U.S. Space & Rocket Center, the Von Braun Civic Center, Broadway Theatre League, Symphony Orchestra, Ballet Company, St. Mark's Evangelical Lutheran Church, and the University of Alabama Huntsville (UAH), all new additions to the community, are often attributed to the efforts of the first group of Germans that arrived in 1950. Real estate companies, travel agents, and the universities like to stress that Huntsville still has the "highest percentage of engineers and more PhDs per capita than any city in the country."[5] Evidence of the main newspaper's perception of its huge debt to the German rocket specialists, especially Wernher von Braun, is revealed in an article naming him "Huntsville's first citizen" and describing the ceremonies at the courthouse to send him and his family off to work for NASA in Washington DC in 1970.[6] Many residents still seem to agree. Alice Tanner, a contributor to a public panel held at Huntsville's main library in 2003 titled "Creating the Rocket City" addressed the influence of the German specialists, who worked on Redstone Arsenal, by asking her audience,

> Does anyone believe we would have a Huntsville Symphony without those arsenal people? I don't think so. I don't think there'd be a Broadway Theater League. I don't think there would be a library like this one. The library that I remember was a tiny, tiny building ... I don't think we'd have a ballet. I don't think we'd have a good many of the wonderful community institutions that we have today.[7]

One of the members of the Etz Chayim Synagogue of Huntsville agreed and explained why the German men's past did not seem to be of much interest to the community.

> They brought a lot of culture into the community. They were very active in organizing the symphony [and] getting various cultural things going. [They] introduced some restaurants, different types of food that hadn't been here. [They were] very active in supporting and initiating theatre.

As far as the interaction between the people in the city, I think, the war was behind us. We all had a goal, you know, when President Kennedy set the goal of going to the moon and coming back by the end of the decade. That was pretty well set.[8]

While the interviewee stated that the goal of going to the moon outweighed questions concerning the men's past, his comment also acknowledged that indeed there is a past in need of being put "behind us." The initial focus on a goal may also be part of the explanation why the German specialists' past was revisited by government officials so much later, that is, when their careers were over and the national and local goal of landing the first human on the moon had long been accomplished. Perhaps the past was not so much "behind us," but the confrontation with it and its investigation simply postponed.

Von Braun is considered instrumental in getting the University of Alabama Huntsville started. Ben Graves, first president of the University of Alabama Huntsville, considers him "the most influential man" on the committee that tried to recruit Graves for UAH. Appearing on the same panel with Alice Tanner, Graves said that von Braun

> spent an unduly amount of time with me. Not only out at his place in the arsenal, but in his home, which I understand was rather unusual, but I spent an entire afternoon in von Braun's home. And, repeatedly, not just once, but repeatedly, he told me that one of his biggest headaches [or] problems here in Huntsville had been the lack of a high-quality University. He said that this was very, very important in recruiting. And, not only that, but when he brought people here, they wanted to have an opportunity to continue their educations at the master's and PhD level.[9]

Wernher von Braun brought more education resources to the town in order to support the space program, which in return presumably benefited Huntsville, or at least many of Huntsville's residents.

High culture and higher education seem to be considered the main influences of the German group on Huntsville, but the prosperity the space program brought to Huntsville was also notable. Presumably the program would not have been executed as quickly and successfully without the expertise of the German group. An article in the *Nashville Tennessean Magazine*, published in the year when the first U.S. satellite, Explorer I, was successfully launched into orbit in 1958, described the changes Huntsville underwent due to the influx of newcomers related to the space program.[10] According to this article, the population had doubled since 1950, the land was selling at very high prices, and the economy had changed from relying almost entirely on cotton to supporting the missile industry. With financial support from the federal government, "the city moved fast to build roads, provide for more utility service and build schools." The churches were expanding and the police found that "most of the new people in Huntsville are educated, family people. There's not much running around and fighting and drunken brawls."[11] The article explains the flipside of this success as well. "The city is a paradox of great employment opportunity and an unemployment problem living side by side. Some of the folks are really hurting ... To the unemployed and to the man who still earns his forty dollars a week in old, local industry, the boom has been a curse ... Food prices are up and housing costs have soared into an orbit of their own."[12]

The Stakes Are High

Despite their seemingly positive influence on most of the community, the specialists' past in World War II Germany seems still to define their reality and that of their families even today. Many media accounts and non-academic books about the approximately 125 German rocket specialists read like hagiographies of a rock star and his supporting band. Wernher von Braun, who not only led the rocket development team in Peenemünde but also in El Paso and later Huntsville, takes centre stage, often referred to as the "father of the United States Space Program"[13] or the "Columbus of Space,"[14] while his German co-workers are uniformly defined as the "von Braun team"[15] and thousands of American co-workers are usually hardly mentioned in these stories or only as supporting vehicles for the German specialists. Contrasting this image is that of Arthur Rudolph, who often functions as a reminder of the threat that the Office of Special Investigations (OSI) might still accuse the German men of being former war criminals.

The stakes still seem high, even today, for those who fear that their freedom, citizenship, reputation, and families are in jeopardy. Even members of the second generation are presumed to be under investigation by the OSI. When the daughter of one of the deceased German specialists moved back to Huntsville in 2000, where she had been raised as part of the German group, she was invited to a gathering at the UAH for the renaming of the Research Institute Building to "Wernher von Braun Research Hall" in April 2000, along with "Officials from UAH, NASA's Marshall Space Flight Center, the U.S. Army, and members of the rocket team that arrived in Huntsville in 1950."[16] Having seen many old friends again, she asked one of the organizers for the mailing list used to invite the members of the second generation. She received the list with the warning to keep the list private because the OSI was supposedly still investigating the group, including the second generation. While it seems unlikely that the second generation is being investigated and this remark may have even been meant as a rather peculiar joke, the daughter took the warning seriously, reflecting a presumably already deep suspicion of government as described by one of the granddaughters of the German specialists in an interview.[17] While discussing the fact that her grandparents and other Germans did not want to be on the church roll of Huntsville's Lutheran Church they had helped found, she explained:

> Well, I think it's more that if your name is on a government list you can be taken off to a concentration camp ... it's a mistrust of government ... I guess, in Germany you don't have that separation of church and state, so that may have been a cultural misunderstanding about who had access to what. But I think that was just a self-preservation instinct that survivors developed. You know, I very much grew up with "don't ever give out any more information to anyone than you absolutely need to, if they have anything to do with the government."[18]

This statement implies not only a general suspicion of government among the first-generation Germans, which has apparently been passed down two generations, but also the perception of being survivors of the war—victims in their own right—which is in stark contrast to accusations of the German specialists being perpetrators and potential war criminals. The distinction between victims and perpetrators is blurred, implying that non-Jewish Germans were primarily victims of the Nazi regime and provoking the following question: How could they possibly be perpetrators at the same time?

Creating a Polarized Worldview

The perception of threat has created an "us versus them" logic, thereby polarizing those who show their undivided support of memorializing the German specialists as U.S. national heroes, and those who want to complicate that notion of monolithic celebrity status by illuminating some of the group members' Nazi past. Constant attempts to set the record straight illustrate the level of concern. At the same time, this concern may have drawn the group closer together in an attempt to demonstrate solidarity with each other and appear united in the face of what has been perceived as unreasonable insinuations, allegations, and "ungratefulness" from outsiders. Members of the German community were and are considered part of an "extended family," especially by the second generation, which did not have grandparents or aunts, uncles, or cousins in the United States to turn to. Oftentimes the rules for family members seem to be different than for non-family members, which might explain the level of emotional intensity produced by a polarized worldview. The word "they" seems to include anyone who does not share the unquestioned celebration of the German rocket specialists as U.S. national heroes and who implies that the men's political position and conduct in the past toward those persecuted by the Nazi regime is still relevant.

This polarizing logic is illustrated in the title of an article by Wilhelm Kreissmann, "Undank ist der Welten Lohn."[19] The article applauds the book *Secrets of the Space Age* by William E. Winterstein for its author's repeated attempts to clear Rudolph's name. The article commends Winterstein for being "a monument of true solidarity" to "his German American coworkers and friends," and for accusing the Office of Special Investigations of having used "Gestapo methods" in trying to label Rudolph as a war criminal.[20] Kreissmann suggests that those accusing Rudolph of being a war criminal and thereby potentially questioning the past of other members of the German group as well are at least as guilty of abusing their power and persecuting defenceless victims as those they accuse.

The article's title refers to the notion articulated in another newspaper piece stating that the United States "government used him [Rudolph] for so many years and then exiled him when they were finished with him."[21] Ten years earlier, the same author, Hugh McInnish, was quoted by the *Huntsville Times* in an obituary for Rudolph: "After Art had given everything we needed from him the same government which was then run by different persons turned on him, using exactly the same information he had always revealed about himself, and hounded him out of the country."[22] Bitterness and resentment seem to dictate these comments, reflecting disappointment and disillusionment in the perceived unreliability of the U.S. government. Their disappointment in the U.S. government stems from the misinterpretation of nation and government as a unified, monolithic, unchanging entity—a common but misleading assumption, especially for democracies.

When the above-mentioned granddaughter of one of the German specialists was asked about the effects of the Rudolph case on the community, she explained:

> It really was a source of grieving and I think a lot of people felt very betrayed, because here, this country had welcomed Rudolph and the whole team had allowed them to spend their whole professional creativity and their lives, you know, building a new home and contributing. And then to suddenly renege and say, oh no, we're going to bow to this pressure of this other group for something that was done, you know, forty or fifty years ago, and you're going to believe their side of the story instead of considering our side too.[23]

In addition, the granddaughter had been told that "our side" of the story was that people like Rudolph joined the Nazi party "in order to be able to have an influence to *improve* the working conditions of the Jewish slave labour." As she explained, this perspective made it "actually an act of integrity and compassion, not something that should be punished."[24] It is possible that the explanation given to her was different than the one repeated in the interview conducted for this study, but what seems important is what the next generation remembers and how it adds to the perception of the German specialists as victims as well as heroes, where a critical reflection of their past appears unjustified and potentially vindictive.

Rudolph had not been accused simply of having joined the Nazi Party. That in itself would not have been considered a war crime. As he testified himself, he had led the production of the V-2 rockets at Mittelwerk Dora, where slave labour was used extensively. The allegations concerned his responsibility for the treatment of the prisoners. However, the allegations never led to a denaturalization hearing in the United States because Rudolph renounced his citizenship and left for Germany instead. According to the then head of OSI, Neal M. Sher, "interviews with witnesses, information from U.S., German and other archives and books about the Dora-Nordhausen camp provided evidence that Rudolph was responsible for the laborer's working condition ... The conditions were utterly outrageous, gruesome, grotesque."[25] Rudolph's supporters claim that the case is fake, that the OSI used "deceptive tactics when questioning him [Rudolph] about his wartime activities" and that the testimonies are worthless because taken from non-credible witnesses.[26]

Whether Rudolph actually tried to help anyone during his time at the Dora-Nordhausen concentration camp has not been publicized. His supporters generally argue that he never was in charge of slave labourers in the first place or postulate that those working at Peenemünde and Mittelwerk Dora had no choice than to do whatever was required of them by the SS because of the threat of severe punishment, or that they were "just serving their country."[27] Thinking of Rudolph as someone who was "acting out of compassion" and trying to "improve the conditions for slave labourers"[28] counters the accusations of having committed war crimes with an alternative interpretation of events. It contrasts with Rudolph's membership in the Nazi party since 1931, long before Hitler was governing Germany and anyone was forced to adhere to Nazism.[29] This explanation, presumably supplied to the next generation, illustrates a need to make sense of a complicated past by creating the notion that Rudolph, and by association his co-workers who came to Huntsville with him, upheld high moral values in the face of an extreme moral dilemma. The idea that Rudolph may not have done anything to incriminate himself as a war criminal, but also nothing to help those in need, is obviously not sufficient to counter the accusations. This interpretation reflects a need to believe that Rudolph, and with him all those the German families and

their descendants loved and relied on for a prosperous future, are mono-
lithically "good people." The tension that would be caused by a realistic
assessment of the German specialists and their pasts is averted and the
situation glossed over with a story of heroism that preserves the overall
notion that these men should be celebrated as national heroes, not questioned and prosecuted for war crimes.

In support of clearing Rudolph's name, some non-German members
of the Huntsville community try to demonstrate their solidarity and counter
criticisms of the German specialists by making exaggerated claims that
"Wernher von Braun and his small team of German scientists helped make
the United States of America what it is today" and postulating that "all
Americans owe a huge debt of gratitude to them for what they have accomplished."[30] Besides the blanket assumption that the accomplishments of
the team are indisputably praiseworthy by an entire nation with a diverse
population and a multitude of interests, this comment is a clear declara-
tion of allegiance with the "us" camp in this ongoing struggle that does
not allow for any doubt, questioning, or complication of the portrayal of
these men. The extreme end of the spectrum is reflected in a review by
Robert Countess[31] of Thomas Franklin's *An American in Exile: The Story of
Arthur Rudolph*[32] in the *Journal of Historical Review,* in which the OSI inves-
tigators are labelled "witch hunters," the Holocaust is described as a "present legend," Hitler is described as having defended Germany against Zion-
ism, which had supposedly "declared war on Germany," and the author of
the Morgenthau Plan is considered to have planned the "genocide of Germans." While it is unlikely that all of those in the "us" camp are Holocaust deniers, being supported by those who do support this notion is
problematic, and the refusal to allow for a more complex view of the German specialists is simply dangerous. It not only ignores and distorts the past
of many other participants of this history, but it also fuels sentiments that
the past is no longer relevant and that the German specialists, who are now
in their eighties and nineties, if still alive, should be left alone, as if the past
and how it is viewed has no bearing on the present and the future. At the
same time, those who do not wish for the men's past to be examined too
carefully are often the same people who are concerned that the rocket
team's accomplishments are not sufficiently acknowledged. Indeed, most
seem quite aware of the importance of the past for the present and the
future.

Conclusion

This chapter attempts to shed light on some of the dynamics
affecting how the German specialists associated with Operation Paperclip and their families living in Huntsville represent themselves and have

been represented by others. Particularly polarizing representations of Wernher von Braun and Arthur Rudolph have already proven to be pivotal in understanding these dynamics. These two men symbolize two extremes of a controversy that affects the German community of Huntsville. Some would like to see the group members celebrated as national heroes whose past has become irrelevant in light of their accomplishments and advanced age. Others insist on a more differentiated view that includes their roles in World War II Germany. Part of the problem might be the conflation of all group members as the "von Braun team," which has been encouraged by members of the group as well as outsiders. While this team spirit has presumably been very useful for concerted technical efforts, it presents a problem when dealing with individual pasts, playing into controversial concepts of collective guilt.

The question of representation hinges on what is at stake. It should not surprise that representations become extremely important when pension payments and citizenship are in jeopardy, but this controversy is part of a much larger discourse about Germany and German American identity in relationship to a Nazi past. The larger investigation of which this chapter forms a part, therefore, explores the specific meaning of *Vergangenheitsbewältigung* in this unique context of Huntsville during the Cold War.

Notes

1 Even though the men are commonly referred to as "rocket scientists," the term "specialists" is used here as most of the men were engineers or technicians.
2 The term "forcibly retired" is used frequently by those affected by the workforce reduction and others who sympathize with them. It is often implied that the German rocket team was the intended target for this action.
3 The oral histories were collected using the "snowball system." The author has access to members of the German community primarily because of her father's marriage to a second-generation German in Huntsville. The author was raised in Germany and the U.S. and is bilingual. For contacts and interviews with other Huntsville residents the author approached diverse cultural institutions in Huntsville.
4 Jones, "German Scientists," 18.
5 McDonald, "Welcome to Huntsville"; "Welcome to Huntsville," 12.
6 Sloat, "Rocket City Launches von Braun."
7 Tanner, "A Century of Flight."
8 Interview with congregation member of Etz Chayim Synagogue.
9 Graves, "A Century of Flight."
10 Barker, "Huntsville."
11 Barker, "Huntsville."
12 Barker, "Huntsville."
13 See, for example, "Wernher von Braun."
14 Freeman, *How We Got to the Moon.*

15 See, for example, MSFC History Office, "Von Braun Team" and also obituaries for various team members.
16 Garner, "UAH Research Institute."
17 In a recent interview with the main investigator at the OSI in Arthur Rudolph's case, Eli Rosenbaum confirmed that the second generation has not been and is not under investigation by that office.
18 Interview with a third-generation member of German community in Huntsville.
19 Kriessmann, "Undank ist der Welten Lohn."
20 Passages translated from German to English by the author.
21 McInnish, "An American in Exile."
22 Peck, "Rudolph dies in Germany."
23 Interview with a third-generation member of German community in Huntsville.
24 Interview with a third-generation member of German community in Huntsville.
25 Thornton, "Rocket Expert Renounces U.S. in Nazi Probe."
26 McInnish, "An American in Exile"; Countess, "Review."
27 This is not a direct quote. Statements to that effect can be found in Gray, "Rocket Man," 5; Frazier, "FBI Files of Wernher von Braun," 14.
28 Interview with a third-generation member of German community in Huntsville.
29 Bower, *The Paperclip Conspiracy*, 204. The negotiations over the Rudolph case are too complicated to be discussed at length here.
30 Gray, "Rocket Man."
31 Countess, "Review."
32 Franklin, *An American in Exile.*

Interview Sources

All interviews conducted by Monique Laney and currently in possession of the author.
Congregation member of Etz Chayim Synagogue, Huntsville, AL, May 2006.
Third-generation member of German community in Huntsville, January 2006,
Eli Rosenbaum, U.S. Department of Justice, Office of Special Investigations, March 2007.

Works Cited

Barker, George. "Huntsville: Bus Stop to the Moon," *Nashville Tennessean Magazine,* 18 May 1958, 10–11, 20–21.
Bower, Tom. *The Paperclip Conspiracy: The Battle for the Spoils and Secrets of Nazi Germany.* London: M. Joseph, 1987.
Carney, Tom. "The FBI Files of Werhner [sic] von Braun—Part 9," reprinted with permission of *Old Huntsville Magazine,* <huntsville.about.com/library/blank/blvonbraum9.htm> (June 2008).
Countess, Robert H. "Review: An American in Exile: The Story of Arthur Rudolph," *Journal of Historical Review,* 8, 1988. <www.ihr.org/jhr/v08/v08p224_Countess.html> (March 2008).
Freeman, Marsha. *How We Got to the Moon: The Story of the German Space Pioneers,* Washington DC: 21st Century Science Associates, 1993.
Franklin, Thomas. *An American in Exile: The Story of Arthur Rudolph,* Huntsville, AL: C. Kaylor Co., 1987.

Garner, Ray. "UAH Research Institute Building Renamed in Honor of Von Braun," University of Alabama in Huntsville, 2000. <www.uah.edu/News/archived News/braun.html> (May 2006).

Graves, Ben (panellist). "A Century of Flight: 'Creating Rocket City.'" Huntsville, AL, Madison Public Library, 2003.

Gray, Jacquelyn Procter. "Rocket Man: The Story of Dr. Wernher von Braun," *Old Tennessee Valley Magazine & Mercantile Advertiser,* n.d., 5–14.

Jones, Joyce. "German Scientists Bring Knowledge and Pumpernickel to Huntsville," *Chattanooga Times,* 11 July 1954, 18.

Kriessmann, Wilhelm. "Undank ist der Welten Lohn," *New Yorker Staatszeitung,* 15 April 2006, 13–14.

McDonald, Holly. "Welcome to Huntsville," Keller Williams Realty. <www.holly mcdonald.com> (March 2008).

McInnish, Hugh. "An American in Exile: The Arthur Rudolph Story," *Old Huntsville Magazine,* 3 January 2006. <www.oldhuntsville.com/formatbox/stories _detail.cfm?ID=18> (December 2007).

MFSC History Office. "Von Braun Team." Marshall Space Flight Centre: Huntsville, AL. <history.msfc.nasa.gov/rocketry/30.html> (March 2008).

Peck, John. "Rudolph Dies in Germany," *Huntsville Times,* 2 January 1996, A1, A4.

Sloat, Bill. "Rocket City Launches von Braun," *Huntsville News,* 25 February 1970, 1–2.

Tanner, Alice (panellist). "A Century of Flight: 'Creating Rocket City.'" Huntsville, AL, Madison Public Library, 2003.

Thornton, Mary. "Rocket Expert Renounces U.S. in Nazi Probe," *Washington Post* 18 October 1984, A1.

"Welcome to Huntsville: It's a Great Place to Live," *Inspired Living: Greater Huntsville Relocation Guide,* Fall/Winter 2005.

"Wernher von Braun," *Wikipedia, The Free Encyclopedia.* <en.wikipedia.org/wiki/ Wernher_von_Braun> (March 2008).

Winterstein, William E. *Secrets of the Space Age.* Bandon, OR: Robert D. Reed Publishers, 2005.

THIRTY-SIX

Brave or Naive?

Memory Work and Vergangenheitsbewältigung in Gertrud Mackprang Baer's In the Shadow of Silence

Doris Wolf

This chapter explores how Gertrud Mackprang Baer's 2002 autobiography, *In the Shadow of Silence—From Hitler Youth to Allied Internment: A Young Woman's Story of Truth and Denial*, takes part in what has been in Germany a long and arduous process: that of *Vergangenheitsbewältigung*. Born in 1925, Baer grew up in Hamburg in an ordinary middle-class family under the Third Reich. She emigrated to the United States in 1957 and settled permanently in Canada four years later. Baer's location in Canada at the turn of the twenty-first century has shaped her published account of mastering the past. By locating Baer's text within the tradition of Mittäterin autobiographies and using feminist historical scholarship on the roles of ordinary German women in the Third Reich as well as autobiographical theory on subjectivity and testimony, this chapter examines the tensions and contradictions that emerge in Baer's text around the questions of guilt and complicity.

There is an inescapable logic that haunts everyone brave—or naive— enough to discuss the Nazi state from first-hand experience rather than through the detached lens of the historian.
— *Gertrud Mackprang Baer*, In the Shadow of Silence

IN HER AUTOBIOGRAPHY, *In the Shadow of Silence—From Hitler Youth to Allied Internment: A Young Woman's Story of Truth and Denial*, Gertrud Mackprang Baer recounts her experiences as a young woman, born in

1925, who came of age in the Third Reich. The introductory Author's Note painstakingly establishes the wider political resonances of what in many respects is a confessional and very personal account. If after the war Germany paid huge monetary sums against its material and moral debts, "the thorny question of the political accountability or moral responsibility of the ordinary German remained unresolved. For decades, it has influenced the country's political culture and marred its tireless efforts to come to terms with the past. It became the defining issue for writing this book."[1] Thus, Baer's autobiography takes part in what has been in Germany the arduous process of *Vergangenheitsbewältigung*. Since World War II, Germans who lived through the Nazi era as well as subsequent generations who inherited this legacy of evil have explored the painful issues of how the Nazi state could have happened and how they should deal with the heavy burden of guilt they carry, nationally and personally, for the atrocities committed under Hitler. Although many Germans hoped that the reunification of their country in 1990 would mark the end of the postwar era, and thus discussions over guilt, these hopes have been unfounded. As Robert C. Holub remarked as recently as 2000, in spite of some revisionary attempts to lay the past to rest, "the uniqueness of the Holocaust and the absolute evil of the Nazi regime have remained the unstated parameters of most official discourses even to the present day."[2]

Baer places before her readers a figure who has become the focus of much recent *Vergangenheitsbewältigung* scholarship: that of the ordinary German woman under National Socialism. For decades after the war, this figure did not arise in historical scholarship written either by men, who were more interested in traditionally male topics of wartime such as military strategy, or by women, who tended to view the Aryan German woman as another victim of Nazi policy because of its overt misogyny. Since the late 1980s, hundreds of historical studies have emerged on both sides of the Atlantic to tease out questions of German women's subjectivity and agency within the Nazi state. German feminist scholars such as Frigga Haug, Christine Thürmer-Rohr, and Karin Windaus-Walser as well as American feminists such as Claudia Koonz, Renate Bridenthal, Marion Kaplan, and Attina Grossman have uncovered much new information about the roles of ordinary women in the Third Reich, resulting in productive although often heated and uncomfortable debates over terminology such as *Täterin, Mittäterin,* and *Mitläuferin*. Ordinary German women, as these labels suggest, are no longer viewed simplistically as victims of an exceptionally patriarchal fascist government.[3]

If formal scholarship in the area did not emerge until well into the 1980s, literary accounts of the period by German women began to emerge in significant numbers a good decade earlier. As Elaine Martin notes, women's earliest writings about the Nazi era are autobiographical, "either directly in autobiographies, diaries, and memoirs, or indirectly in autobiographical novels, short stories, and poetry."[4] Christa Wolf's *Kindheitsmuster*, first published in 1976, stands as the most famous example of this unprecedented surge in autobiographical expression, but other works by her contemporaries appeared, too: Ingeborg Drewitz's *Gestern war Heute: Hundert Jahre Gegenwart* (1978), Ruth Rehmann's *Der Mann auf der Kanzel* (1979), and Eva Zeller's *Solange ich denken kann: Roman einer Jugend* (1981) and its sequel, *Nein und Amen* (1986).[5] While many other women also wrote personal accounts of the period, Wolf, Drewitz, Rehmann, and Zeller share some key characteristics: all were born in the 1920s and came of age in the Third Reich, and none were Nazi activists or opponents but very average in terms of their activities and reactions to Nazi ideology and practice.[6] Yet average does not mean innocent: as Martin comments, their *Mittäterin* literature experiments with various ways of saying, "I was there; I was involved; thus I am guilty."[7]

With its autobiographical form and emphasis on coming to terms with both Germany's and the author's Nazi past, Baer's *In the Shadow of Silence* can usefully be placed alongside the examples cited above. Baer, too, was born in the 1920s and can be considered average in terms of her culpability for the past. Yet significant differences emerge in that Baer published her autobiography a few decades later than Wolf, Drewitz, Rehmann, and Zeller, and did so long after she had left Germany. Baer emigrated to North America in 1957, first going to the United States and then settling permanently in Canada in 1961. Her decision to emigrate occurred instantaneously in 1955, when she learned of the German government's plans for rearmament and general conscription for the new *Bundeswehr*. When asked by friends and relatives why she was leaving Germany, she would reply, "I'm not going to America—I'm leaving Germany."[8] In spite of this harsh assessment, Baer has maintained, as is common among many immigrants and immigrant writers, a strong interest in her homeland and her heritage. For Baer, this interest led her to take on the directorship (1969–77) of the Goethe-Institut in Ottawa, a branch of the worldwide organization for the promotion of the German language and culture. It is precisely this tension between her long-time physical and emotional distance from Germany and her lingering nostalgia for her culture that marks Baer's autobiographical *Mittäterin* literature as so different from that of her contemporaries. The central goal of this chapter is to explore how the intervening factors of time and place, that is, Canada at the turn of the twenty-first century, have shaped Baer's published account of mastering the past.

Locating *In the Shadow of Silence* within the tradition of *Mittäterin* autobiographies and using feminist historical scholarship on the roles of ordinary German women in the Third Reich as well as autobiographical theory on subjectivity and testimony enables an exploration of the tensions and contradictions that emerge in Baer's text over the questions of guilt and complicity. Baer includes two narratives in her autobiography, each with a distinct form. In the well-researched and documented popular history sections (which she labels "Interludes"), she emerges as a rigorous and unbiased critic of the past, telling outsiders—the Canadian reading public—about the way it was for ordinary *Volk* in the Nazi years and what they failed to do afterward. Here she establishes the prevailing heroic persona of the text, which counters the naive persona of the rest of the autobiography, where she recounts the story of the last years of the war and her later internment for her participation in the Sicherheitsdienst, the intelligence service of the SS and a sister organization to the Gestapo. This tension between bravery and naiveté becomes the central motif of the book so that a split that emerges between the older, mature, and brave Baer who tells readers about these events an ocean away and many years later, and her younger naive self who lived the events and whose life she can recall only through memory. This tension is never resolved, and both personas conspire to absolve Baer of her past.

Because her assumptions about her Canadian readers shape so significantly both the format and specific motifs Baer uses throughout *In the Shadow of Silence*, a few comments on her implied readers are in order. Baer's audience, while constructed as solidly middle brow, that is, as intelligent and thoughtful readers, is assumed to be largely ignorant about daily life for average Germans in the Third Reich, as well as about the long tradition of *Vergangenheitsbewältigung*.[9] Baer is quite correct in assuming that most of her readers will hold instead popular conceptions about what Nazism was and what the Nazis did, which tend to come from media images focusing on the worst perpetrators. Here, the exceptional becomes the average in the Canadian mind: all Germans were Nazis, much like Hitler, and thus equally and simplistically bad. Put plainly, the book plays with Canadian readers' naiveté about the "ordinariness" of the Nazi period in ways that would not be possible if Baer had published her text in Germany.

This Canadian naiveté posed distinct challenges for Baer if we consider what it means to write and publish a *Vergangenheitsbewältigung* autobiography in the relative absence of such a tradition in Canada. As Sidonie Smith argues, a formal autobiography is written to be published and thus is addressed to that greatest arbiter of all cultural ideologies, the public reader.[10] Baer may have had the idea of the public reader as supreme judge in mind when she confessed that this "was not an easy book to write. Indeed, it took decades to make a start, and years of rewriting, with the urge to sanitize the text, perhaps to scrap it altogether,... ever present."[11] Unlike in Germany, where everyone, whether they actually do so or not, is perceived as needing to grapple on some level with the Nazi past, in Canada, the experience of the Holocaust is that of being safely on the side of good. Retrospectively, one might question the Canadian government's decision to refuse hundreds of Jewish refugees on board the SS *St. Louis* entry into Canada, but that guilt is easily absolved when one compares Canada's actions to all the nations that did the same or to the horrors actually committed by Germany. Within this context of Canadian innocence, to go public with one's testimony about one's own activities in the Third Reich undoubtedly feels like an especially difficult and risky endeavour.

If the absence of a tradition of coming to terms with the past in Canada created unique difficulties for Baer, it also afforded her some special possibilities in terms of representing herself as heroic. A major component of this self-representation lies in her use of what has been dubbed the "repression thesis," long the most popular view of how Germans have dealt, or more accurately failed to deal, with their Nazi past. Initiated in 1959 when philosopher Theodor Adorno excoriated Germans for failing to come to terms with the past, it gained widespread visibility through the socio-psychological work of Alexander and Margarete Mitscherlich in their influential *Die Unfähigkeit zu trauern* (1967). As Alon Confino stresses, "the myth of repression was, in moral terms, so seductive that even scholars who cited evidence of engagement with the Third Reich ended up interpreting it as a form of denial."[12] When Baer writes that "after the war, the Hitler generation—*das Volk*—instantly and collectively repudiated any personal knowledge of, let alone involvement in, the crimes of the Third Reich," she borrows heavily from this thesis.[13] This borrowing counters both the existence of a strong tradition of *Mittäterin* literature and of newer approaches to *Vergangenheitsbewältigung* that have emerged in recent decades to offer more nuanced ways of reading the often competing discourses around memory, guilt, and responsibility. By continuing to insist on the relevancy of the repression thesis and highlighting her own break with it as unique, Baer implies that she is braver and truer than the Germans who stayed in Germany.

Baer also represents her task as heroic through the German notion of *Gründlichkeit*. To offer background details of daily living under National Socialism, she includes seven "Interludes" in her autobiography along with a postscript on the legacy of postwar Germany, which are dramatically different in content and tone from the personal story she tells about her life from roughly 1941 to 1946. Borrowing from a wide variety of sources, including many popular and academic histories and newspaper articles, both in German and in English, Baer essentially writes her own well-documented and well-informed popular history of the Nazi period in these sections. They are interjected quite evenly throughout her personal narrative and range in topic from the day-to-day life of the ordinary German to the Führer cult to anti-Semitism and to the passivity of the Christian church. Emphasizing Germany's moral failure, these sections are told in a tone best described through the concept of *Gründlichkeit*. If Joyce Marie Mushaben remarks that Germany's women had until the 1980s "failed to confront their own relationship to national history with the same degree of typically German *Gründlichkeit* with which they have traditionally excoriated patriarchy's role in those developments,"[14] that Baer takes up the topic in such a seemingly objective and hard-hitting manner marks her as an especially resolute example of those German women who bravely prevail in their efforts in spite of the difficulties of the subject matter.

Within her personal narrative, Baer shifts in tone from heroic persistence to pervading naiveté. It is not that she completely forecloses the possibility of heroism in the young woman that she was in the final years of the Third Reich and immediate postwar period. In a state that required uncritical devotion to the *Volk*, the state, and the Führer, a willingness to display any signs of individualism became a brave act. Baer constructs herself as a unique individual by insisting on her difference from her friends and peers. For example, early in her personal narrative she comments on her seven months of *Arbeitsdienst*, recalling that "from the beginning, I proved a thoroughly unhappy misfit with the jolly camaraderie and rustic wholesomeness of it all."[15] Positioning herself as a solitary figure against the crowd that seems to have wholeheartedly bought into the system, Baer here establishes the origins of the heroic person who will emerge in Canada decades later to write *In the Shadow of Silence* as an act of courage. There are several moments like this in the book, but overall in this portion Baer maintains her naive persona, afforded her by her youth and gender, as well as family upbringing in an extremely confusing time.

In the first pages of her personal narrative, Baer focuses on her age and gender as the primary factors to blame in her involvement in the Sicherheitsdienst. She reminisces about the crucial moment that will bring her within it: "I wonder now whether even a modest amount of political smarts might have raised in me second thoughts" but "political savvy was not my strong point … and the consequences of that will soon become plain."[16] It was due to youthful love that she fell into this organization, specifically love for a young man named Alex, almost a decade her senior, whom she met at a seaside resort in 1941 and kept in touch with romantically afterward. Madly in love with him from about age sixteen to twenty-one, Baer begins to work for Alex's boss, head of the Sicherheitsdienst in Marburg, in 1944. Within her description of these events, the mature narrator reflects on her younger self's infatuation with Alex: "Years later, while reading Thomas Mann's *Confessions of Con Man Felix Krull,* I was reminded of him and the pivotal role he played in my life during the 1940s."[17] Through her literary reference, Baer retrospectively constructs her younger self as having been conned by a charming older man who was "athletic, blond, with grey mocking eyes, a strong nose and long, dimpled chin" and "oozed quaint old-world courtliness."[18] Baer's inability to see the larger implications of her actions at the time due to her misguided love for Alex is continued in the chapters that follow. Although in one sentence she writes, "it was nobody's fault but my own," in the next she remarks, "ignoring all warnings, I acted out of infatuation and ignorance—as most nineteen-year-olds are wont to do."[19] Her rare moment of conscience and self-blame is mitigated quickly by so-called "normal" female immaturity.

Another motif the mature narrator uses to foreground the naiveté of her younger self is that of family dynamics. Within the traditional patriarchal German family, daughters were afforded few liberties in terms of actions or choices, a point that Ruth Rehmann's *The Man in the Pulpit* emphasizes throughout, not only to work through her relationship with her father but also to explain her own apathy to the Nazi regime. But whereas Rehmann's autobiography looks to the lack of female agency within patriarchy to explain the actions or inactions of the daughter, Baer's looks instead to the breakdown of the German family that occurred in the Third Reich. Scholars have shown how the family unit was eroded throughout the Nazi era, so that one of the greatest ironies of the period was that despite Hitler's attempt to resurrect the traditional nineteenth-century German values represented in *Kinder, Küche,* and *Kirche,* those very values collapsed under the weight of his party's often contradictory policies and practices.[20] A good example was the implementation of a system of German-on-German surveillance for slights against the state, which had a devastating impact on the German *Volk* as well as German family. Evidence shows that the bulk of denunciations had to do with "ordinary" Germans denouncing other "ordinary" Germans, even family members, often for petty reasons.[21] Baer's text reflects how the fear wrought by surveillance could undermine the security of the family unit: apart from his veiled comment that "I believe they spy on people," her father quickly gives up talking her out of taking the job at the Sicherheitsdienst.[22] Through the brevity of the father's warning and emphasis on caution, one can see how the traditional fatherly role as protector is ultimately undermined by Nazi policy, with the result being a daughter left to her own devices.

Through Baer's emphasis on naiveté due to youth, gender, and family, the reader is left to wonder how the younger self could have acted otherwise. Everything is presented as exceptionally reasonable, with clear causes and effects. Yet a crucial question is left unasked: were there no other possibilities available to Baer, no other paths she could have taken either then in living the events or now in recounting them? The range of reactions of writers of autobiographical *Mittäterin* literature suggests that there were. In her discussion of Baer's contemporaries, Elaine Martin outlines how theoretically all could have used their early years as justification and how some did, such as Eva Zeller, who relied on her "alibi of tender years."[23] But others, for example Carola Stern, reproached themselves for failing as human beings, and still others, for example Margarete Hannsman, condemned other women who continued to support Hitler actively or passively: "I hold that against them. I said: You must have had a conscience. I had one at sixteen. Everyone must have had one. Everyone."[24]

Perhaps the major difficulty with Baer's autobiography is how her narrative holds the past against the German people as a collective while at the same time it absolves her of her own personal responsibility. Her construction of the functioning of memory is crucial to this incongruity. In the past couple of decades, autobiographical writers, literary critics, and theorists have been engaged in a rigorous questioning of traditional notions of autobiographical subjectivity, which posit the subject as a unified self produced by linear, progressive development. They have replaced this unified subject with the notion of a decentred one who is a contradictory and fluctuating presence in the text.[25] A conception of memory as a dynamic process of forgetting and remembering is crucial to this newer view of subjectivity. While a writer such as Christa Wolf calls the autobiographical project seriously into question when she has her narrator reinterpret events in several different ways to highlight the unreliability of memory, Baer fixes the past firmly in place through her use of what she calls "memory poles." She defines memory poles as "mental markers, imaginary little flagpoles that clearly say 'from here you may go to there'; and that resist all impulses that want to divert the mind from the outlined road."[26] The notions of clarity and an outlined road suggest an unwillingness to admit the politically conscious woman she is today, the mature narrator, could have acted otherwise as the events transpired. If in Christa Wolf's *Patterns of Childhood*, as Robert C. Holub's claims, we are past the time when ordinary German women are seen as simply going along with National Socialism out of stupidity, naiveté, or habit and rather are seen as conflicted participants in a complex social process, Baer's text reminds us that this view might be rather more hopeful than accurate.[27]

Rather than play with memory or take up notions of individual guilt in any serious way, Baer's autobiography begins with her victim status and ends with her personal absolution. Blaming youth and family for bad choices, the book reads like a story of endless hardships: hunger, loneliness, and emotional despondency stand out throughout her narrative of her internment by the Allied forces after the war. As Baer herself outlined in an article for the *Toronto Star* on the sixtieth anniversary of the liberation of Auschwitz in 2005, the political climate around German discussions of their victimization during the war, especially at the war's end with the relentless Allied bombing raids on German civilians, has changed dramatically in recent years.[28] Whereas earlier any discussion of Germany's losses by Germans themselves was seen as devaluing the monstrous fact of the Holocaust, today Germans are beginning to be allowed to talk about their own traumas in the war. Baer's book takes advantage of this change and helps foster it. Perhaps this is why she feels she can end her book on a note of absolution. After her release from prison, where she was held because of her role in the Sicherheitsdienst, Baer tells us how she had to report to authorities whenever she planned to leave Hamburg for more than three days. A young British civilian who had been employed by her uncle before the war worked in the office that held the files of questionable Germans such as Baer. This young man destroyed Baer's file, eradicating the only official record of her past activities in the Sicherheitsdienst. Baer ends her book asking whether God holds a special place in heaven for people like this family friend. In a book that begins with excuses and continues with her victimization, the forgiveness she emphasizes here through religious imagery seems a fitting, though disappointing, conclusion.

Baer avoids hard-hitting questions about her own guilt through a variety of evasive strategies even while she catalogues Germany's guilt with an appearance of objectivity that verges on and at times crosses into self-righteous indignation. What is especially problematic is how she manages to evince an appearance of coming to terms with the past successfully to her Canadian readers, whose knowledge of the subject is limited and still shaped by the repression thesis. While Baer's *In the Shadow of Silence* provides Canadians with a great deal of valuable and little known information about Nazism, especially in relation to the average German, it also presents a rather skewed picture of Germany's painful process of dealing with the past. It appears that only an outsider located in the German diaspora can interrogate the past with any kind of *Gründlichkeit*. That this outsider in the end does little to interrogate her own individual responsibility leaves us where we began, perhaps even as far back as 1933: wondering where the individual fits into the collective and what collective responsibility really means.

Notes

1   Baer, *In the Shadow*, x.
2   See Holub, "Fact, Fantasy, and Female Subjectivity," 221. Two such revisionary attempts of the 1980s, which ultimately failed, were German chancellor Helmut Kohl's invitation to U.S. president Ronald Reagan to attend a ceremony to honour dead soldiers, including members of the SS, at Bitburg and the *Historikerstreit*, the intellectual and ideological dispute about how the Holocaust should be interpreted, where some of Germany's conservative historians tried to relativize the Holocaust by comparing it to atrocities committed by other nations (e.g., Stalin's terror).
3   For good overviews of the scholarship on German women as more than victims of National Socialism, see Mushaben, "Collective Memory," 14–18; Martin, "Victims or Perpetrators?" 64–66.
4   Martin, "Women Right," 16.
5   Wolf and Rehmann's texts have been translated and published in English: Wolf's as *A Model Childhood* (1980) and then renamed *Patterns of Childhood* (1984), to reflect the German title more accurately, and Rehmann's as *The Man in the Pulpit: Questions for a Father* (1997).
6   Elaine Martin outlines what she calls a "perpetrator-continuum" for Germany's literary women who grappled with their roles in the Second World War. If Melita Maschmann, Renate Finckh, and Carola Stern lie at the most culpable end, she places Wolf, Drewitz, Rehmann, and Zeller at the other end, marked more by apathy, where I also see Baer as falling. Martin, "Victims or Perpetrators?" 65–66.
7   Martin, "Victims or Perpetrators?" 65.
8   Baer, *In the Shadow*, 26.
9   As a middle-brow text, *In the Shadow of Silence* was published by the well-known, mainstream Toronto publisher, HarperCollins, and was shortlisted for the prestigious Charles Taylor Prize for Literary Non-Fiction, which is given annually to the author whose book best demonstrates and combines a command of the English language and elegance of style with a subtlety of thought and perception.
10 Smith, *Poetics of Woman's Autobiography*, 19.
11 Baer, *In the Shadow*, ix.
12 Confino, "Traveling as a Culture of Remembrance," 93.
13 Baer, *In the Shadow*, x.
14 Mushaben, "Collective Memory," 7.
15 Baer, *In the Shadow*, 9.
16 Baer, *In the Shadow*, 6.
17 Baer, *In the Shadow*, 7.
18 Baer, *In the Shadow*, 7.
19 Baer, *In the Shadow*, 15.
20 See Heineman, *What Difference Does a Husband Make?*; Koonz, *Mothers in the Fatherland*.
21 Gellately, *Backing Hitler*, 201–03.
22 Baer, *In the Shadow*, 24.
23 Martin, "Victims or Perpetrators?" 66–67.
24 Margarete Hannsman, quoted in an interview in Martin, "Victims or Perpetrators?" 66–67.
25 Kosta, *Recasting Autobiography*, 4.
26 Baer, *In the Shadow*, 5.
27 Holub, "Fact, Fantasy, and Female Subjectivity," 230.
28 Baer, "Germans Wrestle," A25.

Works Cited

Baer, Gertrud Mackprang. "Germans Wrestle with Culture of Memory," *Toronto Star*, 29 April 2005, A25.

——. *In the Shadow of Silence—From Hitler Youth to Allied Internment: A Young Woman's Story of Truth and Denial*. Toronto: HarperCollins, 2002.

Confino, Alon. "Traveling as a Culture of Remembrance: Traces of National Socialism in West Germany, 1945–1960." *History and Memory* 12, no. 2 (2001): 92–121.

Drewitz, Ingeborg. *Gestern war Heute: Hundert Jahre Gegenwart*. Düsseldorf: Claassen, 1983.

Finckh, Renate. *Mit uns zieht die neue Zeit*. Baden-Baden: Signal, 1979.

Gellately, Robert. *Backing Hitler: Consent and Coercion in Nazi Germany*. Oxford: Oxford University Press, 2001.

Heineman, Elizabeth. *What Difference Does a Husband Make? Women and Marital Status in Nazi and Postwar Germany*. Berkeley: University of California Press, 2003.

Holub, Robert C. "Fact, Fantasy, and Female Subjectivity: *Vergangenheitsbewältigung* in Christa Wolf's *Patterns of Childhood*." In *Facing Fascism and Confronting the Past: German Women Writers from Weimar to the Present*, edited by Elke P. Frederiksen and Martha Kaarsberg Wallach, 217–34. Albany, NY: State University of New York Press, 2000.

Koonz, Claudia. *Mothers in the Fatherland: Women, the Family, and Nazi Politics*. New York: St. Martin's Press, 1987.

Kosta, Barbara. *Recasting Autobiography: Women's Counterfictions in Contemporary German Literature and Film*. Ithaca, NY: Cornell University Press, 1994.

Martin, Elaine. "Victims or Perpetrators? Literary Responses to Women's Roles in National Socialism." In *Facing Fascism and Confronting the Past: German Women Writers from Weimar to the Present*, edited by Elke P. Frederiksen and Martha Kaarsberg Wallach, 61–82. Albany, NY: State University of New York Press, 2000.

——. "Women Right/(Re)Write the Nazi Past: An Introduction." In *Gender, Patriarchy, and Fascism in the Third Reich: The Response of Women Writers*, edited by Elaine Martin, 11–29. Detroit: Wayne State University Press, 1993.

Maschmann, Melita. *Fazit; Mein Weg in der Hitler-Jugend*. Munich: DTV, 1963.

Mitscherlich, Alexander, and Margarete Mitscherlich. *Die Unfähigkeit zu trauern: Grundlagen kollektiven Verhaltens*. 1967. Munich: Piper, 2004.

Mushaben, Joyce Marie. "Collective Memory Divided and Reunited: Mothers, Daughters and the Fascist Experience in Germany." *History and Memory* 11, no. 1 (1999): 7–40.

Rehmann, Ruth. *The Man in the Pulpit: Questions for a Father*. Translated by Christoph Lohmann and Pamela Lohmann. Lincoln, NE: University of Nebraska Press, 1997.

Rehmann, Ruth. *Der Mann auf der Kanzel. Fragen an einen Vater*. Berlin: Evangelische Verlagsanstalt, 1979.

Smith, Sidonie. *A Poetics of Woman's Autobiography: Marginality and the Fictions of Self-Representation*. Bloomington: Indiana University Press, 1987.

Stern, Carola. *In den Netzen der Erinnerung.* Reinbek: Rowohlt, 1986.

Wolf, Christa. *Patterns of Childhood.* Translated by Ursule Molinaro and Hedwig Rappolt. New York: Farrar Straus Giroux, 1984.

Zeller, Eva. *Solange ich denken kann. Roman einer Jugend.* Stuttgart: Deutsche Verlags-Anstalt, 1981.

Zeller, Eva. *Nein und Amen.* Stuttgart: Deutsche Verlags-Anstalt, 1986.

THIRTY-SEVEN

A German Post-1945 Diaspora?

German Migrants' Encounters with the Nazi Past

Alexander Freund

The Germans who immigrated to Canada and the United States after 1945 were a heterogeneous group, but they had one common experience: they had multiple public and private, media and personal encounters and confrontations with Germany's Nazi past in the context of North American society and intercultural relations. This chapter explores whether this common experience was shared among German migrants in such a way that it could become the basis of a diasporic identity. On the basis of oral history interviews, the author concludes that German migrants seldom shared their experiences of encountering the Nazi past in North America and, therefore, did not develop a diasporic identity.

WEST GERMAN NATIONAL IDENTITY AFTER 1945—after National Socialism, war, and the Holocaust—was shaped by *Vergangenheitsbewältigung*, the manifold and diverse ways "of effectively 'working through,' 'coming to terms' with—or eliding—this immediate past, of collectively and individually assimilating and commemorating (or alternatively deflecting, neutralizing or repressing) it."[1] Using Benedict Anderson's idea of "imagined communities,"[2] one can say that Germans had to reimagine the national community of which they believed to be members. Germans' ways of dealing with the Nazi past evolved in diverse ways and directions over the six decades after 1945. At the same time, millions of Germans left Germany to live—temporarily or permanently—in other countries. How did Germans abroad deal with the Nazi past? Did they share their experiences in such a way that they could imagine themselves as members of a diasporic community?

Several oral history projects with German migrants as well as other sources show that throughout the last sixty years, Germans abroad were frequently challenged to deal with the Nazi past, in one way or another, in public and private intercultural encounters. In diverse ways they struggled to make sense not only of the Nazi past, but also of the multiple intercultural encounters shaped by this past. Several factors made *Vergangenheitsbewältigung* abroad a greater challenge than in Germany. They included language problems, cultural differences, and, most important, the fact that at stake for German migrants was not only their German identity but also their attempt to form an identity in their new homeland. If these intercultural encounters of the Nazi past were fairly common and if they raised difficult questions for the migrants, did Germans abroad somehow share them with fellow German migrants in a way that a discourse about this common experience could forge a shared sense of identity? In other words, did this experience of "*Vergangenheitsbewältigung* abroad" forge a diasporic identity among post-1945 German migrants?

From the late 1940s to the early '60s, hundreds of thousands of Germans immigrated to Canada and the United States, tens of thousands more to Australia, New Zealand, Great Britain, and many other countries.[3] Did these migrations constitute a diaspora? For the purposes of this discussion, a diaspora exists if members of an ethnic group reside in at least two countries outside of the home country *and* are linked across political or geographical boundaries through an origin myth, a collective history, or a common religion or ideology. In the broadest sense, they share an identity that does not have to be homogeneous or integrative. Although Dirk Hoerder has pointed to the multiple problems of the concept of diaspora for German worldwide migrations since the eighteenth century,[4] could the concept of diaspora nevertheless be useful in a spatially and temporally more focused application, one that tries to explain German-speaking migrations in North American and possibly elsewhere after 1945?

German migrants were certainly a heterogeneous group. Just among the group of postwar immigrants, they were divided by gender, class, religion and politics, generation and age, region, and even language. They brought with them diverse experiences and memories of the Third Reich, the war, and the postwar years. Most often, they were not connected to other German migrants across national boundaries, and even within national borders many decided to blend in with the dominant society rather than maintain contacts with other Germans. Their connections to Germany were fragile and tenuous, especially for those who had fled eastern Europe or the eastern German territories during or after the war and spent only a few years in western Germany, as well as for those who had few or no relatives left "back home." Any sense of a German "origin myth" had been perverted by the Nazis and thus rendered useless, if not unrecognizable.

Nevertheless, German-speaking immigrants had common experiences that were specific and common to them. They experienced intercultural encounters shaped by memories of the Nazi period, particularly the war and the Holocaust. Excerpt 1 illuminates the kinds of encounters with the Nazi past with which German immigrants could be faced in postwar North America. The interviewee was born in Silesia in 1931 and emigrated to Canada in 1953, aged 22. She soon found "a nice little apartment," recalling:

> Excerpt 1: I didn't know it at first, but I moved in with a Jewish family. And they were so nice to me. And I remember thinking, "How come they're nice to me? How can they be nice to me?" I had to sort of struggle with this. I don't struggle with it any more today, but at that age ... And I remember going to a movie, it was the first American movie I saw where there were Nazis, and I was so upset that they portrayed our soldiers so badly that I ran out half way through, crying. So that was the first time I sort of came face to face with that there was another side, you know ... And this was difficult, because as children all during the war we were sheltered, we weren't told anything that was going on, you know. So I had to, finally—I heard more and more and adjusted more about this problem and I could sort of try to come to grips with it, and I'd tell myself, "Oh, I haven't done anybody any harm, my dad wasn't in the party." But then they all said, "Oh yes, nobody is ever in the party!" That's how the Canadians would talk, you know. [Sara Varsintzky]

Throughout the six decades after 1945, Germans in North America faced two kinds of encounters: confrontations with media representations of World War II and the Holocaust; and personal encounters and relations with other North Americans, including Jewish North Americans. While German migrants disagreed on the meanings of such encounters, confrontations, and relationships, they nevertheless were conscious of the significance of such encounters for their own lives. They came to understand that to be a German abroad, to put it simply and perhaps simplistically, meant to be associated, in one way or another, with the history of Nazi Germany.

Let us first look at media encounters, which can be broken roughly into two periods: the 1950s and '60s focused on representations and interpretations of World War II, while from the 1970s on the focus shifted to the Holocaust. Postwar immigrants were generally not used to North American interpretations of the war. Even though Germans watched U.S.

war movies in postwar Germany, they consumed mostly German-made productions, particularly of the *Heimatfilm* genre. Several postwar immigrants argued that U.S. war movies generated and perpetuated stereotypes of Germans as Nazis among the North American population. While only a few people interviewed for this study said that they personally experienced discrimination with references to such movies,[5] several explained that such movies discriminated against Germans in a more general way.

In the 1960s, several German Canadians protested against the CBS television comedy show *Hogan's Heroes* (1965–71), which depicted the adventures of clever U.S. Air Force officers in a German prisoner of war camp run by cowardly, incompetent, but basically good-hearted German soldiers. Letters to the editor in German Canadian newspapers such as *Der Courier* decried the show as "hate propaganda."[6] At the 1973 annual meeting of the Trans-Canada Alliance for German Canadians (TCA), a national German Canadian umbrella organization founded in 1951, members debated what to do against "*Hetzfilme*" (inflammatory films).[7] While it is unclear which films the members found objectionable, the protest came a year before the TCA, which until then had been dominated by social democrats, was taken over by ultraconservative and extreme right-wing members.[8] According to Peter Hessel, who in the 1980s was a representative to the TCA's successor organization, the German Canadian Congress (GCC, founded in 1984), some German Canadians continued to agitate against such movies.[9] Among them were authors of letters to the editor in the German Canadian newspaper *Kanada Kurier*. Hessel rejected this kind of activity and argued that it damaged the image of German Canadians. Disagreement about how to deal with public discourses about the war thus led to tensions among German Canadians themselves.

A great number of German postwar immigrants were troubled by such North American media discourses. This was so in part because they watched the movies in public, surrounded mostly by non-Germans. In this situation they suddenly became aware of their minority status, their potential vulnerability, and their potential exposure as "the other" in Canadian or U.S. society. Even for those who watched *Hogan's Heroes* at home, at stake was not only their German identity but also their Canadian or American identity. In other words, both truthful and distorted representations of Germans in North American media made it difficult for German migrants to imagine themselves as members of either a German or a North American national community.[10]

Other German migrants saw such movies not as offensive to them, but rather, like the interviewee Sara Varsintzky above, as a learning experience or, in the case of Irma Hiebert, as a teaching tool.[11] When Hiebert, who came to Winnipeg in 1953, saw war movies on television, she became angry and sad because they reminded her of the atrocities committed by her fellow Germans. Although the movies made her upset, she used them to teach her children and grandchildren about the German heritage they shared, which included acknowledging the Nazi atrocities as much as enjoying German culture.

Rather than decreasing in significance over the years, North Americans' interest in the Holocaust grew significantly from the 1970s.[12] Some interviewees saw this new Holocaust awareness as more troubling than the previous focus on the war. Such movies, they argued, revived stereotypes of Germans as Nazis, which now resulted in their children, born in the 1960s and 70s, being taunted at school.[13] Integration now became threatened for themselves as well as for their children. It did so because, as a few argued, such movies implied Germans' trans-generational collective guilt. Some migrants, predominantly those who migrated soon after the war, but also those who migrated later, simply decided not to watch, listen to, or read anything about the Holocaust because they felt it was just too horrible and upsetting for them as Germans or as human beings—an important difference, but too often left unexplored and unexplained in the interviews. As Olaf Jensen and Alexander Freund found in their analysis of an interview with members of three generations of a German Canadian family, in Canada as in Germany the children and grandchildren of those who lived through the Third Reich and emigrated to Canada after the war tended to see their parents as victims and their grandparents as heroes.[14]

As in the case of earlier war movies, other immigrants used this new Holocaust awareness to learn more about the past or to teach their children and grandchildren about it. Thus, German North Americans' responses to the television mini series *Holocaust* (1978), the movie *Schindler's List* (1993), and many other productions were wide-ranging. While this was, in some way, similar to the range of reactions in Germany, German immigrants and their descendents took few cues from the ways in which West German society tried to come to terms with the Nazi past after the 1960s. As the interviews show, German North Americans knew very little about West German/German *Vergangenheitsbewältigung*. Easier forms of transnational communication and travel—from cheaper air fares in the 1970s and cheaper telephone rates in the 1980s, to email, internet and Deutsche Welle TV—seem to have had little impact on this disconnection. Perhaps Germans abroad felt they could not learn much from their cousins in Germany, because, as in the case of the war movies, the situation in which German migrants watched Holocaust movies was decidedly different from the way Germans watched them in Germany. This was particularly true for immigrant children. The situations of watching movies about the war and the Holocaust were more precarious for children than they were for their parents. For example, John and Valerie Werner were born in post-war Austria, came to Toronto in 1949 and 1954 respectively, and married in 1974. Their experiences of watching Holocaust movies in high school were quite different. For Valerie, the experience was positive, because her teacher was "very sympathetic towards the Germans" and she was among several German immigrant children. John, on the other hand, was one of only a few German students in his high school, and his history teacher "just did not distinguish" between Nazis and Germans. As a result, he said, he was harassed and lost friends. At home, he clashed with his father, who said the books did not tell the truth.[15]

While the experience of watching a Holocaust movie could be very much shaped by the social situation, there were also psychological factors. Ethel-Maria Nikesch wrote in 2006 that seeing the movie *Life Is Beautiful* (1997) with her family in Germany had been a good experience, but seeing the Oscar Award–winning Holocaust tragicomedy as an exchange student in Great Britain together with international students was completely different: "All of a sudden, everything changed. [I] could not quite pinpoint the part in the movie when [I] started feeling bad. Was it when the German soldiers in the concentration camps were shouting their commands in German?... For the first time [I] ... realized the burden of what it meant to be German."[16] Nikesch felt everyone was looking at her. Whether anyone actually did is a different question. This self-consciousness was most often articulated by Germans born in the 1970s and '80s who spent some time in North America.

Whatever their response to the growing interest in the Holocaust by North American media products, German migrants felt reminded of their connection with this terrible period in German history. To some degree, the children and even grandchildren of German immigrants felt similarly. German North Americans realized that they could not simply get rid of or away from this link. The "imagined community" was not a matter of individual choice—one could not simply "un-imagine" it from one day to the next.[17]

In sum, with regard to German migrants' encounters with North American media discourses about the war and the Holocaust, while Germans ascribed multiple meanings to public discourses and disagreed about these meanings, it is perhaps even more important that they did not seem to talk about them very much. Some talked about the movies and the bigger questions they raised in their families.[18] But Germans abroad did not talk to other Germans, abroad or in Germany, about their common experiences. The big exception was the fairly small group of Germans who voiced their indignation in German Canadian publications and organizations, but the little response they generated indicates that their sentiments were not widely shared among other Germans migrants. In other words, the experience of being confronted with the Nazi past through media representations of the war and Holocaust may have been common among Germans abroad, but it was not a shared experience. The experience was personal and private, not public and political.

More complex and challenging to deal with than media representations were personal encounters with other North Americans. As mentioned above, Varsintzky met Canadians who ridiculed her solemn vow that her family had not been members of the Nazi party; and she met Jews who, to her great surprise, were nice to her. Germans south of the border in the United States had similar personal encounters.

Of course, most encounters and relations between German immigrants and other North Americans were not influenced by memories of the Nazi past, at least not explicitly. In general, the great majority of Germans in North America felt comfortable in their new homelands.[19] But discrimination and privilege and positive and negative ethnic stereotypes of Germans were nevertheless present and, as the interviewees indicated, memorable.

Privilege was conferred by way of old stereotypes of Germans as hard working and clean. Thus interviewees recounted obtaining jobs because employers assumed they would be good workers simply because they were German. Postwar immigrants felt positive about such stereotypes because they generally agreed with those images. Later generations and later immigrants were more ambivalent: some laughed off such stereotypes; others felt awkwardly reminded of the Nazi past, when they, as Germans, were praised as "orderly and efficient."[20] Negative stereotyping of Germans after 1945 was almost always based on the knowledge of the Nazi period. A minority of interviewees, between 10 percent and 20 percent, reported that they or their children were called Nazis or were otherwise personally identified with the Hitler regime. The interviews contain many striking examples, some as recently as 2003.[21] Several interviewees pointed out, however, that they had never experienced any form of discrimination and others emphasized that their negative experiences were singular or unusual.

Yet there was more to intercultural encounters than simple stereotyping. Especially in the late 1940s and '50s, Germans met Canadians and Americans who had fought in the war or lost relatives in Europe. In a few cases, they met with resentment. To some degree, this has continued to the present, as is evident from the lack of German immigrants' participation in Remembrance Day ceremonies and the lack of invitations from veterans' associations. In Lethbridge, Alberta, "several Canadian war veterans objected to the presence of a German war veteran at their Remembrance Day ceremony" in 1986.[22] In an interview with the *Winnipeg Free Press* in

2003, Wilhelm Kreyes said that he would not feel comfortable at a Remembrance Day ceremony.[23] The newspaper pointed out to its readers that as a medic he had been a "non-combatant," had served on the Eastern Front, and had helped wounded Allied soldiers. Relations in Kitchener-Waterloo, the Canadian region with the highest proportion of German Canadians, were "generally quite amicable" in 1986.[24] Few German immigrants followed the example of Christian Taufberg, a former Wehrmacht soldier, who immigrated to Canada in 1951. He joined "Veterans Against Nuclear Armament," where he shared "great comradeship" with Canadian veterans.[25]

Meeting other Europeans who had suffered under the Nazis was, at least for some German immigrants, a more intense and complex encounter. This ranged from physical violence via accusations, awkward silence, and hesitant inquiries to friendship, love, and marriage, and again the interviews yield many examples.[26] Perhaps most important for German immigrants were encounters and relations with Jews in North America. They met Jewish North Americans who had been in the country for several generations, but also prewar refugees and survivors of the concentration and death camps. Postwar German immigrants, unlike later generations who came in the 1960s and later, were not surprised to meet Jews, but they were surprised that they were, as Varsintzky put it, "nice" to them. In the postwar years, German immigrants often worked for or with Jews. For example, of the 25,000 single German women who came to Canada as domestic servants in the 1950s, many worked in Jewish homes. New York was perhaps the city where most German Jewish relationships developed, and soon after the war there were German Jewish friendships, love, and marriages.

But there were also tensions. Some Jews continued their conscious or subconscious boycott of German goods and German people. Some Germans continued to hold anti-Semitic views. Such negative encounters are much harder to find in German immigrants' life stories because Germans found it difficult to talk about them. The fear of being seen as anti-Semitic explains this only in part. Having a positive relationship with a Jew was seen by some as an "absolution" from collective guilt. For others, particularly migrants after the 1960s, meeting Jews became a learning experience for both sides. Several younger German women who immigrated to New York in the 1990s reported that they confronted Jewish resentment instead of avoiding it. As a result, mutual stereotypes were broken down and sometimes lasting friendships formed.[27]

So far, the interviews with Germans and Jews conducted for this study indicate that German Jewish encounters in post-Holocaust North America were more important for the Germans than for the Jews. This may be why an almost archetypal story among German immigrants of any generation, but perhaps even more so of later generations, has become the one of meeting a Jew for the first time. The other is the general surprise at Jews' friendliness toward Germans; such a perception was of course not unproblematic, but cannot be explored here.[28]

Germans migrants in North America encountered, through the media and personal intercultural relations, representations and memories of the Nazi past that could be even more difficult to deal with than in Germany. Such encounters reminded them of the Nazi past, which challenged not only their ideas of what it meant to be German, but also their attempts to become Canadian or American. They experienced such encounters as roadblocks, but sometimes as new paths to imagining themselves as members of the Canadian or American nation.

Unlike in Germany, *Vergangenheitsbewältigung* abroad was not a shared experience. However they interpreted the past, German migrants dealt with its memories individually, privately, and personally, not collectively, publicly, and politically. If not only nation but also diaspora are understood as an imagined community, it is clear that such a social and cultural sharing—the linking, connecting, networking, and exchanging of experiences, memories, and interpretations—is an integral part of diaspora as an imagined community. There were no German diasporic discourses that would have created a new imagined, German diasporic community. Thus, at least for now, this common experience of intercultural encounters with the Nazi past should not be seen as the grounds for a postwar, post-Holocaust German diasporic identity.

This chapter is based on one hundred and fifty interviews conducted by the author and his research assistants in Canada and the United States between 1993 and 2006 and three hundred interviews with German Canadians from collections at the Multicultural History Society of Ontario and the Manitoba Museum. The author thanks the Rockefeller Foundation, the Columbia University Oral History Research Office, the German Historical Institute in Washington DC, the Johns Hopkins University American Institute for Contemporary German Studies, the University of Winnipeg, his assistants Angela Thiessen and Christine Kampen, and especially the interviewees.

Notes

1   Aschheim, *Culture and Catastrophe*, 17.
2   Anderson, *Imagined Communities*.
3   See Nerger-Focke, *Die deutsche Amerikaauswanderung;* Steinert, *Migration und Politik;* Bönisch-Brednich, *Auswandern;* Freund, *Aufbrüche;* Biedermann, *Eine bezahlte Passage.*
4   Hoerder, "German-Language Diasporas."
5   For example, Dobel, interview.

6   Library and Archives Canada, Manuscript Group 31 H39, Cardinal, Kurt v., vol. 3: Trans-Canada Alliance of German Canadians (TCA), file: "Hate Propaganda."

7   Ontario Archives, Multicultural History Society of Ontario Papers F1405, Series 60, German Canadian Papers, File 060B073, "Protokoll zur Jahreshauptversammlung der Trans-Canada Alliance am 28. und 29. Oktober 1973 im Concordia Club, in Kitchener, Ontario," 6.

8   Wieden, *The Trans-Canada Alliance*. Fritz Wieden, cultural advisor and first vice-president of the TCA from 1969 to 1974 and professor of German at the University of Windsor, was among those ousted by "the right-wing autocracy" (79). According to him, they made the TCA "into a right-wing German organization similar to the old [Nazi-sympathetic] Deutscher Bund Canada," 67.

9   Hessel, interview. For example, "Vierzig Jahre."

10   Anderson, *Imagined Communities*.

11   Hiebert, interview; Pauls (Irma Hiebert's youngest daughter), interview.

12   Novick, *Holocaust in American Life*.

13   See also Chapter 25.

14   Jensen and Freund, "History and Memory."

15   Werner, interview.

16   Nikesch, "*Vergangenheitsbewältigung*," 3.

17   Hegi, *Tearing the Silence*, 15; Reichel, *What Did You Do*, 10.

18   Jensen and Freund, "History and Memory."

19   See Nikesch, "*Vergangenheitsbewältigung*."

20   Hegi, *Tearing the Silence*, 168.

21   See Lippert, interview; Varsintzky, interview; "Schüleraustausch: Ganz rüde Anmache"; Nikesch, "*Vergangenheitsbewältigung*," 22–23.

22   Howitt, "Wounds Largely Healed," 37.

23   Kreyes, interview; Ayers, "Former Medic," B4.

24   Howitt, "Wounds Largely Healed."

25   Taufberg, interview.

26   See Blos, interview; Maatz, interview; Grohsmann, interview; Schulz, interview.

27   See Rosner and Tubach, *An Uncommon Friendship*.

28   See Freund, "'How Come They're Nice to Me?'"

Interview Sources

All interviews conducted by the author and in his possession unless otherwise indicated.

Blos, Magda (pseudonym). Vancouver, March 1993.

Dobel, Helene. Interview by L. Lenze, Winnipeg, 22 January 1997. Interview at Multicultural Historical Society of Ontario Papers A003A.

Grohsmann, Johanna (pseudonym). Vancouver, 26 November 1993.

Hessel, Peter. Waba, ON, 22 March 1998.

Hiebert, Irma. Interview by Angela Thiessen, Winnipeg, 14 July 2005. Interview in author's possession.

Kreyes, Wilhelm. Interview by Angela Thiessen, Winnipeg, 15 July 2005. Interview in author's possession.

Lippert, Karin. New York, NY, 20 June 2000.

Maatz, Mark (pseudonym). Edmonton, 2 and 3 October 1996.

Pauls, Nancy. Interview by Angela Thiessen, Winnipeg, 18 August 2005. Interview in author's possession.

Schulz, Doris (pseudonym). Richmond, BC, 22 September 1993.
Taufberg, Christian and Gitte (pseudonyms). Chelsea, QC, 15 March 1998.
Varsintzky, Sara (pseudonym). Ottawa, 26 March 1998.
Werner, John and Valerie. Interview by R. Zirger, 16 July 1998. Interview at Multicultural Historical Society of Ontario.

Archival Material

Library and Archives Canada. Manuscript Group 31 H39. Cardinal, Kurt v., vol. 3: Trans-Canada Alliance of German Canadians (TCA). File: "Hate Propaganda."
Ontario Archives, Multicultural History Society of Ontario Papers F1405. Series 60. German Canadian Papers. File 060–073. "Protokoll zur Jahreshauptversammlung der Trans-Canada Alliance am 28. und 29. Oktober 1973 im Concordia Club, in Kitchener, Ontario."

Works Cited

Anderson, Benedict. *Imagined Communities: Reflections on the Origin and Spread of Nationalism*. Revised edition. London: Verso, 1991.
Aschheim, Steven E. *Culture and Catastrophe: German and Jewish Confrontations with National Socialism and Other Crises*. Houndmills: Macmillan, 1996.
Ayers, Tom. "Former Medic Quietly Observes Remembrance Day." *Winnipeg Free Press*. 10 November 2003, B4.
Biedermann, Bettina. *Eine bezahlte Passage. Die Auswanderung von Deutschen nach Australien in den 1950er Jahren*. Marburg: Metropolis, 2006.
Bönisch-Brednich, Brigitte. *Auswandern—Destination Neuseeland. Eine ethnographische Migrationsstudie*. Blankenburg: Mana, 2002.
Freund, Alexander. *Aufbrüche nach dem Zusammenbruch: Die deutsche Nordamerikaauswanderung nach dem Zweiten Weltkrieg*. Göttingen: V&R unipress, 2004.
———. "'How Come They're Nice to Me?' Deutsche und Juden nach dem Holocaust in Nordamerika." In *Migration und Erinnerung. Reflexionen über Wanderungserfahrungen in Europa und Nordamerika*, edited by Christiane Harzig. Göttingen: V&R unipress, 2006.
Hegi, Ursula. *Tearing the Silence: On Being German in America*. New York: Simon & Schuster, 1997.
Hoerder, Dirk. "German-Speaking Immigrants: Co-Founders or Mosaic?" *Zeitschrift für Kanada-Studien* 14, no. 2 (1994): 51–65.
———. "The German-Language Diasporas: A Survey, Critique, and Interpretation." *Diaspora: A Journal of Transnational Studies* 11, no. 1 (2002): 7–44.
Howitt, Charles. "Wounds Largely Healed for Canadian, German Vets Here." *Kitchener-Waterloo Record*, 13 November 1986, reprinted in *Canadiana Germanica* 52 (December 1986): 37.
Jensen, Olaf, and Alexander Freund. "History and Memory in the Diaspora: German-Canadian Families Talk about the Nazi Past." Paper presented at the conference on "German Diasporic Experiences," Waterloo Centre for German Studies, University of Waterloo, Waterloo, ON, 25 August 2006.

Nerger-Focke, Karin. *Die deutsche Amerikaauswanderung nach 1945. Rahmenbedingungen und Verlaufsformen*. Stuttgart: Heinz, 1995.

Nikesch, Ethel-Maria. "*Vergangenheitsbewältigung* in the Midwest: Post-War German Immigrants Recall Their Experiences." Senior thesis, Concordia College, 2006.

Novick, Peter. *The Holocaust in American Life*. Boston: Houghton Mifflin, 1999.

Reichel, Sabine. *What Did You Do In the War, Daddy? Growing Up German*. New York: Hill and Wang, 1989.

Rosner, Bernat, and Frederic C. Tubach. *An Uncommon Friendship: From Opposite Sides of the Holocaust*. Berkeley: University of California Press, 2001.

"Schüleraustausch: Ganz rüde Anmache." *Der Spiegel*, 17 March 2003.

Steinert, Johannes-Dieter. *Migration und Politik. Westdeutschland—Europa—Übersee 194–1961*. Osnabrück: Secolo, 1995.

Wieden, Fritz. *The Trans-Canada Alliance of German Canadians: A Study in Culture*. Windsor, ON: Tolle Lege, 1985.

THIRTY-EIGHT

Di Brandt's Writing Breaks Canadian Mennonite Silence and Reshapes Cultural Identity

Natasha G. Wiebe

One cultural storyline of the German-speaking Mennonites—a practice they learn and live by, and express in their discourse—is that of the Mennonites as peacemakers. Admirably, the Mennonites have been opposed to war and conflict for centuries. However, the work of critically acclaimed poet Di Brandt, of Canadian Mennonite heritage, suggests that pacifism, or nonresistance, can silence individual expression and perpetuate abuse in the interest of keeping community peace. In 1987, Brandt challenged the Mennonite storyline of nonresistance and silence by publishing poetry—revolutionary in her patriarchal separatist home community—and by writing about controversial subjects such as religious contradictions, female sexuality, and misogyny. Brandt's collected poetry and prose redefine her cultural identity by relocating it within a storyline of protest and resistance that characterizes the outspoken Mennonite writer as a dissenter like her sixteenth-century Anabaptist ancestors. Her writing also offers insight into the reshaping of the greater Canadian Mennonite cultural identity.

sometimes i just felt i would burst with all of the unanswered questions inside
—Di Brandt

DI BRANDT HOLDS A CANADA RESEARCH CHAIR and is an English professor and a multiple-award-winning poet of Canadian Mennonite heritage. Among the first Mennonite writers and poets in English, Brandt exploded onto the Canadian literary scene in 1987, with *questions i asked my mother*, a book of poetry later shortlisted for the Governor General's Literary Award. Much of this book and subsequent work concern her upbringing in the conservative Russian German Mennonite farming community of Reinland, Manitoba, in the 1950s and '60s. Brandt describes her village as living "with our hearts and souls somewhere halfway between sixteenth-century northern Europe and the Old Testament, and our minds and bodies ... in twentieth-century Canada."[1] Her poetry and prose depict a community that she both loves and hates; a "Family net" she was "happy to have escaped," yet one for which she later "ach[es] with loss."[2] In Reinland, which is filled with "singing and laughter (and also griefs of all sizes),"[3] fathers bear responsibility for the souls[4] within their individual "kingdoms";[5] mothers—with heads properly covered[6]—remain silent in church and find self-expression through canning, gardening, sewing, singing, and irreverent storytelling;[7] and religion is so entwined with daily life that even child's play becomes a metaphor for heaven and hell.[8] At home, the Mennonites speak *Plautdietsch* (Low German), and *Hochdeutsch* (High German) in church. English is learned in school for communication with outsiders, although Brandt rarely encounters *de Englische* during her sheltered childhood.[9] Among Reinland's pleasures are recitations of Goethe, Schiller, and Heine's poetry,[10] but reading anything other than the bible is discouraged since it might distract from God's Word,[11] and the visiting library van is forbidden as "worldly."[12]

These are some images of Reinland drawn primarily from Brandt's early poetry and essays. To date, her published writing spans two decades and includes several collections of poetry, a book of feminist literary criticism, and two of personal essays. She has described her works as "life writing."[13] Her texts with Mennonite themes blend autobiographical and fictional conventions as she shapes key moments from her past and in so doing identifies or constructs different understandings of her self.[14] Life or autobiographical writing in this sense has been embraced by women, since as Sidonie Smith and Julia Watson state,

> before the late twentieth century, patriarchal notions of white women's inherently irrational nature and their primary social role of reproduction severely restricted their access to public space and education. Male distrust and repression of female speech condemned most women to public silence, which in turn qualified their relationship to writing as a means of exploring and asserting an identity publicly.[15]

Writing autobiographically is particularly significant in a traditional Mennonite context since it allows women relegated to the private sphere of domesticity to write themselves into the discourse from which they are excluded, or are less prominent than men, and thereby become culturally significant individuals. However, as this analysis of Brandt's autobiographical writing will show, such writing is problematic in a patriarchal religious community that values community cohesiveness over individual expression. Brandt was among the first Canadian Mennonite women to write autobiographically and be published in English. In fact, she stands among the pioneers of Mennonite literature in English and its emergence in Canada.[16] Critically acclaimed, she stems from a separatist patriarchal religious community and says she was exiled from her home community because of her poetry.[17] This chapter explores how Brandt's autobiographical writing asserts her cultural identity, i.e., her sense of being Mennonite as expressed through her (changing) self-identification in her literary works.

The concept of nonresistance is essential for understanding Brandt's work. For her, nonresistance means silence about issues that might create conflict within the community and threaten its harmony and separatism. One way of dealing with such silence is to relocate it within the context of a "cultural storyline" or, in Brandt's words, an "official communal story" or "cultural script."[18] This can be expanded by describing a cultural storyline as the practices learned and perpetuated by a particular culture and represented in its discourse. In this study, cultural storylines are the practices that have become unquestioned parts of what it means to be Mennonite in Brandt's community and that find support in that community's sermons, conversations, and stories. Brandt's writing identifies the cultural storyline that Mennonites should remain silent, particularly in public and especially to outsiders, about controversial or painful issues such as religious doubt or abuse.

This study is informed by the research of Barbara Kamler, who explores how interrupting cultural storylines by writing new ones can transform a writer's subjectivity or self.[19] For instance, Kamler encouraged a class of senior women to rewrite their experiences of the death of others in the context of a cultural critique. Their stories about the joyousness and sensuality of death, rather than grief alone, challenged societal expectations. She gives examples of how such rewriting facilitated changes in the writer's perspectives, eased her psychological pain, even affected her body, and encouraged more productive interaction with other students. Kamler's method has been distilled into a tripartite approach for this study: identifying how cultural storylines discourage individual stories from being told; exploring how, by interrupting a cultural storyline, one can tell other stories; and discovering how telling these other stories can lead to a reshaping of self.[20] First, using Brandt's writing as a lens, the chapter examines the Mennonite cultural storyline of nonresistance and how it discourages her stories of religious contradictions, misogyny, and abuse from being told. Next, it explores how Brandt's writing resists the storyline of nonresistance by exploring forbidden subjects. Then, it suggests ways that

Brandt's writing helps to reshape her cultural identity as a Mennonite. It concludes by comparing Brandt's expression of cultural identity with that offered by some recent commentaries on the greater Canadian Mennonite community.

Mennonite Nonresistance and Silence

Although the Mennonites have roots in the Anabaptist dissent during the times of Protestant Reformation, Brandt's writing reveals the problems of voicing individual thoughts, particularly those that question or depart from a traditional community's beliefs and norms. Consider an excerpt from the poem "questions i asked my mother," in which a young Brandt unwittingly articulates a contradiction in Reinland's doctrine of the afterlife:

> look when grampa died last week everybody said he's better off
> where he is because he's in heaven now he's with God we should
> be happy he's gone home but yesterday when they put him in the
> ground the minister said he's going to be there till the last trumpet
> raises the quick & the dead for the final judgement now look
> mom i can't figure it out which is true it's got to be either up or
> down ...

Her parents chide and correct her:

> i don't think that's a very
> nice thing to say about grampa she begins
> ... it's your attitude he says I've noticed lately
> everything you say has this questioning tone i don't really think you're
> really interested in grampa or your faith what you really want is to
> make trouble for mom & me you've always been like that you're
> always trying to figure everything out your own way instead of
> submitting quietly to the teachings of the church when are you
> going to learn not everything has to make sense your brain is not
> the most important thing in the world what counts is your attitude
> & your faith your willingness to accept the mystery of God's
> ways.[21]

Brandt's mother sidesteps her daughter's question and defers to the father, the spiritual head of the Mennonite home. The mother's response is not surprising in a community where, Brandt writes, "all the official words, were said by men."[22] But Brandt's father does not answer the question either. Instead, he silences his daughter with a response standard in fundamentalist religious communities: he commands Brandt to put aside her intellectual questioning and accept that there are some questions for which there are no answers. He also tells her to submit quietly to the church's teaching. Perhaps contrary to her father's expectations, Brandt does not repent, but continues to yearn for discussion. But as her father's response suggests, such dialogue would be unacceptable because it would challenge the views espoused by religious leaders. It could also lead to defiance of the community's beliefs and to members leaving or being excommunicated, as Brandt eventually was. To protect the cohesiveness of Brandt's separatist Mennonite community and thus its existence, it is necessary to discourage such potentially divisive questions.

The silencing of controversy is rooted in one of the Mennonites' better-known doctrines, pacifism or nonresistance as it has traditionally been known. This doctrine finds support in biblical passages like Matthew 5:38–48, which express Jesus' teaching to love one's enemies and to "turn the other cheek" if someone strikes you. Living in love would, therefore, also include refusing to go to war, as well as refusing to resort to violence, cruelty, or even unkindness in everyday interaction with others. Mennonite historian Marlene Epp has discussed how the political practice of nonresistance (conscientious objection) privileged male Mennonites in Ontario; women were not conscripted and thus were "left out of the great stories of nonresistance and alternative service."[23] Brandt writes of the psychological and interpersonal effects that nonresistance had for Manitoban Mennonites of both genders, suggesting that the doctrine translated into an unwritten rule that one should not resist "power or authority or painful experiences," that extreme feelings should be left unexpressed, and that conflict and disagreement should be suppressed.[24] Her essays suggest that nonresistance manifested itself through the "emotional depression" of her home community, "where contrary voices were shunned [excommunicated] or heavily disciplined and where no one was ever allowed to be angry or to disagree with men in authority."[25] When community harmony and the "collective good" are valued over self-expression, there is no place for voicing "individual perceptions ... opinions and feelings."[26]

Breaking the Silence

Brandt's writing chooses speaking out over respecting a code of silence. Her early poetry uses run-on sentences without punctuation, creating the sense that pent-up words and questions are spilling onto the page. Brandt articulates the need to express herself:

> I just knew that if I didn't do it, I would surely die, so if I was going to die anyway, I might as well die having tried to do something courageous. So I wrote my first book of poems, *questions i asked my mother*, with absolute fierceness and absolute trepidation. I would say to myself, okay, what's the scariest thing I can think of? And then I'd write that down. I was utterly terrified and full of joy at the same time. I knew I was doing something that none of the women in my culture had dared to do for several

centuries, that learning to speak in public in a woman's voice was going to crack open the Mennonite world, and that it would crack me open, too.[27]

What "scary" things does Brandt write about? Her poetry examines issues about which her community discourages conversation or offers standard responses. *questions* challenges Mennonite doctrine and community lifestyle, including the silencing of women and dissenting voices, and arbitrary rules about women's clothing and "worldly" pursuits. *questions* also pushes against the boundaries of propriety with a suite of "bathroom poems" and poems about sex (such as the "missionary position" collection). Such poems explore subjects that were not to be spoken of in Brandt's village, let alone publicized through writing. Her work also critiques the traditional Mennonite practice of reading the bible literally. She plays with this notion in lines such as "let me tell you what it's like / having God for a father & jesus / for a lover."[28] These lines develop the biblical metaphor of the church as the bride of Christ and shock the reader into realizing that the metaphor is not to be read literally. Later poetry, such as "nonresistance, or love Mennonite style," describes physical and sexual abuse among the Mennonites:

> turn the other cheek when your brother
> hits you & your best friend tells fibs
> about you & the teacher punishes you
> unfairly if someone steals your shirt
> give him your coat to boot this will
> heap coals of fire on his head ...
>   ... where
> it gets tricky is when your grandfather
> tickles you too hard or your cousins
> want to play doctor & your uncle kisses
> you too long on the lips
> ...
> submitting quietly in your grandfather's
> house your flesh smouldering in the
> darkened room as you love your enemy
> deeply unwillingly & full of shame[29]

Perhaps it was telling these particular secrets that led Brandt's family and home community eventually to officially shun her,[30] something that broke her heart[31] and about which her writing is uncharacteristically quiet. While most communities would object to being characterized as Brandt describes Reinland, it must have been especially difficult for the intensely separatist Mennonites to be exposed to outsiders through her publications.

Reshaping Cultural Identity

Brandt's writing helped to break multiple silences in the Canadian Mennonite community. She joined Rudy Wiebe, Patrick Friesen, Sandra Birdsell, and several others in breaking Canadian Mennonite literary "silence" in English and moving Mennonite literature into the Canadian mainstream. *questions i asked my mother* penetrated what Brandt describes as the "centuries-old public silence of women in the Mennonite community where I grew up."[32] Her writing also helped break silence in her home community surrounding controversial and painful issues by exploring female sexuality, misogyny, abuse, and religious contradictions. In short, Brandt's early publications challenged the cultural storyline of nonresistance and silence by expressing her female self publicly in writing[33] and by writing about the forbidden.[34] Kamler suggests that interrupting an official storyline with different ones means that women can be seen not merely as passively shaped by others, but as "capable of taking up discourses through which they are shaped and through which they may reshape themselves."[35] While writing and publishing no doubt changed Brandt's sense of self in multiple ways, most important here is the fact that it helped reshape her cultural identity as a Mennonite.

Brandt's shifting and sometimes contradictory sense of being Mennonite can be traced through works written over twenty years. An essay reveals that even before she published her first collection of poems in 1987, Brandt had decided to leave the Mennonites, believing she could not remain if she wanted to be a writer and speak freely, and "knowing in [her] heart it was forever: I spent the next few years grieving over the huge loss involved in giving up my cultural identity … writing, 'in exile.'"[36] However, an essay published in 1988 suggests that she could not escape her cultural identity because the punitive Mennonite God had stamped himself on her psyche; he followed her wherever she went.[37] Conversely, another essay describes spending about nine years—seemingly from 1987 onward—grieving over her "lost" identity and heritage and, with the help of creative writing and a spiritual healer, "reconstruct[ing] my life out of the shattered bits that were left after my big rebel act of becoming a writer, and my own person."[38] Yet a poem apparently written toward the end of this period of healing suggests that telling her story and "stealing" the English language couldn't make her one of *de Englische*, because the Mennonite history of being "beaten & tortured & killed"[39] is remembered by her very body.

Brandt's recent writing shows a continuing renegotiation of her cultural identity. "Berlin Notes" honours the very traditionalism that once constrained her. After marvelling at how the Mennonites preserved their German customs throughout centuries of exile, one passage concludes,

"I am overwhelmed by the thought of my ancestors' stubborn faithfulness, their anarchistic traditionalism, that crazy beautiful heritage, still flourishing in the old ways in the Canadian prairies, surrounded by Indian history, the resonance of drumbeats on buffalo hide, the modern world of machinery and chemicals gradually moving in."[40] A key phrase in this passage refers to Brandt's ancestors as "anarchistic" in their traditionalism, an interesting descriptor for pacifist Mennonites. The phrase offers a glimpse of a new direction in Brandt's writing. "I'm trying to rewrite the origin of the Mennonites and, therefore, the meaning of the Mennonite movement," said Brandt of her latest book of essays (*So This Is the World and Here I Am In It*, published in 2007). "I'm writing in terms that locate me as a good true heir of the heritage, rather than a good heretic ... Since they've kicked me out, I'm trying to rewrite my history so that I belong!" Writing herself back into the Mennonite community means writing about the history of sixteenth-century Anabaptists—the forerunners of the Mennonites—as an "anti-globalizing, local peasant movement that defended independent land ownership and land use in Northern Europe."[41] A new cultural storyline that Brandt's work is creating for the Mennonites and herself is one of secular activism, not biblically inspired pacifism, of resistance rather than nonresistance.

The storyline of resistance is embodied in the rebelliousness of Brandt's writing, which challenged the "peace" of Reinland by penetrating the public silence of its women and its silence on controversial topics and social problems. The storyline of resistance suggests that the true Mennonite challenges the establishment in these ways. The tradition of Mennonite resistance harkens back to the Protestant Reformation of sixteenth-century Germany, Switzerland, and the Netherlands, when the Anabaptist ancestors of the Mennonites opposed state church dictates by reading and interpreting the scriptures without the guidance of a priest and by practising adult baptism and voluntary church membership. After a period of martyrdom suffered because of these and other "heretical" practices, some survivors embarked on what became centuries of migration in search of religious tolerance, eventually founding the separatist Mennonite communities, like Brandt's Reinland, which have become their most-studied feature.[42] Brandt's writing often alludes to this diaspora. Of particular relevance is an essay that compares the trauma she experienced in leaving home and becoming a writer to her ancestors' traumatic history of "being uprooted and displaced."[43] Other passages describe her fear that the Mennonites would kill her for writing her first book of poetry.[44] While this claim at first seems incredible, given Mennonite pacifism, her other work suggests that this fear is rooted in what Brandt's essays call "the Mennonite psyche."[45] "i came from far away, / & brought everything with me. / the body remembers being / beaten & tortured & killed," claims one of her poems.[46] Brandt's "Berlin Notes" muse on "the collective heritage of our own people's long history of persecution and, yes, cruelty. Martyrs turned perpetrators, the heritage turned inward."[47] When considered together, these and other passages build the paradox of how the Mennonite community, although founded in dissent and strengthened during centuries of forced wanderings, now rejects the outspoken writer and forces her into "official homelessness."[48] Thus, a new cultural storyline embedded within Brandt's writing—resistance rather than nonresistance—characterizes the writer as a "true" Mennonite like the Anabaptists before her.[49]

Brandt's Writing and the Greater Canadian Mennonite Identity

Brandt's autobiographical writing may be seen as a window onto a collective experience as described in several recent commentaries written by scholars of Mennonite heritage.[50] Together, these commentaries tell the story of contemporary Canadian Mennonites, now mostly urban and assimilated like their Anabaptist forebears,[51] resuming Anabaptist attitudes and practices diluted or lost over centuries of migration and separation. These practices include voluntary church membership based on personal commitment and individual interpretation of the scriptures, things that were often suppressed in "old, isolated, rural communities where local leaders sometimes exerted very considerable pressure to achieve conformity."[52] Like Brandt's writing, these commentaries reclaim the cultural storyline of Anabaptism to define a new identity for the Canadian Mennonites, but while Brandt's application is decidedly secular, the commentaries set the new identity within the context of religious faith.

Notes

1 Brandt, *Dancing*, 33.
2 Brandt, *Dancing*, 74.
3 Brandt, "Afterword," 47.
4 Brandt, *questions*, 50.
5 Brandt, *questions*, 13.
6 Brandt, *questions*, 9.
7 Brandt, *Dancing*, 55, 145–46.
8 Brandt, *questions*, 2.
9 Brandt, "Je Jelieda," 10.
10 Brandt, "Je Jelieda"; cf. Wiebe, "Interview."
11 Brandt, *questions*, 17; *Dancing*, 19.
12 Brandt, *questions*, 16.
13 Brandt, "Creating Something."
14 This definition synthesizes ideas from Smith and Watson, *Reading Autobiography*, 6–8, 12–13, 32–35; Buss, *Repossessing the World*, e.g., xiv. Buss writes about memoir,

but her descriptions complement the position given here, and elsewhere, on auto-biographical writing.

15 Smith and Watson, *Reading Autobiography*, 114; cf. Buss, *Repossessing the World*, 186.
16 Hostetler, "Bringing Experience to Consciousness," 138.
17 Brandt, "Afterword," 48–49.
18 Brandt, *Dancing*, 111, 113.
19 Kamler, *Relocating the Personal*, 60–61.
20 As described by Kamler, *Relocating the Personal*, 57. The author thanks Cornelia Hoogland for suggesting this customization of Kamler's approach.
21 Brandt, *questions*, 5–6.
22 Brandt, *Dancing*, 55.
23 Epp, "Nonconformity and Nonresistance," 65.
24 Brandt, *Dancing*, 134–36.
25 Brandt, *Dancing*, 134.
26 Brandt, *Dancing*, 10, 111.
27 Brandt, *Dancing*, 156.
28 Brandt, *questions*, 28.
29 Brandt, *Agnes in the Sky*, 38–39.
30 Nurse, "Di Brandt," 19; Brandt, "Afterword," 48–49.
31 Brandt, "From Berlin Notes," 10.
32 Brandt, *Dancing*, 156.
33 Brandt, "Knacksoet en Communism," paragraph 7.
34 Brandt, *Dancing*, 19.
35 Kamler, *Relocating the Personal*, 57.
36 Brandt, *Dancing*, 51–52.
37 Brandt, "How I Got Saved," paragraph 4.
38 Brandt, *Dancing*, 157.
39 Brandt, *Mother, Not Mother*, 30.
40 Brandt, "Berlin Notes," 16.
41 Wiebe, "Interview," paragraphs 5–6.
42 Regehr, "Communities Transformed," 133.
43 Brandt, *Dancing*, 153.
44 Brandt, *Dancing*, 10; "Afterword," 50–51.
45 Brandt, *Dancing*, 153.
46 Brandt, *Mother*, 30.
47 Brandt, "Berlin Notes," 12.
48 Brandt, *Dancing*, 153.
49 The same comparison was made by Magdalene Redekop, quoted in Reimer, *Mennonite Literary Voices*, 3.
50 Driedger, *Mennonites in the Global Village*, 58, 67, 208, 232; Dyck, *An Introduction to Mennonite History*, 402, 413, 434–35; Regehr, "Communities Transformed," 142, 145; Regehr, *Mennonites*, 192–93, 382–83.
51 Driedger, *Mennonites in the Global Village*, frontispiece, 27–28; Regehr, "Communities Transformed," 131; Regehr, *Mennonites*, 1–2.
52 Regehr, "Communities Transformed," 142–43.

Works Cited

Brandt, Di. "Afterword: You Pray for the Rare Flower to Appear." In *Speaking of Power: The Poetry of Di Brandt*, edited by Tanis MacDonald, 47–53. Waterloo, ON: Wilfrid Laurier University Press, 2006.

———. *Agnes in the Sky.* Winnipeg: Turnstone Press, 1990.

———. *Dancing Naked: Narrative Strategies for Writing Across Centuries.* Stratford, ON: Mercury Press, 1996.

———. "From Berlin Notes." *Prairie Fire* 24, no. 3 (2003): 8–19.

———. "How I Got Saved." In *Why I Am a Mennonite: Essays on Mennonite Identity,* edited by Harry Loewen, 26–33. Kitchener: Herald Press, 1988.

———. "Je Jelieda, Je Vechieda: Canadian Mennonites (Alter)identifications." Paper presented at the Inter-Disciplinary Conference: Canada in the Sign of Migration and Trans-Culturalism, Austria, 2003.

———. "Knacksoet en Communism." In *Rudy Wiebe: A Tribute,* edited by Hildi Froese Tiessen. Kitchener: Pandora Press, 2002.

———. *Mother, Not Mother.* Stratford, ON: Mercury Press, 1996.

———. *questions i asked my mother.* Winnipeg: Turnstone Press, 1987.

———. *So This Is the World and Here I Am In It.* Edmonton: NeWest Press, 2007.

Buss, Helen M. *Repossessing the World: Reading Memoirs by Contemporary Women.* Waterloo, ON: Wilfrid Laurier University Press, 2002.

Driedger, Leo. *Mennonites in the Global Village.* Toronto: University of Toronto Press, 2000.

Dyck, Cornelius J., ed. *An Introduction to Mennonite History: A Popular History of the Anabaptists and the Mennonites.* Second edition. Scottdale, PA: Herald Press, 1981.

Epp, Marlene. "Nonconformity and Nonresistance: What Did It Mean to Mennonite Women?" In *Changing Roles of Women within the Christian Church in Canada,* edited by Elizabeth Gillan Muir and Marilyn Färdig Whiteley, 55–76. Toronto: University of Toronto Press, 1995.

Hostetler, Ann. "Bringing Experience to Consciousness: Reflections on Mennonite Literature, 2004." *Journal of Mennonite Studies* 23 (2005): 137–50.

Kamler, Barbara. *Relocating the Personal: A Critical Writing Pedagogy.* Albany, NY: State University of New York Press, 2001.

Nurse, Donna Bailey. "Di Brandt: Poems of Passionate Accusation." *Quill & Quire* (2004): 18–19.

Regehr, Ted D. "Communities Transformed: The Canadian Mennonite Experience, 1939–1970." In *Realizing Community: Multidisciplinary Perspectives,* 129–61. Saskatchewan: University of Saskatchewan Humanities Research Unit, 1995.

———. *Mennonites in Canada, 1939–1970. Volume 3, A People Transformed.* Toronto: University of Toronto Press, 1996.

Reimer, Al. *Mennonite Literary Voices: Past and Present.* Newton, KS: Mennonite Press, 1993.

Smith, Sidonie, and Julia Watson. *Reading Autobiography: A Guide for Interpreting Life Narratives.* Minneapolis: University of Minnesota Press, 2001.

Wiebe, Natasha G. "Creating Something in Order to Be Somewhere: An Interview with Di Brandt." *Prairie Fire* 27, no. 1 (Spring 2006): 82–85.

———. "Interview with Di Brandt." *Prairie Fire Magazine: Review of Books* <http://www.prairiefire.ca/interview_wiebe_brandt.html>.

THIRTY-NINE

Use It or Lose It?

Language Use, Language Attitudes, and Language Proficiency among German Speakers in Vancouver

Monika S. Schmid

This chapter reports on an investigation into the overall first-language proficiency of a group of long-term German immigrants to Canada. It attempts to link individual scores on a number of language tests as well as performance in free speech to reported language use in daily life and to attitudes toward both German and English. The findings from this study suggest that the use of the first language (L1) for professional purposes may help preserve metalinguistic or explicit knowledge of the language, and so lead to somewhat better performance on more formal language tasks.

Introduction

INVESTIGATIONS INTO THE LANGUAGE behaviour of immigrant communities usually find that the degree of maintenance of the heritage language or shift to the language of the host country differs both by immigrant community and by individual. Some ethnic groups, e.g., Greeks and Italians, have a reputation for long-term maintenance of their first language (L1), and transmission of the language across several generations after immigration, while others tend to blend into the host language community within one generation—the Dutch appear to occupy the extreme position at this end of the continuum. In such investigations, Germans usually take an intermediate position. They do not maintain and transmit their language to the same degree as Greeks and Italians typically do, but neither do they give it up as fast as the Dutch.[1]

Language maintenance and language shift are, however, not only conditioned by group affiliation: investigations of individual linguistic development within groups of immigrants show that there is great variation between speakers of the same origin where the degree of L1 maintenance or deterioration is concerned. Such studies have often remarked that, while there are some speakers who after several decades of immigration have great difficulties completing some tasks in their first language, others still show astonishing fluency and proficiency, and in fact could still pass as native speakers within a native speaker community.[2]

This raises the question of what it is, either in speakers or in their environment, that conditions the degree of deterioration or maintenance of a first language in an immigration setting. Several possible explanations have been put forward. First of all, the degree to which a linguistic system deteriorates—a process usually referred to as language attrition—has been linked to the amount of use speakers make of the language in their daily lives. Second, it has been claimed that maintenance and attrition are conditioned by attitudes toward the language and the language community. And last, it is possible that highly elusive concepts such as individual language aptitude play a role.[3]

This chapter will report on an investigation of language attrition among a group of fifty-three German speakers in the Greater Vancouver area in British Columbia, Canada. It will try to elucidate to what degree the factors of language use and language attitude can be demonstrated to have an effect on language attrition. Unfortunately, it was not possible to include an investigation of language aptitude in the research design, as this highly controversial concept is very difficult and time consuming to measure.

Language Use

The amount to which a potential attriter uses the L1 strikes most researchers intuitively as one of the most important factors in determining the attritional process. Lack of contact leads to attrition, whereas using the L1 on a daily basis prevents loss—that is a widely held view,[4] and one that appears obvious and intuitively convincing. One problem with such assumptions about language is that experimental and empirical data often tell a different story. Another problem is that, because these assumptions seem so obvious and intuitively convincing, people tend to ignore empirical findings and hold on to intuitively obvious beliefs. There is, however, little direct evidence that the degree to which a language system will attrite depends on the amount to which the language is used in everyday life. There are reports stating that participants who use their L1 extremely infrequently show more attrition over time.[5] On the other hand, some studies suggest that attriters who use their L1 on a daily basis actually had more difficulty completing some tasks.[6]

When findings are contradictory, more often than not it is the methodology that is at fault. The mismatch between these studies is likely based on an unwarranted simplification of a set of relationships and speech situations. Language use refers to a complex pattern of behaviour in everyday interaction, and can, therefore, probably not easily be reduced to one dichotomous factor, which is what all of the studies cited above attempt to do. Kees de Bot, Paul Gommans, and Carola Rossing as well as Barbara Köpke make a distinction between "more" and "less" use of the L1, while Jaspaert and Kroon use the L1 of the subject's partner as a measuring stick.

The assumption underlying the idea that attrition and use are linked is that memory is based on reinforcement, and that knowledge (particularly linguistic knowledge) that is not activated over a long period of time becomes difficult to access.[7] Language, however, is not merely a knowledge system but a marker of identity, and linguistic variation is determined by factors such as prestige, solidarity, and identification. This suggests that any investigation of language attrition cannot confine itself to the quantity of the contacts, but has to take into account their quality. In other words, the contacts should be classified and analysed according to speech situations and interlocutors, as the cognitive role that each contact plays for the attriter may be more important in determining the degree of attrition of the L1 than the mere frequency with which the contact occurs.

Furthermore, it may be important whether the persons with whom the L1 is used are themselves bilingual. In such situations, when the interaction is informal, it can be assumed that both language systems are active, and that code-mixing is taking place—a speech setting that has been referred to as the bilingual mode.[8] If, however, bilinguals are using their first language with monolingual speakers, for example, a family member or friend in the country of origin, the situation will require that the second language (L2) be inhibited or deactivated, and that the L1 will be used in a monolingual mode, particularly if the interlocutor is not a speaker of the other language.[9] It has recently been shown that frequent use of the L1 in informal speech situations within the family or with friends in the immigration context does not facilitate lexical access[10] or prevent foreign accent in the first language,[11] while routine use of the L1 in monolingual mode may, to some degree, contravene problems in those areas.

Attitudes

Where second language acquisition is concerned, it has been established that the attitude an individual has toward both the language and the language community will affect success in language learning.[12] A number of studies have made the attempt to link attitudes to the degree of language attrition among individual speakers. From a common-sense perspective, this is a promising area: L1 attrition is a phenomenon that takes place in the context of emigration, a situation that almost invariably involves a reassessment of identity, belonging, and group membership. In this respect, language proficiency and use are among the most immediately obvious defining features,[13] and they are also among the markers of identity that the individual can (to some extent at least) control—unlike, for example, skin colour.

One important factor is that the migrant who may have been part of the main-stream population prior to emigration now is a "foreigner," part of the out-group in the country of immigration. While groups consider themselves as stratified, they are often viewed as homogenous from the outside.[14] Thus, although individuals might have perceived themselves as belonging to a social class with a certain social prestige while still in the country of their origin, after emigration they may find attitudes toward them influenced by stereotyped notions associated with immigrants in general or immigrants of a certain ethnolinguistic background. Almost invariably, the prestige attached to the status of immigrant will be lower than that of their former status.[15]

Being thus suddenly (and often unexpectedly) downgraded by members of the majority community may cause the desire on the part of the immigrants for complete assimilation. In order to achieve that, they may reject their native language in an attempt to acquire native-like competence of their L2, a foreign accent being one of the more notable indications of their immigrant status. If, on the other hand, they still feel comfortable with or even proud of their origins, they may wish to be perceived as members of the community of immigrants from their country of origin, and even flaunt their bilingual competence or non-native command of the dominant language.

Over the past decades, socio- and ethnolinguistics have often concerned themselves with these kinds of situations, as is evident in the works of, among others, Joshua Fishman,[16] R.B. LePage and Andrée Tabouret-Keller, or the scientists associated with the concept of ethnolinguistic vitality.[17] All of these frameworks attempt to measure the slippery and elusive, yet undoubtedly vital, phenomenon of where individuals position themselves within a multilingual or multiethnic community. This includes questions such as what aspects of themselves, their history, loyalty, and association they think most salient and most representative of their "true selves." It seems likely that language attrition will, at least to some extent, be determined by these factors. What is more difficult is the question of how to establish this in a scientifically sound and testable framework.

Several studies have tried, and failed, to relate the degree of individual first language attrition to concepts such as ethnic affiliation[18] or ethnolinguistic vitality.[19] The findings from these studies point to the conclusion that socio- and ethnolinguistic frameworks that rely on subjects' self-reports about their use of and attitude towards their L1 seem to be inadequate tools for the prediction of the linguistic aspects of language attrition. Subjective evaluation reflecting on the past at one point in time cannot establish a link between attrition and concepts such as attitude or identity. The main factor for the difficulty of establishing such a link may be that people's identities, affiliations, and self-concepts do not remain stable across lifespans.[20] Obviously, if a connection between attitudes or identities and attrition is to be found, it would have to be sought at the moment of emigration, i.e., at the possible onset of attrition. This poses an enormous methodological problem for the investigation of a long-term phenomenon such as language breakdown, as it is usually not possible to reconstruct the situation that an attriter experienced several decades ago.

One study that attempted to do this using a historical approach[21] found interesting results in this respect. It investigated L1 attrition among German Jews who emigrated to anglophone countries during the years of the Nazi regime. It divided the speakers who participated in the study into three groups according to the phase during which emigration took place. The study found that the speakers who emigrated at a later stage, and thus were subjected to increasingly drastic anti-Semitic persecution, often came to feel a revulsion for the German language that may have contributed to a higher degree of language loss.

It is, therefore, conceivable that the impact of attitudes on language attrition can only be established on the basis of a longitudinal design, measuring attitude at or before the moment of emigration, and language proficiency several decades later. The methodological difficulties involved with such a design, however, are enormous.[22]

The Participants in the Study

For the present study, data were collected from an experimental group (CA) of fifty-three Germans living in the Greater Vancouver area and a control group (CG) of fifty-three speakers in Germany (in the Rhineland and the lower Rhine area) who had never lived abroad for an extended period of time. Contact with the members of the experimental group, the émigrés (henceforth: attriters), was made through advertisements in both German and English newspapers, through German clubs, churches, libraries, schools, TV channels, and through the "snowball"-method. The control group subjects were approached through advertisements in newspapers, through clubs, and organizations whose members

TABLE 1 Controlling factors across groups for studying German speakers in Vancouver

	Experimental Group (n=53)		Control Group (n=53)	
	Mean	Standard deviation	Mean	Standard deviation
Age	63,23	10,92	60.89	11.60
Age at emigration	26,13	7,07	–	–
Emigration time	37,09	12,25	–	–

were assumed to be in the target age group, and through personal contacts. The attriters had to fit the criterion that they must have lived in an L2 environment for at least ten years (see Table 1).[23]

In addition, an equal distribution of men and women across the two groups was attempted. Although it was not possible to achieve an even distribution of men and women, both groups contained an equal number of thirty-five women and eighteen men. The groups were also controlled for level of education.

Study Design and Results: Language Use, Attitudes, and Language Proficiency

Information on the use of German was elicited by means of semi-structured autobiographical interviews. The interviewer conducted the conversation on the basis of a sociolinguistic questionnaire containing seventy-eight items. For the purpose of the present analysis, answers to a number of questions on language use were taken into account. All answers were on a five-point Likert scale. The points were standardized to a score between 0 and 1 where 1 designates extremely frequent use of or exposure to German and 0 no or very rare use of German (see Table 2).

The relatively high standard deviations here indicate that there was considerable variability among subjects, particularly within the family context. In order to minimize the number of variables used in the statistical analysis and thereby increase the power of the statistical model, superordinate variables were calculated on the basis of these responses in those cases where the speech situations were very similar (e.g., language use within the family) and where a high Cronbach Alpha indicated high reliability within such related blocks of questions. In addition, a distinction was made between informal L1 use in bilingual mode and L1 use in mixed or monolingual mode. The former includes all language-use information that pertains to the family and friends in the immigration context, the latter contact with German speakers in Germany and L1 use for professional purposes.

TABLE 2 Contact with and use of the first language

Experimental Group	Mean	Standard deviation
What language do you speak with your partner?	0.42	0.42
What language do you speak with your children?	0.36	0.35
What language do you speak with your grandchildren?	0.19	0.36
How often do you use German within your family?	0.55	0.35
How often do you use German with your friends?	0.39	0.28
Do you use German for professional purposes?	0.26	0.33
How often do you have contacts with friends or family in Germany?	0.77	0.27
How often do you visit Germany?	0.33	0.17

As was pointed out above, it may not be feasible to relate attitudes and language attrition except in a longitudinal design. A standardized test for the elicitation of attitudes[24] was therefore administered. The items in this test were formulated as statements, with which the participant was invited to agree or to disagree on a five-point Likert scale, as in the following example of one of these statements.

	Strongly disagree	Moderately disagree	Neutral	Moderately agree	Strongly agree
German Canadians are a very sociable, warm-hearted, and creative people.					

The test contains seven items pertaining to speakers of the L1 in immigration, seven items describing speakers of the L1 in the country of origin, nine items on attitude toward speakers of the L2, and nine items eliciting attitudes to foreign language learning. Table 3 sums up average responses in those categories (1 = strongly favourable attitude, 0 = strongly unfavourable attitude).

TABLE 3 Mean responses on attitude and motivation test (n=49)

	Mean	Standard deviation
Attitude toward Germans in Canada	0.61	0.21
Attitude toward Germans in Germany	0.62	0.18
Attitude toward Canadians	0.78	0.13
Attitude toward foreign language learning	0.87	0.13

In order to assess global L1 proficiency among the speakers, the following tests were administered:

1. A grammaticality judgment task (GJ)[25] consisting of forty-seven sentences, of which twenty-two contained a grammatical mistake and twenty-five were grammatically correct filler items. The sentences were presented on a computer screen and accompanied by a recording of the sentence being read out by a native speaker. Subjects were asked to judge whether these sentences were grammatically correct and, if not, to indicate what the correct version would be. Each ungrammatical sentence that was correctly identified was given one point, and the overall result over all twenty-two ungrammatical sentences was then standardized to a score between 0 and 1.

2. A C-Test (CTEST)[26] consisting of five short texts. In the C-Test, parts of words were deleted according to a predetermined scheme, and the subject was then asked to complete these words in order to obtain a coherent text. Each of the texts used contained twenty gaps, and each correctly filled gap was awarded one point, so that the maximum possible score was 100.

3. A Fluency in Controlled Association (FiCA) task,[27] in which the subject was asked to produce as many items of a particular category (e.g., animals) within a limited time span of normally sixty seconds. Two sets of this task were used, one using animals as stimulant, the second using fruit and vegetables.

4. A film-retelling task.[28] Subjects were asked to watch a ten-minute sequence of a silent movie and then asked to retell what they had seen. These retellings were transcribed. Any ungrammatical structure was marked as an error, and the total number of errors per speaker (ERR) was calculated. Furthermore, the lexical diversity measure (D) was calculated using the CHILDES tool package.[29] D is a measure of type-token ratios corrected for text length.

A t-test established that the control group performed significantly better on the C-Test and the FiCA task, and made significantly fewer errors in the film-retelling task than the experimental group (see Table 4 below). There was no significant difference on the grammaticality judgment task and on the lexical diversity measure D.

In order to establish to what degree the independent variables on language use and language attitude might account for the results on the language proficiency tests, bivariate correlations were computed using the data from the Canadian group. The results are summarized in Table 5.

As is evident from this overview, use of German in monolingual mode correlates significantly with the results on the more formal language tasks. The attitude toward Germans, both in Germany and in Canada,

TABLE 4 Language proficiency data, t-test comparison of experimental and control group

	Experimental Group		Control Group		
	Mean	**Standard deviation**	**Mean**	**Standard deviation**	**T-test (2-tailed)**
GJ	0.82	0.12	0.84	0.11	t (104) = 1.099; p=.274
C-Test	75.26	11.61	82.21	8.90	t (104) = 3.456**; p<.01
FiCA	20.44	4.59	24.92	4.67	t (100) = 4.888**; p=.001
D	70.45	17.12	75.35	17.90	t (103) = 1.435; p=.154
ERR	9.02	6.19	1.72	2.50	t (103) = -7.959**; p<.001

D = lexical diversity measure used in film-retelling task; ERR = errors per speaker in film-retelling task; FiCA = Fluency in Controlled Association; GJ = grammaticality judgment task.

** marks a statistically significant difference

Note: The degrees of freedom vary slightly among tests because, for various technical reasons (such as the failure of recording equipment), not all tests were available from all participants.

TABLE 5 Correlating language use, attitude, and proficiency

	GJ	**C-Test**	**FICA**	**D**	**ERR**
Monolingual use	0.385**	0.273*	0.288*	−0.092	−0.193
Bilingual use	0.064	−0.035	0.114	−0.221	−0.107
Attitude toward Germans in Canada	−0.048	−0.162	−0.224	−0.307*	0.121
Attitude toward Germans in Germany	−0.042	−0.209	−0.274	−0.362*	0.128
Attitude toward Canadians	0.181	−0.120	0.101	−0.181	0.044
Attitude toward foreign language learning	0.164	0.217	0.041	0.049	−0.192

* indicates a weak and ** a stronger correlation

correlates significantly with the lexical diversity measure D. However, the correlation is negative, indicating that a more positive attitude is linked with a lower score on D.

Discussion

A noteworthy outcome from the analysis presented above is that while there is a certain amount of correlation between language use data and the results on more formal language tasks on the one hand, on the other attitudes only seem to play a (rather limited) role for performance in relatively free speech. This suggests that using the L1 frequently in formal, professional, or monolingual situations may help retain metalinguistic or explicit knowledge. The findings on attitudes towards the German language and culture are puzzling, as they suggest that a more positive attitude is linked with more restricted lexical access. This result is hard to explain within the framework of attitude and language proficiency, but it may suggest that the test battery used here is unsuitable to capture the interaction between attrition and attitudes.

Interestingly, language use in bilingual settings, that is, the use of German with other bilingual speakers—presumably in situations where code-switching and language mixing occur frequently—does not seem to have any effect whatsoever on the language retention of this group. These findings corroborate some results from similar investigations, including those of studies with native speakers of German in the Netherlands[30] as well as native speakers of Dutch in Canada.[31]

In sum, the findings presented here seem to indicate that the commonly accepted "use it or lose it" tenet does not hold with respect to the target group investigated here. How often immigrants speak their first language may not have a strong impact on whether or not that language is forgotten. In other words, L1 knowledge may to some degree be impervious to frequency of activation.

This allows an intriguing speculation: there is probably no system of human knowledge that is rehearsed as extensively as a first language spoken monolingually until adulthood. While other areas of knowledge and memory are clearly sensitive to frequency of activation, it is possible that in L1 acquisition, a certain "saturation threshold" can be reached. After this threshold, it is possible that activation becomes less important, and that the maintenance or forgetting of the language is affected more by other factors, such as attitude and motivation. This would imply that in order to lose their language, speakers would actively have to want to lose it.

Notes

1   Clyne, "German-Australian Speech Community."
2   For an overview see Köpke and Schmid, "Language Attrition."
3   Paradis, "L1 Attrition Features."
4   For example, Cook, "Changing L1"; Paradis, "L1 Attrition Features."
5   de Bot, Gommans, and Rossing, "L1 Loss"; Köpke, L'attrition de la première langue.
6   Jaspaert and Kroon, "Social Determinants."
7   Paradis, Neurolinguistic Theory.
8   Grosjean, "Bilingual's Language Modes."
9   For a detailed account of languages modes in bilingual individuals see Grosjean, "Bilingual's Language Modes."
10 Schmid, "Role of L1 Use."
11 de Leeuw, Schmid, and Mennen, "Perception of Foreign Accent."
12 Gardner, "Attitude and Motivation."
13 See, for example, Le Page and Tabouret-Keller, Acts of Identity.
14 Breakwell, "Identities and Conflicts," 191.
15 Yağmur, First Language Attrition, 31.
16 Fishman, "Language and Ethnicity."
17 Giles, Bourhis, and Taylor, "Towards a Theory of Language."
18 Waas, Language Attrition Downunder.

19   Hulsen, *Language Loss;* Yağmur, *First Language Attrition.*
20   Breakwell, "Identities and Conflicts," 18.
21   Schmid, *First Language Attrition.*
22   For a more detailed account see Schmid, "Role of L1 Use."
23   One exception was made for a German speaker in Canada who was very eager to participate, but whose emigration was only nine years earlier.
24   Gardner, "Attitude and Motivation Test Battery Manual."
25   See Altenberg and Vago, "Role of Grammaticality Judgments."
26   See Grotjahn, "How to Construct and Evaluate a C-Test."
27   See Goodglass and Kaplan, *Assessment of Aphasia.*
28   See Perdue, *Adult Language Acquisition.*
29   "Child Language Data Exchange System"; see also MacWhinney, *CHILDES Project.*
30   Schmid, "Role of L1 Use"; de Leeuw, Schmid, and Mennen, "Perception of Foreign Accent."
31   Keijzer, *Last In, First Out?*

Works Cited

Altenberg, Evelyn P. and Robert M. Vago. "The Role of Grammaticality Judgments in Investigating First Language Attrition." In *First Language Attrition: Interdisciplinary Perspectives on Methodological Issues,* edited by Monika S. Schmid, Barbara Köpke, Merel Keijzer, and Lina Weilemar, 105–29. Amsterdam: John Benjamins, 2004.

Breakwell, Glynis M. "Identities and Conflicts." In *Threatened Identities,* edited by Glynis M. Breakwell, 189–213. New York: John Wiley, 1983.

"Child Language Data Exchange System." CHILDES/TalkBank database, 2007. <childes.psy.cmu.edu> (March 2008).

Clyne, Michael. "The German-Australian Speech Community: Ethnic Core Values and Language Maintenance." *International Journal of the Sociology of Language* 72 (1988): 67–83.

Cook, Vivian. "The Changing L1 in the L2 User's Mind." Keynote lecture delivered at the 2nd International Conference on First Language Attrition, Vrije Universiteit Amsterdam, 17–18 August 2005.

de Bot, Kees, Paul Gommans, and Carola Rossing. "L1 Loss in an L2 Environment: Dutch Immigrants in France." In *First Language Attrition,* edited by Herbert W. Seliger and Robert M. Vago, 87–98. Cambridge: Cambridge University Press, 1991.

de Leeuw, Esther, Monika S. Schmid, and Ineke Mennen. "Perception of Foreign Accent in Native Speech." *Bilingualism, Language and Cognition,* special issue on First Language Attrition, forthcoming.

Fishman, Joshua A. "Language and Ethnicity." In *Language, Ethnicity and Intergroup Relations,* edited by Howard Giles, 15–57. London: Academic Press, 1977.

Gardner, Robert C. "The Attitude Motivation Test Battery Manual," 1985. University of Western Ontario, London, ON. <publish.uwo.ca/~gardner/AMTB manualforwebpage.pdf> (March 2008).

Giles, Howard, Richard Bourhis, and Donald M. Taylor. "Towards a Theory of Language in Ethnic Group Relations." In *Language, Ethnicity, and Intergroup Relations,* edited by Howard Giles, 307–48. London: Academic Press, 1977.

Goodglass, Harold, and Edith Kaplan. *The Assessment of Aphasia and Related Disorders.* Philadelphia: Lea and Febiger, 1983.

Grosjean, François. "The Bilingual's Language Modes." In *One Mind, Two Languages: Bilingual Language Processing,* edited by Janet L. Nicol, 1–22. Oxford: Blackwell Publishing, 2001.

Grotjahn, Rudiger. "How to Construct and Evaluate a C-Test: A Discussion of Some Problems and Some Statistical Analyses." *Quantitative Linguistics* 34 (1987): 219–53.

Hulsen, Madeleine. *Language Loss and Language Processing: Three Generations of Dutch Migrants in New Zealand.* PhD diss., Radboud Universiteit Nijmegen, 2000.

Jaspaert, Koen, and Sjaak Kroon. "Social Determinants of Language Loss." *ITL: Review of Applied Linguistics* 83/84 (1992): 75–98.

Keijzer, Merel. *Last In, First Out? An Investigation of the Regression Hypothesis in Dutch Emigrants in Anglophone Canada.* PhD diss., Vrije Universiteit Amsterdam, 2007.

Köpke, Barbara. *L'attrition de la première langue chez le bilingue tardif: Implications pour l'étude psycholinguistique de bilingualisme.* PhD diss., Université de Toulouse-Le Mirail, 1999.

Köpke, Barbara, and Monika S. Schmid. "First Language Attrition: The Next Phase." In *First Language Attrition: Interdisciplinary Perspectives on Methodological Issues,* edited by Monika S. Schmid, Barbara Köpke, Merel Keijzer, and Lina Weilemar, 1–45. Amsterdam: John Benjamins, 2004.

Le Page, R.B., and Andrée Tabouret-Keller. *Acts of Identity.* Cambridge University Press, 1985.

MacWhinney, Brian. *The CHILDES Project: Tools for Analyzing Talk. Third Edition.* Mahwah, NJ: Lawrence Erlbaum Associates, 2000.

Paradis, Michel. *A Neurolinguistic Theory of Bilingualism.* Amsterdam: John Benjamins, 2004.

———. "L1 Attrition Features Predicted by a Neurolinguistic Theory of Bilingualism." In *Language Attrition: Theoretical Perspectives,* edited by Barbara Köpke, Monika S. Schmid, Merel Keijzer, and Susan Dostert, 121–34. Amsterdam: John Benjamins, 2007.

Perdue, Clive. *Adult Language Acquisition: Cross-Linguistic Perspectives.* Cambridge: Cambridge University Press, 1993.

Schmid, Monika S. *First Language Attrition, Use, and Maintenance: The Case of German Jews in Anglophone Countries.* Amsterdam: John Benjamins, 2002.

———. "The Role of L1 Use for L1 Attrition." In *Language Attrition: Theoretical Perspectives,* edited by Barbara Köpke, Monika S. Schmid, Merel Keijzer and Susan Dostert, 135–53. Amsterdam: John Benjamins, 2007.

Waas, Margit. *Language Attrition Downunder: German Speakers in Australia.* Frankfurt: Peter Lang, 1996.

Yağmur, Kutlay. *First Language Attrition among Turkish Speakers in Sydney.* Tilburg: Tilburg University Press, 1997.

CONTRIBUTORS

ROLF ANNAS is a senior lecturer in German at the Universiteit Stellenbosch in South Africa. He specializes in foreign language didactics, German in South Africa, and media studies. He has edited a book on the teaching of foreign language and literature and has published a number of articles in academic journals.

JASON TODD BAKER is working with historian James McGrath Morris on a biography of Joseph Pulitzer. He holds a PhD in German literature from Washington University in St. Louis, Missouri, and has studied in Greifswald and Berlin.

KARIN BAUER is an associate professor of German at McGill University in Montreal. She wrote her dissertation on Nietzsche and Adorno and received her PhD in Germanics from the University of Washington in 1992. Her research and publications focus on critical theory, Nietzsche, the Frankfurt School, contemporary German literature, minority literature, and film studies.

BRIGITTE BÖNISCH-BREDNICH is a professor in the anthropology program at the School of Social and Cultural Studies at Victoria University of Wellington in New Zealand. She completed her Habilitation at the University of Göttingen and has published books on German immigration to New Zealand and European ethnology in Silesia as well as many articles and book chapters.

DIETER K. BUSE is Professor Emeritus of History at Laurentian University in Sudbury, Canada, and received his PhD from the University of Oregon. *The Regions of Germany* is the title of his most recently published book. He has also co-edited a well-received encyclopedia of modern German history and published a number of other books and many articles.

JENNY CARL is a research assistant on a project funded by the UK's Arts and Humanities Research Council concentrating on German and Austrian foreign-language policy and German-language practices in Central Europe. She studied European studies at the universities of Osnabrück in Germany and Hull in the United Kingdom and completed her doctorate on representations of European identities in parliamentary discourses in Scotland, Wales, and Northern Ireland at the Universität Osnabrück in 2005.

JAMES CASTEEL is coordinator of the Zelikovitz Centre for Jewish Studies at Carleton University in Ottawa, where he also teaches in the Department of History. He received his PhD from Rutgers University. His publications and conference presentations have focused on encounters with eastern Europe in German culture. He is currently completing a book manuscript on German perceptions of Russia from 1900 to 1945.

JENNIFER DAILEY-O'CAIN is an associate professor of German applied linguistics at the University of Alberta in Edmonton. Her research includes work in language, migration, and identity in both Germany and German-speaking Canada, code-switching in the classroom, the quotative system in English, and language attitudes in post-unification Germany.

STEFAN ENGELBERG is a professor at the Institut für deutsche Sprache in Mannheim. He wrote his Habilitation at the Bergische Universität Wuppertal on lexical and structural aspects of the constitution of sentence meaning. He has co-edited two books and is the author of *Verben, Ereignisse und das Lexikon,* and his research in linguistics is published widely.

NORA FAIRES is a professor of history and the chair of Canadian studies at Western Michigan University in Kalamazoo, Michigan. She has co-authored two award-winning books on the history of immigrants and written a large number of articles and chapters on her research on migration in North America. She also has conducted public history projects, curated a museum exhibit, produced a video, and developed teaching materials for schools.

PATRICK FARGES is an assistant professor at the Université Sorbonne Nouvelle Paris 3. He received his PhD in German from Paris 8 Vincennes—Saint Denis and has presented his research on German migration in papers and at conferences. A book based on his PhD appeared in 2008 in France (Paris, Editions de la MSH).

ALEXANDER FREUND is an associate professor of history and holds the Chair in German-Canadian Studies at the University of Winnipeg in Winnipeg, Canada. He has published a book on German emigration to North America after World War II as well as several articles and chapters on German migration and German migrants' approaches to dealing with the Nazi past.

MÉRI FROTSCHER KRAMER works in the History Department at Universidade Estadual do Oeste do Paraná in Brazil. She wrote her doctoral dissertation at the Universidade Federal de Santa Catarina on nationalism and identity discourses in Blumenau and published it as a book in 2007.

JANET M. FULLER is an associate professor in the Department of Anthropology at Southern Illinois University at Carbondale, Illinois. She studied at Macalester College in Minnesota, the Freie Universität Berlin, and took her PhD in linguistics from the University of South Carolina. She has won many research and professional awards, published in many specialized journals and books, and lectured extensively throughout North America and Europe.

HUGO HAMILTON was born in Dublin of Irish German parentage. He has published a memoir of his Irish German childhood, *The Speckled People*, and its sequel, *The Sailor in the Wardrobe*. He has also written the novels *Surrogate City*, *The Last Shot*, *The Love Test*, *Headbanger*, and *Sad Bastard*, as well as shorter texts. He lives in Dublin.

CHRISTIANE HARZIG was an associate professor of history at Arizona State University. She studied in Berlin and Bremen and completed her habilitation at the Universität Bremen. She edited and co-edited several books on migration and published her research in anthologies and journals. Her book on immigration and politics appeared in 2004. Cancer cut short her life in 2007. She is sadly missed.

GISELA HOLFTER is a senior lecturer in German and the joint director of the Centre for Irish German Studies at the University of Limerick. She obtained her MA from Washington University St. Louis and her PhD in Cologne. Her current research interests include German-speaking exiles in Ireland, and she has published widely on travel writing, German Irish relations, and German literature.

DAVID G. JOHN is a professor of German and the director of the Waterloo Centre for German Studies. His main research focus is on eighteenth-century literature and culture, with an emphasis on theatre. His research on Johann Christian Krüger, the Nachspiel, and Goethe has led to book publications.

SANDRA KIPP has worked and published in the area of Australian language demography since 1991 and has been involved in research on German in Australia since 1969. She is an honorary research fellow at the University of Melbourne working on the maintenance of German in Australia since World War II. Other interests include bilingualism, language contact phenomena, and second-language acquisition.

MONIQUE LANEY is a PhD candidate in American studies at the University of Kansas and received her MA from the J.W. Goethe Universität in Frankfurt. She has published her research comparing German and American newspaper representations of the war in Iraq and presented her research on German Americans after World War II at a number of conferences.

HANS LEMBERG is Professor Emeritus of East European history in the Department of History and Cultural Sciences at Philipps Universität Marburg. He studied and received his doctorate and Habilitation at the University of Cologne and has been professor at the universities of Düsseldorf and Marburg since 1973. His extensive list of articles and book publications focuses inter alia on German minority migration and expulsion in and from Eastern Europe.

CHRISTIAN LIEB received his PhD from the University of Victoria for his research on German immigration to British Columbia between 1945 and 1961. He has MA degrees from the Universität Duisburg and the University of Maine.

GRIT LIEBSCHER is an associate professor of German at the University of Waterloo. She obtained her PhD from the University of Texas at Austin and is a trained sociolinguist with a focus on interactional sociolinguistics and conversation analysis. Her research interests, on which she has published widely, include language use among German Canadians, language and migration in post-unification Germany, and language practices in the bilingual classroom.

ANNE LÖCHTE currently works at the Humboldt Universität in Berlin. She wrote her doctoral dissertation at the Technische Universität Berlin on Gottfried Herder and published it in 2005. During her stay as a guest researcher at the Waterloo Centre for German Studies, she wrote a book on the Canadian German-language newspaper *Berliner Journal*.

PASCAL MAEDER works at the Universität Basel, Switzerland. He completed his PhD at York University, Canada, on the social and cultural integration of expellees in postwar West Germany and Canada. He grew up in Switzerland and studied for his MA at the universities of Basel, Zurich, and Rouen, France.

JÖRG MEINDL is working on his PhD dissertation on communication strategies in Pennsylvania German speech islands in Kansas at the University of Kansas. He received his MA in German philology from the Universität Heidelberg.

MANUEL MEUNE is an associate professor of German at the Université de Montréal. He received his doctorate from the Université Marc Bloch in Strasbourg, France. In 2003, he published a book on the Germans in Quebec. His main research interests are in Canadian German cultural relations and the historical memory of German immigrants to Canada.

BENNO NIETZEL obtained his MA from Humboldt Universität zu Berlin, where he now works in the Department of History as a research assistant for a project on Jewish entrepreneurs in Berlin, Breslau, and Frankfurt between 1929/30 and 1945.

J. OTTO POHL is an associate professor of international and comparative politics at American University of Central Asia in Bishkek, Kyrgyzstan. He received his PhD in history from the School of Oriental and African Studies at the University of London and is the author of two books, *The Stalinist Penal System* and *Ethnic Cleansing in the USSR, 1937–1949*.

CHRISTIN PSCHICHHOLZ completed her PhD on German Protestant communities in the territory of modern-day Turkey between 1843 and 1919 at the Universität Kiel. She is interested in interdisciplinary approaches to European and Oriental history.

ANNE RIBBERT works as a junior researcher at the Radboud University Nijmegen. She is researching the impact of immigration on syntactic change in the Netherlands between 1400 and 1700. Before joining Nijmegen she conducted research in the fields of second-language acquisition, language attrition, and theoretical linguistics at the universities of Amsterdam and McGill.

ANGELIKA E. SAUER is an associate professor of history at Texas Lutheran University. Her PhD in history is from the University of Waterloo. She co-edited *A Chorus of Different Voices: German-Canadian Identities* and has published her research in a large number of articles and chapters.

MONIKA S. SCHMID is a Rosalind Franklin Fellow in the Department of English at Rijksuniversiteit Groningen. She earned her PhD in Düsseldorf with a dissertation entitled "First Language Attrition, Use, and Maintenance: The Case of German Jews in Anglophone Countries," which was published later as a book. She has co-edited books on language history and language attrition, and is published widely in articles and book chapters.

MATHIAS SCHULZE is an associate professor of German at the University of Waterloo. He obtained his PhD in language engineering at the University of Manchester Institute of Science and Technology, co-authored a book on the application of artificial intelligence to computer-assisted language learning, and has published many articles. His research interest in bilingual language structures developed when he moved to Waterloo in 2001.

DORIS SCHÜPBACH is a lecturer in the German program at Monash University in Melbourne, Australia. She received her PhD from the University of Melbourne in 2005 for the thesis entitled "Shared Languages, Shared Identities, Shared Stories: A Qualitative Study of Life Stories by Immigrants from German-Speaking Switzerland in Australia." Her main research interests are in the fields of sociolinguistics, language contact, and language and identity in an immigrant context.

SEBASTIAN SIEBEL-ACHENBACH teaches history at the University of Waterloo. He obtained his DPhil in history from Oxford University and has published a book entitled *The Social and Political Transformation of Lower Silesia, 1943–1948* in English and in German translation.

JAMES M. SKIDMORE is associate professor of German at the University of Waterloo. He wrote his PhD dissertation at Princeton University on Ricarda Huch's historiography during the Weimar Republic and published a revised version as a book. He has also published widely on German literature, German Canadian comparative literature, and university teaching.

HANNO SOWADE is a historian at the Foundation Haus der Geschichte der Bundesrepublik Deutschland in Bonn and an adjunct professor at the Otto Beisheim School of Management. He has consulted on a number of museum exhibitions, co-written the documentation for exhibitions, and published widely on recent German history and society.

JOHANNES-DIETER STEINERT is a professor of modern European history and migration studies at the University of Wolverhampton. He received his habilitation in history from the University of Osnabrück. He has published books on the expellee associations in North Rhine-Westphalia, migration from West Germany between 1945 and 1961, and the relationship between politics and the arts in North Rhine-Westphalia. He has co-authored *Germans in Postwar Britain,* on Germans in Great Britain after World War II, and co-edited two volumes on postwar history, *Labour & Love* and *European Immigrants in Britain 1933–1950.*

PATRICK STEVENSON is a professor of German and linguistic studies at the University of Southampton, where he also obtained his PhD. He authored *The German-Speaking World* and *Language and German Disunity,* has co-authored a book on sociolinguistic perspectives on linguistic variation in German, co-edited two further volumes, and is the editor of *The German Language and the Real World*. His research on sociolinguistics has appeared in numerous articles and book chapters.

ANDREA STRUTZ is a researcher at the Ludwig Boltzmann Institut für Gesellschafts- und Kulturgeschichte having received her PhD from the Universität Graz, where she is also a lecturer at the History Institute. She has published widely on restitution for Holocaust victims in Austria and the role of memory in our understanding of recent history.

INGE WEBER-NEWTH is a principal lecturer in German and applied language studies at London Metropolitan University. Her main research interests are in postwar German and European migration, on which she has published widely. She is co-author or co-editor of, among others, *Labour & Love, European Immigrants in Britain 1933–1950,* and *German Migrants in Postwar Britain*. She also co-organized two conferences entitled "Beyond Camps and Forced Labour" and co-edited two conference proceedings.

NATASHA G. WIEBE is a PhD candidate in educational studies at the University of Western Ontario in London, Canada. Her dissertation project focuses on cultural storylines in the works of Mennonite authors Di Brandt and Miriam Toews. She has published and presented research on the writing of Brandt and Toews, as well as poetry about her own "mennocostal" (Mennonite and Pentecostal) experiences.

DORIS WOLF is an assistant professor at the University of Winnipeg who specializes in contemporary Canadian literature and culture. She has published articles on Suzette Mayr, a Canadian author of Caribbean German descent. She has just completed an examination of Mavis Gallant's German stories, and is currently working on Gertrud Mackprang Baer's *In the Shadow of Silence.*

CARSTEN WÜRMANN is a PhD candidate at the Freie Universität Berlin and is working on a dissertation on literature of the Third Reich. He has published articles, book chapters, book reviews, and encyclopaedia entries on various aspects of German literature and has co-edited five books.

INDEX

occupation zone (Germany), 220, 368, 370, 372–73
Oder (river), 264, 369, 375
Ohio River, 195, 198
Ontario, xviii, 14, 16–17, 74, 107–08, 110–16, 147, 150–52, 177, 205–16, 248, 252, 261, 265–68, 306, 310, 374–75, 475–77, 483, 501, 509
Ontario Journal, 114, 116
Ottoman Empire, 231–34, 239–42

Paarl, xv, 61–72
pacifism, 479, 483, 486
parliament, 36, 111, 214–15, 221, 369, 504
pastor, 64–66, 69, 71, 111, 121, 149–51, 156, 194, 199, 236, 238, 314, 400
Patriotic Fund, 113
Pécs, 26, 32
Pennsylvania Dutch. *See* Pennsylvania German
Pennsylvania German, xvii, 3, 5–9, 14–18, 82, 431, 433–34, 439–41, 507; Pennsylvania German Paradox, 6
Pera (Beyoğlu), 233, 237, 239, 242
Pera-Gesellschaft, 239, 242
pidgin, 317–28
pietism, 194, 198, 216
Pittsburgh (Pa.), xvi, 193–204
Poland/Polish, xvii, 119–20, 124, 186, 234, 247, 263, 307, 359, 363–66, 368–71, 374, 391–402, 408
Pomerania, 69, 152
positioning theory, 23
Potsdam, 152, 286, 368
Prague, 24, 26, 28, 32
Protestant, 163, 188, 193–94, 201, 224–25, 236, 238, 240, 286, 482, 486, 507
Prussia/Prussian, 107–09, 119, 152, 198, 235–36, 239, 241, 286, 297, 346, 392, 395–96, 398, 400–401; church, 236

Red Army, 365, 369
refugee, xvi, 47, 51–54, 60, 83–92, 122, 170, 181–191, 217–18, 220, 226, 228, 245–55, 259, 260–66, 287–88, 293–95, 298–301, 306, 309, 361–62, 367, 369–75, 380, 398, 459, 474; refugee camp, 51, 299, 370; refugee problem, 182, 370, 371
Rehwald, Frank, 256, 263

Reichsdeutsche, 372
Reinland (Man.), 480–86
religion, 6, 9, 25, 99, 182, 189, 194, 196, 202–03, 219, 231–32, 236, 239–40, 367, 393, 407, 468, 480
reparation, 265, 443
restitution, 85, 379, 381, 383–89, 411, 509
Rhodes, Ronald, 148, 156–57
Riemenschneider, Engelhardt, 193–94, 197–98, 202
Rittinger, Friedrich, 108–09
Romania, 234, 307, 366
Russia/Russian, xvi, xvii, 9, 15–16, 19, 53, 117–29, 147, 186, 234, 240, 306, 360, 365, 368, 393–94, 397, 399–400, 402, 405–17, 480, 504; empire, 119, 400, 402, 406; revolution, 119, 123, 365

Salonika, 233
Samoa, 318, 321–29
Samoan Plantation Pidgin, 326
Schleuning, Johannes, 121, 123, 127, 129
Schröder, Heinrich, 125, 127, 129, 292
Schwäbisch, 23, 27, 30–31
Second Great Awakening, 198
Sedan, 109
self-determination of nations, 118
Seliger, Josef, 247, 255–56, 263, 266–68, 278–80, 501
Serbia, 366
shared stories, 35, 42, 45, 508
silence, 350, 474, 479–86
social democracy/social democrats, 245–54, 261–66, 470
Sonderfall, 35, 44–45
South Africa/South African, xv, 13, 61–72, 503
South America. *See* Latin America/South America
southeast Europe, 300, 368
South Pacific, 317–21, 326
South Tyrol, 363–64
Soviet Union/Soviet, 3, 10–11, 118–28, 147, 152–53, 260, 263, 367–69, 371, 394, 395, 405–17, 444, 507
special settlement, 409, 411
SS (Schutzstaffel), 218, 363–65, 401, 450, 458–59, 464
stab-in-the-back myth, 122–23
Stellenbosch, 62, 72, 503